Oil and Gas Federal Income Tax Manual

Thirteenth Edition — 1988

Arthur Andersen & Co.

Editor

J. Ray Jones, CPA
Houston, Texas

Contributing Authors

David W. Blair, CPA
Denver, Colorado

Rees T. Bowen, CPA
Dallas/Fort Worth, Texas

John K. Bywaters, CPA
Houston, Texas

Stephen V. Conrad, CPA
Denver, Colorado

A. Kent Graham, CPA
Houston, Texas

Paul L. Hocevar, CPA
Denver, Colorado

D. Boyd Lovelace, CPA
Houston, Texas

Ted E. McElroy, CPA
Houston, Texas

James W. Miley, CPA
New Orleans, Louisiana

Ross W. Nager, CPA
Houston, Texas

Randy D. Robason, CPA
Dallas/Fort Worth, Texas

Harmon M. Walker, Jr., CPA
Dallas/Fort Worth, Texas

Woody York, CPA
San Antonio, Texas

This manual was produced as a team effort by the editor and members of the Arthur Andersen & Co. Oil and Gas Tax Industry team. We express our deep appreciation and gratitude to the editor and the contributing authors for their tireless endeavors.

Many others outside the industry team also contributed significant time and effort to the completion of this manual. We gratefully acknowledge their efforts.

Arthur Andersen & Co.

Subject File OI 2360, Item 81
88-2002
Library of Congress Catalog Card No. 53-24020

ISBN 0-942319-01-X

Printed in the United States of America

Contents

Case

246 Section V — Disposition of Properties

Preface

This Thirteenth Edition of the *Oil and Gas Federal Income Tax Manual* reflects statutes, regulations, judicial decisions and other pronouncements available through June 30, 1987, with one exception described below.

On September 1, 1987, the Tax Court decided the *Shell Oil Co.* case, regarding the deduction of various costs in determining "taxable income from the property" for purposes of the net income limitation for windfall profit tax purposes. The court addressed the appropriate treatment of several different types of exploration costs as well as interest expense incurred on indebtedness to acquire oil and gas properties. In addition, it held that intangible drilling and development costs, windfall profit tax liability, and current geological and geophysical expenditures were properly includable in the allocation base used to allocate indirect expenses. *(See Cases 90 and 221.)*

This manual discusses our interpretations of the law based on the Committee Reports and other pronouncements available at the time this manual was written. These interpretations may differ substantially from those included in the final regulations that Treasury will release in the future.

Introduction

This is a manual of practical problems, but at the outset users should heed a word of caution. Income tax statutes, administrative rulings and regulations (both final and proposed) and judicial interpretations, particularly as applied to oil and gas operations, are changing continually. In general, this manual attempts to reflect the attitude of the Internal Revenue Service (IRS) as of June 1987. Subsequent shifts in the IRS's position, changes in the tax law or subsequent judicial or administrative interpretations cannot be anticipated or predicted. Many IRS policies do not appear in published rulings but must be obtained by application for a private ruling. For this reason, there never will be a satisfactory substitute for a thorough review of all up-to-date information applicable to a specific transaction. Equally important will be our professional knowledge, gained through experience, of the IRS's current attitude on the various facets of this particular field of tax practice.

Many of our representatives discuss the tax problems of the oil and gas industry with clients who have no previous knowledge of the subject, but who have become interested in making investments in oil and gas properties because they understand that many costs incurred are deductible for tax purposes. We should caution all such prospective investors that the oil and gas business is very complex and that they should either take sufficient time to study thoroughly the problems of this technical business and/or carefully select well-versed, reliable advisers. The fact that losses sustained can be deducted for tax purposes is small comfort to a person who has lost substantial sums of money in ill-advised ventures. For clients investing in the oil business, the most important consideration in many cases is to ensure that a maximum amount of current tax benefits can be obtained and the proper elections are made with respect to claiming those tax benefits.

This manual uses the case method to illustrate a number of common situations in the oil and gas industry where tax considerations are important. The solutions to the problems are developed by reference to fundamental tax principles that frequently have a broader application than the specific illustrative cases. The principles we rely on in answering the tax questions are based on our understanding of the law and regulations as they apply to oil and gas operations, on rulings of the IRS, on court decisions and on actual practice and experience in the handling of tax cases. To the extent any question is dealt with specifically in the Internal Revenue Code or regulations, a court decision or an administrative ruling, a footnote citation is made.

This manual should be used prospectively rather than after the fact. Prior to consummation of a transaction, the taxpayer usually has a choice of methods; afterward, it is too late. In many of the cases where an adverse tax result is indicated, we suggest an alternative method with appropriate cross reference to cases explaining the method. In addition, users should refer to the table of contents and the index for other alternatives that may be appropriate.

During the last several years, many major legislative acts have affected the oil and gas industry, particularly in the areas of the allowance of losses from passive activities, allowance of percentage depletion on lease bonuses and advance royalties, limitation of losses incurred in excess of amounts "at risk," recapture of intangible drilling and development costs (IDC) and depletion as ordinary income on disposition of oil and gas properties, timing of deductions of IDC, treatment of IDC on productive wells as a tax preference item, imputing interest on transactions using less than a market rate of interest, application of the alternative minimum tax to corporations, and provisions requiring the capitalization of indirect costs and interest related to drilling activities. Until regulations, rulings and court decisions clarify applications of these new laws, many questions about them will remain unanswered. This manual discusses the provisions of these laws based on the best information available at the time. Users should understand that it is not intended to represent the rendering of legal, accounting or other professional advice or services. Accordingly, users who require such services or other expert assistance in connection with their specific circumstances should consult competent professional advisers.

Furthermore, this manual is intended to cover only a limited segment of federal income tax practice. Advisedly, we have not considered certain other problems that frequently are encountered in, but not limited to, the oil and gas industry.

The Arthur Andersen Worldwide Organization makes available a number of publications on the taxation and other financial aspects of natural resources around the world. For more information, consult the Arthur Andersen office nearest you.

Section I
The Acquisition and Exploration Period

Before drilling operations begin, the principal tax accounting problem confronting an oil and gas lease operator is the classification of expenditures between deductible expenses and capitalizable costs. Proper classification of expenditures is important because of the varied tax consequences that result from different means of offsetting expenditures against taxable gross income. If an item is an expense, it is deductible either in the year in which it is incurred (if the taxpayer uses the accrual basis of accounting) or in the year in which payment is made (if the taxpayer uses the cash basis of accounting). If an item is a capital expenditure, it may be deducted from gross income only as depreciation, depletion or loss (in the event of worthlessness), or it may be deducted as tax basis in the determination of gain or loss on the sale or exchange of the property. Expenditures resulting in the acquisition, retention or improvement of a mineral property should be capitalized. Most other items may be considered as expenses and claimed as deductions in the year in which they are paid or incurred. Upon receipt of income from the production of oil or gas, an operator is allowed to deduct from his share of gross income an allowance for depletion. This depletion allowance, in many instances, is the larger of cost or percentage depletion determined for each property for each tax year.

Percentage depletion for oil and gas presently is a designated percentage of gross income from each lease or other unit of property, limited to 50% of the net income from that property and further limited to 65% of the taxpayer's taxable income. To the extent percentage depletion is allowable, no tax benefit is derived from cost depletion for regular tax purposes. Additionally, as a result of the alternative minimum tax (AMT) which is now imposed on both individuals and corporations, percentage depletion in excess of the basis of a property will not provide a tax benefit when a taxpayer is subject to this new broader tax. Under prior law, it was especially important from a tax standpoint that an operator reduce to a minimum all costs that were recoverable only in the form of depletion. To this end, most operators elected to deduct intangible drilling and development costs (IDC) and arranged transactions involving the acquisition and exploration of oil and gas properties to minimize capital costs.

The allowance for percentage depletion is significantly limited by provisions of the Tax Reduction Act of 1975. With certain exceptions, percentage depletion is not allowable after a transfer of a proven property. Accordingly, most acquisitions of proven properties will result in the loss of percentage depletion with respect to those properties. Further limitations on percentage depletion for amounts received before production were added by the Tax Reform Act of 1986. The allowance for percentage depletion and the various limitations applicable to it are discussed in Section IV.

Case 1
Option To Acquire Lease and Right To Explore for Oil and Gas

> Operator A pays $50,000 to Lessor R for a one-year option to acquire 10-year primary term leases in blocks of 2,000 acres at $50 per acre on all or part of a ranch of 20,000 acres. Operator A has the right under the option to conduct seismograph surveys on the entire area. Lessor R will retain a one-eighth landowner's royalty in all minerals produced and saved.

Operator A has acquired two specific rights: the right to conduct seismograph work in the area to determine the probable existence of mineral deposits and the right to acquire 10-year primary term leases upon the payment of $50 per acre. Operator A's option covers the entire 20,000-acre tract rather than several smaller tracts. The $50,000 paid by Operator A should be capitalized as the cost of the rights acquired. Although an allocation of cost between the two rights may be possible in certain cases, it generally is not made for the reason that both rights are elements of the cost of any leases acquired.

If Operator A selects acreage and acquires a lease, the entire amount paid for the option generally is considered to be a portion of the aggregate cost of the lease. If more than one lease is acquired, it is customary to allocate the amount paid for the option to the several leases on an acreage basis. If Operator A takes no leases, the amount paid for the option should be charged off as a loss in the year in which the option expires or is relinquished. However, the Internal Revenue Service (IRS) probably will hold that no portion of the $50,000 paid for the option can be written off if a lease is taken on any part of the acreage under option.

If Operator A selects acreage and acquires a lease, the option money received by Lessor R generally is considered to be in the nature of an advance royalty, commonly referred to as a lease bonus. As such, it is considered to be ordinary income which is subject to an allowance for depletion. However, lease bonus income no longer qualifies for percentage depletion for bonuses received or accrued after August 16, 1986.[1] Therefore, only cost depletion will be allowed for bonus income recognized after this date. *(See Case 98 for a discussion of the allowance for depletion on lease bonuses.)* In general, the option money is considered to be a prepayment or a partial payment of the bonus. Although a portion of the amount received may be attributable to the right to conduct seismograph surveys, this is considered to be a normal right granted to a lessee and, therefore, does not alter or affect the right to depletion.

If Operator A allows the option to expire and does not acquire a lease, the $50,000 received by Lessor R is treated as ordinary income, but depletion is not allowable. If depletion was taken as a deduction in a prior year, it must be restored to income in the year the option expires. *(See Case 127.)*

As indicated by the preceding discussion, whether depletion is allowable on the option money cannot be determined until the option is either exercised or allowed to expire. Therefore, the IRS has held in a private ruling that Lessor R's inclusion in income of the option proceeds should be deferred until the option is exercised or expires.[2] This treatment is consistent with that ordinarily applied in situations where the exercise of

1. Comm'r v. Engle, 82 U.S. 599 (1984), 53 AFTR2d 84-415, 84-1 USTC 9134; I.R.C. Sec. 613A(d)(5).
2. IRS Letter Ruling 7949013 (Technical Advice Memorandum).

an option will result in a sale or exchange by the optionor and his receipt of income, which might be treated as a capital gain.[3] In these situations, the character of the income resulting from the receipt of the option money is not fixed until the option is exercised or expires. However, when the owner of an oil and gas mineral interest enters into a lease option arrangement, the receipt of money for granting the option can result only in ordinary income for tax purposes whether the option is exercised or allowed to expire because under either circumstance a sale or exchange has not occurred. Accordingly, at least one court has held that money received for granting an option to acquire oil and gas leases in a leasing transaction is includable in income in the year received.[4]

If Lessor R grants the right to conduct seismograph surveys only (shooting rights), the amount received represents ordinary income not subject to an allowance for depletion.[5] Operator A still will be required to capitalize the amount paid to Lessor R for seismograph rights if he acquires any leases as a result of the seismograph work. *(See Case 5.)* If he acquires no leases, Operator A should deduct the amount he paid to Lessor R as an abandonment loss in the year he abandons any further interest in the project.

Case 2
Bonus Paid to Landowner

> Lessor R owns a 160-acre tract of land on which he grants an oil and gas lease to Operator A for a cash consideration of $5,000. The lease provides for a primary term of five years and as long thereafter as oil or gas is produced; it also provides for annual delay rental payments of $5 per acre. Operator A is required to bear all costs of development and operations and to pay Lessor R one-eighth of the proceeds from the sale of any production from the lease.

Lessor R has retained a continuing economic interest in the minerals by keeping the royalty and, consequently, has made a lease rather than a sale.[6] Accordingly, Lessor R is not entitled to deduct any part of his cost as the cost of property sold or exchanged.

The $5,000 consideration that Lessor R receives commonly is referred to as a lease bonus or as an advance royalty payment for oil and gas to be extracted. It is considered ordinary income subject to depletion.[7] However, lease bonus income no longer qualifies for percentage depletion for bonuses received or accrued after August 16, 1986.[8] Therefore, only cost depletion will be allowed for bonus income recognized after this date. *(See Cases 98 and 127 for a discussion of the allowance for depletion on lease bonus income and the circumstances under which the lessor must restore to his taxable income the amount of depletion claimed on that lease bonus.)*

Lessor R's tax basis in his retained royalty is equal to his basis in the minerals before the lease was granted, and it must be reduced by the amount of the depletion allowable with respect to the bonus.[9]

---

3. Rev. Rul. 69-166, 1969-1 C.B. 37; Comm'r v. Stuart, 300 F.2d 872 (3d Cir. 1962), 9 AFTR2d 1182, 62-1 USTC 9381; Birch Ranch and Oil Co., T.C. Memo Dec. (Apr. 20, 1944).
4. Comm'r v. Pickard, 401 F.2d 615 (10th Cir. 1968), 23 AFTR2d 69-318, 68-2 USTC 9607.
5. Special Ruling, June 18, 1951, 1982 Stand. Fed. Tax Rep. (CCH), Para. 668.614; Wasson v. U.S., 250 F.2d 826 (5th Cir. 1958), 1 AFTR2d 564, 58-1 USTC 9176.
6. Burnet v. Harmel, 287 U.S. 103 (1932), 11 AFTR 1085, 3 USTC 990; Rev. Rul. 69-352, 1969-1 C.B. 34; Rev. Rul. 82-221, 1982-2 C.B. 113.
7. Reg. Sec. 1.612-3(a)(1); Cox v. U.S., 497 F.2d 348 (4th Cir. 1974), 34 AFTR2d 74-5007, 74-1 USTC 9461.
8. I.R.C. Sec. 613A(d)(5).
9. Reg. Sec. 1.612-3(a)(1).

The regulations require that the depletion allowable on the bonus in prior years (whether computed on the cost or percentage basis) be restored to income if and when the entire lease expires, terminates or is abandoned without any income being realized from the extraction of oil or gas from the lease.[10] Because the lease covers a single tract of land, Lessor R will not be required to restore to gross income any depletion taken if only a portion of the acreage under the lease is abandoned without production.[11]

If only a nominal amount of production is obtained from a property and there are no bona fide commercial sales of production, the Internal Revenue Service (IRS) may require the lessor to restore the bonus depletion to income when the lease is terminated, even though the lessor receives payment for his share of the nominal production.[12] *(See Case 127 for further discussion of restoration of depletion.)*

Operator A must capitalize the $5,000 payment as the cost of the mineral rights acquired under the lease.[13] This capitalized cost is deductible only through the allowance for depletion, as a loss on account of worthlessness, as an abandonment loss or as tax basis upon a sale or other disposition of the property.

In calculating the percentage depletion allowance with respect to his share of production from the property, Operator A may be required to exclude from his annual depletable gross income a pro-rata share of the bonus paid to Lessor R.[14] *(See Case 87.)* Based on court cases and IRS pronouncements, the original purpose underlying this "bonus exclusion rule" was to ensure that lease bonus payments were not counted twice in computing percentage depletion.[15] The IRS has held that if the lessor who receives a lease bonus does not take the percentage depletion deduction on the bonus, the lessee must still exclude the income that is allocable to the bonus.[16] Arguably, based on the original purpose of the "bonus exclusion rule," the rule should not be applied if the lessor is not entitled to percentage depletion on the lease bonus. Therefore, since lease bonuses recognized as income after August 16, 1986, no longer qualify for percentage depletion, it appears to be inappropriate to continue to follow the "bonus exclusion rule" on these bonuses. It is hoped that this apparent inconsistency will be rectified by a technical correction or otherwise modified by an administrative pronouncement from the Treasury. *(See Case 98 for a complete discussion of depletion on advance royalties and lease bonus income.)*

Generally, the $5-per-acre rental payments may be deducted currently as paid or accrued, and these rental receipts are taxable as ordinary income not subject to depletion. *(See Case 9 for a discussion of the economic performance rules and other restrictions on the timing of delay rental deductions.)* Accordingly, it is necessary that delay rentals be distinguished from lease bonus payments. The basic distinction is that rental payments are avoidable by abandonment of the property, commencement of development operations or obtaining production,[17] whereas a lease bonus is a fixed obligation of the lessee. *(See Cases 3 and 9.)*

---

10. Reg. Sec. 1.612-3(a)(2).
11. Driscoll v. Comm'r, 147 F.2d 493 (5th Cir. 1945), 33 AFTR 704, 45-1 USTC 9184; Houston Farms Dev. Co. v. Comm'r, 194 F.2d 520 (5th Cir. 1952), 41 AFTR 725, 52-1 USTC 9175.
12. Dolores Crabb, 41 B.T.A. 686 (1940), (NA) 1968-1 C.B. 3; Seth Campbell, 41 T.C. 91 (1963).
13. Sunray Oil Co. v. Comm'r, 147 F.2d 962 (10th Cir. 1945), 33 AFTR 763, 45-1 USTC 9181; Canadian River Gas Co. v. Higgins, 151 F.2d 954 (2d Cir. 1945), 34 AFTR 411, 45-2 USTC 9450; Reg. Sec. 1.612-3(a)(3).
14. Reg. Sec. 1.613-2(c)(5)(ii); Shamrock Oil & Gas Corp. v. Comm'r, 346 F.2d 377 (5th Cir. 1965), 15 AFTR2d 1168, 65-2 USTC 9476; Rev. Rul. 81-266, 1981-2 C.B. 139.
15. Quintana Petroleum Co. v. Comm'r, 143 F.2d 588 (5th Cir. 1944), 32 AFTR 1031, 44-2 USTC 9380; Helvering v. Twin Bell Oil Syndicate, 293 U.S. 312 (1934), 14 AFTR 712, 35-1 USTC 9014; Rev. Rul. 81-266, 1981-2 C.B. 139.
16. Rev. Rul. 81-266, 1981-2 C.B. 139.
17. Reg. Sec. 1.612-3(c)(1).

Case 3
Oil and Gas Lease With Right To Select Acreage for Development

Operator A secures from Lessor R a lease covering 6,400 acres with a primary term of five years and six months for an initial payment of $75,000. Lessor R retains a one-eighth royalty interest. The lease provides that, at the end of six months, Operator A may select acreage for retention in blocks of not less than 640 acres each if an additional payment of $10 per acre is made. This latter payment may not be avoided by the commencement of drilling or by obtaining commercial production from the lease. The lease also contains a provision for an annual rental of $5 per acre beginning one year after the selection date. The rental payment is not required if drilling operations are in progress on the lease at the date the payment becomes due or if production in commercial quantities has been obtained. Operator A may forfeit any or all of the blocks at any time prior to the expiration of the primary term of the lease.

At the end of the six-month period, Operator A has begun a well on one block and pays a total of $25,600 for that and three other blocks.

The initial $75,000 payment constitutes a lease bonus[18] considered to be in the nature of an advance royalty.[19] *(See Case 2.)* Operator A must capitalize the bonus because it is considered to be a payment made for the acquisition of an economic interest in minerals. It is deductible only through the allowance for depletion, as a loss on account of worthlessness, as an abandonment loss or as tax basis in computing gain or loss on disposition.[20]

At the time Operator A made the payment of $25,600 to retain the four blocks, he forfeited a portion of the acreage acquired under the lease. Although there is no ruling directly applicable to a transaction of this nature, the Internal Revenue Service (IRS) probably will hold that Operator A is not entitled to a deductible loss resulting from the forfeiture at the selection date on the theory that Operator A made the original bonus payment for any oil and gas reserves underlying the acreage rather than for the acreage itself. Even if the original payment applies to noncontiguous tracts, the IRS still may contend that no loss is allowable with respect to the acreage not selected. Contrary to this line of reasoning, the Court of Claims has held in a case involving copper deposits[21] that the definition of *separate property units* for depletion purposes also applies for the purpose of determining loss.[22] The court held that it is improper to require reallocation of the tax basis of the separate properties once established if the rights to some of the properties are allowed to expire. In addition, one Tax Court case involving expenses incurred to evaluate prospective leases held that those expenses attributable to leases not acquired should be deducted currently rather than capitalized as a part of the total cost of the leases actually acquired.[23]

18. Herring v. Comm'r, 293 U.S. 322 (1934), 14 AFTR 717, 35-1 USTC 9012; Cox v. U.S., 497 F.2d 348 (4th Cir. 1974), 34 AFTR2d 74-5007, 74-1 USTC 9461.
19. Murphy Oil Co. v. Burnet, 55 F.2d 17 (9th Cir. 1932), 10 AFTR 1028, 3 USTC 1002; Burnet v. Harmel, 287 U.S. 103 (1932), 11 AFTR 1085, 3 USTC 990.
20. Reg. Sec. 1.612-3(a)(3).
21. American Smelting and Ref. Co.-Consol. v. U.S., 423 F.2d 277 (Ct. Cl. 1970), 25 AFTR2d 70-853, 70-1 USTC 9287. *Not being followed by IRS, see* Rev. Rul. 77-187, 1977-1, C.B. 50.
22. Reg. Sec. 1.614-1(a).
23. Vincent T. Larsen, 66 T.C. 478 (1976), (A) 1977-1 C.B. 1.

If the original payment applies to several noncontiguous tracts of land, Operator A probably will be allowed a loss for the cost allocable to any noncontiguous acreage dropped or forfeited during the lease term after the selection date.[24]

Operator A's $25,600 payment for the blocks of acreage retained at the end of six months generally is referred to as a *selection bonus.* The facts surrounding each payment of this type must be scrutinized to determine whether the payment should be deducted as a delay rental or capitalized as a lease bonus.

A delay rental is a payment made for deferring development of mineral lands, which can be avoided by abandonment of the lease, commencement of development operations or by obtaining production.[25] Conversely, to be treated as a lease bonus for tax purposes, an amount must be consideration for a lease and it must be payable in all cases with no conditions precedent or subsequent to subvert the payments. Because the initial payment of $75,000 secures for Operator A all the rights of a lessee and because the $25,600 payment can be avoided by abandonment of the lease, the $25,600 probably is deductible as a delay rental. *(See Case 9.)* A Circuit Court has held that this is true even though the payment may not be avoided by the commencement of drilling operations.[26] On the other hand, if the initial payment was made only to obtain shooting rights *(see Case 5)*, the selection bonus probably would constitute the initial bonus paid to acquire the lease and would not be deductible.

The annual payment of $5 per acre that Operator A must make during the primary term of the lease constitutes a delay rental and generally is deductible by him in the year in which it is paid or accrued. *(See Case 9 for a discussion of economic performance and the impact of the Tax Reform Act of 1986 on delay rental deductions.)*

The initial payment of $75,000 received by Lessor R is a lease bonus, which is subject to the allowance for depletion in the year of receipt.[27] However, lease bonus income no longer qualifies for percentage depletion for bonuses received or accrued after August 16, 1986.[28] Therefore, only cost depletion will be allowed for bonus income recognized after this date. *(See Cases 98 and 127 for a discussion of the allowance for depletion on lease bonus income and the circumstances under which the lessor must restore to his taxable income the amount of depletion (whether computed on the cost or percentage basis) claimed on that lease bonus.)*

If the selection bonus of $25,600 is determined to be a delay rental, it and the $5-per-acre delay rental received by Lessor R constitute ordinary income not subject to an allowance for depletion.[29] If the selection bonus is determined to be a lease bonus, Lessor R treats the $25,600 as ordinary income subject to depletion. As discussed above, only cost depletion will be allowed if the lease bonus is received or accrued after August 16, 1986. *(See Case 98.)*

Case 4
Bonus Paid to Sublessor

> Operator A acquires an assignment of a nonproductive oil and gas lease on 2,500 acres from Lessee E for a consideration of $125,000. Lessee E

24. L. B. Maytag, 32 T.C. 270 (1959).
25. Reg. Sec. 1.612-3(c)(1).
26. White Castle Lumber & Shingle Co. v. U.S., 481 F.2d 1274 (5th Cir. 1973), 32 AFTR2d 73-5549, 73-2 USTC 9590; Houston Farms Dev. Co. v. U.S., 131 F.2d 577 (5th Cir. 1942), 30 AFTR 328, 42-2 USTC 9783.
27. Herring; Reg. Sec. 1.612-3(a)(1).
28. I.R.C. Sec. 613A(d)(5).
29. Reg. Sec. 1.612-3(c)(2).

had leased the land from Lessor R, who retained a one-eighth landowner's royalty interest. Lessee E retains a one-sixteenth overriding royalty interest.

Lessee E has retained a continuing economic interest in the minerals assigned and, consequently, has made a sublease rather than a sale.[30] *(See Case 2.)* To Lessee E, the $125,000 lease bonus represents a payment in advance for oil and gas to be extracted and is considered ordinary income subject to depletion.[31] However, lease bonus income no longer qualifies for percentage depletion for bonuses received after August 16, 1986.[32] Therefore, only cost depletion will be allowed for bonus income recognized after this date. *(See Cases 98 and 127 for a discussion of the allowance for depletion on lease bonus income and the circumstances under which Lessee E must restore to his taxable income the amount of percentage or cost depletion claimed on the bonus.)*

Lessee E's tax basis in the overriding royalty interest is equal to his adjusted tax basis in the oil and gas lease that was assigned, reduced by the amount of any depletion allowable on the lease bonus received (whether computed on the cost or percentage basis).

The consideration of $125,000 paid to Lessee E must be capitalized by Operator A as a lease bonus. Although Operator A classifies this payment as the cost of mineral rights, it also represents royalties paid in advance.[33] Accordingly, the payment represents tax basis for computing cost depletion.

The lease bonus payment may also be an exclusion from Operator A's gross income, pro rata as production is obtained, for computing percentage depletion based on the "bonus exclusion rule." *(See Cases 2 and 87.)* Based on court cases and Internal Revenue Service (IRS) pronouncements, the original purpose underlying this "bonus exclusion rule" was to ensure that lease bonus payments were not counted twice in computing percentage depletion.[34] The IRS has held that if the lessee who receives a lease bonus cannot take the percentage depletion deduction on the bonus, the operator who pays the bonus must still exclude the income that is allocable to the bonus.[35] Arguably, based on the original purpose of the "bonus exclusion rule," the rule should not be applied if the recipient of the bonus is not entitled to percentage depletion on the lease bonus. Therefore, since lease bonuses recognized as income after August 16, 1986, no longer qualify for percentage depletion, it appears to be inappropriate to continue to follow the "bonus exclusion rule" on these bonuses. It is hoped that this apparent inconsistency will be rectified by a technical correction or otherwise modified by an administrative pronouncement from the Treasury.

If Lessee E retains a fraction of the working interest instead of an overriding royalty so that the assignment is a sale rather than a leasing transaction, Operator A will not be required to exclude any portion of the consideration paid to Lessee E from gross income in computing percentage depletion.

30. Palmer v. Bender, 287 U.S. 551 (1933), 11 AFTR 1106, 3 USTC 1026; Rev. Rul. 69-352, 1969-1 C.B. 34; Cox v. U.S., 497 F.2d 348 (4th Cir. 1974), 34 AFTR2d 74-5007, 74-1 USTC 9461; Robert G. O'Connor, 78 T.C. 1 (1982); Rev. Rul. 82-221, 1982-2 C.B. 113.
31. Reg. Sec. 1.612-3(a); Sunray Oil Co. v. Comm'r, 147 F.2d 962 (10th Cir. 1945), 33 AFTR 763, 45-1 USTC 9181.
32. I.R.C. Sec. 613A(d)(5).
33. Reg. Sec. 1.612-3(a)(3); Sunray Oil Co.
34. Quintana Petroleum Co. v. Comm'r, 143 F.2d 588 (5th Cir. 1944), 32 AFTR 1031, 44-2 USTC 9380; Helvering v. Twin Bell Oil Syndicate, 293 U.S. 312 (1934), 14 AFTR 712, 35-1 USTC 9014; Rev. Rul. 81-266, 1981-2 C.B. 139.
35. Rev. Rul. 81-266, 1981-2 C.B. 139; Murphy Oil Corp. v. U.S., 337 F.2d 677 (8th Cir. 1964), 14 AFTR2d 5835, 64-2 USTC 9810.

Case 5
Exploratory Work Resulting in Acquisition of Leases

> **C Company conducts reconnaissance work over an area of 20,000 acres on which it has acquired shooting rights by making a $6,000 payment to Lessor R. The preliminary survey, which costs $16,000, discloses two geographically separate anomalies or areas of interest on which detailed seismograph surveys are conducted. The cost of the seismograph work on the area of interest in the northeast corner is $25,000 and on the area of interest in the south half is $40,000. On the basis of the geological and geophysical data, C Company acquires a commercial lease on 5,000 acres in the south area of interest for a $100,000 bonus.**

The Internal Revenue Service (IRS) will require C Company to allocate all costs relating to the preliminary survey or reconnaissance work equally between the areas of interest that are developed as a result of this work. The allocation of the preliminary survey costs usually is made without regard to the size or probable importance of the several areas of interest. If the preliminary survey discloses only one area of interest on a tract of land, all costs must be allocated to the cost of that one area.[36] When the preliminary survey is conducted on widely separated tracts of land, each separate tract of land should be considered a separate project for accumulating costs.

An *area of interest* has been defined as a separable, noncontiguous portion of the original project area in which there has been identified a specific geological feature having sufficient mineral-producing potential to merit further exploration.[37] Whether more than one area of interest exists sometimes may be determined by rule of thumb. For example, areas that are geographically separated by one mile or more and on which shooting is accomplished may be presumed to be different areas of interest. In addition, if shooting is performed on acreage that has not been shot in the last six months, a new area of interest might be allowed. Rules of thumb, however, should not supplant sound geological and geophysical determinations if available.

C Company should allocate the $16,000 preliminary survey costs equally between the areas of interest disclosed—$8,000 to the area of interest in the northeast corner and $8,000 to the area of interest in the south half. The cost of the shooting permit should be similarly allocated. Until a lease is acquired in one or both of these areas, it appears that the IRS will recognize that the capitalized geological and geophysical costs represent an asset separate and apart from the leasehold.

The detailed survey of the area of interest in the northeast corner does not disclose the existence of any structure that is likely to be productive. If further interest in this area is abandoned, the IRS will permit the deduction as a loss of the cost of the survey of this area of interest.[38] A loss of $36,000 on this area is represented by the sum of the allocated cost of the permit ($3,000), the preliminary work ($8,000) and the cost of the detailed geophysical survey ($25,000). The requirement that these items be capitalized when incurred is predicated on the theory that they constitute exploration costs that are not included within the option either to capitalize or expense the cost of drilling oil and gas wells.[39] The cost of exploratory work that is not included within the option must be deducted as a loss rather than as a current expense.

36. Rev. Rul. 77-188, 1977-1 C.B. 76; Rev. Rul. 83-105, 1983-2 C.B. 51.
37. *Ibid.*
38. *Ibid.*
39. Louisiana Land and Exploration Co., 7 T.C. 507 (1946); Rev. Rul. 80-342, 1980-2 C.B. 99; Rev. Rul. 77-188, 1977-1 C.B. 76.

Negative conclusions reached as a result of the work alone will not be sufficient basis to recognize a loss. It is important that the taxpayer also abandon the respective areas as potential sources of mineral production before the loss can be claimed.[40] This abandonment intent must be clearly evident before the loss will be allowed.[41] Of course, the immediate forfeiture or release of the permit will ensure the allowance of the loss.[42]

When geological and geophysical exploration is conducted offshore, the IRS usually will require capitalization of the costs to areas of interest disclosed by reconnaissance work if there is an indication that the taxpayer plans to bid on any leases or to request that government lands be put up for bids. If any offshore leases are acquired, the previously incurred geological and geophysical costs attributable to the area of interest containing those leases become a part of the leases' cost. If the taxpayer's bid is unsuccessful and no further attempts to acquire properties are contemplated, the geological and geophysical costs should be deducted.[43] If the leases are not offered for sale, the taxpayer cannot deduct costs attributable to that area until there is an identifiable event that justifies the loss. The IRS has indicated that a lease sale, a reasonable indication that the area will not become available for leasing or any event that establishes the worthlessness of the area will be an event that justifies the loss. If no identifiable event occurs, the taxpayer may deduct these costs after 10 years (five years for onshore leases).[44]

On the basis of the information obtained from the exploration of the area of interest in the south half, C Company acquires a lease on 5,000 acres. The cost of the mineral rights obtained through this lease will be the sum of: (1) one-half the cost of the shooting permit—$3,000; (2) one-half the cost of the preliminary survey—$8,000; (3) costs of detailed seismograph work—$40,000 and (4) the lease bonus—$100,000.

C Company has made an investment of $151,000 in the oil or gas to be produced from the lease and may deduct that cost only through the allowance for depletion or as a loss on account of worthlessness, as an abandonment loss or as tax basis upon a sale or other disposition.[45]

Some companies use the shot-point, unit-cost method to identify seismograph survey costs with specific projects or areas of interest. It is customary practice for exploration crews to make their seismograph tests for oil-producing formations at various points throughout the testing areas according to a pre-established plan. Each location where a test is made is referred to as a *shot point.* Under this method, the unit cost per shot point is determined and is multiplied by the number of shot points made in the specific project area or area of interest with respect to which geophysical costs are required to be capitalized. This method of allocation also may be used when a company employs an independent exploration company to conduct its seismograph surveys.

The allocation of geological and geophysical costs to specific land or surface areas often is difficult and arbitrary. Therefore, any reasonable method that is consistently applied should meet with IRS's approval.

40. Rev. Rul. 83-105, 1983-2 C.B. 51. *But see also* Rev. Rul. 54-581, 1954-2 C.B. 112; A. J. Industries v. U.S., 503 F.2d 660 (9th Cir. 1974), 34 AFTR2d 74-5932, 74-2 USTC 9710; Paul Brountas, 73 T.C. 491 (1979); Brountas v. Comm'r, 692 F.2d 152 (1st Cir. 1982), 50 AFTR2d 82-5900, 82-2 USTC 9626; Gulf Oil Corp., 87 T.C. 135 (1986).
41. *Ibid.*
42. Southern Trading Co., T.C. Memo Dec. (Nov. 9, 1956).
43. Vincent T. Larsen, 66 T.C. 478 (1976), (A) 1977-1 C.B. 1; Rev. Rul. 77-188, 1977-1 C.B. 76; Rev. Rul. 83-105, 1983-2 C.B. 51.
44. Rev. Rul. 83-105, 1983-2 C.B. 51.
45. Schermerhorn Oil Corp., 46 B.T.A. 151 (1942); Rev. Rul. 77-188, 1977-1 C.B. 76; Rev. Rul. 80-342, 1980-2 C.B. 99.

Had C Company paid $6,000 to Lessor R for an option to acquire leases rather than for a mere permit to explore, C Company probably would not be permitted to allocate this cost to the several areas of interest on a single contiguous tract of land, as is done with shooting permit costs, but would be required to add the full amount to the cost of any leases taken. *(See Cases 1 and 3 for a more complete discussion of options to acquire leases.)*

With respect to Lessor R, the $6,000 received for the permit to explore is ordinary income in the year of receipt; it is not subject to depletion because it is not in the nature of advance royalties and was not received for any right to produce minerals underlying the property.[46] Had the $6,000 payment been for a permit to explore, coupled with an option to acquire acreage, the income may have been considered in the nature of advance royalties and subject to the allowance for depletion. However, advance royalties no longer qualify for percentage depletion for amounts received or accrued after August 16, 1986.[47] Therefore, only cost depletion will be allowed for advance royalty income recognized after this date. *(See Case 1. See also Cases 98 and 127 for a discussion of the allowance of depletion on those payments and the circumstances under which the lessor must restore to his taxable income the amount of percentage or cost depletion claimed on those payments.)*

Case 6
Exploratory Work on Existing Leases

> **Operator A holds several leases, each constituting a separate unit of property, covering an aggregate of 15,000 acres in an area that has not been tested previously for the presence of minerals. Operator A engages an exploration company to explore the area for probable oil-bearing formations before any rental payments become due. Operator A pays $30,000 for this exploratory work. As a result of studies made, Operator A forfeits the leases on 10,000 acres and, by paying the delay rentals, retains the leases on 5,000 acres.**

If the project contains only one area of interest, the Internal Revenue Service (IRS) will hold that the $30,000 paid for geological and geophysical work must be capitalized by Operator A and added to the cost of the leases retained.[48] The costs previously incurred for the leases on the 10,000 acres, however, may be claimed as a tax deduction in the year the leases are forfeited.

If the exploration company conducts preliminary reconnaissance on the entire acreage (project area) and the work discloses two or more anomalies or areas of interest, the cost of that preliminary work should be divided equally among the several areas of interest disclosed by the survey. *(See Case 5.)* The costs of subsequent detailed surveys should be capitalized as costs of the respective areas of interest. If these detailed surveys indicate that no oil structure exists in one or more of the selected areas of interest, the allocated portion of the preliminary survey and the cost of the subsequent detailed surveys may be written off as a loss in the year the respective areas are abandoned as potential sources of mineral production.[49] Generally, if the costs are claimed as deductions before the year in which title to the leases in the area is forfeited or otherwise released, Operator A would have difficulty proving that he actually

46. Special Ruling, June 18, 1951, 1982 Stand. Fed. Tax Rep. (CCH), Para. 668.614; Wasson v. U.S., 250 F.2d 826 (5th Cir. 1958), 1 AFTR2d 564, 58-1 USTC 9176.
47. I.R.C. Sec. 613A(d)(5).
48. Schermerhorn Oil Corp., 46 B.T.A. 151 (1942); Rev. Rul. 77-188, 1977-1 C.B. 76; Rev. Rul. 83-105, 1983-2 C.B. 51.
49. Rev. Rul. 77-188, 1977-1 C.B. 76; Rev. Rul. 83-105, 1983-2 C.B. 51.

incurred the loss in the earlier year.[50] *(See Case 5 and Case 159.)* However, the IRS has ruled that survey costs attributable to areas of interest that have no potential for producing oil or gas can be deducted prior to abandonment of the lease to which the loss related, provided the taxpayer's intent was to abandon all efforts relating to the area surveyed and the retention of the lease was not attributable to any information obtained from the surveys.[51]

It is very important that the intent to abandon be clearly documented in the taxpayer's records. Based on this ruling, it appears that the IRS now recognizes that geological and geophysical costs represent an asset separate and apart from the leasehold.

The deduction of costs of surveys attributable to an area of interest prior to abandonment of a lease may not be allowed even if separate horizontal strata or sands underlying a single offshore lease are treated as separate areas of interest. The Tax Court ruled that no abandonment deduction was allowed where the taxpayer's only support for its intention to abandon the separate horizontal strata was internal records supporting the decision to abandon.[52] The court was influenced by the fact that the taxpayer paid delay rentals on the lease and retained the right to drill and explore on all portions of the lease. Additionally, since the court reached its conclusion primarily based on what it viewed as inadequate support for an abandonment loss, it did not specifically address the validity of the taxpayer's treatment of separate horizontal strata as separate properties. Arguably, since the IRS apparently recognizes that geological and geophysical costs represent an asset separate and apart from the leasehold,[53] the reasoning of this case should not be applied to these types of costs.

The IRS treats expenditures for geological and geophysical surveys or studies as capital expenditures. Exploratory work of this nature does not come within the option provided by the Internal Revenue Code to expense the costs of drilling wells.[54] If any of the survey costs may be allocated properly to the cost of locating a well site, however, that portion of the costs is properly deductible within the option. *(See Case 7.)*

The capitalization of expenditures for geological and geophysical work as part of the cost of the minerals is required only when the information obtained serves as a basis for a decision to acquire or retain those properties[55] or as a guide for further exploration or development of the properties.[56] The expenditures, when capitalized, are added to the costs of the leases to which they relate. If more than one lease or mineral property is involved, the costs attributed to the area of interest are allocated to the several mineral property units in proportion to their size or acreage.[57]

When geological and geophysical work is performed on leases that are held by production from existing wells, the purpose of the work obviously is not to determine whether to retain or acquire the property. Nevertheless, if the information is useful in determining the nature and extent of further exploration or development of the property, the expenses for the geological and geophysical work should be capitalized as additional costs of the lease.[58]

---

50. A. J. Industries v. U.S., 503 F.2d 660 (9th Cir. 1974), 34 AFTR2d 74-5932, 74-2 USTC 9710; Paul Brountas, 73 T.C. 491 (1979); Brountas v. Comm'r, 692 F.2d 152 (1st Cir. 1982), 50 AFTR2d 82-5900, 82-2 USTC 9626; Gulf Oil Corp., 87 T.C. 135 (1986).
51. Rev. Rul. 83-105, 1983-2 C.B. 51.
52. Gulf Oil Corp., 87 T.C. 135 (1986).
53. Rev. Rul. 83-105, 1983-2 C.B. 51.
54. I.R.C. Sec. 263(c).
55. American Smelting and Ref. Co.-Consol. v. U.S., 423 F.2d 277 (Ct. Cl. 1970), 25 AFTR2d 70-853, 70-1 USTC 9287. *But see also* Rev. Rul. 77-187, 1977-1 C.B. 50; Rev. Rul. 77-188, 1977-1 C.B. 76.
56. Louisiana Land and Exploration Co., 7 T.C. 507 (1946).
57. Rev. Rul. 77-188, 1977-1 C.B. 76.
58. Louisiana Land and Exploration Co.

If the work is performed in an area different from the producing horizon, the costs should be allocated to that area of interest and should be claimed as a loss in the year the decision is made to abandon all efforts relating to that area.

If the information is negative and leads to a decision to abandon further development of the lease, it seems to be reasonable for Operator A to deduct the cost of the geological and geophysical work as an expense in the year paid or incurred. Under these circumstances, the work does not result in any benefits extending substantially beyond the end of the year in which the work is completed, and, accordingly, does not appear to be an improvement or betterment that would qualify as a capital expenditure.[59]

Except when the work is to locate well sites and thus may be classified as intangible drilling costs *(see Case 7)*, the purpose of geological and geophysical work does not determine its ultimate tax treatment. The results of the work, however, will serve either as evidence of a worthless or abandoned capital expenditure or as evidence of an additional investment in the mineral property.

Case 7
Exploratory Work in Locating Well Site

> **Operator A holds leases on 1,000 acres. He has determined through seismograph shooting that there is a likelihood of oil-bearing structures and decides to drill a well to test the formations. He employs a firm of geologists to recommend the location of the initial test well and pays $1,500 for its services.**

Geological costs incurred in connection with the determination of a well location or the supervision of a well are classified as intangible drilling and development costs (IDC).[60] As such, they are subject to the option to be deducted as expenses in the year paid or incurred or to be capitalized as depletable basis.

Expenditures for geological and geophysical work generally are considered to be capital in nature and only those expenditures specifically included in the provisions of the regulations are deductible as expenses. The regulations include as IDC only those geological and geophysical costs connected with the drilling of a particular well or confined to a restricted area that has been tentatively singled out for drilling.[61] The option to deduct as IDC should apply only to costs for preparation for drilling of specific wells after drilling has at least tentatively been decided upon. Therefore, preliminary reconnaissance and detailed surveys probably do not qualify for treatment as IDC.[62] *(See Case 6.)*

The above distinction was illustrated in a District Court Case[63] where a taxpayer treated geological and geophysical costs used for the purpose of locating optimum drill sites as IDC. In this case, prospects had been acquired with the intention to drill one or more wells on structures already known to exist. The taxpayer contended that these costs qualified as IDC, even though in one case no well was ever drilled because no optimal drill site was ever located. The IRS argued that these costs should be treated as IDC only if their sole purpose was to locate the *exact spot* to drill a specific well. The court allowed the IDC deductions since the geological and geophysical costs

59. Louisiana Land and Exploration Co.
60. Reg. Sec. 1.612-4(a).
61. Louisiana Land and Exploration Co., 7 T.C. 507 (1946).
62. *Ibid.*
63. True v. U.S., 603 F. Supp. 1370 (D.C. Wyo. 1985), 56 AFTR2d 85-6208, 86-1 USTC 9193.

incurred related to the drilling of particular wells on restricted areas that had tentatively been singled out for drilling. Therefore, actual drilling may not be necessary to assure these costs can be treated as IDC as long as the facts and circumstances support that a tentative decision to drill had been made prior to performing the geological and geophysical work.

The regulations granting an election to treat as expenses all IDC incurred in the drilling of oil or gas wells and the preparation of those wells for production are discussed in Section II.

Case 8
Cost of Geological and Geophysical Department of Oil Company With Diversified Operations

> **C Company maintains land, scouting, geological and geophysical departments as part of its permanent organization, to locate properties suitable for acquisition. The number and extent of properties leased vary from year to year. A substantial portion of the departmental expenditures represents overhead and supervisory costs of main office personnel. C Company wants to know if it is necessary to allocate overhead and supervisory costs of main office personnel to leases acquired.**

Overhead and supervisory costs are of a recurring nature and generally bear little relation to the intensity of exploratory activities of a company. These expenditures usually remain fairly constant from year to year, even though the leasing and exploratory program expands or contracts.

Expenditures described above should be charged to expense, and only those incurred in connection with actual field operations, including salaries, expenses and supplies of the geological and geophysical field crews, should be screened for possible capitalization. Expenditures that are not directly attributed to specific properties held or acquired should represent costs of a general nature chargeable to expense. Although there is a lack of administrative or judicial guidance dealing with the proper treatment of the expenditures, the oil and gas industry appears to use the method discussed above predominantly.

In addition, the concept of capitalizing the costs of maintaining geological and land departments and the salaries of officers and employees to the extent their efforts result in the acquisition of new properties, while expensing other portions of these costs as overhead applicable to the general business of producing oil and gas, was recognized as an appropriate accounting method by the Internal Revenue Service (IRS) in early pronouncements dealing with the computation of net income for depletion purposes.[64] These rulings occurred prior to the time when formal rules for capitalizing geological and geophysical costs were adopted. As a result, while these pronouncements have never been revoked, the IRS no longer considers these rulings to be determinative with respect to future transactions.[65] However, unless all the geological and geophysical work, including interpretation of the data obtained and recommendation for further action, is performed by an outside contractor or exploration company, the IRS may still require capitalization of a reasonable portion of overhead or general expenses of the department or division performing the service.

---

64. G.C.M. 22689; *superceded by* G.C.M. 22956.
65. Rev. Rul. 68-661, 1968-2 C.B. 607.

A portion of the overhead and supervisory costs of main office personnel may be required to be allocated to the drilling of oil and gas wells and be subject to the uniform cost-capitalization rules. *(See Case 187 for a discussion of which costs must be capitalized under the uniform cost-capitalization rules.)*

Case 9
Delay Rentals

> **Since December 1, 1986, Operator A has held a 2,400-acre lease on which no wells have been drilled. The terms of the lease require the payment of $5 per acre to the lessor on each anniversary date of the lease (December 1), unless drilling operations are in progress on the anniversary date or either oil or gas is being produced in commercial quantities from the lease.**

These payments are termed *delay rentals*, which are defined as sums paid under the terms of an oil or gas lease for the privilege of deferring development of the property and which could have been avoided by abandonment of the lease, commencement of development operations or obtaining production. These expenditures are not in payment for oil and gas to be produced but rather are paid for additional time in which to explore or develop the lease.[66] They are not made for the purpose of increasing the value of the lease.[67] Consequently, delay rentals are treated as rents and may be deducted as an expense by the payor (lessee).[68]

Current law requires certain regular corporations, certain partnerships with corporate partners and all tax shelters (defined below) to report on an accrual basis.[69] However, the above taxpayers can elect to continue to use the cash method for mineral-leasing transactions entered into on or prior to September 25, 1985.[70] Also, corporations and partnerships with average annual gross receipts of less than $5 million in tax years beginning after 1985 can continue to report on a cash basis as long as they are not tax shelters (defined below).[71]

Taxpayers that now must report on the accrual basis[72] are allowed a deduction for items only when economic performance occurs with respect to the item giving rise to the deduction. Economic performance occurs with respect to rental of property as the rental period expires (i.e., day by day in the case of an annual rental period).[73]

For accrual-basis taxpayers that are not tax shelters (defined below), economic performance will be deemed to occur in a tax year if the item meets the special requirements for the recurring-item exception.[74] An item is a recurring item for this purpose if all the following conditions exist:

☐ The "all-events" test is met without regard to the economic performance rules.

☐ Economic performance occurs within the shorter of a reasonable period or 8½ months after yearend.

---

66. Reg. Sec. 1.612-3(c)(1); Rev. Rul. 80-49, 1980-1 C.B. 127.
67. J. T. Sneed, Jr., 33 B.T.A. 478 (1935), (A) XV-1 C.B. 21 (1935).
68. I.R.C. Sec. 162(a)(3); Reg. Sec. 1.612-3(c)(2).
69. I.R.C. Sec. 448(a).
70. P.L. 99-514 (Tax Reform Act of 1986), Sec. 801(d)(2).
71. I.R.C. Sec. 448(b)(3).
72. I.R.C. Sec. 461(h).
73. I.R.C. Sec. 461(h)(2)(A)(iii).
74. I.R.C. Sec. 461(h)(3).

☐ The item is recurring, and the taxpayer consistently treats other similar items as incurred in the tax year when the "all-events" test is met.

☐ Either the item is not material or treating it as incurred provides a better matching with income.

The Committee Reports state that in determining whether an item is recurring in nature and consistently reported by the taxpayer, consideration should be given to the frequency that the item and similar items are incurred (or are expected to be incurred) and the manner in which these items have been reported for federal income tax purposes. This exception is intended to apply to new businesses as well as items that do not occur every year.[75] Thus, it appears that delay rentals generally should qualify as recurring items.

Factors to consider in determining whether an item is material include the size of the item both in the absolute and in relation to the taxpayer's other income and expenses, and whether the item is considered material for financial statement purposes. If it is treated as material for financial statements, it will be considered material for tax purposes. However, if an item is not considered material for financial statement purposes, it still can be material for tax purposes. In determining materiality, the Committee Reports state that items are to be viewed in relation to the activity to which they relate. Thus, an item may not be material when considered with the combined activities of the taxpayer (i.e., combined or consolidated financial statements) but may be material to the separate activity to which it relates (i.e., separate company). Further, to determine whether an item in a partnership or other passthrough entity is material, the test must be made at the entity level and the level to which the item ultimately passes (i.e., partner, S corporation shareholder, etc.). These standards of materiality are solely for purposes of applying the recurring-item exception and are not intended for other purposes of the Internal Revenue Code (the Code).[76] In most cases, delay rentals should be immaterial and, therefore, qualify for treatment as a recurring item.

If the delay rental is a material item, it still could qualify for recurring-item treatment if deducting it currently would result in a better match with the income to which it relates. The Committee Reports state that in determining whether the accrual of an item in a particular year would result in a better matching with income, generally accepted accounting principles will be important guidelines but will not necessarily be definitive.[77] Given these parameters, it is not likely that delay rentals will result in a better matching against income if accrued and deducted prior to the period to which they relate.[78]

Assume Operator A uses the accrual method of accounting and the delay rentals are considered recurring items. Of Operator A's $12,000 payment on December 1, 1987, $9,500 may be deducted in 1987 assuming he is a nontax-shelter taxpayer. The remaining $2,500 attributable to the period September 16, 1988, through November 30, 1988, will be allowed as a deduction in 1988.

For taxpayers considered tax shelters (defined below), the law is more restrictive. These taxpayers may claim a deduction for delay rentals only to the extent economic

75. House Report No. 98-861, 1984-3 C.B. Vol. 2 127.
76. *Ibid.*
77. *Ibid.*
78. General Explanation of the Tax Reform Act of 1984, prepared by the Staff of the Joint Committee on Taxation, p. 264.

performance occurs before yearend.[79] Unlike other accrual-basis taxpayers, the exception for recurring items is not available to a tax-shelter taxpayer.[80] However, tax shelters may elect to continue to use the cash-basis rules (see discussion below) that applied under prior law for leases entered into before September 25, 1985.[81]

The law defines the term *tax shelter* to include: (1) any enterprise (other than a C corporation) that has made an offering required to be registered with any federal or state securities regulating agency; (2) any partnership or other entity (other than a corporation that is not an S corporation) that allocates more than 35% of its losses during the tax year to limited partners or to other persons that did not actively participate in the entity's management or (3) an entity, plan or arrangement if its principal purpose is avoidance or evasion of federal income tax.[82]

Assume Taxpayer A is a taxpayer that meets the definition of a *tax shelter*. Of Taxpayer A's $12,000 payment on December 1, 1987, $1,000 will be deductible in 1987. The remaining $11,000 will be deductible in 1988.

For tax years beginning prior to December 31, 1986, tax shelters were allowed to report on a cash basis. These cash-basis tax shelters could claim a deduction for delay rentals only to the extent economic performance occurred before yearend or within 90 days thereafter.[83] The exception for recurring items was not available for these cash-basis tax shelters. The deduction was further limited to the taxpayers' *cash basis* in the activity.[84]

Assume Taxpayer A is a cash-basis taxpayer that meets the definition of a tax shelter. If Taxpayer A made a payment of $12,000 on December 1, 1986, he would be entitled to deduct $4,000 in 1986. In 1987, Taxpayer A will be required to change to the accrual basis and will not be allowed to use the recurring-item exception. No regulations or other pronouncements have been released that clarify how this change in accounting method should be accomplished for cash-basis tax shelters. It appears that $11,000 of the payment made in 1986 will be deductible in 1987 as economic performance occurs. Due to the change in accounting method, the duplication of $3,000 of deductions in both 1986 and 1987 is required to be restored to income over a period not to exceed four years.

Cash-basis taxpayers not considered tax shelters should deduct delay rentals in the year those rentals are paid, assuming a consistent practice of doing so has been established. Such a practice has been upheld in a case involving minimum royalty payments.[85] However, prepayments of delay rentals that are not due until a later tax year may not be deductible in the year paid unless a substantial business purpose is illustrated.[86] Thus, in this case, since Taxpayer A is required to pay the delay rental on December 1, 1987, he should deduct the full $12,000 in 1987, assuming he is a nontax-shelter, cash-basis taxpayer.

Another type of delay rental is the "shut-in" payment, or "shut-in" royalty, which is made to a lessor to defer production from a lease after a well has been drilled and found to be productive. If the payments are not "in contemplation of production" (i.e., not recoverable from future production) or if failure to make them results in a

79. I.R.C. Sec. 461(i)(1).
80. *Ibid.*
81. P.L. 99-514 (Tax Reform Act of 1986), Sec. 801(d)(2); I.R.C. Sec. 461(i) (*prior to amendment by the Tax Reform Act of 1986*).
82. I.R.C. Sec. 461(i)(3).
83. I.R.C. Sec. 461(i)(1) (*prior to amendment by the Tax Reform Act of 1986*); I.R.C. Sec. 461(i)(2) (*prior to amendment by the Tax Reform Act of 1986*).
84. I.R.C. Sec. 461(i)(2)(B) (*prior to amendment by the Tax Reform Act of 1986*).
85. Zaninovich v. Comm'r, 616 F.2d 429 (9th Cir. 1980), 45 AFTR2d 80-1442, 80-1 USTC 9342.
86. Jack J. Grynberg, 83 T.C. 255 (1984).

termination or forfeiture of the lease, they are in the nature of rental payments and may be deducted by the payor.[87] *(See Case 13.)*

The purpose of a payment and the rights obtained must be examined to determine whether the payment is a delay rental, a royalty or a lease bonus. If the payment is made solely for additional time in which to explore or develop the lease, it is a delay rental.[88] A payment that continues a lease in force for more than one year probably will be treated as a bonus, and a payment that may be avoided by abandonment of the lease has been held to be a delay rental.[89] Payments that are recoverable out of future production generally are in the nature of advance royalties.

In some situations, the original lessee will sublease the working interest to another party under a sublease agreement requiring the sublessee to pay the lessee a rental payment. In that situation, the sublessee will be entitled to a deduction for the delay rentals paid if the contract between the lessee and the sublessee provides that payment is for the privilege of retaining the lease without developing the property in accord with usual rental provisions.[90]

The Code grants taxpayers an election to capitalize carrying charges on property, whether real or personal.[91] In the absence of an election, those carrying charges represent allowable business expenses. The Internal Revenue Service has held that delay rentals are in the nature of carrying charges and, therefore, are subject to the election.[92] Delay rentals are paid to carry unimproved and unproductive real estate; therefore, each year a new election may be exercised as to each lease or unit of property no matter how delay rentals for the same property were treated for a prior year.[93] The election by an accrual-basis taxpayer to capitalize delay rentals may be made for the portion of the rental applicable to the tax year for which the election is made, even though the same treatment is not applied to the portion of the same rental that is applicable to another tax year.[94]

Delay rentals are ordinary income to the recipient and are not subject to the allowance for depletion because they are not received for current or future production.[95] They also have been held to constitute rents for purposes of the definitions of personal holding company income[96] and to constitute passive investment income for S corporations.[97] *(See Case 169 for a discussion of the taxation of S corporations.)*

Case 10
Advance Royalties Recoverable from Production

> Operator A acquires an oil and gas lease from Lessor R, who retains a one-eighth royalty interest with the provision that the royalty payments shall in no case be less than $10,000 per year. Amounts paid in excess of one-eighth of production that are necessary to provide the annual minimum of $10,000 may be accumulated and applied in reduction of the

---

87. Johnson v. Phinney, 287 F.2d 544 (5th Cir. 1961), 7 AFTR2d 860, 61-1 USTC 9307.
88. Houston Farms Dev. Co. v. U.S., 132 F.2d 861 (5th Cir. 1943), 30 AFTR 698, 43-1 USTC 9254.
89. White Castle Lumber & Shingle Co. v. U.S., 481 F.2d 1274 (5th Cir. 1973), 32 AFTR2d 73-5549, 73-2 USTC 9590.
90. Jefferson Lake Sulphur Co. v. U.S., 236 F.2d 542 (5th Cir. 1956), 50 AFTR 39, 56-2 USTC 9875.
91. I.R.C. Sec. 266; Reg. Sec. 1.266-1(b)(1).
92. Reg. Sec. 1.612-3(c)(2).
93. Reg. Sec. 1.266-1(c)(2)(i); Rev. Rul. 55-118, 1955-1 C.B. 320.
94. Rev. Rul. 55-118, 1955-1 C.B. 320. *But see also* Zaninovich.
95. Reg. Sec. 1.612-3(c)(2).
96. Rev. Rul. 70-153, 1970-1 C.B. 139.
97. Opine Timber Co., 64 T.C. 700 (1975).

royalty payments in subsequent years. Royalty payments made to Lessor R are as follows:

Year	Royalties Applicable to Lessor R's One-Eighth of Current Production	Royalties Applicable to Minimum Payment Provision	Actual Payments
One	$ —	$ 10,000	$10,000
Two	4,000	6,000	10,000
Three	30,000	(16,000)	14,000

Operator A's payments to Lessor R are required by a minimum royalty provision in the lease; therefore, Operator A has an election with respect to the treatment of amounts paid in excess of Lessor R's one-eighth share of current production for which Operator A may be reimbursed out of subsequent production.[98] Operator A may claim the excess part of the payments as a deduction from gross income in the year the advance royalties are paid or accrued or in the year the mineral products for which the advance royalties were paid are sold. Although the above election is available, the deduction may also be limited under the economic performance rules. The determination of whether the economic performance rules apply must await future clarification and explanation of the statute.

For payments to be pursuant to a minimum royalty provision and, thus, subject to the election, the provision must require substantially uniform amounts to be paid at least annually over the life of the lease or for a minimum of 20 years in the absence of mineral production requiring greater payments. For these purposes, minimum royalty payments that are adjusted for inflation each year have been held to be "substantially uniform" and, thus, subject to the election.[99] Advance royalties that are not paid pursuant to such a minimum royalty are deductible only in the year the applicable mineral is sold.[100]

To be subject to the election, advance royalties also should be recoverable out of an interest that extends over the entire productive life of the property. In other words, the payments must be recoverable out of the lessor's royalty and not out of a production payment created to cover those payments. *(See Case 143.)*

If Operator A cannot avoid payment of the minimum royalty by forfeiture or reassignments of the lease, the Internal Revenue Service (IRS) may contend that all payments in excess of Lessor R's share of current production constitute a bonus regardless of whether those amounts are recoverable out of future production. *(See Case 12.)* Under this theory, the only payments coming under the election are amounts that are similar to delay rentals but recoverable from future production. *(See Case 13.)*

If Operator A elects to claim deductions equal to the actual payments to Lessor R in the year those amounts are paid or accrued, and Operator A is not subject to the economic performance rules, he will deduct the minimum royalties of $10,000 in years one and two, even though the royalty based on production in these years is less than the minimum payments. The deductibility of these payments does not depend on production but rather on the amounts determined to be paid or payable under the

98. Reg. Sec. 1.612-3(b)(3).
99. Rev. Rul. 81-299, 1981-2 C.B. 138.
100. Reg. Sec. 1.612-3(b)(3).

terms of the minimum royalty provision. In year three, Operator A will deduct the $14,000 paid to Lessor R.

If Operator A elects to deduct the royalties only as the applicable mineral product is produced and sold, he will deduct $4,000 in year two and $30,000 in year three.

The election Operator A exercises in his tax return for the first year in which he makes payments of this type will constitute an election binding for all subsequent years. Operator A will be considered to have made an election in accordance with the manner in which those items are treated in his tax return. If he fails to deduct those advance royalties in his tax return for the first year in which paid or accrued, he will be considered to have made a permanent election to have all those items treated as deductions in the year in which the applicable mineral product is sold.[101]

In 1983, the Tax Court addressed the deductibility of advance minimum royalties.[102] The court held that a valid minimum royalty provision requires that a substantially uniform amount of royalties be paid at least annually. The court did not comment on whether a minimum royalty provision "must" require annual payments in the literal sense or whether it merely "may" establish liability annually for amounts that are not contingent and that must be paid in all events. *(See Case 100 for a complete discussion of this case.)* In 1986, the Tax Court took a more restrictive view and held that the creation of a recourse liability does not satisfy the annual payment requirement.[103]

Complex rules related to the timing of deductions exist for certain accrual-basis taxpayers,[104] certain cash-basis taxpayers[105] and tax shelters.[106] Generally, an item will not be allowed as a deduction under these rules until economic performance has occurred. In addition, certain corporations, certain partnerships with corporate partners and all tax shelters will be required to report on an accrual basis.[107] However, the above taxpayers can elect to continue to report leases entered into prior to September 25, 1985, on a cash basis.[108] Also, corporations and partnerships with less than $5 million in average annual gross receipts for years after 1985 will continue to be allowed to report on a cash basis as long as they are not tax shelters.[109] *(See Case 9 for the definition of tax shelter for these purposes.)* Therefore, many more taxpayers will be subject to the economic performance rules.

For accrual-basis taxpayers, the "all-events" test will not be deemed met until economic performance has occurred unless the item qualifies for the recurring-item exception.[110] *(See Case 9 for a further discussion of the exception.)* For an item to be treated as a recurring item, all the following conditions must be met:

☐ The "all-events" test is met without regard to the economic performance rules.

☐ Economic performance occurs within the shorter of a reasonable period or 8½ months after yearend.

☐ The item is recurring, and the taxpayer consistently treats other similar items as incurred in the tax year when the "all-events" test is met.

101. Reg. Sec. 1.612-3(b)(3).
102. Samuel E. Wing, 81 T.C. 17 (1983).
103. Richard C. Capek, 86 T.C. 14 (1986).
104. I.R.C. Sec. 461(h).
105. I.R.C. Sec. 448(a).
106. I.R.C. Sec. 448(a)(3); I.R.C. Sec. 461(i)(1).
107. I.R.C. Sec. 448(a).
108. P.L. 99-514 (Tax Reform Act of 1986), Sec. 801(d)(2).
109. I.R.C. Sec. 448(b)(3).
110. I.R.C. Sec. 461(h)(3).

□ Either the item is not material or treating it as incurred provides a better matching with income.

The recurring-item exception is not allowed for tax shelters *(see Case 9 for the definition of* tax shelter *for these purposes)*.[111]

However, in addition to the recurring-item exception, the law provides that the economic performance rules will not apply to certain items, the time for deduction of which is determined under other sections of the Internal Revenue Code (the Code).[112] It is possible that the election to deduct advance royalties pursuant to a minimum royalty provision under current regulations[113] may qualify for this exception. This determination must await future clarification and explanation of the statute.

If it is ultimately determined that the election to deduct when accrued does qualify as one of the exceptions for deductions determined under other Code sections, the economic performance rules will have no impact on determining when an advance royalty is deductible by accrual-basis taxpayers. If not, accrual-basis taxpayers will be allowed a deduction only when economic performance occurs unless the recurring-item exception can be met.

For taxpayers that can continue to report on a cash basis, the rules relating to the timing of advance royalty payments are unchanged by the economic performance rules. Thus, the election to deduct as paid or when the mineral is produced still is available. For cash-basis taxpayers considered to be tax shelters and, thus, required to change to accrual-basis accounting in 1987, the election to deduct as paid has been, in effect, modified by changes in the law. Now economic performance is required since these taxpayers do not qualify for the recurring-item exception.[114]

In addition, tax shelters may elect to continue to follow the cash-basis rules that existed under prior law for leases entered into before September 25, 1985.[115] Under prior law for cash-basis taxpayers considered to be tax shelters, the election to deduct as paid was modified by the economic performance rules. Unlike the accrual-basis rules discussed above, the exception for deductions allowed under other Code provisions does not apply to a cash-basis tax-shelter taxpayer. Therefore, prior to 1987, a cash-basis, tax-shelter taxpayer deducted advance royalty payments in the tax year that economic performance occurred with one exception.[116] To the extent economic performance occurred within 90 days after yearend, the deduction was allowed in the preceding year. However, the deduction was limited to the taxpayer's *cash basis* in the activity.[117]

The law sets forth principles to determine when economic performance occurs.[118] For example, economic performance for use of property occurs as the property is used. Likewise, economic performance in connection with providing services occurs as the services are provided. Because the advance royalty is received in connection with a leasing transaction (i.e., use of property), it may be possible that economic performance will occur as the leased property is used (i.e., if annual payments are required, economic performance may occur day by day or month by month). If the advance royalty is not viewed as consideration for the use of the property, economic performance may occur as the mineral is produced and sold.

---

111. I.R.C. Sec. 461(i)(1).
112. I.R.C. Sec. 461(h)(5); House Report No. 98-861, 1984-3 C.B. Vol. 2 128.
113. Reg. Sec. 1.612-3(b)(3).
114. I.R.C. Sec. 461(i)(1).
115. P.L. 99-514 (Tax Reform Act of 1986), Sec. 801(d)(2).
116. I.R.C. Sec. 461(i)(1) *(prior to amendment by the Tax Reform Act of 1986)*.
117. I.R.C. Sec. 461(i)(2) *(prior to amendment by the Tax Reform Act of 1986)*.
118. I.R.C. Sec. 461(h)(2).

The full amount of each payment received by Lessor R is for minerals produced or to be produced. These amounts are subject to an allowance for depletion in the year of receipt (or in the year when payment becomes due if lessor R reports income on the accrual basis of accounting). However, it is not clear whether amounts received by Lessor R that are in excess of his one-eighth share of production will qualify for percentage depletion.[119] This determination must await future clarification and explanation of the statute. Amounts received under the $10,000 minimum requirement that do not qualify for percentage depletion continue to qualify for cost depletion. *(See Case 101 for a discussion of percentage depletion on minimum royalty income.)*

As under prior law, Operator A may be required to exclude from his depletable income all or a portion of the payments made under the minimum royalty provision that are depletable income to Lessor R.[120] Arguably, based on the original purpose of the "advance royalty exclusion rule," the rule should not be applied if the lessor is not entitled to percentage depletion on the lease bonus. *(See Case 101.)* Therefore, since advance royalties recognized as income after August 16, 1986, may no longer qualify for percentage depletion, it appears to be inappropriate to continue to follow the "advance royalty exclusion rule" on these bonuses. *(See Case 101.)* It is hoped that this apparent inconsistency will be rectified by a technical correction or otherwise modified by an administrative pronouncement from the Treasury. This exclusion by Operator A should be made in the respective years in which he deducts the minimum payments.[121] In a controversial 1979 ruling, the IRS held that this exclusion should be made in the years in which the applicable mineral products are produced or sold.[122] This ruling conflicts with the regulations[123] and should be clarified.

If the lease terminates before Operator A recovers all his advance royalty payments through production, Lessor R must restore to income in the year of termination any depletion deducted on the payments not recovered.[124] Although this depletion restoration rule is stated in the regulations, it is inconsistent with a similar rule relating to lease bonuses that requires restoration only if the lease terminates without any commercial production. *(See Case 127.)*

Case 11
Advance Payments Under a Take-or-Pay Gas Purchase Contract

Operator A owns an interest in several producing gas properties and enters into a take-or-pay gas purchase contract with B Company. Operator A agrees to sell or make available 40,000 MCF of gas per year at a price of $2 per MCF, and B Company agrees to take that gas or to pay for it. The contract is for 20 years, and B Company may take make-up gas in any year during each four-year period of the contract after it has taken the minimum 40,000 MCF in that year. The activity for the first four years of the contract is as follows:

119. I.R.C. Sec. 613A(d)(5).
120. Reg. Sec. 1.613-2(c)(5)(i); Reg. Sec. 1.612-3(c)(5)(ii).
121. Reg. Sec. 1.613-2(c)(5)(iii).
122. Rev. Rul. 79-386, 1979-2 C.B. 246.
123. Reg. Sec. 1.613-2(c)(5)(iii).
124. Reg. Sec. 1.612-3(b)(2).

Year	Payment for Gas	Value of Gas Taken	Make-up (Deficiency)
One	$ 80,000	$ 60,000	$(20,000)
Two	80,000	66,000	(14,000)
Three	80,000	87,000	7,000
Four	80,000	93,000	13,000
	$320,000	$306,000	$(14,000)

Provisions of the typical take-or-pay gas purchase contract strongly resemble the substance of a carved-out production payment. In 1986, the Tax Court confirmed that excess payments for gas not taken constitute carved-out production payments as long as the payments can be recovered only from future production from the properties and as long as the other requirements of the regulations for establishing that a production payment exists are met. The other criteria that must be met are: (1) the purchaser must have a right to a specified share of production; (2) the right to recoup amounts paid for gas not taken must have an expected economic life of shorter duration than the term of the contract; (3) the right to recoup must be an economic interest in the minerals in place and (4) the right to recoup must be limited by either a dollar amount, a quantum of material or a period of time.[125]

The case above overruled the previous Internal Revenue Service (IRS) position that rights acquired by the purchasing company from making excess payments under customary take-or-pay gas contracts represent a mere economic advantage derived from a contract to purchase the production. Because the IRS considered customary take-or-pay arrangements to constitute a mere economic advantage rather than an economic interest, the IRS argued that the excess amounts did not create a production payment and could not be treated as mortgage loans.[126] Accordingly, for contracts entered into after August 6, 1969, receipts attributable to gas not actually taken should qualify as a carved-out production payment and, thus, be treated as a mortgage loan for income tax purposes as long as the production payment requirements of the regulations are met.[127] *(See Case 135.)*

Under this approach, Operator A would not report amounts received in excess of the value of the gas delivered as taxable income. Instead, he would treat those amounts as a loan and would report income as make-up gas is taken and applied against the excess. Therefore, over the four-year period Operator A would report taxable income of $306,000 subject to the allowance for depletion. In years one and two, payments for gas in excess of the value of gas taken would be treated as loans. In years three and four, the value of gas taken in excess of the payments for gas would constitute repayments of the loans previously created. The amount of such payments treated as interest would be determined under the original-issue discount rules. If, at the expiration of the make-up period, all the gas paid for has not been taken, Operator A will have ordinary income from cancellation of debt equal to the outstanding principal balance of the loans.

If the excess receipts for gas can be refunded or recovered from sources other than production from the properties burdened by the contract, the receipts do not constitute carved-out production payments.[128] Therefore, payments received under this type of take-or-pay gas purchase contract would be includable in income in the year received,

125. H. J. Freede, 86 T.C. 340, (1986); Reg. Sec. 1.636-3(a)(1); Reg. Sec. 1.636-3(a)(2).
126. Rev. Rul. 80-48, 1980-1 C.B. 99; IRS Letter Ruling 8237001 (Technical Advice Memorandum).
127. I.R.C. Sec. 636; Reg. Sec. 1.636-3; Reg. Sec. 1.636-4.
128. Freede; Reg. Sec. 1.636-3(a)(1).

unless, under the method of accounting used by the taxpayer, those receipts are includable in a different year.[129] For example, an accrual-basis taxpayer could be required to include in income any deficiency payment to which he is entitled at the end of a tax year, but which has not been received.[130] Because Operator A receives the amounts under a claim-of-right, he must report each $80,000 in the year received as taxable income subject to the allowance for depletion. The application of the claim-of-right doctrine to those payments received in these years is based on long-established case law.[131]

If receipts for gas not taken are treated as taxable income under the claim-of-right doctrine, eligibility for percentage depletion with respect to those receipts must be determined. Income recognized for amounts received without regard to production no longer qualifies for percentage depletion if it has been accrued or received after August 16, 1986.[132] *(See Case 98 for a discussion of depletion on income received in advance of production.)*

Under the claim-of-right doctrine, the $80,000 of income should be allocated to the properties that, according to the best estimates at the end of the year, will produce the gas necessary to satisfy the advance payment. If gas is not taken during the make-up period, the IRS may contend that Operator A should restore to income any percentage depletion taken for income recognized prior to August 17, 1986, attributable to that gas.[133] An alternate interpretation is that Operator A should not be required to restore any depletion to income if any gas is sold under the contract because he has received income from the extraction of gas that was actually produced and sold.[134]

If the excess receipts do not qualify as proceeds from a carved-out production payment, they appear to be subject to the limited option available to accrual-basis taxpayers to treat certain advance payments as deferred income in the year received.[135] The option could allow deferral until the last day of the second tax year following the year the payment is received.[136] *(See Case 99.)*

B Company will be required to charge the gas paid for but not taken either to a deferred gas purchase account or to a loan account, as the case may be. As the deficiency is made up in later years, the costs applicable to the make-up gas will be credited to the deferred gas purchase account or to the loan account and charged to purchases. If the gas is not taken within the four-year period and the right to the make-up gas is not assigned, the amount paid for that gas should be deducted as an ordinary loss or a bad debt for the year in which it can be determined that the gas will never be taken and the amount paid will not be refunded.[137]

Case 12
Minimum Royalty Not Recoverable from Production — Liability Certain

> Operator A acquires from Lessor R an oil and gas lease that has a primary term of five years. Lessor R retains a one-eighth royalty interest. The lease agreement provides that the royalty payments shall in no case

129. Rev. Rul. 80-48, 1980-1 C.B. 99.
130. Rev. Rul. 84-31, 1984-1 C.B. 127.
131. North American Oil Consol. v. Burnet, 286 U.S. 417 (1932), 11 AFTR 16, 3 USTC 943.
132. I.R.C. Sec. 613A(d)(5).
133. Reg. Sec. 1.612-3(b)(2).
134. Reg. Sec. 1.612-3(a)(2).
135. Reg. Sec. 1.451-5; IRS Letter Ruling 8237001 (Technical Advice Memorandum).
136. Reg. Sec. 1.451-5(c)(1)(i).
137. Rev. Rul. 66-64, 1966-1 C.B. 97; I.R.C. Sec.166.

be less than $10,000 per year for the primary term of the lease and must be paid even if there is no production from the lease. The payments must be made to Lessor R for five years and may not be avoided by forfeiture of the lease prior to the expiration of the primary term. Amounts paid by Operator A in excess of the amounts attributable to the sale of Lessor R's one-eighth share of current production may not be applied in reduction of the royalty payments in future years.

Any payment to Lessor R that represents his one-eighth of production will constitute a royalty and should be excluded from Operator A's income. Further, if the $10,000 minimum payment exceeds Lessor R's one-eighth share of production, that payment possibly may be treated as a royalty to the extent it does not exceed the total gross income from the property.[138] Any portion of the minimum payment that exceeds the total gross income from the property will represent a lease bonus and not an ordinary royalty because it will not represent a share of actual production nor will it be recoverable from subsequent production. That excess will not be a delay rental because it is not made to secure delay in development of the property and it cannot be avoided by forfeiture of the lease.[139] *(See Case 9.)*

Operator A should capitalize that portion of any annual payment that exceeds the total gross income from the property because it constitutes a lease bonus, even though the payments are made on an installment basis.[140] This treatment is required because the liability for this excess payment may not be avoided by forfeiting the lease prior to the expiration of its primary term and is payable regardless of exploration and development.

Assuming the property was not proven on the date he acquired it, Lessor R may be entitled to percentage depletion on the payments he receives but only to the extent that these amounts do not exceed the total gross income from the property.[141] Amounts in excess of the total gross income from the property are payable without regard to production from the property and represent a lease bonus which no longer qualifies for percentage depletion.[142] Therefore, only cost depletion will be allowed for the excess. Lease bonus income qualified for percentage depletion under prior law, which applies to amounts accrued or received prior to August 17, 1986.[143] *(See Cases 98 and 108.)*

In calculating the percentage depletion allowance with respect to his share of production from the property, Operator A must exclude a pro-rata share of the prior payments to Lessor R that represented lease bonus income.[144] *(See Case 8. See Cases 4 and 98 for discussions of depletion on lease bonus income.)* Based on court cases and Internal Revenue Service (IRS) pronouncements, the original purpose underlying this "bonus exclusion rule" was to ensure that lease bonus payments were not counted twice in computing percentage depletion.[145] The IRS has held that if the lessor who receives a lease bonus does not take the percentage depletion deduction on the bonus,

---

138. Reg. Sec. 1.613-2(c)(5); Rev. Rul. 72-165, 1972-1 C.B. 177; U.S. Steel v. U.S., 445 F.2d 520 (2d Cir. 1971), 28 AFTR2d 71-5053, 71-2 USTC 9505; Handleman v. U.S., 357 F.2d 694 (Ct. Cl. 1966), 17 AFTR2d 609, 66-1 USTC 9310.
139. White Castle Lumber & Shingle Co. v. U.S., 481 F.2d 1274 (5th Cir. 1973), 32 AFTR2d 73-5549, 73-2 USTC 9590; Rev. Rul. 80-49, 1980-1 C.B. 127.
140. James L. C. McFaddin, 2 T.C. 395 (1943); Alice G. K. Kleberg, 43 B.T.A. 277 (1941).
141. I.R.C. Sec. 613A(d)(5).
142. *Ibid.*
143. Comm'r v. Engle, 82 U.S. 599 (1984), 53 AFTR2d 84-415, 84-1 USTC 9134; P. L. 99-514 (Tax Reform Act of 1986), Sec. 412(a)(3).
144. Reg. Sec. 1.613-2(c)(5)(ii); Shamrock Oil & Gas Corp. v. Comm'r, 346 F.2d 377 (5th Cir. 1965), 15 AFTR2d 1168, 65-2 USTC 9476; Rev. Rul. 81-266, 1981-2 C.B. 139.
145. Quintana Petroleum Co. v. Comm'r, 143 F.2d 588 (5th Cir. 1944), 32 AFTR 1031, 44-2 USTC 9380; Helvering v. Twin Bell Oil Syndicate, 293 U.S. 312 (1934), 14 AFTR 712, 35-1 USTC 9014; Rev. Rul. 81-266, 1981-2 C.B. 139.

the lessee must still exclude the income that is allocable to the bonus.[146] Arguably, based on the original purpose of the "bonus exclusion rule," the rule should not be applied if the lessor is not entitled to percentage depletion on the lease bonus. Therefore, since lease bonuses recognized as income after August 16, 1986, no longer qualify for percentage depletion, it appears to be inappropriate to continue to follow the "bonus exclusion rule" on these bonuses. It is hoped that this apparent inconsistency will be rectified by a technical correction or otherwise modified by an administrative pronouncement from the Treasury.

Case 13
Minimum Royalty Not Recoverable from Production — Payment May Be Avoided

> **Operator A acquires from Lessor R an oil and gas lease that has a primary term of five years. Lessor R retains a one-eighth royalty interest. The lease agreement provides that the royalty payments shall in no case be less than $10,000 per year for the primary term of the lease. Operator A may forfeit the lease at any time after the first year by his failure to pay, in advance, the minimum royalty for the succeeding year. Amounts paid by Operator A in excess of the amounts attributable to the sale of Lessor R's one-eighth share of current production may not be applied to reduce the royalty payments in future years.**

Unlike the minimum payments in Case 12, these minimum payments may be avoided by forfeiture of the lease. Thus, the Internal Revenue Service will consider any payments prior to production to be rentals paid for the continued use and possession of the property.[147] As such, the payments are deductible by Operator A in the year in which they are paid or incurred.[148] *(See Case 9 regarding the option to capitalize those costs and for a discussion of the economic performance rules and other restrictions on the timing of delay rental deductions.)* Operator A has no option as to the year of deductibility under the minimum royalty provisions because that option is available to the lessee only when the excess payments are recoverable out of future production.[149] *(See Case 10.)*

After production is obtained, it may be possible to treat any payment made to Lessor R as a royalty to the extent it does not exceed the total gross income from the property; accordingly, Operator A should exclude it from his income.[150] Any excess of the minimum payment over the total gross income from production constitutes a delay rental because it may not be applied by Operator A to reduce any royalties in future years and it could have been avoided by forfeiture of the lease.[151]

If any portion of the minimum payment may be avoided by the commencement of drilling operations on the nonproductive part of a tract or may be avoided by forfeiting all or a part of the nonproductive acreage, that portion of the minimum payment probably will be considered a delay rental with respect to that nonproductive acreage.[152]

---

146. Rev. Rul. 81-266, 1981-2 C.B. 139; Murphy Oil Corp. v. U.S., 337 F.2d 677 (8th Cir. 1964), 14 AFTR2d 5835, 64-2 USTC 9810.
147. Reg. Sec. 1.612-3(c); Rev. Rul. 72-165, 1972-1 C.B. 177.
148. I.R.C. Sec. 162(a)(3); Reg. Sec. 1.612-3(c)(2).
149. Reg. Sec. 1.612-3(b)(3).
150. Reg. Sec. 1.613-2(c)(5); Rev. Rul. 72-165, 1972-1 C.B. 177; U.S. Steel v. U.S., 445 F.2d 520 (2d Cir. 1971), 28 AFTR2d 71-5053, 71-2 USTC 9505; Handleman v. U.S., 357 F.2d 694 (Ct. Cl. 1966), 17 AFTR2d 609, 66-1 USTC 9310.
151. Rev. Rul. 72-165, 1972-1 C.B. 177.
152. Reg. Sec. 1.612-3(c)(1).

A shut-in payment is similar to a minimum royalty, but it is distinguishable in that it is not recoverable from future production. *(See Case 9.)* Accordingly, shut-in payments have been held to be rentals rather than royalties.[153]

Lessor R should report payments that are treated as rentals as ordinary income upon which depletion is not allowable.[154] Lessor R may, however, take depletion on that portion of the payments that is treated as royalty income.[155] *(See Section IV for a discussion of depletion allowances on royalty income.)*

Case 14
Assumption by Sublessee of Lessee's Liability for Installment Bonus Payments — Payments Not Recoverable from Production

> Lessee E acquires from Lessor R a nonproductive oil and gas lease. Lessee E agrees to pay to Lessor R a one-eighth royalty plus $100,000, payable in installments of $20,000 at the beginning of each year during the five-year primary term of the lease, irrespective of production. The payments may not be avoided by forfeiture of the lease prior to expiration of the primary lease. One year after execution of the lease, Lessee E and Sublessee S enter into a contract in the nature of an option and conditional lease. Sublessee S is granted the right to conduct exploratory seismograph operations for a period of six months, after which time S is required to exercise an option either to drill an exploratory well or to abandon all operations on the lease. If Sublessee S elects at the end of the six-month period to drill the well, he agrees to assume the remaining annual payments of $20,000 each and the other royalty obligations contained in the original lease between Lessee E and Lessor R. Sublessee S, however, will make his $20,000 annual payment to Lessee E, who in turn will pay an equal amount to Lessor R. The agreement between Lessee E and Sublessee S further provides that the latter can avoid any remaining payments by failing to exercise the option before expiration of the six-month period or by forfeiting the contract.

Lessee E's payments are installment bonus payments that are capitalized as leasehold costs because he has an unconditional obligation to pay the total amount of the contract to Lessor R and the payments are not recoverable out of subsequent production. The receipts by Lessor R constitute installment bonus income taxable as advance royalties. *(See Case 12 for tax treatment of installment bonus income.)*

Although Sublessee S assumes certain obligations to Lessor R, his contract is not transformed into one with Lessor R. The contract may not actually convey a direct ownership in the minerals to Sublessee S, but it does permit Sublessee S access to the property for purposes of exploration, development and production. Similar contracts have been held to provide a sufficient economic interest to entitle the operator to a deduction for depletion.[156] The possibility of Sublessee S's avoiding the installment payments under certain conditions categorizes those payments by him as delay rentals *(see Case 9)* and precludes their treatment as bonus payments to be capitalized as

153. Johnson v. Phinney, 287 F.2d 544 (5th Cir. 1961), 7 AFTR2d 860, 61-1 USTC 9307.
154. Comm'r v. Wilson, 76 F.2d 766 (5th Cir. 1935), 15 AFTR 1228, 35-1 USTC 9284; Reg. Sec. 1.612-3(c)(2).
155. Reg. Sec. 1.611-1(a).
156. Comm'r v. Mammoth Coal Co., 229 F.2d 535 (3d Cir. 1955), 48 AFTR 914, 56-1 USTC 9286; Weirton Ice and Coal Supply Co. v. Comm'r, 231 F.2d 531 (4th Cir. 1956), 49 AFTR 470, 56-1 USTC 9404.

leasehold costs.[157] The receipt by Lessee E of the $20,000 payment from Sublessee S will be lease rental income not subject to depletion. As discussed above, however, Lessee E's payment of the same amount to Lessor R will be treated as an installment bonus.

Case 15
Payment for Extension of Lease

> **Operator A pays Lessor R $5,000 for the extension of a lease for five years beyond the original termination date. Operator A previously had paid Lessor R a bonus when the lease initially was executed. No wells had been drilled on the lease prior to the original expiration date. None of the payments made may be reimbursed out of future production.**

This type of payment probably will be held to be additional consideration for the lease, particularly if it serves to extend the lease for a period in excess of one year. It also will be accorded the same treatment as the lease bonus paid at the time the lease initially was executed.[158] Even if the $5,000 is payable in installments over the extended term of the lease, it probably will be considered a lease bonus if it is, in fact, consideration for the lease (or the extension of the lease).[159] The treatment of the $5,000 payment made to Lessor R is not affected by the existence or absence of annual rental payments in addition to the consideration paid for the extension of the lease. Any consideration paid for the granting of a lease is considered a lease bonus even though the duration of the lease is materially less than one year.[160]

The continuation of a lease may take a variety of forms. If Operator A allows the original lease to expire before negotiating the new lease, he probably will be allowed to write off the cost of the original lease but will be required to capitalize the bonus paid for the granting of the new lease. However, if the property is top leased (a new lease is executed prior to the expiration of the old lease), any payment will be treated as an additional bonus. In addition, there will be no deduction for the prior costs because the rights do not lapse, even momentarily.

If only part of the acreage is top leased or extended and the remainder surrendered, Operator A should be allowed to write off the portion of the original bonus applicable to any surrender acreage that is not contiguous to the acreage retained. It is doubtful that a writeoff will be allowed if the surrendered acreage is part of a larger tract or is contiguous to the acreage retained. The rationale for not allowing such a writeoff is that the original bonus applicable to a given tract represents an investment in the minerals underlying that tract and, as long as that investment may be recovered from minerals under any part of the tract, no loss has been incurred. In effect, it may be necessary to determine the writeoff by reference to the units of property previously established upon acquisition of the minerals (including any property-unit elections in effect at the time of the extension of the lease).

Operator A should capitalize any payment considered to be in the nature of a lease bonus as a cost of acquisition of the mineral interest.[161] *(See Case 2.)* If a payment is, in fact, a delay rental, it should be charged to expense in the year in which it is paid or

157. Jefferson Lake Sulphur Co. v. U.S., 236 F.2d 542 (5th Cir. 1956), 50 AFTR 39, 56-2 USTC 9875; White Castle Lumber & Shingle Co. v. U.S., 481 F.2d 1274 (5th Cir. 1973), 32 AFTR2d 73-5549, 73-2 USTC 9590.
158. Houston Farms Dev. Co. v. U.S., 131 F.2d 577 (5th Cir. 1942), 30 AFTR 328, 42-2 USTC 9783.
159. Maureen Fitzsimmons, 37 T.C. 179 (1961).
160. Houston Farms Dev. Co.; Rev. Rul. 80-49, 1980-1 C.B. 127.
161. Reg. Sec. 1.612-3(a)(3).

incurred.[162] *(See Case 9 regarding the option to capitalize those costs and for a discussion of the economic performance rules and other restrictions on the timing of delay rental deductions.)*

Lessor R will be required to treat the receipt of a bonus as ordinary income subject to the allowance for depletion.[163] *(See Case 98 for a discussion of the allowance for depletion on lease bonus income.)* However, lease bonus income no longer qualifies for percentage depletion for bonuses received after August 16, 1986.[164] Therefore, only cost depletion will be allowed for bonus income recognized after this date. Lessor R will be required to treat the receipt of a delay rental as ordinary income on which no depletion is allowable. If Operator A allows the old lease to expire, Lessor R will be required to restore to income in the year the lease expires any depletion taken on the initial bonus.[165] *(See Cases 2 and 127 for a discussion of the circumstances under which the lessor must restore to his taxable income the amount of depletion (whether computed on the cost or percentage basis) claimed on that lease bonus income.)*

Case 16
Claims for Insufficient Production

Lessor R and C Company, a natural gas company, enter into a gas lease and operating arrangement whereby C Company agrees to produce one-third of its total requirements from Lessor R's properties upon which Lessor R has retained a one-eighth royalty interest.

Subsequently, Lessor R brings suit against C Company for additional royalties on the grounds that an insufficient proportion of C Company's requirements has been produced from Lessor R's land.

Damages are awarded to Lessor R by judgment of the court, under which C Company makes an additional payment to Lessor R.

C Company's payment to Lessor R is a deductible expense. A settlement for insufficient production or development of oil and gas properties is in the nature of damages; it is not a capital expenditure because no mineral rights are acquired. The payment cannot be considered to be in the nature of a bonus paid as additional consideration for the lease because the suit was based on lack of production and not on production itself.

The payment is not considered to be depletable income to Lessor R because it is not income from production.[166] This rule may be applied even though the claim is based on the general allegation that C Company was producing an excessive amount from adjacent land and, thus, draining the reserves under Lessor R's land. If Lessor R drops his claim as a result of a settlement negotiated with C Company and if the amount applicable to the value of the gas extracted by C Company without payment to Lessor R can be ascertained and segregated from the portion of the payment that is consideration for Lessor R's dropping his claim, that amount may be subject to depletion.[167]

The amount received by a lessee in settlement of a claim against a cycling plant operator for damages to the reservoir has been treated as gain from an involuntary

162. Reg. Sec. 1.612-3(c)(2).
163. Reg. Sec. 1.612-3(a)(1).
164. I.R.C. Sec. 613A(d)(5).
165. Reg. Sec. 1.612-3(a)(2).
166. Crossett Timber & Dev. Co., 29 B.T.A. 705 (1934).
167. Alphonzo E. Bell Corp. v. Comm'r, 145 F.2d 157 (9th Cir. 1944), 32 AFTR 1459, 44-2 USTC 9476.

conversion and thereby subject to capital-gain treatment.[168] The lessee did not lose title to an interest in the lease but merely was compensated for damages to the oil in place.

If Lessor R is on the cash basis, he must report the settlement as income for the year in which it is received. If he is on the accrual basis, the settlement is taxable income for the year in which the settlement is reached.[169]

C Company should deduct the payment in the year in which the amount is ascertained and agreed to or paid, depending on whether the accrual, or cash basis of accounting is used.[170] *(See Case 9 for a discussion of the economic performance rules and restrictions on using the cash basis of accounting.)*

Case 17
Oil and Gas Interest Received for Services

> **Operator A enters into an agreement with E, a lease broker, and F, a geologist. Operator A agrees to reimburse certain of their actual expenses and assign each an agreed share of the mineral interest in any properties that he may acquire as a result of their efforts. During the year, E and F incur various expenses, aggregating $3,000 in connection with a block of leases that Operator A acquires for cash consideration of $25,000. In accordance with their agreement, Operator A reimburses E and F for the $3,000 of expenses and assigns to E a 5% net profits interest and to F a 10% share of the working interest. Operator A also agrees to pay for his share of the initial development costs. In this instance, no partnership is recognized for federal income tax purposes.**

"Pool-of-Capital" Doctrine Defined

Interests in oil and gas properties received for services involve two problems: whether there is present realization of taxable income and how subsequent receipts from the interest acquired should be treated for tax purposes.

In connection with the first problem, the Internal Revenue Service (IRS) has had a longstanding policy that, under certain circumstances (discussed below), the receipt of an interest in an oil and gas property for certain services is not subject to income tax:

- ☐ The interest must be received in return for services rendered in connection with the acquisition, exploration or development of the property.
- ☐ The interest received must be from the same oil and gas property to which the services relate.
- ☐ The property interest must not be received in return for the satisfaction of any liability other than that created by the contract for the assignment of the interest in the property.[171]

The rationale for this policy is that, under these circumstances, a sharing arrangement is created in which the recipient of the oil and gas interest contributes services to the common "pool of capital" necessary for the discovery and development of minerals. Under such a sharing arrangement, no compensatory transfer of property occurs, and

168. Walter A. Henshaw, 23 T.C. 176 (1954).
169. U.S. v. Safety Car Heating & Lighting Co., 297 U.S. 88 (1936), 16 AFTR 1311, 36-1 USTC 9042.
170. Dixie Pine Products v. Comm'r, 320 U.S. 516 (1944), 31 AFTR 956, 44-1 USTC 9127.
171. G.C.M. 22730, 1941-1 C.B. 214.

no taxable income should be attributed to the party who receives an economic interest in the property in return for those services.

The function of the "pool-of-capital" concept is to distinguish transactions that constitute contributions to the "pool of capital" represented by a reservoir of oil and gas from other transactions that represent compensatory transfers of property. In a compensatory transfer of a fractional interest in the property, the interest of the transferor is diminished by the amount by which the interest of the transferee is increased. This contrasts to the sharing of property that occurs in a noncompensatory contribution to capital. In the latter transaction, an oil operator, drilling contractor, geologist, engineer, promoter, landman, financial manager and/or other specialist contributes vital services to the "pool of capital" necessary to develop an oil and gas reserve. The capital represented by this and other contributions converts the bare title to an oil and gas mineral interest into an extremely valuable economic resource, namely a developed oil and gas reserve. As these services are contributed, the "pool of capital" grows, and the related mineral interests grow and change. Each contributor's share of the mineral interest represents his share of the growth resulting from his contribution. It is in one sense a share created by his contribution. It is not a share transferred to him by another participant. To the contrary, if the venture is successful, every participant's share is enlarged by the contributions of others rather than diminished by transfers to them. In effect, all contributors' services are rendered on their own behalf, and their sharing of the growing property is clearly distinguishable from compensatory *transfers* of property for services rendered to the *transferors.*

In these oil and gas situations, each contributor's contribution to the property remains "at risk" in that property until oil and gas is produced or until the contributor disposes of his interest. It is only then that income recognition may be appropriate under Section 61 or any other section of the Internal Revenue Code.

Under the "pool-of-capital" concept as it is applied to a leasing transaction, it is clear that the lessee in the original leasing of a mineral interest does not realize income when he receives a share of that interest in consideration for assuming the obligations to develop the minerals. Likewise, in subsequent transactions, sublessees of that mineral interest do not realize income from receiving fractional interests for assuming fractional shares of those development obligations. These transactions are not distinguishable from more detailed transactions in which shares of the interest are received for assuming designated portions of the development obligations such as performing necessary geological work, drilling specific wells, finding and/or evaluating the properties to be developed, and performing specific legal services, necessary financial planning and management services. If the IRS believes any of these services do not fall within the "pool-of-capital" concept, it should identify them and explain their exclusion from this long-accepted and very important concept of taxation.

The ruling on which the above rationale is based has been in effect since 1941 and has not been formally modified or revoked.

IRS Application of "Pool of Capital"

In a 1977 ruling, the IRS applied this rationale to receipt of an interest in a drill site tract in consideration for drilling a well on that tract.[172] However, in that same ruling, the IRS specifically refused to apply the rationale with respect to an interest in some additional acreage received by the taxpayer in the same transaction.

172. Rev. Rul. 77-176, 1977-1 C.B. 77. *See also* Rev. Rul. 80-153, 1980-1 C.B. 10; IRS Letter Ruling 8311005 (Technical Advice Memorandum).

This refusal was based on the position that the additional acreage constituted a property separate from the property on which the services were rendered and, thus, was not includable in the "pool of capital." This application indicates that the IRS still recognized the validity of the "pool-of-capital" concept. However, it also indicates a tendency to apply the concept much more narrowly than seems to be justified by its substance, its reasonableness and by the length of time it has been relied upon by the oil and gas industry.

In several technical advice memoranda, the IRS has continued to recognize the "pool-of-capital" concept but has applied it very narrowly to the facts involved.[173] In this connection, it has refused to apply the concept to employees who received interests in properties for services rendered not only in connection with those properties but also in connection with other properties in which no interests were received.[174] Further, it has refused to apply the concept where the service rendered related not only to the properties involved but also to the general management and administration of the business.[175]

In a 1983 ruling,[176] the IRS held that income should be recognized in three situations in which, under applications of the "pool-of-capital" concept, taxpayers would not have expected income to be recognized. In these situations, overriding royalties were received by: (1) a corporate promoter for locating oil and gas properties to be acquired and developed by partnerships it syndicated; (2) an attorney for performing legal services related to a corporation's acquisition of oil and gas properties and (3) a corporate executive for arranging financing for the corporation's acquisition and development of oil and gas properties and for overseeing their operation. Information available concerning the background of this ruling indicates an apparent misinterpretation of the "pool-of-capital" concept by the IRS and an intention to restrict its application. The IRS continues to apply the reasoning of this ruling in several technical advice memoranda.[177]

The IRS recognizes that significant judicial and administrative precedents support the application of the "pool-of-capital" concept. Nevertheless, the ruling was issued without any mention of the concept. Apparently, the IRS was extending the same tax treatment to what it believes to be compensatory arrangements involving the acquisition and development of oil and gas properties that it applies to actual compensatory arrangements in which property is received for services rendered. This attempt to correlate compensatory transfers of property in other situations with contributions of services to the acquisition and development of oil and gas properties represents a misinterpretation of, and, consequently, a departure from, the "pool-of-capital" concept.

In 1985, the IRS continued its current ruling policy of recognizing the "pool-of-capital" concept only in extremely narrow factual situations. In a technical advice memorandum, the IRS tried to distinguish the services that qualify for "pool-of-capital" treatment, depending on whether a geologist was acting independently or under a prior arrangement with a drilling contractor.[178] The IRS applied the "pool-

173. IRS Letter Ruling 8014024; IRS Letter Ruling 8047005 (Technical Advice Memorandum); IRS Letter Ruling 8129006 (Technical Advice Memorandum); IRS Letter Ruling 8137006 (Technical Advice Memorandum); IRS Letter Ruling 8146006 (Technical Advice Memorandum); IRS Letter Ruling 8152001 (Technical Advice Memorandum); Internal Revenue Manual Sec. 4232.8, Para. 242(3), April 18, 1985.

174. IRS Letter Ruling 8146006 (Technical Advice Memorandum); IRS Letter Ruling 8152001 (Technical Advice Memorandum).

175. IRS Letter Ruling 8014024.

176. Rev. Rul. 83-46,1983-1 C.B. 16.

177. IRS Letter Ruling 8520005 (Technical Advice Memorandum); IRS Letter Ruling 8636001 (Technical Advice Memorandum).

178. IRS Letter Ruling 8520004 (Technical Advice Memorandum).

of-capital" doctrine only to situations in which a geologist independently acquired leases and subsequently transferred a portion of the mineral interests to a drilling contractor. In contrast, where the same services were rendered under a prior arrangement, the geologist was required to include the value of the mineral interests retained in income. Therefore, it appears that the IRS has tried to add a new standard in determining when the "pool-of-capital" doctrine should be applied. There appears to be no statutory or judicial authority to support that the existence of a prior arrangement causes the "pool-of-capital" doctrine to fail to apply.

Based on the rationale of the "pool-of-capital" concept referred to above and the significant judicial and administrative precedents, it is clear that the IRS's position ignores one of the fundamental principles of oil and gas taxation. It is likely that the conflict concerning the proper application of the "pool-of-capital" concept will have to be judicially resolved.

Consequences to E and F

Under the rationale of the "pool-of-capital" doctrine, E and F should realize no taxable income from the assignment to them of their economic interests in the properties, notwithstanding that the IRS has issued a technical advice memorandum with facts similar to this case which conflicts with this interpretation. They would have no tax basis in those interests unless they incurred unreimbursed costs in connection with the acquisition of the leases. E and F will treat any income they receive from the sale of oil or gas produced from the properties after acquisition as ordinary income subject to the allowance for depletion, similar to income from any oil and gas property they might acquire by any other means.

The IRS may argue that since a prior arrangement was made with E and F regarding the work they would perform, the transfer of mineral interests includes compensatory elements. In the typical industry-sharing arrangement, the parties who contribute services to the "pool of capital" may agree how costs will be shared and to what share of the minerals they will be entitled prior to commencing development of oil and gas reserves. Therefore, the fact that E and F agree to the arrangement before making their contribution of vital services to the pool of capital needed to develop the oil and gas reserves should not convert the transaction into a compensatory transfer.

Consequences to Operator A

Operator A must capitalize the entire $28,000 as his depletable lease investment. All amounts of cash paid to E and F in connection with the acquisition represent lease cost to him. Operator A will not generally be entitled to deduct the cost or value of the interests assigned to E and F; hence, his total cost becomes the tax basis of his remaining net interest.

If Operator A pays intangible drilling and development costs (IDC) attributable to F's 10% share of the working interest, if production is shared with F from first runs and if the arrangement is not treated as a partnership for tax purposes, Operator A will be required to capitalize as additional depletable basis the share of the IDC attributable to F's interest. *(See Case 38.)*

Activities Not Covered by the "Pool-of-Capital" Doctrine

There have been no recent judicial decisions involving factual situations similar to the facts of this case. However, one court decision did hold that a water-flood project was a production activity rather than a development activity and, therefore, the "pool-of-capital" concept did not apply.[179]

This arrangement by which E and F receive a direct property interest in the oil and gas leases in return for their services should not be confused with an arrangement by which a partner receives in return for his services an interest in the capital of a partnership that owns an interest in an oil and gas property. These partnership arrangements are subject to the provisions of the regulations[180] and court decisions[181] pertaining specifically to these matters. *(See Case 18.)*

If E and F are assigned economic interests in properties in return for services not related to acquisition, exploration or development of the properties, the fair market value of any of the interests received will be ordinary income to them.[182] In such a situation, Operator A may be entitled to treat the fair market value of the properties conveyed as payment for the services received and to report a corresponding amount as proceeds from the disposition of oil and gas interests.

Case 18
Interest in Partnership Profits for Services

> **A, B and C enter into a partnership to conduct oil and gas operations. Partners A and B each agree to supply $100,000 of capital, and C, a geologist, agrees to contribute his services to manage the partnership. The agreement provides that initially all losses are to be allocated equally to Partners A and B. All income is to be allocated equally to A and B until the income so allocated equals the losses previously charged. Thereafter, all items of income and deduction will be allocated one-third each to Partners A, B and C. Upon liquidation of the partnership, the agreement provides that all partnership property be valued and the capital accounts be adjusted as if the property had been sold at its fair market value. After this adjustment, the property is to be distributed to the partners in accordance with their adjusted capital account balances. To the extent there is a deficit in a partner's adjusted capital account following the distributions of liquidation proceeds, that partner must restore the deficit by making a corresponding cash contribution to the partnership.**

Under the partnership agreement, Partner C receives an interest only in partnership profits and appreciation, if any, in partnership property. Because Partner C will be taxed on his share of those profits and appreciation at the same time they are realized, he should not recognize any income for services by virtue of his becoming a partner in the ABC partnership. Similarly, he should not recognize any income for services upon liquidation.[183]

---

179. James A. Lewis Eng. Co. v. Comm'r, 339 F.2d 706 (5th Cir. 1964), 15 AFTR2d 9, 65-1 USTC 9122.
180. Reg. Sec. 1.721-1(b)(1).
181. U.S. v. Frazell, 335 F.2d 487 (5th Cir. 1964), 14 AFTR2d 5378, 64-2 USTC 9684, *reh'g denied*, 339 F.2d 885, 14 AFTR2d 6119, 65-1 USTC 9125; Diamond v. Comm'r, 492 F. 2d 286 (7th Cir. 1974), 33 AFTR2d 74-852, 74-1 USTC 9306; Vestal v. U.S., 498 F.2d 487 (8th Cir. 1974), 33 AFTR2d 74-1240, 74-1 USTC 9407, *reh'g denied*, 498 F.2d 495 (8th Cir. 1974), 34 AFTR2d 74-5171, 74-2 USTC 9501. *See also* Richard O. Wheeler, T.C. Memo Dec. (June 7, 1978); Hensel Phelps Construction Co. v. Comm'r, 703 F.2d 485 (10th Cir. 1983), 51 AFTR2d 83-1006, 83-1 USTC 9270.
182. Reg. Sec. 1.61-2(d); Massey v. Comm'r, 143 F.2d 429 (5th Cir. 1944), 32 AFTR 986, 44-2 USTC 9384; Walls v. Comm'r, 60 F.2d 347 (10th Cir. 1932), 11 AFTR 758, 1932 CCH 9400; Rev. Rul. 80-153, 1980-1 C.B. 10.
183. Reg. Sec. 1.721-1(b).

The Internal Revenue Service (IRS) may challenge the above results on the basis of a case[184] that seemed to hold, as an extension of the regulations,[185] that an interest in partnership profits received for services is taxable if the value of the interest is readily determinable. This case held that the value of the partnership interest was readily determinable when the taxpayer sold the partnership interest within 10 days after receipt.

The court acknowledged that taxing the value of a profits interest in a partnership could result in the taxpayer's being taxed twice on the same income—first on the value of the right to participate in future profits, and then on the amount of those profits when they ultimately are realized by the partnership. The court suggested that regulations be promulgated to deal with this and other related problems; however, those regulations have not been proposed. The court also implied that the interest would not be taxed if its value was only speculative.

However, in another case dealing with the transfer of an interest in partnership profits in exchange for services, the Tax Court held that the receipt of an interest in future profits was not taxable.[186] Apparently, the IRS conceded that the receipt of a profits interest was not taxable. Instead, the IRS argued that investors who funded 100% of all lease-acquisition costs and drilling costs on exploratory test wells had transferred an interest in partnership capital to general partners, who received an interest in future production from these test wells. The court held that a transfer of an interest in partnership capital had not occurred and that the receipt of an interest in future profits was not taxable.

In another case, it was held that the right to receive what appeared to be an interest in future partnership profits became currently taxable when the taxpayer's rights were exchanged for corporate stock.[187] The court held that the taxpayer's interest either: (1) "became possessory immediately upon the termination" of his contract so that his interest was received as compensation for services or (2) the corporate stock received "was given in substitution for the partnership interest originally contemplated and therefore that stock received in compensation for services was taxable" to the taxpayer. In denying a petition for rehearing on this decision, the court indicated that the interest in question was an interest in capital rather than an interest in profits only; accordingly, the applicability of this case to a purely profits-interest situation is not entirely clear.

In yet another case, a geologist was taxed on the consideration received for the sale of his right to receive a partnership interest.[188] The court held that the value of the property received at the time the geologist earned his right to receive the partnership interest was not determinable. Therefore, taxation as compensation should have been deferred until the value was either determinable or realized through a closed transaction. In this case, the geologist's services appear to have been rendered to certain partners rather than to the partnership itself.

Pending further clarification by the IRS or the courts on the taxability of an interest in partnership capital or profits in return for services rendered to the partnership, caution should be exercised in entering into arrangements of the type discussed here.

184. Diamond v. Comm'r, 492 F.2d 286 (7th Cir. 1974), 33 AFTR2d 74-852, 74-1 USTC 9306. *See also* Richard O. Wheeler, T.C. Memo Dec. (June 7, 1978); Hensel Phelps Construction Co. v. Comm'r, 703 F.2d 485 (10th Cir. 1983), 51 AFTR2d 83-1006, 83-1 USTC 9270.

185. Reg. Sec. 1.721-1(b).

186. National Oil Company, T.C. Memo Dec. (Dec. 23, 1986).

187. U.S. v. Frazell, 335 F.2d 487 (5th Cir. 1964),14 AFTR2d 5378, 64-2 USTC 9684, *reh'g denied*, 339 F.2d 885, 14 AFTR2d 6119, 65-1 USTC 9125.

188. Vestal v. U.S., 498 F.2d 487 (8th Cir. 1974), 33 AFTR2d 74-1240, 74-1 USTC 9407, *reh'g denied*, 498 F.2d 495 (8th Cir. 1974), 34 AFTR2d 74-5171, 74-2 USTC 9501.

Case 19
Net Profits Interest for Drill Site Location

> **Operator A assembles a block of oil and gas leases within the city limits. Ordinances severely restrict drilling within the city, but by special permit Operator A is allowed to slant drill into his leases from a secluded one-acre industrial parcel near the lease area. For the use of this drill site, Operator A agrees to grant to Landowner R an overriding royalty equal to 15% of net profits derived from the operation of the leases.**

Landowner R has contributed the use of his surface rights in return for a share of net profits from production of oil and gas from Operator A's leases. Because the use of these surface rights is essential to the development of the properties, Landowner R's contribution represents an investment in the oil and gas in place. Landowner R must look solely to the production of that oil and gas for a return on this investment; therefore, Landowner R is deemed to have acquired an economic interest in the properties that entitles him to a deduction for depletion with respect to that production.[189]

Operator A and Landowner R both have made valuable contributions to the common pool of capital necessary to the development of the oil and gas properties, and neither has received any compensatory transfer of property; therefore, neither Operator A nor Landowner R should recognize any income from their arrangement until oil and gas are produced or sold or an interest in the property is disposed of.[190] *(See Case 17.)*

This transaction also may be viewed as a mutual exchange of an interest in Operator A's oil and gas leases for an interest in Landowner R's surface rights in the drill site. This represents an exchange of property for property of like kind to be similarly held. Neither Operator A nor Landowner R should recognize any gain or loss as a result of such an exchange.[191]

If Landowner R had received a working interest and the transaction with Operator A had resulted in a partnership, Landowner R would be considered to have made a capital contribution (the surface rights) to the partnership for a 15% share of the partnership profits.[192]

(For a discussion of a multiple property net profits interest, see Case 173.)

---

189. Comm'r v. Southwest Exploration Co., 350 U.S. 308 (1956), 48 AFTR 683, 56-1 USTC 9304; IRS Letter Ruling 8709007 (Technical Advice Memorandum). *But see* Missouri River Sand Co. v Comm'r, 774 F.2d 334 (8th Cir. 1985), 56 AFTR2d 85-6115, 85-2 USTC 9732, *aff'g* 83 T.C. 193 (1984).
190. G.C.M. 22730, 1941-1 C.B. 214.
191. I.R.C. Sec. 1031.
192. I.R.C. Sec. 721.

Section II
The Drilling and Development Period

Important tax considerations during the drilling and development of oil and gas wells are: (1) distinguishing between capital costs and deductible expenses; (2) determining the year the expenses are deductible and (3) determining which taxpayer is granted the right to deduct the expenses. In recognition of the unique risks involved in drilling for oil and gas, special provisions in the Internal Revenue Code allow persons who bear those risks to elect to deduct certain expenditures that otherwise would be capitalized. These expenditures are designated as intangible drilling and development costs (IDC). The industry commonly refers to these costs as intangibles or IDC.

In drilling oil and gas wells, as in the acquisition and exploration of oil and gas properties before drilling, the taxpayer must classify expenditures as capital costs or deductible expenses. In acquisition and exploration expenditures, the proper classification is determined by certain rules relating to the nature of the charge, and each case is decided on the basis of the facts. These expenditures generally are capitalizable when incurred to acquire or evaluate a particular property. In drilling activities, however, the taxpayer must classify expenditures as: (1) tangible equipment costs, which are subject to depreciation, or (2) intangible drilling and development costs, which either may be deducted as expenses or capitalized and deducted through subsequent depreciation or amortization and depletion allowances.

The general election either to deduct as expenses or to capitalize IDC must be exercised by the taxpayer in the original tax return for the first year in which those costs are paid or incurred. The regulations provide that IDC must be capitalized if a proper election is not made to expense those costs. Once the election to expense is made by claiming the costs as deductions in the return, it is binding for all subsequent years.

If a taxpayer elects to capitalize IDC under the general option, an additional election is available to expense those costs incurred in the drilling of nonproductive wells. A clear statement of election under this second option must be made in the taxpayer's return for the first tax year in which the first nonproductive well is completed. This election, like that made under the general option, is binding for all subsequent years.

The election to deduct IDC does not apply to costs of drilling wells located outside the United States. Such costs are recovered ratably over a 10-year period beginning with the tax year in which such costs are paid or incurred or, at the election of the taxpayer, are included in the basis of the property for computing cost depletion. IDC incurred on nonproductive wells located outside the United States are fully deductible in the year drilling is completed and the well is determined to be nonproductive.

The election to deduct IDC is available only to taxpayers who own operating rights in the properties for which the intangible costs are incurred. The regulations state that

IDC incurred on obligation wells generally may be expensed under the election. However, when the drilling of a well is undertaken to acquire a fractional interest in the operating rights, only that portion of the intangibles attributable to the fractional interest comes under the election. Any costs attributable to the operating rights held by others must be capitalized as depletable leasehold costs of the fractional interest.

IDC incurred on productive wells are treated as a tax preference item for purposes of calculating the alternative minimum tax (AMT).

Taxpayers that have made the general election to expense IDC can make an annual special election to capitalize and amortize any portion of IDC that would have been deductible under the general election. A taxpayer may deduct the capitalized IDC ratably over a 10-year period beginning with the tax year in which the taxpayer paid or incurred the IDC. This capitalized IDC will not be treated as a tax preference item. If the property is disposed of, the IDC recapture rules will apply to the amortization deductions.

Integrated oil companies (corporations that are not independent producers) are required to capitalize 30% of IDC expenditures. Amortization of the capitalized portion is allowed over a 60-month period beginning with the month the cost was paid or incurred. IDC recapture rules apply to the amortization. It appears that the 30% reduction applies to IDC on both productive and nonproductive wells.

In most cases, taxpayers should make the general election to deduct IDC. If the election is not exercised, those costs must be capitalized as leasehold or equipment costs. Once capitalized, the costs are recoverable only through the depletion or depreciation allowance, as tax basis at the time the property is sold or as an abandonment loss if and when the property becomes worthless. Subject to various restrictions (as discussed in Section IV), each taxpayer is granted the percentage depletion allowance (based on gross income from the property) which often exceeds the depletable costs of the property, including the tangibles. Thus, the capitalization of intangibles as leasehold costs in such a situation does not increase the allowable depletion deduction for the property. On the other hand, if a taxpayer expenses intangibles for tax purposes, he may deduct not only the intangibles but also the percentage depletion allowance.

In most cases, even taxpayers that do not qualify for percentage depletion should make the general election to deduct the intangibles. For these taxpayers, the current deduction is an important timing benefit (i.e., it accelerates the total deductions the taxpayer ultimately would be entitled to had the costs been capitalized).

A taxpayer's current deduction for net losses from oil and gas activities (including all intangibles) is limited to the amount of the taxpayer's "at-risk" investment in each such activity. The "at-risk" limitations apply only to individuals and certain closely held corporations. The "at-risk" limitations for partners and S corporation shareholders apply at the individual partner or shareholder level. Generally, these limitations are applied on a property-by-property basis. In addition to the "at-risk" limitations discussed above, the Tax Reform Act of 1986 (the Act) provides extensive new rules that limit the deductibility of passive-activity losses. Generally, income and loss of a taxpayer's passive activities are netted. An aggregate net loss from passive activities cannot be used to offset net income from other sources. Individuals, estates, trusts, closely held C corporations and personal-service corporations are subject to this limitation. The passive-activity provisions are discussed in Section VII.

A number of nonstatutory requirements as well as complex statutory provisions govern the timing of IDC deductions for expenditures paid in advance of economic performance. Generally, an accrual basis taxpayer cannot deduct an item before economic performance occurs. Economic performance occurs when the services or property are provided (i.e., as a well is drilled). In the case of a tax shelter, economic performance with respect to the drilling of an oil or gas well is deemed to occur in the tax year of a prepayment if the well is spudded before the close of the 90th day after the close of the tax year. Cash-basis taxpayers that are not tax shelters are not affected by the economic performance requirement.

The Act adopts new uniform cost-capitalization rules that require the capitalization of direct costs and certain indirect costs to the cost of producing an asset. The drilling of an oil and gas well is considered production of an asset. Therefore, overhead (indirect costs) and interest in certain cases must be capitalized. IDC are specifically excluded, however, from the new capitalization rules.

Case 20
Classification of Expenditures Between Capital and Expense — General

> Operator A, in drilling his first oil and gas well, decides to deduct intangible drilling and development costs (IDC) as expenses in his tax return for the year in which the costs are incurred. Operator A asks his accountant to set up records to classify the drilling costs properly to support the deduction.

The election applies to all expenditures made by an operator for wages, fuel, repairs, hauling, supplies, etc., incident to and necessary for the drilling of wells and the preparation of wells for the production of oil and gas.[1] For this purpose, a well is considered prepared for the production of oil and gas when the casing and the wellhead equipment, including the Christmas tree, have been installed.[2] Generally speaking, expenditures are classified as intangible drilling and development costs if they have, in themselves, no salvage value. Thus, the usual expenses incurred in connection with the installation of tangible equipment up to the wellhead need not be capitalized as a part of the equipment costs because those expenses in and of themselves have no salvage value.[3]

Expenditures subject to the election include wages, fuel, repairs, hauling, supplies, etc., incurred in connection with the following operations, whether undertaken directly by the owner or through an outside contractor:

☐ Clearing of ground, draining, road making, surveying and geological work necessary to prepare for the drilling of wells.

☐ Drilling, shooting and cleaning wells, including the drilling of water wells to furnish water for the drilling operations.

☐ Construction of derricks, tanks, pipelines and other physical structures necessary for the drilling of wells and the preparation of wells for the production of oil and gas.

Other expenditures properly classified as IDC include those for survey and seismic work necessary to determine the location of well sites, drilling muds and chemicals, cement and nonsalvageable cement retainers, the erection of drilling platforms and the

1. Reg. Sec. 1.612-4(a).
2. Rev. Rul. 70-414, 1970-2 C.B. 132.
3. Reg. Sec. 1.612-4(a).

digging of mud pits, damages to crops or to adjoining property during drilling operations, insurance, coring analyses, and electrical or directional surveys of wells.

The Internal Revenue Service (IRS) probably will take the position that the regulations limit the cost of hauling pipe or other material to that for transporting it from the storage yard or rail spur to the drilling location, not including the freight cost from the mill or factory. The cost of hauling pumping equipment, flow lines, separators, storage tanks and other facilities installed beyond the wellhead should not be classified as IDC but should be added to the cost of the facilities installed.[4]

Some operators charge IDC to a "work-in-progress" account during the time of drilling and completing wells. The taxpayer should not overlook the intangibles deduction attributable to expenditures included in such an account.

The election to expense or capitalize IDC does not extend to expenditures for property ordinarily considered to have salvage value,[5] whether or not those items actually may be salvaged after they are installed. The IRS has ruled,[6] and a circuit court has held,[7] that the cost of casing cemented in a well should be capitalized as a depreciable item, even though it has no net salvage value.

Examples of some items the costs of which must be capitalized are:

□ Actual materials used in equipping the wells and structures that are constructed on the property, such as derricks, casing (including casing cemented in the well), tubing, tanks, Christmas trees, pumping units, flow lines, valves and other fittings, separators and compressors.

□ Drilling tools, drill pipe, drilling rig, engines, boilers, machines, tool houses, watchmen's shelter, etc.

□ Wages, fuel, repairs, hauling supplies, etc., in connection with the installation of equipment, facilities or structures not incident to or necessary for the drilling of wells and the preparation of wells for the production of oil and gas, such as oil well pumps, separators, flow lines, salt water disposal equipment, storage tanks, etc. Because these items are installed beyond the wellhead, the costs of installation constitute capital costs.[8]

The purpose for which a lease road is constructed determines whether its cost should be capitalized or expensed.[9] The costs of a road constructed to obtain access to the drilling location may be classified as IDC, even though the road later is devoted to the producing operation. The costs of a road constructed after the completion of the well for the purpose of operating the lease must be capitalized and recovered through depreciation deductions.

The IRS has taken the position that the portions of a taxpayer's general overhead expenses that are clearly related to or identified with drilling and development activities must be characterized as IDC. Each item of overhead expense must be analyzed to determine if it is related to a drilling and development activity.[10] *(See Case 187 for a discussion of additional cost-capitalization requirements enacted by the Tax Reform Act of 1986.)*

4. Rev. Rul. 70-414, 1970-2 C.B. 132.
5. Reg. Sec. 1.612-4(c)(1).
6. Rev. Rul. 70-414, 1970-2 C.B. 132.
7. Harper Oil Co. v. U.S., 425 F.2d 1335 (10th Cir. 1970), 25 AFTR2d 70-996, 70-1 USTC 9330.
8. Rev. Rul. 70-414, 1970-2 C.B. 132.
9. Amherst Coal Co. v. U.S., 295 F. Supp. 421 (S.D. W.Va. 1969), 23 AFTR2d 69-863, 69-1 USTC 9215, *aff'd per curiam* (4th Cir. 1971), 27 AFTR2d 71-460, 71-1 USTC 9223.
10. IRS Letter Ruling 8406006 (Technical Advice Memorandum); IRS Letter Ruling 8622005 (Technical Advice Memorandum); IRS Letter Ruling 8640006 (Technical Advice Memorandum).

The election to expense IDC does not apply to ordinary lease operating expenses incurred after production has begun. Lease operating expenses are deductible only as ordinary and necessary business expenses.[11]

Although the election with respect to IDC is provided in a separate subsection of the Internal Revenue Code,[12] those costs, when expensed, are deductible as ordinary and necessary business expenses.[13]

(See Cases 21 and 22 for a discussion of the classification of expenditures for stratigraphic wells and offshore drilling platforms.)

Case 21
Classification of Expenditures Between Capital and Expense — Stratigraphic or Expendable Wells

> **C Company conducts a survey of certain offshore areas to evaluate the possible existence of oil or gas. After the survey discloses promising prospects, C Company successfully bids for leases within the area and now plans to conduct drilling operations. C Company inquires as to the tax treatment of various costs that will be incurred in connection with this offshore project, including the drilling of test wells to determine the most desirable locations for the drilling platforms. All test wells will be drilled in a potential platform location and will be completed if production is economically feasible.**

The rules governing the tax treatment of inland operations apply equally to offshore operations. Consequently, no special treatment applies to payments of lease bonuses or costs incurred in connection with the usual geological or geophysical work. Sometimes, however, special problems arise that are peculiar to offshore operations.

Because it generally is more feasible to drill all the wells in a particular offshore area from a central platform or island than to drill each well independently, it often is necessary to drill stratigraphic (sometimes referred to as expendable) wells to test the underlying geological structure to determine the most desirable location for the drilling platform or island. The Internal Revenue Service (IRS) originally took the position[14] that those wells were drilled primarily to obtain geological information and that, unless the taxpayer had an "intention to produce" oil or gas from the wells, the costs of drilling must be capitalized as leasehold cost. *(See Case 5.)*

The courts consistently have rejected IRS's position. They have held that the regulations do not require that a taxpayer intend to complete and produce a well to deduct related intangibles. Further, the courts have held that the dominant purpose of onshore and offshore "wildcat" wells is identical. The dividing line between "exploratory" work (geological and geophysical expenditures) that must be capitalized and "development" activities coming within the intangibles option is the point at which preparation for drilling begins and not when the decision to produce is made, as the IRS originally contended.[15] The IRS has announced its acquiescence[16] to all three

11. Reg. Sec. 1.612-4(c)(2).
12. I.R.C. Sec. 263(c).
13. Island Gas, Inc., 30 T.C. 787 (1958).
14. IRS Letter Ruling 7834002; IRS Letter Ruling 7837004; Rev. Rul. 80-342, 1980-2 C.B. 99.
15. Standard Oil Co. (Indiana), 68 T.C. 325 (1977); Gates Rubber Co., 74 T.C.1456 (1980), *aff'd* 694 F.2d 648 (10th Cir. 1982), 51 AFTR2d 83-628, 82-2 USTC 9702; Sun Company, Inc. and Subsidiaries (Consolidated) v. Comm'r, 677 F.2d 294 (3d Cir. 1982), 49 AFTR2d 82-1206, 82-1 USTC 9336.*See also* IRS Announcement 1983-1 C.B. 1, in which the IRS acquiesced to decisions of the Tax Court in Standard Oil Co. (Indiana), Gates Rubber Co. and Sun Company.
16. IRS Announcement 1983-1 C.B. 1.

cases in this area and concluded that it will not continue to litigate the issue.[17] Accordingly, C Company is entitled to a current deduction for the intangible drilling and development costs (IDC) incurred in drilling the test wells whether or not C Company intends to or does produce from those wells.

The IRS apparently continues to take the position that the deduction for IDC does not extend to the costs of drilling shafts (core drilling, for example) that, due to their design or the manner in which they are drilled, will not be capable of production but only of yielding geological information.[18] In certain situations, however, these shafts may be drilled primarily to determine the best location for the platform or island and not to determine the existence and extent of the reserves. It should follow that those costs are incurred to locate the drill site or are incident to and necessary for drilling and, therefore, are properly within the option to deduct IDC. They are similar to costs incurred to determine the most favorable location for a single well on land. Those costs, arguably, constitute IDC *(see Case 7)*, and offshore operations should not be handled differently.

Case 22
Classification of Expenditures Between Capital and Expense — Drilling Platforms

> C Company is engaged in oil and gas exploration activities in the Gulf of Mexico. C Company uses two different types of platforms from which to perform its drilling and production operations. C Company designs and fabricates templet-type platforms and transports them in component form to the drill site for installation. In most instances, these platforms can be dismantled and the templates can be used again at other platform sites.
>
> In addition to templet-type platforms, C Company uses a jacket-type platform. C Company is not capable of fabricating this type of platform, but it provides the design and engineering specifications to an independent marine contractor for the fabrication. C Company's employees witness, inspect and test the various aspects of the construction process performed by the contractor. Neither the jacket-type platform nor any of its components are used for any other purpose and, in fact, generally are towed away and sunk at the end of their useful lives.

The tax treatment of costs incurred in the drilling and completion of wells in onshore and offshore operations generally is the same.[19] However, special problems arise that are peculiar to offshore operations. One such problem is the continuing disagreement between the Internal Revenue Service (IRS) and taxpayers about the classification of expenditures incurred in the construction and erection of drilling platforms used both for the drilling of wells and for operating the well or wells during the productive life of the property.

The option for intangible drilling and development costs (IDC) applies only to those drilling and development expenditures that, in themselves, have no salvage value and are incident to and necessary for the drilling of wells and the preparation of wells for the production of oil or gas.[20] The costs of labor, hauling, fuel, supplies and similar expenses incurred in transporting a platform to the drilling site, positioning and

17. G.C.M. 38976.
18. Gates Rubber Co.; Sun Company; Miller v. U.S., (C.D. Cal. 1977), 41 AFTR2d 78-376, 78-1 USTC 9127.
19. Rev. Rul. 70-596, 1970-2 C.B. 68.
20. Reg. Sec. 1.612-4(a).

erecting the platform, and anchoring it clearly are within the option. However, it is the IRS's position that certain costs associated with the onshore fabrication of a platform and fabrication performed during its transportation to the well site are not within the option and, accordingly, must be charged to depreciable property accounts.[21] The regulations, however, provide that labor, fuel, hauling and similar costs are not considered to have a salvage value, even though they are used in the installation of physical property that has a salvage value. The Court of Claims,[22] therefore, has held that the labor, fuel, repairs, supplies and similar costs of building templates used to construct an offshore platform come within the scope of the option, even though those costs are incurred through an unrelated contractor. In a position apparently at variance with the published ruling previously noted, the IRS also contended before the court that the expenditures did not come within the option because the platform would be used in future production activities if the wells were productive. The court, however, rejected this reasoning, noting that this position could lead to the inaccurate conclusion that none of the costs relating to platform construction are deductible.

The Tax Court[23] has held that similar costs associated with a jacket-type platform come within the option, but has developed its own test for making the determination. The intangible costs of integrating materials into an ordinarily salvageable component of a platform are not subject to the option to deduct. The intangible costs of integrating salvageable materials into an unsalvageable component do fall within the option. The Tax Court questioned the Court of Claims' reasoning and probably will require capitalization of those intangibles incurred for fabrication of the salvageable parts (templates) of the templet-type platforms. A District Court in the Fifth Circuit has applied the Tax Court's rationale.[24]

The intangible costs incurred by C Company in connection with the jacket-type platforms should fall within the option to deduct because these platforms and components thereof are not salvageable by C Company. Also, C Company should consider claiming deductions for the intangible costs incurred in the templet-type platforms. However, it should be aware that the Tax Court has indicated it probably will require capitalization of intangible costs incurred in developing and constructing the salvageable tangible components of a templet-type platform.

Off the coast of California, the use of manmade islands has been more prevalent than the use of self-contained drilling platforms. The construction of these islands usually involves the sinking of wooden or steel pilings to enclose a desired area and then filling the enclosed area with rocks, sand and other materials. The islands sometimes are linked to the mainland by causeways constructed in a similar manner. The tax treatment of the expenditures for constructing a drilling island should follow that appropriate for a self-contained drilling platform. However, because the materials used in the construction of the island may not have any appreciable salvage value, the capitalizable portion of the costs may be relatively small.

In some instances, canals are dug to move drilling rigs and other drilling equipment into marshy lands. The cost of such a canal usually will come within the intangibles option if it can be shown that the canal is incident to and necessary for the drilling of the wells and the preparation of the wells for the production of oil or gas.[25] However,

21. Rev. Rul. 70-596, 1970-2 C.B. 68; G.C.M. 39564.
22. Exxon Corp. v. U.S., 547 F.2d 548 (Ct. Cl. 1976), 39 AFTR2d 77-442, 77-1 USTC 9114; Exxon Corp. v. U.S., (Ct. Cl. Trial Judges Op. 1976), 37 AFTR2d 76-730, 1976-1 USTC 9205.
23. Standard Oil Co. (Indiana), 77 T.C. 349 (1981).
24. Texaco, Inc. v. U.S., 598 F. Supp. 1165 (S.D. Tex. 1984), 54 AFTR2d 84-6308, 84-2 USTC 9866.
25. Reg. Sec. 1.612-4(a).

if any of the costs can be attributed solely to the producing phases of the operation (such as deeper dredging for oil barges or dredging for the creation of islands to support oil storage and treatment equipment or for constructing levees to protect the wellhead equipment), they will be treated as capital costs of depreciable assets.

Another area of controversy concerns offshore drilling platforms. The question is whether a taxpayer using the accrual method of accounting may accrue and deduct the estimated cost of removing offshore platforms and well fixtures currently as the oil or gas is produced on an estimated cost-per-unit basis, as opposed to when the costs actually are incurred. The issues involved are substantially the same in determining whether reclamation costs associated with strip mining can be accrued and deducted as the coal or ore is mined.

The IRS has ruled that the reclamation costs[26] and platform removal costs[27] cannot be accrued and deducted until they actually are incurred. Although the courts have not ruled on platform removal costs, the reclamation costs issue has been litigated numerous times. The courts have held that these costs can be currently accrued in situations where the liability for reclaiming the land is fixed either under state law or by the terms of the lease, and the costs can be reasonably estimated.[28] However, the courts have denied a current deduction in situations where they concluded the estimated amount was not reasonably determinable.[29]

The controversy concerning accrual of platform removal costs was resolved in favor of the IRS by a 1984 amendment to the Internal Revenue Code. Generally, the law provides that the "all-events" test applicable to accrual-basis taxpayers is not met until economic performance occurs with respect to the item of expense.[30] Since economic performance occurs as property or services are provided, the deduction for platform removal costs would be allowed in the year the platform is dismantled. Taxpayers may elect to accrue certain qualified mine and waste disposal reclamation and closing costs in advance of economic performance.[31] However, no exception to the economic performance requirement has been provided for platform removal costs.

Case 23
General Election Pertaining to Intangible Drilling and Development Costs

> **C Company begins preparation of its federal income tax return for the fiscal year during which it has drilled its first oil and gas well. Before the due date of the return, the company realizes that it has insufficient data to complete the return and files Form 7004 to obtain an automatic extension of time to file the return. C Company plans to expense intangible drilling and development costs (IDC) for tax purposes.**

C Company has made no election with respect to the treatment of IDC by obtaining an extension of time in which to file its return. By extending the period within which

26. IRS Letter Ruling 7831003.
27. Rev. Rul. 80-182, 1980-2 C.B. 167.
28. Harrold v. Comm'r, 192 F.2d 1002 (4th Cir. 1951), 41 AFTR 442, 52-1 USTC 9107; Denise Coal Co. v. Comm'r, 271 F.2d 930 (3d Cir. 1959), 4 AFTR2d 5815, 59-2 USTC 9769.
29. Patsch v. Comm'r, 208 F.2d 532 (3d Cir. 1953), 44 AFTR 857, 54-1 USTC 9124, *aff'g* 19 T.C. 189; Jenkins v. Comm'r, 217 F.2d 951 (3d Cir. 1955), 46 AFTR 1415, 55-1 USTC 9150; Comm'r v. Gregory Run Coal Co., 212 F.2d 52 (4th Cir. 1954), 45 AFTR 1368, 54-1 USTC 9342, *aff'g* 19 T.C. 501, *cert. den.* 348 U.S. 828 (1954).
30. I.R.C. Sec. 461(h).
31. I.R.C. Sec. 468.

to file a timely return, C Company also has extended the period within which to make its election to expense IDC.

C Company's election to expense IDC must be made in its return for the year in which it first has paid or incurred those costs. The election is made by claiming the IDC as a deduction in the return.[32] Failure to deduct those costs as expenses in this return will be deemed to be an election to capitalize and recover the costs through depreciation and depletion.[33] If a taxpayer elects to capitalize IDC, an additional election is available to permit the deduction of IDC incurred in drilling nonproductive wells. Such an election must be stated clearly in the return for the first tax year in which a nonproductive well is completed.[34] The classification of certain IDC as dry-hole losses has been held to indicate an election to expense only those costs on nonproductive wells.[35]

If a taxpayer elects to capitalize IDC on productive wells and to expense IDC on nonproductive wells, the deduction for the costs of the nonproductive wells is allowable only in the year in which the nonproductive wells are completed as dry holes. Even if some of the costs of the dry holes are incurred and capitalized in a prior year and the outcome of the well is known before the tax return is filed for the year in which the costs were incurred, the costs still may not be deducted until the year in which the well is abandoned.[36]

The taxpayer should take extreme care in the year an election is to be made to ascertain that no IDC paid or incurred remain deferred at yearend. Thus, any IDC carried in "work in progress" should be reclassified as a deduction in the federal income tax return.

Although no formal statement of election is required, attaching to the return a statement similar to the following eliminates any questions as to the intent to deduct IDC:

> Taxpayer hereby elects, under the provisions of Regulations Section 1.612-4, pursuant to Section 263(c) of the Internal Revenue Code, to deduct as expenses all intangible drilling and development costs incurred in the drilling of both productive and nonproductive oil or gas wells and the preparation of wells for production.

This form of election may be modified in many instances for use in state income tax returns for those states in which an election is required.

The election made by the taxpayer in the first year that IDC are paid or incurred is binding for all subsequent years;[37] therefore, care must be exercised in properly classifying those expenditures in the return for the first year in which they are incurred.

The Internal Revenue Scrvice (IRS) has taken the position that each member of an affiliated group filing a consolidated return must continue to treat IDC in accordance with its previous election. Any member of an affiliated group filing a consolidated return must make its own election in the year in which it first incurs any IDC, irrespective of any election made previously by the common parent corporation.[38] Also,

32. Reg. Sec. 1.612-4(d).
33. Reg. Sec. 1.612-4(d); California Coast Oil Co., 25 B.T.A. 902 (1932); Boone v. U.S., 374 F. Supp. 115 (D.C. N.D. 1973), 33 AFTR2d 74-541, 74-1 USTC 9180.
34. Reg. Sec. 1.612-4(b)(4).
35. Hawkeye Petroleum Corp., 18 T.C. 1223 (1952).
36. Great Western Petroleum Corp., 1 T.C. 624 (1943); Ravencliffs Development Co. v. U.S., 144 F. Supp. 131 (S.D. W.Va. 1956), 50 AFTR 350, 56-2 USTC 9873.
37. Reg. Sec. 1.612-4(e).
38. Rev. Rul. 69-590, 1969-2 C.B. 170.

partnerships and trusts must make their own elections, regardless of any elections previously made by their partners or beneficiaries.

In the past, there had been informal indications that the IRS would not recognize an election to expense intangibles if made in a delinquent return even though the regulations require only that the election be made in the return for the taxpayer's first tax year in which those costs are paid or incurred.[39] There is no requirement in the regulations that the return for that year be filed timely for the election to be effective. The IRS has issued several private letter rulings[40] that confirm the conclusion that the election need not be made in a timely filed return. Therefore, an election to expense intangibles made in a delinquent return should be valid. Care should be exercised, however, until the IRS expresses its opinion publicly.

In situations where a request for an extension of time to file an election[41] still may be appropriate, the IRS has expressed, informally, a willingness to issue a favorable ruling when the failure to elect was caused by persons not employed by the taxpayer, such as outside consultants, tax advisors or attorneys.

The IRS also takes the position that a valid election cannot be made or changed in an amended return. A court has held that a taxpayer exercised his option to capitalize IDC when those costs were not deducted in his original return; therefore, the costs were not allowed as deductions in an amended return filed approximately two years later.[42] The courts also have denied taxpayers the right to use amended returns either to exercise the option to deduct IDC or to change an election.[43] However, one court has held that the election could be made in an amended return if the taxpayer did not have all the material facts required to make a deliberate choice at the time of filing the original return. Under those circumstances, the initial return was regarded as tentative, and any election made therein was not binding.[44]

If a taxpayer has elected erroneously to capitalize IDC, consideration should be given to conducting future oil and gas operations in the partnership form. A new partnership, being a new tax reporting entity, has the right to make a separate election with respect to the deduction of IDC.[45] This is true whether the partnership is legally constituted as such or is a co-owned oil and gas property for which the co-owners do not elect to be excluded from the partnership provisions of the tax law. *(See Case 163.)* If a corporate taxpayer has erroneously elected to capitalize IDC, a new subsidiary can be formed to conduct future exploration and development activities. The new subsidiary then can make its own election.

Except in very limited circumstances, the elections of both independent producers and integrated oil companies to expense IDC do not apply to amounts paid or incurred after December 31, 1986, for IDC with respect to wells located outside the United States.[46] Such amounts are required to be capitalized and amortized ratably over a 10-year period beginning with the tax year in which such costs were paid or incurred[47] or, at the election of the taxpayer, included in the basis of a property and recovered through cost depletion.[48] For this purpose, the United States includes the 50 states, the District of Columbia and the continental shelf areas that are adjacent to U.S.

---

39. Reg. Sec. 1.612-4(d).
40. IRS Letter Ruling 8341032; IRS Letter Ruling 8341053; IRS Letter Ruling 8341054; IRS Letter Ruling 8341055; IRS Letter Ruling 8341056.
41. Reg. Sec. 1.9100-1; Rev. Proc. 79-63, 1979-2 C.B. 578; IRS Letter Ruling 8636041; IRS Letter Ruling 8701058.
42. Titus Oil & Investment Co. v. Comm'r, 132 F.2d 969 (10th Cir. 1943), 30 AFTR 716, 43-1 USTC 9249.
43. Burford Oil Co. v. Comm'r, 153 F.2d 745 (5th Cir. 1946), 34 AFTR 1055, 46-1 USTC 9185; Oils, Inc., 41 B.T.A. 1338 (1940).
44. Lucas v. Sterling Oil & Gas Co., 62 F.2d 951 (6th Cir. 1933), 12 AFTR 90, 1933 CCH 9076.
45. Reg. Sec. 1.703-1(b)(1).
46. I.R.C. Sec. 263(c); I.R.C. Sec. 263(i)(1).
47. I.R.C. Sec. 263(i)(2)(B).
48. I.R.C. Sec. 263(i)(2)(A).

territorial waters and over which the United States has exclusive rights with respect to the exploration and exploitation of natural resources.[49] The Committee Reports under the Tax Reform Act of 1986 indicate that foreign dry-hole costs are fully deductible in the year the dry hole is "completed."[50] Presumably, this means that the costs may be deducted in the year drilling is completed and the well is determined to be nonproductive.

(See Case 25 for a discussion of the requirement for integrated oil companies to capitalize and amortize 30% of IDC expenditures after 1986. The 30%-capitalization requirement for IDC expenditures of integrated oil companies does not apply to foreign IDC since all foreign IDC expenditures after 1986 must be capitalized.[51])

(See Case 181 for a discussion of when taxpayers that make the general election to expense IDC have a further annual election to capitalize and amortize any portion of the IDC.)

Case 24
Treatment of Intangible Drilling Costs by Integrated Oil Companies

In June 1987, Corporation A incurred $3 million of intangible drilling costs. Corporation A owns major refining operations and is not an "independent producer" within the meaning of the windfall profit tax provisions. Corporation A's accountant wants to know the impact of Corporation A's integrated company status on the corporation's intangible drilling cost deduction in its year ended December 31, 1987, and future years.

The Tax Reform Act of 1986 (the Act) requires integrated oil companies to capitalize 30% of intangible drilling and development costs (IDC) after December 31, 1986.[52] The amount so capitalized is allowable as a deduction ratably over the 60-month period beginning with the month in which the costs are paid or incurred.[53] The term *integrated oil company* means, with respect to any tax year, any producer of crude oil other than an independent producer. The terms *producer* and *independent producer* have the same meanings as used in the windfall profit tax provisions.[54] *(See Case 216.)* Only corporations other than S corporations are subject to these provisions.[55]

Under the facts of this case, Corporation A is entitled to a total deduction for 1987 of $2,205,000, determined as follows:

70% of IDC ($3,000,000) incurred		$2,100,000
Ratable amortization of capitalized portion:		
30% of IDC incurred	$900,000	
Seven months' amortization over 60-month period	× 7/60	
Allowable amortization		105,000
Total deduction for 1987		$2,205,000

49. House Report No. 99-426, 1986-3 C.B. Vol. 2 203.
50. Conference Committee Report, No. 99-841, 1986-3 C.B. Vol. 4 121.
51. House Report, No. 99-426, 1986-3 C.B. Vol. 2 203.
52. I.R.C. Sec. 291(b)(1).
53. I.R.C. Sec. 291(b)(2).
54. I.R.C. Sec. 291(b)(4).
55. I.R.C. Sec. 291(b)(4); I.R.C. Sec. 4996(a)(1)(C)[D].

Corporation A may continue to amortize the capitalized costs at the rate of $15,000 per month ($900,000 ÷ 60 months) until fully deducted.

The capitalized portion of the IDC is not included in the adjusted basis of the property for purposes of cost depletion.[56] The provisions apply to all costs deductible as IDC,[57] presumably including IDC relating to dry holes. The 30%-capitalization requirement for IDC does not apply to IDC incurred with respect to wells located outside the United States.[58] *(See Case 23 for a discussion of the treatment of foreign IDC expenditures after 1986.)*

If Corporation A subsequently disposes of a property and is required to recapture IDC,[59] amounts deducted under the ratable amortization provision must be included with the 70% deductible portion for purposes of computing recapture.[60] *(See Case 131 concerning recapture of IDC.)*

Before the Act, integrated oil companies were required to capitalize 20% of the IDC expenditures after December 31, 1984.

For tax years beginning after December 31, 1986, IDC incurred in drilling a productive well are a tax preference item for corporations. The amortization deductions of integrated oil companies under the 30%-capitalization requirement are included as a tax preference item in the year incurred. *(See Case 181 for a discussion of the election to capitalize and amortize IDC over a 10-year period to avoid having IDC treated as a tax preference item.)*

For the purpose of computing earnings and profits, corporations are required to capitalize IDC (other than costs incurred in connection with a nonproductive well) and deduct those costs ratably over 60 months beginning with the month in which production from the well begins. This rule applies to amounts paid or incurred in tax years beginning after September 30, 1984.[61] The 30% of the IDC capitalized and amortized by integrated oil companies is not subject to further adjustment for earnings and profits computations because the amortization deduction is not considered to be IDC deductible under Section 263(c).[62]

Case 25
Subchapter K and Intangibles Elections by Co-Owners

Operators B and C enter into a joint operating agreement with Operator A. Each of the co-owners owns title to an undivided interest in an oil and gas lease. Among other things, the agreement gives Operator A full control over development and operation of the property. The agreement further provides that each party has the right to take in kind or separately dispose of his share of any production that may be obtained. Each of the co-owners previously has elected to expense intangible drilling and development costs (IDC) with respect to his separately owned properties.

Although the corporate characteristics of continuity of life and centralized management may exist under this operating agreement, each party has retained ownership of his undivided interest in the lease and control over the marketing of his share of

56. I.R.C. Sec. 291(b)(5).
57. I.R.C. Sec. 291(b)(1)(A).
58. House Report No. 99-426, 1986-3 C.B. Vol. 2 203.
59. I.R.C. Sec. 1254.
60. I.R.C. Sec. 291(b)(3).
61. I.R.C. Sec. 312(n)(2).
62. I.R.C. Sec. 291(b)(2); I.R.C. Sec. 312(n)(2).

production. Under these circumstances, present regulations do not classify the joint operation of the property as an association taxable as a corporation.[63] *(See Case 161.)* Such an operation of an oil and gas property by co-owners through an agent or operator comes within the statutory definition of a partnership.[64] However, when the owner of a mining claim farmed it out, retaining an overriding royalty interest that would convert into a working interest at payout, the Internal Revenue Service (IRS) held in a technical advice memorandum that the particular facts did not constitute a partnership.[65] Factors relied on by the IRS in reaching this conclusion were: (1) no intent by the parties to form a partnership; (2) no present sharing of profits and losses; (3) no business conducted in the joint names of the parties and (4) no mutual control over operations. It should be noted that a technical advice memorandum may not be relied upon as a precedent by taxpayers not directly involved in the specific situation. A slight change in the sharing arrangement or subjective intent of the parties may be sufficient to cause the arrangement to be a partnership. For example, a farmout in which the farmor is "carried" to casing point customarily is treated as a joint venture taxable as a partnership unless the Subchapter K election discussed below is made. *(See Case 163.)*

Under the partnership regulations,[66] the co-owners in the typical joint operation of an oil and gas property are granted an election to be excluded from the application of all or part of the provisions of Subchapter K of the Internal Revenue Code (the Code). The election may be made by filing a partnership return (Form 1065) for the first year the unincorporated organization elects to be excluded. The return must contain only the name or other identification of the organization, its address and a statement containing the following information:

- ☐ Names, addresses and identification numbers of all members of the organization.
- ☐ A statement that the organization qualifies for the election under the appropriate provisions of the regulations.
- ☐ A statement that all the members of the organization elect that it be excluded from all of Subchapter K.
- ☐ A statement indicating where a copy of the agreement under which the organization operates is available.[67]

If the operator elects to exclude the organization from the partnership provisions of the Code, each co-owner's share of the IDC incurred in the joint operation must be treated in accordance with that co-owner's prior election.

If the co-owners do not elect to be excluded from the provisions of Subchapter K or if they form a general or limited partnership to own and operate the properties, the partnership, as owner of the operating rights, can make a separate election to expense its IDC. Even though a partnership, as such, is not a taxpayer, the regulations provide that the partnership must make the election.[68] The election by the partnership will have no effect on the treatment of similar costs incurred by the partners on their separately owned properties.[69] Partners have an additional annual election to capitalize and amortize any portion of the IDC elected to be expensed by the partnership. *(See Case 181.)*

---

63. Reg. Sec. 301.7701-2.
64. I.R.C. Sec. 761(a); Reg. Sec. 1.761-1(a).
65. IRS Letter Ruling 8302002 (Technical Advice Memorandum).
66. Reg. Sec. 1.761-2(a).
67. Reg. Sec. 1.761-2(b)(2)(i).
68. Reg. Sec. 1.703-1(b)(1).
69. Bentex Oil Corp., 20 T.C. 565 (1953).

According to current regulations, even though co-owners in the joint operation of an oil and gas property do not elect to be excluded from the provisions of Subchapter K, the venture, nevertheless, will be deemed to have made the election if it can be shown that the co-owners intended from inception of the venture to secure exclusion from Subchapter K.[70] Among the facts that may be used to show this intent are: (1) an agreement among the co-owners at the time the venture is formed to exclude the venture from Subchapter K or (2) reporting by the co-owners on their respective returns of their pro-rata shares of income, deductions and credits of the venture and the making of appropriate elections in a manner consistent with the exclusion of the venture from Subchapter K. This is in the nature of a relief provision for taxpayers that have done everything except the actual filing of the election. If taxpayers are uncertain about the provision's application, however, they should file the proper election to avoid later controversy over the actual intent of the co-owners.

This "deemed" election provision apparently does not apply to co-owners in the joint operation of foreign oil and gas properties.[71]

The right of participants to elect out of the partnership provisions is subject to certain requirements, one of which is that the parties "reserve the right separately to take in kind or dispose of their shares of any property produced, extracted or used. . . ." The IRS has issued a technical advice memorandum that addresses a factual situation wherein a right of first refusal or call on production existed.[72] It provides that such a call is inconsistent with the right to take in kind and separately dispose of production. This technical advice memorandum is an indication that the IRS may construe the requirements narrowly for electing out of Subchapter K. In the absence of judicial interpretation and clear statutory or regulatory authority and when a right of first refusal or call on production exists, consideration should be given to filing a partnership return of income to protect the validity of certain elections required of the partnership (such as the election to deduct IDC).

Case 26
Issues Affecting Decisions of Co-Owners To Make Subchapter K Elections

Operator A has entered into a joint operating agreement with Operators B and C. The joint operating agreement meets all the qualifications for electing to be excluded from the provisions of Subchapter K of the Internal Revenue Code (the Code). Operator A asks for assistance in determining if and when the election should be made.

Subchapter K of the Code contains the various code sections relating specifically to the taxation of partnerships. Thus, an election to be excluded from all the provisions of Subchapter K means they will not apply to the joint venture.

Many joint ventures elect to be excluded from the partnership provisions of Subchapter K. This election generally provides the co-owners with maximum tax flexibility, requires less coordinated tax planning and eliminates the need to prepare an annual partnership income tax return. Once the election is made, each of the co-owners reports his share of the operations, using his own accounting methods and tax year.

70. Reg. Sec. 1.761-2(b)(2).
71. Reg. Sec. 1.6031-1(d)(2).
72. IRS Letter Ruling 8226014 (Technical Advice Memorandum).

Despite these advantages, the number of joint ventures choosing not to be excluded from the partnership provisions has increased significantly in recent years. Subjecting the joint venture to the partnership provisions of Subchapter K may effectively: (1) avoid capitalization of intangibles when sharing of cost is disproportionate to the relative ownership of the working interests *(see Case 38)*; (2) avoid capitalization of intangibles when payout is computed on a composite basis for multiple properties *(see Case 46)*; (3) avoid possible income recognition in a farmout involving a carved-out drill site situation *(see Case 41)* and (4) enable a taxpayer to use a method of accounting (e.g., cash basis) for a particular property that is different from the taxpayer's general accounting method.

The joint venture is not required to make the election to be excluded from the partnership provisions effective for the first year of its existence. The election can be made at the time of filing the return for any tax year for which exclusion is first desired. Such a subsequent-year election is retroactive to the beginning of the tax year for which the return containing the election applies. The joint venture then will be subject to Subchapter K for all years prior to the year the election is made.[73]

The co-owners should consider carefully the consequences of making the election in a subsequent year, both in terms of the pertinent provisions of the joint venture agreement and tax consequences.

An effective election to be excluded from the provisions of Subchapter K does not cause a joint venture to lose its characterization as a partnership for other purposes. For example, it has been held that the exclusion election is ineffective with respect to the computation of the limitation on used property for investment credit purposes[74] and to the capitalization of startup costs.[75] The Internal Revenue Service (IRS) even has held that fractional working interests are separate partnership interests (even though all partners had elected to be excluded from Subchapter K), with each interest constituting a separate and distinct closely held business. As a result, the IRS held that a taxpayer was not entitled to an extension of time for payment of estate tax because the percentage ownership of each "partnership" was insufficient to meet the qualifying tests.[76] However, the IRS reached the opposite conclusion in a subsequent technical advice memorandum, which held that for purposes of installment payment of estate tax, it was not necessary for each working interest to qualify as a separate partnership.[77]

Although the consent of all co-owners who are members of a joint venture is required to make an exclusion election effective,[78] it often is difficult to determine which co-owners are members of a particular joint venture. The IRS apparently has held in at least one situation[79] that when co-owners are covered by two separate operating agreements, the co-owners comprise two separate joint ventures, each of which has a separate exclusion election available.

The regulations provide that a partnership return must be filed for the first tax year in which the participants, by a formal agreement, undertake to engage in joint operations. In the absence of a formal agreement, a partnership return must be filed for the first tax year in which the participants jointly make or incur any expenditures treated

73. Reg. Sec. 1.761-2(b)(1).
74. Rev. Rul. 65-118, 1965-1 C.B. 30; Olin Bryant, 46 T.C. 848 (1966), *aff'd* 399 F.2d 800 (5th Cir. 1968), 22 AFTR2d 5375, 68-2 USTC 9521.
75. Madison Gas and Elec. Co., 72 T.C. 521 (1979), *aff'd* 633 F.2d 512 (7th Cir. 1980), 46 AFTR2d 80-5955, 80-2 USTC 9754.
76. IRS Letter Ruling 8042011.
77. IRS Letter Ruling 8419002.
78. I.R.C. Sec. 761(a); Reg. Sec. 1.761-2(b)(3).
79. IRS Letter Ruling 7951080.

as deductions for federal income tax purposes.[80] In interpreting this regulation, the IRS has held that the payment of exploration expenditures incurred in connection with the acquisition of property or the payment of delay rentals is not an expenditure requiring the filing of a return. However, the payment of any development costs, including geological costs incurred in locating a drill site, does require the filing of a return.[81]

Case 27
Deduction Allowable When Drilling Is Done by Operator for His Own Account

> **Operator A keeps his books and files his tax return on the accrual basis and has elected to expense intangible drilling and development costs (IDC). During 1987, Operator A drills one producing oil well and is drilling another well at the close of the year. Operator A uses his own drilling rigs and personnel on the wells. The IDC incurred during the year are $400,000 on the completed well and $75,000 on the well in progress. The costs are carried on Operator A's books as "intangible drilling and development costs" and "work in progress," respectively.**

The regulations provide that a taxpayer using the accrual method of accounting must deduct IDC in the year incurred if he has elected to treat those costs as expenses.[82] Because Operator A is drilling the well himself, using his own equipment and personnel, his costs are incurred as the drilling progresses. Accordingly, Operator A should deduct the $475,000 incurred for IDC in his 1987 return. The portion of the costs carried on the books as "work in progress" was incurred during the current year and, therefore, the deduction cannot be postponed until the succeeding year when the well is completed.[83]

The Supreme Court has held that depreciation on equipment used to construct a taxpayer's capital assets is a capital cost of the asset being constructed and not a current depreciation deduction.[84] However, Operator A should claim depreciation on the drilling rigs and other drilling tools used in connection with drilling the wells as a current deduction because the purpose of the election to expense IDC is to allow as a current deduction amounts that otherwise would be capital costs.[85]

The Internal Revenue Service has taken the position that the portions of a taxpayer's general overhead expenses that are clearly related to or identified with drilling and development activities must be characterized as IDC. Each item of overhead expense must be analyzed to determine if it is related to a drilling and development activity.[86] *(See Case 187 for a discussion of additional cost-capitalization requirements enacted by the Tax Reform Act of 1986.)*

80. Reg. Sec. 1.6031-1(a)(2).
81. Rev. Rul. 56-500, 1956-2 C.B. 464.
82. Reg. Sec. 1.446-1(c)(1)(ii).
83. Great Western Petroleum Corp., 1 T.C. 624 (1943).
84. Idaho Power Co. v. Comm'r, 94 U.S. 2757 (1974), 34 AFTR2d 74-5244, 74-2 USTC 9521.
85. I.R.C. Sec. 263(c).
86. IRS Letter Ruling 8406006 (Technical Advice Memorandum); IRS Letter Ruling 8622005 (Technical Advice Memorandum); IRS Letter Ruling 8640006 (Technical Advice Memorandum).

Case 28
Deduction for Drilling Done by Outside Contractor

Driller D contracts with Operator A to drill a well on Operator A's lease at a contract price of $12 per foot. The drilling is to begin in 1987. The well is to be drilled to a depth of 6,000 feet unless oil or gas is found at a shallower depth. Operator A has no obligation to make payment unless the well reaches contract depth. At the end of the year, the well is in progress and drilling at 4,000 feet. Operator A files his tax return on a calendar-year basis and reports on the accrual method of accounting.

An accrual-basis taxpayer is allowed a deduction when all events have occurred that determine the fact of liability and the liability can be determined with reasonable accuracy.[87] In addition, an accrual-basis taxpayer that is not a tax shelter may not deduct any item until economic performance has occurred, with an exception for certain recurring items. Economic performance is deemed to occur when property or services are provided.[88] *(See Case 9 for a discussion of economic performance.)*

Because Operator A's liability is contingent upon Driller D's drilling to a depth of 6,000 feet, the intangible drilling and development costs (IDC) relative to the 4,000 feet of hole drilled by the end of the tax year will not be deductible until the year in which contract depth is reached and the liability is fixed. Although the economic performance test would be met with respect to the 4,000 feet of hole drilled, the "all-events" test would not be met.

However, when a taxpayer consistently accrues his estimated liability for drilling costs incurred on outstanding drilling contracts over a period of time, this method may be accepted as properly reflecting income.[89] The contingency that the contractor will be unable to complete his contract is considered remote in most situations because of improvements in the techniques of drilling. When the number of outstanding contracts is material or substantial and a reasonable estimate of the liability can be made, proper accounting requires that liability be reflected in the accounts, even though it may not be deductible for tax purposes until the next year.

If the contractor has reached contract depth by the end of the tax year or is drilling on a "daywork" basis, Operator A should deduct the IDC for which he is liable. If the drilling contract provides that Operator A's liability becomes fixed on a "footage basis," he can deduct the IDC applicable to the depth drilled by yearend in his return for 1987.

Operator A can obtain a deduction for amounts accrued for drilling to the depth reached by yearend by releasing Driller D from liability to that depth. The release of Driller D from liability to the depth attained removes the contingency of Operator A's liability at yearend and permits the deduction in 1987.

Case 29
Year in Which Expenses Are Deductible

Operator A, an accrual-basis, calendar-year taxpayer, owns a three-fourths undivided interest in an oil and gas lease. Operator B, a cash-

87. Reg. Sec. 1.461-1(a)(2).
88. I.R.C. Sec. 461(h).
89. Terminal Drilling & Production Co., 32 T.C. 926 (1959).

basis, calendar-year taxpayer, owns the remaining one-fourth interest. Neither operator owns any drilling equipment.

Operators A and B enter into an agreement for the drilling and completion of a well before December 31, 1987. They agree to share proportionately all costs and expenses of drilling and completing the well, with Operator A acting as operator for purposes of negotiating with the driller, paying the costs and expenses, etc.

At yearend, the well is drilled and completed, and Operator B has advanced to Operator A sufficient funds to cover his share of the costs of the well to casing point, but he has not paid Operator A for his share of the completion costs of the well. At yearend, Operator A had paid some of the costs and expenses of drilling and completing the well but does not pay several bills, including the amount payable to the drilling contractor, until 1988.

Operators A and B elect to be excluded from the partnership provisions of the Internal Revenue Code.

Under the circumstances, Operator A, an accrual-basis taxpayer, is entitled to deduct his entire share of the intangible drilling and development costs (IDC) and other expenses incurred before yearend, assuming a proper election to deduct those costs is or has been made.[90] *(See Case 9 for a discussion of the impact of the "all-events" test and economic performance requirement on the deductibility of accrued expenses.)*

The rules concerning the timing of the deduction to Operator B as a cash-basis nonoperator are unclear. The uncertainty is due to whether an operating agreement creates a principal/agency relationship between the operator and the nonoperators. *(See Case 9 for a discussion of taxpayers that are required to report on an accrual basis.)*

The Internal Revenue Service (IRS) apparently has adopted in its audit guide the position that a principal/agency relationship generally exists between the operator and the nonoperator.[91]

The concept of the agency relationship originally was established by the courts in a case involving unusual facts.[92] Because of these facts and the lack of adequate explanation by the courts of their conclusions, the use of the case as general precedent has been questioned by the courts[93] and even by the IRS itself.[94]

As is the case with numerous areas of oil and gas taxation, the actual industry practice varies among taxpayers and is influenced significantly by the limits of practicality. The general lack of judicial or administrative developments with regard to this issue is evidence that the IRS generally has been willing to accept the varying approaches used thus far by taxpayers. However, the IRS generally requires that a taxpayer's approach be reasonable and that it be applied on a consistent basis from year to year.

If Operator B has access to the necessary information and has followed the agency approach consistently, he should deduct only his share of the IDC and other expenses actually paid by Operator A prior to yearend. Under this rationale, Operator A, as

90. Great Western Petroleum Corp., 1 T.C. 624 (1943); I.R.C. Sec. 461(h).
91. Internal Revenue Manual—Audit Sec. 4232.8-12, Para. 257.5 (Apr. 18, 1985).
92. McAdams v. Comm'r, 198 F.2d 54 (5th Cir. 1952), 42 AFTR 310, 52-2 USTC 9373; Irving Segall, 30 T.C. 734 (1958).
93. Rife v. Comm'r, 356 F.2d 823 (5th Cir. 1966), 17 AFTR2d 367, 66-1 USTC 9239. *See also* Levy v. Comm'r, 732 F.2d 1435 (9th Cir. 1984), 53 AFTR2d 84-1435, 84-1 USTC 9470.
94. IRS Letter Ruling 7808253250D (Technical Advice Memorandum).

operator, is considered to be acting as Operator B's agent in the drilling of the well. Because payment by an agent is construed to be payment by the principal, the current deductibility of these costs and expenses by Operator B depends solely on whether Operator A, the agent, has made payment. This is true whether or not Operator B, the principal, has reimbursed him. Thus, even if Operator B has made no payment to Operator A, Operator B should be entitled to deduct his share of the deductible costs and expenses paid by Operator A and charged to the joint account *(however, see the following discussion of the "at-risk" rules)*. Payment by Operator A of Operator B's share of the costs results in a constructive loan arrangement as though the latter had obtained a loan from an outside source to pay the expenses directly. This treatment should not be confused with the general concept that the issuance of a note, which merely evidences an indebtedness, in payment of an expense normally will not permit a cash-basis taxpayer to deduct that expense because there has been no actual payment during the year.[95]

If Operator A is an unrelated third-party operator, Operator B may find it difficult, if not impossible, to determine when Operator A paid the various costs. In such a situation, Operator B may not be able to apply the agency approach and, thus, must claim his deductions on the basis of the timing of his reimbursements to Operator A. However, although this approach may be the practical solution, the IRS could question deductibility until Operator B proves that Operator A paid the contractor.

When Operators A and B are related parties, the information concerning the timing of Operator A's payment of third-party invoices generally will be readily available. If an agency relationship exists between the related parties and if the needed information with regard to date of payment by the operator is available, it appears that the taxpayers should adhere to the agency principles and Operator B should claim his deductions based on the timing of Operator A's payment of the third-party invoices *(however, see the following discussion of the "at-risk" rules)*.

Operating expenses incurred by Operator A after the well has been completed and is in production may be treated somewhat differently. In operating the well, Operator A generally acts as an independent contractor rather than as agent for the co-owners. If Operator A is an independent contractor, operating expenses will be deductible by Operator B only when he pays Operator A for his share of the expenses. The legal relationship between the parties should be examined to determine the proper timing of the deduction for operating expenses.

In this case, Operator B is "at risk" because he has advanced his share of the costs to Operator A. However, if Operator B had not made the advance, he would not be "at risk" with regard to the funds Operator A constructively loaned to him because Operator A owns an interest in the activity. Thus, if Operator B had not made the advance, his deduction of the expenses would be disallowed, in whole or in part, until he reimbursed Operator A. This would be true whether or not Operator B would be entitled to a deduction under his general method of accounting. *(See Case 32 for a discussion of the "at-risk" rules.)*

For purposes of computing cost depletion, depreciation, abandonment losses, or gain or loss on sale, both Operators A and B have tax basis in the leasehold and in any lease and well equipment installed on the property. The tax basis in the depletable and the depreciable property includes the amount of any outstanding liability for both

95. Quinn v. Comm'r, 111 F.2d 372 (5th Cir. 1940), 24 AFTR 927, 40-1 USTC 9403. *See also* Levy v. Comm'r; Chapman v. U.S., 527 F. Supp. 1053 (D.C. Minn. 1981), 49 AFTR2d 82-443, 82-1 USTC 9119, involving a note and a letter of credit; Eckert v. Burnet, 283 U.S. 140 (1931), 9 AFTR 1413, 2 USTC 714; Helvering v. Price, 309 U.S. 409 (1940), 24 AFTR 657, 40-1 USTC 9336; G.C.M. 39096; Stanley Halle, T.C. Memo. Dec. (Dec. 19, 1983); Stinnett's Pontiac Service, Inc. v. Comm'r, 730 F.2d 634 (11th Cir. 1984), 53 AFTR2d 84-1197, 84-1 USTC 9406.

accrual- and cash-basis taxpayers.[96] However, if the purchase price of the property exceeds a reasonable estimate of its fair market value and part of the price is represented by nonrecourse debt, that debt probably will not be considered to represent bona fide indebtedness. Accordingly, it may be ignored in determining basis of the property and deductibility of interest.[97] If Operator B had not advanced his share of costs to Operator A, the "at-risk" rules could limit Operator B's depreciation and depletion deductions.[98]

IDC and operating expenses should be deducted in the year paid or incurred, even though they may be reimbursed in a later year. This situation may occur, for example, when there is pending litigation concerning a title dispute and the right of reimbursement is contingent on the outcome of the suit.[99]

The Tax Reform Act of 1986 provides new limitations on the deductibility of passive-activity losses. These limitations may not affect the taxpayers in the factual situation presented in this case because the term *passive activity* does not include a working interest that a taxpayer owns directly or through an entity which does not limit the liability of the taxpayer with respect to the working interest. *(See Case 182 for a discussion of how the new passive-activity limitations may limit the deductibility of losses of certain taxpayers.)*

Case 30
Use of Nonrecourse Notes for Partial Payment of Intangible Drilling Costs

> Corporation A and Corporation B form a partnership, P, to explore for oil and gas. Corporations A and B are equal partners in Partnership P, which is an accrual-basis partnership.
>
> Partnership P purchases two oil and gas leases from Driller D for $25,000 on June 1, 1987, and at the same time enters into a turnkey contract whereby D agrees to drill two wells on the leases for $250,000. Consideration paid to Driller D for the leases is $10,000 cash and a $15,000 nonrecourse promissory note. The consideration for the turnkey drilling obligation is $100,000 cash and a $150,000 nonrecourse note. Corporations A and B each contribute $55,000 to Partnership P. The wells are completed in 1987.
>
> The nonrecourse notes are dated June 1, 1987, and are payable on December 1, 1990. Interest at 10% per annum is due on the unpaid balance of the notes. The only collateral securing the notes consists of Partnership P's interest in the two oil and gas leases, the lease and well equipment thereon and 80% of any future oil and gas production from the wells completed on the two leases.

Generally, an accrual-basis taxpayer is allowed to deduct amounts paid with a note provided the note is a "true" loan and the "all-events" test[100] is met. Accrual-basis

96. Crane v. Comm'r, 331 U.S. 1 (1947), 35 AFTR 776, 47-1 USTC 9217.
97. Fortune Odend'hal, Jr., 80 T.C. 588 (1983); Max E. Wildman, 78 T.C. 943 (1982). *See also* CRC Corporation v. Comm'r, 693 F.2d 281 (3d Cir. 1982), 50 AFTR2d 82-6105, 82-2 USTC 9677; Gibson Products Co. v. U.S., 637 F.2d 1041 (5th Cir. 1981), 47 AFTR2d 81-863, 81-1 USTC 9213; Brannen v. Comm'r, 722 F.2d 695 (11th Cir. 1984), 53 AFTR2d 84-579, 84-1 USTC 9144; Carolina, Clinchfield, and Ohio Railway Company, 82 T.C. 888 (1984); William J. Law, 86 T.C. 1065 (1986).
98. I.R.C. Sec. 465(b)(3).
99. Mel Dar Corp. v. Comm'r, 309 F.2d 525 (9th Cir. 1962), 10 AFTR2d 5845, 62-2 USTC 9793.
100. Reg. Sec. 1.461-1(a)(2); U.S. v. Anderson, 269 U.S. 422 (1926), 5 AFTR 5674, 1 USTC 155.

taxpayers must also meet the economic performance test to claim a current deduction.[101] *(See Case 31 for a discussion of the economic performance rules as they apply to drilling deductions.)*

However, in a fact situation similar to the above, the Fifth Circuit Court[102] held that Partnership P would be allowed to deduct only an amount equal to the cash portion of the consideration. The court concluded that the nonrecourse note was not a "true" loan because repayment thereof was contingent upon production. The court held that the nonrecourse note was so lacking in the essential economic realities and financial expectations of a true lending transaction that it had to be reclassified for tax purposes as a transaction other than a "true" loan. The most important factor in the decision was that the total value of the assets securing the notes was not sufficient to pay the notes absent production from the leases.

In a similar case, the Tax Court[103] determined that the note was the economic equivalent of a production payment. *(See Case 135.)* Thus, the Tax Court, while recognizing the contingent nature of such a note, concluded that the note was a "true" loan because production payments are considered loans for tax purposes.[104] On appeal, the First Circuit Court[105] overruled the Tax Court and concluded it was not necessary to determine whether the notes constituted production payments because the application of I.R.C. Section 636 could not be used to recharacterize a contingent loan into a "true" loan for this purpose.

In the instant case, it is unlikely that the note will be considered a "true" loan because of its contingent nature. Thus, Partnership P will be allowed to deduct only $100,000 of intangible drilling costs attributable to the turnkey drilling contract. Because the $150,000 of intangible drilling and development costs (IDC) attributable to the nonrecourse note will not be allowed at the partnership level, Operators A and B will not be allowed to deduct their pro-rata share of those costs. *(See the discussion below regarding production payment implications.)*

Many of the cases decided in this area have involved "wildcat" leases. Thus, the conclusion reached could be different in the case of partially developed properties when production is established and the fair market value of the leases is more certain. A nonrecourse loan by the driller can be regarded as "true" debt in those cases where it can be concluded there is reasonable certainty at the time the loan is created that the loan will be repaid.[106] For example, assume that Partnership P paid cash to drill the first well on a lease. Assume further that Partnership P drilled a successful well on the property and the value of the leases increased significantly. Then, assume Partnership P borrowed money to develop the property further on a nonrecourse basis, using the lease as the sole collateral. In this situation, if the loan did not exceed the fair market value of the property and is not considered a production payment pledged for development *(see Case 150)*, Partnership P should be allowed to deduct IDC paid with funds obtained from nonrecourse borrowing.[107] *(However, see the discussion below regarding the "at-risk" rules.)* The conclusion becomes less clear if the nonrecourse note balance is more than the value of the leases and the leases have more than a nominal value.

---

101. I.R.C. Sec. 461(h).
102. Gibson Products Co. v. U.S., 637 F.2d 1041 (5th Cir. 1981), 47 AFTR2d 81-863, 81-1 USTC 9213. *See also* Brountas v. Comm'r, 692 F.2d 152 (1st Cir. 1982), 50 AFTR2d 82-5900, 82-2 USTC 9626; CRC Corp. v. Comm'r, 693 F.2d 281 (3d Cir. 1982), 50 AFTR2d 82-6105, 82-2 USTC 9677; G.C.M. 39488.
103. Paul P. Brountas, 73 T.C. 491 (1979).
104. I.R.C. Sec. 636; Reg. Sec. 1.636-1.
105. Paul P. Brountas. *See also* CRC Corp.; Carolina, Clinchfield, and Ohio Railway Company, 82 T.C. 888 (1984).
106. Dillingham v. U.S., (W.D. Okla. 1981) 48 AFTR2d 81-5815, 81-2 USTC 9601; IRS Letter Ruling 8614033.
107. *Ibid.*

In the case of a cash-basis taxpayer, it has been well settled that the payment of an expense with a note does not give rise to a deduction.[108] In addition, the Tax Court in two decisions[109] disallowed deductions to cash-basis taxpayers that paid for the disallowed deductions with an advance from a third party. Such an advance was obtained in an arrangement not considered to be a "true" loan. The Tax Court held that the rationale in the cases that have disallowed deductions for accrual-basis taxpayers because the amounts were paid by nonrecourse, "contingent" loans applies equally to cash-basis taxpayers. Thus, the nature of the loan transaction is important in determining whether a cash-basis taxpayer will be allowed deductions if funds used to pay expenses are from loans that may not be considered "true" loans.

The use of nonrecourse notes in a turnkey drilling arrangement may suggest an unreasonable markup of the turnkey price. If the turnkey price has been inflated, a portion of the IDC may not be deductible as such.[110] *(See Case 49.)*

The facts and circumstances of each case must be examined to determine whether a "true" loan exists. Thus, care should be taken in structuring any arrangement involving a nonrecourse note to assure that the note will be considered a "true" loan.

In addition to the impact of the "true" loan issue on the amount the partners could deduct, if any of the partners were subject to the "at-risk" rules, their losses will be limited to their amount "at risk." Generally, the "at-risk" provisions apply to individuals and closely held corporations. *(See Case 32.)* For example, if the nonrecourse loan is a "true" loan and Corporation A is subject to the "at-risk" rules, its deduction will be equal to the cash invested in Partnership P ($55,000). On the other hand, if the nonrecourse loan is not a "true" loan and Corporation A is subject to the "at-risk" rules, its deduction will be equal to its share of the $100,000 of IDC deductible by Partnership P ($50,000).

Complex rules exist that impute interest in certain situations involving debt instruments having interest rates below certain levels. *(See Case 55 for the possible application of those rules to the facts of this case.)*

Case 31
Prepayment of Intangible Drilling and Development Costs

Partnership P, an oil and gas exploration limited partnership with approximately 75 partners, was organized in July 1987. Partnership P complied with registration requirements of the SEC and also with applicable state "Blue Sky" laws.

Many of the drilling contractors used by the partnership required advance payments of estimated drilling costs upon execution of the drilling contracts. Five wells for which the drilling costs were prepaid in 1987 were commenced after December 31, 1987. Three were commenced between January 1, 1988, and March 30, 1988. The remaining two will not be spudded by March 30, 1988, and probably will not be spudded before October 1988.

---

108. Quinn v. Comm'r, 111 F.2d 372 (5th Cir. 1940), 24 AFTR 927, 40-1 USTC 9403. *See also* Helvering v. Price, 309 U.S. 409 (1940), 24 AFTR 657, 40-1 USTC 9336; Eckert v. Burnet, 283 U.S. 140 (1931), 9 AFTR 1413, 2 USTC 714; Stinnett's Pontiac Service, Inc. v. Comm'r, 730 F.2d 634 (11th Cir. 1984), 53 AFTR2d 84-1197, 84-1 USTC 9406.
109. Werner Graf, 80 T.C. 944 (1983); Ernest J. Saviano, 80 T.C. 955 (1983). *See also* Richard L. Burns, 78 T.C. 185 (1982).
110. Bernuth v. Comm'r, 470 F.2d 710 (2d Cir. 1972), 31 AFTR2d 73-388, 73-1 USTC 9132; Rev. Rul. 73-211, 1973-1 C.B. 303; Internal Revenue Manual—Audit Sec. 4236-15, Para. 584 and 590 (June 27, 1985).

The partnership intends to elect to deduct currently all intangible drilling and development costs (IDC) and will file its partnership income tax returns on a calendar-year basis.

The general partner must determine the appropriate tax treatment to be accorded the various advance payments to drilling contractors. In connection with preparing the U.S. partnership income tax return for 1987, he has asked whether the partnership should adopt the accrual or cash method of accounting. He also has requested assistance in determining the amount of prepaid IDC that is deductible in the 1987 partnership income tax return.

In certain situations, taxpayers may deduct intangible drilling and development costs in the year paid, even though the work is not performed until the following year. However, there is no comprehensive authority defining precisely the conditions to be satisfied for prepaid IDC to be deducted currently. Accordingly, any general summary of "required" conditions must be developed by reviewing and comparing the various cases and rulings that have dealt with the deductibility of prepaid intangibles under various factual situations. In addition, accrual-basis taxpayers must meet specific accounting method statutory requirements to deduct prepaid expenses or certain accrued expenses. The specific statutory provisions do not override any of the general limitations under existing case law. They merely add additional requirements limiting the deductibility of prepayments for accrual-basis taxpayers.

General Nonstatutory Requirements for Prepayments

Several factors appear to be pertinent to the determination of whether prepaid IDC are deductible in the year of payment; however, the relative importance of these factors varies significantly. Some appear to be absolutely required, while the necessity of others is less certain. Many taxpayers have claimed, and the Internal Revenue Service (IRS) has allowed, deductions for prepaid drilling costs in situations where one or more of the factors were not present. The IRS also has challenged the deductions for prepaid drilling costs in various factual situations. Although the deductibility of prepaid drilling costs in the year of payment never is absolutely assured, the more closely the facts of a given situation parallel the facts in the various cases and rulings in which the deduction has been allowed, the better the chances for immediate deductibility.

Following is a summary of the various factors that are pertinent to the determination of deductibility:

Executed Drilling Contract — The drilling contract under which the prepayment is made must be executed prior to yearend and must contain a requirement that the prepayment be made before the end of the year. The IRS has ruled that a partial payment for IDC made before the date payment was required under the drilling contract and before the performance of any work is not deductible in the year paid.[111] However, the Tax Court has allowed the deduction in the year paid, even though prepayment was not required in the contract when substantial services were rendered in the year of payment.[112]

Identification of Wells To Be Drilled — The drilling contract should identify specifically the wells to be drilled. Additionally, if possible, the specific well site should

111. Rev. Rul. 71-579, 1971-2 C.B. 255; William B. Scheidt, T.C. Memo Dec. (July 26, 1982).
112. Ronald R. Levy, T.C. Memo Dec. (July 26, 1982).

be defined and staked, the necessary drilling permits obtained and other activities (such as obtaining a drill site title opinion or clearing the location) completed.[113] These activities help to demonstrate the taxpayer's preparedness to drill.

Courts have held that the ability of a taxpayer to change the location of the wells to be drilled[114] or to increase the number of wells to be drilled[115] under the contract is an acceptable contract provision and does not affect the current deductibility of the related IDC.

Payment to the Drilling Contractor — The payment must be made to the drilling contractor and not simply to the operator of the property because the operator normally is considered to be the participant's agent during the drilling period.[116] *(See Case 29.)* Payment to a general partner of a partnership also may not be sufficient to secure the deductions because the general partner generally is treated as an agent of the partnership.

An operator or general partner (or a related entity) also can be a drilling contractor with respect to the partnership's well(s). In such a case, payment to the operator or general partner in his role as a drilling contractor should be acceptable.[117] However, in the case of these payments between related parties, it may be difficult to convince the IRS that a bona fide business purpose exists for a prepayment.

The requirements for making a true payment are discussed further below.

Commencement of Drilling — The drilling contract should provide a specified date by which drilling operations will commence. The IRS apparently views the absence of such a provision as an indication that there was no business purpose for prepayment.[118]

Although an early case[119] and ruling[120] contained factual situations in which the wells were commenced within the first month following the taxpayer's yearend, the IRS and the courts have not held taxpayers to any arbitrary date by which drilling must be commenced.[121] In fact, it is common simply to provide in the drilling contract that the commencement date will be as soon as possible, depending on the availability of the desired rig. This may mean that the wells will not be spudded for several months.[122] In the *Keller* case,[123] no issue was raised concerning the commencement date of drilling, even though the facts indicated that the wells were spudded as late as 12 months following the year of prepayment.

In general, it is difficult to demonstrate a business purpose for the prepayment without providing for the commencement of the drilling operations at the earliest reasonable time, subject to availability of a drilling rig, acceptable weather conditions or other unforeseen delays.

Expenditures Must Be Payments Rather Than Refundable Deposits — The term *payment* has a special meaning for tax purposes. It does not mean a simple transfer of

113. Rev. Rul. 71-252, 1971-1 C.B. 146; Pauley v. U.S., (S.D. Cal. 1963), 11 AFTR2d 955, 63-1 USTC 9280; IRS Letter Ruling 8232008.
114. Keller v. Comm'r, 725 F.2d 1173 (8th Cir. 1984), 53 AFTR2d 84-663, 84-1 USTC 9194, *aff'g* 79 T.C. 7 (1982).
115. George Cheroff, T.C. Memo Dec. (Apr. 21, 1980).
116. Scheidt.
117. Dillingham v. U.S., (W.D. Okla. 1981) 48 AFTR2d 81-5815, 81-2 USTC 9601; IRS Letter Ruling 8232008.
118. Rev. Rul. 71-252, 1971-1 C.B. 146; Rev. Rul. 80-71, 1980-1 C.B. 106.
119. Pauley.
120. Rev. Rul. 71-252, 1971-1 C.B. 146.
121. IRS Letter Ruling 8232008.
122. IRS Letter Ruling 8111055.
123. Keller.

money by a taxpayer, even if that transfer is pursuant to a binding contract. A payment occurs only when the taxpayer's money is "irretrievably out-of-pocket." If by express, implied or customary terms a taxpayer retains a unilateral power to get the money back, the transfer is a "deposit" rather than a payment. The Tax Court used this logic in denying a deduction to a taxpayer in a situation where the drilling contracts allowed the taxpayer, by unilateral action, to terminate the contracts and receive a full refund of the prepaid amounts. The court held that the prepayments thus constituted a deposit instead of a payment of IDC.[124]

It does not appear that this requirement should be interpreted to mean that any payments made to the drilling contractor must be absolutely nonrefundable. The IRS has issued private letter rulings that hold that prepayments are deductible as IDC when the amount required to be prepaid under footage and daywork contracts will not be in excess of a reasonable estimate of the amount to be payable under the contract, and when the difference between the prepayment and the amount ultimately due the contractor will be adjusted on completion of the well.[125] However, when partial refunds ultimately are received under this type of contract, the burden of proof will be on the taxpayer to show that the estimated amount was reasonable.

Additionally, for a transfer of funds to be treated as a payment, the funds must not be escrowed under any arrangement whereby the subsequent disbursement of the funds is subject to the taxpayer's control.

Nontax Business Purpose — The IRS has ruled that a prepayment must have a bona fide, nontax business purpose before the taxpayer can take a deduction in the year of payment.[126] However, the Tax Court has held that, insofar as cash-basis taxpayers are concerned, the business-purpose test must be considered in conjunction with the distortion-of-income test (discussed below) and not as an independent requirement for deductibility.[127]

This case also serves as evidence that both the IRS and the courts will look closely at the business purpose and will not necessarily accept without question the terms of the drilling contract. For example, the IRS was successful in refuting the taxpayer's stated business purpose of "ensuring rig availability" by introducing oral testimony of the drilling contractors that they would have provided the services without the prepayments and that the prepayment provisions were included in the contracts at the taxpayer's request.

The cases and rulings in this area discuss at least four possible nontax business purposes:

☐ To ensure that the drilling contractor will have operating funds necessary for drilling.

☐ To allow the drilling contractor to take advantage of cash discounts.

☐ To allay concern on the part of the drilling contractor over the taxpayer's willingness or ability to pay at a later date.

☐ To fix the costs of drilling the well.

124. Keller; Scheidt.
125. IRS Letter Ruling 8012060; IRS Letter Ruling 8111055.
126. Rev. Rul. 71-252, 1971-1 C.B. 146; Rev. Rul. 80-71, 1980-1 C.B. 106.
127. Keller. *See also* Scheidt; Ronald E. Jolley, T.C. Memo Dec. (Feb. 13, 1984); Leonard T. Ruth, T.C. Memo Dec. (Sept. 22, 1983).

Distortion-of-Income Test — The requirement that a prepayment must not result in a substantial and material distortion of the taxpayer's income first was established formally by the IRS in a 1980 revenue ruling.[128] The distortion-of-income test has since been adopted in a somewhat modified form by the Tax Court, and this decision was affirmed on appeal.[129]

The Tax Court also addressed the deductibility of that portion of prepayments under footage or daywork contracts that was attributable to the completed portion of partially drilled wells and the deductibility of prepayments under turnkey contracts. The court held that the payments were currently deductible because they were nonrefundable and that they did not materially distort income. The court held that the nonbusiness motivation for paying the amounts was irrelevant because a cash-basis taxpayer's income is reflected clearly if he deducts an expense in the same year he pays for and receives his bargained-for benefits (e.g., drilling that had already occurred at yearend) since the transaction is closed at that point.

It is unclear at this time how the courts will apply the material distortion-of-income test in situations involving prepayments by cash-basis taxpayers under footage or daywork contracts that qualify as payments and not as refundable deposits.

Requirement of 100% Prepayment Participation — The IRS takes the position that there cannot be a business purpose for prepaying IDC unless 100% of the working interest owners are required to prepay.[130] This position does not seem to consider the realities of many situations. For example, if a prepayment is required from a working interest owner with limited financial resources and is not required of other working interest owners with more substantial resources, it appears that the prepayment is being required for a valid business reason.

Prepayment of Third-Party Expenditures — Prepayments of estimated costs of services and materials to third-party well-servicing contractors should be deductible, subject to the above criteria,[131] when the drilling contract provides that the drilling contractor will arrange for those services and the drilling contract requires that the amount be prepaid to the drilling contractor. In certain situations, it also may be possible to make separate prepayment arrangements with the various third-party supplies.

Specific Accounting Method Requirements

In addition to the general criteria discussed above, a taxpayer must also meet certain additional statutory requirements to be able to deduct prepaid IDC in the year it is paid.

Limitations on Use of Cash Method of Accounting — Current law generally requires regular corporations, partnerships with corporate partners and all tax shelters (defined below) to report on the accrual basis.[132] However, corporations and affected partnerships with average annual gross receipts of less than $5 million in tax years beginning after 1985 can report on a cash basis, as long as they are not tax shelters (defined below).[133]

128. Rev. Rul. 80-71, 1980-1 C.B. 106.
129. Keller.
130. Tax Shelter Audit Techniques Guidelines; IRS Letter Ruling 8012060; IRS Letter Ruling 8111055.
131. Keller.
132. I.R.C. Sec. 448(a).
133. I.R.C. Sec. 448(b)(3).

The term *tax shelter* is defined to include: (1) any enterprise other than a C corporation that has made an offering required to be registered with any federal or state securities regulating agency; (2) any partnership or other entity (other than a corporation that is not an S corporation) that allocates more than 35% of its losses during the tax year to limited partners or to other persons that did not actively participate in the entity's management or (3) any entity, plan or arrangement if its principal purpose is avoidance or evasion of federal income tax.[134]

In the factual situation presented in this case, Partnership P is a tax shelter. Therefore, the partnership will be required to report on the accrual basis and must meet the economic performance requirement discussed below to be able to deduct prepaid IDC.

Economic Performance Requirement — Generally, an accrual-basis taxpayer may not deduct any item until it meets the accrual method of accounting "all-events" test and until economic performance occurs with regard to the expenditure.[135] The "all-events" test is met when all events have occurred that determine the fact of liability and when the liability can be determined with reasonable accuracy.[136] Economic performance occurs when the services or property are provided.[137] Economic performance occurs with respect to the drilling of an oil or gas well as the well is drilled. The Conference Committee Report[138] indicates that burdensome additional recordkeeping to substantiate economic performance is not intended and that usually the existence of a valid contract requiring performance by a specified date will be sufficient.

For accrual-basis taxpayers that are not tax shelters, there is a limited exception to the requirement that economic performance take place before yearend. This "recurring-item" exception allows certain items to be deducted when all events have occurred that determine the fact of liability and the amount can be determined with reasonable accuracy, even though economic performance has not occurred. To be deductible under this exception, (1) the item must be recurring in nature; (2) the item must meet the "all-events" test without regard to the economic performance rules; (3) economic performance must occur within the shorter of a reasonable period or 8½ months following the close of the tax year; (4) either the item must not be material or accrual of the item in the tax year must result in a better matching with income than would accruing it when economic performance occurs and (5) similar items must be treated consistently by the taxpayer.[139] The purpose of this exception is to avoid disruption of normal business and accounting practices for certain recurring items. The taxpayer's treatment of these items in its financial statements will be considered in determining if it qualifies for this exception.[140]

Special rules apply for taxpayers considered tax shelters. Unlike for other accrual-basis taxpayers, the exception for recurring items is not available to tax-shelter taxpayers.[141] However, for tax-shelter taxpayers, there is a special definition of economic performance with respect to the drilling of an oil or gas well. Economic performance in this case is deemed to occur in the tax year of prepayment if drilling of the well commences before the close of the 90th day after the end of the tax year.[142] Therefore, a tax-shelter taxpayer may deduct an item in the year paid if it meets the

134. I.R.C. Sec. 461(i)(3).
135. I.R.C. Sec. 461(h).
136. I.R.C. Sec. 461(h)(4).
137. I.R.C. Sec. 461(h)(2).
138. House Report No. 98-861, 1984-3 C.B. Vol. 2 130.
139. I.R.C. Sec. 461(h)(3)(A).
140. I.R.C. Sec. 461(h)(3)(B).
141. I.R.C. Sec. 461(i)(1).
142. I.R.C. Sec. 461(i)(2).

accrual method of accounting "all-events" test, the well is spudded before the close of the 90th day after the close of the tax year and the other nonstatutory requirements (discussed above) are met. A technical correction to the statute has been proposed that provides that the 90-day grace period applies only to the portion of the prepaid IDC that does not exceed a partner's cash basis in a partnership.[143] A partner's cash basis is equal to the adjusted basis of his partnership interest determined without regard to: (1) any partnership liability, (2) any amount borrowed by the partner that was secured by any assets of the partnership and (3) any borrowing arranged by the partnership or by any person who participated in the organization, sale or management of the partnership (or by certain related persons).[144] The technical correction indicates that similar cash-basis limitations will apply to tax shelters other than partnerships.

The effect of the economic performance rules may be summarized as follows:

- ☐ Cash-basis taxpayers are not affected by the economic performance requirement. However, cash-basis taxpayers are required to meet the nonstatutory requirements discussed above in order to be able to deduct prepaid IDC.

- ☐ All accrual-basis taxpayers, whether or not tax shelters, are required to meet the economic performance requirements as well as the "all-events" test and the other nonstatutory criteria discussed above in order to be able to deduct prepaid IDC.

- ☐ For accrual-basis taxpayers that are not tax shelters, economic performance occurs as the well is drilled, not when the well is spudded.[145] The 90-day exception discussed below does not apply to accrual-basis taxpayers that are not tax shelters.

- ☐ For tax shelters, there is a special rule that economic performance is deemed to occur in the year of a prepayment of IDC with respect to specific wells that are spudded before the close of the 90th day after the tax year.[146]

- ☐ There is a possibility that the accrual-basis taxpayer recurring-item exception discussed above may apply to prepayments of IDC by accrual-basis taxpayers that are not tax shelters. However, it probably will be difficult to establish that the prepaid IDC is immaterial at both the partnership and partner level or is more clearly matched against income if deducted before economic performance.[147] The recurring-item exception does not apply to tax shelters.

In the factual situation presented in this case, Partnership P is a tax shelter and, therefore, must report on the accrual basis. Prepaid IDC with respect to the three wells spudded before March 30, 1988, should be deducted in 1987. The prepaid IDC applicable to the two wells that were not spudded by March 30, 1988, should be deducted in 1988 as long as the wells are spudded on or before the 90th day following December 31, 1988.

After applying the prepayment rule explained above, the partnership and its partners must consider the passive-activity limitations. (*See Case 182.*)

---

143. Technical Corrections Bill of 1987, Sec. 108(a)(3), *amending* I.R.C. Sec. 461(i)(2)(B).
144. Technical Corrections Bill of 1987, Sec. 108(a)(3), *amending* I.R.C. Sec. 461(i)(2)(C).
145. I.R.C.Sec. 461(h)(2)(A); House Report No. 98-861, 1984-3 C.B. Vol. 2 138.
146. I.R.C. Sec. 461(i)(2).
147. House Report No. 98-861, 1984-3 C.B. Vol. 2 138-139.

Case 32
Application of "at-Risk" Limitations

In 1987 Operator A, who owns the entire working interest in a lease, enters into an arrangement with Individuals B, C and D, who agree to drill a well free of cost to Operator A. Operator A assigns a one-third working interest in the lease to Individuals B, C and D in exchange for their agreement to pay one-third each of the costs to drill and equip the well. A 30% working interest will revert to Operator A after B, C and D have recovered all their costs of drilling and completing the well from the net cash profits from production.

The parties elect to be excluded from the partnership provisions of the Internal Revenue Code. Individual B agrees to act as operator under the terms of the joint operating agreement.

The total costs of developing the property are $1,500,000, of which $1,200,000 represents intangible drilling and development costs; the $300,000 balance is capitalizable as lease and well equipment costs. Individuals B, C and D incur no leasehold cost. There were no other items of income or expense during the year.

Individual B's obligation was satisfied by $100,000 cash, which he had on hand, and $400,000, which he borrowed from his brother. Individual C's payment of $500,000 was funded from $50,000 of available cash and $450,000 of bank financing, for which he is personally liable. The $450,000 note is payable over 10 years and is to be paid from Individual C's share of the net revenue from the property. The balance of the note, if any, is payable in full after 10 years, regardless of the amount of net production income. Individual D's payment of $500,000 consisted of $250,000 cash, which D had on hand, and a $250,000 nonrecourse loan from Individual B. Individual D pledged his 25% working interest in another oil property with an estimated fair market value of $350,000 as security for the $250,000 nonrecourse loan.

The "at-risk" limitations apply to individuals and most closely held corporations (other than S corporations) that meet the stock-ownership test used for determining personal holding company status.

Amounts considered to be "at risk" include the amount of cash and the adjusted basis of other property contributed by the taxpayer to the activity, amounts borrowed for use in the activity for which the taxpayer has personal liability and amounts borrowed (when the taxpayer is not personally liable) for use in the activity that are secured by the taxpayer's property other than property used in the activity (to the extent of the net fair market value of the taxpayer's property).[148]

Amounts borrowed from any person who has an interest in the activity other than as a creditor never can qualify as being "at risk" irrespective of the nature or terms of the debt.[149] Similarly, a taxpayer will not be considered "at risk" on amounts protected against loss through guarantees, stop-loss agreements or other similar arrangements.[150]

148. I.R.C. Sec. 465(b)(1); I.R.C. Sec. 465(b)(2).
149. I.R.C. Sec. 465(b)(3); Prop. Reg. Sec. 1.465-8; Prop. Reg. Sec. 1.465-20.
150. I.R.C. Sec. 465(b)(4); Prop. Reg. Sec. 1.465-6.

Losses generated from operations financed by all types of indebtedness, including normal trade payables, are subject to "at-risk" limitations.[151] Accordingly, amounts owed to an operator by a co-owner will not be considered "at risk" in situations in which the operator owns an interest in the property. Each situation should be analyzed carefully to determine whether the liability is payable to the operator or to a third-party vendor.

For purposes of applying the "at-risk" limitations, each unit of property generally is treated as a separate activity.[152] For tax years beginning after December 31, 1983, a taxpayer's oil and gas activities are aggregated and treated as a single activity if they constitute a trade or business and the taxpayer actively participates in the management of that trade or business.[153] The determination of whether a person actively participates in the management of the business depends on the facts and circumstances. According to applicable Congressional Committee Reports,[154] factors evidencing active participation include participating in decisions involving the operation or management of the activity, actually performing services for the activity, or hiring and discharging employees. Factors indicating a lack of active participation include lack of involvement in management and operation of the activity, having authority only to discharge the manager of the activity, or having a manager of the activity who is an independent contractor rather than an employee. The Committee Reports further state that two or more properties may be aggregated only if the taxpayer actively participates in the management of each individual property. Special rules apply in determining "at-risk" limitations applicable to a taxpayer's interest in a partnership or S corporation. *(See Case 33.)*

Loss from the activity is defined as the excess of deductions over the income therefrom for the tax year.[155] The amount "at risk" is increased by the excess of the deductions for depletion over the basis of the property.[156]

Any loss disallowed by the "at-risk" limitation carries over and becomes a deduction attributable to the activity for the next succeeding tax year, subject to the application of the "at-risk" rules for the subsequent tax year.[157] There is no limit to the number of years to which a disallowed loss can be carried forward.[158]

The following three paragraphs assume that Individuals B, C and D are not required for "at-risk" purposes to aggregate their respective interests in the subject lease with their other oil and gas activities.

In the instant case, Individual B will be "at risk" for $500,000. Borrowings from related parties (including brothers) are considered to be "at risk." Therefore, Individual B's deduction in 1987 will be $400,000 of intangible drilling and development costs (IDC) plus his share of depreciation because his total amount "at risk" is $500,000.

Individual C also will be entitled to deduct the $400,000 of IDC plus his share of depreciation in 1987 limited to a maximum of $500,000 because Individual C is liable personally for the loan and the borrowing is not otherwise "tainted." The fact that the loan is to be repaid from net production income does not "taint" the borrowing. The

151. General Explanation of the Tax Reform Act of 1976, prepared by the Staff of the Joint Committee on Taxation, 1976-3 C.B. Vol. 2 51.
152. I.R.C. Sec. 465(c)(2).
153. I.R.C. Sec. 465(c)(3)(B).
154. House Report No. 98-861, 1984-3 C.B. Vol. 2 375.
155. I.R.C. Sec. 465(d); Prop. Reg. Sec. 1.465-11.
156. Prop. Reg. Sec. 1.465-45(d); Prop. Reg. Sec. 1.465-95.
157. I.R.C. Sec. 465(a)(2); Prop. Reg. Sec. 1.465-2(b).
158. I.R.C. Sec. 465(b)(5); Prop. Reg. Sec. 1.465-2(b).

bank will not be deemed to have an interest in the activity other than as a creditor simply because the repayment schedule is based on the amount of the cash flow from production.[159]

Individual D's deduction for IDC in 1987 will be limited to $250,000 because the $250,000 loan from Individual B, a co-owner of the property, constitutes a borrowing from one who has an interest in the activity other than as a creditor. Had Individual B not had an interest in the activity other than as a creditor, Individual D would have been able to deduct his share of the IDC ($400,000) plus depreciation (limited in total to $500,000) because the nonrecourse debt was collateralized by "other" property with sufficient fair market value.

The results may be different if any of the individuals is required to aggregate his oil and gas activities. Aggregation is required if the subject property and other oil and gas activities constitute a trade or business in which the taxpayer actively participates in management. If Individual B must aggregate, he must combine his $400,000 (plus depreciation) loss with the income and losses from his other oil and gas business activities. If the combined activity generates a net loss, he may deduct that loss to the extent of his combined "at-risk" basis in the oil and gas activities. In effect, the $100,000 (less depreciation) excess "at-risk" basis in the subject property may permit deduction of losses from other properties for which he has insufficient "at-risk" basis. The same comments apply to Individual C if he must aggregate his oil and gas activities.

If Individual D is required to aggregate, his $400,000 (plus depreciation) loss is combined with income and losses of his other oil and gas business activities. The combined net loss, if any, then is limited to his combined "at-risk" basis in his oil and gas business activities. In effect, an excess of "at-risk" basis in his other oil and gas business activities may permit him to deduct more than the $250,000 amount that is allowable if the subject property is treated as a separate activity.

In the situations discussed above where the deduction is limited, the taxpayers can carry over the disallowed loss indefinitely until the "at-risk" amount is sufficiently increased to absorb the carryover.[160]

The "at-risk" rules present taxpayers with many tax planning possibilities. For example, in situations where there is a possibility of losing net operating loss deductions due to the expiration of the carryover period, taxpayers often can finance development activities with nonqualifying debt and, thus, definitely defer the related deductions. It also is possible to generate current taxable income through the application of the "at-risk" provisions. *(See Case 34.)*

(See Case 185 for a discussion of the passive-activity provisions as they apply to working interest owners like Individuals B, C and D.)

Case 33
Deduction for Losses Limited to the Amount "at Risk" — Operation as a Partner or as an S Corporation Shareholder

Investor L participates in oil and gas operations as a limited partner in partnerships and as a stockholder in S corporations. The results of his activities for 1987 were as follows:

159. IRS Letter Ruling 8215012 (Technical Advice Memorandum).
160. I.R.C. Sec. 465(a)(2).

Partnership A
Investor L's share of the partnership's loss was $14,200, net of gross receipts from oil and gas production of $1,000. No percentage depletion was allowable on the partnership properties. Investor L's total commitment was a $10,000 contribution to capital. Losses in excess of capital contributions were financed with nonrecourse debt.

Partnership B
Investor L's share of the partnership's loss was $6,200, net of his share of gross receipts from oil and gas production of $400. No percentage depletion was allowable on the partnership properties. Investor L contributed $5,000 in cash to this partnership and was unconditionally committed to contribute an additional $5,000 on call. Losses in excess of capital contributions actually received by the partnership were paid with the proceeds of nonrecourse debt incurred in 1987 and secured only by partnership oil and gas properties.

X Corporation
Investor L's share of this S corporation's loss was $2,200. Investor L's remaining tax basis in the stock of this corporation, before considering the results of 1987 operations, was $3,000. The loss is attributable to properties for which all expenditures were paid with the proceeds of nonrecourse debt incurred in 1987 by X Corporation.

Y Corporation
Investor L's share of this S corporation's loss was $1,400. Investor L's basis in the stock of Y Corporation, before considering 1987 operations, was $10,000. Investor L has funded $9,000 of his equity investment in Y Corporation through borrowings from a wholly owned C corporation. The C corporation does not have an interest in any of Y Corporation's oil and gas activities.

At the end of 1987, Investor L had no personal indebtedness of any type, other than the commitment to Partnership B and the $9,000 payable to his wholly owned corporation.

The "at-risk" provisions apply to individuals and most corporations (other than S corporations) that meet the stock-ownership tests used for determining personal holding company status.[161] *(See Case 32 for a general discussion of the "at-risk" provisions.)*

Investor L's activities in Partnerships A and B, and X and Y Corporations may also be subject to limitation by the passive-activity provisions. *(See Section VII for a discussion of the passive-activity provisions.)*

Generally, for tax years beginning after December 31, 1983, partners and S corporation shareholders determine their amounts "at risk" in partnership and S corporation oil and gas activities on a unit-of-property basis.[162] However, oil and gas activities of a partnership or an S corporation are aggregated and treated as a single activity if those activities constitute a trade or business and 65% or more of the losses for the tax year is allocable to persons who actively participate in the management of that trade or business.[163] *(See Case 32 concerning active participation in management.)*

161. I.R.C. Sec. 465(a)(1).
162. I.R.C. Sec. 465(c)(2).
163. I.R.C. Sec. 465(c)(2)(B)(ii); I.R.C. Sec. 465(c)(3)(B).

For the tax years beginning prior to January 1, 1984, a partner's or S corporation shareholder's interest in the entity was treated as a single activity, meaning that the entity's oil and gas activities were aggregated. The Internal Revenue Service (IRS) has delayed implementation of the rules requiring partners and S corporation shareholders to make "at-risk" computations on a unit-of-property basis for every year since the rules were enacted in 1984.[164] Therefore, it is not certain that unit-of-property computations will be required in 1987.

It appears the statutory language[165] also may require aggregation of a taxpayer's interest in a partnership's or S corporation's oil and gas activities if the 65% requirement is not met but the taxpayer actively participates in the management of those activities. However, Congressional intent is unclear.

A partner's "at-risk" amount is increased by his share of partnership income.[166] If cash or property representing that income then is applied to reduce nonrecourse debt, the partner's basis is reduced, but the amount "at risk" is not affected.[167] However, if the income is distributed, the partner's amount "at risk" in the partnership is reduced.[168] The same rules apply to a shareholder in an S corporation. In the case of a partnership, a partner's amount "at risk" generally includes his share of any partnership debt for which the partner is personally liable.[169]

The determination of whether a partner is personally liable with respect to partnership debt has been the subject of several recent Tax Court cases. In the first case,[170] limited partners in oil and gas exploration partnerships executed various partnership agreements obligating themselves to make additional capital contributions if the partnership was not able to make payments on partnership recourse debt. The court held that since the limited partners' obligations were contingent upon future partnership cash flow and whether the general partners would call for additional capital contributions, the limited partners were not "at risk" for their share of the partnership recourse debt. In contrast, in another Tax Court decision,[171] the court held that limited partners who guarantee what would otherwise be partnership nonrecourse debt may increase their amount "at risk" in the activity by the pro-rata amount of their guarantee. These cases illustrate that caution must be exercised when using guarantees and cash-call provisions to ensure that limited partners receive an increase in their "at-risk" amounts for situations when they are ultimately liable for partnership debt.

One other method commonly used to increase a limited partner's amount "at risk" for partnership recourse debt was discussed in a recent technical advice memorandum.[172] The ruling dealt with a situation where limited partners contributed irrevocable and transferable bank letters of credit which were pledged to the lender on partnership recourse debt. In addition, the limited partners executed assumption agreements by which each agreed to assume unconditional personal liability for his share of the partnership loan, limited to the amount of his letter of credit. The IRS held that the limited partners who used the letter of credit and assumption-agreement method of

164. I.R.C. Sec. 465(c)(2) *(prior to amendment by Tax Reform Act of 1984)*; Temp. Reg. Sec. 1.465-1T; IRS Announcement 86-35, 1986-12 I.R.B. 27.
165. I.R.C. Sec. 465(c)(3)(B).
166. General Explanation of the Tax Reform Act of 1976, prepared by the Staff of the Joint Committee on Taxation, 1976-3 C.B. Vol. 2 50.
167. Prop. Reg. Sec. 1.465-25(c).
168. Prop. Reg. Sec. 1.465-22(b).
169. Prop. Reg. Sec. 1.465-24(a)(2).
170. Jerry E. Pritchett, 85 T.C. 580 (1985).
171. Edwin D. Abramson, 86 T.C. 360 (1986).
172. IRS Letter Ruling 8636003 (Technical Advice Memorandum).

making their capital contribution were "at risk" for their pro-rata share of the partnership debt.

A shareholder in an S corporation is not generally considered to be "at risk" for corporate debt other than to the shareholder.[173] However, based on an Eleventh Circuit Court case, S corporation shareholders who guarantee corporate debt may have an argument to support inclusion of that debt in their amount "at risk" for claiming losses.[174]

A partner who lends money to a partnership increases his amount "at risk" by the amount his basis in the partnership is increased because the partnership incurs that liability. However, the amount "at risk" of any other partner does not increase as a result of the loan.[175]

Neither the statutory provisions nor the applicable Congressional Committee Reports provide guidance as to how a partner's or S corporation shareholder's "at-risk" basis is allocated among the entity's oil and gas properties if the partner or shareholder is not allowed to aggregate those properties. It is hoped the IRS will provide this guidance in the near future.

If the "at-risk" rules must be applied to an entity's properties on a unit-of-property basis, Investor L presumably must obtain additional property-by-property information and allocate his "at-risk" amounts among the properties in some reasonable manner. Pending further guidance, it is unclear how the process should be performed.

Assuming the IRS allows aggregation for 1987, Investor L's amount "at risk" in Partnership A for 1987 is $10,000, which consists solely of his cash contribution. Although Investor L's share of gross income is $1,000, this is not considered as cash contributed to the activity but is "allowed" in computing the net loss of $14,200 for the tax year. At the end of the year, Investor L is not considered to be "at risk" beyond his capital contribution of $10,000. Therefore, he should be entitled to claim $10,000 of the $14,200 loss allocable to him, with the balance of $4,200 to be carried forward.

The circumstances of Investor L's interest in Partnership B are different. In this case, he paid $5,000 in cash and is irrevocably committed to pay an additional $5,000 on call, a recourse-type of commitment. Nevertheless, Investor L may not be considered "at risk" beyond the $5,000 paid in cash. Arguably, Investor L should be "at risk" to the extent of up to $5,000 of his share (based on his ratio for sharing partnership losses) of any recourse debt at the partnership level since he is ultimately liable and in the same economic position as the general partner on the partnership recourse debt.[176] However, based on a recent Tax Court decision dealing with a similar transaction, the IRS may argue that Investor L is not "at risk" for an obligation to make future capital contributions.[177] Accordingly, Investor L's 1987 deductible loss, calculated on an aggregate basis, will be $5,000 (assuming the partnership has no recourse indebtedness), and $1,200 will be deferred to subsequent years pending an increase in the amount "at risk."

There is no "at-risk" limitation at the S corporation level. Therefore, assuming the "at-risk" rules are applied on an aggregate basis, Investor L may claim the entire $2,200 loss from X Corporation because his "at-risk" basis is $3,000. The use of nonrecourse debt proceeds to fund the loss is not relevant as long as Investor L has sufficient "at-risk" basis. If Investor L must calculate his "at-risk" limitation on a separate basis, it is possible that the association of nonrecourse debt with a particular property may result in some limitation with respect to that property.

---

173. Prop. Reg. Sec. 1.465-24(a)(3).
174. Selfe v. U.S., 778 F.2d 769 (11th Cir. 1985) 57 AFTR2d 86-464, 80-1 USTC 9115. *But see* Lewis Bader, T.C. Memo Dec. (Jan. 14, 1987).
175. Prop. Reg. Sec. 1.465-7.
176. I.R.C. Sec. 465(b)(1)(A).
177. Jerry E. Pritchett.

In connection with the activities of Y Corporation, Investor L's 1987 deductible loss will be $1,400, assuming an aggregate calculation. Investor L's "at-risk" investment in Y Corporation includes the $9,000 loan from the related corporation. Related-party borrowings are included as an amount "at risk," as long as the lender or a person related to the lender has no interest in the activity.[178]

The facts of this case indicate that percentage depletion was not allowable with respect to any of the properties. If any depletion was allowable, it would be considered a deduction in computing the taxpayer's loss from the activity. However, a taxpayer's amount "at risk" in an activity is increased by the excess of the depletion deduction over the basis of the depletable property used in the activity.[179]

Case 34
Recapture of Losses as a Result of Decrease in Amount "at Risk"

In 1986, Individual C made a cash investment of $400,000 in an oil and gas lease. He incurred $325,000 of intangible drilling costs to drill a well, $25,000 of leasehold costs and $50,000 of lease and well equipment. In 1987, the lease had net income of $20,000. The net income amount was after deducting depreciation of $7,500 and percentage depletion of $20,000. During 1987, Individual C also sold a production payment carved out of this lease for $250,000.

Individual C is a cash-basis taxpayer and has elected to deduct intangible drilling costs currently.

A taxpayer must include in gross income the amount of losses previously deducted from an activity if the taxpayer has a negative amount "at risk" in that activity at the end of a tax year. The amount included in gross income will be treated as a deduction allocable to the activity in future years to the extent the taxpayer has an increase in his amount "at risk" with respect to that activity.[180]

The amount of income to be recognized under these provisions shall not exceed the total losses deducted by the taxpayer for the activity for all prior tax years beginning after December 31, 1978.[181]

(See Case 32 for a general discussion of the "at-risk" rules, including the definitions of various terms such as activity *and* amount "at risk."*)*

Applying these rules to the above facts, Individual C will be required to include $155,000 in taxable income for 1987 computed as follows:

Initial cash investment	$ 400,000
Loss — 1986	(325,000)
Amount "at risk" — December 31, 1986	$ 75,000
Income — 1987	20,000
Distribution of cash from sale of carved-out production payment	(250,000)
Amount "at risk" — December 31, 1987	$(155,000)

178. I.R.C. Sec. 465(b)(3).
179. Prop. Reg. Sec. 1.465-45(d).
180. I.R.C. Sec. 465(e)(1).
181. I.R.C. Sec. 465(e)(2).

Percentage depletion of $20,000 is less than the tax basis in the property; accordingly, it does not increase the amount "at risk." As a result of Individual C's carving out a production payment, he effectively has borrowed funds on a nonrecourse basis and has secured borrowing with property used in the activity. Therefore, because Individual C's amount "at risk" is less than zero (by $155,000), he will be required to recognize $155,000 of ordinary income in 1987. The $155,000 will be available as a deduction in future years if Individual C's amount "at risk" increases.

The carved-out production payment may be subject to the original-issue discount rules. *(See Case 138 for discussion of the original-issue discount rules.)*

(See Section VII for a discussion of the application of the passive-activity provisions to Individual C's oil and gas activities.)

Case 35
Well Drilled Prior to Formal Assignment

> **C Company agrees to assign the full working interest in a lease, subject to a retained one-eighth net profits interest, to Operator A as consideration for the drilling of a well to 10,000 feet. Under the contract, the lease will be assigned formally only after completion of the obligation well. Operator A may request assignment of the lease whether or not the obligation well is completed as a producer. Operator A has elected to expense intangible drilling and development costs (IDC) on both productive and nonproductive wells. C Company also contracts to drill the well for a cash consideration of $12 per foot ($120,000), which is considered a reasonable price for the drilling. Operator A is to furnish the casing and is to pay C Company for the actual costs of completing and equipping the well if it is productive.**

Operator A is entitled to deduct IDC incurred by him, whether the formal grant or assignment of the operating rights or working interest in the lease is made to him before or after the drilling of the well.[182] Even though the drilling of the well is the sole consideration for the lease and Operator A receives the formal assignment of the lease after he has completed the well, his right to the deduction is not affected. Consequently, Operator A may take the deduction in the tax year in which costs are paid or incurred, depending on the method of accounting used. *(See Case 31 for a discussion of the economic performance rules.)*

The regulations clearly permit the deduction of IDC incurred in the drilling of an obligation well to the extent of the operator's ownership in the entire working or operating interest.[183] Because a net profits interest is considered a type of royalty interest, Operator A will own all the working interest in the lease and may deduct the entire $120,000 of IDC in the year paid or incurred. Any additional IDC incurred in completing and equipping the well also will be deductible. Operator A's right to the deduction is not affected by the outcome of the well because his election to charge IDC to expense was made with respect to both productive and nonproductive wells.

Operator A may have no capitalized costs for his depletable investment, except for legal and other costs relating to the acquisition of the property, because all expenditures will be classified either as depreciable tangible equipment costs or currently

182. Reg. Sec. 1.612-4(a).
183. *Ibid.*

deductible IDC. *(However, see Case 187 for a discussion of additional cost-capitalization requirements of the Tax Reform Act of 1986.)*

The Internal Revenue Service (IRS) has ruled that Operator A's treatment of the costs incurred would be the same as summarized above, even if Operator A was entitled to an assignment of the lease only if the obligation well was completed successfully as a producing well.[184]

C Company's original investment in the lease becomes its tax basis for the retained net profits interest. The drilling of the well does not result in current income to C Company, except for the profits earned on the drilling contract.

When, as here, the sublessor also contracts to drill the well, the price charged must stand the test of reasonableness.[185] The contract price must be comparable to the going rate in the area. If the price appears excessive under the circumstances, the IRS may contend that a portion of the contract price should be treated as consideration for the lease. *(See Case 49.)*

Case 36
Working Interest Acquired Subsequent to Commencement of Well on Lease

> **Operator A is considering acquiring a 25% working interest in a lease from Operator B. Under the terms of the proposed arrangement, Operator A will make a cash payment of $50,000 and also will pay 25% of all costs previously incurred, or to be incurred, in the drilling of a test well on the lease.**
>
> **Operator B currently owns the entire working interest in the lease and has commenced the drilling of a 6,000-foot test well. The well is being drilled by an independent contractor under a "daywork" contract. At the time of the offer to Operator A, the well is drilling at 3,000 feet but has not encountered any potentially productive formations.**
>
> **Operator A's 25% share of the intangible drilling and development costs (IDC) incurred and paid by Operator B to 3,000 feet is $40,000. Operator A's 25% share of tangible equipment costs incurred to date is $5,000.**
>
> **Operator A is a cash-basis taxpayer and has elected to deduct IDC. Operator A asks how the various costs involved will be treated for income tax purposes. He also asks if the farmout can be structured differently for a more favorable tax treatment.**

A circuit court[186] has held that costs paid for drilling a well to a depth that had been attained before the taxpayer acquired its operating interest were not IDC incurred and expended by the taxpayer. The court held that the costs represented a capital investment in the oil and gas leases. Although the regulations allow the deduction of IDC incurred prior to the formal grant or assignment of operating rights, a taxpayer does not incur expenses or the risk of loss as an operator before acquiring any right to the operating interest.

---

184. Rev. Rul. 69-332, 1969-1 C.B. 87.
185. Bernuth v. Comm'r, 470 F.2d 710 (2d Cir. 1972), 31 AFTR2d 73-388, 73-1 USTC 9132; Rev. Rul. 73-211, 1973-1 C.B. 303.
186. Platt v. Comm'r, 207 F.2d 697 (7th Cir. 1953), 44 AFTR 530, 53-2 USTC 9560.

Accordingly, if the above-described farmout arrangement were consummated as proposed, Operator A would be required to capitalize the $40,000 payment for the intangibles previously incurred and paid for by Operator B. The capitalization would be required for any expenses Operator A pays that were incurred and paid before he acquires his interest, whether or not Operators A and B elected to be excluded from the partnership provisions of the Internal Revenue Code. The portion of the $40,000 that represents the installation costs of tangible equipment would be capitalized, along with the $5,000, as tangible equipment costs subject to depreciation. The balance of the $40,000 and the $50,000 initial cash consideration would be capitalized as leasehold cost.

The arrangement possibly can be structured so that Operator A will pay a disproportionate share of future costs to be incurred rather than having to reimburse Operator B (or otherwise pay) for the costs previously incurred. In this situation, the disproportionate sharing arrangement should be structured to require Operator A to pay 100% of the next $60,000 of costs incurred in drilling the test well and 25% of all subsequent costs, with Operator B paying the remaining 75% of subsequent costs.

This alternative approach assumes that Operators A and B do not elect to be excluded from the partnership provisions of the Internal Revenue Code and that their joint venture agreement contains appropriate provisions to specially allocate deductions to the party bearing the related costs. *(See Case 165.)* The resulting partnership generally can elect either the cash or accrual method of accounting for tax purposes. *(However, see Case 9 for a discussion of restrictions on use of the cash method of accounting by certain taxpayers.)* Assuming the special allocation provisions satisfy the substantial economic effect test, Operator A should be entitled to deduct the expenses specially allocated to and funded by him. *(For a discussion of special allocations, see Case 165.)*

(See Case 37 for a discussion of another type of arrangement that may be considered in similar situations.)

Case 37
Working Interest Assigned to Partnership by General Partner Subsequent to Commencement of Well on Lease

Operator A acquires a 10% interest in a lease from Operator B for a cash consideration of $12,000. Operator A also agrees to pay its 10% share of all costs to be incurred in developing the property.

Operator A acquires the lease with the intention of reassigning it to its 1987-A Drilling Partnership P, of which Operator A will be the general partner. However, the formation of Partnership P was delayed unexpectedly, and it did not come into existence until 20 days after a test well had been spudded on the lease. The lease was immediately thereafter assigned to Partnership P. During that 20-day period, Operator A incurred intangible drilling and development costs (IDC) of $25,000, none of which were billed or paid by the operator until after the interest was assigned to Partnership P. Partnership P assumed liability for all the intangibles that had been incurred and reimbursed Operator A for the initial $12,000 paid to acquire the lease. The well did not penetrate any potentially productive sands until after the lease was assigned to Partnership P.

Under the terms of the operating agreement, the various co-owners elect to be excluded from the partnership provisions of the Internal Revenue Code.

Partnership P inquires as to the proper treatment to be accorded the $25,000 payment to Operator A. Partnership P intends to elect to deduct all IDC currently. Partnership P is not a tax shelter and, therefore, intends to use the cash method of accounting.

A partnership is separate and distinct from its general partner and cannot acquire a lease before it exists as an entity. Thus, Partnership P will be treated as having acquired an interest in a partially drilled well.

These facts are similar to those in Case 36. Accordingly, Partnership P will be required to capitalize the $25,000 paid for IDC incurred prior to the date it acquired the interest in the lease. This capitalization will be required regardless of Partnership P's method of accounting.

The result in this case will not be any different even if Operators A and B agree not to elect to be excluded from the partnership provisions, thus, creating a tax partnership in which Partnership P becomes a partner.[187] Additionally, the result will not be different if a tiered partnership arrangement is used because certain so-called cash items, including: (1) interest, (2) taxes, (3) payments for services or use of property or (4) other amounts to be specified by regulations, must be prorated over the period to which attributable and be allocated to partners in proportion to their interests on a daily basis. The Committee Reports indicate that regulations will permit a monthly convention for making the daily calculations. Tiered partnerships are made subject to the daily proration rules by looking through the upper-tier partnership to the lower-tier partnership.[188] (*See Case 165 for a discussion of special allocations.*)

Case 38
Drilling as Consideration for a Fractional Interest in a Lease

Operator B receives from Operator A an assignment of a two-thirds interest in an oil and gas lease, for which he agrees to drill and equip one well free of cost to Operator A. If the well is completed as a producer, the income and operating expenses will be shared one-third by Operator A and two-thirds by Operator B.

Operators A and B elect to be excluded from the partnership provisions of the Internal Revenue Code.

The agreement between Operators A and B commonly is referred to as a *free-well arrangement.*

Operator A realizes no taxable gain or loss upon assignment of two-thirds of his working interest to Operator B because the successful development of the lease merely enhances the value of his retained interest in the lease.[189]

187. Cecil R. Richardson, 76 T.C. 512 (1981). Richardson was affirmed on another issue by the Fifth Circuit, 693 F.2d 1189 (5th Cir. 1982), 51 AFTR2d 83-418, 83-1 USTC 9109. *See also* Williams v. U.S., 680 F.2d 382 (5th Cir. 1982), 50 AFTR2d 82-5323, 82-2 USTC 9467; Kenneth E. Lipke, 81 T.C. 689 (1983); William J. Silberman, T.C. Memo Dec. (Dec. 28, 1983); Hawkins v. Comm'r, 713 F.2d 347 (8th Cir. 1983), 52 AFTR2d 83-5616, 83-2 USTC 9475.

188. I.R.C. Sec. 706.

189. G.C.M. 22730, 1941-1 C.B. 214; E. C. Laster, 43 B.T.A. 159 (1940).

When drilling is undertaken for the grant or assignment of a fraction of the operating rights, only that portion of the intangible drilling and development costs (IDC) attributable to the fractional interest acquired may be deducted.[190] IDC and tangible equipment costs allocable to operating rights held by others must be capitalized as the cost of the operating rights acquired.[191] For many years, this rule has been interpreted to allow Operator B to deduct only two-thirds of the IDC incurred in drilling the well and to require him to capitalize the remaining one-third of those costs as leasehold cost. Operator B must capitalize two-thirds of the tangible costs as depreciable lease and well equipment and one-third as leasehold cost.

Operator A may not deduct the IDC paid by Operator B that are allocable to his one-third working interest because he has not incurred these costs, nor may he allocate a portion of his tax basis in the lease to the equipment or claim depreciation because he has no investment in the tangible equipment.[192]

Operator B is required to capitalize one-third of his intangible and tangible costs of drilling the well as leasehold cost even if the well is dry.[193] If Operator B continues to hold the interest after drilling a dry hole, he may deduct the leasehold cost as a loss in the tax year in which the property is surrendered, abandoned or otherwise proved worthless. *(See Case 160.)* If a successful well subsequently is drilled on the property, these capitalized costs will be recovered through depletion. *(See Section IV.)* If the property is sold, these capitalized costs will be taken into account in determining Operator B's gain or loss. *(See Section V.)*

If the well is productive, Operators A and B each should report their shares of the production income as ordinary income subject to an allowance for depletion, and each should deduct his share of the operating expenses.

To obtain a similar economic effect with different tax results, the parties should consider treating the joint venture as a partnership for federal income tax purposes, with a special allocation to Operator B of the total deduction for IDC. Treating the venture as a partnership may require a change in the overall economics of the arrangement to ensure that the special allocations have substantial economic effect. *(See Cases 161, 163 and 165.)*

The tax consequences resulting from an arrangement similar to the above may vary significantly in situations where the assignee earns an interest in property other than the property on which the drill site is located *(see Case 41)* or in situations where the assignee pays a cash consideration in addition to assuming the obligation to drill the test well.

If the arrangement were structured to provide Operator B with all the operating rights during the drilling and development period, with the right to recoup his costs from the entire working interest's net cash profits before Operator A would receive any of the net cash profits, Operator B would be entitled to deduct all the IDC incurred in drilling the well. *(See Case 39.)*

190. Reg. Sec. 1.612-4(a).
191. Reg. Sec. 1.612-4(a); Rev. Rul. 70-657, 1970-2 C.B. 70.
192. U.S. v. Cocke, 399 F.2d 433 (5th Cir. 1968), 22 AFTR2d 5267, 68-2 USTC 9502.
193. Reg. Sec. 1.612-4(a); Rev. Rul. 69-332, 1969-1 C.B. 87.

Case 39
Intangible Drilling and Development Cost Deduction When Drilling for an Interest Under a Carried-Interest Arrangement With the Right To Complete Payout

Operator A, who owns the entire working interest in a 40-acre lease, enters into an arrangement with Operator B, who agrees to drill a well free of cost to Operator A. Operator A assigns the full working interest in the lease to Operator B until the latter has recovered all his costs of drilling and completing the well from the net cash profits from production. After recoupment, one-half the working interest in the lease reverts to Operator A, and the working interest thereafter is owned one-half by each.

Operators A and B elect to be excluded from the partnership provisions of the Internal Revenue Code.

The arrangement between Operators A and B commonly is referred to as a "carried-interest" arrangement, with Operator A as the carried party and Operator B, the carrying party.

The period during which the carrying party is entitled to recover his costs commonly is referred to as the *recoupment* or *payout period*, and the point at which the carrying party has recovered all costs is referred to as *payout*. The interest that remains with the carrying party after payout is referred to as a *permanent interest*. The carried party's interest after payout is referred to as a *residual* or *reversionary interest*.

Operator A realizes no taxable gain or loss on assignment of the working interest to Operator B because the successful development of the lease merely enhances the value of Operator A's residual interest.[194] Operator A's basis in the interest retained is his adjusted basis in the lease prior to the assignment.

Operator B should deduct all intangible drilling and development costs (IDC) incurred in drilling the well because he owns all the operating rights while the well is being drilled and is entitled to all the net cash profits from the entire working interest until he has recouped all his costs of drilling and equipping the well.[195] Operator B should capitalize the expenditures for tangible equipment as depreciable costs.[196]

Operator B should report all the production income and operating expenses throughout the payout period.[197] After payout, Operators A and B each should report one-half the production income and expenses from the well.

The Internal Revenue Service (IRS) has ruled that upon reversion of one-half the interest to Operator A, Operator B is required to capitalize as depletable leasehold cost one-half his remaining unrecovered depreciable cost of lease and well equipment.[198] Operator B also may be required to add to his tax liability in the year of the reversion a portion of the investment credit previously claimed.[199] Operator A will not be permitted to allocate a portion of his tax basis in the lease to the equipment upon

194. G.C.M. 22730, 1941-1 C.B. 214; E. C. Laster, 43 B.T.A. 159 (1940).

195. Reg. Sec. 1.612-4(a); Rev. Rul. 69-332, 1969-1 C.B. 87; Rev. Rul. 71-207, 1971-1 C.B. 160; Rev. Rul. 75-446, 1975-2 C.B. 95.

196. Rev. Rul. 69-332, 1969-1 C.B. 87; Rev. Rul. 71-207, 1971-1 C.B. 160.

197. Weinert v. Comm'r, 294 F.2d 750 (5th Cir. 1961), 8 AFTR2d 5417, 61-2 USTC 9644; Manahan Oil Co., 8 T.C. 1159 (1947).

198. Rev. Rul. 69-332, 1969-1 C.B. 87; Rev. Rul. 71-207, 1971-1 C.B. 160. *Compare* Choate v. Comm'r, 324 U.S. 1 (1945), 33 AFTR 297, 45-1 USTC 9153; Rev. Rul. 68-361, 1968-2 C.B. 264.

199. Reg. Sec. 1.47-2(c).

payout or to claim depreciation with respect to the equipment because he has no investment in it.[200]

The concept of recoupment of cost assumes that all the costs of drilling, completing, equipping and operating the well will be recovered from the gross income from the production and sale of oil or gas.[201] Recoupment does not include acquisition costs or related expenditures that normally would be considered leasehold cost. Any windfall profit tax paid with respect to production logically should be treated as an operating expense in computing the amount of net cash income from production because the windfall profit tax is similar in nature to a severance, or production, tax and should be accorded similar treatment. The windfall profit tax amount used in the computation of net cash income should be reduced by any refunds received as a result of the 90% of net income limitation.

The term *gross income attributable to the operating mineral interest in the well* has not been defined specifically for purposes of computing recoupment or payout. Generally, the practice has been to include in gross income the proceeds of the sales of oil and gas at the wellhead. One court decision and numerous revenue rulings have indicated that only income subject to the depletion allowance can be included as gross income for purposes of determining the return on the oil and gas well investment.[202]

Although not entirely clear, it appears that the production proceeds from existing producing wells located on the same taxable unit of property may be included in computing payout with respect to the costs incurred in developing the well or wells subject to the carried interest. *(See Case 46.)* Proceeds from sales of salvaged equipment on the well or wells subject to the carried-interest arrangement generally are considered a reduction of the cost of equipment charged to the carried-interest account. Working interest income attributable to the carried interest should be determined by excluding royalties, overriding royalties and net profits interests reserved or assigned at the time of or prior to the carried-interest arrangement *(see Case 47)* and also excluding production payments pledged for development assigned by the carrying party.

The IRS has ruled that a bottom-hole contribution constitutes income for the service of providing geological information to the payor. *(See Case 53.)* Accordingly, the IRS ruled that the recipient is not permitted to reduce or offset drilling or exploration costs but rather must include the bottom-hole contribution in gross income.[203] Although the ruling does not discuss specifically the effect of dry-hole or bottom-hole contributions on payout computations, it is logical to assume that the IRS will conclude that the contributions should not be considered a reduction of recoupable costs (or as production income) in making the payout computation.

The reversion of one-half the working interest to Operator A upon payout should not constitute a transfer of a proven property so as to deny future percentage depletion on the reassigned fraction of the working interest. *(See Cases 108 and 109.)*[204] Also, the reassignment to Operator A should not constitute a disposition that requires Operator B to recapture any of the IDC. *(See Case 131.)*[205]

The IRS has held that payout must be computed on a property-by-property basis. *(See Case 46.)*[206]

200. U.S. v. Cocke, 399 F.2d 433 (5th Cir. 1968), 22 AFTR2d 5267, 68-2 USTC 9502.
201. Rev. Rul. 69-332, 1969-1 C.B. 87; Rev. Rul. 70-336, 1970-1 C.B. 145; Rev. Rul. 71-207, 1971-1 C.B. 160.
202. Weinert; Rev. Rul. 70-336, 1970-1 C.B. 145; Rev. Rul. 71-206, 1971-1 C.B. 105; Rev. Rul. 71-207, 1971-1 C.B. 160.
203. Rev. Rul. 80-153, 1980-1 C.B. 10.
204. Prop. Reg. Sec. 1.613A-3(h)(2), Example 5; Prop. Reg. Sec. 1.613A-3(h)(2), Example 6.
205. Prop. Reg. Sec. 1.1254-1(a)(4).
206. Rev. Rul. 80-109, 1980-1 C.B. 129.

Case 40
Drilling in Consideration of Full Interest in Well Site — Overriding Royalty Convertible into Share of Working Interest

Operator A assigns the full working interest in a 40-acre lease to Operator B in consideration of Operator B's agreement to drill and complete one well on the lease. Operator A retains a one-eighth overriding royalty interest in the property, with an option to convert that interest into an undivided one-half working interest after Operator B has recovered all his costs of drilling and completing the well from the net cash profits from production.

Operators A and B elect to be excluded from the partnership provisions of the Internal Revenue Code.

Operator B owns the full working or operating interest in the property during the drilling period. Before any portion of the working interest is transferable to Operator A, Operator B is entitled to recoup his tangible and intangible drilling and development costs (IDC), plus the costs of operating the well, out of the gross income attributable to the well. Accordingly, Operator B should deduct all the IDC incurred in drilling the well and should capitalize as depreciable basis the cost of the equipment installed on the property.[207]

Operator A should not recognize any taxable income if he exercises the option to convert the overriding royalty interest to a one-half working interest because that conversion should qualify for nontaxable treatment. *(See Cases 131, 146 and 147.)* Operator A's tax basis in the working interest after the conversion will be his remaining tax basis, if any, in the retained overriding royalty interest. The other tax consequences to Operators A and B are substantially the same as in a "carried-interest" arrangement providing for full recoupment of drilling costs. *(See Case 39.)*

Many variations of this so-called "convertible-override" arrangement are encountered in practice. The overriding royalties may be convertible to working interests at the assignor's option at casing point or at some future date, such as 90 days after completion of the well. If the conversion privilege is exercisable by the carried party before the carrying party has recouped all its costs, the Internal Revenue Service (IRS) likely will require the carrying party to capitalize as leasehold cost that portion of the costs attributable to the working interest that may have to be reassigned to the carried party. *(See Cases 38 and 45.)* The IRS has ruled that this capitalization is required even if the conversion privilege is not actually exercised.[208]

Case 41
Drilling as Consideration for Carved-Out Drill Site

Operator A owns the full working interest in a 640-acre oil and gas lease. Operator A assigns to Operator B the full working interest in a 40-acre drill site and an undivided one-half working interest in the remaining 600 acres as consideration of Operator B's agreement to drill and complete

207. Reg. Sec. 1.612-4(a); Rev. Rul. 69-332, 1969-1 C.B. 87.
208. Rev. Rul. 80-109, 1980-1 C.B. 129.

one well on the 40-acre drill site. Operator A retains a one-eighth overriding royalty in the 40-acre drill site, convertible to a 50% working interest upon payout of the initial test well.

Operators A and B elect to be excluded from the partnership provisions of the Internal Revenue Code.

This situation is the same as Case 40, except that Operator B receives an undivided interest in the acreage surrounding the drill site property in addition to the operating interest in the drill site acreage itself.

The tax consequences to both Operators A and B are substantially the same as in Case 40. The only additional tax consequences are associated with Operator A's transfer of the interest in the surrounding acreage to Operator B.

The Internal Revenue Service (IRS) has ruled with respect to a similar situation[209] that the transfer of the surrounding acreage represents compensation to Operator B in the form of property for undertaking the development project on the drill site. The IRS held that because the rights of Operator B to receive the assignment of the acreage were conditioned upon the abandonment or completion of the test well, the fair market value of the acreage, determined as of the date of the transfer to Operator B, is includable in his gross income in the year the well is completed or when he receives the acreage, whichever is earlier.

The IRS further reasoned that Operator A should be taxed as though he sold the surrounding acreage for its fair market value on the date of transfer and paid Operator B the resulting cash proceeds as compensation for developing the drill site. Based on the ruling, Operator A should recognize the taxable gain or loss in the year of transfer. The nature of that gain or loss, i.e., whether it is ordinary or results from the sale or disposition of real property used in a trade or business, will depend on whether Operator A held the acreage primarily for sale to customers in the ordinary course of his trade or business or for development.

Operator A's adjusted basis in the retained overriding royalty interest reserved in the drill site would be increased by the fair market value of the interest in the surrounding acreage that was transferred to Operator B.

The IRS's overall conclusions appear to be correct only if its interpretation of the term *property*, as used in the "pool-of-capital" concept, is correct and if the interests Operator B receives constitute two separate properties.

The IRS, in fact, concluded that the acreage Operator B received under the farmout agreement consisted of two separate properties. Although the IRS did not offer any support for its conclusion, it held that the entire working interest in the drill site was a property separate from the undivided one-half working interest in the surrounding acreage. The validity of the IRS's conclusion is questionable. (*See Section III for a discussion of the unit-of-property concept.*)

The IRS then attempted to limit the scope of the "pool-of-capital" concept by concluding that property, as the term is used in that concept, should be interpreted to mean the unit of property as determined for depletion purposes rather than the prospect or area of interest, as was commonly accepted prior to these rulings.

Because the IRS held that the "pool-of-capital" concept applies to the transfer of the acreage in the drill site property, the transfer of that property interest should not

209. Rev. Rul. 77-176, 1977-1 C.B. 77 (provisions applicable only to transfers made on or after Apr. 27, 1977). *See also* IRS Letter Ruling 8311005 (Technical Advice Memorandum); IRS Letter Ruling 8317043.

result in the recognition of any income to Operators A or B. The transferred working interest is in the same property to which Operator B makes his "contribution" and, therefore, the receipt of the working interest in the drill site should not represent payment for services but rather a capital interest acquired through Operator B's agreement to make a contribution to the "pool of capital." Operator A should not realize taxable income from the transfer of the working interest in the drill site because under the "pool-of-capital" concept Operator A is not regarded as having parted with a capital interest.[210]

The IRS reasoned that the "pool-of-capital" concept does not apply to the interest in the surrounding acreage because Operator B did not make any contribution toward the development of that property. Accordingly, Operator A is treated as having sold the interest on the date of its transfer and as having paid the cash proceeds to Operator B as compensation for the drilling of the obligation well on the other property.

These conclusions should be applicable equally to any farmout situation in which an interest is received in a unit of property other than the drill site unit of property as consideration for the drilling of a well. For example, it is not necessary that Operator B receive a lesser interest in the surrounding acreage, as long as that acreage consitutes a separate unit of property (e.g., a farmout involving multiple underlying leases).

In a private letter ruling,[211] the IRS applied the reasoning of the ruling discussed above to a subleasing transaction whereby the working interest owner transferred a producing lease to an unrelated party and retained a net profits interest. The IRS ruled that the unrelated party recognized income to the extent of the fair market value of the equipment because the equipment was additional compensation (i.e., not part of the drill site acreage).

The ruling has been questioned with respect to its restriction of the "pool-of-capital" concept to a single taxable unit of property. Traditionally, the "pool of capital" has been considered to include the area of interest or prospect. However, in spite of considerable public debate and discussion concerning the ruling, it has not been modified or revoked. No litigation of the issue has been reported, even though the ruling is effective for transfers made on or after April 27, 1977.

Various techniques may be considered to eliminate or minimize the possible application of this ruling to a transaction without substantially altering the transaction's overall economics. For example, Operators A and B could structure the transaction as a legal or tax partnership, with a special allocation to Operator B of the IDC incurred in drilling the obligation well. Income recognition would be avoided because the partnership would be considered to own all the property for tax purposes and no actual or "deemed" exchange of properties would take place between the partners, Operators A and B.[212] However, the economic sharing arrangement may require alteration so that the special allocations have substantial economic effect.[213] *(See Cases 161, 163 and 165.)*

Because the IRS held that the amount of income is determined by reference to the fair market value of the surrounding acreage at the date of transfer or when the drilling

210. Reg. Sec. 1.612-4(a); Rev. Rul. 69-332, 1969-1 C.B. 87; Rev. Rul. 71-207, 1971-1 C.B. 160; Rev. Rul. 75-446, 1975-2 C.B. 95.
211. IRS Letter Ruling 8317043.
212. I.R.C. Sec. 721(a).
213. I.R.C. Sec. 704(b); Prop. Reg. Sec. 1.704-1.

obligation is completed, whichever occurs first,[214] income will be minimized if the acreage can be assigned before the well is drilled. This approach will yield particularly favorable results when the first well is successful. In practice, however, this approach probably is of limited use because Operator A generally is unwilling to transfer the acreage to Operator B until the latter has fulfilled his development obligation. It generally will be acceptable to make the assignment prior to the drilling of the obligation well if the agreement requires Operator B to reassign the acreage if the obligation well is not completed as agreed. In such a case, however, the IRS probably will view the assignment as a forfeitable right until the obligation well is completed.

It may be possible under certain circumstances to use a Section 83(b) election to minimize the amount of income to be recognized. The parties can use other methods to void the potential detrimental impact of the ruling (e.g., having Operator B purchase an interest in the surrounding acreage); however, doing so will change the economics of the basic agreement.

Case 42
Intangible Drilling and Development Cost Deduction When Drilling for an Interest Under a Carried-Interest Arrangement, With Payout Defined as a Specific Amount

> **Operator A, who owns the entire working interest in a lease, enters into an arrangement with Operator B, who agrees to drill a well free of cost to Operator A. Operator A assigns the full working interest in the lease to Operator B until the latter recovers $400,000 out of the net cash profits from production, after which one-half the working interest reverts to Operator A. Operator B expends $360,000 for intangible drilling and development costs (IDC) and $80,000 for tangible lease and well equipment costs for a total of $440,000.**
>
> **Operators A and B elect to be excluded from the partnership provisions of the Internal Revenue Code.**

The owner of an operating interest has an option to expense IDC except that, if drilling is undertaken for an assignment of a fraction of the operating rights, only the costs attributable to the fraction of the operating rights acquired are within the option.[215] *(See Case 38.)* To deduct all IDC incurred in drilling the well, a carrying party must own the operating rights in the well for which he pays the costs during both the drilling period and the complete payout period.[216] *(See Case 39.)* If the carrying party owns the entire working interest for less than the complete payout period, he must capitalize as leasehold cost the portion of the IDC and tangible lease and well equipment costs that is applicable to the carried party's residual interest in the lease.[217]

In this case, Operator B is not entitled to recover all his drilling and equipping costs prior to the reversion of one-half the operating rights to Operator A. Therefore, Operator B is not considered to own all the operating rights during the complete payout period. Accordingly, the free-well rules apply *(see Case 38)*, and Operator B

214. Rev. Rul. 77-176, 1977-1 C.B. 77.
215. Reg. Sec. 1.612-4(a).
216. Rev. Rul. 71-207, 1971-1 C.B. 160; Rev. Rul. 75-446, 1975-2 C.B. 95.
217. Rev. Rul. 70-336, 1970-1 C.B. 145; Rev. Rul. 71-206, 1971-1 C.B. 105; Rev. Rul. 80-109, 1980-1 C.B. 129.

must capitalize as depletable leasehold cost one-half the tangible and intangible costs ($220,000) incurred in drilling the well.[218] Operator B should deduct one-half the IDC ($180,000) and capitalize as depreciable cost of the equipment one-half the tangible costs ($40,000).

In a ruling involving another type of payout situation, the Internal Revenue Service (IRS) held that the mere possibility that the carried party will receive a portion of the permanent operating interest before the carrying party achieves complete payout is sufficient to limit the intangible deduction to the portion attributable to the carrying party's permanent interest.[219]

To avoid any exposure to possible capitalization of a portion of the carrying party's costs when recoupment is to be measured by a specific amount (or by a specific time period), the agreement should provide that the reversion of a fractional part of the operating rights to the carried party will not occur until the recoupment of the specified amount or of the actual cost of drilling and equipping the well, whichever is larger. *(See Case 39.)* Of course, such a provision could change the economic arrangement between the parties. As an alternative, the parties could elect to be treated as a partnership for federal income tax purposes. *(See Case 163.)* This election too could require a change in the economic arrangement to meet the "substantial economic effect" requirements of the partnership special allocation rules.

Operator B, as the owner of all the operating rights until he has recouped $400,000, should report, as ordinary income subject to depletion, all production income and should deduct all operating expenses during the payout period. Thereafter, as owner of one-half the operating rights, he should report his one-half share of the proceeds from production and deduct his one-half share of the operating expenses. Operator B should compute cost depletion based on 100% of the reserves prior to the projected date at which 50% of the interest is to revert to Operator A and on 50% of the reserves after that date. *(See Case 79.)*.

The reassignment of one-half the working interest to Operator A should not constitute a disposition that requires Operator B to recapture any of the IDC[220] *(see Case 131)*, nor should that reassignment constitute the transfer of a proven property so as to deny future percentage depletion.[221] *(See Cases 108 and 109.)*

The tax consequences to Operator A are the same as in a carried-interest arrangement that provides for complete recoupment. *(See Case 39.)*

Case 43
Intangible Drilling and Development Cost Deduction When Drilling for an Interest That Consists of an Undivided Interest and an Interest in the Nature of a Mortgage Until Payout

> Operator A, who owns the entire working interest in a lease, enters into an agreement with Operator B for the drilling and equipping of a well on the lease. The agreement provides that Operator B will advance all funds necessary for the drilling, equipping and testing of the well. On completion of the well as a commercial producer, Operator A will assign a one-half interest in the lease to Operator B. In addition, Operator B will receive an

218. Rev. Rul. 70-336, 1970-1 C.B. 145; Rev. Rul. 80-109, 1980-1 C.B. 129.
219. Rev. Rul. 80-109, 1980-1 C.B. 129.
220. Prop. Reg. Sec. 1.1254-1(a)(4).
221. Prop. Reg. Sec. 1.613A-3(h)(2), Example 5; Prop. Reg. Sec. 1.613A-3(h)(2), Example 6.

assignment in the nature of a mortgage for the remaining one-half interest in the lease until the net cash profits from production from the mortgaged interest equal the costs of drilling and equipping allocable to that interest. When Operator B has recouped these costs, he will reassign that one-half interest to Operator A. Operator A has no personal liability for any drilling or operating costs until the reversion of the mortgaged interest.

If the well is completed as a dry hole, Operator B will receive an assignment of a one-half interest in the lease.

The parties elect to be excluded from the partnership provisions of the Internal Revenue Code.

Operator B is obligated to drill and equip a well at his sole cost and risk in return for all the rights and burdens of ownership until he has recouped his costs (intangible and tangible) and, subsequent to recoupment, one-half the operating rights. The substance of this arrangement does not differ from the carried-interest arrangement that provides for an outright assignment of the entire operating rights to the carrying party for the complete payout period. Accordingly, Operator B should be entitled to deduct all the intangible drilling and development costs (IDC) incurred in drilling the well.

To deduct the IDC, Operator B need not hold title to the interest at the time the well is being drilled.[222] Also, receiving an assignment for only a one-half interest in the lease if the well is completed as a dry hole will not affect Operator B's right to deduct all the IDC. The fact that only the permanent interest is transferred to Operator B in the case of a dry hole should have no effect on the recoupment provisions of the agreement because the agreement provides for complete payout if the well is productive.[223]

The method or legal means of the conveyance of a portion of the operating rights during recoupment (in this case, in the form of a mortgaged interest) should not determine the tax consequences of the transaction.[224] However, this type of arrangement was the subject of a Tax Court decision[225] in which the court held that the conveyance to the carrying party consisted of two separate property interests: a one-half interest in the operating rights that continued over the life of the property and a production payment[226] to the extent of the costs advanced attributable to the carried party's residual interest in the lease. Under the two-property concept, Operator B would be entitled to deduct only one-half the IDC. The remaining half of those costs and one-half the tangible lease and well equipment costs would constitute an investment in a production payment pledged for development.[227] Under this concept, Operator B would report one-half the gross income and operating expenses as attributable to his one-half working interest and the remaining one-half as production payment income during the recoupment period. *(See Cases 86 and 150 for a detailed discussion of a production payment pledged for development.)* Although this decision has not been overruled by a higher court, it generally is not followed by other courts or the Internal Revenue Service.

Operators A and B may treat the co-ownership as a partnership for federal income tax purposes. *(See Case 163.)* However, doing so may require a change in economic

222. Reg. Sec. 1.612-4(a).
223. Rev. Rul. 69-332, 1969-1 C.B. 87.
224. Palmer v. Bender, 287 U.S. 551 (1933), 11 AFTR 1106, 3 USTC 1026; Kirby Petroleum Co. v. Comm'r, 326 U.S. 599 (1946), 34 AFTR 526, 46-1 USTC 9149; U.S. v. Cocke, 399 F.2d 433 (5th Cir. 1968); 22 AFTR2d 5267, 68-2 USTC 9502.
225. Herndon Drilling Co., 6 T.C. 628 (1946).
226. I.R.C. Sec. 636; Reg. Sec. 1.636-3(a).
227. Reg. Sec. 1.636-1(b).

arrangement to meet the "substantial economic effect" requirements of the partnership special allocation rules. If partnership treatment is not desired, it appears to be prudent, at least from a tax standpoint, to change the agreement to provide for the assignment to the carrying party of his permanent operating interest and the right of recoupment from the entire operating interest before the carried party has a share of the operating income.[228] *(See Case 39.)*

The reversion of one-half the working interest to Operator A upon payout should not constitute the transfer of a proven property so as to deny future percentage depletion on the reassigned fraction of the working interest.[229] *(See Cases 108 and 109.)* Also, the reassignment to Operator A should not constitute a disposition that requires Operator B to recapture any of the IDC.[230] *(See Case 131.)*

Case 44
Intangible Drilling and Development Cost Deduction When Drilling for an Interest With Recoupment from a Portion of the Operating Rights

> Operator B agrees to pay all the costs to drill and equip a well on a lease owned by Operator A. If the well is productive, Operators A and B will own the operating rights and will share the income and operating expenses one-fourth and three-fourths, respectively, until Operator B has recouped all his costs of drilling and equipping the well. After recoupment, Operators A and B will own the operating rights and will share equally the income and operating expenses.
>
> Operators A and B elect to be excluded from the partnership provisions of the Internal Revenue Code.

Operator B is entitled to recoup all his costs of drilling and equipping the well from production; however, recovery is limited to the production attributable to a fraction of the operating interest, which is less than the portion Operator B is obligated to pay for drilling and equipping the well.

Operator B has the obligation to drill the well and incurs the incident risks and hazards of three-fourths of the operating rights in the lease with the right to three-fourths of the net cash profits from the well until recoupment of drilling, equipping and operating costs. When Operator B has recovered his costs, assuming the productive life of the well is sufficient to produce net cash profits of 133⅓% of the costs of drilling and equipping the well, Operator B's ownership of the operating rights is reduced to 50%. If the well does not produce sufficient income to allow full recovery of Operator B's costs, he will own three-fourths of the operating rights during the drilling and the productive life of the well.

Because the carrying party will recoup his costs from a fractional share of operating interest income that is less than his fractional share of costs for drilling and equipping the well, the free-well rules apply *(see Case 38)* and the deduction for intangible drilling and development costs (IDC) will be limited. However, it is not clear whether the deduction will be limited to the carrying party's permanent share of the operating

228. Rev. Rul. 69-332, 1969-1 C.B. 87; Rev. Rul. 71-207, 1971-1 C.B. 160; Rev. Rul. 75-446, 1975-2 C.B. 95.
229. Prop. Reg. Sec. 1.613A-3(h)(2), Example 5; Prop. Reg. Sec. 1.613A-3(h)(2), Example 6.
230. Prop. Reg. Sec. 1.1254-1(a)(4).

interest income (50%) or to the fractional interest of the recoupment period (75%). Published rulings and litigated cases do not specifically cover this issue.

The Internal Revenue Service (IRS) may require that the deduction for the IDC be limited to the taxpayer's permanent share of the operating interest income (50%). The various IRS rulings regarding the payout concept generally require ownership of "the entire working interest throughout the complete payout period."[231] This treatment means the carrying party does not have the right to complete recoupment. *(See Case 38.)*

To the contrary, it appears reasonable to allow Operator B to deduct the portion of the IDC attributable to the fractional interest of the operating rights owned during the recoupment period. In that case, Operator B should deduct three-fourths of the IDC and capitalize as depreciable costs three-fourths of the tangible costs. Operator B should capitalize as depletable leasehold cost one-fourth of both the tangible and the intangible drilling and development costs incurred in drilling the well. Other federal income tax consequences will be the same as discussed in Case 42.

Due to the capitalization required (of either 25% or 50% of total costs incurred), Operators A and B may wish to have the co-ownership treated as a partnership for federal income tax purposes. However, doing so may require a change in the economic arrangement to meet the substantial economic effect requirements of the partnership special allocation rules. *(See Case 165.)*

The tax consequences to Operator A are the same as in a carried-interest arrangement that provides for complete recoupment. *(See Case 39.)*

Case 45
Intangible Drilling and Development Cost Deduction When Drilling for an Interest and the Carried Party Has an Option To Pay Completion Costs

> **Operator A assigns all the operating rights in a lease to Operator B, who agrees to pay all costs of drilling and testing a well and, if the well is capable of commercial production, all completion costs, including those for the tangible equipment. Operator B is entitled to recoup all drilling, testing and completion costs from the net cash profits from the entire operating interest. After recoupment, Operators A and B will own the operating rights equally.**
>
> **Operator A has an option to pay one-half the completion costs. If Operator A exercises that option, Operator B immediately will reassign one-half the working interest to Operator A, and both will share production income and operating expenses equally. Operators A and B elect to be excluded from the partnership provisions of the Internal Revenue Code.**

Whether or not Operator A exercises his option, the free-well rules apply. *(See Case 38.)* Operator B should deduct one-half his expenditures for intangible drilling and development costs (IDC) and capitalize as depletable leasehold cost one-half his expenditures of drilling the well to the point that Operator A joins in the completion

231. Rev. Rul. 69-332, 1969-1 C.B. 87; Rev. Rul. 70-336, 1970-1 C.B. 145; Rev. Rul. 71-206, 1971-1 C.B. 105; Rev. Rul. 71-207, 1971-1 C.B. 160; Rev. Rul. 75-446, 1975-2 C.B. 95; Rev. Rul. 80-109, 1980-1 C.B. 129.

effort.[232] Operator B should capitalize as depreciable costs one-half of any expenditures for tangible equipment incurred during the drilling period and capitalize the other half of those tangible costs as depletable leasehold cost. Operator B should be allowed to deduct all his expenditures that are classified as IDC after Operator A joins in the completion effort and should capitalize as depreciable costs his expenditures for tangible equipment incurred during the completion period.

Before 1980, it generally was accepted that Operator A's option to reacquire one-half of the operating rights did not affect the tax consequences of the transaction if Operator A, in fact, did not exercise the option to join the completion attempt. If Operator A did not elect to share in the completion, Operator B continued to own all the operating rights during both the completion and complete payout periods. If the well was dry and no completion attempt was made, Operator A's option would not have been exercisable nor would his option have had any effect on Operator B's ownership during the drilling period.[233]

During 1980, the Internal Revenue Service (IRS) modified its position concerning the effectiveness of payout computations in these situations.[234] Specifically, the IRS ruled that it is no longer sufficient for taxpayers to hold the initial fraction of the operating interest through the complete payout period. Rather, the carrying arrangement must state that the carrying party will (in all events) hold the initial fraction through the complete payout period. Thus, the mere possibility that a portion of the operating rights may revert to the carried party before payout is sufficient to require capitalization of a portion of the carrying party's costs as leasehold cost, even if the reversion does not actually occur.

The IRS apparently has recognized that its ruling represented a change of prior policy. Accordingly, the ruling will not be applied adversely to taxpayers that executed carrying arrangements before April 21, 1980, or that had entered into written binding agreements to execute carrying arrangements before that date if those taxpayers do, in fact, hold the initial fraction of the operating interest through the complete payout period.

If the arrangement in this case example was entered into after April 20, 1980, the IRS will apply the free-well rules *(see Case 38)* and will require Operator B to capitalize one-half of all expenditures incurred as leasehold cost, even if Operator A does not elect to share in the completion attempt.

Operator A should deduct his one-half share of any IDC incurred after joining the completion effort and should capitalize as depreciable costs his one-half of the tangible equipment costs because he will possess one-half of the operating rights and will be obligated to pay one-half of all completion costs.

If Operator A elects not to pay his one-half of the completion costs, it appears Operator B should be allowed to deduct all IDC incurred after Operator A's right to elect to pay completion costs expires. Further, Operator B should be allowed to capitalize as depreciable costs all tangible equipment costs incurred after that election date. Once Operator A's election is made, he gives up his right to obtain a share of the operating interest before payout; accordingly, the terms of the carrying arrangement make it clear that thereafter Operator B holds the full operating rights throughout the complete payout period.

---

232. Rev. Rul. 70-657, 1970-2 C.B. 70; Rev. Rul. 70-336, 1970-1 C.B. 145; Rev. Rul. 71-206, 1971-1 C.B. 105.
233. Reg. Sec. 1.612-4(a); Rev. Rul. 69-332, 1969-1 C.B. 87; Rev. Rul. 71-207, 1971-1 C.B. 160; Rev. Rul. 75-446, 1975-2 C.B. 95.
234. Rev. Rul. 80-109, 1980-1 C.B. 129.

As an alternative, the parties may elect to be treated as a partnership for tax purposes. Special allocation provisions can assure Operator B's deduction of the drilling costs and eliminate the potential reclassification of one-half of tangible costs to leasehold cost. However, the special allocation provisions must have "substantial economic effect," which could change the economics of the arrangement.[235] *(See Cases 161, 163 and 165.)*

Case 46
Intangible Drilling and Development Cost Deduction When Drilling for an Interest in Multiple Leases With Recoupment from the Combined Production of All Wells

> **Operator A assigns the entire working interest in three leases to Operator B, who agrees to drill and equip a test well on each lease at his sole cost and expense. Operator B is entitled to recoup the expenses of drilling and equipping the three wells out of the net cash profits from the combined production of all three wells. After recoupment, one-half the working interest in each lease reverts to Operator A. Each lease constitutes a separate unit of property. Operators A and B elect to be excluded from the partnership provisions of the Internal Revenue Code.**

This arrangement differs from the carried-interest arrangement *(see Case 39)* because Operator B, the carrying party, is entitled to recoup the cost of drilling on a particular property from sources other than the production from the well on that property. Generally, the carrying party in a carried-interest arrangement is entitled to deduct all intangible drilling and development costs (IDC) incurred in drilling a well only if he owns all the operating rights in the property on which the well is located during the drilling and the complete payout period.[236] In this situation, Operator B may recoup a portion of the costs of drilling the well on one lease from the production from wells on one or both of the other leases. Thus, Operator B may not own the operating rights in each particular property until he has recovered the costs of drilling and equipping the well on that property solely from the production attributable to that property.

In this type of situation, which involves an aggregate payout computation (commonly referred to as basket payout), at least one of the properties will reach payout (as computed on a property-by-property basis) before the carrying party's interest in the properties is reduced. However, it is not possible to determine in advance which property (or properties) will reach payout and which will not.

The Internal Revenue Service (IRS) has ruled that payout computations must be made on a property-by-property basis.[237] The IRS held that the mere possibility that the carrying party may not hold the entire operating interest in a particular property through the complete payout period is sufficient to require capitalization under the free-well rules. Thus, the IRS will require capitalization even if the carrying party ultimately holds the initial fraction of the operating interest through the complete payout period. Accordingly, in this situation, Operator B will be required to capitalize as leasehold cost one-half of both the IDC and the tangible equipment costs incurred in drilling each of the wells under the free-well rules. *(See Case 38.)*

---

235. I.R.C. Sec. 704(b); Reg. Sec. 1.704-1.

236. Reg. Sec. 1.612-4(a); Rev. Rul. 69-332, 1969-1 C.B. 87; Rev. Rul. 71-207, 1971-1 C.B. 160; Rev. Rul. 75-446, 1975-2 C.B. 95.

237. Rev. Rul. 80-109, 1980-1 C.B. 129.

The IRS apparently recognized that this ruling represents a change of prior policy; accordingly, the ruling will not be applied adversely to taxpayers subject to carrying arrangements executed before April 21, 1980, (or subject to written binding agreements before that date) if those taxpayers do, in fact, hold the initial fraction of the operating interest through the complete payout period.

Operators A and B should consider having the joint venture treated as a partnership for federal income tax purposes. However, the partnership alternative with the appropriate special allocation provisions may result in a change in the economic arrangement. *(See Cases 161, 163 and 165.)*

Alternatively, they could change the arrangement to provide that the reversion to Operator A of the one-half interest in any property will not occur until Operator B has recovered the costs of drilling all wells from the production attributable to all properties and that in no event will the interest in any particular property revert to Operator A until Operator B has recovered the costs of drilling and equipping the wells on that property from the production from that property. Under this modified arrangement, Operator B should be allowed to deduct all IDC incurred because he would own the operating rights in each property until he recovered his costs of drilling the well on that property from the production from that property. However, this definition of payout may result in the carrying party receiving a larger share of the production income than he would have otherwise.

If all the wells covered by the agreement are located on a *single unit of property* and a portion of the working interest reverts to Operator A when Operator B has recovered all costs of drilling from the cash profits from the combined production of all wells covered by the agreement, Operator B should not be required to capitalize any portion of the costs of drilling the wells because the determination is made on a unit-of-property basis.[238]

Case 47
Intangible Drilling and Development Cost Deduction When Drilling for an Interest and a Third Party Retains an Overriding Royalty

C Company assigns the entire working interest in a lease to Operator A as consideration for Operator A's obligation to drill and equip one well at his sole risk and expense. One-half the working interest will revert to C Company when Operator A recovers his drilling and equipping costs from the net cash profits from the property.

Operator A assigns all rights in the agreement with C Company to Operator B for a cash consideration of $5,000. In addition, Operator A retains an overriding royalty consisting of a one-sixteenth net profits interest (measured by production income less production expenses) payable from Operator B's permanent one-half interest in the lease.

The parties elect to be excluded from the partnership provisions of the Internal Revenue Code.

238. Rev. Rul. 80-109, 1980-1 C.B. 129; Rev. Rul. 71-207, 1971-1 C.B. 160; Rev. Rul. 69-332, 1969-1 C.B. 87.

The tax consequences of this arrangement are uncertain because the regulations and litigation do not specifically define complete payout and the published rulings that deal with payout situations do not specifically cover this particular fact situation.

The arrangement between Operator A and C Company provides for complete payout of the well before any interest reverts to C Company. That agreement, standing alone, permits the carrying party to deduct all the intangible drilling and development costs (IDC) because the drilling obligation was undertaken for the assignment of all the operating rights during the payout period.[239] The arrangement between Operators A and B does not affect C Company's rights because B acquired only Operator A's rights and assumed his obligations. Also, because Operator A retained an overriding royalty interest and not a share of the operating interest, Operator B acquired all the operating rights. However, the gross income attributable to the operating rights has been reduced by the overriding royalty retained by Operator A.

If Operator B spends $100,000 to drill and equip the well, a one-half interest in the well will revert to C Company when the net cash profits from the production, including amounts attributable to Operator A's overriding royalty interest, equal $100,000. Operator B, however, will have received only $93,750 because B will have paid $6,250 to Operator A for his net profits interest.

If *complete payout period* is interpreted to mean recovery of all costs applicable to the carried party's reversionary interest from the net cash income applicable to that interest, Operator B will have recovered all these costs because the overriding royalty interest is payable only from his permanent share of the working interest. In the example, Operator B incurred costs of $50,000 applicable to C Company's reversionary share (one-half) of the well and recouped $50,000 from C Company's reversionary share of the net cash profits from the well. Under this interpretation, Operator B should be allowed to deduct all the IDC because he owns all the operating rights during the period in which he recovers the costs attributable to the carried party's reversionary interest.[240] The balance of the tax consequences to Operator B also should be the same as in any carried-interest arrangement that provides for complete recoupment. *(See Case 39.)* This interpretation appears to meet the criteria of the regulations and rulings when the total arrangement is viewed with respect to the economics and interests of each party.

On the other hand, if *complete payout period* is interpreted to mean the recovery of all costs of drilling and equipping the well from the net cash profits from the operating rights attributable to both the carried party's reversionary interest and the carrying party's permanent interest, Operator B will not have recovered his costs at the time the one-half interest reverts to C Company. Under this interpretation, Operator B will be required to capitalize part of the expenditures for drilling and equipping the well as additional leasehold cost under the free-well rules.[241] *(See Case 38.)*

Until the Internal Revenue Service has clarified its position, Operators A and B should consider changing their arrangement to provide that the net profits interest will not be effective until the time one-half the working interest reverts to C Company. Operator B then should be entitled to deduct all IDC, as he will own all the operating rights during the complete payout period. Such a change, however, could alter the underlying economic arrangement of the parties.

---

239. Reg. Sec. 1.612-4(a); Rev. Rul. 71-207, 1971-1 C.B. 160; Rev. Rul. 75-446, 1975-2 C.B. 95.
240. *Ibid.*
241. Rev. Rul. 70-336, 1970-1 C.B. 145; Rev. Rul. 71-206, 1971-1 C.B. 105.

To obtain a similar economic effect with different tax results, the parties should consider treating the joint venture as a partnership for federal income tax purposes, with a special allocation to Operator B of the total deduction for IDC. In the partnership alternative, it may be necessary to change the overall economics of the arrangement to ensure the special allocation has substantial economic effect.[242] *(See Cases 161, 163 and 165.)*

Operator A actually has made a sublease because he has retained a nonoperating interest that continues over the life of the property, and he should report the lease bonus of $5,000 as ordinary income. Any amounts Operator A receives with respect to the retained net profits interest should be reported as ordinary income subject to an allowance for depletion.

Case 48
Intangible Drilling and Development Cost Deduction When Drilling for an Interest and All the Operating Rights Revert to the Carried Party for a Limited Period After the Carrying Party Has Obtained Payout

> **Operator A assigns the entire working interest in a lease to Operator B in consideration for which Operator B agrees to pay all costs of drilling and equipping a well. The agreement provides that the entire working interest will revert to Operator A after Operator B has recouped all his costs from the net cash profits from production. When Operator A has received a like amount, each party will own a one-half working interest.**
>
> **Operators A and B elect to be excluded from the partnership provisions of the Internal Revenue Code.**

This arrangement differs from the carried-interest arrangement discussed in Case 42 because the entire working interest reverts to the carried party for a limited period after the carrying party has recouped his cost of drilling and equipping the well. If the well produces sufficient income to pay out Operators A and B and then reverts to equal ownership, the income they receive over the life of the property will be the same as in a free-well arrangement. *(See Case 38.)* However, the economic substance differs from the free-well arrangement because Operator A is not assured of any proceeds from the well until Operator B has recovered all his costs of drilling and equipping the well from the net cash profits from the well. For example, if Operator B pays $400,000 to drill and equip the well and recovers $380,000 from the net cash profits from operating it, at which time the well ceases to produce and is plugged, Operator A will not receive any of the net cash profits, nor will Operator B have obtained payout. Alternatively, if the well produces $600,000 of net cash profits before it ceases to produce and is plugged, Operator B will receive $400,000 (cost of drilling and equipping the well) and Operator A, $200,000. In the latter example, Operator B recovered his investment, but his interest effectively terminated at that time due to the limited productivity of the well.

The Internal Revenue Service has ruled that a taxpayer who agreed to pay all the costs to drill and equip a well on a lease in return for the entire working interest in the lease until he had recouped 200% of his costs to drill and equip the well from the operating cash profits of the well was entitled to the deduction for intangible drilling

242. I.R.C. Sec. 704(b); Reg. Sec. 1.704-1.

and development costs (IDC), even though the taxpayer retained no continuing interest in the lease after recouping 200% of the costs.[243] Under the rationale of this ruling, Operator B should be entitled to claim a full deduction for the IDC incurred. The lack of clarity in the production payment regulations causes some uncertainty as to the tax consequences of this type of arrangement.[244] *(See Case 43 for a discussion of the possible application of the production payment rules to certain carried-interest situations.)*

Case 49
Turnkey Drilling Arrangement on Jointly Owned Lease

> **Operator B, a cash-basis taxpayer, purchases a one-half interest in a nonproducing oil and gas lease from Operator A for a cash consideration of $25,000. Simultaneously, Operators A and B enter into an agreement by which Operator A will make the arrangements for and supervise the drilling of a well on the property. The agreement provides that Operator B will pay $200,000 to Operator A as his share of the cost of drilling the well to a depth of 5,000 feet. Operator B also agrees to pay one-half the actual amount of any completion and equipment costs. The cost to Operator A of having the well drilled to 5,000 feet is $350,000.**

Operator A has sold a one-half interest in an oil and gas lease and simultaneously has contracted to drill a well to the extent of a one-half interest in the well. The $200,000 Operator A receives from Operator B is, therefore, gross income from a turnkey drilling contract. From that amount Operator A may deduct one-half the drilling costs ($175,000), leaving him a net profit of $25,000 on the contract. The other one-half of the drilling costs ($175,000) represents intangible drilling and development costs (IDC) to Operator A, which is subject to the election to expense those costs as provided by the regulations,[245] and tangible costs, which must be capitalized and depreciated. Operator A may not adjust his share of the IDC by the profit on the contract with Operator B. In other words, Operator A may not reduce the $350,000 paid to drill the well by the $200,000 received from Operator B and deduct only the difference as IDC in computing net income from the property to determine his percentage depletion allowance. Such a "net" approach also would affect incorrectly the computation of the net income limitation with respect to the windfall profit tax, the amount of the intangibles to be treated as a tax preference item and the amount of intangibles subject to recapture upon a subsequent disposition of the property interest.

Operator B's portion of the well cost is the contract cost rather than one-half the actual costs incurred by Operator A.[246] Therefore, Operator B should treat the entire $200,000 as IDC except for his share of the cost of any tangible costs and recover these tangible costs through depreciation.

If the co-owners stipulate an unreasonably high price for the turnkey contract and a relatively low price for the interest in the lease, the Internal Revenue Service (IRS) and the courts[247] probably will hold that Operator B should treat a portion of the contract price for the drilling of the well as additional leasehold cost.

---

243. Rev. Rul. 75-446, 1975-2 C.B. 95.
244. Reg. Sec. 1.636-3(a)(2).
245. Reg. Sec. 1.612-4(a).
246. Reg. Sec. 1.612-4(a); G. F. Hedges, Jr., 41 T.C. 695 (1964); Erwin H. Haass, 55 T.C. 43 (1970).
247. Bernuth v. Comm'r, 470 F.2d 710 (2d Cir. 1972), 31 AFTR2d 73-388, 73-1 USTC 9132; Rev. Rul. 73-211, 1973-1 C.B. 303.

In any situation involving the receipt of a leasehold interest and the concurrent execution of a turnkey drilling contract, all the facts and circumstances must be examined carefully to determine that the overall consideration paid is reasonably allocated between the acquisition of the leasehold and the drilling of the well. The primary facts to consider are the market value of comparable leases in the area and the reasonableness of the turnkey contract, which can be evaluated by comparison with the going rate for footage and daywork contracts in the area or, if possible, with the turnkey price that would have been incurred in an arm's-length transaction with an unrelated drilling contractor.

Taxpayers should avoid using a "standard" acceptable percentage turnkey markup or profit factor computed with respect to estimated costs. The amount of a reasonable markup will vary significantly from well to well depending on the precise terms of the drilling contract, the depth to which the well is being drilled and the geological characteristics of the area involved.

If the consideration for the lease and the well is stipulated as a single sum, it will be necessary to allocate the consideration between the lease and the well. The taxpayer has the burden of proof if the IRS questions the allocation.[248] In addition, a contract of this type should be drawn up carefully to avoid an IRS contention that the transaction, in effect, constitutes the purchase of a lease with a well on it.[249] *(See Case 36.)*

Operator A should not be considered as acting as an agent for Operator B because Operator A has contracted to drill the well for a fixed price. Therefore, Operator B should claim a deduction for the IDC in the year in which he pays Operator A. *(See Case 31 for a discussion of the tax treatment applicable if Operator B makes the payment in a year prior to that in which the well is drilled. See Case 31 for a discussion of economic performance and its impact on IDC deductions.)*

Case 50
Drilling and Other Costs in Connection With Water Flooding and Salt Water Disposal Programs

> Operator A owns the working interests in an oil field. A water-flooding program is necessary to develop the field for production in commercial quantities because the natural reservoir energy in this area is inadequate. Operator A develops the field by drilling a pattern of wells and pumping water under pressure into the input wells to stimulate the flow of oil. Operator A previously has elected to expense intangible drilling and development costs (IDC) for tax purposes.

Input wells, such as those described above, drilled to stimulate oil production are treated the same for tax purposes as oil wells.[250] Thus, under his election, Operator A may expense the IDC of the input wells. To compute net income from the property for the percentage depletion limitation, and for other purposes, Operator A should apportion the costs of those input wells to all properties benefited by the repressuring operation.

The costs of drilling wells for the disposal of salt water probably are not included in the option to expense IDC because that drilling is not considered generally to be

248. H. Patricia Roby, T.C. Memo Dec. (Nov. 21, 1983).
249. Platt v. Comm'r, 207 F.2d 697 (7th Cir. 1953), 44 AFTR 530, 53-2 USTC 9560.
250. Page Oil Co., 41 B.T.A. 952 (1940); Rev. Rul. 69-583, 1969-2 C.B. 41; Rev. Rul. 84-65, 1984-1 C.B. 229; G.C.M. 39224; G.C.M. 39619.

incident to and necessary for the preparation of wells for the production of oil and gas. The cost of a salt water disposal system, including equipment and any wells, should be capitalized and recovered in the form of depreciation.[251] If an operator drills a well in exploring for oil or gas and later converts it to a salt water disposal well, the IDC incurred prior to the decision to convert the well should be subject to Operator A's option to expense.

The costs of drilling a well or reworking an existing well to inject salt water to stimulate production will be treated as being similar to the costs of an injection well and, therefore, deductible for tax purposes to the extent allowable under the option. If the operator drills a fresh water well to supply water for drilling an oil or gas well, the intangible costs incurred in drilling the water well are includable in the option because those costs are incident to and necessary for the drilling of oil and gas wells. *(See Case 20.)*

The intangible drilling costs of water wells drilled solely to provide a source of water for the secondary recovery of oil probably are not within the option to expense IDC because that drilling is not considered generally to be incident to and necessary for the preparation of the wells for the production of oil or gas. This is consistent with an Internal Revenue Service ruling that held that the costs of drilling wells to supply carbon dioxide for use in a tertiary project are not within the option to expense IDC.[252] If this treatment is correct, all costs of drilling and equipping the source water wells should be capitalized as depreciable property and the annual depreciation deduction should be apportioned for percentage depletion purposes among the leases benefited by the water injection.

Case 51
Drilling Under a Footage Contract

Driller D arranges to drill a well for Operator A, who agrees to furnish the casing, tubing and all other tangible lease and well equipment and to pay Driller D $12 per foot for a well drilled to a depth of 5,000 feet unless oil or gas is found above that depth. Driller D agrees to furnish the rig and other drilling equipment and the labor and tools necessary to perform the drilling. Operator A previously has elected to expense intangible drilling and development costs (IDC).

The situation explained above is a common type of nonturnkey footage drilling contract. Operator A may expense his payments to Driller D as IDC because he properly elected to do so.[253] *(See Case 23.)* Operator A should capitalize his payments for the casing and tubing and for all other lease and well equipment as depreciable assets. However, the costs of installing certain equipment are deductible as IDC. *(See Case 20.)*

Driller D's receipts are ordinary income, and his expenses in drilling the well are deductible as ordinary and necessary business expenses.[254]

(See Case 31 for a discussion of the tax treatment applicable if Operator A makes the payment in a year prior to that in which the well is drilled. Also see Case 31 for a discussion of economic performance and its impact on IDC deductions.)

251. Rev. Rul. 70-414, 1970-2 C.B. 132.
252. Rev. Rul. 82-17, 1982-1 C.B. 95.
253. Reg. Sec. 1.612-4(a).
254. G.C.M. 22332, 1941-1 C.B. 228.

Case 52
Drilling Under a Turnkey Contract

> **Operator A, who has elected to expense intangible drilling and development costs (IDC), enters into a contract with Driller D in which the latter agrees both to drill and to equip a well on Operator A's property. The contract provides that if the well is completed as a producer, Operator A will pay Driller D $200,000 of which $40,000 will be for equipment and $160,000 for labor, drilling, testing, etc. If a dry hole results, Operator A will pay $140,000 to Driller D, who agrees to plug and abandon the well.**

Pursuant to Operator A's prior election, he may expense the portion of the payments attributable to IDC.[255] He must also capitalize and depreciate any payments made for tangible equipment. *(See Case 20.)*

If a turnkey contract does not contain provisions that specifically allocate the total consideration between tangible lease and well equipment costs and IDC, Operator A must allocate the contract price between the two elements. The usual method is to value the tangible equipment and treat the remainder of the consideration as IDC. The cost or value of the equipment may be furnished by the driller or determined by a physical inventory.

Because Driller D is a stranger to the lease and has no part of the working interest or royalty in the property, Operator A should be entitled to the appropriate deductions for IDC under the contract. In other situations *(see Case 49)*, when the parties stipulate an unreasonably high-priced turnkey contract, the Internal Revenue Service (IRS) and the courts will seek to determine the purpose for such a high price. To the extent that price does not relate to drilling, including the risk involved with accepting a turnkey contract, different treatment for income tax purposes may be necessary.[256] The burden of proof is on the taxpayer if the IRS or court questions the amount allocated to IDC.[257]

(See Case 182 for a discussion of the passive-activity limitations and their effect on oil and gas operations.)

Case 53
Bottom-Hole and Dry-Hole Contributions

> **Operator A prepares to drill a well to a considerable depth on a lease in "wildcat" territory to determine the geological formations and producing possibilities. The information Operator A obtains will be beneficial to Operator B's evaluation of his adjoining lease. Operator B agrees to pay $75,000 to Operator A toward the cost of the well because he is interested in having a test well drilled and in the geological information Operator A will obtain.**

Operator B's payment constitutes a "bottom-hole contribution" because payment is due regardless of whether the well is dry or productive.

---

255. Reg. Sec. 1.612-4(a).
256. Bernuth v. Comm'r, 470 F.2d 710 (2d Cir. 1972), 31 AFTR2d 73-388, 73-1 USTC 9132; Rev. Rul. 73-211, 1973-1 C.B. 303.
257. H. Patricia Roby, T.C. Memo Dec. (Nov. 21, 1983).

The Internal Revenue Service (IRS) has ruled that a bottom-hole contribution must be capitalized as additional leasehold basis in the payor's adjoining acreage. The IRS reasoned that Operator B has received information relating to the retention of his interest in the adjoining lease, that this qualifies the payment as a capital expenditure under the Internal Revenue Code and that the expenditures do not fall within the option to be expensed as intangible drilling and development costs (IDC).[258]

A "dry-hole contribution" is similar except that it is payable only if the drilling results in a dry hole. Although the recent ruling does not specifically discuss dry-hole contributions, they should be treated in the same manner as bottom-hole contributions.

It is common practice to deduct currently both dry-hole and bottom-hole contributions if the related well was a dry hole. The deduction is claimed in the tax year in which the obligation to pay is determined, or is paid, depending on the method of accounting the taxpayer used. *(See Case 31 for requirements concerning economic performance.)* This treatment is based on the presumption that the payment is of no benefit to the payor and adds nothing to the value of his lease.[259] Bottom-hole contributions paid with respect to producing wells always have been capitalized as additional leasehold cost.

This ruling also holds that the recipient of the bottom-hole contribution must include the contribution in income and is not permitted to use the contribution to reduce or offset the cost of drilling the well. This is contrary to longstanding industry practice, which was to reduce ratably all costs the recipient incurred in drilling the well.[260] The effect of this change will impact numerous computations, including the net income limitations with respect to percentage depletion and windfall profit tax, the amount of IDC subject to recapture, the amount of IDC to be treated as a tax preference item and the amount of depreciable basis.

If, in lieu of cash, property such as an interest in a lease outside the drill site unit of property is contributed to Operator A, he should record that property at its fair market value. The fair market value of that property is treated the same as a cash payment. Operator B should treat the transaction as a taxable exchange of an interest in his lease for geological information.

In this case, Operator B has no ownership interest in the well to be drilled by Operator A; nor does Operator B acquire any interest in the well or in any other acreage. The payment is made to induce the drilling of a test well and in consideration for information that will be obtained by the drilling and not for any property rights in the well to be drilled.

Several types of transactions may be referred to as contributions but are not treated as such for tax purposes. For example, assume Operator B assigns Operator A two-thirds of the working interest in certain acreage in consideration for Operator A's agreement to drill a test well on the property. In addition, Operator B agrees to contribute $75,000 toward the drilling of the well. Because under these conditions Operator B is the owner of a one-third interest in the property, he should treat the $75,000 as a payment of a portion of the costs of developing the property and not as a bottom-hole or dry-hole contribution.

To illustrate further, assume that Operator A agrees that Operator B may recoup his $75,000 out of oil if the well is productive or assume Operator A agrees to assign to Operator B, on completion of the well, one-eighth of the working interest in the well

258. Rev. Rul. 80-153, 1980-1 C.B. 10.
259. IRS Letter Ruling dated May 4, 1945, 1945 P.H. Sec. 76,209, *cited in* P.H. 1976 Federal Taxes at Sec. 22, 178(10).
260. Coats v. U.S., 258 F. Supp. 1 (E.D. Tex. 1966), 18 AFTR2d 5465, 66-2 USTC 9567.

site or to assign to Operator B some fractional working interest in other adjoining acreage. In all these illustrations, Operator B's $75,000 payment represents consideration paid for the acquisition of a property interest or for B's participation in the well. It should not be treated as a bottom-hole or dry-hole contribution.

If the well is dry and also condemns Operator B's adjoining lease, he should claim a deduction for a loss on worthless property for the tax year in which the dry hole is completed. *(See Case 160.)*

Case 54
Basis if Intangible Drilling and Development Costs Are Capitalized

> **Operator A first incurs intangible drilling and development costs (IDC) in 1987 and is contemplating capitalizing those costs for tax purposes. Operator A inquires as to the segregation required of his capitalized costs to calculate depreciation and depletion.**

Operator A should follow the same rules for segregation of equipment and IDC *(see Case 20)* as one who has elected to expense those costs, except for the installation costs (wages, fuel, repairs, hauling, supplies, etc.) of casing, equipment, derricks and other physical structures incident to the production of oil or gas. If an election is made to expense IDC, installation costs of the tangible equipment up to the wellhead are treated as intangible costs.[261] However, Operator A elects to capitalize IDC, and he should treat well equipment installation costs as part of the cost of tangible property recoverable through depreciation.[262] In every instance, installation costs of lease equipment installed beyond the wellhead must be added to the cost of that equipment.[263]

Capitalized IDC (except installation costs of physical equipment) are recoverable only through depletion and may not be amortized or depreciated.[264] If percentage depletion for a particular unit of property exceeds depletion based on cost, the percentage depletion amount becomes the allowable depletion for that unit. In such a case, no additional depletion deduction is allowed by reason of the capitalization of the IDC. IDC that are currently deducted and that are attributable to productive properties constitute a tax preference item. *(See Case 174.)* However, if the taxpayer capitalizes that IDC for income tax purposes, the preference tax will not apply.[265]

Case 55
Advance Payments Received To Finance Development of Properties

> **Operator A enters into a gas purchase agreement and an advance payment agreement with C, a public utility company. Company C agrees to purchase gas that will be produced from Operator A's property at fluctuating market prices. To finance the development of his property, Operator A enters into an advance payment contract, which calls for Company C to**

261. Reg. Sec. 1.612-4(a)(3).
262. Reg. Sec. 1.612-4(b)(2).
263. Reg. Sec. 1.612-4(c)(1); Reg. Sec. 1.611-5(b)(4); Philadelphia Steel & Iron Corp., T.C. Memo Dec. (Apr. 13, 1964), *aff'd* 344 F.2d 964 (3d Cir. 1965), 15 AFTR2d 609, 65-1 USTC 9308.
264. U.S. v. Dakota-Montana Oil Co., 288 U.S. 459 (1933), 12 AFTR 18, 3 USTC 1067.
265. I.R.C. Sec. 57(a)(2).

advance him $3 million. Operator A is to repay the advance, free of interest, within five years after deliveries of gas to Company C commence.

Before the Tax Reform Act of 1984, the Internal Revenue Service (IRS), in factual situations similar to those of this case, sought to impute taxable income to the operator measured by the amount of interest the operator would have had to pay if he had borrowed the amount of the advance from commercial lending institutions. However, the Tax Court and a number of Circuit Courts of Appeal consistently held that interest-free loan arrangements in general[266] and an interest-free advance similar to the one in this case[267] do not result in taxable income to the borrower. Despite the overwhelming magnitude of judicial opinion to the contrary, the IRS did not change its position on this issue.

Under similar factual situations, the IRS has issued technical advice memoranda dealing with whether advance payments should be treated as payments for "contract rights" under a gas contract,[268] as advance payments for gas[269] or as proceeds on the sale of a royalty interest rather than as loan transactions.[270] Two of these rulings concluded that the transactions should be treated as loans. None of the rulings dealt with the tax implications of the interest-free character of these advances.

Current law[271] effectively adopts the IRS's position for interest-free or below-market loans. The proposed regulations provide that the term *loan* will be interpreted broadly for purposes of these provisions.[272]

The Tax Reform Act of 1984 substantially changed the income tax consequences of below-market or interest-free loans for transactions that are in the nature of dividends or compensation or are for tax avoidance.[273] Loans between a corporation and its shareholders and between employers and their employees (which also can include a corporation and its shareholder who also is an employee) will be treated as below-market loans unless the aggregate amount of loans between the corporation/shareholder or employer/employee does not exceed $10,000.[274] Additionally, the below-market loans where a principal purpose for the below-market interest arrangement is tax avoidance will be subject to below-market loan treatment.[275] The Treasury has regulatory authority to subject other below-market loans to these provisions if the interest arrangements have a significant effect on the tax liability of the lender or borrower.[276] The proposed regulations do not, however, include provisions to accomplish this.

The proposed regulations[277] provide that certain loans are exempt from the below-market interest loan provisions. The more prominent exemptions from these provisions are as follows:

□ Loans made available by the lender to the general public on the same terms and conditions that are consistent with the lender's customary business practices;

266. J. Simpson Dean, 35 T.C. 1083 (1960); Herman M. Greenspun, 72 T.C. 931 (1979), *aff'd* 670 F.2d 123 (9th Cir. 1982), 49 AFTR2d 82-937, 82-1 USTC 9218; Martin v. Comm'r, 649 F.2d 1133 (5th Cir. 1981), 48 AFTR2d 5537, 81-2 USTC 9534; Beaton v. Comm'r, 664 F.2d 315 (1st Cir. 1981), 49 AFTR2d 82-368, 81-2 USTC 9789; Suttle v. Comm'r, 625 F.2d 1127 (4th Cir. 1980), 46 AFTR2d 80-5413, 80-2 USTC 9534; Baker v. Comm'r, 677 F.2d 11 (2d Cir. 1982), 49 AFTR2d 82-1082, 82-1 USTC 9318; Parks v. Comm'r, 686 F.2d 408 (6th Cir. 1982), 50 AFTR2d 82-5508, 82-2 USTC 9584; Hardee v. U.S., 708 F.2d 661 (Fed. Cir. 1983), 52 AFTR2d 83-5022, 83-1 USTC 9353, *rev'g* Hardee v. U.S. (Ct. Cl. 1982), 50 AFTR2d 82-5252, 82-2 USTC 9459.

267. IRS Letter Ruling 8130013 (Technical Advice Memorandum); IRS Letter Ruling 8130017 (Technical Advice Memorandum); Charles E. Marsh, II, 73 T.C. 317 (1979).

268. IRS Letter Ruling 8202014 (Technical Advice Memorandum).

269. IRS Letter Ruling 8246016 (Technical Advice Memorandum).

270. IRS Letter Ruling 8248011 (Technical Advice Memorandum).

271. I.R.C. Sec. 7872.

272. Prop. Reg. Sec. 1.7872-2(a)(1).

273. I.R.C. Sec. 7872(c)(1); Prop. Reg. Sec. 1.7872-4(c); Prop. Reg. Sec. 1.7872-4(d).

274. I.R.C. Sec. 7872(c)(3); Prop. Reg. Sec. 1.7872-9.

275. I.R.C. Sec. 7872(c)(1)(D); Prop. Reg. Sec. 1.7872-4(e).

276. I.R.C. Sec. 7872(c)(1)(E); Prop. Reg. Sec. 1.7872-4(f) (Reserved).

277. Prop. Reg. Sec. 1.7872-5(b).

□ Acquisitions of publicly traded debt obligations for an amount equal to this public trading price at the time of acquisition;

□ Certain employee relocation loans and

□ Certain loans to foreign persons.

The Committee Reports provide that a below-market loan has an effect on the tax liability of the borrower or lender if, among other things, it results in the conversion of a nondeductible expense into the equivalent of a deductible expense.[278] For example, if a member of a club makes a noninterest-bearing refundable deposit to the club in lieu of part or all of the membership fee, the member is paying the fee with the interest earned by the club on the deposit, which is not being included in the member's income. Other situations apparently are contemplated but must await regulations.

The statute authorizes the Treasury to prescribe regulations to exempt lending transactions from the below-market interest provisions where the arrangement has no significant effect on any federal tax liability of the lender or borrower.[279] The proposed regulations[280] provide that the following factors will be applied in making this determination:

□ Whether items of income and deduction generated by the loan offset each other;

□ The amount of those items;

□ The cost to the taxpayer of complying with the provision *and*

□ Any nontax reasons for deciding to structure the transaction as a below-market loan rather than as a loan with interest at a rate equal to or greater than the applicable federal rate and a payment by the lender to the borrower.

A demand loan will be treated as a below-market loan if interest is payable at a rate less than the Applicable Federal Rate (AFR).[281] A term loan will be so treated if the amount loaned exceeds the present value of all payments due under the loan (including interest payments), using a discount rate equal to the AFR.[282] For term loans made after June 30, 1985, and demand loans outstanding after that date, a monthly determination of the AFR must be used in making these interest calculations.[283] For term loans, the AFR is the AFR in effect on the day the loan was made, compounded semiannually.[284] For demand loans, the AFR is the federal short-term rate in effect for which the foregone interest (discussed below) is being determined, compounded semiannually.[285] The IRS publishes blended annual rate calculations to derive inputed interest amounts for demand loans outstanding for the entire year.[286]

The treatment of the unstated or below-market interest element differs depending on whether the loan is a demand loan or a term loan.

For demand loans, the excess of the interest that would have been payable at a rate equal to the applicable federal rate over any interest payable on the loan is treated as first being transferred from the lender to the borrower and then retransferred by the borrower to the lender as interest.[287] This excess is referred to as *foregone interest.*[288] This transfer and retransfer are deemed to occur on the last day of the calendar year to which the foregone interest relates.[289] Thus, in a situation involving an interest-free

278. House Report No. 98-861, 1984-3 C.B. Vol. 2 273-274.
279. I.R.C. Sec. 7872(h)(1)(C).
280. Prop. Reg. Sec. 1.7872-5(c)(3).
281. I.R.C. Sec. 7872(e)(1)(A); Prop. Reg. Sec. 1.7872-3(a)(1).
282. I.R.C. Sec. 7872(e)(1)(B); Prop. Reg. Sec. 1.7872-3(a)(2); I.R.C. Sec. 7872(f)(1); Prop. Reg. Sec. 1.7872-7(a)(5).
283. I.R.C. Sec. 7872(f)(2).
284. I.R.C. Sec. 7872(f)(2)(A).
285. I.R.C. Sec. 7872(f)(2)(B).
286. Rev. Rul. 86-17, 1986-1 C.B. 377 (1985 blended rate); Rev. Rul. 86-94, 1986-31 I.R.B. 20 (1986 blended rate).
287. I.R.C. Sec. 7872(a)(1); Prop. Reg. Sec. 1.7872-1(a).
288. I.R.C. Sec. 7872(e)(2); Prop. Reg. Sec. 1.7872-6(c).
289. I.R.C. Sec. 7872(a)(2); Prop. Reg. Sec. 1.7872-6(b).

loan by an employer to an employee, the foregone interest for each year will be treated as being transferred to the employee as compensation on the last day of the year. The retransfer by the employee to the employer will be deemed to occur on the last day of the year and will be treated as interest income by the employer and interest expense by the employee.

For term loans, however, the rules are very different. In the case of a term loan, the excess of the amount loaned over the present value of all payments (including interest) due on the loan will be treated as original-issue discount (OID).[290] The full amount of OID will be treated as transferred to the borrower by the lender on the date the loan is made.[291] Subsequently, the lender will recognize interest income, and the borrower will claim an interest deduction as the OID is amortized over the life of the loan on the basis of a constant interest rate. *(See Case 146 for a discussion and illustration of the OID rules.)* Thus, in the example of the employer/employee discussed above, if the loan had been a term loan, the total amount of OID would be treated as being transferred to the employee as compensation on the date the loan was made. Thus, over the term of the loan, the employee would be entitled to an interest deduction and the employer would recognize interest income as the OID is amortized.

The proposed regulations provide for the reporting of interest income and expense and other recharacterized items (such as compensation or dividends) by the lender and borrower, respectively, in connection with below-market loans.[292] All applicable information and reporting requirements (Forms W-2 and 1099) must be satisfied.[293]

Because the facts of this case deal with an interest-free loan, it appears the provisions discussed above will apply unless the effect on Operator A's and Company C's tax liabilities is not significant. In addition, the loan in this case probably is a term loan because the loan is not payable at any time upon demand by the lender. It is not clear, however, how the computation of the amount of OID should be made because the beginning of the term is unknown at the date the loan is made. Additionally, the terms of the loan are such that Operator A could pay the entire amount of the loan in the first year, an equal amount each year, an unequal amount each year or the entire amount in the fifth year. Due to these unknown factors, Operator A cannot possibly compute the present value on the date the loan is made. One possible solution may be to treat these loans as demand loans and follow the rules discussed above. Another possible solution might be to use the contingent payment rules for OID instruments with contingencies as to time of payment. Resolution must await further regulations since the proposed regulations fail to address this issue.[294]

Once a method to compute the present value of such a loan is determined, the amount of OID deemed transferred by Company C to Operator A on the date the loan is made presumably will be treated as an advance payment for gas due to the nature of the transaction between them.

290. I.R.C. Sec. 7872(b)(2); Prop. Reg. Sec. 1.7872-7.
291. I.R.C. Sec. 7872(b)(1); Prop. Reg. Sec. 1.7872-7(a)(1).
292. Prop. Reg. Sec. 1.7872-11(g).
293. Prop. Reg. Sec. 1.7872-11(g)(4).
294. Prop. Reg. Sec. 1.7872-10(a)(4) (Reserved).

Section III
The Unit of Property

Before any computation of depletion can be made, mineral interests must be separated into proper units of property. This separation is necessary because allowable depletion is the greater of cost or percentage depletion computed separately for each such property.

The Internal Revenue Code defines the term *property* as "each separate interest owned by the taxpayer in each mineral deposit in each separate tract or parcel of land," or a permissible aggregation or combination of those interests. The term *interest* means an economic interest in a mineral deposit and includes a working interest, royalty, overriding royalty, net profits interest and certain production payments.

The term *tract or parcel of land* is used to describe the physical scope of the land and means an area delineated by metes and bounds, lot and block description, or otherwise. A separate tract or parcel of land does not include or encompass areas that are not contiguous. Tracts or parcels of land may be separated by conveyance, as well as by geography; thus, even though two areas are contiguous, they may be separate tracts or parcels of land if they were leased to an operator either by different persons or in different transactions. If contiguous areas are separate properties because they initially were leased from different persons or in different transactions, those properties remain separate even if later they are assigned simultaneously to another taxpayer.

If two or more operating mineral interests are held within a single tract or parcel of land, the entire group of interests will be combined for depletion purposes unless the taxpayer affirmatively elects to treat one or more of them separately.

A deduction for depletion is allowed only to the owner of an economic interest in a mineral deposit. An economic interest is held when the taxpayer has acquired by investment an interest in mineral in place and is entitled, through any form of legal relationship, to income derived from the extraction of the mineral to which he must look for a return of his capital. The taxpayer's investment in the mineral deposit may be made in the form of money, property or services. However, if the taxpayer obtains a mere economic advantage to be derived from the production of the mineral, such as a right to purchase or process the mineral after it is produced, this mere advantage will not constitute an economic interest in the mineral deposit and will not entitle the holder to a deduction for depletion.

The concept of property discussed above also is used when making certain computations in connection with the recapture of intangible drilling and development costs (IDC), the determination of IDC as an item of tax preference and the windfall profit tax (WPT). However, in other instances a different unit of property concept is used for WPT purposes. See Section IX for a discussion of these principles for WPT.

Case 56
Leases Geographically Separated

Operator A acquires from the same individual two producing oil leases in two geographically separated areas. The transfer is made by one assignment for a lump-sum consideration. Each lease contains only one known mineral deposit.

Even though Operator A's acquisition was from one owner in a single transaction, he has two separate properties because the leases are geographically separated.[1] To determine the tax basis of each property acquired, Operator A should allocate the total amount paid between the two leases and between depreciable equipment and depletable reserves on the basis of the relative fair market values of the assets at date of purchase.

Any depletion allowable to Operator A must be determined separately for each property; therefore, Operator A should maintain continuing records reflecting his tax basis and depletion previously allowed or allowable with respect to each property.

Case 57
Contiguous Leases Separately Acquired

Operator A simultaneously acquires from two separate owners leases on two contiguous tracts of land. Operator A later assigns the two leases to Operator B. The same mineral deposit underlies both tracts. No other mineral deposits are known to exist under the leases.

Operator A has acquired two separate leases, each of which constitutes a separate property even though the two tracts are contiguous and contain part of the same mineral deposit. The fact that they are acquired from different persons causes them to be treated as separate properties.[2]

Operator B also is required to treat the two leases as separate properties.[3] If more than one mineral deposit is discovered on the leases, Operator B may elect to treat each separate mineral deposit as a separate unit of property. *(See Case 58.)*

The regulations distinguish the lease and sublease situation presented above from a purchase of the mineral fee with a subsequent granting of a lease. If Operator A had acquired the mineral fee in two contiguous tracts and then leased both tracts to Operator B by a single lease, Operator B normally would have only one property.[4] The regulations, however, restrict this method of combining contiguous tracts. If Operator B determines his basis by reference to Operator A's basis in the lease (for example, if Operator B received the property as a gift from Operator A), Operator B will have the same number of properties as Operator A.[5]

The term *contiguous tracts* means tracts that have a common boundary. Tracts that touch only at a common corner are not contiguous.[6]

---

1. I.R.C. Sec. 614(a); Reg. Sec. 1.614-1(a)(5), Example 4.
2. Reg. Sec. 1.614-1(a)(3); Reg. Sec. 1.614-1(a)(5), Example 8.
3. Reg. Sec. 1.614-1(a)(3); Reg. Sec. 1.614-1(a)(5), Example 9.
4. Reg. Sec. 1.614-1(a)(3); Reg. Sec. 1.614-1(a)(5), Example 6; Norman and Ernestine H. Freeman, 48 T.C. 96 (1967).
5. Reg. Sec. 1.614-1(a)(4); Reg. Sec. 1.614-1(a)(5), Example 7.
6. Berkshire Oil Co., 9 T.C. 903 (1947).

Case 58
Election To Treat Operating Mineral Interests Separately or in Combination

> **Operator A purchases the working interest in noncontiguous tracts X and Y; producing sands M, N and O lie under each. He plans to drill another well on Lease Y next year to determine if sand P exists. Operator A inquires whether he can combine sands M and N in Lease X and combine O and P in Lease Y, treating all others separately. He also inquires about treating Leases X and Y as one property, to simplify administration.**

All operating mineral interests in a single tract will be combined unless Operator A elects to treat one or more of them separately.[7] Operating mineral interests that are discovered in later years may be added to an existing combination or treated separately,[8] but there can be only one combination in each tract or parcel.[9] For example, with respect to Lease X, Operator A may combine sands M and N and elect separate treatment for sand O. Similar combination elections are available for Lease Y. If Operator A discovers sand P on Lease Y in the following year, he can elect to combine sands O and P for Lease Y. If a well is drilled to sand P on Lease X, the well can be added to the M-N combination of Lease X or treated separately, but it cannot be combined with sand O because of the one combination limit. Leases X and Y cannot be treated as one property.[10]

The election to treat each property as a separate property or to make proper combinations must be made for the first year the taxpayer makes an expenditure for development or operation of the property interest.[11] For this purpose, a development expenditure includes intangible drilling and development costs but does not include delay rentals or amounts paid for lease options.[12] If the property subject to the election is held by a partnership, the election is made at the partnership level and each individual partner is bound by the treatment so elected by the partnership.[13] The election is made by attaching a specific statement to the income tax return for the year in which it is made. The statement must describe the tract, the facts that justify its treatment as a single and entire tract, all the operating interests owned in the tract, and which operating interests are being combined and which ones are being kept separate. However, if the taxpayer wishes to treat all operating interests in a given tract as separate properties, a blanket election may be made for all such interests held at that time in that tract and only the tract itself need be identified.[14]

An election to treat operating mineral interests separately or in combination is binding for the year made and all subsequent years and is effective for all tax computations relating to mineral property interests; however, such an election will not prevent the proper election to combine a newly discovered or later acquired property with a previously held property or combination of properties as long as only one combination is elected within a single tract or parcel of land.

---

7. I.R.C. Sec. 614(b); Reg. Sec. 1.614-8(a)(1).
8. Reg. Sec. 1.614-8(a)(2).
9. Reg. Sec. 1.614-8(a)(1).
10. I.R.C. Sec. 614(b)(1)(B).
11. I.R.C. Sec. 614(b)(4).
12. Reg. Sec. 1.614-8(a)(3)(i).
13. Rev. Rul. 84-142, 1984-2 C.B. 117.
14. Reg. Sec. 1.614-8(a)(3)(ii).

Case 59
Leases Acquired by Competitive Bidding

Operator A acquires two contiguous offshore leases from the United States Department of the Interior as a result of two successful competitive bids. The leases are granted on the same day through two separate documents.

Generally, if two contiguous leases are acquired at the same time from one lessor, the two leases will constitute one property, whether the conveyances are made by a single document or separate ones.[15] However, the Internal Revenue Service has held that the term *at the same time* is not synonymous with *on the same date*. Rather, it contemplates simultaneous acts that are mutually or reciprocally dependent upon each other. Even though executed on the same date, the government leases are not considered to be acquired simultaneously because they are granted as a result of separate and independent competitive bids. Therefore, Operator A must treat the leases as two separate properties, even though the leases are contiguous and were acquired on the same day from the same assignor.[16]

Case 60
Aggregation of Nonoperating Mineral Interests

Operator A assigns Lease X to Operator B, retaining a one-eighth overriding royalty interest. Subsequently, Operator A acquires an additional one-sixteenth overriding royalty in Lease X. The property is not productive on the date of either assignment.

Operator A has two separate nonoperating properties. He may aggregate these interests and treat them as one property only if he obtains the prior consent of the Internal Revenue Service (IRS).[17] Consent will be granted if Operator A establishes that the principal purpose for the aggregation is not tax avoidance.[18] Reasons for aggregation may exist if: (1) it is impossible for Operator A to determine the boundaries, source or cost of his acquisition of separate interests; (2) the financial returns from more than one property are economically interrelated; (3) an aggregation will simplify accounting procedures or (4) if Operator A, as an owner of a single royalty, net profits interest or other nonoperating interest, cannot determine the separate deposits from which his payments will be derived. If tax saving is the principal purpose, the IRS will not grant consent.

Nonoperating interests may be aggregated only if located in the same tract or in adjacent tracts or parcels of land. For this purpose, adjacent tracts must be reasonably close to each other but need not be contiguous.[19] The IRS has ruled in connection with the creation of a royalty trust that multiproperty net profits interests should be treated as a single unit of property for depletion purposes if the amounts attributable to the holders' interest in each lease were interdependent on the costs and revenues on other leases included in the net profits interests. Accordingly, permission to aggregate the interests was not required.[20] *(See Case 173.)*

---

15. Reg. Sec. 1.614-1(a)(3).
16. Rev. Rul. 68-566, 1968-2 C.B. 281.
17. I.R.C. Sec. 614(e)(1).
18. IRS Letter Ruling 8603080; IRS Letter Ruling 8611002 (Technical Advice Memorandum); IRS Letter Ruling 8614013.
19. Reg. Sec.1.614-5(d).
20. IRS Letter Ruling 8312019.

Application for inclusion of a newly acquired nonoperating mineral interest in a pre-existing aggregation must be filed within 90 days of the date of acquisition.[21] However, when such an application is filed after the 90-day period, the IRS will regard it as an application to change an existing aggregation. If the inclusion is granted, it will be effective as of the first day of the tax year succeeding the year of acquisition if filed within 90 days of the beginning of that tax year.[22]

Case 61
Fraction of Same Working Interest Acquired at Separate Times

> **Operator A acquires one-half of the working interest in Lease X from Operator B. Mineral deposits M, N and O underlie Lease X. Operator A later acquires an additional one-fourth of the working interest in Lease X after the lease is partially developed.**

Operator A has a minimum of two separate mineral interests because he has acquired the separate fractions of the working interest at different times.[23] However, unless Operator A properly elects to treat the newly acquired interest as a separate property, both interests must be combined and treated as one property.[24] If Operator A's cost basis in the original one-half interest is fully depleted or is relatively low compared to his cost basis in the newly acquired interest, it normally will be beneficial to elect to treat the interests as separate properties because Operator A then may be able to take percentage depletion on his low-basis property and cost depletion on his high-basis property.

Because deposits M, N and O are separate mineral interests,[25] Operator A's treatment of each deposit in the original one-half interest in prior years must be examined to determine what alternatives are available regarding the newly acquired one-fourth interest. The various alternatives are:

- Operator A did not file an election to treat the original interests in mineral deposits M, N and O as separate properties; therefore, they have been combined under the general rule. *(See Case 58.)* If Operator A makes no election with respect to the newly acquired interest, it must be added to the original combination.[26] Alternatively, Operator A may elect either: (1) to treat each deposit as a separate property or (2) to combine any one or two of the newly acquired deposits with the original interest and to treat as a separate property each deposit not combined with the original interest.

- Operator A properly elected to treat each deposit as a separate property. Operator A's prior election prohibits a combination of all deposits in the old and new interests. Therefore, Operator A must make a new election with respect to the new interest. He may elect any of the following alternatives:

  - Each deposit in the new interest may be treated as a separate property.

  - All deposits in the new interest may be treated as one separate property.

---

21. Reg. Sec. 1.614-5(e)(1).
22. Rev. Rul. 67-205, 1967-1 C.B. 158.
23. I.R.C. Sec. 614(a).
24. I.R.C. Sec. 614(b)(1)(A).
25. Reg. Sec. 1.614-1(a)(5), Example 1.
26. I.R.C. Sec. 614(b)(1).

- ☐ All deposits in the new interest may be combined with any one of the deposits in the original interest.
- ☐ Any one or more of the new deposits may be combined with any one of the old deposits; each deposit not combined will be treated as a separate property.

☐ Operator A previously elected to treat his original interest in deposits M and N as one property and deposit O as a separate property. Because he has made a prior election, Operator A must make a new election for the new interest. Operator A may have only one combination in one tract or parcel of land,[27] and he has one combination by the earlier election. Therefore, he may combine all or any of the newly acquired deposits with his original interest in M and N and treat all deposits not included in this combination as separate properties. Operator A may not make any combination involving his original interest in deposit O, nor may he treat the newly acquired interest as a separate property because to do so would create two combinations.

If Operator A acquires a royalty or other nonoperating mineral interest rather than an additional working interest in the same lease, he cannot elect to combine the two interests because operating and nonoperating mineral interests may not be combined.[28]

Case 62
Royalties Reserved Under Leases on Adjoining Acreage

Lessor R inherits a ranch that has prospects for production of oil or gas. During 1987, he grants several leases to separate parties on contiguous tracts for separate lease bonuses and reserved royalties. Lessor R retains his full interest in other tracts not leased.

By granting separate leases, Lessor R has created separate properties out of the inherited mineral rights for purposes of computing depletion and gain or loss upon disposition.[29] Unless Lessor R obtains consent from the Internal Revenue Service (IRS), he will not be allowed to aggregate his contiguous royalty interests and treat them as one depletable property.[30] *(See Case 60.)* When several leases are granted at the same time to one lessee, all contiguous leases will be treated as one property. *(See Case 59 for a discussion of leases being granted at the same time.)*

Even though Lessor R may have made an allocation of basis between surface and mineral rights when he inherited the ranch, he probably will not be allowed a loss because of worthlessness of the minerals if the leases prove nonproductive and are abandoned without production. One court has held that even when such an acquisition is made by purchase and an allocation between surface and mineral rights is made, the worthlessness of the minerals is considered to cause only a shrinkage of value of the entire fee interest and there is no closed transaction as long as the surface has value.[31] However, another court has held that if the surface and minerals are valued separately in the estate tax return, a deduction is allowable when the minerals are proven worthless.[32]

27. Reg. Sec. 1.614-8(a)(1).
28. Reg. Sec. 1.614-2(b).
29. Reg. Sec. 1.614-1(a)(5), Example 3.
30. Reg. Sec. 1.614-5(d).
31. Louisiana Land and Exploration Co. v. Comm'r, 161 F.2d 842 (5th Cir. 1947), 35 AFTR 1388, 47-1 USTC 9266.
32. Pool, Exec. and Trustee v. U.S., 119 F. Supp. 202 (Ct. Cl. 1954), 45 AFTR 706, 54-1 USTC 9263.

The lease bonus and royalty income received by Lessor R is considered ordinary income subject to depletion. However, lease bonus income no longer qualifies for percentage depletion for bonuses received or accrued after August 16, 1986. Therefore, only cost depletion will be allowed on the bonus income received by Lessor R in 1987. *(See Case 2.)*

If the depletion allowed on the lease bonus and on the royalty income exceeds the allocated basis applicable to the retained mineral interests, the excess will not reduce Lessor R's basis in the surface rights.

Case 63
Property Units When Fee Title Is Obtained in Separate Acquisitions

> **Operator A secures from Lessee E the entire working interest in a lease for $2,000. Lessee E previously had leased the interest from Lessor R, who retained a one-eighth royalty. At a later date, Operator A acquires Lessor R's one-eighth royalty for $2,500. Operator A incurs no expenditures for drilling or exploration with respect to the lease until after acquisition of the full mineral interest.**

The Internal Revenue Service probably will hold that the separately acquired mineral interests merge and become a single unit of property for computing the depletion allowance because Operator A then owns the entire mineral interest in the tract before the drilling operations commence.[33]

The theory of merging probably will apply if Operator A subsequently disposes of only the leasehold interest that he originally acquired. In this situation, it will be held that Operator A has made a lease rather than a sale.

The rationale for this tax treatment is that an individual cannot be both a lessor and a lessee with respect to the same tract of real property, and, consequently, the lessee interest disappears or merges with the lessor interest when fee title to the minerals is owned.

It is uncertain whether a merging of the property interests will occur if Operator A obtains production from the lease prior to his acquisition of the royalty interest from Lessor R. *(See Case 66.)*

If Operator A acquires less than the full royalty interest, he should treat the two interests as separate properties.[34]

Case 64
Two or More Minerals Produced from One Lease

> **Operator A acquires a lease upon which he drills several wells that produce oil, gas and distillate.**

Each mineral deposit of oil, gas and distillate constitutes a separate property to Operator A.[35] The Internal Revenue Code (the Code) specifically defines a *property*

33. Henry Boos, 30 B.T.A. 882 (1934); Herzberg v. Alexander, 5 F. Supp. 334 (W.D. Okla. 1933), 13 AFTR 112, 3 USTC 1156.
34. Herndon Drilling Co., 6 T.C. 628 (1946); Badger Oil v. Comm'r, 118 F.2d 791 (5th Cir. 1941), 26 AFTR 910, 41-1 USTC 9386.
35. Reg. Sec. 1.614-1(a)(1).

as "each separate interest owned by the taxpayer in each mineral deposit in each separate tract or parcel of land."[36]

Under the laws of certain states, oil, gas and other hydrocarbons are severable from one another for purposes of assignment. Even though they contain substantially the same basic chemical elements, they generally are recognized as separate properties, whether they are produced from the same or different producing horizons. However, the Internal Revenue Service may hold that oil, gas and distillate produced from the same formation are produced from one property.[37]

Even though, by definition, each mineral deposit constitutes a separate property, the Code provides that when two or more operating mineral interests are held within a single tract or parcel of land, those interests will be combined and treated as one property unless the taxpayer elects to treat one or more of those interests as separate properties.[38] Thus, Operator A's interests in the oil, gas and distillate under this lease will be combined and treated as a single property unless he elects otherwise. *(See Case 58.)* In this connection, Operator A may elect one of the following alternatives:

□ To treat each mineral deposit under the lease as a separate property.

□ To combine any two or more of the interests as one property.

□ To have all the mineral interests treated as one property.

Operator A should study the projections of income and expenses so that he can make the election that will give him the maximum benefit considering the impact on his percentage depletion allowance and windfall profit tax calculations. *(See Cases 105 and 212 for discussion of the impact of separate property elections on depletion and windfall profit tax, respectively.)*

Case 65
Sublease of a Fraction of the Working Interest

> **Lessee E acquires the full working interest in a lease through an assignment. Lessee E then assigns three-fourths of his working interest to another party for development purposes. Lessee E retains an overriding royalty that is equivalent to one-eighth of the three-fourths working interest assigned. He also retains a one-fourth share of the working interest.**

Lessee E apparently has retained two separate properties. An overriding royalty and a working interest are dissimilar properties that cannot be combined.[39] Even though Lessee E acquired the original lease by one assignment and the economic effect of the subsequent assignment is simply to retain a share in the gross income larger than the agreed-upon share of expenses, E should treat the royalty interest and the working interest as separate properties.[40]

---

36. I.R.C. Sec. 614(a).
37. Hudson Engineering Corp. v. Comm'r, 183 F.2d 180 (5th Cir. 1950), 39 AFTR 646, 50-2 USTC 9371.
38. I.R.C. Sec. 614(b); Reg. Sec. 1.614-8.
39. Reg. Sec. 1.614-1(a)(5), Example 3.
40. Sence v. U.S., 394 F.2d 842 (Ct. Cl. 1968), 21 AFTR2d 1309, 68-1 USTC 9368; IRS Letter Ruling 8311005 (Technical Advice Memorandum). *See also* Rev. Rul. 77-176, 1977-1 C.B. 77.

Case 66
Outstanding Production Payment Purchased by Owner of Working Interest

Operator A, the owner of an oil and gas lease, assigns to Driller D a $50,000 production payment out of a lease in consideration for D's drilling a well on the lease. The well is productive. After Driller D has received $10,000 from his production payment, Operator A purchases D's right to the remaining $40,000 of oil for the sum of $30,000. Operator A had no obligation to purchase Driller D's interest.

Operator A has two separate properties—the working interest and the production payment. Therefore, depletion should be computed separately for each. The assignment of the production payment to Driller D created a separate property subject to the allowance for depletion because this production payment was pledged for development.[41] The Internal Revenue Service (IRS) has ruled that when an economic interest is created by the assignment of a production payment out of the leasehold estate, the reacquisition of the production payment by the assignor in a subsequent transaction does not merge the two interests into a single property.[42] Although this ruling has been declared obsolete,[43] the IRS has not stated the reason for its action nor expressed its current view with respect to this question. Operator A may not elect to combine the two interests because they are unlike properties.

Operator A will be entitled only to cost depletion with regard to the production payment because the property was proven when he acquired the production payment. He may deduct the higher of cost or percentage depletion with respect to the working interest provided he otherwise qualifies for percentage depletion thereon.[44]

It should be noted that the production payment in the above discussion is treated as a depletable interest in the minerals because it was pledged for exploration or development of the property.[45] An entirely different result will occur if the production payment is treated as a mortgage loan on the property. *(See Case 135.)*

Case 67
Unitization of a Portion of a Productive Lease

Operator A owns a 160-acre lease. Two producing wells are located on the west 80 acres. No wells ever have been drilled on the east 80 acres of the lease. Operator A enters into a unitization agreement with C Company and Operator B by which the east 80 acres of Operator A's lease are combined with portions of contiguous leases owned by C Company and Operator B. The operating mineral interests covered by the agreement are in the same deposit, and the production and expenses of the block are apportioned among the three parties on the basis of acreage contributed by each to the unitized block.

Operator A will be considered to have converted the working interest in the east half of his lease into an undivided interest in the unitized block, regardless of whether

41. Reg. Sec. 1.614-1(a); Reg. Sec. 1.636-1(b).
42. G.C.M. 24094, 1944 C.B. 250.
43. Rev. Rul. 70-277, 1970-1 C.B. 280.
44. I.R.C. Sec. 613(a); I.R.C. Sec. 613A(c).
45. I.R.C. Sec. 636(a); Reg. Sec. 1.636-1(b); Reg. Sec. 1.614-1(a).

unitization is accomplished by cross-assignments or by a contract among the parties. In effect, Operator A has divided his lease into two properties upon unitization of the east half, and the two properties will be treated as separate units for computing depletion.[46] The transaction with C Company and Operator B is not viewed as an acquisition of undivided interests in their properties but as the acquisition of a single, undivided interest in a unitized property. *(See Case 68.)*

An exchange of the working interest in 80 acres for an undivided interest in a larger tract, being an exchange of like properties, will not result in any recognized gain or loss.[47] Even if under state law, Operator A is required to make the exchange, the transaction is tax free and not treated as an involuntary conversion.[48]

If one or more producing wells are located on the acreage contributed by C Company and Operator B, Operator A still will not realize a taxable gain or loss on the exchange of interests. In this type of situation the Internal Revenue Service generally treats the equipment on the wells, although not permanently affixed and, therefore, removable to some extent, as an improvement to the real estate. Operator A should allocate a portion of his basis to any interest he acquires in any tangible equipment on the unitized property at the time of the unitization. It should be noted that if producing wells are located on a portion of the acreage contributed by some of the participants in the unitization, possible recapture of depreciation, depletion, intangible drilling and development costs, and investment tax credit may be required. *(See Cases 146 and 148 for discussions of possible recapture requirements resulting from various exchanges and unitizations.)*

Unitization agreements are used frequently in the development of natural gas fields and in the secondary recovery of oil. Such a pooling of acreage makes possible efficient planning of well spacing to yield maximum production with minimum cost. If the project involves the cycling of gas, unitization also permits the spacing of input wells to provide maximum recovery of liquid hydrocarbons from the gas reserves.

If Operator A incurs any costs in connection with the formation of a producing unit, he should deduct the costs as current expenses in his tax return.[49]

Transfers of property in accordance with unitization agreements are not treated as transfers of proven properties under proposed regulations; therefore, if deductions for percentage depletion are allowable under the independent-producer exemption before the unitization, they will continue to be allowable after the unitization.[50]

Case 68
Several Leases Treated as One Property After Unitization

Operator A owns a fraction of the working interest in two producing leases in the same area. One lease has been held for several years, and allowable depletion exceeds Operator A's basis in that lease. The other lease was acquired recently, and Operator A has a remaining basis of $20,000 in both depletable and depreciable property. To expedite and facilitate development and operations of the field that includes Operator A's leases, all owners of the minerals sign a unitization agreement in 1987

46. Reg. Sec. 1.614-8(b)(4).
47. E. C. Laster, 43 B.T.A. 159 (1940).
48. Eugene H. Koziara, 86 T.C. 999 (1986).
49. Campbell v. Fields, 229 F.2d 197 (5th Cir. 1956), 48 AFTR 859, 56-1 USTC 9233.
50. Prop. Reg. Sec. 1.613A-7(o).

under which the entire block of leases is to be developed and operated as a single unit.

A voluntary unitization or pooling arrangement results in one property if the operating mineral interests included in the agreement are in tracts that are contiguous or in close proximity. If the agreement covers more than one deposit, the several deposits must be ones that are logical for joint development or production from the standpoint of geology, convenience, economy or conservation (without taking tax benefits into account).[51] Compulsory unitizations are treated as one property without limitation.

If an operating interest has been combined previously with other operating interests in the same tract *(see Case 61)*, its participation in that combination is suspended for the period it is included in the unitization or pooling arrangement. When the unitization or pooling arrangement is terminated, the interest automatically reverts to its status as part of the prior combination.[52]

If a portion of an operating mineral interest is included in a unit and the remaining portion is surrendered, no writeoff of the cost attributable to the surrendered portion will be allowed.[53] Additionally, no depletion allowable on lease bonuses (whether computed on the cost or percentage basis) attributable to the portion surrendered should be restored.[54] *(See Case 127 for further discussion of restoration of depletion on lease bonuses.)* If, however, the portion is sold, the cost attributable to the surrendered portion should be considered for purposes of computing gain or loss on the sale. *(See Case 148 for further discusssion of unitization agreements.)*

51. I.R.C. Sec. 614(b)(3).
52. Reg. Sec. 1.614-8(b)(5).
53. Reg. Sec. 1.614-8(b)(4).
54. Rev. Rul. 68-78, 1968-1 C.B. 294.

Section IV
The Production Period

Tax consequences during the production period relate mainly to the proper accounting for depreciation and depletion. Because the amount of income, expenses and depreciation affects the computation of allowable depletion, it also is important for the taxpayer to record these items properly to maximize his depletion allowance.

Depreciation

Because the tax rules for depreciable properties are very complex, the discussion in this section is limited to the more general problems applicable to depreciation of oil and gas properties.

The Tax Reform Act of 1986 (the Act) substantially modifies the accelerated cost recovery system (ACRS) that was enacted in 1981. Instead of providing statutory depreciation allowances, the modified ACRS specifies methods, lives and averaging conventions to be used for property placed in service after 1986. The modified ACRS produces lower deductions in the earlier years of an asset's useful life than the original ACRS, but it still permits more generous depreciation allowances than could be obtained under the pre-1981 rules. Property placed in service before 1987 will continue to be depreciated as it was in the past, except that a taxpayer may elect to use modified ACRS for property placed in service between July 31, 1986, and January 1, 1987. *(See Case 69.)*

Under the modified ACRS, personal property is assigned to one of six classes, while real property is assigned to one of two classes. The double-declining balance method is used for 10-year and below classes with a switch to the straight-line method when needed to optimize the deductions. Assets in the 15- or 20-year classes are depreciated using the 150% declining-balance method with a switch to the straight-line method at the optimum time. The straight-line method must be used for all real estate and may be elected for use with personal property. The component method is prohibited for all recovery property. Generally, a half-year averaging convention applies to first-year and last-year allowances for personal property, and a mid-month convention applies to real property. A special rule requires the use of a mid-quarter convention for all additions within the year when more than 40% of the additions is placed in service in the last quarter. *(See Case 70.)*

The Act also provides an alternative depreciation system that is mandatory in some instances and that may be elected in others. The alternative depreciation system is generally effective for property placed in service after 1986. The alternative depreciation system is mandatory for property used outside the United States, tax-exempt use property, property financed with tax-exempt bonds, designated imported property, and for calculating corporate earnings and profits. Under the alternative depreciation system, depreciation is calculated for personal property using the straight-line method and the mid-point Asset Depreciation Range (ADR) life. If there is no mid-point life, a 12-year life is used. For real property (except for low-income housing), the alternative system requires use of a 40-year life and the straight-line method. *(See Case 70.)*

The modified ACRS and the alternative depreciation system do not apply to property that the taxpayer elects to depreciate using the unit-of-production method or any other method not expressible in years. Use of the unit-of-production method requires that salvage value be considered; both the modified ACRS and the alternative cost recovery system, on the other hand, ignore salvage value. *(See Case 70.)*

Property placed in service after 1986 will be depreciated under three basic altenatives: (1) modified ACRS, (2) alternative depreciation system or (3) a method not expressible in years such as the unit-of-production method. Depreciation otherwise to be calculated under modified ACRS by use of the declining-balance method may be calculated using the straight-line method if the taxpayer elects to do so in a particular year on a class-by-class basis. Regardless of the depreciation alternative used, taxpayers (other than an estate or trust) may elect annually to expense a portion of the cost of certain property placed in service each year. The maximum amount that may be expensed is $5,000 for tax years beginning in 1982 through 1986 and $10,000 for tax years beginning after 1986. After 1986, each dollar of investment in qualifying property in excess of $200,000 reduces the $10,000 ceiling by one dollar. The amount expensed is further limited to taxable income from any trade or business of the taxpayer. *(See Case 73.)*

The alternative used in calculating the depreciation allowance will affect the property-by-property 50% of net income limitation and overall 65% of taxable income limitation for percentage depletion calculations. It also will affect the 90% of net income windfall profit tax limitation.

For both corporate and individual alternative minimum tax (AMT) purposes, regular tax depreciation computations as described above must be adjusted. Generally, AMT depreciation is calculated using the applicable ADR midpoint life (40 years in the case of most real property) which is the same life used for the alternative depreciation system in the chart below. For AMT depreciation, the 150% declining-balance method is used for property other than: (1) Section 1250 property and (2) property for which the taxpayer elects or is required to use a straight-line method (over an extended life) for regular tax purposes. No adjustment is made for property depreciated under the unit-of-production or income-forecast methods.

Depreciation with respect to property placed in service before 1987 (unless the taxpayer elected the new modified ACRS for regular tax purposes) is treated as a tax preference item only to the extent that it constituted a tax preference item under prior law. Previously, only certain leased personal property and certain real property depreciated by an accelerated method gave rise to a depreciation preference. *(See Case 69.)*

The chart below shows the prescribed depreciable lives under the modified ACRS and alternative depreciation system, and the methods of depreciation for assets common to the oil and gas industry:

Type of Asset	Depreciable Lives: Modified ACRS (See Footnotes for Method)	Depreciable Lives: Alternative Depreciation System (Straight-Line Method)
Automobiles and trucks (both light and heavy general purpose)	5*	5
Drilling equipment, including assets used in exploration and field services but not including assets used in the performance of these activities by integrated petroleum and natural gas producers for their own account	5*	6
Offshore drilling equipment and other assets used in offshore drilling for oil and gas	5*	7.5
Drilling equipment used in exploration and field services by integrated petroleum and natural gas producers for their own account	7*	14
Lease and well equipment, including gathering pipeline and related storage equipment	7*	14
Natural gas production plant	7*	14
Liquified natural gas plant	15**	22
Office furniture and fixtures	7*	10
Crude oil refining equipment	10*	16
Transmission pipeline and related equipment	15**	22
Building (does not include residential or low-income housing)	31.5***	40***

Methods:

* 200% declining-balance switching to the straight-line method when appropriate or straight line.

** 150% declining-balance switching to the straight-line method when appropriate or straight line.

*** Straight-line method used for all real estate (both modified and alternative depreciation system) and for all assets under alternative ACRS.

If depreciable personal property is disposed of at a gain, all or part of the depreciation and ACRS recovery allowance must be recaptured as ordinary income. Special recapture rules apply to dispositions of depreciable real property. For 1988, capital gains are taxed at the same rate as ordinary income; nevertheless, the distinction between capital gains and ordinary income is still important because of the limitation on the amount of capital loss that can be used to offset ordinary income.

Before 1981, the tax accounting rules for depreciable property were fairly broad and gave taxpayers considerable leeway in choice of depreciable method and in classification of items of property. Four methods were generally available: (1) straight-line method, (2) declining-balance method, (3) sum of the years-digits method and (4) unit-of-production and operating-day methods.

Investment Tax Credit

The Act repeals the investment tax credit (ITC) generally for assets placed in service after December 31, 1985. Transition rules are provided for assets subject to a binding contract on December 31, 1985. Assets that qualify for ITC as transition property are subject to full-basis reduction for depreciation purposes. Full-basis reduction applies to all assets placed in service after 1985. Pre-1986 law required a 50%-basis reduction. Before 1986, a reduced credit in lieu of a basis reduction could be elected. This election is no longer available. Special rules allow upward basis adjustments to reflect recapture on disposition of assets.

ITC carryovers from pre-1986 years are allowed as under prior law except that the carryovers are reduced by 35% (17½% in 1987 and 17½% in 1988) to correlate with the reduction in the tax rates.

Generally, for tax years beginning after 1983, the investment tax credit was combined with certain other nonrefundable credits. The combined credit, referred to as the "general business credit," was limited to $25,000 plus 85% of the taxpayer's tax liability (as reduced by certain other credits). For tax years beginning after 1985, the 85% limitation is reduced to 75%.

Depletion

The federal income tax concept of percentage depletion recognizes that substantial risks are involved in obtaining oil and gas production and that oil and gas properties are wasting assets that eventually will be exhausted through production. To be entitled to a deduction for percentage depletion, the owner of an oil and gas property must determine the specific unit of property. Moreover, he must establish that he has an economic interest in that property. These problems are treated at some length in Section I, *The Acquisition and Exploration Period,* and in Section III, *The Unit of Property.*

With certain exceptions, percentage depletion on oil and gas produced after December 31, 1974, is repealed. The exceptions include an allowance for percentage depletion for: (1) certain domestic gas wells from which natural gas is sold under a fixed contract in effect on February 1, 1975, and at all times thereafter and (2) oil and gas produced by certain independent producers and royalty owners. Percentage depletion is not allowable for oil and gas production outside the territorial limits of the United States. Independent producers and royalty owners are entitled to percentage depletion on a "depletable oil quantity" of a maximum of 1,000 barrels of oil per day or its equivalent in natural gas (determined by treating 6,000 cubic feet of gas as the equivalent of one barrel of oil). Taxpayers may elect to include natural gas as part of their depletable oil quantity. The percentage depletion deduction for oil and gas may not exceed 65% of the taxable income of the taxpayer computed without regard to the deduction for percentage depletion and certain other items. Any depletion disallowed as the result of the 65% of taxable income limit may be carried forward indefinitely and claimed in future years to the extent the total percentage depletion claimed in those years does not exceed 65% of the taxable income of those years.

The allowance for depletion represents the higher of the results obtained from two alternative computations—cost depletion or percentage depletion. Cost depletion involves writing off the capitalized cost of the mineral property (bonus, exploration cost, legal fees, etc.) over the life of the property on a pro-rata basis as the oil and gas are produced. *(See Case 79.)* Percentage depletion applicable to oil and gas production is calculated at a statutory percentage of gross income from the property, but cannot exceed 50% of the taxable income from the property before the deduction for depletion. *(See Case 87.)* Both cost depletion and percentage depletion must be calculated for each unit of property. The determination of which is greater is made on a property-by-property basis.

Percentage depletion in excess of basis calculated on a property-by-property basis is a tax preference item for alternative minimum tax purposes. *(See Cases 175 and 176.)*

Case 69
Accelerated Cost Recovery System Allowances (Depreciation)—Lease and Well Equipment Placed in Service Before 1987

> **During 1985, C Company completed 10 producing wells on 10 separate leases. The cost of the equipment installed was $1 million. In addition, C Company constructed a gasoline extraction and processing plant at a cost of $750,000. C Company requests information concerning allowable depreciation methods and the effect of the depreciation deduction on percentage depletion.**

The accelerated cost recovery system (ACRS) generally is required for depreciable property placed in service after 1980 and before January 1, 1987.[1] ACRS is a mandatory cost recovery system requiring taxpayers to compute the cost recovery allowance on the unadjusted basis of recovery property according to tables provided by law. Recovery property is new or used tangible property subject to the allowance for depreciation. The term *recovery property* does not include: (1) property placed in service before 1981; (2) property the taxpayer elects to depreciate under the unit-of-production method or any other depreciation method not expressed in terms of years; (3) certain public utility property; (4) motion picture films and videotape and (5) certain properties described in the antichurning rules.[2] The ACRS is substantially changed by the Tax Reform Act of 1986 (the Act), effective generally for property placed in service after December 31, 1986. *(See Case 70.)*

Before the Act, there were six classes of property under ACRS:

□ Three-year property, defined as Section 1245 property with a present class life of four years or less. This category consists primarily of automobiles, light duty trucks, and research and development property.[3]

□ Five-year property, defined as all Section 1245 property not specifically included in the 3-, 10- and 15-year classes. This category covers most oil and gas exploration equipment, refining and marketing equipment, including offshore drilling equipment and platforms, marine construction assets and facilities used to store petroleum and its primary products.[4]

□ Ten-year property, defined as public utility property with a present class life of more than 18 years but not more than 25 years, and Section 1250 property with a present class life of 12.5 years or less.[5]

□ Fifteen-year public utility property, defined as certain public utility property with a present class life greater than 25 years.[6]

---

1. I.R.C. Sec. 168 *(prior to amendment by the Tax Reform Act of 1986).*
2. I.R.C. Sec. 168(e) *(prior to amendment by the Tax Reform Act of 1986).*
3. I.R.C. Sec. 168(c)(2)(A) *(prior to amendment by the Tax Reform Act of 1986).*
4. I.R.C. Sec. 168(c)(2)(B) *(prior to amendment by the Tax Reform Act of 1986).*
5. I.R.C. Sec. 168(c)(2)(C) *(prior to amendment by the Tax Reform Act of 1986).*
6. I.R.C. Sec. 168(c)(2)(E) *(prior to amendment by the Tax Reform Act of 1986).*

☐ Nineteen-year real property, defined as Section 1250 property that does not have a present class life of 12.5 years or less and is not low-income housing. This class includes most depreciable real estate.[7]

☐ Low-income housing that is specifically described in Clause (i), (ii), (iii) or (iv) of Section 1250(a)(1)(B).

Unless C Company elects to depreciate under a method not based on a term of years, both the lease and well equipment and the gasoline plant are 5-year recovery property subject to the ACRS provisions. *(See Case 71 for a discussion of the unit-of-production method.)* C Company computes its recovery allowance by multiplying the unadjusted basis of the property by a statutory percentage found in tables provided in the law. The tables automatically contain the half-year convention. Thus, C Company obtains a half-year's writeoff regardless of the time of year it places the assets in service.

Unadjusted basis is the basis of property without adjustment for prior depreciation.[8] Salvage value is ignored.[9] The applicable percentages for 5-year recovery property are summarized below:[10]

Recovery Year	Applicable Percentage
1	15
2	22
3	21
4	21
5	21

Assuming C Company elects a reduced investment tax credit, it will claim a cost recovery allowance in 1985 equal to 15% of $1,750,000, or $262,500. In 1986, the recovery allowance will be 22% of $1,750,000 (the unadjusted basis), or $385,000. C Company will determine the cost recovery allowances for the remaining three years in a similar manner.

This example assumes that C Company is in existence for the full calendar year 1985. If C Company has a short tax year in 1985, it must prorate the ACRS deduction on a 12-month basis, calculated from the beginning of the short tax year.[11] Deductions for years 1986 through 1989 will use the applicable percentages from the table above, and the balance of the unrecovered basis will be deducted in 1990, the sixth year.[12]

A taxpayer may elect to use the straight-line method over the regular recovery period or optional longer recovery periods. For 5-year recovery property, the taxpayer may elect a recovery period of 5, 12 or 25 years.[13] Under this election, a taxpayer must use the half-year convention by claiming a half year in the year he places the property in service and another half-year in the year following the end of the recovery period, assuming he holds the property for the entire period.[14] The straight-line election, made on a class-by-class basis, applies to all property (except real property) of the particular class placed in service in the tax year of the election. It also applies to the property throughout its recovery period.[15] The election does not apply to property in other classes or to any property placed in service in another tax year.

7. I.R.C. Sec. 168(c)(2)(D) *(prior to amendment by the Tax Reform Act of 1986).*
8. I.R.C. Sec. 168(d) *(prior to amendment by the Tax Reform Act of 1986).*
9. I.R.C. Sec. 168(f)(9) *(prior to amendment by the Tax Reform Act of 1986).*
10. I.R.C. Sec. 168(b)(1) *(prior to amendment by the Tax Reform Act of 1986).*
11. I.R.C. Sec. 168(f)(5) *(prior to amendment by the Tax Reform Act of 1986).*
12. Prop. Reg. Sec. 1.168-2(f)(2); Prop. Reg. Sec. 1.168-2(f)(3).
13. I.R.C. Sec. 168(b)(3)(A) *(prior to amendment by the Tax Reform Act of 1986).*
14. I.R.C. Sec. 168(b)(3)(B) *(prior to amendment by the Tax Reform Act of 1986).*
15. *Ibid.*

Under this election, C Company may elect to depreciate the lease and well equipment and the gasoline plant, using the straight-line method over a 5-, 12- or 25-year life. This election will apply to all 5-year recovery property C Company places in service during 1985. C Company may revoke the election only with consent from the Internal Revenue Service (IRS). In 1986 and later years, C Company must continue to depreciate 1985 additions over the original period elected. However, C Company may use the recovery allowance tables or a straight-line recovery period for 5-year property placed in service in 1986. For property placed in service after July 31, 1986, and before January 1, 1987, that is not transition-rule property, C Company may elect to use the modified ACRS prescribed by the Tax Reform Act of 1986. Unless transition rules apply, the modified ACRS must be used for eligible property placed in service after December 31, 1986. Lease and well equipment is placed in service when an oil or gas zone is found and the well is made capable of production.[16] *(See Case 70.)*

Using the recovery allowance tables gives the taxpayer larger cost recovery allowances in the earlier part of the recovery period of the equipment. A taxpayer should consider the effect of the depreciation deduction or recovery allowance on the percentage depletion limitations. Because percentage depletion is limited to 50% of the net income from the particular oil and gas property, the use of the recovery allowance tables may accelerate cost recovery deductions at the expense of a reduced percentage depletion allowance. The taxpayer also should consider the effect of increased recovery allowances on the overall percentage depletion limitation, based on 65% of taxable income for the year. Increased deductions will reduce taxable income and can limit the amount of percentage depletion available to the taxpayer as a current deduction.

A taxpayer also should consider the ramifications of the recovery allowance in computing the net income per barrel of crude oil for determining the 90% of net income limitation provided by the Crude Oil Windfall Profit Tax Act of 1980. An increased deduction may contribute to a taxpayer's receiving a credit or refund of windfall profit tax because the windfall profit on a barrel of oil may not exceed 90% of the net income attributable to that barrel. *(See Section IX for a discussion of the Windfall Profit Tax Act.)*

C Company must weigh all the various factors involved when deciding whether to use the unit-of-production method, the recovery allowance tables or the straight-line method for the equipment it placed in service in 1985. Taxpayers with numerous properties will have difficulty determining the best method to use for a given year. A detailed property-by-property analysis may be necessary to maximize net income from properties for percentage depletion purposes and minimize net income from properties with a potential windfall profit tax net income limitation.

In addition, the ACRS rules do not provide flexibility on a property-by-property basis because all current-year additions within the same class must use the same recovery rate or percentage. For example, if C Company makes a straight-line election to recover costs over five years or over a longer period, the election is binding not only on all lease and well equipment placed in service in 1985 but on all other 5-year class property C Company places in service in 1985. It appears that a taxpayer can elect the unit-of-production method on a property-by-property basis, beginning with the first year the property is placed in service.[17] Any lease and well equipment for which the unit-of-production method is not elected will be placed in the 5-year class. *(See Case 71 for a further discussion of this method.)*

---

16. Rev. Rul. 78-13, 1978-1 C.B. 63.
17. I.R.C. Sec. 168(e)(2) *(prior to amendment by the Tax Reform Act of 1986).*

Case 70
Modified Accelerated Cost Recovery System Allowances (Depreciation) — Lease and Well Equipment Placed in Service After 1986

> D Company completed a producing well in June 1986, a second in August 1986 and a third producing well in February 1987. All of the wells were drilled within the United States. D Company requests information on how depreciation is to be calculated on the equipment installed on each of the three wells. None of the equipment was installed pursuant to a contract binding on March 1, 1986, nor was it otherwise qualified under the general transition rule.

Property placed in service after 1980 and before January 1, 1987, generally is required to be depreciated under the former accelerated cost recovery system (ACRS). *(See Case 69.)* The Tax Reform Act of 1986 (the Act) substantially modified the ACRS for property placed in service after December 31, 1986, except for property covered by transition rules. Additionally, property that is not transition-rule property and that is placed in service after July 31, 1986, and before January 1, 1987, may, at the election of the taxpayer on an asset-by-asset basis, be depreciated under the modified ACRS rules.[18]

The modified ACRS abandons the statutory tables used by the former ACRS to calculate depreciation; instead, it prescribes depreciation methods, recovery periods, and either a mid-year, mid-quarter or mid-month convention. Generally, depreciation is faster under the new method, but this advantage is more than offset by the longer recovery period. The mid-year convention should normally be used for lease and well equipment unless the basis of ACRS property placed in service during the last three months of the year exceeds 40% of the basis of all ACRS property placed in service during the tax year, in which case a mid-quarter convention applies.[19] As under prior law, antichurning rules apply to prevent certain properties acquired from related persons from being depreciated under ACRS.[20] If the antichurning rules apply, the affected property will be depreciated by the acquirer using the rules applicable when the property was originally acquired by the transferor.

An alternative depreciation system is required for: (1) property used predominantly outside the United States; (2) tax-exempt use property; (3) property financed with tax-exempt bonds; (4) designated imported property and (5) computing earnings and profits of a domestic corporation.[21] A taxpayer may elect to use the alternative depreciation system for all property additions otherwise qualifying for modified ACRS depreciation within a particular class.[22] The alternative depreciation system provides longer lives for assets and requires use of the straight-line method. However, the Technical Corrections Bill of 1987 allows the use of the method of depreciation required for alternative minimum tax purposes. If such election is made for lease and well equipment, depreciation is calculated by either the straight-line or the 150%

18. P.L. 99-514 (Tax Reform Act of 1986), Sec. 203(a)(1)(B); Conference Committee Report No. 99-841, 1986-3 C.B. Vol. 4 39.
19. I.R.C. Sec. 168(d)(3)(A).
20. I.R.C. Sec. 168(f)(5).
21. I.R.C. Sec. 168(g).
22. I.R.C. Sec. 168(g)(7).

declining-balance method over 14 years, using the same conventions as for modified ACRS.[23] This election is available in addition to the election to use straight-line depreciation with the modified ACRS life that is described below.

The date property is placed in service determines whether it is to be depreciated under the former ACRS or modified ACRS.[24] Lease and well equipment is placed in service when an oil or gas zone is found and the well is made capable of production.[25] Since the first well in the above example was completed before January 1, 1987, and also before July 31, 1986, and did not meet the general transition rule[26] (i.e., the March 1, 1986, binding contract exception or March 1, 1986, substantial construction exception), the former ACRS applies. Since the second well was completed between July 31, 1986, and January 1, 1987, and did not meet the transition rule, the former ACRS applies unless D Company elects to use modified ACRS.[27] The third well was completed after December 31, 1986, and, accordingly, modified ACRS applies. In lieu of using ACRS, D Company could depreciate the equipment on any of these wells under some method not expressed in terms of years, such as the unit-of-production method.[28]

The classification of property under the Act is determined by reference to its class life.[29] Lease and well equipment has a class life of 14 years,[30] therefore, it is classified as 7-year property.[31] The applicable recovery period is seven years,[32] and the applicable method of depreciation is 200% declining-balance, switching to the straight-line method for the first year in which the switchover would produce a larger allowance.[33] In lieu of using the double declining-balance method, the taxpayer may make an irrevocable election to use the straight-line method with respect to all property in the same class placed in service during the year.[34] Under either the declining-balance or straight-line method, salvage value is treated as zero.[35] The applicable convention is the half-year convention unless the aggregate basis of ACRS property placed in service during the last three months of the tax year exceeds 40% of the basis of all ACRS property placed in service during the tax year; in such case, the mid-quarter convention must be used.[36]

Following is a comparison of the depreciation deduction for regular income tax purposes with respect to the well drilled in August 1986 under the former ACRS and modified ACRS, assuming the following: (1) the equipment costs $100,000; (2) the mid-year convention applies and (3) no election to use straight-line depreciation is made.

---

23. I.R.C. Sec. 168(g)(2).
24. P.L. 99-514 (Tax Reform Act of 1986), Sec. 203(a).
25. Rev. Rul. 78-13, 1978-1 C.B. 63.
26. P.L. 99-514 (Tax Reform Act of 1986), Sec. 203(b).
27. P.L. 99-514 (Tax Reform Act of 1986), Sec. 203(a)(1)(B).
28. I.R.C. Sec. 168(f)(1).
29. I.R.C. Sec. 168(e).
30. I.R.C. Sec. 168(i)(1); Rev. Proc. 83-35, 1983-1 C.B. 745.
31. I.R.C. Sec. 168(e).
32. I.R.C. Sec. 168(c).
33. I.R.C. Sec. 168(b).
34. I.R.C. Sec. 168(b)(5).
35. I.R.C. Sec. 168(b)(4).
36. I.R.C. Sec. 168(d)(3)(A).

Year	Depreciation Expense	
	Former ACRS	Modified ACRS
1986	$ 15,000	$ 14,286
1987	22,000	24,488
1988	21,000	17,492
1989	21,000	12,494
1990	21,000	8,925
1991	—	8,925
1992	—	8,925
1993	—	4,465
Total	$100,000	$100,000

The foregoing discussion describes how depreciation is required by the Act to be computed for regular income tax purposes. A separate calculation of depreciation with respect to property eligible for modified ACRS will be required for alternative minimum tax (AMT) purposes for tax years beginning after 1986 unless the taxpayer has elected or is required to use the straight-line method, the 150% declining-balance method (as provided in the Technical Corrections Bill of 1987), unit-of-production method or another method not expressed in a term of years.[37] Depreciation in tax years beginning after 1986 with respect to property placed in service before 1987 that is not depreciated under modified ACRS is treated as a tax preference item only to the extent that it constituted a tax preference item under the rules applying under pre-1986 Act law.[38]

If D Company calculates depreciation on the third well (completed in 1987) under modified ACRS using the 200% declining-balance method and a 7-year life, it will have to make a separate calculation using the 150% declining-balance method and a 14-year life for AMT purposes.[39] By electing to depreciate equipment on the third well using: (1) the straight-line method and a 7-year life, (2) the straight-line method or the 150% declining-balance method (as provided in the Technical Corrections Bill of 1987) and a 14-year life (alternative depreciation system) or (3) the unit-of-production method, D Company could avoid having to adjust its regular tax depreciation deduction in calculating the AMT.[40] An election by D Company to use the straight-line method under either modified ACRS or the alternative depreciation system would apply to all 1987 property additions within that class.[41] The unit-of-production election can be made on a property-by-property basis.

If D Company elects for regular income tax purposes to use the modified ACRS for the second well completed after July 31, 1986, its 1987 depreciation on that well will have to be recomputed for the AMT in the same manner as for the third well.

Case 71
Unit-of-Production Method of Computing Depreciation

In 1987, C Company acquires producing oil properties for $450,000; $150,000 is allocable to lease and well equipment, and $300,000 is

37. I.R.C. Sec. 56(a).
38. Conference Committee Report No. 99-841, 1986-3 C.B. Vol. 4 251-252; General Explanation of the Tax Reform Act of 1986, prepared by the Staff of the Joint Committee on Taxation, p. 440.
39. I.R.C. Sec. 56(a).
40. I.R.C. Sec. 56(a)(1).
41. I.R.C. Sec. 168(b)(5); I.R.C. Sec. 168(g)(7).

allocable to leaseholds. The producing formations are such that the oil reserves are expected to be recovered during the first three years following purchase.

Because of the relatively short economic lives of the properties, C Company should consider electing to use the unit-of-production method for calculating the annual allowance for depreciation on the equipment.[42] Even though the accelerated cost recovery system (ACRS) as modified by the Tax Reform Act of 1986 is mandatory for eligible property placed in service after December 31, 1986, an exception applies to property the taxpayer elects to depreciate under the unit-of-production method or any method of depreciation not expressed in terms of years.[43] This election will apply to lease and well equipment and can be made on a property-by-property basis.[44] This election gives the taxpayer flexibility in determining the depreciation deduction for a particular property without affecting the recovery allowances claimed on all other eligible property the taxpayer may place in service in a given year. Use of ACRS or the alternative depreciation system election is binding on all eligible property in a particular class placed in service by the taxpayer in a given year.[45] *(See Cases 69 and 70 for a discussion of ACRS provisions.)*

The unit-of-production method may be used advantageously to accelerate depreciation deductions for equipment when the estimated productive life of any property is less than the 7-year period provided by the modified ACRS. Such a rapid writeoff is desirable if the income tax savings (regular and alternative minimum tax) and potential windfall profit tax savings (from the 90% net income limitation) outweigh the effects of any potential loss of percentage depletion from the 50% of net income limitation. (The 65% of taxable income limitation also may be affected.) Likewise, for oil and gas properties with longer than 7-year estimated lives, the unit-of-production method may reduce depreciation deductions claimed on particular properties without affecting faster recovery allowances claimed on other 7-year properties. This may be particularly desirable if the slower recovery rates will result in an increased percentage depletion on a particular property due to the 50% of net income limitation. Electing straight-line ACRS recovery over the 7-year period (or 14-year period under the alternative depreciation system) may produce similar results on a particular property; however, such a straight-line election will be binding on all property within that particular class placed in service by the taxpayer in that year.

C Company will calculate its depreciation deduction much as it computes cost depletion. *(See Case 79.)* The adjusted basis of the equipment is divided by the estimated recoverable reserves as of the beginning of the year. The resulting unit cost is multiplied by the production for the current year to determine the allowable depreciation. In this computation of depreciation, the adjusted basis of the equipment is reduced by estimated salvage value to the extent that salvage value exceeds 10% of original cost.[46]

The estimated recoverable reserves C Company uses in calculating unit-of-production depreciation should be limited to the amount of oil and gas that the existing well equipment will produce.

---

42. Reg. Sec. 1.611-5(a); Golconda Oil Co., 7 B.T.A. 955 (1927).
43. I.R.C. Sec. 168(f)(1).
44. I.R.C. Sec. 168(f)(1); Prop. Reg. Sec. 1.168-4(b).
45. I.R.C. Sec. 168(g)(7).
46. Reg. Sec. 1.167(f)-1.

As C Company drills new wells, the reserves used to calculate depreciation will increase to include any newly developed reserves.[47] To depreciate equipment that serves an entire lease, C Company must include the total commercial production it expects to recover from the entire lease.[48]

C Company is entitled to compute a reasonable depreciation allowance due to obsolescence and decay during periods when the oil properties are not producing or are producing at a rate below their normal capacity.[49]

If C Company treats the equipment installed in more than one well on a lease as a single group of assets, it generally may not claim a tax deduction for a loss on the normal retirement of equipment from any well on the lease.[50] As long as other wells on the same lease are producing, the cost (net of any salvage) of abandoned equipment should be charged to the accumulated reserve for depreciation for that particular unit.[51] However, if the abandonment is attributable to extraordinary circumstances (abnormal retirement), C Company may claim a deduction for the loss in the year of the abandonment.[52]

The unit-of-production method may be used for both regular income tax and alternative minimum tax purposes, thereby simplifying tax-basis recordkeeping.[53]

Case 72
Operating-Day Method of Computing Depreciation

In 1987, Driller D, an independent producer, purchases a rotary drilling rig having a depreciable basis of $1,250,000 and an estimated salvage value of $125,000. The estimated useful life of the rig is eight years; however, it is anticipated that the rig will be used more during the first few years of its useful life than later.

Driller D may compute his annual charge for depreciation on the rig by the operating-day method because wear and tear from use are major factors in determining the useful life of the asset to the taxpayer.[54]

The accelerated cost recovery system (ACRS) as modified by the Tax Reform Act of 1986 is mandatory for eligible property placed in service after December 31, 1986. However, instead of ACRS, a taxpayer may elect to use a depreciation method not expressed in terms of years. The operating-day method qualifies for that election and can be elected on a property-by-property basis without jeopardizing ACRS depreciation allowances claimed on other eligible property in a particular class placed in service that year.[55]

Driller D may compute the annual charge for depreciation by prorating the cost of the rig over its estimated useful life (expressed in total operating days) and multiplying the resulting daily rate by the number of days the rig is in use during the year. The operating-day method tends to match the charge for depreciation with the revenue earned by use of the rig. Under the stated facts, no reduction of cost for estimated salvage value need be made because that value does not exceed 10% of the cost of the rig.[56]

---

47. Dulup Oil Co., B.T.A. Memo Dec. (Aug. 14, 1940).
48. Reg. Sec. 1.611-2(c).
49. Reg. Sec. 1.611-5(b)(2).
50. Mohawk Petroleum Co. v. Comm'r, 148 F.2d 957 (9th Cir. 1945), 33 AFTR 1226, 45-1 USTC 9265.
51. Reg. Sec. 1.167(a)-7(b).
52. Reg. Sec. 1.167(a)-8.
53. I.R.C. Sec. 56(a)(1).
54. Rev. Rul. 56-652, 1956-2 C.B. 125.
55. I.R.C. Sec. 168(g)(7).
56. Reg. Sec. 1.167(f)-1(a).

The drilling rig will be 5-year property eligible for the double declining-balance method if Driller D does not elect to use the operating-day method of computing depreciation.[57] In this example, use of modified ACRS may provide larger deductions in the earlier years of the recovery period of the equipment than would the use of the operating-day method. *(See Case 70 for a discussion of modified ACRS.)*

If Driller D adopts the operating-day method of computing depreciation, he cannot change to another method in a later year without securing the prior approval of the Internal Revenue Service.[58]

The depreciation deduction computed by use of the operating-day method will be the same for both regular and alternative minimum tax purposes.[59]

Case 73
Election To Expense the Cost of Certain Depreciable Assets

C Company purchased new lease and well equipment for $150,000 on July 1, 1987. For tax purposes, C Company wants to depreciate the cost of the equipment as rapidly as possible.

C Company will use the accelerated cost recovery system (ACRS), as modified by the Tax Reform Act of 1986 (the Act), that generally prescribes the 200% declining-balance method with a 7-year life. *(See Case 70.)*

For property placed in service in tax years beginning after 1981, a taxpayer may elect to deduct a limited amount of the cost of qualifying property as an expense, rather than capitalizing and depreciating the property. The Act makes several important changes in the expensing rules, which are generally effective with respect to property placed in service after December 31, 1986.[60]

Under the new rules, the maximum amount eligible for expensing is increased from $5,000 to $10,000 of qualifying property in any particular tax year.[61] If a taxpayer's total investment in qualifying property in a tax year exceeds $200,000, each dollar of qualifying property in excess of $200,000 reduces the $10,000 ceiling by one dollar.[62] As an additional limitation, the aggregate amount expensed within a tax year cannot exceed the aggregate amount of taxable income computed without this expensing deduction derived by the taxpayer from the active conduct of any trade or business during such tax year.[63] Any unused deduction caused by this net income limitation may be carried forward and added to the amount allowable in the subsequent year.[64] If the expensed property is converted to personal use at any time before the end of its ACRS recovery period, the difference between the amount expensed and modified ACRS depreciation must be recaptured as income.[65]

Married persons filing separate returns are treated as one taxpayer, and the annual ceiling of $10,000 (or lesser amount if over $200,000 is placed in service) is allocated equally between the two spouses, unless they elect otherwise.[66]

57. I.R.C. Sec. 168(e).
58. Reg. Sec. 1.167(e)-1(a); Reg. Sec. 1.167(a)-11(c)(1)(iii).
59. I.R.C. Sec. 56(a)(1)(B).
60. P.L. 99-514 (Tax Reform Act of 1986), Sec. 203(a)(2).
61. I.R.C. Sec. 179(b)(1).
62. I.R.C. Sec. 179(b)(2).
63. I.R.C. Sec. 179(b)(3)(A).
64. I.R.C. Sec. 179(b)(3)(B).
65. I.R.C. Sec. 179(d)(10).
66. I.R.C. Sec. 179(b)(4).

To qualify for the expense election, the property must be recovery property purchased for use in the active conduct of a trade or business.[67] Property will not qualify if it is acquired from a related taxpayer or another member of a controlled group or if the acquiring taxpayer's basis is determined by reference to the basis of the property exchanged in the hands of the transferor.[68] Cost eligible for the expense election does not include any portion of the basis of an asset that is determined by reference to any other asset held at any time by the taxpayer.[69] For example, property received in a like-kind exchange will not qualify to the extent the basis in the property is determined by reference to the basis of the property exchanged.

In determining the annual dollar limit on the expense election, all members of a controlled group are treated as one taxpayer, with the dollar limit apportioned among the members.[70] The limitation also applies both at the partnership and the partner level.[71] In 1987, for example, a partnership is allowed a maximum current-dollar expense deduction of $10,000 which would be allocated among the partners of the partnership. Each partner is permitted to expense qualifying costs from other businesses, up to the maximum limitation of $10,000, including each partner's share of the qualifying costs of each partnership ($5,000 for a married individual filing separately). Thus, a 10% partner may deduct up to $1,000 as his share of the partnership deduction and is entitled to deduct up to $9,000 from other partnerships or other businesses. A similar rule applies to S corporations and their shareholders.[72] Trusts and estates are not eligible to make the election to expense items currently.[73]

The election to expense property currently must be made in the taxpayer's income tax return for the tax year. The election is made by showing as a separate item on the taxpayer's income tax return the total Section 179 expense deduction and the portion of that deduction allocable to each specific item.[74] An election may not be revoked without the consent of the Internal Revenue Service.[75] Proposed regulations would allow the election to be made in a delinquent return or in an amended return filed by the due date of the return (including extensions).[76]

The lease and well equipment purchased by C Company in 1987 qualifies for the special expensing provisions. Assuming C Company is a calendar-year taxpayer and uses the double declining-balance method of depreciation and the mid-year convention under modified ACRS, the maximum deduction available to C Company in 1987 is as follows:

	Asset	Deduction
Cost of property	$150,000	
Special expense provisions	(10,000)	$ 10,000
Remaining basis subject to modified accelerated cost recovery	$140,000	
Recovery allowance 1/2 (1/7th of $140,000 × 200%)		20,000
Total 1987 deduction		$ 30,000

67. I.R.C. Sec. 179(d)(1).
68. I.R.C. Sec. 179(d)(2).
69. I.R.C. Sec. 179(d)(3).
70. I.R.C. Sec. 179(d)(6).
71. I.R.C. Sec. 179(d)(8).
72. *Ibid.*
73. I.R.C. Sec. 179(d)(4).
74. I.R.C. Sec. 179(c)(1); Prop. Reg. Sec. 1.179-4(a).
75. I.R.C. Sec. 179(c)(2).
76. Prop. Reg. Sec. 1.179-4(a).

In making the decision whether to expense, consideration should be given to the effect on the percentage depletion limitations, the 90% of net income limitation on the windfall profit tax and the alternative minimum tax. The deduction resulting from the election to expense is not a tax preference item for alternative minimum tax purposes.[77]

Case 74
Depreciation of Pipeline Rights-of-Way, Clearing and Grading Costs and Line Pack

> C Company owns a number of pipelines, including both trunk and gathering lines. C Company has expended $2.5 million in acquiring rights-of-way on which the pipelines are constructed.
>
> In 1980, C Company constructed a 900-mile, large-diameter pipeline and added a second loop line in 1987. C Company incurred clearing and grading costs of $.95 per linear foot for construction of the original pipeline. In 1987, it incurred additional clearing and grading costs of $.90 per linear foot for the second line. C Company wants to know the general rules for depreciating these costs.
>
> C Company also wants to know how to account for the cost of natural gas required to fill the second loop line.

The pipeline builder must obtain an easement, or right-of-way agreement, from the owner of the land on which he is to build the line. The landowner usually will charge a roddage fee as the initial consideration for granting the easement. Other costs incurred for the acquisition of an easement typically include salaries and travel expenses of employees or agents who deal with the landowners, legal and recording fees, severance and other damage costs and the costs of right-of-way surveys. If an additional loop line or replacement line is constructed, it usually is placed at a distance from the original line. The costs of obtaining additional rights-of-way generally duplicate those for original rights-of-way.

Rights-of-way are considered to be intangible assets[78] and must have an ascertainable life to be subject to depreciation.[79] Rights-of-way typically have no usefulness except for the operation of the pipeline to which they are related; thus, the costs of rights-of-way generally are depreciable over the estimated useful life of the related pipeline.[80]

The depreciation of the cost of rights-of-way has been the subject of considerable litigation. Generally, the courts have allowed depreciation using the straight-line method over the estimated life of the related pipeline, whether the line is a gathering line or a trunk line system.[81] The Internal Revenue Service (IRS) has announced it will no longer contend that these costs are not subject to depreciation unless the facts and circumstances clearly differ from those prevalent in the industry. For example, if the taxpayer plans to replace all or a part of an existing pipeline on the original right-

---

77. I.R.C. Sec. 56(a)(1)(A)(i); I.R.C. Sec. 168(g)(1); Senate Report No. 99-313, 1986-3 C.B. Vol. 3 522, Footnote 5.
78. Rev. Rul. 71-120, 1971-1 C.B. 79; Rev. Rul. 71-448, 1971-2 C.B. 130.
79. Reg. Sec. 1.167(a)-3.
80. Rev. Rul. 71-120, 1971-1 C.B. 79; Rev. Rul. 71-448, 1971-2 C.B. 130.
81. Northern Natural Gas Co. v. O'Malley, 277 F.2d 128 (8th Cir. 1960), 5 AFTR2d 1246, 60-1 USTC 9395; Commonwealth Natural Gas Corp. v. U.S., 395 F.2d 493 (4th Cir. 1968), 21 AFTR2d 1353, 68-1 USTC 9391; Shell Pipe Line Corp. v. U.S., 267 F. Supp. 1014 (S.D. Tex. 1967), 19 AFTR2d 1269, 67-1 USTC 9396; Southern Natural Gas Co. v. U.S., 412 F.2d 1222 (Ct. Cl. 1969), 23 AFTR2d 69-1714, 69-2 USTC 9473.

of-way (or actually follows such a practice), the IRS will continue to contest depreciation of the right-of-way costs.[82]

Attempts by a taxpayer to use an accelerated depreciation method for these costs generally have been unsuccessful.[83] Taxpayers must compute allowable depreciation on right-of-way costs under the straight-line method because a right-of-way is an intangible asset. Before repeal of the investment tax credit by the Tax Reform Act of 1986 (the Act), rights-of-way costs were ineligible for the credit.[84]

In some instances, it may be difficult to distinguish between direct pipeline costs and the costs of acquiring rights-of-way. It is important that a proper allocation be made because accelerated cost recovery is allowable for direct pipeline costs. For example, an easement agreement may provide that damages will be paid to the landowner for the permanent diminution in the value of his land and for the temporary injury to the land caused by the construction and repair of the pipeline. In several cases, the taxpayer contended that the damages measured by the temporary injury to the land should be properly classified as part of the cost of the pipeline because that temporary injury was caused solely by the construction of the line. The courts have held that those damage payments constitute costs of constructing the pipeline because the obligation to pay those amounts under an easement contract is only created if and when a pipeline is constructed.[85]

A small part of the clearing and grading costs is to provide access to the property. Most costs, however, are connected with providing a foundation for the pipeline and a suitable construction site. The clearing and grading require the removal of boulders and trees, leveling of hills, filling of gullies and other similar work. These costs also include excavating, backfilling and regrading to restore the land to its original configuration.

Clearing and grading costs incurred in the construction of one pipeline are seldom of material benefit in the construction of any subsequent line. The taxpayer often duplicates many of these costs (excavating and refilling the land) even when he places another line in the same trench. Due to economic considerations, it generally is not feasible to use the same trench; therefore, construction of a loop line or a replacement line usually duplicates most of the clearing and grading costs incurred for the construction of the original line.

The clearing and grading costs are not permanent improvements to the land and are not a part of the cost of rights-of-way. They represent construction costs, and the taxpayer should capitalize these costs and depreciate them over the useful life of the related pipeline.[86] The IRS has stated, however, that the asset guideline classes do not include the useful life of the initial clearing and grading costs.[87]

C Company may elect to use the double declining-balance method or another accelerated method of depreciation for the clearing and grading costs attributable to pipelines placed in service before January 1, 1981. C Company must use ACRS recovery allowances as modified by the Act for costs incurred on the second line placed in

82. Rev. Rul. 71-120, 1971-1 C.B. 79; Rev. Rul. 71-448, 1971-2 C.B. 130.
83. Tenneco, Inc. v. U.S., 433 F.2d 1345 (5th Cir. 1970), 26 AFTR2d 70-5780, 70-2 USTC 9695.
84. Rev. Rul. 71-120, 1971-1 C.B. 79; Rev. Rul. 71-448, 1971-2 C.B. 130.
85. Mapco Inc. v. U.S., 556 F.2d 1107 (Ct. Cl. 1977), 40 AFTR2d 77-5144, 77-2 USTC 9476; True v. U.S., 603 F. Supp. 1370 (D.C. Wyo. 1985), 56 AFTR2d 85-6208, 86-1 USTC 9193.
86. Commonwealth Natural Gas; Tenneco, Inc. v. U.S., 301 F. Supp. 598 (S.D. Tex. 1969), 23 AFTR2d 69-1123, 69-1 USTC 9274, *rev'd on other issues* 433 F.2d 1345 (5th Cir. 1970), 26 AFTR2d 70-5780, 70-2 USTC 9695.
87. Rev. Rul. 72-403, 1972-2 C.B. 102.

service after December 31, 1986, unless certain exceptions under the general transition rule apply.[88] *(See Case 70.)* Since the pipeline facilities have a class life of 22 years, the exceptions under the general transition rule could apply. An exception to the general effective date of December 31, 1986, applies in the case of property constructed, reconstructed or acquired pursuant to a written contract that was binding as of March 1, 1986.[89] Another exception to the general effective date applies to self-constructed property if: (1) the lesser of $1 million or 5% of the cost of the property was incurred or committed as of March 1, 1986, and (2) the construction or reconstruction began by that date.[90] A further exception to the general effective date is provided where construction of an equipped building or plant facility began before March 2, 1986, and more than one-half the cost (including machinery and equipment) was incurred or committed before such date.[91] For any of the three exceptions under the general transition rule to apply, the property also must be placed in service before January 1, 1991.[92]

If C Company's property is public utility property, a normalization method of accounting must be used for ratemaking purposes if ACRS is to be used.[93]

In cases where the construction of additional lines or the replacement of existing lines in the original trench clearly is contemplated or is the practice of the taxpayer, the IRS may contend that the nonrecurring clearing and grading costs have an indeterminable life and are not subject to depreciation.[94]

Clearing and grading costs were eligible for the investment tax credit before its repeal, generally effective for property placed in service after December 31, 1985, but subject to certain transition rules. *(See Case 76.)*

The IRS has held that the cost of gas that must be present at all times in a pipeline (i.e., line pack) is inventory.[95] The Court of Claims, however, has held that line pack is depreciable.[96] Line pack is similar to nonrecoverable cushion gas in an underground storage facility which, as the IRS has ruled, is depreciable.[97]

Case 75
Impact of Technical Termination of Partnership on Subsequent Depreciation Deductions

Partnership P is a partnership whose ownership units are traded on an established securities exchange. It is referred to as a master limited partnership (MLP). During the 12-month period from July 1986 through June 1987, sales and exchanges of its limited partnership interests caused a 51% change of ownership in partnership capital and profits. The depreciable assets of the partnership consist of lease and well equipment that was acquired at various times which, for convenience, may be classified as pre-1981 assets, post-1980 to pre-1987 assets depreciated under the accelerated cost recovery system (ACRS) and post-1986

88. P.L. 99-514 (Tax Reform Act of 1986), Sec. 203(b)(2).
89. P.L. 99-514 (Tax Reform Act of 1986), Sec. 203(b)(1)(A).
90. P.L. 99-514 (Tax Reform Act of 1986), Sec. 203(b)(1)(B).
91. P.L. 99-514 (Tax Reform Act of 1986), Sec. 203(b)(1)(C).
92. P.L. 99-514 (Tax Reform Act of 1986), Sec. 203(b)(2)(A).
93. I.R.C. Sec. 168(f)(2).
94. Rev. Rul. 71-120, 1971-1 C.B. 79; Rev. Rul. 71-448, 1971-2 C.B. 130.
95. Rev. Rul. 68-620, 1968-2 C.B. 199.
96. Transwestern Pipeline Co. v. U.S., 639 F.2d 679 (Ct. Cl. 1980), 46 AFTR2d 80-6113, 80-2 USTC 9800.
97. Rev. Rul. 75-233, 1975-1 C.B. 95. *But see* Arkla, Inc. v. U.S., 765 F.2d 487 (5th Cir. 1985), 56 AFTR2d 85-5446, 84-2 USTC 9740.

assets depreciated under the modified accelerated cost recovery system. The depreciation methods and useful lives used by Partnership P before its technical termination are as follows:

> **Pre-1981 assets—11-year double declining-balance method (DDB), switching to straight-line (SL) method**
> **Post-1980 to pre-1987—5-year ACRS**
> **Post-1986—7-year DDB, switching to SL**

Partnership P wants to know what effect the technical termination will have on the methods of depreciation it has been using.

Because within a 12-month period there has been a sale or exchange of 50% or more of the total interest in partnership capital and profits, Partnership P is considered to have terminated for tax purposes and to have distributed all of its assets to its partners.[98] Since the partnership, in fact, did not actually terminate, all the partners are deemed to have recontributed the assets to the reconstituted partnership.[99]

Partnership P, as reconstituted, cannot depreciate the pre-1981 assets under the modified accelerated cost recovery system.[100] The pre-1981 assets should be depreciated under the facts-and-circumstances method or over the Asset Depreciation Range (ADR) life using either the straight-line method or the 150% declining-balance method or unit-of-production method.[101] The pre-1981 assets will be considered used property in the hands of reconstituted Partnership P and no longer will be eligible for the 200% declining-balance method under nonmodified accelerated cost recovery system rules.[102] The ADR life for lease and well equipment ranges from 11 to 17 years.[103]

The post-1980 to pre-1987 assets may be depreciated by reconstituted Partnership P using the ACRS prescribed rates[104] unless the depreciation calculated under ACRS on a property-by-property basis for the first full tax year the property is placed in service exceeds the depreciation that would be allowable by the modified ACRS using the half-year convention.[105] If the ACRS deduction is greater than the modified ACRS deduction, the property must be depreciated under a method allowable under I.R.C. Section 168 (including the modified ACRS double declining-balance method, the modified ACRS straight-line method, the alternative depreciation system straight-line method, the alternative depreciation system 150% declining-balance method (as provided in the Technical Corrections Bill of 1987) or unit-of-production method). *(See Cases 69, 70 and 71.)*

The post-1986 properties are not subject to the antichurning rules.[106] Therefore, after a technical termination of a partnership, the remaining basis of the post-1986 assets will be eligible for use of the modified ACRS double declining-balance method, the modified ACRS straight-line method,[107] the alternative depreciation system straight-line method, alternative depreciation system 150% declining-balance method (as

98. I.R.C. Sec. 708(b).
99. Reg. Sec. 1.708-1(b)(1)(iv).
100. I.R.C. Sec. 168(f)(5)(A)(i).
101. I.R.C. Sec. 167(b); Reg. Sec. 1.167(a)-11; Rev. Rul. 57-352, 1957-2 C.B. 150; Rev. Rul. 59-389, 1959-2 C.B. 89; Rev. Rul. 67-248, 1967-2 C.B. 98.
102. I.R.C. Sec. 167(c).
103. Rev. Proc. 83-35, 1983-1 C.B. 745.
104. I.R.C. Sec. 168(f)(5)(A)(i); I.R.C. Sec. 168(e)(4)(D) *(prior to amendment by the Tax Reform Act of 1986).*
105. I.R.C. Sec. 168(f)(5)(B)(ii).
106. I.R.C. Sec. 168(i)(7)(B).
107. I.R.C. Sec. 168(a).

provided by the Technical Corrections Bill of 1987),[108] or the unit-of-production method.[109] *(See Case 70.)*

Case 76
Credit for Increasing Research Activities and Investment Tax Credit After December 31, 1985

Taxpayer A owns an interest in a producing oil lease classified as a tier-1 property for purposes of the windfall profit tax. The property currently is under a water-flood program. During 1987, Taxpayer A and the other working interest owners in the lease decide to initiate a polymer-augmenting water-flood project (a qualified tertiary recovery method under the energy regulations) and employ Engineer B, who is an expert in tertiary recovery techniques. Engineer B has been experimenting with a special chemical additive he believes will improve the horizontal and vertical sweep efficiency of the polymer slug.

On July 1, 1987, the polymer slug (with the experimental special chemical additive) was injected into the producing reservoir. Taxpayer A's share of the tangible lease and well equipment expenditures made during 1987 on the newly drilled producing wells is $1 million. His share of the cost of the unrecoverable polymer slug is $350,000, and his share of the cost of raw materials necessary to produce the special chemical additive is $150,000. Taxpayer A incurs $100,000 of unreimbursed laboratory costs to develop the special chemical additive.

Credit for Increasing Research Activities

The Tax Reform Act of 1986 (the Act) extends the research tax credit, which was scheduled to expire at the end of 1985, for an additional three years.[110] The Act modifies the definition of eligible expenditures and reduces the rate from 25% to 20%.[111] The extension of the credit is effective for tax years ending after December 31, 1985. The modifications to the credit are effective for tax years beginning after December 31, 1985, except the modifications relating to the qualifying organization basic research credit are effective for tax years beginning after December 31, 1986.[112]

The research credit is equal to 20% of the excess of the "qualified research expenditures" during the year over the "base-period research expenditures."[113] The research credit has been made subject to the general limitation on business credits (i.e., it cannot exceed $25,000 of tax liability plus 75% of excess).[114] Where an individual owns an interest in a proprietorship, partnership, estate, trust or S corporation, the research credit attributable to each such interest is limited to that portion of his tax attributable to the income from the entity that generated the credit.[115]

The term *qualified research* means research with respect to which expenditures may be treated as expenses under I.R.C. Section 174 and that is undertaken to discover

108. I.R.C. Sec. 168(g)(7).
109. I.R.C. Sec. 168(f).
110. I.R.C. Sec. 41(h).
111. I.R.C. Sec. 41(a).
112. Conference Committee Report No. 99-841, 1986-3 C.B. Vol. 4 76.
113. I.R.C. Sec. 41(a).
114. I.R.C. Sec. 38(b)(4).
115. I.R.C. Sec. 41(g).

information that is technological in nature and that pertains to functional aspects of products.[116] Specifically excluded from the term *qualified research* is any research: (1) conducted after the beginning of commercial production of the business component, (2) related to adaptation of an existing business component to a particular customer, (3) that duplicates an existing business component, (4) consisting of a survey or study involving efficiency, management, marketing, routine data collection or routine quality control, (5) consisting of computer software unless for use in qualified research or a production process involving a credit-eligible component, (6) conducted outside of the United States, (7) involving the social sciences, arts or humanities or (8) that is funded by another person.[117] Rental payments for use of personal property are ineligible unless for computer time used in connection with qualified research.[118]

For tax years beginning after 1986, the research credit of a corporation that is not an S corporation, a personal holding company or a service organization described in I.R.C. Section 414(m)(3)[119] may include a new basic research credit[120] for amounts paid to a qualifying organization (most colleges, universities and tax-exempt research organizations would qualify).[121] Generally, the basic research credit is equal to 20% of all basic research expenses in excess of a special base amount.[122] Basic research expenses that do not exceed the special base amount, and, thus, are ineligible for the basic research credit, may be added to the qualified research expenses eligible for the regular 20% credit.[123]

The term *base-period research expenditures* generally means the average of qualified research expenditures for the three tax years immediately preceding the year of change.[124] In computing the research credit for tax years beginning after December 31, 1985, base-period expenditures for tax years beginning before January 1, 1986, are to be determined under the credit definition of qualified research that was applicable in such base-period years and are not to be redetermined under the amended definition of qualified research.[125]

Costs paid or incurred for the purpose of ascertaining the existence, location, extent or quality of any deposits of ore or other minerals (including oil and gas) are not included in the term *qualified research expenditures*.[126] However, Taxpayer A's expenditures to develop new methods for extracting oil from the formation should constitute "qualified research expenditures" eligible for the credit.

It appears that the cost of the polymer slug and the special chemical additive constitute "supplies used in the conduct of qualified research" if they are used by an employee of Taxpayer A in the conduct of qualified services (testing the effectiveness of Engineer B's special chemical additive in actual application in a producing oil reservoir).[127] As such, they will be eligible for the credit, even though the $350,000 cost of the polymer slug is specifically deductible in the year in which it is injected,[128] and is not property subject to the allowance for depreciation. The $100,000 of unreimbursed laboratory costs incurred by Taxpayer A may be deducted currently as research and

116. I.R.C. Sec. 41(d).
117. I.R.C. Sec. 41(d)(4).
118. I.R.C. Sec. 41(b)(2).
119. I.R.C. Sec. 41(e)(7)(E).
120. I.R.C. Sec. 41(a)(2).
121. I.R.C. Sec. 41(e)(6).
122. I.R.C. Sec. 41(e)(1)(A).
123. I.R.C. Sec. 41(e)(1)(B).
124. I.R.C. Sec. 41(c)(2).
125. Conference Committee Report No. 99-841, 1986-3 C.B. Vol. 4 76, Footnote 5.
126. I.R.C. Sec. 174(d).
127. I.R.C. Sec. 41(b)(2)(A)(ii); Prop. Reg. Sec. 1.44F-2(b)(1).
128. I.R.C. Sec. 193.

experimental expenses, and also should qualify for the credit. The $150,000 of chemical additive expenditures is deductible either as research and experimental expenses or as qualified tertiary injection expenses. *(See Case 229 for a discussion of the windfall profit tax aspects of oil produced and recovered through the application of a tertiary process.)*

The Committee Reports make it clear that even though commercial production had been obtained before the initiation of the polymer-augmenting water flood project, the expenditures in question should be eligible for the credit since they would result in significant improvements in an existing process.[129]

Investment Tax Credit

The Tax Reform Act of 1986 repeals the investment tax credit for property placed in service after December 31, 1985.[130] Therefore, the $1 million of lease and well equipment installed in 1987 will not qualify for the investment tax credit unless the transition rules apply. The equipment would qualify under the transition rules if it had been acquired pursuant to a written contract binding on December 31, 1985, and is placed in service by January 1, 1989. Other transition rules are provided that appear not to apply to the facts of this case.[131]

Case 77
Credit for Producing Gas from a Tight Formation

> **Taxpayer A has a natural gas property that produced gas having a fuel content of 119,000 MM BTUs during 1987. This property is a "qualified tight sand formation" producing from a zone above the 5,000-foot depth. Taxpayer A filed for dual Federal Energy Regulatory Commission (FERC) determinations under Sections 103 and 107 of the Natural Gas Policy Act (NGPA). Taxpayer A sold gas with 3,000 MM BTUs at the Section 107 price during November and December. Due to weak demand for natural gas, Taxpayer A received substantially less than the maximum lawful Section 107 price for gas sold during the first 10 months of 1987. The price that A received never exceeded the maximum lawful price for gas under Section 103. Taxpayer A wants to know if he is entitled to any credit for producing fuel from nonconventional sources. If so, how is the credit calculated?**

The law provides for special tax credits for qualified fuels produced from nonconventional sources. The purpose of the credit is to encourage the development of energy from certain nonconventional sources in the event of a decline in the price of domestic crude oil. Some of the qualified fuels for which the credit is available are as follows:[132]

- Oil produced from shale and tar sands.
- Gas produced from geopressured brine, Devonian shale, coal seams, tight formations or biomass. (Gas from tight formations is included if it is regulated by the United States and entitled to a maximum lawful NGPA price equal to at least 150% of the NGPA Section 103 ceiling price.)
- Liquid, gaseous or solid synthetic fuels produced from coal.

129. Conference Committee Report No. 99-841, 1986-3 C.B. Vol. 4 74, Footnote 4.
130. I.R.C. Sec. 49(a).
131. I.R.C. Sec. 49(b).
132. I.R.C. Sec. 29(c).

The credit is computed by multiplying the "barrel of oil equivalent" of qualified fuels produced by the taxpayer and sold to an unrelated person by $3.[133] Cash-basis taxpayers may be required to claim the credit in the year in which revenue from the sale of production is recognized.[134] The amount of fuel required to equal the BTU content of one barrel of oil (5.8 million BTU or 5.8 MM BTU) is one barrel-of-oil equivalent.[135] The credit, however, is reduced as the price of oil increases. Essentially, the statute provides that, as the national average annual price of oil (the "reference price") increases above $23.50 per barrel, the credit begins to phase out.[136] When the reference price goes above $29.50 (a $6 increase), the available credit is zero. Since the date of enactment, the $23.50, $6 and $3 amounts have been adjusted for inflation.[137]

The following formula illustrates how the credit is calculated:

$$\text{Allowable Credit} = \$3 \times I - \left(\frac{R - (\$23.50 \times I)}{\$6 \times I} \times (\$3 \times I) \right)$$

Where: R = Reference price
I = Inflation factor

The reference price and the inflation factors are provided annually in an announcement by the Internal Revenue Service (IRS). The reference price and inflation adjustment factors for nonconventional fuels produced and sold in 1980,[138] 1981,[139] 1982,[140] 1983,[141] 1984,[142] 1985[143] and 1986[144] are as follows:

Year	Reference Price	Inflation Adjustment Factor
1980	$33.03	1.08976
1981	32.19	1.19000
1982	28.50	1.26760
1983	26.19	1.31970
1984	25.88	1.36730
1985	24.08	1.42110
1986	12.66	1.45550

The only exception to this general formula is that the $3 credit amount is not adjusted for inflation when computing the credit for gas from a tight formation.[145] For example,

133. I.R.C. Sec. 29(a)
134. IRS Letter Ruling 8532016.
135. I.R.C. Sec. 29(d)(6).
136. I.R.C. Sec. 29(b); I.R.C. Sec. 29(d)(2).
137. I.R.C. Sec. 29(b)(2); I.R.C. Sec. 29(d)(2).
138. IRS Notice 81-7, 1981-1 C.B. 615.
139. IRS Notice 82-6, 1982-1 C.B. 356.
140. IRS Notice 83-8, 1983-1 C.B. 536.
141. IRS Publications, *Inflation Adjustment Factor and Reference Price for Calendar Year 1983,* 51 F.R. 9992, March 16, 1984.
142. IRS Publications, *Inflation Adjustment Factor and Reference Price for Calendar Year 1984,* 50 F.R. 11043, March 19, 1985.
143. IRS Publications, *Inflation Adjustment Factor and Reference Price for Calendar Year 1985,* 51 F.R. 8271, March 10, 1986.
144. IRS Publications, *Inflation Adjustment Factor and Reference Price for Calendar Year 1986,* 52 F.R. 7365, March 10, 1987.
145. I.R.C. Sec. 29(b)(2).

the credit that would be available to Taxpayer A had the production in this situation been removed during 1986 is calculated as follows:

$$\text{Credit/Equivalent Barrel} = \$3 - \left(\frac{\$12.66 - (\$23.50 \times 1.4555)}{\$6 \times 1.4555} \times \$3 \right)^{*}$$

$$= \$3 - 0^{*}$$

$$= \$3$$

$$\text{Available Credit} = \$3 \times (116{,}000 \div 5.8)$$

$$= \$60{,}000$$

*The phase-out portion of the formula cannot result in an amount less than zero.

Only 116,000 MM BTUs were included in this credit calculation because the credit cannot be claimed on any production that is sold at the Section 107 ("incentive") price.[146] This limitation is applied on a sale-by-sale basis rather than an annual basis.[147] If the reference price for 1986 does not exceed at least $34.20 ($23.50 X 1.4555), the taxpayer qualifies for the full $3 credit on all eligible production. Production through June 30, 1987, should clearly be eligible, but whether production from July 1, 1987 through October 31, 1987, is eligible for the credit is less certain even though such production was not sold at the Section 107 ("incentive") price.

Before 1985, if a producer received the incentive price for only a portion of his qualified production for the year, he still was eligible for the Section 29 credit on any gas sales that were made at a price that did not exceed the maximum lawful price otherwise available for that type of gas under the NGPA (typically Section 102 or Section 103).[148]

For sales of gas made after 1984, the answer is not as clear. The statute[149] provides that tight formation gas must be "regulated" to qualify for the credit. Section 121 of the Natural Gas Policy Act eliminated price controls as of January 1, 1985, on many categories of Section 102 and Section 103 gas from below 5,000 feet. Section 103 gas from formations above 5,000 feet is decontrolled as of July 1, 1987. Gas produced from a tight formation that qualifies under Section 107 of the NGPA must generally meet the qualification criteria for "new gas" under either Section 102 or Section 103 of the NGPA.

In interpreting the decontrol provisions of the NGPA, the FERC ruled[150] that gas is deregulated if it falls into (or could fall into) two or more categories, any one of which is a deregulated category. Based on this FERC ruling, the IRS ruled that the Section 29 credit was not available after December 31, 1984, for tight formation gas (Section 107), which remains forever regulated, that otherwise fell into (or could fall into) a Section 102 or Section 103 deregulated category.[151] Subsequently, the IRS modified its ruling to recognize that not all Section 102 and Section 103 gas was deregulated as of January 1, 1985; specifically, Section 103 gas from a formation 5,000 feet or shallower remained regulated until July 1, 1987.[152]

A recent decision of the 10th Circuit Court of Appeals rejected as unreasonable the FERC's ruling that if a sale of natural gas qualifies for both a regulated category and

146. I.R.C. Sec. 29(e).
147. Rev. Rul. 86-2, 1986-1 C.B. 3; IRS Letter Ruling 8422132; IRS Letter Ruling 8422134; IRS Letter Ruling 8422137.
148. *Ibid.*
149. I.R.C. Sec. 29(c)(2)(B)(i).
150. FERC Order 406, 49 F.R. 46874 (1984).
151. Rev. Rul. 86-19, 1986-1 C.B. 4.
152. Rev. Rul. 86-127, 1986-44 I.R.B. 4.

a deregulated category, then the deregulated category would control.[153] Pending a possible Supreme Court review of this decision, the Section 29 credit should be available for qualifying Section 107 tight formation gas production after December 31, 1984, that is treated as "regulated" where an "incentive" price is not received. In making the determination whether an "incentive" price is received after December 31, 1984, it appears that the maximum NGPA prices that continue to be published monthly for the otherwise applicable gas category may not be exceeded, notwithstanding that such categories are deregulated.[154]

The credit is limited to qualified fuels produced and sold within the United States and its possessions before January 1, 2001,[155] from wells drilled or from facilities placed in service between December 31, 1979, and January 1, 1990.[156] A property producing gas from Devonian shale, coal seams, geopressured brine or a tight formation is not eligible for the credit if gas was produced from that property in marketable quantities before January 1, 1980.[157] For tax years beginning before January 1, 1987, the credit is limited to the taxpayer's tax liability after being reduced by nonrefundable personal credits, the foreign tax credit and the qualified clinical testing credit.[158]

For tax years beginning after December 31, 1986, the credit allowed may not exceed the excess of the regular income tax as reduced by the applicable credits (see above) over the tentative minimum tax.[159] Any unused credit is not available for carryback or carryforward to other tax years. If a taxpayer does not claim the credit on his initial tax return, he may claim the credit by filing an amended tax return. If the taxpayer is in a minimum tax position, the credit may be useful in demonstrating that a portion of the tax preferences produced no regular tax benefit.[160]

The IRS has ruled that the Section 29 credit is available for gas produced from a Section 107 coal seam well in a situation where the otherwise applicable gas category was Section 103.[161] The well was producing at a completion depth of less than 5,000 feet, and, thus, the Section 103 category was price regulated until July 1, 1987. Section 107 coal seam wells were deregulated on November 9, 1979. The IRS held that the Section 29 credit was available before July 1, 1987, provided the taxpayer received a price for the gas that was below the regulated Section 103 price. The IRS also ruled that the Section 29 credit remained available after July 1, 1987, without regard to the price received for the gas since both the Section 103 and Section 107 categories were deregulated, thus affording no possibility for "double dipping" (i.e., "incentive" price and tax credit). The IRS's interpretation of the statute[162] should be equally applicable in determining eligibility for the Section 29 credit in the case of gas produced from Section 107 Devonian shale and geopressured brine, which were also deregulated on November 9, 1979.

The IRS takes the position that the Section 29 credit is determined at the partnership level and then apportioned to persons who are partners on the last day of the partnership's tax year.[163] This method of apportionment seems inconsistent with other partnership rules that require apportionment to recognize changes in ownership during the year. Similar rules are applicable for S corporations, except that the credit

153. Martin Exploration Management Co. v. Federal Energy Regulatory Commission, 813 F.2d 1059 (10th Cir. 1987).
154. I.R.C. Sec. 29(e)(1).
155. I.R.C. Sec. 29(d)(1); I.R.C. Sec. 29(f)(1).
156. I.R.C. Sec. 29(f)(1).
157. I.R.C. Sec. 29(d)(4)(A).
158. I.R.C. Sec. 29(b)(5) *(prior to amendment by the Tax Reform Act of 1986)*.
159. I.R.C. Sec. 29(b)(5).
160. First Chicago Corp., 88 T.C. No. 37 (Mar. 24, 1987).
161. IRS Letter Ruling 8642052; G.C.M. 39481.
162. I.R.C. Sec. 29(e)(1).
163. Instructions to Form 1065 (1986), Schedule K, Line 17; IRS Letter Ruling 8422132.

is apportioned to shareholders in accordance with stock ownership.[164] Both the partnership and S corporation allocation methods ignore the fact that Congress apparently intended for the credit to be allocated among taxpayers with an interest in a qualified property based on their respective shares of gross income from that property.[165]

Royalty owners also should be eligible for the credit. Typically, they will have to request additional information before they can determine which properties have production eligible for the credit, the time period during which the credit can be claimed and any other information necessary for the statement required to be attached to their tax returns.

At this time, an official form does not exist for the calculation of the Section 29 credit. Even so, the instructions to the partnership and S corporation tax returns require the taxpayer to attach a separate schedule showing the computation of the Section 29 credit. Additionally, this statement must show the time period for which an election to take the credit is made, and records must be maintained to substantiate the price for which the gas is sold.[166] Presumably, these same requirements would be applicable to any taxpayers claiming the credit.[167]

For fiscal-year taxpayers, the reference price for purposes of calculating the credit is determined by the year in which the gas is sold.[168]

Before the Tax Reform Act of 1986 (the Act), the credit was not available for sales of qualified fuel to another member of an affiliated group that ultimately sold the qualified fuel (or a product thereof) to an unrelated third party. The Act retroactively changed the definition of a related party to exclude members of an affiliated group that files a consolidated return.[169]

Case 78
Investment Tax Credit Recapture — Dissolution of Partnership

> **A, a limited partnership, owns working interests in various oil and gas leases. A majority of the limited partners vote (in accordance with the partnership agreement) to dissolve the partnership and distribute undivided interests in the oil and gas leases and related tangible property to the respective limited partners. Individual B, a partner in A, had claimed investment tax credit for his proportionate share of the limited partnership's investment in qualified property. Individual B wants to know if investment tax credit recapture is required upon dissolution of the limited partnership for qualifying property that has not been held for the requisite period.**

Investment tax credit recapture occurs when a taxpayer disposes of qualifying property (or the property ceases to qualify) before he has held the property for the required period.[170] One important exception to investment tax credit recapture, however, applies when there is a "mere change in the form of conducting the trade or

164. Instructions to Form 1120S (1986) Schedule K, Line 11.
165. I.R.C. Sec. 29(d)(3); Senate Report No. 96-394, 1980-3 C.B. 106.
166. IRS Letter Ruling 8422132.
167. IRS Letter Ruling 8422137.
168. I.R.C. Sec. 29(b)(1)(A); I.R.C. Sec. 29(b)(2).
169. I.R.C. Sec. 29(d)(8).
170. I.R.C. Sec. 47(a).

business."[171] The regulations state four conditions a taxpayer must meet for the disposition to be considered a "mere change in the form of conducting the trade or business:"[172]

- □ The property is retained as qualifying property in the same trade or business.
- □ The transferor (the partner in the case of a partnership transferor) retains a substantial interest in the trade or business.
- □ Substantially all the assets (including nonqualifying property) necessary to conduct the trade or business are transferred to the transferee.
- □ The basis of the qualifying property in the hands of the transferee is determined in whole or in part by reference to the basis in the hands of the transferor.

Here, the transfer to Individual B probably meets the first three conditions imposed by the regulation. Satisfaction of the fourth requirement is questionable because the partnership basis rules relating to distributions in liquidation[173] require Individual B to determine his basis in qualifying and other property received in the liquidation by referring to his basis in his partnership interest. Individual B uses the partnership's basis in the property only to allocate the basis in his partnership interest among the properties received in the liquidation.[174]

The Internal Revenue Service (IRS) once issued a private letter ruling concluding that a partnership's pro-rata distribution of qualified property to its partners in complete liquidation did not cause investment tax credit recapture.[175] Subsequently, the IRS revoked its earlier ruling and held that recapture did occur in those circumstances, presumably because of failure to meet the last condition of the regulation.[176] Apparently, it did not matter that the statute itself does not incorporate the last condition into the test for a "mere change in the form of conducting the trade or business."[177]

In a situation involving an S corporation, one district court has questioned the validity of that specific requirement in the regulation.[178] The Sixth Circuit, however, reversed the district court and upheld the condition as properly restricting the recapture exception to situations in which there is a carryover of basis of the property.[179] The Tax Court has followed the Sixth Circuit in a similar case involving an S corporation.[180] The issue will be again considered in a pending Tax Court case involving a partnership.[181]

It is not clear whether investment tax credit recapture is required by the "dissolution" of or election out of Subchapter K by a tax partnership, in which the co-owners (not the partnership) hold title as tenants in common to undivided interests in the oil and gas leases and related tangible property. The IRS has held and a court has ruled[182] that a partnership still exists for purposes of the investment tax credit even though the

171. I.R.C. Sec. 47(b).
172. Reg. Sec. 1.47-3(f)(1)(ii).
173. I.R.C. Sec. 732(b).
174. I.R.C. Sec. 732(c)(2).
175. IRS Letter Ruling 7952066.
176. IRS Letter Ruling 8127060.
177. I.R.C. Sec. 47(b).
178. Long v. U.S. (W.D. Tenn. 1979), 44 AFTR2d 79-5888, 79-2 USTC 9612.
179. Long v. U.S., 652 F.2d 675 (6th Cir. 1981), 48 AFTR2d 81-5517, 81-2 USTC 9537, *rev'g* (W.D. Tenn. 1979), 44 AFTR2d 79-5888, 79-2 USTC 9612.
180. Erwin W. Gorton, T.C. Memo Dec. (Jan. 30, 1985).
181. Siller Brothers, Inc., 89 T.C. No. 33 (1987).
182. Rev. Rul. 65-118, 1965-1 C.B. 30; Bryant v. Comm'r, 399 F.2d 800 (5th Cir. 1968), 22 AFTR2d 5375, 68-2 USTC 9521.

co-owners of oil and gas properties elect out of the partnership provisions of Subchapter K. In addition, the IRS has ruled[183] that oil and gas properties are partnership properties even when the taxpayers own the properties in undivided interests as tenants in common and elect to be excluded from the partnership provisions. Accordingly, the IRS did not allow a buyer of an undivided interest to claim investment tax credit on the "used" property so acquired because the "partnership" was the user of the property both before and after the acquisition. Yet, the seller was required to recapture his investment tax credit because he sold more than one-third of his ownership interest.[184]

Distributions in partial liquidation of a legal partnership may meet all four conditions set out in the regulations so that the taxpayer will not have to recapture investment tax credit. If the partner's basis in his partnership interest exceeds the basis to the partnership of assets distributed, the partnership's basis becomes the partner's basis.[185] Hence, the fourth requirement may be met.[186]

The IRS may question whether the distribution of one or more working interests in oil and gas leases in partial liquidation meets the third test: that substantially all the assets necessary to conduct the trade or business are transferred.[187] The ownership and operation of a single working interest can be considered sufficient to permit the partner to conduct the trade or business. The IRS's interpretation of this aspect of the regulation remains unclear.

Case 79
Computation of Cost Depletion in General

> Operator A, who is on the accrual basis of accounting, owns an oil and gas lease for which he paid a bonus of $8,000 to the landowner. Operator A also spent $1,000 for title work, $500,000 for intangible drilling and development costs and $200,000 for lease and well equipment for the first well, which is a producer. He estimates the recoverable oil reserves applicable to the working interest to be 150,000 barrels, of which 20,000 barrels are sold for $400,000 during the first year. Operating and other expenses on or attributable to the property were $150,000. Pursuant to a prior election, Operator A expenses the intangible drilling and development costs for tax purposes.

The total basis of Operator A's depletable property is computed as follows:

Bonus paid to lessor	$8,000
Title work	1,000
	$9,000

Operator A is entitled only to cost depletion in the first year because the deduction of intangible drilling and development costs and other expenses causes a net loss from the property, thereby precluding the allowance of percentage depletion.[188] The first step in calculating cost depletion is to determine the depletion unit (cost per barrel) by dividing the total unrecovered depletable cost by the estimated recoverable barrels of oil. The allowance for cost depletion is the depletion unit multiplied by the total

183. Rev. Rul. 74-64, 1974-1 C.B. 12.
184. Reg. Sec. 1.47-6(a)(2).
185. I.R.C. Sec. 732(a).
186. Reg. Sec. 1.47-3(f)(1)(ii)(d).
187. Reg. Sec. 1.47-3(f)(1)(ii)(c).
188. I.R.C. Sec. 613(a).

barrels sold.[189] *(For computation of depletion if income is reported on the cash basis, see Case 85.)* Reduced to a formula, the calculation is as follows:

$$\frac{\text{Unrecovered depletable costs}}{\text{Estimated recoverable reserves at beginning of year}} \times \text{Barrels sold} = \text{Cost depletion}$$

$$\frac{\$9{,}000}{150{,}000} \times 20{,}000 = \$1{,}200$$

In the case of natural gas, the customary unit for measuring either reserves or production is MCF (thousand cubic feet).

Another method often used multiplies the unrecovered depletable cost by the percentage of estimated recoverable reserves sold during the year. This method may be expressed by the following formula:

$$\frac{\text{Barrels sold}}{\text{Estimated recoverable reserves at beginning of year}} \times \text{Unrecovered depletable cost} = \text{Cost depletion}$$

$$\frac{20{,}000}{150{,}000} \times \$9{,}000 = \$1{,}200$$

Both methods will result in the same depletion allowance.

Case 80
Adjustment of Depletable Cost for Prior Years' Depletion

Operator A owns a lease in which he has an unadjusted tax basis of $4,500. In the first year, he claims cost depletion of $600, and, in the second year, he claims percentage depletion of $5,500.

The basis for computing cost depletion is the basis of the property,[190] reduced by the higher of: (1) the amount of depletion allowed to the extent the deduction reduces the taxpayer's income taxes or (2) the amount of depletion allowable.[191] Operator A has no remaining tax basis for depletion after the second year because the original cost of $4,500 was fully recovered by cost depletion of $600 for the first year and by percentage depletion of $5,500 for the second year. His depletable tax basis in the lease is not reduced below zero, even though he deducts percentage depletion in excess of the cost of the lease. The $1,600 ($5,500 − $3,900) excess of percentage depletion allowed for the second year over the adjusted tax basis of the property ($4,500 − $600) is a tax preference item that may be subject to the alternative minimum tax.

Case 81
Subsequent Investment When Prior Years' Depletion Exceeds Original Cost

Operator A has deducted $20,000 of percentage depletion in excess of his tax basis in an oil and gas lease. He employs a seismograph crew to explore an undeveloped portion of the lease. The cost of this geophysical work is $30,000, all of which Operator A must capitalize as leasehold cost.

---

189. Reg. Sec. 1.611-2(a).
190. I.R.C. Sec. 612.
191. I.R.C. Sec. 1016(a)(2); Granger v. U.S. (S.D. Cal. 1958), 3 AFTR2d 361, 59-1 USTC 9151; Cranberry Improvement Co. v. Smith, 222 F.2d 706 (3d Cir. 1955), 47 AFTR 929, 55-1 USTC 9457.

The excess of percentage depletion over the cost or other basis of one property does not reduce the basis for cost depletion on other properties, nor does it reduce the basis for computing depreciation. The Internal Revenue Service, however, has ruled that the excess does reduce the recoverable depletable cost of subsequent capital additions to the same property.[192] Under this ruling, after the geophysical work is completed, Operator A's tax basis in the lease for cost depletion is $10,000. *(See Case 6 for a discussion of when the cost of geophysical work on an existing lease must be capitalized.)*

The absence of any cost or other basis in a property does not affect the allowance of percentage depletion.[193] Moreover, the basis for computing gain on disposition of a property does not become a negative amount. If the amount of depletion previously allowed exceeds the sum of the original cost and the cost of subsequent additions, the adjusted basis is zero.[194]

If an operator acquires an additional working interest in a lease on which previously deducted percentage depletion exceeds the tax basis of his original interest, he may be able to avoid offsetting the excess depletion against the acquisition cost of the additional working interest by making a separate property election.[195] *(See Case 58.)* A separate property election in this instance also may be necessary to preserve percentage depletion on the original working interest held by the operator in the leasehold.[196]

Case 82
Revision of Estimated Recoverable Reserves

Operator A is the owner of an oil and gas lease on which he has drilled a productive oil well. At the end of the first year, geological reports indicate reserves of 475,000 barrels of recoverable oil underlying the lease. Operator A produced and sold 25,000 barrels in the first year. His original depletable cost in the lease is $10,525, and he claims $525 of cost depletion the first year, leaving an unrecovered tax basis of $10,000. In the second year, Operator A drills two additional productive wells on the lease and sells a total of 50,000 barrels of oil from all the wells. At the end of the second year, a revised geological report indicates estimated reserves of 950,000 barrels.

The depletion unit is calculated on the basis of the estimated reserves at the end of the year plus the oil sold during the year.[197] The cost depletion on this property for the second year will be $500, calculated as follows:

$$\frac{\$10{,}000}{950{,}000 + 50{,}000} \times 50{,}000 = \$500$$

If operations or development lead to a materially different estimate of remaining recoverable reserves, the revised estimate must be used to compute cost depletion.[198] As long as the taxpayer made the previous estimate of recoverable reserves on the best information then obtainable, the courts have held that he may not go back and revise

192. Rev. Rul. 74-451, 1976-2 C.B. 330.
193. Reg. Sec. 1.611-2(b)(2).
194. Rev. Rul. 75-451, 1975-2 C.B. 330.
195. I.R.C. Sec. 614(b)(2); IRS Letter Ruling 7743002 (Technical Advice Memorandum).
196. I.R.C. Sec. 613A(c)(9)(A).
197. Reg. Sec. 1.611-2(a)(3).
198. Reg. Sec. 1.611-2(c)(2); Wylie v. U.S., 281 F. Supp. 180 (N.D. Tex. 1968), 21 AFTR2d 972, 68-1 USTC 9287.

the depletion unit for any year before the reserve estimate was revised.[199] It does not matter that he later determines the original estimate was materially wrong.[200]

A taxpayer must use the revised estimate for the year in which he taps a new formation or some other event occurs to revise the previous estimate.[201] He may not defer the change until the year in which an engineer actually determines the revised estimate. The estimates should include only the reserves available for commercial production, excluding reserves for which recovery is not feasible.[202] However, the Internal Revenue Service (IRS) will not permit a taxpayer to reduce the total estimated recoverable reserves due to speculative factors, such as remoteness of the time of production, or speculative increases in recovery costs.[203] If it is known that the wells will produce more oil than underlies the lease because of a water drive, the estimated reserves should include the oil that will be drained from the adjacent areas.[204]

In practice, revisions of estimated recoverable reserves often are applied by IRS engineers to all years still open under the statute of limitations. Often, it is difficult for the taxpayer to prove the year in which the facts occurred resulting in the reserve revision. If a question arises as to the proper allowance for depreciation or depletion, the burden of proof is on the taxpayer to show that the IRS is in error.[205] For this reason, the IRS engineers' determination typically will prevail unless the taxpayer's facts clearly indicate the year when a reserve adjustment should be made.

Case 83
Cost Depletion When Royalty and Production Payments Are Retained on a Lease of Property

> In 1987, Operator A obtains a lease for which he pays a $10,000 bonus to Lessor R. Lessor R reserves a one-eighth royalty and an additional sum of $600,000 payable solely out of one-fourth of seven-eighths of the first oil or gas produced. Operator A also pays legal fees and commissions of $4,000. After completion of the development program, the estimated reserves are 560,000 barrels. In addition, payments in 1987 to Lessor R applied against the retained production payment amount to $367,500. Because of drilling results on adjacent acreage, it is reasonably estimated that the lease contains sufficient reserves (after completion of the development program) to cover the production payment retained by Lessor R.

A lessee must treat a production payment retained by a lessor in a leasing transaction as a bonus payable to the lessor in installments.[206] Accordingly, in 1987, Operator A must include in his gross income the $367,500 that he pays to Lessor R and applies against the production payment. He also must capitalize that same amount as a cost of acquiring the lease.[207] *(See Case 230 on computation of the windfall profit tax net*

199. Kehota Mining Co. v. Lewellyn, 30 F.2d 817 (3d Cir. 1929), 7 AFTR 8506, 1929 CCH D-9110, *aff'g* 28 F.2d 995 (W.D. Pa. 1928), 7 AFTR 8270, 1 USTC 320; Petit Anse Co. v. Comm'r, 155 F.2d 797 (5th Cir. 1946) 34 AFTR 1415, 46-1 USTC 9260; Ah Pah Redwood Co. v. Comm'r, 251 F.2d 163 (9th Cir. 1957), 1 AFTR2d 456, 58-1 USTC 9153.
200. McCahill v. Helvering, 75 F.2d 725 (8th Cir. 1935), 15 AFTR 304, 35-1 USTC 9100.
201. Big Four Oil & Gas Co. v. Comm'r, 83 F.2d 891 (3d Cir. 1936), 17 AFTR 1209, 36-1 USTC 9210; Wylie; Reg. Sec. 1.611-2(c)(2).
202. Black Gold Petroleum Co., T.C. Memo Dec. (Mar. 21, 1944).
203. Rev. Rul. 67-157, 1967-1 C.B. 154.
204. J.B. Cage, T.C. Memo Dec. (Sept. 28, 1950).
205. Reinecke v. Spalding, 280 U.S. 227 (1930), 8 AFTR 10255, 2 USTC 452.
206. I.R.C. Sec. 636(c).
207. Reg. Sec. 1.636-2(a).

income limitation when a property is burdened by a production payment.) Therefore, Operator A's depletable basis in the lease at December 31, 1987, is as follows:

Lease bonus	$ 10,000
Legal fees and commissions	4,000
Payments to Lessor R in satisfaction of production payment	367,500
Depletable basis	$381,500

The current production and estimated recoverable reserves attributable to the working interest are 49,000 and 490,000 barrels, respectively. Thus, Operator A's cost depletion with respect to the property is $38,150.

$$\frac{49,000}{490,000} \times \$381,500 = \$38,150$$

In addition, as Operator A makes payments to Lessor R in 1988 and subsequent years in satisfaction of the production payment, he must capitalize each payment and add the amount he pays to his adjusted basis of the property to compute cost depletion for that year and for other purposes.[208]

If the production payment Lessor R retains includes a secondary amount equivalent to interest (for example, an amount equivalent to interest at 10% per annum on the outstanding primary amount), Operator A will have to capitalize as cost of the lease the total payments made to Lessor R to discharge both the primary amount and the interest element of the production payment. These amounts also should be included in Operator A's gross income.[209]

The regulations concerning the computation of cost depletion are not consistent with regulations concerning the computation of the "bonus exclusion" used to determine gross income subject to the percentage depletion allowance. When computing his share of income subject to the percentage depletion allowance, Operator A is to use the entire amount of the production payment ($600,000) to compute the pro-rata portion he must exclude from gross income.[210] *(See Case 88.)* In computing cost depletion, Operator A should use only the amount actually paid to date ($367,500). He may be able, by following a Supreme Court decision,[211] to increase the amount of cost depletion available for 1987. Retention of a production payment in a leasing transaction is essentially the same as the creation of an indebtedness secured only by the property. Following the court decision, Operator A will consider the total production payment, paid and payable, as the basis for computing cost depletion. In that case, Operator A's cost depletion will be $61,400 (10% × ($600,000 + $10,000 + $4,000)).

Because Lessor R retained the production payment in a leasing transaction, it constitutes an economic interest and he is entitled to claim depletion on the receipt of the $367,500.[212] Lessor R also can deduct depletion for the $10,000 bonus received in 1987. However, it is not clear whether amounts received by Lessor R that exceed his one-eighth royalty share of production qualify for percentage depletion. The statute provides that gross income for purposes of computing percentage depletion does not include any lease bonus, advance royalty or other amount payable without regard to

208. Reg. Sec. 1.636-2(c).
209. Reg. Sec. 1.636-2(a).
210. Reg. Sec. 1.613-2(c)(5)(ii), Example 2.
211. Crane v. Comm'r, 331 U.S. 1 (1947), 35 AFTR 776, 47-1 USTC 9217.
212. Reg. Sec. 1.636-2(b).

production for amounts accrued or received after August 16, 1986.[213] Lessor R's gross income for depletion purposes may include the gross receipts of the lease bonus, the royalty and the production payment to the extent the $10,000 and the $367,500 payments do not exceed current production from the property.[214] Arguably, these payments are payable with regard to production and may constitute depletable gross income. The Internal Revenue Service (IRS) may contend that amounts received in excess of Lessor R's one-eighth share of production constitute "lease bonuses" or "advance royalties" and, therefore, do not qualify for percentage depletion. This determination must await future clarification and explanation of the statute. Amounts received for the bonus and for the production payment that do not qualify for percentage depletion continue to qualify for cost depletion. *(See Case 98 for a discussion of depletion of lease bonuses.)*

Operator A must exclude payments attributable to the royalty from his gross income because these payments are depletable gross income to Lessor R. As under prior law, Operator A may be required to exclude from his depletable income all or a portion of both the $10,000 lease bonus and the $600,000 production payment that is depletable income to Lessor R.[215] Under the argument made above, payments to Lessor R that do not exceed the total production from the property may constitute royalties, which constitute depletable income for percentage depletion purposes. If they are royalties, Operator A is required to exclude from his depletable income the payments made under the lease bonus and the production payment that are depletable to Lessor R.[216] However, since payments to Lessor R that are in excess of his one-eighth share of production may be treated as lease bonus, Operator A may be required to exclude from his annual depletable gross income a pro-rata share of the bonus paid to Lessor R.[217]

Based on court cases and IRS pronouncements, the original purpose underlying this "bonus exclusion rule" was to ensure that lease bonus payments were not counted twice in computing percentage depletion.[218] The IRS has held that if the lessor who receives a lease bonus is not allowed the percentage depletion deduction on the bonus, the lessee must still exclude the income that is allocable to the bonus.[219] Arguably, based on the original purpose of the "bonus exclusion rule," the rule should not be applied if the lessor is not entitled to percentage depletion on the lease bonus. Therefore, since lease bonuses recognized as income after August 16, 1986, no longer qualify for percentage depletion, it appears to be inappropriate to continue to follow the "bonus exclusion rule" on these bonuses. It is hoped that this apparent inconsistency will be rectified by a technical correction or otherwise modified by an administrative pronouncement from the Treasury. *(See Cases 88 and 221.)*

The facts of this case state that it is reasonably estimated that the nonproducing lease contains sufficient reserves to cover the retained production payment because of drilling results on adjacent acreages. Recently, the IRS ruled that a production payment payable from a nonproducing lease was in substance a royalty interest where the only basis for expecting the presence of oil and gas was geological and geophysical studies and there were no successful exploratory wells on the leased area or adjacent

213. I.R.C. Sec. 613A(d)(5).
214. Reg. Sec. 1.612-3(b)(1); Rev. Rul. 72-165, 1972-1 C.B. 177.
215. Reg. Sec. 1.613-2(c)(5)(i); Reg. Sec. 1.613-2(c)(5)(ii).
216. Reg. Sec. 1.613-2(c)(5)(i).
217. Reg. Sec. 1.613-2(c)(5)(ii).
218. Quintana Petroleum Co. v. Comm'r, 143 F.2d 588 (5th Cir. 1944), 32 AFTR 1031, 44-2 USTC 9380; Helvering v. Twin Bell Oil Syndicate, 293 U.S. 312 (1934), 14 AFTR 712, 35-1 USTC 9014; Rev. Rul. 81-266, 1981-2 C.B. 139.
219. Rev. Rul. 81-266, 1981-2 C.B. 139; Murphy Oil Corp. v. U.S., 337 F.2d 677 (8th Cir. 1964), 14 AFTR2d 5835, 64-2 USTC 9810.

tracts.[220] If the facts of this case had been the same as in this recent ruling, presumably the IRS's position would be that the retained production payment should be treated as a retained royalty and Operator A would have excluded from income the $367,500 cash payments applied against the so-called production payment. However, the correctness of this ruling may be subject to question. *(See Case 143 for a further discussion of the ruling.)*

(See Case 88 for a discussion of the potential effects of the windfall profit tax attributable to a production payment retained in a leasing transaction.)

Case 84
Cost Depletion When Properties Are Purchased With Noninterest-Bearing Installment Notes

> **In January 1987, Operator A acquired from Individual R a fully developed gas lease for a consideration of $3 million, payable in installments of $300,000 annually for 10 years. The consideration is represented by noninterest-bearing notes secured by the property and for which Operator A has personal liability. The lease is estimated to have recoverable reserves of 6 million MCF.**

Because the notes do not bear an adequate rate of interest, Operator A must allocate the $3 million consideration between imputed interest (also referred to as original-issue discount or OID) and principal.[221] The principal portion is based on the present value of all payments due under the contract, using a discount rate equal to the applicable federal rate (AFR). The AFR for a note payable over 10 years is the federal long-term rate[222] based on compounding consistent with the accrual period.[223] For transactions occurring after June 30, 1985, the AFR is the lowest AFR (determined by the Treasury based on average market yields) in effect for any month in the three-calendar-month period ending with the first calendar month in which there is a binding contract in writing for the sale or exchange of property. The federal long-term rate for January of 1987 with annual compounding is 7.41%.[224] Once calculated, the principal portion must be allocated between leasehold cost and lease and well equipment costs based on their relative fair market values. In this case the principal portion of the consideration is calculated to be $2,067,713. If the sales price had not exceeded $250,000,[225] the computation of the imputed interest would have been made under a different set of rules but with similar results.[226] The imputed interest (or OID) is deductible as interest expense by Operator A and is treated as interest income by Individual R. The annual amount of interest expense to Operator A and interest income to Individual R is the sum of the daily portions of OID for each day of each tax year. The daily portion is each day's ratable portion of the increase in the adjusted issue price during the accrual period. This increase is the excess of: (1) the adjusted issue price (as adjusted for prior accrual periods) multiplied by the yield to maturity over (2) the sum of amounts payable as interest during the accrual period.[227] *(See Case 138 for a more detailed discussion of the original-issue discount rules.)*

---

220. Rev. Rul. 86-119, 1986-41, I.R.B. 8.
221. I.R.C. Sec. 1274.
222. I.R.C. Sec. 1274(d).
223. I.R.C. Sec. 1274(b)(2)(B).
224. Rev. Rul. 86-158, 1986-52 I.R.B. 16.
225. I.R.C. Sec. 1274(c)(3)(C).
226. I.R.C. Sec. 483.
227. I.R.C. Sec. 1272(a).

Operator A will compute cost depletion by multiplying each year's gas sales by the unit cost per MCF. Assuming that $300,000 is allocable to depreciable equipment, the unit cost per MCF is determined by dividing $1,767,713 (the amount of the total obligation allocated to leasehold cost) by the total estimated recoverable reserves of 6 million MCF, thus obtaining a unit cost expressed in cents per MCF.[228] *(See Cases 69 and 70 for a discussion of depreciation methods.)*

Any amount recharacterized as interest also reduces the total sales price and contract price for purposes of calculating Individual R's gain.

The complexities involved in accounting for imputed interest can be avoided by providing for interest at least equal to the AFR and by providing that such interest is to be paid currently on an unconditional basis. The discount rate for calculating OID or unstated interest shall not exceed 9% if the principal amount of the debt does not exceed $2,800,000, and it was not given as consideration for new Section 38 property within the meaning of Section 48(b). In addition, if the stated principal amount of the debt is less than $2 million, under certain circumstances taxpayers can elect to report the imputed interest on a cash basis.[229]

Because this property was proven at the date of transfer, Operator A is not entitled to percentage depletion with respect to the property. *(See Case 108.)*

Case 85
Cost Depletion Under the Cash Basis of Accounting

> **Operator A owns a lease with a depletable cost of $10,000. The oil reserves attributable to Operator A's interest are estimated at 200,000 barrels. In the first year, 30,000 barrels of Operator A's oil are produced, of which 25,000 barrels are sold. The remainder is retained in Operator A's storage tanks. Payment for December runs of 4,000 barrels is received in January of the next year. Operator A files his tax returns on a calendar-year basis and uses the cash basis of accounting.**

Operator A computes cost depletion with reference only to that portion of the production for which he receives payment during the year (21,000 barrels). This treatment is proper for the cash basis of accounting. The depletion unit is $.05 per barrel, determined by dividing the cost of $10,000 by the estimated recoverable reserves of 200,000 barrels. This unit is multiplied by the 21,000 barrels for which payment was received to obtain allowable cost depletion.[230] The 4,000 barrels for which payment was not received and the 5,000 barrels in storage tanks will be subject to cost depletion in a succeeding period when Operator A receives payments from the purchaser.

The owner of an oil and gas lease may use the cash basis of accounting for tax purposes because oil stored in lease tanks generally is not considered to be a material income-determining factor. Oil stored in lease tanks is disregarded in computing depletable gross income of a cash-basis taxpayer. The Tax Reform Act of 1986 generally requires regular (subchapter C) corporations, partnerships that have a C corporation as a partner and tax shelters to use the accrual method of accounting.[231]

228. Reg. Sec. 1.611-2(a)(1).
229. I.R.C. Sec. 1274A(c).
230. Reg. Sec. 1.611-2(a)(2)(i); National Oil & Gas Co., 6 B.T.A. 399 (1927).
231. I.R.C. Sec. 448(a).

An exception to the accrual method requirement is provided for entities that are not tax shelters and have average annual gross receipts of less than $5 million.[232]

The principle that depletion is allowable in the same year as that in which income is returned also applies to a royalty owner reporting income on the cash method of accounting.[233]

A taxpayer reporting income on the accrual method of accounting computes depletion using the number of barrels of oil sold. *(See Case 79.)*

(See Case 94 for a discussion of the computation of percentage depletion under the independent-producer and royalty-owner provisions for a cash-basis taxpayer.)

Case 86
Cost Depletion of Production Payment Pledged for Development

> Operator A acquires a lease from Lessor R in 1987 for a $5,000 bonus and a one-eighth royalty, but he requires funds to drill a test well on the property. Investor L advances $500,000, which Operator A pledges to use for drilling the test well. Operator A agrees to pay Investor L the sum of $900,000 out of three-fourths of the first oil and gas produced (net of severance and windfall profit tax). He also agrees to return to Investor L any portion of the money not expended in the drilling of the well, with the production payment being reduced proportionately. After completion of the development program, the estimated reserves applicable to the working interest are 360,000 barrels of oil. The lease is a tier-3 property for purposes of the windfall profit tax.
>
> In 1987, the production attributable to the working interest and the production payment was 10,000 barrels, which were sold for $30 a barrel net (after production or severance taxes and windfall profit tax). (The $30 price of oil net of taxes is used to facilitate discussion of the windfall profit tax aspects of this case.) The parties agree that Investor L will reduce the balance of the production payment by any windfall profit tax refund he receives. It is reasonably estimated that the reserves committed to the lease are sufficient to discharge fully the production payment before the end of the property's productive life.

Under the general rule, a production payment carved out of a mineral property will be treated as a mortgage loan on the property.[234] However, an exception to this rule provides that a production payment carved out of a mineral property for exploration or development of the property will qualify as an economic interest in the property and will not be subject to mortgage loan treatment.[235] In this situation, the interest assigned to Investor L constitutes a production payment pledged for the exploration and development of the property. Because Investor L's interest constitutes an economic interest, he is treated as a producer for purposes of the windfall profit tax.[236] *(See Case 230.)* Assuming that Operator A expends the entire proceeds to explore and develop the property, Investor L's cost basis in the production payment is $500,000. In the first year, Investor L realizes depletable gross income of $225,000 (¾ × 10,000 × $30)

232. I.R.C. Sec. 448(b)(3).
233. R. M. Waggoner, 5 B.T.A. 1191 (1927); Rev. Rul. 68-565, 1968-2 C.B. 263.
234. I.R.C. Sec. 636(a).
235. I.R.C. Sec. 636(a); Reg. Sec. 1.636-1(b).
236. I.R.C. Sec. 4986(b); I.R.C. Sec. 4996(a)(1)(A).

plus the amount of any severance and windfall profit taxes that represent his liability. *(See Case 89 and the comment below concerning the possible effects of these taxes attributable to the production payment.)*

Investor L's cost basis in the production payment is high in relation to the total amount of income he expects to receive, so cost depletion probably will exceed percentage depletion. Because the production payment agreement does not provide for an amount equivalent to interest, Investor L should compute cost depletion by using the "sum-of-the-dollars" method. The method chosen in the first year must be used consistently over the life of the production payment unless permission to change methods is obtained from the Internal Revenue Service (IRS).[237]

Cost depletion using the "sum-of-the-dollars" method is computed by multiplying the remaining tax basis of the production payment at the end of the year (before adjustment for depletion for the current year) by a fraction, the numerator of which is the total amount of the receipts for the year and the denominator of which is the total expected amount remaining to be received as of the beginning of the year. Cost depletion allowable to Investor L in 1987 using this method is $125,000, computed as follows:

$$\frac{\$225,000}{\$900,000} \times \$500,000 = \$125,000$$

Assuming that $200,000 is received in 1988, cost depletion allowable to Investor L in that year will be:

$$\frac{\$200,000}{\$900,000 - \$225,000} \times (\$500,000 - \$125,000) = \$111,111$$

If subsequent operations or events indicate that the original estimate of gross receipts is erroneous, the depletion computation for subsequent years should be adjusted to reflect the revised estimate. If the production payment agreement provided for the payment of interest, Investor L could elect to compute cost depletion by either the "decline-in-principal" method or the "sum-of-the-dollars" method. The method chosen in the first year must be used consistently over the life of the production payment unless permission to change methods is obtained from the IRS.

Assume Investor L pays Operator A $50,000 and receives a production payment of $50,000 plus 15% interest. If Investor L uses the "decline-in-principal" method, he will compute cost depletion by applying first the payments to interest and the remainder to principal as if the production payment is a loan on the property. Cost depletion for the year then will be the reduction in the principal amount remaining.

When cost depletion is calculated under the "sum-of-the-dollars" method for an interest-bearing production payment, the amount of interest remaining to be received as of the beginning of each year must be estimated. This amount is added to the denominator of the fraction, which is multiplied by the remaining tax basis of the production payment as discussed above. The numerator of this fraction will include amounts of both interest and principal received on the production payment during the year.

237. Rev. Rul. 65-10, 1965-1 C.B. 254.

If a production payment is expressed in terms of units to be recovered (barrels (bbls.) or MCF), cost depletion should be computed by multiplying the unrecovered basis by a fraction, the numerator of which is the total units sold during the year applicable to the production payment and the denominator of which is the total estimated recoverable units applicable to the production payment at the beginning of the year.

The $500,000 Operator A receives as consideration for the assignment of the production payment is not taxable income to him but is applied to reduce the cost of drilling the well. *(See Case 150.)* The amount paid to Investor L in satisfaction of the production payment, including interest, if any, is excluded from Operator A's income.

Investor L may not be willing to enter into the production payment arrangement unless he is reimbursed for his severance and windfall profit tax associated with the payment in addition to receiving his $900,000. No authoritative pronouncements have been made as to how any such reimbursements (i.e., the payments of Investor L's taxes) are treated by either Investor L or Operator A in a production payment arrangement. It appears that these reimbursements may be treated as additional amounts due under the production payment. If so, the reimbursements should be excluded from Operator A's depletable gross income (similar to the interest element of the production payment). Investor L should include the reimbursements in his depletable gross income and should be entitled to deduct the taxes. Resolution of this issue must await further developments in this area. *(See Case 88 regarding similar arrangements for royalties; Case 230 concerning Operator A's and Investor L's computation of the windfall profit tax net income limitation; and Case 151 concerning a production payment pledged for development used for the purchase of equipment.)*

Case 87
Computation of Percentage Depletion in General

Operator A, who is on the accrual basis of accounting, owns a producing U.S. oil and gas lease for which he originally paid $29,000 as a bonus and $1,000 for title work. The recoverable reserves under the lease applicable to the working interest have been estimated at 94,000 barrels. During 1987, 9,400 barrels attributable to the working interest are produced and sold at $20 per barrel. The purchaser deducts transportation charges of $.25 per barrel and production taxes of $1.25 per barrel, remitting a net amount of $173,900. Depreciation for the year amounts to $6,000. The purchaser pays the royalty directly to Lessor R. The operating and overhead expenses and intangible drilling and development costs (IDC) attributable to the property amount to $150,000.

Gross income from the property for purposes of depletion is the value of the oil or gas in the immediate vicinity of the well.[238] Therefore, to arrive at gross income for computing percentage depletion, Operator A must subtract the transportation charges, but not the production taxes, from the total sales value. Similarly, if the windfall profit tax had been applicable, it would be deducted as an expense and not treated as a reduction of gross income.

Operator A also must reduce gross income from the property by an allocable portion of the bonus of $29,000.[239] He computes this reduction by multiplying the bonus by

238. Reg. Sec. 1.613-3(a).
239. Reg. Sec. 1.613-2(c)(5)(ii).

the ratio of the lessee's production sold during the tax year to the total estimated reserves recoverable by the lessee. For example:

$$\frac{\$\ 9,400}{\$94,000} \times \$29,000 = \$2,900$$

The lessor is entitled to claim cost depletion if applicable with respect to the lease bonus he receives; therefore, this reduction serves to prevent duplicating "depletable gross income from the property" by the amount of the lease bonus. *(See Case 98 for a discussion of depletion on lease bonus income.)* However, the Internal Revenue Service (IRS) will not distinguish between a bonus paid to a taxable lessor versus a bonus paid to a governmental or other nontaxable organization.[240] Since percentage depletion on lease bonuses payable without regard to production from the property is eliminated by the Tax Reform Act of 1986 *(see Case 98)*, the bonus exclusion rule should not equitably apply.

In computing his taxable income, Operator A should not exclude or deduct from his gross income the reduction attributable to the bonus payment.[241]

Following the treatment outlined above, Operator A determines his gross depletable income from the property as follows (the royalty is paid directly to the landowner by the purchaser of the oil):

Sale of 9,400 barrels at $20 per barrel	$188,000
Less: Transportation at $.25 per barrel	(2,350)
Gross income at the well	$185,650
Less: Allocable portion of bonus	
$\frac{9,400}{94,000} \times \$29,000$	(2,900)
Gross income for depletion	$182,750
15% of gross income	$ 27,413

(See Case 94 for percentage depletion rates.)

Gross income for purposes of computing percentage depletion includes only the income received or accrued from oil sold or transported off the lease; the determination of gross income should disregard variations in inventories of oil on the lease. A royalty owner is not allowed the depletion deduction on oil or gas used as fuel in the lease operations if the lease agreements provide that he is not to be compensated for that oil or gas.[242]

Although the 1987 allowance for percentage depletion is 15% of gross depletable income from each unit of property, it may not exceed 50% of the taxable income (before depletion) from each property.[243] The IRS has ruled that the exclusion of the bonus from gross income applies both in the determination of gross income for the 15% calculation and the determination of taxable income from the property for purposes of the 50% limitation.[244] This appears to be an extreme interpretation by the IRS because the bonus exclusion is not a deduction for determining taxable income for

240. Murphy Oil Corp. v. U.S., 337 F.2d 677 (8th Cir. 1964), 14 AFTR2d 5835, 64-2 USTC 9810.
241. Reg. Sec. 1.613-2(c)(5)(ii); Shamrock Oil and Gas Corp. v. Comm'r, 346 F.2d 377 (5th Cir. 1965), 15 AFTR2d 1168, 65-2 USTC 9476.
242. Le Danois Land & Stone Co. v. Comm'r, 215 F.2d 475 (5th Cir. 1954), 46 AFTR 520, 54-2 USTC 9573.
243. I.R.C. Sec. 613(a).
244. Rev. Rul. 79-73, 1979-1 C.B. 218.

the year. The IRS's position in this regard is inconsistent with its position that net income is not reduced by the bonus exclusion for purposes of the windfall profit tax 90% net income limitation.[245] In accordance with the IRS's interpretation, however, Operator A's taxable income from the property is computed as follows:

Sales value		$188,000
Less: Transportation		(2,350)
Gross income at the well		$185,650
Less: Allocable portion of bonus		(2,900)
Gross income for depletion		$182,750
Less:		
Depreciation	$ 6,000	
Production taxes	11,750	
Windfall profit tax	0	
Expenses	150,000	(167,750)
Taxable income from the property		$ 15,000
50% of taxable income from the property		$ 7,500

Because 50% of the taxable income from the property ($7,500) is less than 15% of gross income ($27,413), the net income limitation limits the percentage depletion allowance to $7,500. Percentage depletion is greater than cost depletion in this year (cost depletion is $3,000); therefore, Operator A should claim depletion in the amount of $7,500.[246]

This case assumes that Operator A is an independent producer of oil and gas and that his average daily production in 1987 does not exceed 1,000 barrels *(see Case 96)*; that the property was not proven when he purchased it *(see Case 108)*; and that Operator A's percentage depletion deduction does not exceed the overall 65% of taxable income limitation. *(See Cases 115, 116 and 117.)*

Since percentage depletion of $7,500 does not exceed the unrecovered tax basis in the property of $30,000, such depletion is not a tax preference item. If the allowable percentage depletion had been $32,000 for example, the $2,000 of depletion in excess of the $30,000 would have been a tax preference item subject to the alternative minimum tax. A portion of the intangible drilling and development costs may also be treated as a tax preference item. *(See Cases 174 and 175.)*

Individuals and certain closely held corporations engaged in oil and gas activities can deduct a loss from those activities only up to the aggregate amount each taxpayer has "at risk" with respect to those activities at the close of the tax year.[247] *(See Case 33 for a discussion of the "at-risk" provisions.)* However, percentage depletion in excess of the basis of the property subject to depletion does not reduce a taxpayer's amount "at risk."[248]

If the taxpayer does not sell the oil or gas in the immediate vicinity of the well but manufactures or converts the oil or gas into a refined product prior to sale, the value of the production in the immediate vicinity of the well is a question of fact and must be determined. That value is assumed to be the equivalent of the representative market or field price of the oil or gas before conversion or transportation.[249]

245. IRS Letter Ruling 8543005 (Technical Advice Memorandum); G.C.M. 39423.
246. Reg. Sec. 1.613-1.
247. I.R.C. Sec. 465(a)(1).
248. Prop. Reg. Sec. 1.465-45(d).
249. Reg. Sec. 1.613-3(a).

Case 88
Gross Income from Property With Production Payment and Royalty Outstanding

> In October 1987, Operator A pays a $20,000 bonus to Lessor R for Lease B in which the lessor retains, in addition to a one-eighth royalty, an $800,000 production payment payable out of one-fourth of the working interest income (net of severance and windfall profit tax (WPT)). Production is found on the lease, and the recoverable reserves under the lease are estimated to be 560,000 barrels of oil. Gross production for the year amounts to 56,000 barrels. Operator A sells the production for $30 a barrel (before WPT). The parties agree that Lessor R will reduce the balance of the production payment by the amount of any refund of WPT he receives.
>
> Lease B is a tier-1 property for purposes of the windfall profit tax. The state in which Lease B is located does not impose a severance or production tax. The adjusted base price (adjusted for inflation) of the oil is $18.72. The first purchaser pays Lessor R directly for his royalty interest. Operator A computes and pays the amount owing to Lessor R on the production payment on an annual basis at the end of the calendar year. Operator A's average daily production is 700 barrels a day in 1987.
>
> Operator A is not engaged in retailing or refining activities and qualifies for percentage depletion under the independent-producer and royalty-owner exemption.
>
> It was reasonably estimated at the time the lease was executed that there would be sufficient reserves (after completion of the development program) to cover the production payment retained by Lessor R.
>
> (The $30-per-barrel price for oil and the $18.72 adjusted base price are used to facilitate discussion of the WPT aspects of this case.)

Operator A's gross income (the amount applicable to his working interest) is determined by excluding the gross revenues attributable to Lessor R's royalty interest (56,000 × ⅛ × $30, or $210,000).[250] Lessor R is responsible for the royalty share of the WPT ($210,000 − (⅛ × 56,000 × $18.72) × .70, or $55,272). Lessor R also is subject to the windfall profit tax on the production payment because it is treated as an economic interest.[251] *(See Case 230.)* Lessor R is not entitled to the lower WPT rates (applicable to independent producers) on his share of the production (royalty and production payment) because these interests are not working interests.[252] *(See Case 216.)*

250. I.R.C. Sec. 613(a); Reg. Sec. 1.613-2(c)(5).
251. I.R.C. Sec. 636(c); Reg. Sec. 1.636-2(b); I.R.C. Sec. 4986(b); I.R.C. Sec. 4996(a)(1)(A); Reg. Sec. 51.4996-1(b)(1).
252. I.R.C. Sec. 4992(d)(1)(D); I.R.C. Sec. 4992(d)(2)(A).

Operator A's payment to Lessor R with respect to the retained production payment is computed as follows:

Gross payment (¼ × ⅞ × 56,000 × $30)		$367,500
Windfall profit tax:		
Gross payment	$ 367,500	
Adjusted base price (¼ × ⅞ × 56,000 × $18.72)	(229,320)	
Windfall profit	$ 138,180	
Windfall profit tax rate	.70	
Windfall profit tax		(96,726)
Net payment		$270,774

With respect to a production payment retained by the lessor in a leasing transaction (including a sublease or the exercise of an option to acquire a lease or sublease), the lessee treats payments made toward the production payment as if the latter were a bonus granted by the lessee to the lessor payable in installments.[253] The Internal Revenue Service has ruled that where the only basis for expecting oil or gas in sufficient quantities to effect payout of the production payment is geological and geophysical studies, the production payment is in substance a royalty interest.[254] *(See Case 83 for a further discussion of this ruling and the tax consequences of such characterization.)*

The lessee reports the amount (including any interest and any amounts added to the production payment other than amounts for which the lessee would be liable in the absence of the production payment) applied in satisfaction of the production payment as gross income and capitalizes each payment as depletable basis attributable to the acquired working interest.[255] The lessor is treated as holding an economic interest, and payments in discharge of the production payment constitute ordinary income subject to depletion.[256]

It appears that Operator A should include the $367,500 in gross income in 1987 and capitalize it as part of his depletable basis in the acquired working interest. *(See the discussion below on the effect of the WPT.)*

Operator A holds the division order for the working interest and production payment. However, he should certify only his own share of production as independent-producer oil. Otherwise, Lessor R will owe additional WPT if the purchaser has been withholding pursuant to an incorrect certification that all the production qualifies for the lower independent-producer rates.[257] If Lessor R cannot or does not pay the additional WPT, either the first purchaser or Operator A may be held liable for the additional WPT.[258] *(See Case 230 for a discussion of the WPT net income limitation computation when a property is burdened by a production payment, and Case 235 for a discussion of the qualified disburser election.)*

To determine gross income for the computation of percentage depletion, Operator A must exclude the production attributable to the royalty and, under the "bonus exclusion rule," he also must exclude an allocable portion of both the lease bonus ($20,000) and the production payment.[259] *(See Case 87.)*

253. I.R.C. Sec. 636(c); Reg. Sec. 1.636-2(a).
254. Rev. Rul. 86-119, 1986-41 I.R.B. 8.
255. *Ibid.*
256. I.R.C. Sec. 636(c); Reg. Sec. 1.636-2(b).
257. I.R.C. Sec. 4992(a); I.R.C Sec. 4987(b)(2).
258. I.R.C. Sec. 4995(a).
259. I.R.C. Sec. 613(a); Reg. Sec. 1.613-2(c)(5)(ii).

Under the facts of the case, the parties intend that Lessor R will receive, with respect to the production payment, $800,000 after payment of all WPT associated with the production payment. It is not clear how the payment of Lessor R's WPT affects Operator A or Lessor R. It appears that payment probably will be treated as an additional amount due under the production payment arrangement. If so, as indicated above, the gross payment attributable to Lessor R's production payment ($367,500) will be included in Operator A's depletable gross income and capitalized as part of Operator A's depletable cost basis. *(See Case 141.)* Lessor R will treat the gross amount as payment in discharge of the production payment and will include it as ordinary income subject to depletion. Lessor R will be entitled to deduct the WPT attributable to the production payment. In connection with this issue, as noted earlier, the regulations provide that the lessee should capitalize each payment paid or incurred with respect to the production payment (including any interest and any amounts added to the production payment *other than amounts for which the lessee would be liable in the absence of the production payment)*.[260] Under the facts of this case, in the absence of the production payment, Operator A will be liable for WPT on amounts otherwise applicable to the production payment. Therefore, it may be argued that even though Operator A's WPT on these amounts may be different from Lessor R's, the regulations indicate that the WPT actually paid or incurred need not be capitalized by Operator A. In that case, Operator A will not be required to include the full $367,500 in income in 1987. Resolution of this issue must await further developments in this area.

For 1987, Operator A's gross income for computing percentage depletion, assuming the WPT is considered an additional payment under the production payment arrangement, is as follows:

Gross income (⅞ × 56,000 bbls. × $30)	$ 1,470,000
Less: Bonus exclusion—	
56,000 / 560,000 × $ 20,000 = $ 2,000	
56,000 / 560,000 × $800,000* = 80,000*	
	(82,000)
Gross income for computing percentage depletion	$ 1,388,000

* To be increased by any additions to the production payment attributable to the WPT (see discussion above).

No guidance is available as to a method for determining the amount by which the production payment is to be increased for additions attributable to the WPT. Presumably, this can be done by: (1) increasing each year's bonus exclusion by the amount of that year's WPT or (2) estimating each year the total tax remaining to be paid and adjusting that estimate for variations between actual and estimated taxes of prior years.

Further, assuming the WPT is considered an additional payment under the production payment arrangement, Operator A's basis for cost depletion is the $20,000 bonus plus the $367,500 gross amount applicable to the production payment, less any prior depletion. *(See Case 83.)*

260. Reg. Sec. 1.636-2(a).

Case 89
Effect of Production and Ad Valorem Taxes on Depletable Income When Taxes Are Paid by Lessee

Lessor R owns certain oil and gas royalties on which he receives payments from a purchasing oil company under division orders. The purchasing oil company withholds $1.50 per barrel purchased as a production and severance tax to be remitted to the state treasurer and $4 windfall profit tax (WPT) payable to the federal government.

Under the leasing agreement between Lessor R and Lessee E, E is required to pay all ad valorem property taxes accruing to the property during the period the lease remains in force.

In determining gross income for depletion purposes, Lessor R should add to the amounts received from the purchasing oil company the production and WPT withheld and the ad valorem taxes Lessee E paid on the property.[261] Lessor R's percentage depletion calculation then results in a greater depletion allowance than would result if he had computed depletion only on the net amounts received. Although Lessee E pays the ad valorem taxes, they represent Lessor R's liability. Lessor R should claim those taxes as a deduction rather than reducing depletable gross income.

It is a well-established industry practice for the purchaser of oil or gas to deduct from the amount due the owner the applicable production taxes levied by the state and the WPT due the federal government and to remit these taxes directly to the proper authority. The liability for the taxes is not shifted, however, and the procedure is merely a convenient method of reporting and paying the taxes.

The courts have held[262] that ad valorem taxes for which the lessor is liable but paid by the lessee are considered additional royalties to the lessor. However, if the amount of those payments exceeds the total amount of production, the excess does not constitute depletable gross income.[263] The Internal Revenue Service has ruled that it will follow the court decisions and recognize taxes the lessee pays as additional royalties to the lessor except in the absence of production or to the extent that taxes paid exceed current income from production. In those cases, the taxes paid will be treated as delay rentals taxable to the lessor and deductible by the lessee.[264]

Case 90
Allocation of Indirect Expenses in Determining Taxable Income from the Property

C Company has producing and nonproducing oil and gas properties and also owns a cycling plant. C Company wants information concerning the allocation of overhead for computing the percentage depletion allowance.

C Company also is a limited partner in X Partnership, an oil and gas drilling fund that pays guaranteed salary payments to the managing general partner of the fund. C Company does not participate in the

261. Myrtle J. Wood, 31 T.C. 528 (1958); Louisiana Land and Exploration Co. v. Donnelly, 394 F.2d 273 (5th Cir. 1968), 21 AFTR2d 1254, 68-1 USTC 9356.
262. Burt v. U.S., 170 F. Supp. 953 (Ct. Cl. 1959), 3 AFTR2d 848, 59-1 USTC 9288; Byron H. Farwell, 35 T.C. 454 (1960); U.S. Steel v. U.S., 445 F.2d 520 (2d Cir. 1971), 28 AFTR2d 71-5053, 71-2 USTC 9505.
263. Handelman v. U.S., 357 F.2d 694 (Ct. Cl. 1966), 17 AFTR2d 609, 66-1 USTC 9310.
264. Rev. Rul. 72-165, 1972-1 C.B. 177; Rev. Rul. 75-182, 1975-1 C.B. 176.

management of this partnership. C Company wants information concerning the partnership's overhead allocation method used on the tentative depletion schedules it receives from the partnership.

(Pertinent financial data are summarized in the exhibit following the discussion.)

In computing taxable income from the property for the 50% limitation on percentage depletion, a taxpayer must reduce his gross income from each depletable property, including royalty interests, not only by costs directly associated with that property but also with a fair proportion of the indirect costs expensed by the taxpayer.[265] A taxpayer must fairly apportion indirect expenses among the oil- and gas-producing activity and any other activities in which the taxpayer may be engaged.

A company engaged exclusively in oil and gas exploration and production may determine it is involved solely in two activities—a producing activity and a nonproducing activity. However, this finding may not be appropriate for all taxpayers as each taxpayer must consider its particular factual situation. The number of activities will depend on the taxpayer's organizational structure, business objectives, actual operations, etc. Identifying activities is important because this will ultimately affect the allocation of indirect costs to each depletable property.

While C Company must consider all items of income and expense reported in its tax return for the tax year for this purpose, it should begin by attributing direct expenditures to each respective activity. Costs directly related to the oil- and gas-producing activity should be further attributed to each specific property on which the expenditure occurred. Examples include production or severance tax, ad valorem tax, crude oil windfall profit tax (WPT), lease operating expense, depreciation (or cost recovery) on lease and well equipment and intangible drilling and development costs (IDC) where the taxpayer properly elects to deduct these costs as paid or incurred.

After determining the costs directly related to the producing activity, C Company should determine the items that are directly related to other activities. Amounts directly attributable to these activities will be excluded from indirect expenses to be allocated. In this example, C Company will allocate revenue from cycling operations and expenses directly related to the cycling plant to the nonproducing activity.

After all costs that can be directly related to an activity have been properly classified, indirect costs should be considered next. Certain items of an indirect nature previously have been held to be unrelated to and, therefore, nonallocable to the oil and gas operations. For this reason, in determining the percentage depletion limitation, C Company need not consider contributions,[266] net operating loss carryovers and carrybacks,[267] premiums for business interruption insurance[268] or damage payments resulting from a breach of contract due to lack of production.[269] The Tax Court recently held that certain exploration costs were only attributable to the abandoned or nonproducing properties on which they were incurred and, consequently, were not allocable to producing properties. However, a portion of certain exploration and land department indirect expenses were held allocable to producing and nonproducing properties.[270]

---

265. Reg. Sec. 1.613-5(a).
266. F.H.E. Oil Co., 3 T.C. 13 (1944); U.S. Potash Co., 29 T.C. 1071 (1958); Rev. Rul. 60-74, 1960-1 C.B. 253.
267. Rev. Rul. 60-164, 1960-1 C.B. 254.
268. Island Creek Coal Co. v. Comm'r, 382 F.2d 35 (4th Cir. 1967), 20 AFTR2d 5391, 67-2 USTC 9632.
269. Rev. Rul. 80-317, 1980-2 C.B. 202.
270. Shell Oil Co., 89 T.C. No. 33 (1987).

Indirect items that have been specifically held to be allocable, all or in part, to producing operations for depletion purposes include general and administrative overhead,[271] administrative salaries,[272] interest and amortization of bond discount and expenses,[273] state income and franchise taxes,[274] foreign taxes claimed as a deduction,[275] interest on federal income tax deficiencies for prior years,[276] association dues, legal and professional fees,[277] receivership fees,[278] payments to a pension plan for services on properties no longer in operation[279] and payments of back wages for prior years.[280] To the extent miscellaneous income is not treated as a separate activity, it should reduce the indirect expenses to be allocated.

It may be possible to attribute interest expense directly to the property or activity to which the indebtedness relates, although facts and circumstances may suggest that an allocation approach would be more appropriate. The Tax Court recently held that interest expense incurred on indebtedness to acquire oil and gas properties where the properties were not collateral for the debt, should be treated as financial overhead and allocable, in part, to producing properties.[281] Generally, any interest expense not directly attributed to an activity should be included with other indirect costs to be allocated to all activities. However, to determine properly "actual" interest cost, a taxpayer should net any interest expenses incurred to borrow funds with interest income earned, if any, by temporarily investing such funds until they are used.[282] Alternatively, in some situations the process of making investments to earn interest or other miscellaneous income may, in fact, be a separate activity to which direct and indirect expenses should be attributed. To sustain separate activity status, the taxpayer must be able to demonstrate that the investment or other activity is not related to the oil and gas activity. Otherwise, the Internal Revenue Service (IRS) may conclude that interest income and expense should be netted because temporary investments have been made to minimize the "carrying" cost of liquid assets that could otherwise have been used to retire debt.

The IRS has accepted a variety of methods for allocating indirect costs, if consistently followed. Two such methods are the allocation of indirect costs among the producing activity and other activities based on either gross receipts or direct expenditures. A taxpayer may further allocate indirect costs within the producing activity among the several producing mineral properties based on relative production, gross income or direct expenditures. It also is acceptable to allocate a portion of such costs on the basis of income and the remaining portion on the basis of direct expenditures. In a recent decision, the Tax Court held that IDC, WPT, and current year geological and geophysical expenditures were properly includable in the allocation base used to allocate indirect expenses in the calculation of taxable income from the property.[283]

271. Senate Report No. 1622, 83d Cong., 2d Sess. (1954) 330; Occidental Petroleum Corp., 55 T.C. 115 (1970).
272. Rocky Mountain Oil Co., 36 B.T.A. 365 (1937).
273. Sheridan-Wyoming Coal Co. v. Helvering, 125 F.2d 42 (D.C. Cir. 1941) 28 AFTR 908, 42-1 USTC 9194; St. Louis, Rocky Mountain & Pacific Co., 28 T.C. 28 (1957).
274. Montreal Mining Co., 2 T.C. 688 (1943); Grison Oil Corporation, 42 B.T.A. 1117 (1940).
275. Kern Oil Co., Ltd., 9 T.C. 1204 (1947).
276. Holly Development Co., 44 B.T.A. 51 (1941).
277. Lumaghi Coal Co. v. Helvering, 124 F.2d 645 (8th Cir. 1942), 28 AFTR 847, 42-1 USTC 9216; Crews v. Comm'r, 89 F.2d 412 (10th Cir. 1937), 19 AFTR 365, 37-1 USTC 9196.
278. C.A. Hughes & Company, T.C. Memo Dec. (March 9, 1955).
279. IRS Letter Ruling 7842008 (Technical Advice Memorandum); G.C.M. 39099; Rev. Rul. 84-46, 1984-1 C.B. 146.
280. Rialto Mining Corp., T.C. Memo Dec. (June 25, 1946).
281. Shell Oil Co. *See also* St. Mary's Oil and Gas Co., 42 B.T.A. 270 (1940); Mirabel Quicksilver Co., 41 B.T.A. 401 (1940); IRS Letter Ruling 8551002 (Technical Advice Memorandum).
282. General Portland Cement Co. v. U.S., 628 F.2d 321 (5th Cir. 1980), 46 AFTR2d 80-5864, 80-2 USTC 9720, (A) AOD 86-023 (Feb. 26, 1986); Ideal Basic Industries, Inc., 82 T.C. 352 (1984), (A) AOD 86-022 (Feb. 26, 1986).
283. Shell Oil Co.

From a conceptual standpoint, the allocation of indirect costs should take into consideration the relative effort involved. An allocation based solely on relative direct expenditures may be unsatisfactory. For example, the drilling costs may be much greater than operating costs in terms of total dollars expended, but managing ongoing operations may require more effort in terms of personnel resources and indirect costs incurred by the taxpayer. To use absolute dollars could distort the amount of indirect costs ultimately attributed to various activities, resulting in an allocation that may not properly apportion the indirect costs. There is no universal allocation method that is proper for all situations. When more than one activity exists, the appropriate method to use is one in which the indirect costs of the business are reasonably associated with each activity. The appropriate method for each taxpayer is the allocation that produces a fair apportionment for that taxpayer's circumstances. The IRS was granted authority to prescribe regulations to dictate an allocation approach for indirect costs and chose to issue only very broad guidelines. As a result, the Tax Court[284] has held that the IRS does not also have the authority to propose alternate specific apportionment methods that the taxpayer must prove to be improper. If the IRS wishes to change the taxpayer's allocation, it will be necessary to demonstrate that a different approach will produce a fairer apportionment in that taxpayer's circumstances than the taxpayer's method. Any allocation method will necessarily involve the use of accepted accounting principles, but it is not an accounting method that cannot be changed or modified from one year to the next if changes occur in the make-up of the indirect costs or in the conduct of operations.

Recently, the IRS has been re-examining the taxpayer treatment of indirect costs to determine whether some portion of these costs should be reclassified as IDC. In one ruling,[285] the taxpayer used direct expenditures as a basis for allocating indirect expenses such as officers' salaries, interest and administrative expenses for purposes of computing the 50% of net income limitation. The IRS held that the portion of the indirect costs allocated to each property based on relative IDC deducted on each property should be reclassified and considered as IDC. The issue, addressed by a technical advice memorandum, arose during the audit of a claim for refund of WPT. The effect such a reclassification would have on the WPT claim was a major concern. (IDC for purposes of the 90% of net income limitation calculation must be capitalized and amortized rather than taken as a current deduction, thereby reducing the potential for a WPT refund.)

The IRS recently followed this rationale in yet another ruling[286] dealing with IDC recapture. In this ruling, the IRS recognized that all indirect costs were not necessarily allocable in precisely the same manner. Rather, each indirect item may be allocated on a different basis. For example, it was suggested that relative floor space could be used to allocate rent, or relative time could be used to allocate items such as legal fees. Once allocated, these items would be considered to be "incident to and necessary" for drilling to the extent they facilitate the conduct of drilling operations and, therefore, should be treated as IDC rather than overhead. Further clarifying its current position, the IRS ruled[287] that administrative and financial overhead directly related to drilling should be reclassified as IDC before determining the 50% of net income limitation. The IRS recognized there are no rigid rules for making allocations and that a major oil company may need a different method than a small independent producer. Regardless of the method used, the IRS view is that if any item of overhead such as

284. Occidental Petroleum Corp.; Shell Oil Co.
285. IRS Letter Ruling 8406006 (Technical Advice Memorandum).
286. IRS Letter Ruling 8622005 (Technical Advice Memorandum).
287. IRS Letter Ruling 8640006 (Technical Advice Memorandum).

rent, clerical staff, legal fees, etc., can be related in some manner to the drilling activity, it is incident to and necessary for drilling and should be considered to be IDC.

For depletion purposes, whether allocated indirect costs are treated as IDC or overhead may have no impact on the 50% of net income limitation since they are deducted currently in either case. However, the taxpayer should carefully consider the impact the indirect cost allocation method may have on IDC recapture, the IDC preference amount for alternative minimum tax purposes and the WPT. As discussed above, the method chosen should, to the extent possible, match in the fairest and most reasonable way the indirect costs incurred to the activity necessitating such costs. Various items of costs may need to be allocated in different ways such as square footage (rent), time spent (salaries), passage of time (interest), etc. Due to the complexities involved, simplified approaches have been used by taxpayers to approximate the proper allocation. Although these approaches traditionally have been accepted by the IRS, the taxpayer has the burden of demonstrating that the allocation is reasonable. The IRS would probably be allowed to change the taxpayer's approach if it can be demonstrated that a different approach would be fairer.

For indirect costs incurred after December 31, 1986, current law requires that the uniform cost-capitalization rules be considered for self-constructed property.[288] The Committee Report[289] indicates that the drilling of an oil and gas well is considered the production of an asset. Therefore, indirect costs and interest expense, if applicable, must be capitalized.[290] Interest expense is required to be capitalized only if it is applicable to a long-lived asset, the construction period exceeds two years or if the construction period exceeds one year and the cost exceeds $1 million.[291] Intangible drilling costs are specifically excluded from the new capitalization rules.[292] Still, it is unclear how the indirect costs required to be capitalized as part of an oil and gas well would be allocated between the lease and the equipment. *(See Case 187.)*

In the example that follows this discussion, C Company allocates its net indirect expenses of $85,000 among producing activities and other activities on the basis of direct expenditures. *(See Cases 174 and 221 for additional considerations regarding treatment of a portion of general overhead as IDC.)* C Company includes depreciation on lease and well equipment and the cycling plant in direct costs for purposes of the indirect cost allocation to give effect to the capital investment in the various operations. If depreciation on lease and well equipment has no direct relationship to the indirect costs incurred, then it will be proper to exclude depreciation when making the indirect cost allocation. The IRS historically has accepted either treatment if consistently followed.

X Partnership is required to provide C Company with all the information it needs to compute depletion with respect to the producing properties of the partnership because depletion is computed at the partner level. *(See Case 104.)* C Company should receive tentative depletion schedules, prepared by the partnership, that compute the net income by producing property. These schedules should consider C Company's share of direct expenses attributable to each producing property as well as C Company's share of the partnership's indirect expenses that are reasonably allocated to the various properties of the partnership. If any of C Company's expenses incurred outside the partnership relate to C Company's investment in that partnership, C

288. P.L. 99-514 (Tax Reform Act of 1986), Sec. 803(d).
289. Senate Report No. 99-313, 1986-3 C.B. Vol. 3 141.
290. I.R.C. Sec. 263A(a)(2); I.R.C. Sec. 263A(f).
291. I.R.C. Sec. 263A(f)(1).
292. I.R.C. Sec. 263A(c)(3).

Company also should reasonably allocate those expenses to the producing and non-producing properties of the partnership. In this example, it is assumed that C Company has not incurred any such expenses. Therefore, C Company, as a passive investor in X Partnership, will use the tentative allowable depletion schedules provided by the partnership to determine its depletion deduction resulting from its partnership investment.

A guaranteed salary payment to a partner is recognized as an item of income to the partner and as an expenditure, although not necessarily a deductible expenditure, to the partnership.[293] The IRS has ruled that the nature of the services performed by the partner receiving the guaranteed payment determines whether all or a part of the guaranteed payment represents a capital expenditure rather than a deductible expense to the partnership. The IRS also has ruled that a limited partnership's payments to one of its general partners for services rendered in organizing the partnership are capital expenditures.[294] Similarly, a finder's fee paid to a general partner for obtaining a loan is capitalized and amortized over the lives of the loans to the applicants.[295] If a management fee that qualifies as a startup expenditure of the partnership is paid to a partner, it also must be capitalized and amortized.[296]

One district court[297] has held that a partner's guaranteed salary should not be treated as a deduction for computing the 50% of net income limitation for percentage depletion purposes. The court stated in this case that the purpose of the guaranteed payment was to distribute to a service partner a larger share of the partnership income than was distributed to the other partners who made no service contributions.

A producer entitled to percentage depletion under the independent-producer and royalty-owner provision should consider the interaction between the WPT 90% of net income limitation *(see Case 221)* and the percentage depletion deduction on properties with substantial production income. The allocation of significant amounts of indirect costs to producing properties may reduce the WPT through the 90% limitation, but it also may reduce percentage depletion through the 50% limitation and thus increase the income tax burden. When the WPT 90% of net income limitation applies to a property on which percentage depletion is limited to 50% of taxable income, the reduction of the WPT in turn increases net income for purposes of the 50% of taxable income limitation, thereby increasing allowable percentage depletion.

The method for allocating indirect costs should be chosen carefully and consistently applied. Percentage depletion (in excess of the basis of the property) results in a permanent income tax savings. The WPT savings resulting from the application of the net income limitation also is permanent. The taxpayer's income tax bracket and the rate of the WPT are both factors to consider in selecting an allocation method.

293. Jackson E. Cagle, Jr., 63 T.C. 86 (1974), *aff'd* 539 F.2d 409 (5th Cir. 1976), 38 AFTR2d 76-5834, 76-2 USTC 9672.
294. Rev. Rul. 75-214, 1975-1 C.B. 185.
295. Rev. Rul. 80-234, 1980-2 C.B. 203.
296. Rev. Rul. 81-150, 1981-1 C.B. 119.
297. Mallary v. U.S., 238 F. Supp. 87 (M.D. Ga. 1965), 15 AFTR2d 384, 65-1 USTC 9224.

An example of a method used in the allocation of indirect costs between oil and gas operations and other activities is presented following this case. Differing facts and circumstances may suggest or require varying approaches.

C Company Allocation of Indirect Expenses for Percentage Depletion

Description	Total	Directly Related to Operations: Producing	Directly Related to Operations: Nonproducing	Expenses To Be Allocated	Unallocable Items
Income:					
Oil and gas sales	$ 725,000	$725,000	$ —	$ —	$ —
Receipts from royalties and net profits interests	180,000	180,000	—	—	—
Cycling plant revenue	102,000	—	102,000	—	—
Lease bonuses	35,000	35,000	—	—	—
Rent	5,000	—	—	—	5,000
Dividends	1,000	—	—	—	1,000
Interest income	18,000	—	—	18,000	—
Partnership income	2,000	—	—	—	2,000
Total income	$1,068,000	$940,000	$ 102,000	$ 18,000	$ 8,000
Deductions:					
Lease operating expense	$ 112,000	$112,000	$ —	$ —	$ —
Intangible drilling and development costs	178,000	60,000	118,000	—	—
Lease rentals	20,000	—	20,000	—	—
Taxes, including windfall profit taxes	121,000	104,000	7,000	10,000	—
Interest expense (not directly allocable)	20,000	—	—	20,000	—
Cycling plant operations	50,000	—	50,000	—	—
Depreciation	71,000	58,000	10,000	3,000	—
Contributions	1,500	—	—	—	1,500
Surrendered and expired leases	13,000	—	—	—	13,000
General and administrative expenses	70,000	—	—	70,000	—
Subtotal	$ 656,500	$334,000	$ 205,000	$103,000	$14,500
Allocation of net indirect expense ($85,000):					
Producing ($334,000 ÷ $539,000 = 61.97%)	—	52,675	—	(52,675)	—
Nonproducing ($205,000 ÷ $539,000 = 38.03%)	—	—	32,325	(32,325)	—
Subtotal	$ 656,500	$386,675	$ 237,325	$ 18,000	$14,500
Depletion	126,500	126,500	—	—	—
Total Deductions	$ 783,000	$513,175	$ 237,325	$ 18,000	$14,500
Taxable Net Income (Loss)	$ 285,000	$426,825	$(135,325)	$ —	$ (6,500)

Note: The above method of allocating indirect expenses in some cases may give unrealistic results. In those cases, a more realistic allocation should be used.

Case 91
Depletable Gross Income in an Integrated Gas Operation

C Company, an integrated gas company, owns all the working interest in certain gas leases and a fractional share of the working interest in other leases. C Company is the owner of a gasoline extraction and processing plant in which it processes its own gas (using some for fuel). It also purchases and processes gas for others. To maintain adequate reservoir pressure and to prevent retrograde condensation in certain formations, the residue gas from the formation is not sold but is cycled and injected into the reservoir. By agreement, the landowner's royalty is compounded and paid on a flat basis for each type of product sold.

C Company is entitled to percentage depletion under the independent-producer and royalty-owner exemption.

C Company is both a producer and a processor of petroleum products, but it may claim depletion only on the income attributable to its economic interest in the minerals in place.[298] The regulations provide that "gross income from the property," for computing percentage depletion, is the amount for which the taxpayer sells the oil or gas in the immediate vicinity of the well. If the oil or gas is not sold on the premises but is converted or transported prior to sale, the gross income is assumed to be equivalent to the representative market or field price of the oil or gas before conversion or transportation.[299] If there is a current posted field price for production, the portion of the proceeds from the sale of the plant products equal to the posted price will represent depletable income. However, in many cases, a current posted market price is not available, and a taxpayer must use some other means to determine the income from production and the income from manufacturing. The determination of what is equivalent to the market or field price of the production in the immediate vicinity of the well and of what constitutes income from a production or manufacturing operation is a question that must be decided in each case in light of all relevant circumstances.

In a cycling operation, the operator extracts the heavier hydrocarbons, such as propane, butane and other natural gasoline constituents, from the wet gas and sells them. The operator then injects the dry or residue gas into the reservoir (except for a small portion that is consumed in the process). C Company's production is converted prior to sale, so its gross income from the property is equivalent to the representative market or field price of the gas prior to conversion. C Company also must give consideration to the dry gas injected into the reservoir because all the mineral is not sold. In determining gross income from the property, C Company includes the value of the wet gas that goes into the production of the dry gas consumed in the process or used as plant fuel; however, C Company does not include in gross income from the property the value of dry gas that is injected into the formation.[300]

When a taxpayer does not sell the product at the well, he computes gross income from the property for depletion purposes by using the "market comparison" method.[301] Under this method, the gross income is assumed to be the weighted average of prices received for comparable gas, both as to quality and quantity, in the local area. In

298. Reg. Sec. 1.611-1(b).
299. Reg. Sec. 1.613-3(a); Brea Cannon Oil Co. v. Comm'r, 77 F.2d 67 (9th Cir. 1935), 15 AFTR 1335, 35-1 USTC 9339.
300. Rev. Rul. 68-665, 1968-2 C.B. 280; G.C.M. 39132.
301. Shamrock Oil and Gas Corp., 35 T.C. 979 (1961), *aff'd* 346 F.2d 377 (5th Cir. 1965), 15 AFTR2d 1168, 65-2 USTC 9476; Hugoton Production Co. v. U.S., 315 F.2d 868 (Ct. Cl. 1963), 11 AFTR2d 1198, 63-1 USTC 9393; Panhandle Eastern Pipe Line Co. v. U.S., 408 F.2d 690 (Ct. Cl. 1969), 23 AFTR2d 69-933, 69-1 USTC 9276; Hugoton Production Co. v. U.S., 349 F.2d 418 (Ct. Cl. 1965), 16 AFTR2d 5296, 65-2 USTC 9566.

determining the weighted average of prices received for comparable gas in the local area, a taxpayer should adjust the original contract price for increases allowed by the Federal Energy Regulatory Commission (FERC), even though the increases are under temporary orders. If the temporary price increase is redetermined in subsequent years, a taxpayer should make the proper adjustment for the change of price in the year FERC issues the order. A taxpayer should compute the weighted average price using only prices working interest owners receive; he should not include the prices received by royalty owners.[302] After determining the wellhead price, the working interest owner must exclude from the assumed income the actual amounts paid to the royalty owners, even though the royalty owners receive an amount that may be attributable to the manufacturing process.[303] In one case, it was held that there was no representative market for purposes of computing percentage depletion. Instead, the court determined fair market value in the vicinity of the well by looking to prices paid under orders of the applicable regulatory authority, weighted sales prices in other fields and a prior settlement with the Internal Revenue Service (IRS).[304] In certain situations (such as the production of oil on the Alaskan North Slope), there is not a representative market price in the local area. When there are insufficient sales in the vicinity of the well to establish a market price, the "wellhead price" is calculated from the actual sales price of the oil or gas in the market area to which the production is delivered, reduced for the cost of transporting the production to the point of sale.[305]

In determining depletable income when a taxpayer converts the oil and gas prior to sale, the taxpayer must distinguish the processes that represent conversion or manufacturing processes from those that represent production or extraction activities. The production vs. manufacturing issue has no clear definition. Therefore, a taxpayer must examine any processing activity very closely. Generally, any processes to prepare petroleum and natural gas for sale or use in crude form are production or extractive processes. Those processes include mechanical separation and removal of water by absorption. The courts have not established a clear cutoff point. One court held that the production process continues through separation and absorption and that manufacturing begins with fractionation.[306] However, in a later decision, another court held that the separation of liquid hydrocarbons by absorption is a manufacturing process.[307] The IRS ruled that the compression of natural gas to meet a purchaser's specifications is a manufacturing process and the value added by compression does not constitute gross income from the property for purposes of computing percentage depletion.[308] However, when the absorption process is essential to the production of both hydrocarbons and sulfur from a sour gas reservoir, the IRS has ruled informally that the absorption process is a part of production. In this ruling, the IRS stated that when no representative market or field price for the sour gas exists, the costs of the separating process and the absorption process are considered production functions and, therefore, are not deducted from the sale of the sulfur in computing gross income from the property.[309] *(See Case 95 for a discussion of the availability of percentage depletion for gas production.)*

302. Panhandle Eastern Pipe Line.
303. Mesa Petroleum Co., 58 T.C. 374 (1972).
304. Petroleum Exploration v. U.S., 404 F. Supp. 93 (N.D. W.Va. 1975), 37 AFTR2d 76-461, 76-1 USTC 9136.
305. Rev. Rul. 83-161, 1983-2 C.B. 202.
306. Scofield v. La Gloria Oil and Gas Co., 268 F.2d 699 (5th Cir. 1959), 3 AFTR2d 1631, 59-2 USTC 9522; Weinert v. Comm'r, 294 F.2d 750 (5th Cir. 1961), 8 AFTR2d 5417, 61-2 USTC 9644.
307. Mountain Fuel Supply Co. v. U.S., 449 F.2d 816 (10th Cir. 1971), 28 AFTR2d 71-5833, 71-2 USTC 9681.
308. Rev. Rul. 75-6, 1975-1 C.B. 178.
309. IRS Letter Ruling 7908005 (Technical Advice Memorandum).

Case 92
Depletable Gross Income When Produced Gas Is Not Sold

> Corporation A owns a lease producing both oil and gas from the same geological formation. It also owns a widget manufacturing plant located near the lease. The oil is sold currently as it is produced. A relatively small amount of the gas is used for fuel in operating the lease, and substantial amounts of gas are used for fuel in the widget plant. The remaining gas is reinjected into the producing formation.

The Tax Court has ruled[310] that coal produced by and consumed in production or development activities on the same property is not subject to the allowance for depletion. However, a district court allowed percentage depletion based on comparable market prices in a situation where coal was mined by a taxpayer and then used in its manufacture of iron.[311] In another hard mineral case,[312] a Circuit Court of Appeals held that depletable gross income should include amounts attributable to the mineral used in a manufacturing or refining process. In agreeing with the district court, the Circuit Court distinguished its finding from the Tax Court decision, in part, by noting that the cost of coal consumed in the mining operation is actually reflected in the ultimate sales price of the coal. The coal producer will ultimately get depletion based on the full sales price of the total coal produced, but a manufacturer does not receive a similar deduction when its product (pig-iron in this case) is sold. The Internal Revenue Service (IRS) acknowledges this distinction and strictly limits the application of the Tax Court decision.[313]

Minerals consumed in a refining process also may be reflected in the value of the refined product, but the value of the refined product is not included in depletable gross income. *(See Case 91 for the calculation of depletion when oil or gas is converted or transported prior to sale.)* When oil or gas is not sold on the premises but is manufactured into a refined product prior to sale, *gross income from the property* is assumed to be determinable by reference to the representative market or field price.[314] The IRS has ruled that the value of that portion of produced wet gas refined into dry gas is not included in gross income from the property to the extent that dry gas is reinjected into the producing formation. However, the value of produced wet gas refined into dry gas is included in gross income from the property to the extent that dry gas is consumed as fuel in the processing of liquid products for sale.[315] Accordingly, the IRS probably would rule that Corporation A is not entitled to depletion with respect to the portions of the gas used in the operation of the lease or reinjected into the producing formation.

The above authorities do not specifically address depletion attributable to the value of oil and gas consumed by a taxpayer in connection with a manufacturing operation unrelated to oil and gas. The concept of percentage depletion is to provide for capital recovery due to the exhaustion of oil and gas reserves. These authorities recognize that exhaustion occurs without regard to the sale of raw mineral produced. Accordingly, it appears that Corporation A should be allowed percentage depletion with respect to the value of gas consumed in its manufacturing plant.

---

310. The Roundup Coal Mining Co., 20 T.C. 388 (1953).
311. Woodward Iron Company v. Patterson, 173 F. Supp. 251 (D.C. Ala. 1959), 3 AFTR2d 1427, 59-1 USTC 9454.
312. U.S. v. Henderson Clay Products, 324 F.2d 7 (5th Cir. 1963), 12 AFTR2d 5816, 63-2 USTC 9780.
313. G.C.M. 39132.
314. Reg. Sec. 1.613-3(a); Prop. Reg. Sec. 1.613A-1(a).
315. Rev. Rul. 68-665, 1968-2 C.B. 280.

To avoid any possible issue regarding the lack of an actual sale, Corporation A should consider transferring its manufacturing plant to a subsidiary that would purchase its gas from Corporation A at the prevailing market price. This arrangement would clearly establish the amount of depletable gross income. Obviously, other business and legal ramifications must be considered before forming a subsidiary for this purpose.

Case 93
Percentage Depletion of Natural Gas Sold Under a Fixed Contract, Regulated Natural Gas and Natural Gas from Geopressured Brine

> **Operator A owns working interests in various leases in a producing gas field in the United States. The gas is sold intrastate to a single purchaser under a fixed contract in effect on February 1, 1975. The contract contains a clause providing that, if the purchaser pays any other working interest owner in the area a price for gas in excess of that provided for in Operator A's contract, the purchaser must pay Operator A the same price. Operator A wants to know what effect a price escalation under this clause will have on his right to percentage depletion with respect to gas properties.**

Domestic natural gas sold under a fixed contract in effect on February 1, 1975, remains subject to percentage depletion at a 22% rate, computed without regard to the limitations on percentage depletion provided by the independent-producer exemption provisions.[316] A fixed contract is one under which the price of that gas cannot be adjusted to reflect, to any extent, the increase in the seller's liabilities for income tax by reason of the repeal of percentage depletion for gas. Any price increase after February 1, 1975, will be presumed to reflect the repeal of percentage depletion unless the taxpayer can prove otherwise by clear and convincing evidence.[317]

Many gas contracts contain specific provisions allowing escalation in the price of the gas for an increase in severance or real property taxes. An increase in price solely attributable to such a provision should not preclude the seller from claiming percentage depletion on production sold pursuant to the higher prices. Other acceptable price increases include those to reflect additional operating costs (such as costs of secondary and tertiary processes), increases for additional drilling and related costs, and a change in the quality of gas produced. In addition, an escalation clause designed solely to project the estimated effects of inflation will not result in a loss of percentage depletion.[318]

Proposed regulations indicate that when a contract provides for an increase in price to the highest price paid to a producer in the area, gas sold after a price increase will not be gas sold under a fixed contract. If the contract permits renegotiation of the price, gas sold after the time renegotiation *can* occur will not qualify as fixed-contract gas, whether or not an increase or renegotiation actually occurs. However, the disqualification as a fixed-contract applies only on and after the date the renegotiation or price increase may occur.[319] If the renegotiation provision is limited to permit renegotiation of prices solely to reflect price increases that are allowable under the fixed-contract provision (i.e., to reflect increases in operating costs, change in quality, etc.), the provision should not affect qualification as a fixed contract. Because all price increases

316. I.R.C. Sec. 613A(b)(1).
317. I.R.C. Sec. 613A(b)(3)(A); Prop. Reg. Sec. 1.613A-7(d).
318. Prop. Reg. Sec. 1.613A-7(d).
319. Prop. Reg. Sec. 1.613A-7(d); Prop. Reg. Sec. 1.613A-2(b).

are presumed to take into account the repeal of percentage depletion, the taxpayer must demonstrate by clear and convincing evidence that the price increase in fact does not reflect the loss of percentage depletion. For example, even though the proposed regulations permit a price increase pursuant to an escalation clause reflecting inflation, it may be difficult to establish that a renegotiated price increase relates solely to the effects of inflation. The seller should fully document the reason for any price increase through cost studies and memoranda describing the factors considered in the negotiations.

To claim percentage depletion, it is not necessary that all production from a property qualify as fixed contract production because the determination is made with respect to each sale of the mineral production.[320]

Based on the proposed regulations, it appears that the potential for Operator A's contract price to increase based on prices paid to other working interest owners will result in loss of status as a qualified fixed contract as of the time a price increase actually occurs.

If it is determined that Operator A's production after a price increase is not sold pursuant to a fixed contract, he will be entitled to elect to include that gas in his depletable oil quantity when computing percentage depletion as long as he otherwise qualifies under the independent-producer exemption provisions.

Several technical advice memoranda have been issued on whether certain natural gas was sold under a fixed contract. One ruling[321] involved gas purchase and sale contracts between producing and utility subsidiaries in a consolidated group. The taxpayer could not rebut the presumption that certain price escalations pursuant to modifications in the contracts after February 1, 1975, took into account increased tax liabilities that resulted from the loss of percentage depletion. However, sales made prior to those modifications did qualify as natural gas sold under a fixed contract. This conclusion was reached even though the parties to the contract were related and could have agreed to change the contract terms at any time. Further, the purchasing party could have increased its price to third parties and, thus, made up for any loss suffered by the consolidated group from the loss of percentage depletion by the producing member. The Internal Revenue Service (IRS) indicated that "the literal language of the Code is concerned with the contract entered into by the producer; the language does not address other increases by the consolidated group."

In another memorandum,[322] the IRS ruled that a contractual gas royalty payment to the lessor by a lessee, which depended upon a complex three-pronged fair market formula based on certain price levels for the gas, was not a fixed contract under the statute.

In still another memorandum,[323] the IRS considered a natural gas producer who sold natural gas to operators of natural gas processing plants based on a pricing formula that depended on the operator's sales to buyers of the natural gas liquids and residue. The IRS ruled that his agreement was not a fixed contract.

Depletion computed with respect to fixed-contract gas production is computed as it was under the law prior to 1975.[324] This depletion is not subject to the various limitations of the independent-producer exemption, including the limitations on the

320. Prop. Reg. Sec. 1.613A-7(d).
321. IRS Letter Ruling 8015047 (Technical Advice Memorandum).
322. IRS Letter Ruling 8041015 (Technical Advice Memorandum).
323. IRS Letter Ruling 8129007 (Technical Advice Memorandum).
324. I.R.C. Sec. 613A(b).

amount of production on which depletion may be claimed, the transfer of proven property rules[325] and the limitation of the deduction to 65% of taxable income. In addition, taxpayers engaged in the retailing of petroleum or petroleum products or in the refining of crude oil may deduct percentage depletion on fixed-contract gas sales.

Qualified natural gas from geopressured brine is subject to depletion at 10%, computed without regard to the limitations on percentage depletion of the independent-producer provisions.[326] *Qualified natural gas from geopressured brine* means any natural gas that is determined, in accordance with Section 503 of the Natural Gas Policy Act of 1978, to be produced from geopressured brine that is extracted from a well, the drilling of which began after September 30, 1978, and before January 1, 1984.[327] *(See Case 77 concerning when gas produced from geopressured brine may qualify for the alternative fuels credit.)*

Case 94
Percentage Depletion Allowable to Independent Producers of Oil and Gas

> **Operator A, a calendar-year taxpayer, is engaged in the business of exploring for, developing and producing oil and gas properties. Operator A owns numerous leases, and in calendar year 1987 the production from those leases was 255,500 barrels of oil and 438,000 MCF of gas. Operator A wants to know if he is entitled to a deduction for percentage depletion in 1987. His taxable income in 1987, computed on an accrual basis before deducting depletion, is $10,000.**

Percentage depletion generally is not allowed with respect to income from oil and gas properties.[328] Exceptions include domestic gas sold pursuant to a qualifying fixed contract and qualified natural gas from geopressured brine produced from wells, the drilling of which began after September 30, 1978, and before January 1, 1984.[329] *(See Case 93.)* Certain producers and royalty owners may claim percentage depletion, subject to limitations, on a specified quantity of oil and gas production pursuant to the provisions of the independent-producer exemption.[330] *(See Case 98 relative to percentage depletion on lease bonus income.)*

Operator A first should determine if any of his 1987 gas production is sold pursuant to a qualifying fixed contract or is qualified natural gas from geopressured brine. That production is not subject to the independent-producer limitations.[331] Operator A computes percentage depletion on fixed-contract gas, using a 22% depletion rate.[332] With respect to qualified natural gas from geopressured brine, Operator A's percentage depletion rate is 10%.[333]

He will be entitled to deduct percentage depletion with respect to his domestic production not qualifying for the fixed-contract or geopressured-brine exceptions only if he qualifies for the benefits of the independent-producer exemption. Percentage depletion is denied on all foreign production.The maximum quantity of production for

325. IRS Letter Ruling 8208213.
326. I.R.C. Sec. 613A(b)(2).
327. I.R.C. Sec. 613A(b)(3)(C).
328. I.R.C. Sec. 613A(a).
329. I.R.C. Sec. 613A(b)(2).
330. I.R.C. Sec. 613A(c).
331. I.R.C. Sec. 613A(c)(12).
332. I.R.C. Sec. 613A(b)(1).
333. I.R.C. Sec. 613A(b)(2).

which percentage depletion is allowable (depletable oil quantity) is an average daily production of 1,000 barrels.[334]

The percentage depletion rate for production after 1983 of oil and gas from primary, secondary or tertiary processes is 15%.[335] *(See Case 103.)*

A taxpayer determines his average daily production by dividing his production for that tax year by the number of days in the year.[336] A taxpayer may elect to deduct percentage depletion on gas production by converting all or a portion of his gas production to equivalent barrels of oi1, using a ratio of 6,000 cubic feet of gas to one barrel of oil.[337] The taxpayer may make the annual gas election by claiming percentage depletion deductions for the tax year based on that election. The election may be made, on an original or amended return or a claim for credit or refund, at any time before the expiration of the statutory period (including extensions) for the filing of a claim for credit or refund by the taxpayer. No separate election statement is required.[338]

If average daily production of oil and gas exceeds 1,000 barrels per day, a taxpayer must prorate percentage depletion among his properties according to stated rules.[339] *(See Case 96.)* In addition, certain related taxpayers and business entities under common control as well as certain controlled groups of corporations must allocate the depletable oil quantity among themselves.[340] *(See Cases 106 and 107.)*

Producers that directly or indirectly engage in the retailing of petroleum or petroleum products,[341] or in the refining of crude oil,[342] are not entitled to claim percentage depletion under the independent-producer exemption. *(See Cases 113 and 114.)*

Generally, if the combined gross receipts from the sale of oil, natural gas or products derived therefrom for the tax year of all retail outlets do not exceed $5 million, the taxpayer will not be considered to be engaged in retailing and will not lose the benefits of the independent-producer exemption.[343] Similarly, unless a taxpayer's refining facility has throughput in excess of 50,000 barrels on any day during the tax year, the taxpayer will not be considered to be a refiner.[344]

Percentage depletion under the independent-producer exemption generally is not available with respect to the production of a proven property transferred after December 31, 1974.[345] *(See Cases 108 and 109.)*

If Operator A is entitled to claim percentage depletion under the provisions of the independent-producer exemption with respect to all his production in 1987, he should compute his average daily production in the following manner:

Gas—(438,000 MCF ÷ 6) ÷ 365	200 barrels
Oil—255,500 barrels ÷ 365	700 barrels
Average daily production	900 barrels

334. I.R.C. Sec. 613A(c)(3)(B).
335. I.R.C. Sec. 613A(c)(5).
336. I.R.C. Sec. 613A(c)(2)(A); Prop. Reg. Sec. 1.613A-7(f).
337. I.R.C. Sec. 613A(c)(4); Prop. Reg. Sec. 1.613A-7(i).
338. Reg. Sec. 1.613A-5.
339. I.R.C. Sec. 613A(c)(7)(A); I.R.C. Sec. 613A(c)(7)(B).
340. I.R.C. Sec. 613A(c)(8).
341. I.R.C. Sec. 613A(d)(2).
342. I.R.C. Sec. 613A(d)(4).
343. I.R.C. Sec. 613A(d)(2).
344. I.R.C. Sec. 613A(d)(4).
345. I.R.C. Sec. 613A(c)(9).

Because Operator A's average daily production of oil and gas does not exceed the maximum depletable quantity of 1,000 barrels, he should compute percentage depletion with respect to the production from each property, including the computation of the limitation based on 50% of the taxable income from the property. *(See Case 87.)* By claiming percentage depletion on his gas production, Operator A is properly electing to convert his gas production to equivalent barrels of oil.[346]

The deduction for percentage depletion computed in this manner is limited to 65% of taxable income computed without the deduction for percentage depletion allowable under the independent-producer exemption, and certain other items.[347] *(See Cases 115, 116 and 117.)* Accordingly, the amount of percentage depletion Operator A can deduct in 1987 is limited to $6,500, which is 65% of his taxable income (before computing that depletion) of $10,000. If percentage depletion computed without regard to the 65% limitation exceeds $6,500, he may deduct the excess in future years, subject to certain limitations.[348] *(See Case 96.)*

Case 95
Percentage Depletion With Respect to Natural Gas Under the Independent-Producer Exemption

Operator A owns numerous properties located in the United States that produce oil and gas. During 1987, Operator A's production, none of which is from secondary or tertiary processes, is as follows:

Oil produced	438,000 barrels
Gas produced	547,500 MCF

None of the gas is sold pursuant to a qualifying fixed contract or is qualified natural gas from geopressured brine.

Operator A, who is entitled to claim depletion under the independent-producer exemption provisions, wants information concerning the election with respect to natural gas as it relates to the computation of percentage depletion.

The independent-producer exemption provision allows taxpayers to claim percentage depletion, subject to the limitation based on 65% of taxable income, with respect to limited quantities of average daily production (depletable oil quantity) of certain domestic crude oil or natural gas. The total depletable oil quantity is 1,000 barrels per day.[349] For this purpose, production of natural gas is converted into equivalent barrels at the ratio of 6,000 cubic feet to one barrel.[350]

Under the independent-producer exemption, no percentage depletion is allowable on natural gas production unless the taxpayer elects to have the exemption apply to that production. If this election is made, the number of equivalent barrels covered by the election reduces the 1,000-barrel-per-day depletable oil quantity otherwise applicable to crude oil production.[351]

---

346. Reg. Sec. 1.613A-5.
347. I.R.C. Sec. 613A(d)(1).
348. I.R.C. Sec. 613A(d)(1); Prop. Reg. Sec. 1.613A-7(q).
349. I.R.C. Sec. 613A(c)(3)(B).
350. I.R.C. Sec. 613A(c)(4).
351. *Ibid.*

The amount of gas, if any, subject to the independent-producer exemption is termed the *daily depletable natural gas quantity*. It is equal to 6,000 cubic feet multiplied by the number of barrels of the taxpayer's depletable oil quantity that the taxpayer elects to have transferred to natural gas production. The election is made in the tax return by claiming percentage depletion on the natural gas production that the taxpayer elects to include in filling the depletable oil quantity.[352] The election may be made in the original or amended tax return, or through a claim for credit or refund at any time before the expiration (including extensions) of the statute of limitations.[353] The taxpayer may change the election by filing an amended return or a claim for credit or refund.[354]

Operator A's average daily production of domestic crude oil or natural gas for any tax year is determined by dividing his aggregate production of domestic crude oil or natural gas by the number of days in that tax year.[355] *(See Case 94.)* In this case, Operator A's average daily production of oil is 1,200 barrels per day (438,000 ÷ 365 days), and his average daily production of gas is 250 barrels ((547,500 MCF ÷ 6) ÷ 365).

Because Operator A's combined average daily production of oil and gas exceeds his 1,000-barrel-per-day depletable quantity, he should make computations to determine whether it is advantageous to elect to convert a portion (or all) of his natural gas to equivalent barrels for the depletable quantity limitation. Factors affecting the decision to convert natural gas to equivalent barrels include variations in price, the 50% of net income limitation on percentage depletion, the amount of available cost depletion and the effect of the reduction in depletion due to the excess of actual daily production over the depletable quantity.

Natural gas sold pursuant to a qualifying fixed contract or qualified natural gas from geopressured brine is subject to the allowance for depletion without regard to the independent-producer exemption provisions.[356] *(See Case 93.)* Consequently, any such gas production should not be considered in computing the average daily production of natural gas.[357] The production of that gas does not reduce the quantity available for depletion under the independent-producer exemption, and no election is necessary to claim percentage depletion on that gas production. *(See Case 103 for a discussion of secondary or tertiary gas production as it relates to the depletable quantity limitations.)*

352. Reg. Sec. 1.613A-5.
353. *Ibid.*
354. *Ibid.*
355. I.R.C. Sec. 613A(c)(2); Prop. Reg. Sec. 1.613A-7(f).
356. I.R.C. Sec. 613A(b).
357. I.R.C. Sec. 613A(c)(12).

Case 96
Computation of Percentage Depletion Under the Independent-Producer Exemption

During calendar year 1987, Operator A has oil and gas production as follows:

	Type of Production	1987 Gross Production	Percentage Depletion Carryforward from 1986
United States			
Lease A	Primary oil	160,000 bbls.	$ 50,000
Lease B	Secondary oil	100,000 bbls.	100,000
Lease C	Fixed-contract gas	200,000 MCF	None
Lease D	Primary oil	391,920 bbls.	50,000
Lease E	Primary oil	50,000 bbls.	25,000
Foreign			
Lease F	Primary oil	100,000 bbls.	None

Operator A's taxable income for 1987 before any depletion deduction is $240,000. His accountant requests information as to the steps to be followed in computing percentage depletion under the independent-producer exemption.

Operator A is not engaged in refining, nor does he operate any retail outlet that markets petroleum products. None of the properties was proven when acquired.

Operator A cannot deduct any percentage depletion on the foreign oil production *(see Case 94)* but may deduct cost depletion. Operator A may claim percentage depletion on at least a portion of his domestic oil production under the independent-producer exemption.

The steps in the computation of percentage depletion under the independent-producer exemption are as follows:

1. Compute cost depletion for each property. *(See Case 79.)*
2. Identify production (if any) from fixed-contract gas. This production is subject to the 22% depletion rate and is not subject to the depletable quantity limitations.[358] Also, for production from wells drilled between September 30, 1978, and January 1, 1984, segregate qualified natural gas from geopressured brine, which is subject to the 10% depletion rate and is not subject to the depletable quantity limitations.[359] Compute percentage depletion on this production in the customary way, considering the 50% of net income limitation. *(See Case 87.)* The allowable depletion deduction for each property with respect to fixed-contract gas and qualified natural gas from geopressured brine equals the greater of cost depletion or percentage depletion computed in this Step 2.

358. I.R.C. Sec. 613A(b)(1); I.R.C. Sec. 613A(c)(12).
359. I.R.C. Sec. 613A(b)(2); I.R.C. Sec. 613A(c)(12).

3. Compute tentative percentage depletion on all the remaining production at the rate of 15%, considering the 50% of net income limitation. If cost depletion (Step 1) exceeds tentative percentage depletion thus computed with respect to a particular property, that cost depletion represents the allowable deduction for that property. If the average daily production from all properties subject to the independent-producer exemption exceeds the depletable quantity, apply the depletable-quantity limitation by adjusting the tentative percentage depletion (other than for properties for which cost depletion exceeds percentage depletion) as follows:[360]

Depletable quantity / Average daily production from all domestic properties**	×	Tentative percentage depletion on each property*	=	Tentative adjusted percentage depletion*

* Excluding properties for which cost depletion exceeds tentative percentage depletion.

** Excluding fixed-contract gas, natural gas from geopressured brine and production from properties ineligible for percentage depletion as a result of the proven property transfer rules. (Note that this fraction in effect allocates a portion of the depletable quantity to properties for which cost depletion exceeds percentage depletion.)

4. Determine the maximum percentage depletion allowable under the 65% of taxable income limitation for the current year. Taxable income for this purpose is computed without regard to any depletion allowable under the independent-producer exemption. It is computed, however, by deducting percentage or cost depletion on natural gas production that is not subject to the independent-producer exemption (i.e., natural gas sold under a qualified fixed contract and natural gas from geopressured brine) and by deducting cost depletion on any oil production to which the independent-producer exemption does not apply (i.e., foreign production and transferred production).[361] Net operating loss carrybacks and capital loss carrybacks are not considered, nor is the deduction for trust distributions (except in certain circumstances).

   The Congressional Committee Reports and proposed regulations indicate that if the cost depletion deduction allowable on one or more of a taxpayer's oil or gas properties subject to the independent-producer exemption is greater than the percentage depletion deduction allowable without regard to the 65% limitation or the depletable quantity limitation, a taxpayer also must deduct the entire amount of that allowable cost depletion in computing taxable income for purposes of the 65% limitation.[362]

   The maximum percentage depletion allowable under the independent-producer exemption is 65% of taxable income thus computed. If the maximum amount allowable exceeds the aggregate amount determined in Step 3, the amount determined in Step 3 will be the percentage depletion allowable and Steps 5 and 6 will not be necessary.

5. If 65% of taxable income as determined in Step 4 is less than the aggregate tentative percentage depletion (or tentative adjusted percentage depletion if applicable) determined in Step 3, the 65% limit applies and must be allocated to properties. Allocate the 65% of taxable income to those properties for which the tentative percentage depletion (or tentative adjusted percentage depletion if applicable) determined in Step 3 exceeds cost depletion. Note, do not allocate any of the

360. I.R.C. Sec. 613A(c)(7)(A); I.R.C. Sec. 613A(c)(7)(B).
361. I.R.C. Sec. 613A(d)(1).
362. General Explanation of the Tax Reform Act of 1976, prepared by the Staff of the Joint Committee on Taxation, 1976-3 C.B. Vol. 2 638; Prop. Reg. Sec. 1.613A-4(a)(1).

65% limit to depletion on gas from fixed contracts or from geopressured brine and do not allocate any to properties on which cost depletion exceeds percentage depletion determined without the 65% limit (Step 3). Allocate the 65% limit in accordance with the relative amounts of tentative (or tentative adjusted) percentage depletion on applicable properties as determined in Step 3.

6. Compare the percentage depletion determined in Step 5 to cost depletion determined in Step 1 for each property. If cost depletion exceeds the percentage depletion on any property, the depletion deductible with respect to that property will be the cost depletion.[363]

   Also, if cost depletion exceeds percentage depletion for any of the properties, reallocate the amount of the 65% limit among the remaining properties in the manner prescribed under Step 5.[364] This reallocation results in the apportionment of the total 65% limit computed in Step 4 among only those properties for which the percentage depletion exceeds cost depletion. *(See Case 115.)* The percentage depletion on each property will be the amount resulting from this reallocation.

7. Determine if any percentage depletion carryovers from prior years may be utilized. The amount of those carryovers that may be utilized is equal to the excess of 65% of taxable income for the current year as determined in Step 4 over the percentage depletion otherwise allowable for the year as determined in Step 3 or after the reallocation in Step 6, whichever is applicable.[365] Note that, in making this comparison, the aggregate 65% limit is compared only to percentage depletion allowable under the independent-producer exemption (i.e., percentage depletion other than on gas from fixed contracts and geopressured brine and on properties other than those for which cost depletion exceeds percentage depletion).

   For purposes of determining the adjusted basis of oil and gas properties, to the extent a carryover is used as a deduction, the amount so used is allocated to properties in proportion to the amounts disallowed on the respective properties in the year of disallowance.[366] Presumably, percentage depletion carryovers are utilized on a first-in, first-out basis.

8. Determine the deduction for allowable depletion by computing the sum of:

   a. Cost depletion on properties for which cost depletion (Step 1) exceeds percentage depletion as determined in Steps 3, 5 or 6, as the case may be;

   b. Percentage depletion on fixed-contract gas and on gas from geopressured brine as determined in Step 2;

   c. Percentage depletion on current-year production under the independent-producer exemption (i.e. the lesser (on a property-by-property basis) of the amounts determined under Step 3 or the 65% limit determined under Steps 5 or 6); and

   d. Any usable portion of the carryover from prior years determined under Step 7.

9. Determine the percentage depletion carryover from the current year by computing for all properties subject to the independent-producer exemption the excess of the greater of cost depletion (Step 1) or tentative (adjusted) percentage depletion (Step 3) for each property over the allowable depletion for each property, whether based on percentage or cost (Step 8). In determining this carryover, depletion applicable

363. I.R.C. Sec. 613(a); I.R.C. Sec. 613A(d)(1); Prop. Reg. Sec. 1.613A-4(a)(1).
364. Prop. Reg. Sec. 1.613A-4(a)(1).
365. Prop. Reg. Sec. 1.613A-7(q).
366. Prop. Reg. Sec. 1.613A-4(a)(1).

to fixed-contract gas and qualified gas from geopressured brine should not be considered.

Under the steps outlined above, the tax basis of properties is reduced (but not below zero) only to the extent of the percentage depletion actually deducted within the 65% of taxable income limitation. Under this approach, any percentage depletion included in a carryover amount will not reduce tax basis in the specific properties to which it relates until the year in which the carryover becomes deductible within the 65% of taxable income limitation. In that year, the taxpayer adjusts the basis of the property downward (but not below zero) by the amount of the allowable depletion.[367]

If a particular property is disposed of prior to the beginning of the year in which the carryover depletion is deducted, proposed regulations require the taxpayer to reduce the amount of the carryover depletion deduction by the lesser of the adjusted basis in the property at the date of disposition or the difference between that basis and the taxpayer's adjusted basis in the property in the absence of the 65% limitation. (If this difference is the lesser amount, it will be equal to the carryover depletion on that property.)[368]

Assume the following in 1987 with respect to Operator A's property:

Property	Cost Depletion (Step 1)	Tentative Percentage Depletion* (Step 3)
Lease A	$50,000	$ 40,000
Lease B	15,000	60,000
Lease C	10,000	70,000
Lease D	20,000	120,000
Lease E	3,000	10,000
Lease F	40,000	N/A

* After the 50% of taxable income limitation, but before application of the depletable quantity limitation.

The allowable deduction for Lease C (fixed-contract gas) is not subject to the 65% or depletable quantity limitations. Operator A is entitled to deduct the full percentage depletion ($70,000), which exceeds cost depletion (Step 2). The cost depletion on Lease A ($50,000) exceeds the tentative percentage depletion ($40,000); therefore, that cost depletion will become the allowable deduction with respect to Lease A. However, as illustrated below, the production on Lease A still must be considered in applying the depletable quantity limitation.

Operator A's average daily production from properties subject to the independent-producer exemption exceeds his depletable quantity; therefore, the depletable quantity limitation applies, and the tentative percentage depletion for Operator A's properties must be adjusted as follows (Step 3):

367. Prop. Reg. Sec. 1.613A-4(a)(1).
368. Prop. Reg. Sec. 1.613A-4(a)(1); Prop. Reg. Sec. 1.613A-4(a)(2), Example 5.

$$\text{Limitation Ratio} = \frac{\text{Depletable quantity (365,000 barrels)}}{\text{Aggregate production (701,920 barrels)*}} = .520$$

Property	Tentative Percentage Depletion	Limitation Ratio	Tentative Adjusted Percentage Depletion
Lease A	$ 40,000	N/A	$ N/A
Lease B	60,000	.520	31,200
Lease C	N/A	N/A	N/A
Lease D	120,000	.520	62,400
Lease E	10,000	.520	5,200
Total			$98,800

* Aggregate production (in barrels) includes Lease A + Lease B + Lease D + Lease E, or 160,000 + 100,000 + 391,920 + 50,000.

Operator A's taxable income for applying the 65% of taxable income limitation is computed as follows (Step 4):

Taxable income before depletion	$240,000
Cost depletion on Lease A (where cost exceeded percentage depletion before application of the depletable quantity limitation)	(50,000)
Allowable depletion on Lease C (fixed-contract gas)	(70,000)
Cost depletion on Lease F (foreign production)	(40,000)
Taxable income for purposes of 65% of taxable income limitation	$ 80,000
	× 65%
Maximum allowable percentage depletion under 65% of taxable income limitation	$ 52,000

The $52,000 maximum percentage depletion is allocated initially among Leases B, D and E as follows (Step 5):

Property	Cost Depletion	Tentative Depletion (before 65% limitation)	Relative Percent	Allocated Percentage Depletion Limitation
Lease B	$15,000	$31,200	31.6%	$16,432
Lease D	20,000	62,400	63.2	32,864
Lease E	3,000	5,200	5.2	2,704
	$38,000	$98,800	100.0%	$52,000

After allocation of the allowable percentage depletion of $52,000, cost depletion of $3,000 on Lease E exceeds percentage depletion of $2,704 (Step 6). The regulations[369] provide that, in this case, the allowable percentage depletion deduction should be

369. Prop. Reg. Sec. 1.613A-4(a)(1).

reallocated between the remaining properties (Leases B and D) as shown below (Step 7):

Property	Tentative Depletion (before 65% limitation)	Relative Percent	Allocated Percentage Depletion Limitation
Lease B	$31,200	33.3%	$17,333
Lease D	62,400	66.7	34,667
	$93,600	100.0%	$52,000

Operator A's 1987 depletion deduction may be summarized as follows:

Property	Type of Depletion	1987 Depletion Deduction
Lease A	Cost	$ 50,000
Lease B	Percentage	17,333
Lease C	Percentage (fixed-contract gas)	70,000
Lease D	Percentage	34,667
Lease E	Cost	3,000
Lease F	Cost	40,000
		$215,000

Operator A's percentage depletion carryforward from 1987 is computed as follows (Step 8):

Property	Allowable Depletion (before 65% limitation)	1987 Allowable Depletion	Percentage Depletion Carryover from 1987
Lease A	$ 50,000*	$ 50,000*	$ None
Lease B	31,200	17,333	13,867
Lease C	70,000**	70,000**	None
Lease D	62,400	34,667	27,733
Lease E	5,200	3,000*	2,200
Lease F	40,000***	40,000***	None
	$258,800	$215,000	$43,800

* Cost Depletion
** Fixed-Contract Gas
*** Cost Depletion on Foreign Production

In this case, Operator A cannot use any of his percentage depletion carryforward from 1986. Assume, however, that Operator A's taxable income before depletion in 1987 had been $500,000 rather than $240,000. Operator A's allowable depletion deduction would have been computed as follows:

Taxable income before depletion	$500,000
Cost depletion on Lease A (where cost exceeded percentage depletion before application of the depletable quantity limitation)	(50,000)
Allowable depletion on Lease C (fixed-contract gas)	(70,000)
Cost depletion on Lease F (foreign production)	(40,000)
Taxable income for purposes of 65% of taxable income limitation	$340,000
	× 65%
Allowable percentage depletion	$221,000

In this case, Operator A will be able to use fully the percentage depletion of $98,800 he generated in 1987 (Lease B, $31,200; Lease D, $62,400; Lease E $5,200) and $122,200 ($221,000 less $98,800) of his $225,000 percentage depletion carryforward from 1986. Operator A also will have a remaining carryforward to 1988 of $102,800 ($225,000 less $122,200) with respect to Leases A, B, D and E, computed as follows:

Property		Utilized in 1987 (Step 9)	Carryforward to 1988
Lease A:	$\frac{50,000}{225,000} \times \$122,200 =$	$ 27,156	$ 22,844
Lease B:	$\frac{100,000}{225,000} \times \$122,200 =$	54,311	45,689
Lease D:	$\frac{50,000}{225,000} \times \$122,200 =$	27,156	22,844
Lease E:	$\frac{25,000}{225,000} \times \$122,200 =$	13,577	11,423
		$122,200	$102,800

Operator A reduces the depletable basis in his oil and gas properties by the carryforward percentage depletion when that depletion is used in his tax return.[370]

Case 97
Depletable Quantity and Rates for Fiscal-Year Taxpayers

X Corporation is in the business of exploring for, developing and producing oil and gas in the United States. It is neither directly nor indirectly engaged in refining or retailing activities. X Corporation is not a personal-service corporation, but it does use the accrual method of accounting and has adopted a fiscal year ending May 31. For its fiscal year ended May

370. Prop. Reg. Sec. 1.613A-4(a)(1).

31, 1987, its oil and gas production, all from primary processes, and gross income from production are as follows:

	June 1-Dec. 31, 1986	Jan. 1-May 31, 1987	Total
Oil production	192,600 bbls.	120,800 bbls.	314,200 bbls.
Gas production	642,000 MCF	362,400 MCF	1,006,800 MCF
Oil sales	$3,852,000	$2,416,000	$6,268,000
Gas sales	$1,284,000	$ 724,800	$2,008,800

None of the producing properties was acquired in a disqualifying transfer after December 31, 1974. The corporation is not a member of a controlled group of corporations, nor is it a business entity under common control.

X Corporation's taxable income for its fiscal year ended May 31, 1987, is $6 million before any percentage or cost depletion deductions.

If none of X Corporation's gas production is sold under a fixed contract or qualifies as natural gas from geopressured brine *(see Case 93)*, the allowable percentage depletion is limited to the amount computed under the independent-producer exemption provisions. In computing allowable percentage depletion under these provisions, fiscal-year taxpayers must treat each part of a fiscal year that falls within a calendar year as if it were a separate, short tax year.[371] Even though the depletion rate would be the same for both periods, the barrel-per-day limitation can be different. For this reason, X Corporation must make two separate percentage depletion computations: one covering production during the period from June 1, 1986, through December 31, 1986, and another covering production during the period from January 1, 1987, through May 31, 1987.

Assuming that the 50% of net income limitation does not limit the percentage depletion computed on any of X Corporation's oil and gas properties, X Corporation's tentative percentage depletion for the fiscal year ended May 31, 1987, (before applying the independent-producer quantity limitation) is $1,241,520, computed as follows:

	Gross Income	Applicable Rate	Tentative Percentage Depletion
1986 Oil	$3,852,000	15%	$ 577,800
1986 Gas	1,284,000	15%	192,600
1987 Oil	2,416,000	15%	362,400
1987 Gas	724,800	15%	108,720
	$8,276,800		$1,241,520

371. I.R.C. Sec. 613A(c)(11).

X Corporation should maintain records to show the actual amount of production attributable to each period.

In this situation, X Corporation's average daily production for 1986 is:

Oil—192,600 barrels ÷ 214 (days)	900 barrels
Gas—(642,000 MCF ÷ 6) ÷ 214 (days)	500 barrels
Total average daily production	1,400 barrels

The average daily production attributable to 1987 is:

Oil—120,800 barrels ÷ 151 (days)	800 barrels
Gas—(362,400 MCF ÷ 6) ÷ 151 (days)	400 barrels
Total daily average production	1,200 barrels

X Corporation may claim percentage depletion only on oil production unless it properly elects to include all or a portion of its gas production in the computation.[372] *(See Case 95.)* Because only 1,000 barrels per day are eligible for percentage depletion under the independent-producer exemption for both 1986 and 1987 production *(see Case 96)*, X Corporation should determine the amount of gas that will maximize the percentage depletion deduction for each of the short periods contained in its tax year.

Assuming that X Corporation wants to take percentage depletion on all its oil production in each period, X Corporation must reduce the percentage depletion computations on its gas production for each short period because total average daily production exceeds 1,000 barrels in each period. X Corporation computes the limitation ratio for gas production for each period as follows:

	1986 Average Daily Production	1987 Average Daily Production
Tentative depletable oil quantity for 1986 and 1987 (in barrels)	1,000	1,000
Less: Average daily oil production per period	900	800
Remaining depletable quantity available for gas	100	200
Average daily gas production per period	500	400
Limitation ratio for gas production (Remaining quantity ÷ gas production)	100/500 20%	200/400 50%

Applying these limitation percentages to the tentative percentage depletion computed for primary gas production for both short periods of its fiscal year, X Corporation will

372. I.R.C. Sec. 613A(c)(4); Reg. Sec. 1.613A-5.

calculate the adjusted percentage depletion of $1,033,080 as follows for the fiscal year ended May 31, 1987:

	Tentative Percentage Depletion	Limitation Ratio	Adjusted Percentage Depletion
1986 Oil	$ 577,800	—	$ 577,800
1986 Gas	192,600	100/500	38,520
1987 Oil	362,400	—	362,400
1987 Gas	108,720	200/400	54,360
Total	$1,241,520		$1,033,080

X Corporation may elect to apply more of its gas production to its 1,000-barrel-per-day depletable oil quantity at the expense of limiting the percentage depletion claimed on its oil production. When determining the amount of gas to apply to the depletable quantity limitation, X Corporation should consider the effect of the 50% of net income limitation as well as the gross selling price per barrel (or equivalent unit) when trying to maximize depletion. For example, it may be desirable for a taxpayer to elect to apply more gas production to the limitation quantity when the 50% depletion limitation applies to oil properties. X Corporation should also consider the effect of cost depletion when making the election.

After X Corporation reduces its tentative percentage depletion by taking into consideration the depletable quantity limitation adjustments, the deduction for percentage depletion is limited further to 65% of taxable income prior to the deduction for that depletion.[373]

Even though a fiscal-year taxpayer must compute percentage depletion (subject to the 50% of net income limitation) separately for each short period in the fiscal year, that taxpayer apparently should compute cost depletion for each property based on the production for the entire fiscal year. According to proposed regulations, this is true for fiscal-year taxpayers with oil and gas production attributable to periods before January 1, 1975, that was not subject to the independent-producer exemption provisions.[374]

X Corporation first will compare cost depletion computed on each property for the entire fiscal year with the sum of the percentage depletion amounts computed for the two short periods that are attributable to the property. The percentage depletion computations will consider the 50% of net income limitation but will not consider the depletable quantity limitation or the 65% of taxable income limitation. On those properties for which cost depletion exceeds the sum of the percentage depletion amounts so calculated, the cost depletion amounts will be deductible and will reduce the income of X Corporation in determining the 65% of taxable income limitation.[375]

Fiscal-year taxpayers apply the 65% limitation to taxable income for the entire fiscal year and not to each short period included in the fiscal year.[376]

In this example, X Corporation's percentage depletion deduction for the fiscal year ended May 31, 1987, would be limited as follows, assuming that X Corporation has

373. I.R.C. Sec. 613A(d)(1).
374. Reg. Sec. 1.613A-1.
375. Prop. Reg. Sec. 1.613A-4(a)(1).
376. *Ibid.*

cost depletion of $100,000 on properties exceeding percentage depletion before applying the depletable quantity limitation or 65% limitation:

Taxable income for the year before considering any depletion deduction	$6,000,000
Cost depletion on properties that exceeds percentage depletion (before any limitations)	(100,000)
Taxable income for purposes of computing 65% limitation	$5,900,000
Maximum percentage depletion allowable on production for the year ($5,900,000 × 65%)	$3,835,000

If X Corporation's percentage depletion as adjusted for the depletable quantity limitation exceeds 65% of its taxable income as adjusted, the 65% limitation is allocated to each property for which percentage depletion exceeds cost depletion. *(See Case 115 for further discussion of the mechanics of applying the 65% of taxable income limitation on a property-by-property basis.)*

In this case, X Corporation's percentage depletion deduction as adjusted for the depletable quantity limitation ($1,033,080) does not exceed 65% of taxable income as adjusted ($3,835,000). Accordingly, for its fiscal year ended May 31, 1987, X Corporation will claim a depletion deduction on a particular property equal to the greater of cost depletion computed on that property for the entire fiscal year or the sum of the percentage depletion amounts (adjusted for the quantity limitation) computed on that property for the two short periods.

Case 98
Computation of Depletion on Lease Bonus Income

In 1987, Lessor R assigns 100% of the working interest in a 1,280-acre oil and gas lease to Lessee S in consideration of an initial payment (lease bonus) of $100,000. Lessor R retains an overriding royalty interest of 4% of all the minerals produced from the oil and gas lease. No development or production takes place during 1987. Lessor R has a $15,000 adjusted tax basis in the oil and gas lease. The nearest commercial production is approximately 30 miles away.

Lessor R actually has made a sublease of the oil and gas lease by virtue of retaining a continuing economic interest in the property in the form of an overriding royalty interest. The $100,000 constitutes ordinary income to Lessor R, subject to an allowance for depletion.[377]

Percentage Depletion

Percentage depletion under the independent-producer and royalty-owner exemption is computed with respect to as much of a taxpayer's average daily production as does not exceed a specified amount.[378]

For amounts received or accrued before August 17, 1986, taxpayers were permitted to claim percentage depletion allowances on lease bonuses and advance royalties for the

377. Berg v. Comm'r, 33 F.2d 641 (D.C. Cir. 1929), 7 AFTR 9195, 1929 CCH D-9256; Cox v. U.S., 497 F.2d 348 (4th Cir. 1974), 34 AFTR2d 74-5007, 74-1 USTC 9461; Rev. Rul. 69-352, 1969-1 C.B. 34.
378. I.R.C. Sec. 613A(c)(1).

year those payments were included in income.[379] The depletable quantity limitation was applied by simply converting those payments into units of production at the same price received for production from the property during the year.[380] If there was no production from the property during the year, or if the product was not sold before conversion or transportation from the premises, the conversion into units of product was to be based on a representative market or field price for production in the area.[381] If percentage depletion has been claimed in prior years, the units of production calculated in this manner should continue to be excluded from actual production in subsequent years to prevent double counting.[382]

Lease bonuses, advance royalties and other payments without regard to production no longer qualify for percentage depletion for income received or accrued after August 16, 1986.[383] Therefore, only cost depletion will be allowed for bonus income recognized after this date. Also, if the lease expires without production, cost depletion previously claimed must be returned to income.[384] Should the lease expire without production, restoration of the cost depletion on the lease bonus may be avoided if Lessor R disposes (by any means) of his retained royalty prior to termination of the lease.[385] *(See Case 127.)* To the extent cost depletion claimed on the bonus is restored to income, the taxpayer should increase his basis in the lease.

Cost Depletion

Lessor R's allowable cost depletion is an amount equal to the portion of his adjusted basis of the oil and gas lease that the bonus bears to the sum of the bonus and the royalties expected to be received, without reduction of the royalties to present value.[386] To make this computation, Lessor R must secure geological information sufficient to make a reasonable estimate of the amount of royalties expected to be received from the retained interest. The cost depletion formula may be expressed mathematically as follows:

$$\text{Cost depletion} = \text{Adjusted basis} \times \frac{a}{a + b} \quad \text{where}$$

a = Lease bonus

b = Royalties expected to be received in the future

The *Collums* decision[387] held that a zero estimate of royalties to be received in the future is "reasonable" in circumstances where the lease is in a "wildcat" area and where there is no evidence to indicate there will be future oil and gas production during the term of the lease. The burden of proof is on the taxpayer to demonstrate the reasonableness of the estimate of the royalties to be received in the future.[388] Because Lessor R's lease is 30 miles away from the nearest commercial production, it may be possible for him to assert that a reasonable estimate of the royalties expected to

379. IRS Announcement 84-59, 1984-23 I.R.B. 58.
380. *Ibid.*
381. *Ibid.*
382. *Ibid.*
383. I.R.C. Sec. 613(e)(4); I.R.C. Sec. 613A(d)(5).
384. Reg. Sec. 1.612-3(a)(2).
385. Mary F. Waggoner, 47 B.T.A. 669 (1942).
386. Reg. Sec. 1.612-3(a).
387. Collums v. U.S., 480 F. Supp. 864 (D.C. Wyo. 1979), 45 AFTR2d 80-751, 80-1 USTC 9203.
388. F-K Land Company v. Comm'r, 90 F.2d 484 (9th Cir. 1937), 19 AFTR 862, 37-2 USTC 9346.

be received is zero. In that case, using the formula above, Lessor R will compute a cost depletion deduction as follows:

$$\$15{,}000 \times \frac{\$100{,}000}{\$100{,}000 + 0} = \$15{,}000$$

It should be noted that the Internal Revenue Service (IRS) has been reluctant to apply broadly the finding in the *Collums* decision. In a subsequent technical advice memorandum,[389] the IRS ruled that a 100% cost depletion rate was inappropriate with respect to certain overriding royalty interests retained on various wildcat leases. The IRS reasoned that a determination that no future production was likely was equivalent to arguing no mineral deposit exists. In that case, the IRS argued that a deduction for cost depletion cannot be claimed when there is no mineral deposit present. This ruling fails to make any reference to the *Collums* decision in reaching its conclusion, and it does not appear that its position is a correct interpretation of the regulations. For example, the ruling states that the regulations that allow cost depletion on a bonus presume the existence of depletable mineral deposits. Arguably, these regulations contemplated that no mineral deposit may exist when cost depletion is claimed by requiring that any cost depletion claimed be restored to income if the lease expires, terminates or is abandoned before obtaining production.[390]

When the adjusted basis of the lease exceeds the lease bonus, the cost depletion deduction should not exceed the amount of the lease bonus.[391]

Case 99
Percentage Depletion on Amounts Received With Respect to Take-or-Pay Gas Contracts

Operator A owns working interests in several gas properties and enters into a 20-year take-or-pay gas purchase contract with B Company. Operator A agrees to sell or make available a minimum of 100,000 MCF of gas per year at a price of $2 per MCF (with escalation provisions), and B Company agrees to take that gas or pay for it. B Company may take make-up gas in any year after taking the minimum of 100,000 MCF for that year. The payments by B Company are considered to be nonrecourse to Operator A. The activity for the first four years of the contract is as follows:

Year	Payment for Gas	Value of Gas Delivered	Make-up (Deficiency)
1	$200,000	$ 80,000	$ (120,000)
2	200,000	160,000	(40,000)
3	200,000	40,000	(160,000)
4	200,000	40,000	(160,000)
	$800,000	$320,000	$ (480,000)

389. IRS Letter Ruling 8532011 (Technical Advice Memorandum).
390. Reg. Sec. 1.612-3(a)(2).
391. Murphy Oil Co. v. Burnet, 287 U.S. 299 (1932), 11 AFTR 1095, 3 USTC 1002.

Operator A is entitled to percentage depletion under the independent-producer exemption.

The Internal Revenue Service (IRS) has ruled[392] that payments received for gas to be taken in the future are not mineral production payments and must be included in taxable income for the year in which received. The IRS would have allowed percentage depletion for the year in which the advance payment was received to the extent the advance payment was received before August 17, 1986, and when converted to equivalent units of production, it did not exceed the depletable quantity limitation.[393] However, the Tax Reform Act of 1986 does not allow percentage depletion on amounts payable without regard to production.[394] *(See Case 98 for a discussion of the right to percentage depletion on lease bonuses.)*

Before the ruling, many practitioners believed that the production payment rules applied to payments taxpayers received for gas not actually taken.[395] This conclusion was based on the premise that take-or-pay contracts give the buyer of the gas the implied right to minerals in place equal to the quantity of gas for which the buyer had paid but had not taken. In a fact pattern very similar to this case, the Tax Court recently concluded that a taxpayer making payments pursuant to a take-or-pay contract had created a production payment.[396] *(See Case 11 for a further discussion of take-or-pay gas purchase contracts.)*

A taxpayer following the Tax Court decision will treat as nonrecourse loans payments received for gas the buyer does not take and will report taxable income when the buyer takes the gas in a subsequent tax year. This treatment will result in the taxpayer's reporting taxable income coincident with the actual production, which should also result in the proper allowance of percentage depletion since the payment would then be attributable to actual production. *(See Case 88 concerning treatment of production payments retained in leasing transactions.)*

The regulations define a production payment as the right to a specified share of the production from minerals in place (if, as and when produced) or the proceeds from that production. This right must be an economic interest in the minerals in place and may be payable out of more than one property.[397] In addition, the regulations state that any right that is in substance economically equivalent to a production payment shall be treated as a production payment.[398] Based on this definition, it appears that taxpayers receiving payment for gas the buyer does not take may properly classify that amount as a production payment to be treated as a nonrecourse loan for income tax purposes. This was the very analysis made by the Tax Court in reaching the conclusion that the purchaser had acquired by investment (i.e., the advance payments) an interest in the mineral in place which could be satisfied solely by production from the property.[399] Although the payment for gas not taken was considered the economic equivalent to a production payment, the IRS (consistent with its prior ruling) argued that the take-or-pay situation merely involved the contractual right to receive the gas upon production and, therefore, did not constitute economic interest. The IRS believed the payment created at best an "economic advantage," not an "economic interest."

392. Rev. Rul. 80-48, 1980-1 C.B. 99; IRS Letter Ruling 8237001 (Technical Advice Memorandum).
393. Comm'r v. Engle, 82 U.S. 599 (1984), 53 AFTR2d 84-415, 84-1 USTC 9134; IRS Announcement 84-59, 1984-23 I.R.B. 58.
394. I.R.C. Sec. 613A(d)(5); I.R.C. Sec. 613(e)(4); P.L. 99-514 (Tax Reform Act of 1986), Sec. 412(a)(1); P.L. 99-514 (Tax Reform Act of 1986), Sec. 412(a)(2).
395. I.R.C. Sec. 636; Reg. Sec. 1.636-3.
396. H. J. Freede, 86 T.C. 340 (1986).
397. Reg. Sec. 1.636-3(a)(1).
398. Reg. Sec. 1.636-3(a)(2).
399. Freede.

The Tax Court did not agree, believing the taxpayers had satisfied the definitional requirement, and held in their favor.

The regulations provide an accounting method election that may apply to advance payments received for goods and long-term contracts by accrual-basis taxpayers.[400] Whether these rules may be elected for payments received under take-or-pay gas contracts depends on whether gas is an inventoriable product[401] and, if it is, whether there must be an actual inventory of produced and unsold gas at the end of the tax year. Although gas in place is not considered inventory, nevertheless, it should be considered inventoriable because it will be included in inventory if produced and stored for sale to customers. If gas is inventoriable, accrual-basis taxpayers receiving payments for gas under take-or-pay contracts generally can defer reporting the income until the earliest of: (1) the second year after the tax year of the receipt of payment for gas not taken if (generally) the gas is on hand and properly includable in inventory; (2) the year the buyer actually takes the make-up gas or (3) the year the taxpayer reports the income in his financial reports to shareholders, partners, beneficiaries or other proprietors or for credit purposes.

Based on the facts in this case, it appears that B Company has acquired an economic interest in the property via the take-or-pay contract payments under the reasoning of the recent Tax Court decision. Therefore, Operator A should treat the excess payments as a production payment. In that event, he will report income and claim depletion as the gas is delivered. *(See Case 11.)* If the excess payments are treated as a production payment, the original-issue discount rules may recharacterize a portion of those payments as interest. *(See Case 135 concerning the original-issue discount rules.)*

In contrast, if B Company did not acquire rights economically equivalent to an interest in the properties due to other provisions in the contract, then Operator A would report all receipts as taxable income. Income recognized for amounts received without regard to production no longer qualifies for percentage depletion for income accrued or received after August 16, 1986.[402] To the extent the payments received can be attributed to actual production, percentage depletion can be claimed, subject to the application of the depletable quantity limitations.

Case 100
Treatment of Advance Minimum Royalties Paid in Computing Percentage Depletion

On December 1, 1987, Operator A acquires an oil and gas lease on a contiguous 640-acre tract from Lessor R, who retains a one-eighth royalty interest. The lease contains a stipulation that in no event can the royalty payment in any year be less than $12,000. The $12,000 minimum payment is subject to an annual price adjustment to reflect changes in the U.S. Consumer Price Index (CPI). The lease also provides that amounts paid by Operator A in excess of one-eighth of production that are necessary to provide the annual minimum of $12,000 may be accumulated and applied to reduce future royalty payments to Lessor R in years in which one-eighth of the production exceeds $12,000. On December 1, 1987, Operator A pays Lessor R the $12,000 advance minimum royalty due under the agreement for the first annual leasing period (December 1, 1987-

400. Reg. Sec. 1.451-5; IRS Letter Ruling 8237001 (Technical Advice Memorandum).
401. Reg. Sec. 1.451-5(a)(1).
402. I.R.C. Sec. 613A(d)(5).

November 30, 1988). Production royalties otherwise due during each leasing period are to be reduced by the $12,000 minimum payment made at the commencement of each such leasing period. Based on geological and geophysical work, it is reasonable to expect that the mineral reserves committed to the lease are sufficient to cover the advance minimum royalty payments over the life of the lease. In the first year of the leasing period (December 1, 1987-November 30, 1988), total production from the lease is sold for $24,000. Operator A is a C corporation qualified to use a cash-basis accounting method and uses a calendar year for tax reporting.

The regulations[403] provide that the payor of recoupable advance royalties generally must treat those payments (in connection with the mineral property) as deductions from gross income in the year in which the mineral product that relates to those payments is sold. In the case of advance royalties paid in connection with a minimum royalty provision, however, the payor may elect to deduct those payments from gross income in the year those royalties are paid or accrued.[404] To qualify for the deduction, advance royalty payments under a minimum royalty provision must be payable in "substantially uniform" amounts at least annually over the life of the lease or for a period of at least 20 years.[405] If the lease may be renewed or extended, the additional period is treated as being part of the term of the original lease to qualify under the minimum royalty provisions.[406] The purpose of the "substantially uniform" clause ostensibly is to prohibit the lessee from being able to manipulate (particularly in the early years of the lease) the advance royalty to maximize the tax benefits from the deduction in a given year.

The Internal Revenue Service (IRS) has ruled[407] that an advance royalty computed according to a formula based on prior-year production is not "substantially uniform" within the meaning of the regulation. Additionally, in a recent court decision, it was held that, even though the regulations do not define "substantially uniform," it was clear that a schedule of payments that varied from $1 million in the initial year to $500,000 annually was not "substantially uniform."[408] However, in another ruling,[409] the IRS held that a provision in a lease calling for an annual adjustment to the advance royalty based on the CPI does not violate the "substantially uniform" requirement. Based on the literal language of the subsequent ruling, it appears that other advance royalty adjustments might be incorporated in the lease, provided those provisions are "outside the control of the parties to the lease" and do not "give rise to large aggregated payments in the earlier years."

Because the advance royalty provision in the agreement between Lessor R and Operator A satisfies the "substantially uniform" provision of the regulation and because annual payments are required over the life of the lease, Operator A may elect to treat the December 1, 1987, payment in excess of one-eighth of current production in either of the following ways:

☐ As a deduction from gross income in the year paid or accrued.

403. Reg. Sec. 1.612-3(b)(3); Redhouse v. Comm'r, 728 F.2d 1249 (9th Cir. 1984), 53 AFTR2d 84-995, 84-1 USTC 9311; Robert P. Wendland, 79 T.C. 355 (1982), *aff'd* 739 F.2d 580 (11th Cir. 1984), 54 AFTR2d 84-5851, 84-2 USTC 9746.
404. *Ibid.*
405. *Ibid.*
406. *Ibid.*
407. Rev. Rul. 79-381, 1979-2 C.B. 244.
408. Long, Jr. v. U.S., 10 Cl. Ct. 46 (Ct. Cl. 1986) 57 AFTR2d 86-1431, 86-1 USTC 9415.
409. Rev. Rul. 81-299, 1981-2 C.B. 138; IRS Letter Ruling 8106045; IRS Letter Ruling 8337019.

□ As a deduction from gross income in the year the mineral products for which the advance royalties were paid are sold.

If Operator A elects to defer the deduction of that portion of the royalty that represents an advance on future production, he will exclude only $3,000 (one-eighth of $24,000) as royalty payments and compute percentage depletion on gross income of $21,000 ($24,000 - $3,000). Operator A will exclude (as royalty and in computing gross income from the property for percentage depletion) the remaining $9,000 ($12,000 - $3,000) in future years when he recovers that advance royalty from Lessor R's share of production.[410]

If Operator A elects to claim the advance royalty as a deduction in the year in which it is paid, he will deduct $12,000 in 1987.[411] In a 1979 revenue ruling,[412] the IRS took the position that the lessee's "gross income from the property" for the purpose of computing percentage depletion should be reduced by the advance minimum royalty when the mineral product is produced and sold, even though the lessee had elected to deduct the advance minimum royalties in the year paid. This revenue ruling is inconsistent with the regulations which state that the amount excluded from "gross income from the property" for depletion purposes on account of advanced royalties paid is equal to the deduction taken in that year with respect to those payments.[413]

The IRS may take the position that Operator A is entitled to deduct only an allocable portion (one-twelfth) of the advance minimum royalty in 1987 should he elect to deduct the advance minimum royalty when paid.[414] The principal case[415] on which the IRS relied in reaching its conclusion in this ruling was reversed on appeal.[416] If Operator A were an accrual-basis taxpayer, the IRS also may contend that he would be limited to the portion of the advance minimum royalty allocable to 1987 (one-twelfth).[417]

In a ruling[418] where a lease provided for annual payment (involving both an accrual- and cash-basis taxpayer) of advance royalties over the life of the lease through the use of cash and nonrecourse, noninterest-bearing notes with no maturity dates, the IRS held the payment was not deductible as advance minimum royalties. The amount was not considered paid as the payment on those notes was contingent upon extraction of the underlying mineral and did not constitute a "fixed liability."

In 1983, the Tax Court addressed the deductibility of advance minimum royalties.[419] In the fact situation involved, the accrual-method taxpayer acquired a 10-year coal mining lease, pursuant to which he was required to prepay minimum royalties of $6,000 a year. Accordingly, in the initial year, the taxpayer paid the lessor $60,000, consisting of $10,000 in cash and a $50,000 nonrecourse interest-bearing note secured by the lease. Payment was to be made from all proceeds received by the project at the rate of $.50 per ton of coal sold. All unpaid principal and interest on the note were payable following the expiration of the lease in 10 years. The taxpayer claimed the entire $60,000 payment as a deduction on his tax return for the initial year, although no coal was mined in that year.

---

410. Reg. Sec. 1.613-2(c)(5)(iii).
411. Reg. Sec. 1.612-3(b)(3).
412. Rev. Rul. 79-386, 1979-2 C.B. 246.
413. Reg. Sec. 1.613-2(c)(5)(iii).
414. Rev. Rul. 80-70, 1980-1 C.B. 104; Rev. Rul. 77-489, 1977-2 C.B. 177.
415. Martin J. Zaninovich, 69 T.C. 605 (1978).
416. Zaninovich v. Comm'r, 616 F.2d 429 (9th Cir. 1980), 45 AFTR2d 80-1442, 80-1 USTC 9342.
417. Rev. Rul. 80-70, 1980-1 C.B. 104.
418. Rev. Rul. 80-73, 1980-1 C.B. 128.
419. Samuel E. Wing, 80 T.C. 537 (Mar. 14, 1983), *decision withdrawn, revised opinion* 81 T.C. 17 (Jul. 11, 1983).

In its original decision, the Tax Court held that the taxpayer could not claim any deduction to the extent the royalties were paid with the $50,000 note. The Tax Court withdrew this original decision and, in its substituted opinion, held that the taxpayer was not entitled to any deduction whatsoever, either for the $50,000 note or the $10,000 cash contribution because neither was paid pursuant to a valid minimum royalty provision. The court noted that a valid minimum royalty provision requires that a "substantially uniform" amount of royalties be paid at least annually. The court then agreed with the IRS that under the facts of the case there was no requirement for the taxpayer to make a payment on an annual basis because payment of the $50,000 would not be made for 10 years, if at all (except to the extent that annual royalties were paid out of production). In summary, the court concluded that the obligation to pay $10,000 the first year and possibly $50,000 after 10 years did not satisfy the requirement of "substantially uniform" annual payments.

In its substituted opinion, the court made no reference to the government's argument in its brief that when interpreting the words "paid at least annually" in the regulations, the word "paid" should be taken literally. However, in subsequent decisions the court has made it clear that it believes a minimum royalty provision "must" require annual payments in the literal sense.[420] Merely establishing the liability via annual nonrecourse or otherwise contingent obligations will not be sufficient to qualify as a minimum royalty provision.

In a 1978 decision, a federal district court in Oklahoma held that: (1) the term *royalty* in the context of advance royalty provisions includes an advance "overriding royalty" paid by a sublessee to the lessee of the mineral interest and (2) advance royalty payments covering multiple "units of property" may be recoupable out of more than one unit of property and still constitute advance royalties under the regulations.[421] Accordingly, if Lessor R's acreage was noncontiguous and thereby constituted more than one unit of property, Operator A's advance royalties (covering all properties) could be recoupable out of the combined production from all such properties without affecting his ability to deduct those amounts when paid. This decision allows flexibility in negotiating the terms of the agreement without necessarily affecting the lessee's (sublessee's) ability to deduct advance royalties when paid. The decision, however, does not necessarily reconcile neatly with the multiple property payout problem as it relates to the deductibility of intangible drilling and development costs.[422] *(See Case 46.)*

The treatment of advance minimum royalties in the tax return for the first year in which that payment is made constitutes an election to use that same treatment for all subsequent payments.[423] In the case of a partnership, the election to deduct advance minimum royalties when paid is made by the partnership, not the individual partners.[424]

Advance minimum royalties that are not recoverable out of future production are not subject to the treatment discussed above. *(See Cases 12 and 13.)*

In addition to the above, special rules exist for accrual-basis taxpayers,[425] cash-basis taxpayers and tax-shelter taxpayers[426] relating to the timing of deductions. Generally,

420. James Maddrix, 83 T.C. 613 (1984), *aff'd* 780 F.2d 946 (11th Cir. 1986), 57 AFTR2d 86-690, 86-1 USTC 9189; Dorothy Vastola, 84 T.C. 969 (1985); Richard C. Capek, 86 T.C. 14 (1986).
421. Aven v. U.S. (W.D. Okla. 1978), 42 AFTR2d 78-6120, 78-2 USTC 9729.
422. Rev. Rul. 80-109, 1980-1 C.B. 129.
423. Reg. Sec. 1.612-3(b)(3).
424. Reg. Sec. 1.612-3(b)(3); I.R.C. Sec. 703(b); Paul Elkins, 81 T.C. 669 (1983).
425. I.R.C. Sec. 461(h).
426. I.R.C. Sec. 461(i).

an item will not be allowed as a deduction under these rules until economic performance has occurred. *(See Case 10 for a discussion of when economic performance occurs with respect to advance minimum royalty payments.)*

For accrual-basis taxpayers, the "all-events" test will not be deemed to have been met until economic performance has occurred, unless the item qualifies for the recurring-item exception.[427] *(See Case 10 for this and other exceptions that may apply to accrual-basis taxpayers.)* The recurring-item exception is not allowed for tax shelters. *(See Case 9 for the definition of tax shelter for these purposes.)*

For taxpayers that can continue to report on a cash basis, the rules relating to the timing of advance royalty payments are unaffected by changes in the law. Thus, the election to deduct as paid or when the mineral is produced still is available. For cash-basis taxpayers considered to be tax shelters that were required to change to the accrual basis in 1987, the election to deduct as paid has been, in effect, modified by the economic performance requirement since tax shelters cannot utilize the recurring-item exception. *(See Case 10 for a discussion of the applicable transition rules for advance royalty payments under leases entered into by cash-basis tax shelters before September 25, 1985.)*

It appears that a lessor is treated as the producer[428] for purposes of the windfall profit tax (WPT) when advance minimum royalties are recouped through actual production. In connection with the WPT net income limitation[429] *(see Case 221)*, it is not clear how the computation is made when income and barrels attributed to the lessor are not closely matched. Resolution of these WPT issues must await further developments.

Case 101
Percentage Depletion on Minimum Royalty Recoverable from Future Production

In 1987, Lessor R grants an oil and gas lease in the United States to Operator A and retains a one-eighth royalty interest in the property with the provision that the royalty payment shall in no case be less than $5,000 per year. Amounts paid in excess of one-eighth of production that are necessary to provide the annual minimum payment of $5,000 may be accumulated and applied in reduction of royalty payments due in future years in excess of the annual minimum. Royalty payments for oil production for the year 1987 are as follows:

Lessor R's one-eighth of current production of $16,000	$2,000
Minimum payment provision	3,000
Total	$5,000

The estimated reserves underlying the lease substantially exceed those required for complete recoupment of the minimum payment.

427. I.R.C. Sec. 461(h)(3).
428. I.R.C. Sec. 4986(b); I.R.C. Sec. 4996(a)(1)(A).
429. I.R.C. Sec. 4988(b).

Percentage depletion under the independent-producer exemption is allowable on lease bonuses and advance royalties received or accrued before August 17, 1986.[430] *(See Case 98 for a discussion of the application of the depletable quantity limitations.)* However, it is not clear whether amounts received by Lessor R in 1987 that exceed his one eighth share of production will qualify for percentage depletion. The statute provides that gross income for purposes of computing percentage depletion does not include any lease bonus, advance royalty or other amount payable without regard to production for amounts accrued or received after August 16, 1986.[431] Lessor R's gross income for depletion purposes may include the gross receipts of the royalty, including amounts received in addition to his one-eighth share of current production necessary to meet the $5,000 minimum requirement to the extent the $5,000 payment does not exceed current production from the property.[432] Arguably, these payments are payable with regard to production and may constitute depletable gross income. However, amounts received in excess of Lessor R's one-eighth share of production may constitute "advance royalties" and, therefore, may not qualify for percentage depletion. This determination must await future clarification and explanation of the statute. Amounts received under the $5,000 minimum requirement that do not qualify for percentage depletion continue to qualify for cost depletion.

Lessor R may consider the total minimum royalty of $5,000 in computing his allowance for cost depletion.[433] For example, if the $5,000 received in 1987 is the equivalent to production of 250 barrels of oil, the estimated recoverable reserves at the beginning of the year attributable to Lessor R's royalty interest are 25,000 barrels of oil and his basis in the royalty interest is $60,000, Lessor R will be entitled to claim cost depletion in 1987 of $600, computed as follows:

$$\frac{\text{Unrecovered depletable costs}}{\text{Estimated recoverable barrels at beginning of year}} \times \text{Barrels sold} = \frac{\$60{,}000}{25{,}000} \times 250 = \$600$$

As under prior law, Operator A may be required to exclude from his depletable income all or a portion of the payments made under the minimum royalty provision which are depletable income to Lessor R.[434] Under the argument made above, payments to Lessor R that do not exceed the total production from the property may constitute royalties which constitute depletable income for percentage depletion purposes. If they do constitute royalties, Operator A is required to exclude from his depletable income the payments made under the minimum royalty provision that are depletable to Lessor R.[435] However, since payments to Lessor R that are in excess of his one-eighth share of production may be treated as an advance royalty, Operator A may be required to exclude from his annual depletable gross income a pro-rata share of the advance royalty paid to Lessor R.[436] This exclusion by Operator A should be made in the respective year in which he deducts the minimum payments.[437] In a controversial 1979 ruling, the IRS held that this exclusion should be made in the years

430. Comm'r v. Engle, 82 U.S. 599 (1984), 53 AFTR2d 84-415, 84-1 USTC 9134; IRS Announcement 84-59, 1984-23 I.R.B. 58.
431. I.R.C. Sec. 613A(d)(5); I.R.C. Sec. 613(e)(4); P.L. 99-514 (Tax Reform Act of 1986), Sec. 412(a)(1); P.L. 99-514 (Tax Reform Act of 1986), Sec. 412(a)(2).
432. Reg. Sec. 1.612-3(b)(1); Rev. Rul. 72-165, 1972-1 C.B. 177.
433. Reg. Sec. 1.612-3(b); Prop. Reg. Sec. 1.613A-7(f); Prop. Reg. Sec. 1.613A-3(a)(4), Example 4.
434. Reg. Sec. 1.613-2(c)(5)(i); Reg. Sec. 1.612-3(c)(5)(iii).
435. Reg. Sec. 1.613-2(c)(5)(i).
436. Reg. Sec. 1.613-2(c)(5)(iii).
437. I.R.C. Sec. 611(b)(1); Reg. Sec. 1.613-2(c)(5)(iii).

in which the applicable mineral products are produced or sold.[438] This ruling conflicts with the regulations[439] and should be clarified.

Based on court cases and IRS pronouncements, the original purpose underlying the "advance royalty exclusion rule" was to ensure that advance royalty payments were not counted twice in computing percentage depletion.[440] The IRS has held that if the lessor who receives a lease bonus (which is treated as an advance royalty) does not take the percentage depletion deduction on the bonus, the lessee must still exclude the income that is allocable to the bonus.[441] Arguably, based on the original purpose of the "advance royalty exclusion rule," the rule should not equitably be applied if the lessor is not entitled to percentage depletion on the advance royalty. Therefore, since advance royalties recognized as income after August 16, 1986, no longer qualify for percentage depletion, it appears to be inappropriate to continue to follow the "advance royalty exclusion rule" on these payments. It is hoped that this apparent inconsistency will be rectified by a technical correction or otherwise modified by an administrative pronouncement from the Treasury.

If the lease terminates before Operator A recovers all his advance royalty payments through production, Lessor R must restore to income in the year of termination any depletion deducted on the payments not recovered.[442] Although this depletion restoration rule is stated in the regulations, it is inconsistent with a similar rule relating to lease bonuses, which requires restoration only if the lease terminates without any commercial production. *(See Case 127.)*

If the amount received by Lessor R that is not in excess of his share of current production from the lease is the only amount that constitutes depletable income, the percentage depletion available to Lessor R would be \$300 (\$2,000 × 15%). In this case, he would deduct the cost depletion amount of \$600 since it is greater. *(See Cases 12 and 13 for a discussion of the treatment by the payor of any excess payments.)*

In contrast, if Lessor R is allowed percentage depletion on the total amounts received since such amounts do not exceed the current production from the property, the percentage depletion available to Lessor R would be \$750 (\$5,000 × 15%). In this case, he would deduct the percentage depletion amount of \$750 since it exceeds the cost depletion of \$600.

Case 102
Depletion of a Net Profits Interest

In 1987, Lessor R assigns an undeveloped oil and gas lease in the United States to Operator A for \$25,000 consideration and retains a net profits interest measured by one-sixteenth of the gross proceeds less one-sixteenth of the direct cash operating expenses. During the year, the lease produced 37,500 barrels of oil which sold for \$750,000. Cash operating expenses were \$294,000. Lessor R received \$28,500 with respect to his net profits interest. The agreement between Lessor R and Operator A provides that Lessor R may elect to take his share of production in kind and, if he does, the number of barrels to which he is entitled in any one month is determined by the estimated net income

438. Rev. Rul. 79-386, 1979-2 C.B. 246.
439. Reg. Sec. 1.613-2(c)(5)(iii).
440. Quintana Petroleum Co. v. Comm'r, 143 F.2d 588 (5th Cir. 1944), 32 AFTR 1031, 44-2 USTC 9380; Helvering v. Twin Bell Oil Syndicate, 293 U.S. 312 (1934), 14 AFTR 712, 35-1 USTC 9014; Rev. Rul 81-266, 1981-2 C.B. 139.
441. Rev. Rul. 81-266, 1981-2 C.B. 139; Murphy Oil Corp. v. U.S., 337 F.2d 677 (8th Cir. 1964), 14 AFTR2d 5835, 64-2 USTC 9810.
442. Reg. Sec. 1.612-3(b)(2).

divided by the estimated price per barrel received by the operator. Differences in estimated and actual figures, if any, are to be adjusted annually.

Lessor R has granted a lease and retained an interest in the minerals measured by the profits to be derived from production.[443] A net profits agreement is a contract providing that the owner shall receive a share of gross production measured by the net profits generated from the operations of the property, computed in accordance with the agreement's terms.

The $25,000 received by Lessor R when the lease was granted constitutes a lease bonus. If Lessor R has tax basis in the net profits interest, he may claim a deduction for cost depletion with respect to the lease bonus income he receives. Percentage depletion was formerly available in some situations for independent producers with respect to lease bonus payments.[444] *(See Case 98 for a discussion of the computation of depletion on lease bonus income.)* However, it is not clear whether the lease bonus received by Lessor R, which is paid in addition to the one-sixteenth net profits interest, will qualify for percentage depletion. The statute provides that gross income for purposes of computing percentage depletion does not include any lease bonus, advance royalty or other amount payable without regard to production for amounts accrued or received after August 16, 1986.[445] Lessor R may be entitled to percentage depletion on the lease bonus payments he receives since the total payments he receives in 1987 do not exceed the current production from the property.[446] Arguably, these payments are payable with regard to production and may constitute depletable gross income. However, since the amounts received may constitute a "lease bonus," they may not qualify for depletion. This determination must await future clarification and explanation of the statute.

Assuming that Lessor R is entitled to the benefits of the independent-producer exemption *(see Case 94)*, he should consider the $28,500[447] proceeds from the net profits interest in his computation of percentage depletion. Assuming applicable limitations do not apply, Lessor R's percentage depletion deduction in 1987 would be $4,275, or 15% of $28,500. If the $25,000 lease bonus received in 1987 is also eligible for percentage depletion, Lessor R's percentage depletion deduction would be $8,025, or 15% of $53,500.

If, under local law, Lessor R is obligated for the production taxes and the ad valorem taxes applicable to his interest, he should increase net receipts by the taxes paid by Operator A attributable to Lessor R's interest to determine gross income subject to the percentage depletion rates.[448] Lessor R should deduct the same amount in computing the 50% of net income limitation on percentage depletion. Lessor R does not "gross up" his net receipts for operating expenses. As a producer, he is liable for windfall profit tax on his share of the production. *(See Case 212.)*

443. Comm'r v. Felix Oil Co., 144 F.2d 276 (9th Cir. 1944), 32 AFTR 1186, 44-2 USTC 9434; Burton-Sutton Oil Co. v. Comm'r, 328 U.S. 25 (1946), 34 AFTR 1017, 46-1 USTC 9243; Kirby Petroleum Co. v. Comm'r, 326 U.S. 599 (1946), 34 AFTR 526, 46-1 USTC 9149.

444. Comm'r v. Engle, 82 U.S. 599 (1984), 53 AFTR2d 84-415, 84-1 USTC 9134; IRS Announcement 84-59, 1984-23 I.R.B. 58.

445. I.R.C. Sec. 613A(d)(5); I.R.C. Sec. 613(e)(4); P.L. 99-514 (Tax Reform Act of 1986), Sec. 412(a)(1); P.L. 99-514 (Tax Reform Act of 1986), Sec. 412(a)(2).

446. Reg. Sec. 1.612-3(b)(1); Rev. Rul. 72-165, 1972-1 C.B. 177.

447. Byron H. Farwell, 35 T.C. 454 (1960); IRS Letter Ruling 7937015 (Technical Advice Memorandum).

448. Louisiana Land and Exploration Co. v. Donnelly, 394 F.2d 273 (5th Cir. 1968), 21 AFTR2d 1254, 68-1 USTC 9356; Farwell.

Lessor R's deduction for percentage depletion will be limited if his average daily production from oil and gas production subject to the independent-producer exemption exceeds 1,000 barrels a day. *(See Case 96.)* In addition, the deduction is subject to the 65% of taxable income limitation. *(See Cases 115, 116 and 117.)*

For purposes of calculating his average daily production, Lessor R determines his share of the production from the property by multiplying the total production of that property by his percentage participation in the revenues of that property.[449] The proposed income tax regulations provide that the production attributable to a net profits interest owner is deemed to be that portion of production that produced the same fraction of the property's gross income as the taxpayer's fractional interest in the net profits from the property.[450] Using this formula, Lessor R's production from the property is 2,344 barrels, computed as follows:

$$\text{Net profits ratio} \times \text{Total barrels of production} = 1/16 \times 37{,}500 = 2{,}344 \text{ barrels}$$

The formula provided by the proposed regulations treats a net profits interest owner similar to a working interest owner rather than a royalty owner. This treatment seems inconsistent with the characterization of such an interest as a royalty. An alternative interpretation of the statute provides that the holder of a net profits interest is deemed to have an interest in the gross income from the property equal to the amount of net profits received. Using this rationale, Lessor R will determine his share of production from the property by multiplying his percentage participation in revenues by the total production from the property as follows:

$$\frac{\text{Net profits interest proceeds}}{\text{Total production proceeds}} \times \text{Total barrels of production} = \frac{\$\ 28{,}500}{\$750{,}000} \times 37{,}500 = 1{,}425 \text{ barrels}$$

The second calculation correlates the net profits treatment with that of the working interest owner, who excludes the net profits payment from his gross income. *(See Case 231 for a discussion of the methods prescribed for allocating production to the net profits interest holder for windfall profit tax purposes.)*

Operator A should exclude from gross income as royalties the amounts actually paid to Lessor R and also any taxes paid by Operator A on behalf of Lessor R that represent depletable income to Lessor R.[451] Operator A also should exclude from the computation of his average daily production the barrels of production attributable to Lessor R's net profits interest.

Had Lessor R purchased a net profits interest in another property, he must capitalize the consideration he paid for the economic interest as the depletable cost of the interest acquired. Lessor R will claim the greater of cost or percentage depletion with respect to the receipts from the net profits interest. He cannot claim percentage depletion if the property was proven at the date of acquisition. *(See Case 108.)* In addition, Lessor R will own no interest in the lease and well equipment on the lease so he may not allocate any of the consideration to the depreciable tax basis.

449. I.R.C. Sec. 613A(c)(2)(B).
450. Prop. Reg. Sec. 1.613A-7(f)(3).
451. Reg. Sec. 1.613-2(c)(5); IRS Letter Ruling 8317043.

Case 103
Percentage Depletion Resulting from Secondary Operations

Operator A has production from various oil leases in the United States. In 1987, to stimulate additional production, Operator A commenced water-flooding operations in a field that had been producing for many years. During 1987, Operator A had the following daily production from his properties:

Primary oil production	2,000 barrels
Secondary oil production	500 barrels

For years before 1984, to compute percentage depletion under the independent-producer exemption provisions, production of oil and gas from secondary and tertiary processes had to be segregated from primary production. For production subsequent to 1983, the distinction between primary and secondary or tertiary production as it relates to depletable oil quantity is no longer significant. Accordingly, 15% is the percentage depletion rate applicable to all such production, and the 1,000-barrel-per-day depletable quantity limit applies to the aggregate production from primary, secondary and tertiary methods.

Properties having secondary or tertiary production are subject to the transfer of proven property disqualification provisions for years after 1983 with respect to transfers after 1974.[452] Thus, percentage depletion is not allowable on secondary or tertiary properties that have been transferred after 1974 if they were proven properties at the date of transfer. In addition, secondary and tertiary properties have been subject to the retailer and refiner exceptions and to the 65% of taxable income limitation for all years after 1974.

Secondary and tertiary production is defined in proposed regulations as the increased production of crude oil or natural gas from a domestic well after the application of enhanced recovery techniques.[453] The increased production is the "excess of actual production over the maximum primary production which would have resulted during the tax year if such process had not been applied."[454] The increased production may be due to an increase in either the rate or duration of recovery. It is not clear how, in a practical context, the Internal Revenue Service will apply that rule in determining a taxpayer's secondary production in a given tax year. Taxpayers that claimed the higher percentage depletion for secondary or tertiary production before 1984 must maintain records of the secondary or tertiary processes applied and the resulting increased production.[455] Presumably, the determination of "increased production" from secondary or tertiary processes is applied on a unit-of-property basis (typically in a unitized area) as opposed to a reservoir-by-reservoir (deposit-by-deposit) basis,[456] but this is not entirely clear.

Common secondary or tertiary production methods include water flooding; "in situ" combustion (fire flooding, in which combustible gases are ignited in the reservoir); and the injection of air, carbon dioxide, polyethylenes or various other chemicals or additives into the reservoir. However, if a process must be introduced early in the

452. I.R.C. Sec. 613A(c)(9)(A).
453. Prop. Reg. Sec. 1.613A-7(k).
454. *Ibid.*
455. Reg. Sec. 1.613A-6(b).
456. Prop. Reg. Sec. 1.613A-3(a)(4), Example 6.

productive life of the mineral property to be reasonably effective (such as cycling of gas in the case of a gas-condensate well), the process is not considered a secondary or tertiary process.[457]

Operator A's total average daily production for 1987 of 2,500 barrels exceeds his depletable oil quantity of 1,000 barrels per day, so he will be allowed to claim percentage depletion, subject to the 65% limitation based on taxable income, at a rate of 15% of gross income (limited to 50% of net income) on only a portion of his production during 1987. *(See Case 96.)* Even though the water-flooding operations constitute secondary recovery activities, Operator A's limited amount of percentage depletion will be determined with respect to all his properties without regard to the primary or secondary nature of the production methods.

Case 104
Partner and Partnership Computations of Percentage Depletion Under the Independent-Producer Exemption

X Corporation is the general partner of numerous limited partnerships engaged in the business of exploring for, developing and producing oil and gas from properties located in the United States. Several of the partnerships have more than 200 partners, and one has in excess of 3,000 partners. The corporate controller of X Corporation is beginning the work necessary to prepare the tax information schedules for 1987 and requests information as to the data required to permit the partners to compute their allowable deduction for depletion.

The partners, and not the partnership, must separately compute the depletion allowance (cost or percentage) on oil and gas properties.[458]

X Corporation, as general partner responsible for preparing the tax information schedules, must supply each partner with complete depletion information relating to his share of partnership oil and gas operations. X Corporation must allocate the adjusted depletable basis of each property to each partner on the basis of each partner's interest in partnership capital or income.[459] In the case of property contributed to the partnership by a partner, this allocation must take account of the difference between the partnership's basis in the property and its fair market value at the time of contribution.[460]

X Corporation should classify each partner's share of oil and gas production into the following groups:

- ☐ Foreign production (eligible for cost depletion only).
- ☐ Proven properties acquired after December 31, 1974, including the effect of sales or exchanges of partnership interests (eligible for cost depletion only).
- ☐ Natural gas sold under a qualifying fixed contract and qualified natural gas from geopressured brine (eligible for cost or percentage depletion, whichever is greater, not subject to the limitations of the independent-producer exemption).

---

457. Prop. Reg. Sec. 1.613A-7(k).
458. I.R.C. Sec. 613A(c)(7)(D).
459. *Ibid.*
460. I.R.C. Sec. 613A(c)(7)(D); I.R.C. Sec. 704(c).

□ Production from properties that may be eligible for the independent-producer exemption (eligible for cost depletion or percentage depletion, whichever is greater, subject to the independent-producer exemption rules and limitations).

For the last classification, information must be provided for oil and gas production separately.

The proposed regulations require that each partnership producing crude oil or natural gas must provide each partner with all the information in its possession necessary to determine the amount of the partner's depletion deduction allowable with respect to that crude oil or natural gas.[461] The information required for depletion purposes includes each partner's share of the following items with respect to each property:[462]

□ Gross income.

□ Operating expenses.

□ Production taxes.

□ Windfall profit tax.

□ Intangible drilling and development costs (IDC).

□ Allocated overhead.

□ Depreciation (cost recovery allowance).

□ Estimated reserves.

□ Production in barrels or cubic feet for the tax year.

□ The partner's original share of the partnership adjusted basis of properties producing domestic crude oil or domestic natural gas, and the partner's allocable share of any subsequent adjustments made to the basis of those properties by the partnership.

□ The amount realized from the sale of any such property.

□ Possibly, information to allow the partners to compute the net income limitation for windfall profit tax. *(See Section IX.)*

□ Possibly, information to allow the partners to compute the "at-risk" basis on an activity-by-activity basis. *(See Case 33.)*

Each partner must determine separately whether he qualifies for percentage depletion under the independent-producer exemption. Thus, with certain exceptions, a partner who is a retailer or a refiner, as defined in the statute, will be entitled only to cost depletion.[463] Retailers and refiners will be entitled to percentage depletion with respect to qualified natural gas from geopressured brine and natural gas sold under a qualified fixed contract.[464] *(See Cases 93 and 114.)* In addition, a partner who acquired his partnership interest by transfer at a time when all or part of the partnership properties were proven will be entitled, with certain exceptions, only to cost depletion on his share of the production from those proven properties.[465] *(See Case 108.)* Even though partnership properties may have been proven at the time he acquired his partnership interest, such a partner will be entitled to percentage

461. Prop. Reg. Sec. 1.613A-3(j).
462. *Ibid.*
463. I.R.C. Sec. 613A(c)(1); I.R.C. Sec. 613A(d)(2); I.R.C. Sec. 613A(d)(3); I.R.C. Sec. 613A(d)(4).
464. I.R.C. Sec. 613A(b).
465. I.R.C. Sec. 613A(c)(9).

depletion for natural gas from geopressured brine and natural gas sold under qualified fixed contracts.[466]

If a partner qualifies for percentage depletion under the independent-producer exemption, he must consider all his oil and gas activities from all sources, including his share of any partnership operations, in computing any adjustment due to production in excess of the depletable oil quantity. He also must separately apply the 65% of taxable income limitation, if applicable.

At a minimum, X corporation should make the necessary percentage depletion computations (15% of gross income limited to 50% of net income) on a 100% basis at the partnership level and supply each partner with a copy of the schedules showing the computations to which the partner can apply his percentage interest to determine his share. If certain income and expense items are specifically allocated to the various partners, X Corporation should supply each partner with tentative allowable depletion computations, taking into account the special allocations. Cost depletion data should be furnished separately. Partnerships with many partners may find it both practical and desirable to use computers to make the computations and supply copies of the printed schedules to the partners.

If the partnership acts on behalf of its partners with respect to the determination, assessment and collection of the windfall profit tax,[467] presumably the partnership will consider each partner's windfall profit tax deduction in the percentage depletion computations. *(See Case 225.)* If the partnership does not so act, each partner also must consider his windfall profit tax deduction in computing or modifying the 50% of net income limitation on each property.

Due to the length and complexity of the data to be furnished to the limited partner, the partnership should provide comprehensive instructions describing further work the limited partner must do to complete his depletion computation. Some partnerships may assist partners with the computations of the depletable oil quantity limitation, the 65% of taxable income limitation and the "at-risk" limitations.

For general partners furnishing the limited partners with data concerning the depletable cost basis of each property owned by the partnership, the statute[468] requires that a partner determine his proportionate share of the adjusted basis of the partnership's property (including his share of the adjusted basis of any property contributed to the partnership by the partner) in accordance with his interest in partnership capital or income. The allocation is to be made as of the later of the date the partnership acquired the oil or gas property or January 1, 1975. Each partner is to keep separate records of his share of the adjusted basis for any depletion taken on that property and use that adjusted basis each year in the computation of his gain or loss on the disposition of that property by the partnership.[469]

The proposed regulations provide that a partner shall determine his proportionate share of the adjusted basis of each property in accordance with his interest in partnership capital. However, a partner's share of the adjusted basis shall be determined in accordance with his interest in partnership income if the partnership agreement so provides, unless: (1) written provision has been made for any partner's share in partnership income to be reduced for any purpose other than merely to reflect the admission of a new partner or (2) at the time of allocation any partner expects his income interest to be reduced pursuant to an understanding with another partner or

466. I.R.C. Sec. 613A(b).
467. I.R.C. Sec. 6232; Reg. Sec. 51.6232(c)-1; Reg. Sec. 51.6232(c)-2.
468. I.R.C. Sec. 613A(c)(7)(D).
469. *Ibid.*

partners. However, in the case of property contributed to the partnership, the statute requires that a partner's share of the adjusted basis be determined by applying the provisions requiring income, gain, loss and deductions with respect to the property to take into account the variation between the basis of the property to the partnership and its fair market value at the time of contribution.[470] The statute also requires that income, gain, loss and deduction with respect to property contributed to the partnership by a partner shall be shared so as to take into account the variation between the basis of the property to the partnership and its fair market value at the time of contribution.[471]

The application of this allocation of basis rule is not clear, particularly when, for example, a general partner contributes all the capital necessary to cover the costs to the partnership of producing leases and equipment and the limited partners contribute the capital necessary to pay for the IDC. In these cases, the deductions arising from the expenditure of partnership funds generally have been allocated to the partners supplying the funds from which the expenditures were made—IDC deductions to the limited partners and depreciation and cost depletion deductions to the general partner. If these allocations have substantial economic effect, they should be effective for tax purposes. Partnerships should consider the effect of these tangible/intangible provisions in allocating items of deduction to the properties to allow each partner to compute his share of depletion on partnership properties.

It appears reasonable to allocate all the depletable basis to the general partner in these tangible/intangible arrangements because such an allocation is in accordance with the interests in partnership capital. Further, if special allocations of items such as IDC or depreciation have substantial economic effect, these should be allocated to the respective groups of partners and taken into account in percentage depletion computations to determine the 50% of net income limitations. *(See Case 165 for a discussion of special allocations of partnership items among partners.)*

Regulations dealing with partnership special allocations provide additional, though limited, provisions concerning the allocation of the adjusted basis of an oil and gas property among partners. Specifically, the regulations provide that any allocation of the adjusted basis of an oil or gas property among the partners shall be deemed to be in accordance with the partners' interest in partnership capital or income provided that all the partnership's allocations of income, gain, loss and deduction (or item thereof) are recognized as having substantial economic effect.[472] Otherwise, this adjusted basis must be allocated in accordance with the partners' actual interests in partnership capital or income. Like the existing proposed depletion regulations, the special allocation regulations do not provide any definitive guidance as to the practical application of this general provision.

Case 105
Depletion When Both Oil and Gas Are Produced from a Lease

> **Corporation A, a calendar-year, accrual-basis taxpayer, owns a lease on which primary oil is produced from one sand and primary gas from a different sand. Oil reserves are valued at $4 million. Gas reserves are valued at $2 million. Investment in the leasehold is $75,000. Production in the current year (1987) is 20,000 barrels of oil and 100,000 MCF of gas. Gross revenues attributable to the 20,000 barrels are $400,000. Gross**

470. I.R.C. Sec. 613A(c)(7)(D); I.R.C. Sec. 704(c).
471. I.R.C. Sec. 704(c).
472. Reg. Sec. 1.704-1(b)(4)(v).

revenues attributable to the 100,000 MCF are $200,000. Direct and indirect expenses attributable to operating the lease are as follows:

Lease operating expenses	$280,000
Depreciation expense	100,000
Production tax—oil	24,000
Production tax—gas	16,000
Windfall profit tax	—
Allocated overhead	60,000

Corporation A's accountant seeks advice on computing depletion on the lease. Corporation A elects to include the gas production in its depletable quantity for 1987. Corporation A is not engaged in retailing or refining, and 1987 production does not exceed the depletable quantity limitations under the independent-producer and royalty-owner provisions. The 65% of taxable income limitation does not apply to Corporation A.

Corporation A has two mineral deposits on a single tract or parcel of land, and it may elect to treat each deposit separately.[473] *(See Case 58.)* If Corporation A fails to make the election, the two deposits will be treated as one property.[474]

When oil is the principal income-producing factor and a separate property election is not made, the Internal Revenue Service (IRS) probably will allow the taxpayer to disregard incidental gas reserves in the computation of cost depletion, even though occasional sales of the gas are made.

In the present case, assuming a separate property election is made, $50,000 of the leasehold cost is allocated to the oil reserves ($.25 per barrel) and $25,000 is allocated to the gas reserves ($.025 per MCF), computed as follows:

$$\text{Tax basis of oil} = \frac{\$4{,}000{,}000}{\$6{,}000{,}000} \times \$75{,}000 = \$50{,}000$$

$$\text{Tax basis of gas} = \frac{\$2{,}000{,}000}{\$6{,}000{,}000} \times \$75{,}000 = \$25{,}000$$

Cost depletion attributable to the current year's production is $5,000 for oil (20,000 barrels × $.25) and $2,500 for gas (100,000 MCF × $.025), a total of $7,500.

If a separate property election is not made, Corporation A normally will combine the oil and gas production and reserves (because other-than-incidental gas production and reserves are present) and make the cost depletion computation using $75,000 as the depletable basis for its entire interest. In making this computation, it may be possible for Corporation A to convert its gas production and reserves to equivalent barrels in a manner similar to that prescribed for computing the windfall profit net income limitation.[475] *(See Case 223.)*

Corporation A also may elect to convert natural gas production into equivalent barrels to compute percentage depletion.[476] *(See Case 95.)* The election is made by claiming

473. I.R.C. Sec. 614(b)(2).
474. I.R.C. Sec. 614(b)(1)(A).
475. Reg. Sec. 51.4988-2(b)(4).
476. I.R.C. Sec. 613A(c)(4).

percentage depletion on the natural gas production in Corporation A's income tax return.[477]

In computing the 50% of taxable income limitation on percentage depletion,[478] even though a separate property election is not made, Corporation A is required to allocate the taxable income from the property[479] between oil and gas production in proportion to the gross income from each during the tax year.[480] The taxable income from the lease is computed as follows:

Gross revenues—oil	$400,000
Gross revenues—gas	200,000
Lease operating expense	(280,000)
Depreciation expense	(100,000)
Production tax—oil	(24,000)
Production tax—gas	(16,000)
Windfall profit tax	—
Allocated overhead	(60,000)
Taxable income from the property	$120,000

The $120,000 taxable income from the property is allocated between oil production and gas production as follows:

$$\textbf{Oil:}\quad \frac{\$400{,}000}{\$600{,}000} \times \$120{,}000 = \$80{,}000$$

$$\textbf{Gas:}\quad \frac{\$200{,}000}{\$600{,}000} \times \$120{,}000 = \$40{,}000$$

If Corporation A elects to treat the oil and gas sands as separate properties,[481] the allowable depletion deduction (greater of percentage or cost) can be summarized as follows:

Oil		**Gas**	
Gross revenues	$400,000	Gross revenues	$200,000
Applicable rate	× .15	Applicable rate	× .15
(A) Tentative percentage depletion	$ 60,000	(A) Tentative percentage depletion	$ 30,000
(B) 50% of taxable income limitation (50% × $80,000)	40,000	(B) 50% of taxable income limitation (50% × $40,000)	20,000
Allowable percentage depletion:		Allowable percentage depletion:	
(C) (Lesser of A or B)	40,000	(C) (Lessor of A or B)	20,000
(D) Cost depletion	5,000	(D) Cost depletion	2,500
Allowable depletion (greater of C or D)	40,000	Allowable depletion (greater of C or D)	20,000

To make this computation for a separate property election, it is assumed that expenses allocable to the property are reasonably apportionable to the oil and gas production

477. Reg. Sec. 1.613A-5.
478. I.R.C. Sec. 613(a).
479. Reg. Sec. 1.613-5.
480. I.R.C. Sec. 613A(c)(7)(C); Prop. Reg. Sec. 1.613A-3(d)(3).
481. I.R.C. Sec. 614(b)(2).

based on the relative gross income, although other reasonable allocation methods presumably will be acceptable to (or perhaps even required by) the IRS.

If Corporation A does not treat the oil and gas sands as separate properties, thus falling under the general rule,[482] total cost depletion is compared with total percentage depletion based on the combined gross income from the oil and gas production. The total allowable depletion here is the same regardless of whether Corporation A makes a separate property election; however, the answer can vary depending on the amount of leasehold cost, the allocation of that cost between oil and gas, the relative production rates, lifting costs and other expenses and relative prices of the two mineral products.

When oil and gas are produced from a property and the gas qualifies as fixed-contract gas *(see Case 93)*, but the taxpayer is not eligible for percentage depletion on the oil production (for example, a retailer), the regulations prescribe that the taxable income from the property (for the 50% of taxable income limitation) is computed with respect to the entire taxable income from the property.[483] To determine the allowable depletion deduction the percentage depletion (for the gas production only) is compared with the cost depletion for the entire property.

For purposes of the 50% of taxable income limitation, the statute provides that when a separate property election is made, taxable income from the property is allocated between the oil and gas production based on relative gross income.[484] However, this allocation does not correspond to economic reality when certain expenses (such as the windfall profit tax and possibly severance taxes) are directly traceable to one or the other mineral product. The windfall profit tax regulations provide that direct expenses may be apportioned specifically to the mineral product to which they are allocable and only indirect expenses are allocated based on relative gross income.[485] *(See Case 223.)* Accordingly, if a separate property election is made, these direct expenses may be allocable directly to the mineral to which they relate for both depletion and windfall profit tax purposes.

Case 106
Percentage Depletion of Component Members of a Controlled Group of Corporations

Operator A, an individual, owns 100% of the stock of X Corporation. X Corporation has a wholly owned subsidiary, Y Corporation, and both corporations are engaged in the exploration, development and production of oil and gas. Operator A also owns 60% of the stock of Z Corporation, which also is engaged in the exploration, development and production of oil and gas. Each corporation is on the calendar year for tax purposes. Operator A has significant personal income from the ownership of oil and gas royalties. All the oil and gas properties are located in the United States and during 1987 produced as follows:

Operator A's royalty share	200 barrels per day
X Corporation	1,200 barrels per day
Y Corporation	400 barrels per day
Z Corporation	600 barrels per day

482. I.R.C. Sec. 614(b)(1)(A).
483. Reg. Sec. 1.613-2(c)(2), Example 2.
484. I.R.C. Sec. 613A(c)(7)(C).
485. Reg. Sec. 51.4988-2(b)(2).

The percentage depletion statute requires members of a controlled group of corporations to share a single depletable oil quantity.[486] A similar rule applies to a group of business entities under common control.[487] Under a literal reading of the statute, Corporations X, Y and Z meet both statutory definitions and must share a single depletable oil quantity. Operator A will not be required to share his depletable oil quantity with X, Y and Z Corporations.

There are three types of controlled groups of corporations: a parent-subsidiary group, a brother-sister group and a combined group.[488]

A parent-subsidiary controlled group consists of one or more chains of corporations if the common parent owns more than 50% (combined voting power or total value) of at least one of the other corporations, and one or more of the other corporations, or any combination thereof, owns more than 50% of each of the other corporations.[489]

A brother-sister controlled group consists of one or more corporations if five or fewer persons who are individuals, estates or trusts own directly or indirectly more than 50% (combined voting power or total value) of the stock of each corporation, taking into account the stock ownership of each corporation.[490]

A combined group consists of three or more corporations, each of which is a member of a parent-subsidiary group or a brother-sister group, and one of which is a common parent of a parent-subsidiary group.[491] Corporations X, Y and Z are members of a combined group of controlled corporations.

Component members of a controlled group of corporations are treated as one taxpayer for purposes of the depletable quantity limitation.[492] Consequently, the depletable oil quantity is allocated among the corporations based on each member's proportionate share of production.[493]

Business entities under common control also must share a single depletable oil quantity. Included in the definition of *business entities under common control* are two or more corporations, 50% or more of the beneficial interest in which is owned by the same or related persons.[494] *(See Case 107 for a description of other types of entities included in the definition.)* These entities share the depletable oil quantity in proportion to their respective production of domestic crude oil and natural gas equivalent.[495] Corporations X, Y and Z meet the definition of *business entities under common control.*

Percentage depletion is now determined without any distinction between primary production and secondary or tertiary production. Accordingly, characterization of a group of corporations as a controlled group of corporations or as business entities under common control no longer can affect the allocation of the depletable quantity in cases where one or more members of the group have secondary or tertiary production.

486. I.R.C. Sec. 613A(c)(8)(A); I.R.C. Sec. 1563(a).
487. I.R.C. Sec. 613A(c)(8)(B).
488. I.R.C. Sec. 1563(a).
489. I.R.C. Sec. 1563(a)(1); I.R.C. Sec. 613A(c)(8)(D)(i).
490. I.R.C. Sec. 1563(a)(2); I.R.C. Sec. 613A(c)(8)(D)(i).
491. I.R.C. Sec. 1563(a)(3).
492. I.R.C. Sec. 613A(c)(8)(A).
493. I.R.C. Sec. 613A(c)(3); I.R.C. Sec. 613A(c)(8).
494. I.R.C. Sec. 613A(c)(8)(B).
495. I.R.C. Sec. 613A(c)(8)(B); I.R.C. Sec. 613A(c)(8)(D)(iv).

Thus, the depletable oil quantity of each of the corporations for 1987 is as follows:

Corporation X:	$\frac{1{,}200}{2{,}200} \times 1{,}000 =$	545
Corporation Y:	$\frac{400}{2{,}200} \times 1{,}000 =$	182
Corporation Z:	$\frac{600}{2{,}200} \times 1{,}000 =$	273
		1,000

After the corporations determine their respective portions of the depletable quantity, each corporation will compute its allowable percentage depletion on a property-by-property basis before considering the 65% of taxable income limitation. *(See Cases 115, 116 and 117.)*

If Corporations X, Y and Z use different fiscal years for income tax purposes, it appears that the group will have to determine its depletable quantity limitation for each part of each fiscal year of each corporation included within a calendar year and then allocate the depletable quantity to each corporation as described above.[496]

Case 107
Percentage Depletion of Business Entities Under Common Control

> **Operators A, B and C are brothers, engaged in the business of exploration, development and production of oil and gas from properties located in the United States. Each owns one-third of the stock of Corporation X, which also is engaged in oil and gas operations in the United States. The brothers are beneficiaries of a testamentary trust under their father's will (Trust M), which owns royalties in oil and gas properties located in the United States.**
>
> **Operator D owns 50% of the stock of Corporation Y and is the grantor of a trust (Trust N) for the benefit of his minor daughter. For 1987, Corporation Y's average daily production of domestic crude oil is 1,000 barrels, and Trust N's domestic crude oil production is 600 barrels per day.**
>
> **None of the persons or entities is involved in refining or retailing.**
>
> **Operators A, B, C and D ask what effect their ownership in the corporation and interest in the trusts will have on their allowable percentage depletion under the independent-producer exemption.**

To apply the depletable quantity limitation, the component members of a controlled group of corporations are treated as a single taxpayer.[497] *(See Case 106.)* Further, business entities under common control[498] and members of the same family[499] are required to share a single depletable quantity. Common control exists when 50% or more of the beneficial interest in two or more corporations, trusts or estates is owned by the same or related persons, taking into account only persons owning at least 5% of

496. I.R.C. Sec. 613A(c)(11); Prop. Reg. Sec. 1.613A-3(i).
497. I.R.C. Sec. 613A(c)(8)(A); Prop. Reg. Sec. 1.613A-3(g)(1).
498. I.R.C. Sec. 613A(c)(8)(B).
499. I.R.C. Sec. 613A(c)(8)(C).

that beneficial interest. The word *same* should be read as referring to one person. In all cases applicable to determining allocation requirements for the independent-producer exemption, *family relationship* includes only the individual's spouse and minor children.[500]

Businesses under common control must allocate among themselves a single tentative depletable quantity for a tax year in proportion to the respective production of barrels of domestic crude oil and natural gas equivalent.[501] This provision does not require an allocation of the exemption between the entity (or entities) and the individual or beneficial owners, but rather requires an allocation only at the entity level.

Members of the same family also must allocate a single depletable quantity among the family in proportion to the respective production of each member.[502] A family includes only an individual, his spouse and minor children.[503] The Internal Revenue Service (IRS) has indicated that state law determines when a child attains majority.[504]

In this example, Operators A, B and C (brothers) are not considered "related" for purposes of determining common control. Accordingly, the ownership of Corporation X and the beneficial interests in Trust M will not affect the entities' or the brothers' computations of percentage depletion under the independent-producer exemption.

However, Corporation Y and Trust N are entities under common control and must share the maximum depletable oil quantity of 1,000 barrels per day.

In this example, Corporation Y and Trust N allocate the tentative depletable quantity of 1,000 barrels per day as follows:

Entity	Actual Average Daily Production	Maximum Depletable Quantity
Corporation Y	1,000 bbls. per day	625 bbls. per day
Trust N	600 bbls. per day	375 bbls. per day
	1,600 bbls. per day	1,000 bbls. per day

The IRS has indicated that the tentative quantity is not to be allocated among the beneficiaries of 10 testamentary trusts of a decedent or the adult beneficiaries.[505] The IRS also has indicated that, at the partnership level, allocation of the depletable oil quantity is not made among related partnership members.[506]

Case 108
Percentage Depletion Following the Transfer of a Proven Property

During 1987, Operator A sold oil and gas properties in the United States and a partnership interest to Operator B (who is not a retailer or refiner) as follows:

- ☐ Leases on which there are 20 producing wells.

500. I.R.C. Sec. 613A(c)(8)(D)(ii); I.R.C. Sec. 613A(c)(8)(D)(iii).
501. Prop. Reg. Sec. 1.613A-3(g)(2).
502. Prop. Reg. Sec. 1.613A-3(g)(3).
503. Prop. Reg. Sec. 1.613A-3(g)(4)(i).
504. IRS Letter Ruling 8142179.
505. IRS Letter Ruling 7805007 (Technical Advice Memorandum).
506. *Ibid.*

□ Nonproducing leases in a separate area containing 20,000 acres (no production within one mile).

□ A nonproducing lease in a producing field immediately adjacent to a lease that has three producing wells near the border of the property. That lease had a fair market value of $100,000 on the date of sale.

□ Nonproducing deposits or horizons underlying a tract of land containing a producing well.

□ All his interest in Partnership X that is engaged in oil operations in the United States and holds producing properties.

If an interest in a proven oil or gas property (including an interest in a partnership or trust) is transferred (including the subleasing of a lease), the independent-producer and royalty-owner exemption is not available to the transferee for production of crude oil or natural gas attributable to that interest. The transferee will not take into account that production for any percentage depletion computations relating to the independent-producer and royalty-owner exemption.[507] Production qualifying as natural gas sold under a fixed contract is not subject to the transfer of proven property rules.[508]

The term *transfer* means any change in legal or equitable ownership by sale, exchange, gift, lease, sublease, assignment, contract or other disposition.[509] *(See Case 109 for a detailed discussion of the various exceptions to the transfer rules provided by the Internal Revenue Code (the Code), the proposed income tax regulations and various published and private letter rulings of the Internal Revenue Service.)*

The term *transferee* includes the original transferee of a proven property and his successors in interest.[510] A person *is not* a transferee of an interest in a proven oil or gas property if he was entitled to a percentage depletion deduction allowance on minerals produced from that property immediately before the transfer. However, a person *is* a transferee of an interest in a proven property if the interest that person receives is greater than the interest in the property held immediately before the transfer.[511] For example, if Operator A transferred the 20 producing wells to a partnership, he may claim percentage depletion (subject to the independent-producer exemption rules) on subsequent production from the wells if there is an effective allocation of the income from those wells to him. He also will be entitled to a continuing depletion allowance if he had transferred the wells pursuant to a unitization or pooling agreement.

A property is a *proven* oil or gas property if at the time of the transfer the principal value of the property has been demonstrated by prospecting, exploration or discovery work.[512] The proposed income tax regulations[513] provide that such a demonstration occurs only if at the time of transfer:

□ Any oil or gas has been produced from a deposit, whether or not produced by the taxpayer or from the property transferred;

□ Prospecting, exploration or discovery work indicates that it is probable that the property will have gross income from oil or gas from the deposit sufficient to justify development of the property; and

---

507. I.R.C. Sec. 613A(c)(9)(A).
508. IRS Letter Ruling 8208213.
509. Prop. Reg. Sec. 1.613A-7(n).
510. Prop. Reg. Sec. 1.613A-7(o).
511. *Ibid.*
512. I.R.C. Sec. 613A(c)(9)(A).
513. Prop. Reg. Sec. 1.613A-7(p).

☐ The fair market value of the property is 50% or more of the fair market value of the property, minus actual expenses of the transferee for equipment and intangible drilling and development costs, at the time of the first production from the property subsequent to the transfer and before the transferee transfers his interest.

The proposed income tax regulations also provide that seismographic surveys and other geological and geophysical activity are included in the term *prospecting, exploration or discovery work.*[514]

The interpretation of identical phrasing in a former Code section dealing with the sale of oil and gas properties indicated that an oil and gas property should not be considered *proven* until it can be shown that in-place reserves exist in commercial quantities.[515] Although certain types of geological and geophysical work may increase the speculative value of an oil and gas prospect, the proven nature of the property cannot be demonstrated until the existence of in-place oil and gas reserves is confirmed by drilling. The term *proven*, as used in the oil and gas industry, also means that known reserves exist in commercial quantities. Presumably, the Treasury will consider the history and industry practice when it promulgates final regulations under this section of the Code.

The transferee of a proven property must keep records showing the terms of the transfer, any geological and geophysical data in the possession of the transferee or other exploratory data for the property transferred and any other information that bears on the question of whether at the time of the transfer the principal value of the property had been demonstrated by prospecting, exploration and discovery work.[516]

If Operator A transfers one of the above interests to Operator B prior to proving the principal value of the particular oil and gas property, the transfer will not negate Operator B's right to claim percentage depletion on that property under the independent-producer exemption. Operator B must analyze each of the sales from Operator A in light of the above requirements to determine whether he may claim percentage depletion on the production from those properties under the independent-producer exemption.

The sale of Operator A's leases when there are 20 producing wells is a transfer of a proven property for the producing horizons. Therefore, Operator B will not be able to claim percentage depletion under the independent-producer exemption on production from these leases. On the other hand, Operator A's sale of nonproducing leases located at least one mile away from any other production may not constitute the transfer of a proven property, particularly if no commercially productive wells ever have been drilled on these leases. Thus, if Operator B is able to complete a producing well on these leases, he may be able to claim percentage depletion under the independent-producer exemption.

Operator A's sale of a nonproducing lease that is contiguous to leases containing three producing wells and located in a producing field may or may not constitute a transfer of a proven property. Based on the proposed regulations, the property will be considered proven if the three tests discussed above are met.[517] The first test, production from a deposit, may be met if it is expected that the transferred property may produce from the same deposits from which wells on neighboring leases are producing. This test will apparently not be met for a deposit that exists under but has not been produced from neighboring leases (i.e., lower horizons). The second test may be met if

514. Prop. Reg. Sec. 1.613A-7(p).
515. I.R.C. Sec. 632 *(repealed by the Tax Reform Act of 1976).*
516. Reg. Sec. 1.613A-6(a).
517. Prop. Reg. Sec. 1.613A-7(p).

prospecting, exploration or discovery work indicates the probability that the property will generate oil or gas income sufficient to justify development of the property. Operator B must consider any such work performed with respect to the transferred lease. Although unclear from the regulations, the work done on neighboring leases may be sufficient to meet this test unless the geology of the transferred lease differs significantly from the surrounding leases. Satisfaction of the third test, relating to the value of the property before the transfer compared to the value (reduced by drilling and equipment costs) at the time of first production, can be determined only after Operator B drills a well or wells on the transferred property.[518]

Operator A's sale of a lower deposit or horizon should not constitute a transfer of a proven property. Although a higher deposit or horizon contains a producing well, other horizons may not be considered proven even though they underlie the same tract or parcel of land. If Operator A sells Operator B the entire tract, containing a well producing in a shallow zone, Operator B will not be entitled to percentage depletion on the gross income from the shallow zone. However, he will be entitled to percentage depletion on gross income from the deeper zone.[519]

Operator A's sale of his interests in Partnership X to Operator B is a transfer of any proven properties that the partnership owns at the time of sale.[520] Operator B may not claim percentage depletion under the independent-producer exemption for production attributable to proven properties owned by Partnership X at the time of transfer. Operator B may claim percentage depletion on production attributable to properties proven subsequent to his purchase of the partnership interests from Operator A.

Under the proposed regulations, the date of the transfer is the date when the parties involved execute a binding contract to transfer the property or, if they do not execute a contract, on the date they execute a document that causes the title to pass.[521] For example, the date of transfer of a property as a result of the settlement of litigation is when the parties are bound by a settlement agreement as opposed to a later date when their agreement is approved by the courts.[522] State law should determine the transfer date. If state law provides that the mere execution of a deed without delivery does not give the transferee any rights in the property, the date of transfer will be the delivery date.[523]

When parties enter into a partnership agreement for the acquisition of oil and gas leases, the transfer of the right to production from those leases occurs on the date the partnership agreement becomes applicable to the specific property.[524] If those leases are unproven when the partnership acquires them, a partner will be allowed percentage depletion on his share of production, even if his share increases at a later date because of a special allocation provision in the partnership agreement, provided the provision of his increased share of income is made part of the partnership agreement before the date the property becomes proven.[525]

When an individual places a property in a trust for the benefit of a particular beneficiary and executes a trust agreement that requires the trustee of the trust to transfer the oil property to the beneficiary on a particular date, the transfer occurs on the date the property is placed in trust.[526] If the agreement gives the trustee discretion

518. Prop. Reg. Sec. 1.613A-3(h)(2), Example 9.
519. Prop. Reg. Sec. 1.613A-3(h)(2), Example 8.
520. Prop. Reg. Sec. 1.613A-3(h)(2), Example 17.
521. Prop. Reg. Sec. 1.613A-7(n).
522. IRS Letter Ruling 8624028.
523. Prop. Reg. Sec. 1.613A-3(h)(2), Example 14.
524. Prop. Reg. Sec. 1.613A-3(h)(2), Example 11.
525. Prop. Reg. Sec. 1.613A-3(h)(2), Example 5; Prop. Reg. Sec. 1.613A-3(h)(2), Example 11.
526. IRS Letter Ruling 8710003 (Technical Advice Memorandum).

in selecting the date of transfer of the property to the beneficiary, the transfer still will be deemed made at the time the property is placed in trust. However, if the trustee can make at his discretion a transfer to the beneficiary (but was not under an obligation to do so), the date of the actual transfer of the property to the beneficiary governs.[527]

When an oil and gas property owner grants an option to buy that property, the date of transfer is the date that the transferee exercises his option and both parties become bound to the agreement.[528]

When a lease is farmed out before it is proven and the individual farming out the lease retains an overriding royalty that automatically will convert to a fraction of the working interest at payout, the conversion is not a transfer of a proven property. Similarly, when the conversion of the overriding royalty to a working interest is optional, rather than automatic, the conversion is not a transfer.[529]

Case 109
Percentage Depletion — Exceptions to the Transfer of Proven Property Rules

> **A, an individual, is involved in numerous oil and gas activities in the United States. He directly owns royalty interests and operating interests. He also is the sole shareholder of a corporation involved in oil and gas exploration and development activities, and is a partner in several partnerships that own producing properties in the United States. Individual A seeks general information regarding exceptions to the general rule that percentage depletion is disallowed to transferees following transfers of proven oil or gas properties.**

Generally, if an interest in a proven oil or gas property is transferred, the independent-producer and royalty-owner exemption is not available to the transferee for production of oil or gas attributable to that interest, and that production will not be taken into account for any computation by the transferee regarding its independent-producer and royalty-owner exemption.[530] *(See Case 108 for a discussion of the definition of a proven property.)*

The Internal Revenue Code lists the following exceptions to the transfer rules:

- ☐ A transfer of property at death.[531]
- ☐ A transfer in an exchange to which Section 351 applies if, following the exchange, the tentative depletable quantity is required to be allocated between the transferee and transferor.[532]
- ☐ A change of beneficiaries of a trust by reason of the death, birth or adoption of any vested beneficiary if the transferee was a beneficiary of that trust or is a lineal descendent of the settlor or any other vested beneficiary of the trust (with one narrow exception).[533]

---

527. Prop. Reg. Sec. 1.613A-3(h)(2), Example 12.
528. Prop. Reg. Sec. 1.613A-3(h)(2), Example 13.
529. Prop. Reg. Sec. 1.613A-3(h)(2), Example 6.
530. I.R.C. Sec. 613A(c)(9)(A).
531. I.R.C. Sec. 613A(c)(9)(B)(i).
532. I.R.C. Sec. 613A(c)(9)(B)(ii).
533. I.R.C. Sec. 613A(c)(9)(B)(iii).

□ A transfer of property between corporations that are members of the same controlled group, but only as long as the tentative quantity is allocated between the transferor and transferee.[534]

□ A transfer of property between business entities under common control or between related persons in the same family, but only as long as the tentative quantity is allocated between the transferor and transferee.[535]

□ A transfer of property between a trust and members of the same family if: (1) the beneficiaries of that trust are, and continue to be, members of the family that transferred the property and (2) the tentative quantity is allocated among the family members.[536]

For these purposes, a *controlled group of corporations* includes both parent and subsidiary groups of corporations involving more than 50% intercompany control.[537] *Business entities under common control* exist where 50% or more of the beneficial interest in two or more corporations, trusts or estates is owned by the same or related persons, taking into account only persons who own at least 5% of that beneficial interest.[538] Members of the same *family* include only the taxpayer, his spouse and his minor children.[539]

The proposed income tax regulations are comprehensive in their coverage of the transfer of proven property rules and expand on the exceptions listed in the statute. These proposed regulations specify the following types of transfers that do not result in a loss of percentage depletion to the transferee:

□ A sale of proven oil or gas properties from a parent to its wholly owned subsidiary as long as the tentative depletable quantity is allocated between the two corporations.[540]

□ A transfer of a proven property from an individual upon his death to his estate, then from the estate to a trust and then from the trust to an individual, pursuant to provisions in the will.[541] (The distribution does not have to be pro rata.)

□ A transfer of secondary and tertiary production property for production before 1984.[542]

□ The reversion of a portion of a working interest in a carried-interest arrangement provided the property was not proven when the carried party entered into the agreement.[543]

□ The optional conversion of a retained overriding royalty to a fraction of the working interest provided the property was not proven when acquired originally.[544]

□ A transfer of a proven property producing from a shallow zone to the extent of production from subsequent wells the transferee drills to a deeper reservoir or zone.[545] The transferee may claim percentage depletion with respect to production

534. I.R.C. Sec. 613A(c)(9)(B)(iv).
535. I.R.C. Sec. 613A(c)(9)(B)(v).
536. I.R.C. Sec. 613A(c)(9)(B)(vi).
537. I.R.C. Sec. 613A(c)(8)(D)(i).
538. I.R.C. Sec. 613A(c)(8)(B).
539. I.R.C. Sec. 613A(c)(8)(D)(iii).
540. Prop. Reg. Sec. 1.613A-3(h)(2), Example 2.
541. Prop. Reg. Sec. 1.613A-3(h)(2), Example 3.
542. Prop. Reg. Sec. 1.613A-3(h)(2), Example 4; IRS Letter Ruling 8723073.
543. Prop. Reg. Sec. 1.613A-3(h)(2), Example 5.
544. Prop. Reg. Sec. 1.613A-3(h)(2), Example 6.
545. Prop. Reg. Sec. 1.613A-3(h)(2), Example 8.

from the deeper zone, even though he is not entitled to percentage depletion on the gross income from the shallow zone.

- ☐ The maturity of a remainder interest in a trust holding producing oil and gas properties provided the properties were not proven at the time the remainder interest in trust was created.[546]
- ☐ A transfer of a proven property to a revocable trust in which the transferor is treated as the owner under Section 676 ("grantor" trust) provided the transferor was entitled to percentage depletion on the production from that property before the transfer.[547]
- ☐ A transfer of interest in a proven property to a partnership in which the transferor was entitled to percentage depletion on that interest before the transfer provided any other partner's interest in the producing property does not increase as a result of the transfer.[548]
- ☐ A distribution of a proven property from a partnership to a partner provided the partner was entitled to percentage depletion immediately before the distribution and his interest in the property does not increase as a result of the distribution.[549]
- ☐ A transfer of proven properties by two transferors to a partnership provided a special allocation provision in the partnership agreement allocates the gross income from production of each property to the respective original transferor. However, if no special allocation of income is made, each partner may claim percentage depletion based only on his share of the production for the property he had contributed.[550]

The Internal Revenue Service (IRS) also has issued a number of published revenue rulings and private letter rulings that supplement the proposed regulations, including:

Corporations

- ☐ The transfer of proven royalty interests by an individual to a newly formed S corporation is not a disqualifying transfer of proven properties. Thus, the individual transferor, as sole shareholder, is entitled to percentage depletion on the proportion transferred to the extent that he was so entitled before the transfer.[551] *(See Case 111 for further discussion of percentage depletion in situations involving S corporations.)*
- ☐ A transfer of proven oil or gas properties from a corporation to its wholly owned subsidiary and a transfer of proven properties from a wholly owned subsidiary to its parent are not disqualifying transfers as long as the members of the controlled group share one depletable quantity.[552]
- ☐ A sale of overriding royalties on various oil and gas leases by a corporation to its wholly owned subsidiary is not a disqualifying transfer of proven properties as long as one depletable oil quantity is allocated between the corporations.[553]
- ☐ The transfer of properties pursuant to either a type "A" reorganization (statutory merger) or an I.R.C. Section 332 liquidation of wholly owned subsidiaries does not

546. Prop. Reg. Sec. 1.613A-3(h)(2), Example 10.
547. Prop. Reg. Sec. 1.613A-3(h)(2), Example 15.
548. Prop. Reg. Sec. 1.613A-3(h)(2), Example 18; IRS Letter Ruling 8310079; IRS Letter Ruling 8632035.
549. Prop. Reg. Sec. 1.613A-3(h)(2), Example 19; IRS Letter Ruling 8310079; IRS Letter Ruling 8632035.
550. Prop. Reg. Sec. 1.613A-3(h)(2), Example 20.
551. IRS Letter Ruling 8350088.
552. IRS Letter Ruling 7713005; IRS Letter Ruling 8510033.
553. IRS Letter Ruling 7726051.

constitute a transfer of proven properties when the parties to the reorganization were members of a controlled group of corporations required to allocate the depletable quantity immediately before the reorganization.[554] Although the technical requirement of allocating the depletable quantity between transferor and transferee cannot be met because only one corporation remained after the transfer, the allowable percentage depletion from the properties transferred will be subject to the same limitations in the surviving entity as they were subject to within the former controlled group. In addition, a statutory merger qualifying under I.R.C. Section 368(a)(2)(E) (commonly referred to as a reverse triangular merger) should not constitute a disqualifying transfer if the surviving corporation owns the properties because there has been no transfer and no change in the legal or equitable ownership of the properties.

☐ The statutory downstream merger of a parent corporation into its wholly owned subsidiary does not constitute a disqualifying transfer of proven oil and gas properties.[555] In addition, the dropdown of proven properties from the subsidiary to a lower-tier, wholly owned subsidiary following that merger is not a disqualifying transfer.[556]

☐ A type "B" reorganization (stock-for-stock) does not constitute a transfer of proven properties because immediately after the reorganization the participants will be members of the same controlled group and must share the depletable quantity.[557] (Because a transfer of stock normally does not constitute a transfer of properties, the ruling's significance is not clear.)

☐ A tax-free spin-off of stock in an existing subsidiary (with no prior transfer of properties) should normally constitute a transfer of stock and not properties. Accordingly, percentage depletion should survive such a spin-off. However, if properties are transferred to the subsidiary before the spin-off (and after 1974), the spin-off will constitute a transfer if the two corporations are not required to allocate the independent-producer's exemption after the spin-off.[558]

☐ A dividend distribution of proven oil or gas properties from one member of a controlled group of corporations to its parent, followed by a contribution of these properties to a subsidiary member of the group, does not constitute a disqualifying transfer of proven properties.[559]

☐ The contribution of stock in a corporation owning proven oil or gas properties by two joint shareholders to a transferee corporation also owned jointly by the same shareholders, followed by a statutory merger of the first corporation into the transferee corporation, does not constitute a transfer of proven properties.[560]

☐ An "F" reorganization involving a single entity does not constitute a disqualifying transfer of proven oil and gas properties.[561]

☐ The transfer of properties by a trust to a corporation in which the trust retains the right to income from the production of oil and gas from the properties in an amount equal to the greater of a fixed proportion of all the net proceeds of production from the properties or a specified minimum amount is a lease for federal income tax

554. Rev. Rul. 83-167, 1983-2 C.B. 104; IRS Letter Ruling 7945095; IRS Letter Ruling 8126061; IRS Letter Ruling 8250026; IRS Letter Ruling 8337022.
555. IRS Letter Ruling 8216045.
556. IRS Letter Ruling 8208017.
557. IRS Letter Ruling 7838107; IRS Letter Ruling 8229072.
558. I.R.C. Sec. 613A(c)(9).
559. IRS Letter Ruling 7952066; IRS Letter Ruling 8031082.
560. IRS Letter Ruling 8152060; IRS Letter Ruling 8229072.
561. Rev. Rul. 83-62, 1983-1 C.B. 113.

purposes. The trust will be entitled to percentage depletion on its retained share of the production and, although the ruling holds otherwise, the trust also would have been entitled to percentage depletion on the specified minimum payment for amounts accrued or received before August 17, 1986.[562] *(See Case 100.)*

Partnerships

- ☐ The distribution of proven properties in the liquidation of a partnership does not disqualify properties for future percentage depletion when distributions are pro rata to all partners.[563]

- ☐ The technical termination of a partnership resulting from a more-than-50% change in ownership does not disqualify percentage depletion for the remaining partners in the partnership provided their interests in the successor partnership are identical with their *interests* in the predecessor partnership.[564]

- ☐ The contribution of oil or gas properties by individuals to a limited partnership, when the limited partners are entitled to the same gross income from each property after the contributions as before, is not a transfer of proven properties.[565]

Estates

- ☐ The transfer of a primary life estate in a proven oil or gas property by a husband to his wife, with a secondary life estate (should the husband survive the wife) retained by the husband (remainder interest was assigned to an adult son), is not a disqualifying transfer of proven property.[566]

- ☐ The allocation of the entire community property interest in producing oil and gas properties to the estate of the decedent and the allocation of an equivalent value of other community property to be allocated to the surviving spouse do not constitute a disqualifying transfer of proven properties. The estate, as well as the heirs, will be entitled to percentage depletion on the properties because the allocations are considered part of a transfer of property at death.[567] Under applicable state law, the surviving spouse's ownership is one-half the total value of the community property, not one half-of each community asset.

Trusts

- ☐ The transfer of proven oil or gas properties back to the grantor of a revocable trust upon revocation of that trust is not a disqualifying transfer when the grantor was entitled to percentage depletion during both the term of and after termination of the trust.[568]

- ☐ In the case of a transfer of proven royalty interests to a trust that is amendable and revocable during the lifetime of the settlor and that becomes irrevocable upon the death of the settlor, the settlor will continue to be entitled to percentage depletion,

562. IRS Letter Ruling 8337019; Comm'r v. Engle, 82 U.S. 599 (1984), 53 AFTR2d 84-415, 84-1 USTC 9134; I.R.C. Sec. 613A(d)(5).
563. IRS Letter Ruling 7913012; IRS Letter Ruling 7824062.
564. IRS Letter Ruling 8026071.
565. IRS Letter Ruling 8205044; IRS Letter Ruling 8205048; IRS Letter Ruling 8239021; IRS Letter Ruling 8310079; IRS Letter Ruling 8421043.
566. IRS Letter Ruling 8149078.
567. IRS Letter Ruling 8005042.
568. IRS Letter Ruling 7937057.

even if the properties were transferred back to him before his death, as long as the settlor is treated as the owner of the trust under I.R.C. Sections 671-679.[569]

- Neither the establishment nor termination of Clifford trusts constitutes transfers of proven property when the trust agreement requires the trustee to maintain reserves for depletion. The grantor is required to include in taxable income all oil and gas income that each trust sets aside for the depletion reserve and is entitled to the depletion deduction during the term of each trust.[570]

- When Clifford trusts are established under trust agreements requiring the trustee to distribute all income to the beneficiaries and there is no provision in the agreements (or local law) requiring or permitting the trustee to maintain a reserve for depletion, only beneficiaries who are members of the grantor's family (spouse or minor children) are entitled to the percentage depletion allowances during the terms of the trusts. After the oil and gas interests revert back to the grantor (at the end of the trust period), the grantor will be entitled to the percentage depletion allowance.[571] Note that the taxation of Clifford trusts funded on or after March 1, 1986, has changed substantially under the Tax Reform Act of 1986. *(See Case 112 for a discussion of the taxation of Clifford trusts after the Tax Reform Act of 1986.)*

Case 110
Percentage Depletion After Transfer of Property by Individuals to Corporations

X, an individual, has been conducting oil and gas operations as an individual proprietor. Individual X desires to incorporate his oil and gas interests because he is concerned about the liability exposure associated with individual operations. Individual X desires advice on the various income tax consequences resulting from a transfer of his operating interests to a corporation that will be controlled by him and his wife. In particular, he is interested in the availability of percentage depletion for proven properties transferred to a controlled corporation.

Production from a proven oil or gas property that is transferred generally is not eligible for percentage depletion.[572] *(See Case 108.)* This general rule does not apply to situations in which the transferor and transferee are required to allocate the independent-producer's exemption following the transfer.[573] The rules requiring allocation of the depletable quantity among businesses under common control or among members of the same family do not require an allocation between an individual and a controlled corporation.[574] However, effective for production after December 31, 1979, from property transferred after December 31, 1974, a taxpayer may transfer proven oil or gas properties to a controlled corporation without loss of percentage depletion only if the following requirements are met:

- The transferor shareholder (or shareholders) must be an individual who elects to share his depletable quantity with the transferee corporation. Such election must be

569. IRS Letter Ruling 8337023.
570. Rev. Rul. 84-14, 1984-1 C.B. 147; IRS Letter Ruling 7938028; IRS Letter Ruling 8102027; IRS Letter Ruling 8128096; IRS Letter Ruling 8133081; IRS Letter Ruling 8227047; IRS Letter Ruling 8230135; IRS Letter Ruling 8307022; IRS Letter Ruling 8414057.
571. IRS Letter Ruling 8142179.
572. I.R.C. Sec. 613A(c)(9)(A).
573. I.R.C. Sec. 613A(c)(9)(B)(ii).
574. I.R.C. Sec. 613A(c)(8).

made by all the individual transferors on or before the due date, including extensions, for filing the corporation's income tax return for its first tax year ending after the transfer date.[575] The statement should be filed with the District Director of the Internal Revenue Service Center where each transferor files his tax return. The individual transferor must provide the corporation with a copy of the statement of election which the corporation shall attach to its income tax return.[576]

☐ All the corporation's outstanding stock must be issued to individuals solely in exchange for qualified property held by those individuals.[577] The stock received must also be in proportion to the relative value of the properties transferred.[578] Note that if a corporation subsequently issues stock for services, the election is retroactively voided.[579]

☐ The properties transferred include only: (1) oil or gas properties that have not been transferred previously in a "disqualifying" transfer[580] and (2) $1,000 cash in the aggregate.[581] The term *oil or gas property* includes necessary production equipment for that property that is in place when the property is transferred.[582] The term *necessary production equipment* includes, for example, the Christmas tree, casing, pumping jacks and other equipment essential for the efficient and effective production of oil and gas from a well.[583] It is not clear whether the term includes related equipment such as a gas-gathering system or a gas-processing plant.

☐ All transferors must be individuals. The stock is treated as issued to and held by the transferor if it is issued to and held by himself, his spouse and his minor children.[584]

☐ The transferor(s) or his spouse or minor children must continue to hold the stock in the corporation.[585] If at any time during his lifetime the transferor disposes of stock outside the family, the depletable quantity of the corporation is reduced by an amount that bears the same ratio to the depletable quantity as the fair market value of the stock transferred bears to the aggregate fair market value of all stock on the date transferred.[586] Also, the spouse and minor children are included in the transferor's "family" only as long as they remain the spouse and minor children.

If Individual X desires a nontaxable incorporation of his qualified oil and gas interest and meets the above requirements, he may transfer those properties to a qualified controlled transferee corporation. The tentative quantity (1,000 barrels per day) for the corporation is determined in the normal manner.[587] The transferor's tentative quantity is reduced by his pro-rata share of the corporation's depletable quantity.[588] For this purpose, the corporation's *depletable quantity* for any tax period is the lesser of its tentative depletable quantity (i.e., 1,000 barrels a day after 1979) or its actual average daily production for the period.[589] The transferor's *pro-rata share* is the sum of: (1) the corporation's depletable quantity allocable to production from property transferred to the corporation under this exception[590] and (2) the depletable quantity

575. I.R.C. Sec. 613A(c)(10)(I); IRS Announcement 81-67, 1981-15 I.R.B. 47; Prop. Reg. Sec. 1.613(A)-3(i)(9).
576. Prop. Reg. Sec. 1.613A-3(i)(9).
577. I.R.C. Sec. 613A(c)(10)(D).
578. Prop. Reg. Sec. 1.613A-3(i)(4).
579. *Ibid.*
580. I.R.C. Sec. 613A(c)(10)(E)(i).
581. I.R.C. Sec. 613A(c)(10)(E).
582. *Ibid.*
583. P.L. 97-448 (Technical Corrections Act of 1982), Sec. 202(d)(1); Prop. Reg. Sec. 1.613A-3(i)(5).
584. I.R.C. Sec. 613A(c)(10)(G).
585. I.R.C. Sec. 613A(c)(10)(F).
586. *Ibid.*
587. I.R.C. Sec. 613A(c)(10)(B).
588. I.R.C. Sec. 613A(c)(10)(C).
589. I.R.C. Sec. 613A(c)(10)(C)(iii).
590. I.R.C. Sec. 613A(c)(10)(C)(ii)(II).

allocable to all properties, (other than those transferred under this exception) multiplied by a fraction, the numerator of which is the fair market value of the transferor's stock and the denominator of which is the fair market value of all stock of the corporation.[591]

Where there is more than one transferor, the proposed regulations require that all transferors must reduce their depletable quantity by all production from properties that are proven at the time of transfer. For example, if A and B each transfer a property with 100 barrels per day of production to Corporation X, both are required to reduce their depletable quantity by 200 barrels per day.[592]

If the transferor disposes of the stock to anyone other than his spouse or minor children during his lifetime, the corporation's depletable oil quantity must be reduced for all periods on or after the date of transfer. The reduction is computed by multiplying the corporation's depletable oil quantity by a fraction, the numerator of which is the fair market value of the disposed stock and the denominator of which is the fair market value of all the corporation's stock on the date of disposition.[593]

The lower windfall profit tax (WPT) independent-producer rates may apply to production from the property transferred to the qualified transferee corporation. The independent-producer transfer rules (for WPT purposes) will not apply if the transferee establishes that the property has always been held by an independent-producer and the owner(s) has never had qualified production in excess of the independent-producer amount.[594]

Although Individual X wants to retain percentage depletion on the properties he transfers to his controlled corporation, the tax savings from the percentage depletion deduction allowed may be offset by other factors. The sharing of one depletable quantity between transferor and transferee may be costly with respect to future production of the transferee corporation. When an individual transfers unproven property to a qualified transferee corporation and the corporation has significant amounts of production in future years, the individual transferor may reduce or eliminate his depletable oil quantity through operation of the allocation provisions. If only unproven properties are transferred to the corporation, the election under I.R.C. Section 613A(c)(10) should *not* be made.

To qualify under the special exception, only stock (and up to $1,000 cash) may be received in exchange for oil or gas property.[595] It is sometimes desirable to structure a corporation with a combination of debt and equity. However, if the corporation issues debt securities in connection with the exchange, it appears the exception will not apply. It is not entirely clear whether the corporation may purchase (with debt) oil and gas or other property in connection with the exchange.

A double tax applies to the earnings and profits of any corporation if they are distributed as a dividend to the shareholder. This double tax can be mitigated by electing under Subchapter S not to be subject to the corporate income tax, whereby the corporation's income is taxed directly to the shareholders.[596] *(See Case 111 for a discussion concerning the interplay of deductions for depletion for S corporations.)*

Two other alternatives (or combination thereof) available to Individual X are a tax-free incorporation of the properties without making the special election to share one

591. I.R.C. Sec. 613A(c)(10)(C)(ii)(I).
592. Prop. Reg. Sec. 1.613A-3(i)(3)(iii), Example 1.
593. I.R.C. Sec. 613A(c)(10)(F).
594. I.R.C. Sec. 4992(d)(3)(B).
595. I.R.C. Sec. 613A(c)(10)(A).
596. I.R.C. Sec. 1366; I.R.C. Sec. 1363(a).

depletable quantity and a taxable sale of the oil and gas properties to a corporation to be controlled by Individual X and his wife. In both these situations, neither Individual X nor the corporation may claim percentage depletion on any proven property he transfers to the newly formed corporation (or corporations).

If Individual X already has production in excess of his depletable oil quantity, he should consider transferring some of his marginal properties to a controlled corporation in a regular tax-free transfer or a taxable transfer to the corporation. Properties that should be considered are those subject to the 50% of net income limitation and those for which the oil and gas sales prices are relatively low compared with the sales price of production from other properties. Even though the corporation is not allowed percentage depletion on those properties, such a transfer may increase the percentage depletion deduction available to Individual X with respect to his retained properties. By transferring those properties, Individual X's depletable oil quantity may be applied to his remaining production without a "wastage" of the depletable oil quantity on the marginally profitable properties.

It may be more advantageous for Individual X to sell his oil and gas properties to a corporation in a taxable transaction rather than effecting a tax-free exchange. Individual X will recognize gain on the transaction equal to the excess of the fair market value of the properties transferred over his adjusted basis in those properties. *(See Case 131 for a discussion of the character of gains on such a sale.)* Individual X may structure the sale using the installment method and defer recognition of gain until he receives payment.[597] *(See Case 138.)*

Even though the corporation is not allowed percentage depletion on any proven property it acquires from Individual X through a taxable sale, the corporation may claim cost depletion based on the purchase price allocated to those properties. In addition, the corporation will not have any preference depletion on those properties whereas, in a qualified tax-free exchange, percentage depletion in excess of the corporation's depletable basis in a given property will be a tax preference item subject to the alternative minimum tax provisions.

Many factors, tax and nontax, are involved in a decision on whether to use a corporation to explore for and produce oil and gas. Individual X should make computations, including the income tax effects based on his specific circumstances, to determine the best method or combination of methods for incorporating or not incorporating his oil and gas interests. No general rule will apply to all situations. Factors to consider in comparing a tax-free incorporation (with or without the special election to share the depletable quantity) with a taxable sale include the current volume of Individual X's production, the fair market value of the properties at the date of transfer, estimated future revenues, estimated rate of production, the various tax brackets of Individual X and the newly formed corporation, and the time value of money. Individual X also should consider electing S corporation status to reduce the "double tax" problem inherent in regular corporations.

Case 111
S Corporations — Effects on Determination of Percentage Depletion and on Transfers of Proven Properties

X, an individual, conducts oil and gas operations as an individual proprietor and as a shareholder in various S corporations. Individual X has

597. I.R.C. Sec. 453.

requested a summary analysis of the rules concerning the calculation of percentage depletion in situations involving S corporations.

Determination of Percentage Depletion

With the exception of certain "qualified oil corporations" (discussed below), an S corporation does not generate earnings and profits from current operations as a result of claiming percentage depletion in excess of cost depletion. Items of income, expense, gain, loss, etc., affect the shareholders' basis of their corporate stock. The shareholders compute their depletion allowance separately in a manner essentially like partners in partnerships.[598] Each shareholder is considered as producing his pro-rata share of the S corporation's oil and gas production. For purposes of calculating cost depletion, each shareholder is allocated his pro-rata share of the adjusted basis in each oil and gas property held by the S corporation.[599] The shareholder's portion of the adjusted basis then must be adjusted for any depletion allowed or allowable to the shareholder. The adjusted basis is to be used not only by the shareholder for the calculation of subsequent cost depletion but also by the S corporation for determining gain or loss on the disposition of that property.

Although the above rules have been in effect for S corporation tax years beginning after December 31, 1982, certain "qualified oil corporations" can continue to compute allowable depletion at the S corporation level. *Qualified oil corporations* are defined as: (1) those corporations that were electing small business S corporations as of September 28, 1982, that had average daily production of domestic crude oil or natural gas that, when combined with the production of any one of their substantial shareholders (one who owns more than 40% of the value of the stock at July 1, 1982), was in excess of 1,000 barrels per day for the calendar year 1982 and (2) those corporations that elected to have the Subchapter S rules in effect as of July 1, 1982, continue to apply.[600] The election was required to be filed with an S corporation's tax return for its tax year beginning in 1983.[601] However, the Internal Revenue Service (IRS) has allowed taxpayers to perfect this election at a later date when their 1983 returns failed to include such an election.[602] If this election were made, the S corporation would continue to be treated as a corporation for purposes of the depletion calculations, transfer-of-property rules, etc. (as opposed to the "partnership-like" treatment under current law). Terminating the S corporation election, for example, would not be deemed to be a transfer of oil and gas properties since the corporation has continued to hold the properties.

To illustrate how the depletion rules were changed, assume Corporation Y (an S corporation in existence at September 28, 1982) is owned 100% by Individual X and 1987 average daily production (ADP) is 400 barrels for Corporation Y and 1,400 barrels for Individual X. If Corporation Y is not an electing "qualified oil corporation," Individual X will be deemed to have 1,800 barrels ADP (1,400 barrels from other interests and 400 barrels from Corporation Y). Individual X will be allowed percentage depletion on only 1,000 barrels in 1987. He will not be allowed additional percentage depletion as a result of the production from Corporation Y because he is already over the 1,000-barrel-per-day limit.

598. I.R.C. Sec. 613A(c)(13)(A); I.R.C. Sec. 1379(d).
599. I.R.C. Sec. 613A(c)(13)(B).
600. P.L. 97-354 (Subchapter S Revision Act of 1982), Sec. 6(c)(3).
601. Temp. Reg. Sec. 18.1379-1(c).
602. IRS Letter Ruling 8524096.

If Corporation Y has made the election, even though Individual X does not claim the depletion in his personal return, Individual X receives a current benefit for the depletion attributable to Corporation Y's production because his net taxable income from Corporation Y is reduced by the corporation's percentage depletion deduction. This benefit will continue unless Corporation Y terminates its election. The remainder of this discussion assumes the S corporation is not a "qualified oil corporation."

Transfers of Proven Properties

Election of S Corporation Status by an Existing C Corporation

An S corporation election by an existing C corporation is treated as a disqualifying transfer of all the C corporation's proven properties as of the date the election first takes effect.[603]

Contribution of Proven Property to an S Corporation

Shareholders of S corporations are treated as partners, and the S corporation is treated as a partnership with respect to contributions of proven properties to the corporation.[604] Under proposed regulations, a partner (and similarly, therefore, a shareholder of an S corporation) is allowed percentage depletion with respect to the contributed property, based on the lesser of his interest in the partnership (S corporation) or his interest in oil and gas production from that property before the transfer.[605] Other partners (shareholders, in the case of an S corporation) are not entitled to percentage depletion with respect to production attributable to the transferor's interest in that property before the transfer.[606] The corporation's adjusted basis in the property is equal to the adjusted basis of the transferor shareholder(s) at the time of the transfer. *(See Case 110 for a detailed discussion of the requirements that are applicable to transfers of proven properties to S corporations that are qualified oil corporations.)*

Termination of S Corporation Election

Each shareholder of an S corporation that terminates its S corporation election is treated for percentage depletion purposes as having transferred to the C corporation his pro-rata share of all the assets of the S corporation.[607] The shareholders' combined adjusted tax bases in the properties as of the end of the corporation's last S corporation tax year become the corporation's adjusted tax basis in its properties. This transfer of properties by individuals to a corporation constitutes a disqualifying transfer of proven properties unless specific statutory requirements for an exception are met and an election is made.[608] Termination of an S corporation election in most instances will probably not qualify under this exception because all the S corporation's assets are deemed to be transferred when the S election is terminated.

Distribution of Proven Property by an S Corporation

A transferee shareholder will be entitled to claim percentage depletion based on the lesser of his pro-rata interest in the property before the transfer or on his interest in the property immediately after the transfer.[609] However, a distribution of appreciated

603. I.R.C. Sec. 613A(c)(13)(C)(ii).
604. I.R.C. Sec. 613A(c)(13)(C)(i); IRS Letter Ruling 8510054.
605. Prop. Reg. Sec. 1.613A-3(h)(2), Example 18.
606. Prop. Reg. Sec. 1.613A-7(o).
607. I.R.C. Sec. 613A(c)(13)(D).
608. I.R.C. Sec. 613A(c)(10).
609. Prop. Reg. Sec. 1.613A-3(h)(2), Example 19; IRS Letter Ruling 8510054.

property to the S corporation's shareholder(s) is treated as though the property were sold at its fair market value, and gain is recognized by the corporation.[610] The shareholder's adjusted basis in the distributed property is equal to the fair market value of the property on the date of distribution. Therefore, even though percentage depletion is available to the shareholder, cost depletion on the stepped-up basis generally may exceed any available percentage depletion. *(See Case 169 for a further discussion of S corporations.)*

Case 112
Percentage Depletion Following the Placement of Oil and Gas Properties in Trust

> On February 28, 1986, X, an individual, transfers a separate, undivided fractional interest in oil and gas royalty interests to each of three separate Clifford trusts for the benefit of his children—A, B and C. A and B are adults; C is a minor. Individual X's brother is the trustee for each of the children's trusts. Each of the three trusts will terminate at the expiration of 10 years and one month or upon the earlier death of the trust's beneficiary. Upon each trust's termination, all principal will revert to Individual X (or his estate if he is not living upon termination). The terms of the trusts include the following:
>
> - Trust A (for the benefit of A): The trustee shall distribute to A sums from trust income as he deems appropriate, less an annual reserve for depletion equal to an amount deductible in the tax year for federal income tax purposes. The annual reserve for depletion will be allocated to the trust corpus.
> - Trust B (for the benefit of B): The trustee shall distribute quarterly all the trust income to B. The trust agreement does not contain a provision for a depletion reserve.
> - Trust C (for the benefit of C): The trustee shall distribute at least annually all the trust income to or for the benefit of C. The trust agreement does not contain a provision for a depletion reserve.
>
> Before the transfer, Individual X was entitled to percentage depletion under the independent-producer and royalty-owner exemption on his royalty interests. Individual X wants to know whether the above three transfers will result in a loss of percentage depletion because the royalty interests were proven at the time of transfer to the various trusts.

A trust may claim a depletion deduction only to the extent not allowable to beneficiaries.[611] If a mineral property is held in trust, the allowable deduction for depletion is to be apportioned among the income beneficiaries and the trustee on the basis of the trust income allocable to each, unless the governing instrument (or local law) requires or permits the trustee to maintain a reserve for depletion.[612]

If a depletion reserve is maintained, the depletion deduction first is allocated to the trustee to the extent income is set aside for the reserve. The trustee then apportions any excess deductions among the income beneficiaries and the trustee on the basis of

610. I.R.C. Sec. 1363(d).
611. I.R.C. Sec. 642(e).
612. Reg. Sec. 1.611-1(c)(4).

trust income (in excess of the income set aside for the reserve) allocable to each.[613] If the amount authorized or required as a reserve is greater than the allowable deduction, the trustee may claim no deduction for the excess.

Specific provisions within a trust instrument generally prevail in determining the allocation of a depletion deduction among the trustee and income beneficiaries. Absent a specific provision in the trust instrument, state or local law prevails. Many states are concerned with the preservation of corpus and require the trustee to maintain a reserve for depletion for the benefit of a remainderman. If the trust instrument does not contain a specific provision and state or local law does not provide for a depletion reserve, the depletion deduction follows the general rule of apportionment.

With certain exceptions, percentage depletion allowances are not available to the transferee of an interest in a proven oil or gas property.[614] *(See Case 108.)* Individual X must examine each of the three transfers he made when forming the short-term Clifford trusts to determine whether the trustees and/or beneficiaries may claim percentage depletion for oil and gas production on the undivided interests in proven properties transferred to each trust.

The Trust A agreement provides that the trustee must maintain an annual depletion reserve equal to the amount allowed as a deduction to the trust for federal income tax purposes. The agreement also provides that the reserve become part of the trust corpus, which will revert to Individual X, the grantor, when the trust terminates. The Internal Revenue Service has ruled that, in such a situation, the grantor is entitled to the entire depletion deduction on the trust's income from oil and gas production because the entire amount of the depletion deduction was added to the trust's reserve for depletion.[615] Neither the conveyance of the interest in oil and gas royalties to the trustee when Trust A is established nor the conveyance of the corpus of Trust A to Individual X when the trust terminates will constitute a disqualifying transfer of proven oil and gas properties. Because Individual X was entitled to percentage depletion before the transfer, he will remain entitled to it during the existence of the trust and will continue to be entitled to it after the trust terminates.

During each year that Trust A exists, Individual X must include in his taxable income all oil and gas royalty receipts that Trust A sets aside for the depletion reserve. To the extent of the amount set aside, he will be allowed the deduction for depletion. The amount of taxable income of the trust allocable to Individual X (the depletion reserve) is completely offset by the depletion deduction available to him.

Unlike Trust A, Trust B's instrument does not authorize or require the trustee to maintain any type of depletion reserve. If state or local law requires the trustee to maintain a depletion reserve (even if the trust instrument does not), Individual X will include in his taxable income the amount of income set aside for the depletion reserve and will be entitled to a deduction for depletion allowable to the extent the amount allowable does not exceed the amount of income set aside. The same rules applicable to Trust A will apply because local law, by requiring maintenance of a depletion reserve, will govern the transfer.

If state or local law does not require the maintenance of a depletion reserve, the results will be different. The provisions of Trust B require all income to be distributed to the beneficiary. When there is a conveyance of property in trust, the percentage depletion is available only to beneficiaries who are and continue to be related persons in the

613. Reg. Sec. 1.611-1(c)(4).
614. I.R.C. Sec. 613A(c)(9)(A).
615. Rev. Rul. 84-14, 1984-1 C.B. 147; IRS Letter Ruling 7938028; IRS Letter Ruling 8128096; IRS Letter Ruling 8133081; IRS Letter Ruling 8227047; IRS Letter Ruling 8230135; IRS Letter Ruling 8307022; IRS Letter Ruling 8414057.

family of the transferors and only as long as the tentative oil quantity is allocated among the members of the family.[616] The family of an individual includes only his spouse and minor children.[617] Because B is not a minor child of Individual X, he may not claim percentage depletion on the oil and gas royalty income allocated to him in accordance with the provisions of the trust instrument.[618]

C, on the other hand, is a minor child of Individual X. Because there is no provision in the trust instrument for a depletion reserve, and assuming local law does not require such a reserve, all royalty income will be allocated and distributed to C. As long as C is a minor child of Individual X and continues to share the depletable oil quantity with him, C may claim percentage depletion on the oil and gas income from the property held in trust.[619] State law shall control as to when a child reaches majority.[620]

As for Trust A, the corpus of Trusts B and C will revert to Individual X at the end of the trust period. Because Individual X will have a reversionary interest in the corpus, which will be the same interest he had in the oil and gas properties prior to their being conveyed to the trusts, these conveyances are not disqualifying transfers. Individual X will be entitled to the deduction for percentage depletion on the income after the corpus is conveyed to him when the trusts terminate.[621]

The 65% of taxable income limitation must be considered by the grantor and the beneficiaries in calculating their respective allowable depletion deduction after applying the allocation rules discussed above. *(See Case 96 concerning the 65% limitation.)*

The results of the transfer to each of the above trusts would have been significantly different if it was made after March 1, 1986, and the value of the reversionary interest retained by Individual X had exceeded 5% of the value of each trust when it was formed. Under these circumstances, Individual X would be taxed on all of the income of the trusts under the grantor trust rules.[622] The transfer of a proven property to a grantor trust in which the grantor is treated as the owner will not be considered a transfer that causes the loss of percentage depletion.[623] Since X would recognize all royalty income earned on these properties, he would be apportioned all these percentage depletion deductions from each of the trusts.[624]

Case 113
Percentage Depletion for Retailers — Producing Subsidiary Owned by Retailer Parent Company

Corporation A is a publicly traded gas utility company providing residential energy to various communities. Corporation A's sales of natural gas to residential end-users in 1987 exceeded $75 million. Corporation B, an 85%-owned subsidiary of Corporation A, is involved in oil and gas exploration in the western United States. Corporation B's average daily production of oil and equivalent gas in 1987 is 950 barrels. Corporations A and B file a consolidated federal income tax return, using a calendar year. None

616. I.R.C. Sec. 613A(c)(9)(B)(vi).
617. I.R.C. Sec. 613A(c)(8)(D)(iii).
618. IRS Letter Ruling 8142179.
619. Prop. Reg. Sec. 1.613A-3(h)(2), Example 7.
620. IRS Letter Ruling 8142179.
621. *Ibid.*
622. I.R.C. Sec. 673(a).
623. Prop. Reg. Sec. 1.613A-3(h)(2), Example 15.
624. Reg. Sec. 1.611-1(c)(4).

of Corporation B's production is sold to Corporation A for use in Corporation A's utility operations. In 1987, Corporation B sold 1.7 million MCF of natural gas to 50 unrelated industrial end-users in large-volume transactions during the year for $3.4 million. On December 1, 1987, Corporation B acquired 1 million common shares (representing 6% in value of all outstanding stock) of Corporation A in open market purchases. Corporation A's tax manager wants to know whether Corporation B is entitled to claim percentage depletion in the 1987 consolidated federal income tax return.

The independent-producer and royalty-owner exemption does not apply to taxpayers who directly (or through a related person) sell oil or natural gas (excluding bulk sales of oil or gas to commercial or industrial users), or any product derived therefrom:

- ☐ Through a retail outlet operated by the taxpayer or a related person or
- ☐ To any person given authority under an agreement or contract with the taxpayer or a related person to occupy any retail outlet owned, leased or controlled by the taxpayer (or a related person) or obligated under an agreement or contract with the taxpayer to use a trademark, trade name, service mark or name owned by the taxpayer (or a related party) in marketing or distributing oil or natural gas (or products derived therefrom).[625]

The statute provides that the retailer rules apply only if the combined gross receipts from all retail outlets exceed $5 million during the tax year. For this purpose, gross receipts include all sales of oil and natural gas, except for bulk sales to industrial or commercial users (before conversion to a refined product) and all sales of products derived from oil and natural gas except for bulk sales of aviation fuels to the Department of Defense (after September 18, 1982). Sales of oil or natural gas (or products derived therefrom) do not include sales of these items outside the United States if no domestic production of the taxpayer (or a related person) is exported during the current or immediately preceding tax year.[626]

A person is a *related person* with respect to the taxpayer if a significant ownership interest (5% or more) in either the taxpayer or that person is held by the other, or if a third person holds a 5%-or-more interest in both the taxpayer and that person.[627] An interest owned by a corporation, partnership, trust or estate is considered to be owned directly by itself and proportionately by its shareholders, partners or beneficiaries, as the case may be.[628] For purposes of the retailer provisions of the statute, a husband and wife are not considered to be related persons.[629]

Products derived from oil or natural gas include gasoline, kerosene, number 2 fuel oil, refined lubricating oils, diesel fuel, methane, butane, propane and similar products recovered from petroleum refineries or field facilities.[630] There is no statutory definition provided for the term *retail*. The proposed regulations define a *retail outlet* as any place where sales of oil and natural gas (or products derived therefrom) accounting for more than 5% of the gross receipts from all sales made at that place during the tax year are "systematically made to any person or persons other than for resale."[631]

625. I.R.C. Sec. 613A(d)(2); Prop. Reg. Sec. 1.613A-7(r).
626. *Ibid.*
627. I.R.C. Sec. 613A(d)(3); Prop. Reg. Sec. 1.613A-7(m).
628. *Ibid.*
629. Prop. Reg. Sec. 1.613A-4(b)(2), Example 9; Prop. Reg. Sec. 1.613A-4(b)(2), Example 10.
630. Prop. Reg. Sec. 1.613A-7(r).
631. Prop. Reg. Sec. 1.613A-7(r); Prop. Reg. Sec. 1.613A-4(b)(2), Example 6; Prop. Reg. Sec. 1.613A-4(b)(2), Example 8.

Although the proposed regulations do not specifically define the term *systematically,* it appears the term *retail* is being defined to include all sales to end-users or consumers.

The Appeals Court has adopted a more restrictive definition for the term *retail.*[632] The court held, based on a dictionary definition, that retail sales include only those sales made in small quantities to ultimate consumers to meet personal needs. They do not include sales to commercial and industrial accounts, distributors for resale or to political subdivisions (such as municipalities and county governmental agencies). The court's decision appears to be consistent with Congressional intent based on Committee Reports that stated " . . . the retailer exclusion should be applied only in the case of retail sales as that term is commonly used. Thus, bulk sales of oil and natural gas directly to industrial or commercial users should not be treated as retail sales through a retail outlet."[633] The Appellate Court stated that sales made by owner-operated retail outlets and sales to retail outlets owned by a taxpayer but leased to third parties are to be included in the computation of total retail sales. However, the court determined that sales made by leased retail outlets should be excluded from the computation.

The case also held that a taxpayer should not include retail sales made by a third person under a trademark, trade name, service mark or name owned by the taxpayer (or a related person) for purposes of determining whether the taxpayer's gross receipts from all retail outlets exceed $5 million during the tax year.[634] The decision appears to be predicated on the findings that the taxpayer's sales of those products were made to distributors for resale and those purchasers were not obligated to use the taxpayer's trademark or trade name. The court concluded that Congress intended to include only those contractual obligations that *explicitly* require the use of the taxpayer's trademark in marketing or distribution.

For purposes of the windfall profit tax (WPT), the retailer status is determined on a calendar-year basis.[635] Thus, for calendar-year taxpayers, the test for determining retailer status will be the same for both depletion and WPT purposes. However, for fiscal-year taxpayers, the test will be applied on a fiscal-year basis for depletion purposes and a calendar-year basis for WPT purposes.

In situations where a subsidiary such as Corporation B is not otherwise a retailer and does not sell its production through its retailer parent (A), the statute[636] and proposed regulations[637] indicate that Corporation B should not be classified as a retailer. Although ownership percentages (5% and 50%) in examples supporting this conclusion in the proposed regulations are insufficient to permit the filing of a consolidated income tax return, the statutory language expressly supports the conclusion that retailer status should be determined at the separate-company level, even though consolidated returns may be filed. The consolidated return regulations accept as their central premise the concept that each member's separate taxable income is determined and then appropriate intercompany adjustments are made to arrive at consolidated taxable income.[638] Retailer status is determined at the separate-company level, even though the 65% of taxable income limitation is applied to consolidated taxable

632. Witco Chemical Corp. v U.S., 742 F.2d 615 (Fed. Cir. 1984), 54 AFTR2d 84-5795, 84-2 USTC 9751.
633. Senate Report No. 94-938, 1976-3 C.B. Vol. 3 463.
634. Witco Chemical Corp.
635. I.R.C. Sec. 4992(b)(2).
636. I.R.C. Sec. 613A(d)(2).
637. Prop. Reg. Sec. 1.613A-7(r); Prop. Reg. Sec. 1.613A-4(b)(2), Example 2; Prop. Reg. Sec. 1.613A-4(b)(2), Example 11.
638. I.R.C. Sec. 613A(c)(8)(A); Prop. Reg. Sec. 1.613A-3(g)(1).

income.[639] *(See Case 116.)* Component members of a controlled group of corporations are treated as one taxpayer for purposes of the depletable quantity limitation[640] *(see Case 106)*, but that appears to be the only purpose for which the single-taxpayer treatment is intended. Because no similar language is present under the retailer provisions of the statute, the existence of the controlled group is not relevant to the determination of Corporation B's status as a retailer.

It is clear that a corporation is a retailer if it owns a 5%-or-more interest in a retailer (and thereby benefits from the retailer's retail sales)[641] or sells its production through a related-party retailer.[642] However, retailer status should not be imputed to a taxpayer from a brother-sister related corporation or from a parent corporation if the taxpayer does not actually sell its production to or through such related-party retailers.[643] This conclusion is properly in contrast with the language in the refiner provisions,[644] whereby mere related-party affiliation with a refiner causes disallowance of percentage depletion under the independent-producer and royalty-owner provisions. *(See Case 114.)*

In private letter rulings,[645] the Internal Revenue Service (IRS) has ruled that the retailer status of a sister corporation does not preclude percentage depletion for another member in the consolidated group provided none of that member's production is sold through the sister retailer corporation's retail outlets. Subsequently, the IRS also has issued a private letter ruling in which it considered a fact situation very similar to that presented in this case.[646] In that ruling, the IRS held that the producer, a wholly owned subsidiary of a retailing parent, was eligible for percentage depletion provided none of its production was sold to or through the parent company. Accordingly, Corporation B should be eligible for percentage depletion under the independent-producer and royalty-owner provisions.

It appears that a retailer's production is not counted in determining the 1,000-barrel depletable quantity limitation in a controlled group situation, even though the members of the controlled group are treated as one taxpayer for purposes of the depletable quantity limitation. This conclusion is drawn from the provision in the statute that the independent-producer provisions do not apply in the case of a retailer.[647]

Corporation B's sale of 1.7 million MCFs of natural gas to 50 unrelated industrial end-users in large-volume transactions should constitute bulk sales and not sales through retail outlets or to any person that would classify Corporation B as a retailer.[648] In a private letter ruling,[649] the IRS held that similar sales to 102 industrial end-users under contracts calling for the taxpayers to deliver specified maximum quantities of natural gas subject to curtailment or interruption by the seller during

639. Reg. Sec. 1.1502-12.
640. Reg. Sec. 1.1502-44(a); Reg. Sec. 1.1502-12(p).
641. I.R.C. Sec. 613A(d)(2); Prop. Reg. Sec. 1.613A-7(r); Prop. Reg. Sec. 1.613A-4(b)(2), Example 1; Prop. Reg. Sec. 1.613A-4(b)(2), Example 3.
642. I.R.C. Sec. 613A(d)(2); Prop. Reg. Sec. 1.613A-7(r); Prop. Reg. Sec. 1.613A-4(b)(2), Example 5; Prop. Reg. Sec. 1.613A-4(b)(2), Example 14.
643. I.R.C. Sec. 613A(d)(2); Prop. Reg. Sec. 1.613A-7(r); Prop. Reg. Sec. 1.613A-4(b)(2), Example 2; Prop. Reg. Sec. 1.613A-4(b)(2), Example 4; Prop. Reg. Sec. 1.613A-4(b)(2), Example 11; Rev. Rul. 85-12, 1985-1 C.B. 181; IRS Letter Ruling 8009001 (Technical Advice Memorandum).
644. I.R.C. Sec. 613A(d)(4); Prop. Reg. Sec. 1.613A-7(s); Prop. Reg. Sec. 1.613A-4(c)(1); Prop. Sec. 1.613A-4(c)(2), Example 1.
645. IRS Letter Ruling 8204217; IRS Letter Ruling 8336088; IRS Letter Ruling 8340019; IRS Letter Ruling 8602003 (Technical Advice Memorandum).
646. IRS Letter Ruling 8250014 (Technical Advice Memorandum).
647. I.R.C. Sec. 613A(d)(2); Prop. Reg. Sec. 1.613A-4(b).
648. I.R.C. Sec. 613A(d)(2); Prop. Reg. Sec. 1.613A-7(r); Prop. Reg. Sec. 1.613A-4(b)(2), Example 12.
649. IRS Letter Ruling 8207011 (Technical Advice Memorandum).

periods when natural gas is in short supply constituted "bulk sales" under the statute. The IRS noted that the Committee Reports accompanying the Tax Reform Act of 1976 indicate that the definition of *retail sale* should be applied based on a common usage of the term. "Bulk sales" of oil or natural gas directly to industrial or commercial end-users should not be treated as sales through a retail outlet. It is not entirely certain whether specific clauses in the contracts with industrial end-users in the private letter ruling influenced the IRS's conclusion that such sales were "bulk sales." In an earlier private letter ruling,[650] however, the IRS indicated that sales to industrial end-users were to be treated the same as sales to residential end-users because the taxpayer did not demonstrate that sales to industrial users were made in bulk quantities.

In one private letter ruling,[651] the IRS denied independent-producer status to a producer marketing refined products to industrial and commercial end-users because the exclusion for bulk sales to industrial and commercial users does not apply for bulk sales of refined products.

The proposed regulations provide that a taxpayer will be deemed to be selling oil, gas or derivative products through a related person's retail outlets if those sales by the related person produce gross income from which the taxpayer may benefit by virtue of its direct or indirect ownership interest in that related person. Because Corporation B acquired an ownership interest in Corporation A on December 1, 1987, under these proposed regulations Corporation B will be classified as a retailer at that time. The proposed regulations also provide that if a taxpayer is a retailer for a portion of the tax year, a proportionate part of the gross income and taxable income from the taxpayer's oil and gas properties (based on the portion of the year a taxpayer is a retailer) will not be eligible for percentage depletion under the independent-producer and royalty-owner provisions.[652] Accordingly, a proportionate part (31/365) of Corporation B's gross income and taxable income from all oil and gas properties (otherwise eligible for percentage depletion under the independent-producer and royalty-owner provisions) will not be eligible for percentage depletion in 1987. A literal reading of the statute[653] suggests this provision is not intended to allow taxpayers who are *prima facie* retailers to compute percentage depletion to the date during the tax year the $5 million limitation is reached.

Corporation B should consider a dividend distribution of the Corporation A stock to Corporation A to remove the retailer "taint" in subsequent tax years. Such a dividend will not result in federal income taxation because intercompany dividends in a consolidated return are eliminated,[654] but the corporations must consider the possible state tax and other legal implications of this approach.

Because the retailer exclusion disallows only the benefits of the independent-producer exemption, a retailer qualifies for percentage depletion for natural gas sold under a qualified fixed contract and qualified natural gas from geopressured brine.[655] *(See Case 93.)*

650. IRS Letter Ruling 8005008 (Technical Advice Memorandum).
651. IRS Letter Ruling 8337001.
652. Prop. Reg. Sec. 1.613A-7(r); Prop. Reg. Sec. 1.613A-4(b)(2), Example 13.
653. I.R.C. Sec. 613A(d)(2).
654. Reg. Sec. 1.1502-14(a)(1).
655. I.R.C. Sec. 613A(d)(2); I.R.C. Sec. 613A(b).

Case 114
Percentage Depletion With Respect to Certain Refiners

> During 1987, X Corporation had 800 barrels per day of oil and equivalent gas production from properties located in the United States. A, an individual, owns 8% in value of the outstanding stock of X Corporation. No other shareholder of X Corporation owns more than 5% in value of the outstanding stock of X Corporation. Individual A owns a 30% capital and profits interest in a general partnership (Z) that owns a refinery which sells its products only to wholesalers. Partnership Z's refining capacity is 60,000 barrels per day, but normal refinery runs seldom exceed 45,000 barrels. On one day in June 1987, Partnership Z's refinery run is 52,000 barrels. None of X Corporation's production is sold to Partnership Z.

Percentage depletion under the independent-producer and royalty-owner provisions is not available to a taxpayer if the taxpayer or a related person engages in the refining of crude oil and if, on any day during the tax year, the refinery runs of the taxpayer and that person exceed 50,000 barrels.[656] The Internal Revenue Service defines *refinery runs* as the volume of crude oil input into the refining process. The term does not include products of natural gas or products of crude oil refineries such as reduced crude or gas oil.[657] The 50,000-barrel-per-day test is applied for each tax year. Thus, a taxpayer ineligible for percentage depletion in a given tax year due to a refinery run in excess of 50,000 barrels may become eligible for percentage depletion in a subsequent tax year provided that on no one day do refinery runs exceed 50,000 barrels. Refining is any process by "which the physical or chemical characteristics of crude oil or crude oil products are changed."[658] Refining, however, does not include "passing crude oil through separators to remove gas, placing crude oil in settling tanks to recover basic sediment and water, and dehydrating crude oil."[659] The mining and processing of oil shale into refined products should not constitute "refining" because the term *crude oil* does not include oil shale.[660]

For purposes of the refiner provisions, a person is related to the taxpayer if a significant ownership interest in either the taxpayer or that person is held by the other or if a third person has a significant ownership interest in both the taxpayer and that person.[661] A 5%-or-more ownership interest is deemed to be significant. For purposes of determining a significant ownership interest, an interest owned by or for a corporation, partnership, trust or estate shall be considered as owned directly both by itself and proportionately by its shareholders, partners or beneficiaries, as the case may be.[662] For purposes of the related-person rules, a husband and wife are not considered to be related persons.[663]

Because Individual A owns a significant (5% or more) ownership interest in Partnership Z, he is deemed to be a refiner and is ineligible for percentage depletion under the independent-producer provisions. Furthermore, because Individual A has a significant (5% or more) ownership interest in both X Corporation and Partnership Z, X

656. I.R.C. Sec. 613A(d)(4); Prop. Reg. Sec. 1.613A-7(s).
657. IRS Letter Ruling 8328039; IRS Letter Ruling 8405012.
658. Prop. Reg. Sec. 1.613A-7(s).
659. *Ibid.*
660. Prop. Reg. Sec. 1.613A-7(g).
661. I.R.C. Sec. 613A(d)(3); Prop. Reg. Sec. 1.613A-7(m).
662. *Ibid.*
663. Prop. Reg. Sec. 1.613A-4(b)(2), Example 9; Prop. Reg. Sec. 1.613A-4(b)(2), Example 10.

Corporation is deemed to be a related person with respect to Partnership Z and will be ineligible for percentage depletion, even though none of its production is sold to Partnership Z.

A number of alternatives may be open to X Corporation, Partnership Z and Individual A to remove the refiner "taint" and thereby allow X Corporation to claim percentage depletion in subsequent tax years. Individual A can give half his shares to his spouse, thereby keeping an 8% ownership interest in X Corporation within the family unit. As previously noted, a husband and wife are not considered to be related persons for purposes of the refiner provisions. Because Individual A and his spouse are not related persons, a 4% ownership by each in X Corporation will not cause Partnership Z to be a related party to X Corporation. This same result occurs for taxpayers in community property states where each spouse is deemed to own a one-half interest in the holdings of the family unit.[664] Second, Individual A and the other general partners in Partnership Z can agree that on no day will the refinery runs of the partnership exceed 50,000 barrels. Because the partnership's refinery runs average 45,000 barrels per day, this agreement should not be difficult for Individual A to arrange. Nevertheless, the agreement will be ineffective for this purpose if the refinery runs ever exceed 50,000 barrels. Individual A also could insist that Partnership Z confine its sales of products to wholesalers to avoid classifying X Corporation as a retailer. *(See Case 113.)*

For purposes of the retailer provisions *(see Case 113)*, sales of oil, natural gas or any product derived from oil or natural gas do not include sales of those items outside the United States if no domestic production of the taxpayer or a related person is exported during the tax year or the immediately preceding tax year.[665] No corresponding language is contained in the refiner provisions;[666] accordingly, even if Partnership Z's refinery operations are located outside the United States, X Corporation will not be allowed percentage depletion on its production.

Because of the unfortunate consequences of being deemed a refiner, corporations otherwise entitled to percentage depletion under the independent-produce and royalty-owner provisions should (if possible) monitor their 5%-or-more stockholders to make certain these persons are not refiners or do not own a significant ownership interest in an entity classified as a refiner.

A partnership owning producing oil and gas properties in which one of the partners is a refiner does not cause nonrefiner partners to be classified as refiners, even when all the partnership production is sold to the refiner partner.[667]

Because the refiner exclusion disallows only the benefits of the independent-producer exemption, a refiner qualifies for percentage depletion for natural gas sold under a qualified fixed contract and qualified natural gas from geopressured brine.[668] *(See Case 93.)*

---

664. IRS Letter Ruling 8042070; IRS Letter Ruling 8042080.
665. I.R.C. Sec. 613A(d)(2); Prop. Reg. Sec. 1.613A-7(r).
666. I.R.C. Sec. 613A(d)(4); Prop. Reg. Sec. 1.613A-7(s).
667. I.R.C. Sec. 613A(d)(4); Prop. Reg. Sec. 1.613A-6(c)(2), Example 2.
668. I.R.C. Sec. 613A(d)(4); I.R.C. Sec. 613A(b).

Case 115
Computation of 65% of Taxable Income Limitation — Reallocation of Limitation When Cost Depletion Exceeds PercentageDepletion After Initial Allocation of 65% of Taxable Income Limitation

Operator A, a cash-basis, calendar-year taxpayer, has taxable income of $240,000 in 1987 before any deduction for depletion (cost or percentage). Operator A's average daily production is 300 barrels per day. Operator A's cost depletion and tentative percentage depletion (limited to 50% of the net income from the property) are as follows:

Property	Cost Depletion	Tentative Percentage Depletion
A	$40,000	$ 20,000
B	35,000	60,000
C	10,000	100,000
D	5,000	120,000

Operator A is neither directly nor indirectly involved in retailing or refining operations. He wants to know his allowable depletion deduction for 1987. Production from all the properties qualifies for percentage depletion under the independent-producer and royalty-owner exemption.

The deduction for percentage depletion under the independent-producer and royalty-owner exemption cannot exceed 65% of the taxpayer's taxable income determined without regard to:

☐ Depletion on production from an oil or gas property subject to the independent-producer exemption.[669]

☐ Net operating loss carrybacks to the tax year under Section 172.[670]

☐ Capital loss carrybacks to the tax year under Section 1212.[671]

☐ Distributions to beneficiaries (with certain exceptions) in the case of a trust.[672]

The aggregate percentage depletion disallowed as a deduction for the tax year due to the 65% of taxable income limitation is available for carryforward to subsequent years, subject to the 65% of taxable income limitation in those later years.[673] For fiscal-year taxpayers, the 65% of taxable income limitation is applied for the entire fiscal year, not each short period included within that year.[674] *(See Case 116 for the rules applicable to corporations filing a consolidated return.)*

Depletion on oil and gas properties for which percentage depletion is not deductible under the independent-producer exemption, such as natural gas sold under a fixed

669. I.R.C. Sec. 613A(d)(1)(A); Prop. Reg. Sec. 1.613A-4(a)(1)(i).
670. I.R.C. Sec. 613A(d)(1)(B); Prop. Reg. Sec. 1.613A-4(a)(1)(ii).
671. I.R.C. Sec. 613A(d)(1)(C); Prop. Reg. Sec. 1.613A-4(a)(1)(iii).
672. I.R.C. Sec. 613A(d)(1)(D); Prop. Reg. Sec. 1.613A-4(a)(1)(iv); Prop. Reg. Sec. 1.613A-4(a)(2), Example 4; IRS Letter Ruling 8252013 (Technical Advice Memorandum).
673. I.R.C. Sec. 613A(d)(1); Prop. Reg. Sec. 1.613A-7(q); Prop. Reg. Sec. 1.613A-4(a)(1); Prop. Reg. Sec. 1.613A-4(a)(2), Example 2.
674. Prop. Reg. Sec. 1.613A-4(a)(1); Prop. Reg. Sec. 1.613A-4(a)(2), Example 3.

contract, natural gas from geopressured brine *(see Case 93)*, foreign oil and gas properties *(see Case 94)* or production from transferred proven oil and gas properties *(see Case 108)*, reduces taxable income for purposes of applying the 65% of taxable income limitation.[675] In the case of natural gas sold under a fixed contract or natural gas from geopressured brine, however, the entire production (oil or gas) from the property must qualify under the provisions before depletion on those properties reduces taxable income for purposes of the 65% of taxable income limitation.[676] The proposed regulations[677] take the position that taxable income for purposes of the 65% of taxable income limitation also must be reduced by cost depletion when that depletion is greater than percentage depletion before application of the depletable quantity limitation *(see Case 96)* or the 65% of taxable income limitation.

Operator A's taxable income for purposes of the 65% of taxable income limitation is computed as follows:

Taxable income before depletion	$240,000
Cost depletion on property A (when cost depletion exceeds percentage depletion before the 65% of taxable income limitation)	(40,000)
Taxable income for purposes of the 65% of taxable income limitation	$200,000
	× .65
Maximum amount of percentage depletion allowable	$130,000

The $130,000 limit on allowable percentage depletion is allocated among properties B, C and D as follows:

Property	Tentative Percentage Depletion	Percentage	Allowable Depletion
B	$ 60,000	21.4	$ 27,820
C	100,000	35.7	46,410
D	120,000	42.9	55,770
	$280,000	100.0%	$130,000

Because cost depletion ($35,000) exceeds percentage depletion ($27,820) on property B after allocation of the 65% of taxable income limitation, the proposed regulations[678] provide that the limitation ($130,000) must be reallocated among the remaining properties (C and D) as follows:

Property	Tentative Percentage Depletion	Percentage	Allowable Depletion
C	$100,000	45.5	$ 59,150
D	120,000	54.5	70,850
	$220,000	100.0%	$130,000

675. I.R.C. Sec. 613A(d)(1)(A); Prop. Reg. Sec. 1.613A-4(a)(1)(i).
676. Prop. Reg. Sec. 1.613A-4(a)(1)(i); Prop. Reg. Sec. 1.613A-4(a)(2), Example 6.
677. *Ibid.*
678. Prop. Reg. Sec. 1.613A-4(a)(1); Prop. Reg. Sec. 1.613A-4(a)(2), Example 1.

It is possible for the percentage depletion deduction reallocated to a property to exceed the tentative percentage depletion allocable to that property before the depletable quantity limitation or the 65% of taxable income limitation is applied. Because the proposed regulations do not address this possibility, it is unclear whether the realloca-tion should be limited to the amount of the tentative percentage depletion calculated before applying the two limitations.

Operator A's 1987 depletion deduction may be summarized as follows:

Property	Total Cost Depletion	Tentative Percentage Depletion	Allowable Depletion without Regard to 65% Limitation	Allowable Depletion
A	$40,000	$ 20,000	$ 40,000	$ 40,000
B	35,000	60,000	60,000	35,000
C	10,000	100,000	100,000	59,150
D	5,000	120,000	120,000	70,850
		$300,000	$320,000	$205,000

Operator A's percentage depletion carryover to 1988 and subsequent years is as follows.[679]

Depletion allowable (whether cost or percentage) without regard to the 65% limitation	$320,000
Depletion allowable after the 65% limitation	(205,000)
Amount disallowed—available for carryover	$115,000

For the purpose of ultimately adjusting the basis of properties, the amount disallowed is allocated to the properties as follows:

Property B:

Percentage depletion before limitation	$60,000	
Cost depletion allowed	(35,000)	
Adjustment for Property B		$ 25,000

Property C:

$$\$90{,}000 \times \frac{\$100{,}000}{\$100{,}000 + \$120{,}000} = \quad 40{,}950^{*}$$

Property D:

$$\$90{,}000 \times \frac{\$120{,}000}{\$100{,}000 + \$120{,}000} = \quad 49{,}050^{*}$$

Total adjustment $115,000

* Rounded

679. I.R.C. Sec. 613A(d)(1); Prop. Reg. Sec. 1.613A-4(a)(1).

Operator A's adjusted basis in his oil and gas properties is reduced by the amount of the depletion carryforward only when he uses the carryforward as a deduction.[680] Should Operator A generate sufficient taxable income in 1988 to use his 1987 percentage depletion carryforward (in whole or in part) after taking into account any percentage depletion generated in 1988, the basis in properties B, C and D must be reduced (but not below zero) by the amount of the 1987 carryover used in proportion to the amount of percentage disallowed for those properties in the year of disallowance.[681]

Should Operator A dispose of an oil and gas property before using the percentage depletion carryforward for that property, Operator A's depletion carryforward (but not the basis in the property for determining gain or loss) must be reduced by the lesser of: (1) his adjusted basis in the property or (2) the difference between that basis and the adjusted basis he would have in the property, absent the 65% of taxable income limitation.[682] For example, if Operator A sells property D when the property has an adjusted basis of $20,000, Operator A's percentage depletion carryforward will be reduced by $20,000, as follows:

Lesser of:	
Adjusted basis in property	$20,000
Adjusted basis in property less adjusted basis absent the 65% of taxable income limitation: $20,000–0 (because $20,000-$49,050 is less than zero)	$20,000

Operator A must maintain records, by property, of the origin of the percentage depletion carryforward and its subsequent use in future tax years.

Case 116
Application of the 65% of Taxable Income Limitation — Consolidated Tax Returns and Carryovers in Corporate Acquisitions

Corporation A is engaged in contract drilling operations. Its taxable income for 1986 is $200,000. Corporation B, a wholly owned subsidiary of Corporation A purchased for cash and notes in March 1985, is engaged in the business of exploring for, developing and producing oil and gas in the United States. Corporation B's taxable income for 1986 (before the deduction for percentage depletion) is $100,000, and it has no tax basis in its oil and gas leases. Corporation B's tentative allowable percentage depletion deduction (after application of the 50% of net income limitation) for 1986 is $200,000. Corporations A and B file a consolidated return for calendar year 1986. B has a percentage depletion carryforward of $150,000 from years prior to affiliation. Corporation B is not engaged in retailing or refining activities. Corporation A's corporate accountant wants to know the allowable percentage depletion deduction that may be claimed in the 1986 consolidated tax return.

In 1987, Corporation A acquired unrelated Corporation C (engaged in the business of exploring for, developing and producing oil and gas in the United States) in a Type A statutory merger. Corporation C has a

680. Prop. Reg. Sec. 1.613A-4(a)(1).
681. *Ibid.*
682. Prop. Reg. Sec. 1.613A-4(a)(1); Prop. Reg. Sec. 1.613A-4(a)(2), Example 5.

percentage depletion carryforward of $100,000. Corporation A's corporate accountant wants to know whether the $100,000 percentage depletion carryforward of Corporation C will be available as a carryforward item to the consolidated group in 1987.

Consolidated Tax Returns

The deduction for percentage depletion under the independent-producer and royalty-owner exemption cannot exceed 65% of the taxpayer's taxable income, determined without regard to:

☐ Percentage depletion for production from an oil and gas property subject to the independent-producer exemption.[683]

☐ Net operating loss carrybacks to the tax year under Section 172.[684]

☐ Capital loss carrybacks to the tax year under Section 1212.[685]

☐ Distributions to beneficiaries in the case of most trusts.[686]

For an affiliated group of corporations filing a consolidated tax return, the limitation is applied to the group's adjusted consolidated taxable income.[687] The group's adjusted consolidated taxable income is its taxable income determined without regard to the first three items noted above, computed at the consolidated return level.[688] The maximum allowable percentage depletion deduction is apportioned to all oil and gas properties held by members of the consolidated group under the prescribed allocation rules.[689] *(See Case 115.)* The carryover of disallowed percentage depletion to subsequent years is governed by the general rules.[690] In the case of a carryover from a separate return limitation year (SRLY), a carryover is allowed to the current year only to the extent that 65% of the adjusted taxable income of the SRLY member exceeds the otherwise allowable percentage depletion allocable to the SRLY member for the year.[691]

683. I.R.C. Sec. 613A(d)(1)(A); Prop. Reg. Sec. 1.613A-4(a)(1)(i).
684. I.R.C. Sec. 613A(d)(1)(B); Prop. Reg. Sec. 1.613A-4(a)(1)(ii).
685. I.R.C. Sec. 613A(d)(1)(C); Prop. Reg. Sec. 1.613A-4(a)(1)(iii).
686. I.R.C. Sec. 613A(d)(1)(D); Prop. Reg. Sec. 1.613A-4(a)(1)(iv).
687. Reg. Sec. 1.1502-44(a).
688. Reg. Sec. 1.1502-44(b).
689. Reg. Sec. 1.1502-44(c).
690. Reg. Sec. 1.1502-44(d).
691. Reg. Sec. 1.1502-44(d)(2); Reg. Sec. 1.1502-44(d)(3).

The computation of the allowable percentage depletion for the consolidated group in 1986 is as follows:

Overall limitation	
Corporation A—adjusted taxable income	$200,000
Corporation B—adjusted taxable income	100,000
Adjusted consolidated taxable income	$300,000
65% thereof (maximum deduction)	$195,000
Determination of use of SRLY depletion carryforward of Corporation B	
Adjusted consolidated taxable income	$300,000
Adjusted consolidated taxable income without Corporation B	(200,000)
Adjusted consolidated taxable income attributable to Corporation B	$100,000
65% thereof	$ 65,000
Percentage depletion allocable to Corporation B without regard to SRLY depletion carryforward (lesser of $195,000 or $200,000)	(195,000)
Allowable use of SRLY depletion carryforward of Corporation B	-0-
Summary	
Percentage depletion deduction in 1986	$195,000
Percentage depletion carryforward to 1987:	
Non-SRLY ($200,000 − $195,000)	$ 5,000
SRLY	$150,000

Percentage Depletion Carryovers in Corporate Acquisitions

In certain tax-free liquidations and reorganizations, the acquiring corporation succeeds to certain carryover attributes of the acquired corporation,[692] subject to certain statutory limitations.[693] However, percentage depletion carryover of the transferor is not one of the enumerated items specified in the statute.[694] In two revenue rulings,[695] the Internal Revenue Service (IRS) applied case law in effect prior to enactment of the 1954 Internal Revenue Code and allowed foreign tax credits (an item not then designated in the statute as a carryforward attribute to which the acquiring corporation succeeds) to carry over to the transferee in certain tax-free reorganizations. Although the regulations[696] indicate that no inference regarding carryover of a tax attribute should be drawn from the regulations when an item is not enumerated in the statute, the IRS allowed the carryover of foreign tax credits on the premise that the foreign tax credit carryover provisions of the law were added subsequent to the enactment of Section 381. The IRS has held[697] that a parent corporation succeeds to its subsidiary's percentage depletion carryover after a liquidation of the subsidiary into the parent in a distribution to which I.R.C Sections 332 and 334(b)(1) apply when the parent and the subsidiary filed consolidated returns for all the tax years in which the depletable production occurred. Arguably, the same rationale referred to above to foreign tax credits and liquidation of subsidiaries should apply in the case of

692. I.R.C. Sec. 381(a).
693. I.R.C. Sec. 382; I.R.C. Sec. 383.
694. I.R.C. Sec. 381(c).
695. Rev. Rul. 68-350, 1968-2 C.B. 159, *declared obsolete by* Rev. Rul. 80-144, 1980-1 C.B. 80; Rev. Rul. 72-452, 1972-2 C.B. 438, *declared obsolete by* Rev. Rul. 80-144, 1980-1 C.B. 80.
696. Reg. Sec. 1.381(a)-1(b)(3).
697. G.C.M. 38966; IRS Letter Ruling 8310082; IRS Letter Ruling 8510033.

percentage depletion carryovers. Until clarified, the status of Corporation C's SRLY depletion carryover is uncertain. *(See Case 109 for a discussion of the transfer of proven property rules in the context of a statutory merger.)*

Case 117
Computation of Allowable Percentage Depletion Deduction When Charitable Contribution Limitation and 65% of Taxable Income Limitation Occur Simultaneously

Operator A, a calendar-year, cash-basis, married taxpayer, has the following income and expenses in 1987:

Oil and gas sales—one property	$200,000
Production tax	(8,000)
Windfall profit tax	None
Lease operating expense	(28,000)
Depreciation expense	(20,000)
Allocated overhead	(14,000)
Net oil and gas sales	$130,000
Interest and dividends	30,000
Long-term capital gain from sale of stock	20,000
Farm loss	(120,000)
Exemptions and itemized deductions (other than charitable contributions and miscellaneous itemized deductions)	(23,400)
	$ 36,600

Operator A is entitled to no deduction for miscellaneous itemized deductions in 1987 due to the 2% floor. During 1987, Operator A gave $30,000 in cash to his church. He also has no tax basis in his producing oil and gas lease. Operator A's tentative allowable depletion is $30,000 (15% × $200,000) because the 50% of net income limitation is not applicable ($30,000 is less than 50% × $130,000, or $65,000). Operator A is not directly or indirectly involved in retailing or refining operations. Assume Operator A's farming operations are not subject to the limitations on passive losses. Operator A wants to know his allowable percentage depletion and charitable contribution deductions in 1987.

Operator A's deduction for percentage depletion cannot exceed 65% of taxable income for the year, determined without regard to:

- ☐ The deduction for depletion on production from oil and gas properties subject to the independent-producer and royalty-owner provisions.[698]
- ☐ Net operating loss carrybacks to the tax year under Section 172.[699]
- ☐ Capital loss carrybacks to the tax year under Section 1212.[700]
- ☐ Distributions to beneficiaries in the case of most trusts.[701]

698. I.R.C. Sec. 613A(d)(1)(A); Prop. Reg. Sec. 1.613A-4(a)(1)(i).
699. I.R.C. Sec. 613A(d)(1)(B); Prop. Reg. Sec. 1.613A-4(a)(1)(ii).
700. I.R.C. Sec. 613A(d)(1)(C); Prop. Reg. Sec. 1.613A-4(a)(1)(iii).
701. I.R.C. Sec. 613A(d)(1)(D); Prop. Reg. Sec. 1.613A-4(a)(1)(iv).

Operator A's charitable contribution deduction is limited to 50% of his contribution base (adjusted gross income without regard to net operating loss carrybacks to the year).[702]

Based on Operator A's taxable income situation in 1987, he will be limited by both the 65% of taxable income limitation for the percentage depletion deduction and the 50% of adjusted gross income limitation for the charitable contribution deduction. There is no statutory, judicial or administrative authority that directly addresses the question of which limitation should be applied first or whether both limitations should be considered as occurring simultaneously.

Similar corporate situations involving the interaction of the 80% dividends-received deduction and the percentage limitations with respect to charitable contributions and percentage depletion have been addressed. The Internal Revenue Code (the Code) specifically provides that when a corporation is entitled to deductions for both charitable contributions and dividends received, taxable income for purposes of computing the percentage limitation for charitable deductions is computed without regard to the dividends-received deduction. In other words, the charitable deduction is taken first.[703]

The situation involving the interaction of the 80% dividends-received deduction and the 65% of taxable income limitation for percentage depletion has been considered both by the Internal Revenue Service (IRS) and the Tax Court, with conflicting results. The IRS ruled[704] that, because the statute does not designate which limitation should be applied first, those limitations should be considered as occurring simultaneously. Accordingly, the IRS held that taxpayers must compute the allowable deductions with respect to dividends received and percentage depletion through the use of a simultaneous equation or by trial and error.

The courts[705] considered the same factual situation that was the subject of the above-referenced technical advice memorandum and concluded, contrary to the position taken by the IRS, that the proper method is to rank the deductions, with the dividends-received deduction being taken last. Thus, the courts held that the 65% of taxable income limitation for percentage depletion should be computed based on taxable income before any deduction for dividends received.

The court decisions provide little guidance as to how Operator A should compute his allowable percentage depletion and charitable contribution deductions. The court based its decision to "rank" the deductions on the belief that it was legislative intent that: (1) the dividends-received deduction was not to be limited in the event of a net operating loss and (2) the dividends-received deduction was not intended to reduce the amount of other deductions in the Code.[706]

Because such a legislative intent has not been attributed to deductions for charitable contributions and percentage depletion, it seems reasonable, pending further developments, for limitations on deductions for charitable contributions and percentage depletion to be computed through the use of simultaneous equations.

702. I.R.C. Sec. 170(b)(1)(A); I.R.C. Sec. 170(b)(1)(F).
703. I.R.C. Sec. 170(b)(2)(B).
704. Rev. Rul. 79-347, 1979-2 C.B. 122; IRS Letter Ruling 7902021 (Technical Advice Memorandum).
705. Lastarmco, Inc. v. Comm'r, 737 F.2d 1440 (5th Cir. 1984), 54 AFTR2d 84-5726, 84-2 USTC 9719, *aff'g* 79 T.C. 810 (1982).
706. I.R.C. Sec. 170(b)(2)(B).

Based on the IRS's approach in its 1979 rulings,[707] an equation to compute Operator A's 1987 allowable percentage depletion deduction and charitable contribution deduction may be derived as follows:

C = .50 (AGI - D)
D = .65 (TI - C)
C = allowable charitable contribution
D = allowable percentage depletion
AGI = adjusted gross income (before percentage depletion)
TI = taxable income (before depletion or charitable contributions)

Substituting the mathematical equation for C in the depletion equation yields the following:
D = .65(TI - .5O(AGI - D))
D = .65(TI - .5AGI + .5D)
D = .65TI - .325AGI + .325D
D = .65($36,600*) - .325($60,000**) + .325D
.675D = $23,790 - $19,500
.675D = $4,290
D = $6,356

Since D is equal to $6,356, C is $26,822, solved as follows:
C = .5(AGI - D)
C = .5($60,000 - $6,356)
C = $26,822

The accuracy of this equation may be proven as follows:

Interest and dividends	$ 30,000
Long-term capital gain from sale of stock	20,000
Net oil and gas sales	130,000
Allowable depletion	(6,356)
Farm loss	(120,000)
Adjusted gross income	$ 53,644
Exemptions and itemized deductions (other than charitable contributions and miscellaneous itemized deductions)	(23,400)
Allowable charitable contributions	(26,822)
Taxable income	$ 3,422

C = $53,644 × .5, or $26,822
D = .65 [$3,422 (taxable income) + $6,356 (allowable depletion)]
D = .65($9,778)
D = $6,356

Operator A has a percentage depletion carryforward[708] of $23,644 ($30,000 - $6,356) and a charitable contribution carryforward of $3,178 ($30,000 - $26,822).[709]

*TI = $36,600
**AGI = ($30,000 + $20,000 + $130,000 - $120,000) = $60,000

The equations may be very complex if an individual also has charitable contributions subject to the 30% and 20% limitations in the same tax year.[710] Similar equations may be derived for other deductions, such as medical expenses and miscellaneous itemized deductions, based on a percentage of taxable income or adjusted gross income.[711]

707. Rev. Rul. 79-347, 1979-2 C.B. 122; IRS Letter Ruling 7902021 (Technical Advice Memorandum).
708. I.R.C. Sec. 613A(d)(1); Prop. Reg. Sec. 1.613A-4(a)(1).
709. I.R.C. Sec. 170(d)(1)(A).
710. I.R.C. Sec. 170(b)(1)(B); I.R.C. Sec. 170(b)(1)(C); I.R.C. Sec. 170(b)(1)(D).
711. I.R.C. Sec. 213(a); I.R.C. Sec. 213(b).

In the 1979 rulings cited herein,[712] the IRS applied a simultaneous equation to a corporate taxpayer involving the interaction of the 85% dividends-received deduction[713] and the 65% of taxable income limitation for percentage depletion. Use of a simultaneous linear equation also may be necessary for corporate taxpayers having a percentage depletion deduction and a charitable contribution deduction, due to the limitation on charitable contributions as a percentage of taxable income.[714]

Case 118
Depletion When Gas Is Transported from One Lease and Stored in Another Lease

> C Company, an accrual-basis taxpayer, owns a producing gas lease. The company also transports produced gas to wholesale customers in distant markets where the gas is used principally as heating fuel. Because of the heavy seasonal demand on the pipeline facilities in cold months, C Company acquires a lease near its marketing area and develops and equips it for gas storage. The purchased lease has some native gas in the reservoir. C Company produces gas from its own lease and transports and injects the gas into the acquired lease for storage pending the seasonal demand. C Company qualifies for percentage depletion under the independent-producer exemption.

If gas produced from a lease is transported to and stored in a separate lease, C Company has made no sales of gas and no taxable income should result. *(See Case 92.)* The Internal Revenue Service (IRS) ruled[715] that an accrual-basis taxpayer that produces oil but transports it to a storage tank located off the lease must compute the percentage depletion deduction in the year the oil is sold. The IRS stated that the regulations[716] that define *gross income from the property* for purposes of the percentage depletion deduction apply in determining the amount of gross income but not in determining the time for claiming the percentage depletion deduction. However, the proposed regulations under the independent-producer and royalty-owner provisions state that, in a similar situation, production quantities are included in a taxpayer's average daily production in the year the gross income is reported for tax purposes.[717] The same principles apply if C Company stores its produced gas in a geographically separate reservoir for sale in subsequent tax years. It appears the same rules should apply if C Company is a cash-basis taxpayer.

C Company's gas lifting and transportation costs should be treated as deferred charges to match the deduction of these items with the income. The IRS may contend that cash-basis taxpayers should likewise defer these expenditures until the product is sold, particularly if that product is not sold within the subsequent tax year. The gross income for computing taxable income and percentage depletion should be the field price of the gas in the immediate vicinity of the well when sold. *(See Case 92.)* At this time, deferred lifting and transportation costs will be deducted and accounted for in computing the net income limitation on percentage depletion. If C Company stores gas from other leases in the reservoir, pending ultimate sale, careful records must be

712. Rev. Rul. 79-347, 1979-2 C.B. 122; IRS Letter Ruling 7902021 (Technical Advice Memorandum).
713. I.R.C. Sec. 243(a)(1).
714. I.R.C. Sec. 170(b)(2).
715. Rev. Rul. 76-533, 1976-2 C.B. 189; *citing* Rev. Rul. 68-565, 1968-2 C.B. 263.
716. Reg. Sec. 1.613-3(a).
717. Prop. Reg. Sec. 1.613A-3(a)(4), Example 7.

maintained that identify each lease's specific volume of gas. Allowable depletion then can be computed separately for each property.

If the storage lease is not empty, the reservoir's native gas will mingle with the storage gas and cause a depletion problem. When gas is withdrawn, it is customary to treat the withdrawals as coming first from the injected gas and then from the native gas. If other working interest or royalty owners have reservoir storage contracts with the other owners, an accounting for withdrawals will determine the portion of native and injected gas. Because the purchased lease is a separate unit of property, the depletion allowance applicable to native gas sold must be computed separately.

An interesting situation arises when taxpayers produce oil, transport it to a storage tank located off the property and sell that production in a subsequent tax year. As previously noted, the IRS has ruled that taxpayers realize taxable income and compute percentage depletion in the year the production is sold, not the year of production.[718] The windfall profit tax (WPT), however, is imposed when oil is "removed from the premises."[719] Accordingly, if oil is produced and transported more than a short distance away from the lease and stored, the WPT is imposed, even though the revenues are not included in taxable income until an actual sale is made. Thus, taxpayers may be able to secure a refund of WPT due to the net income limitation[720] *(see Case 221)* in the year of production because taxable revenues are unreported (for both accrual- and cash-basis taxpayers) until the actual sale. A bunching of income for the net income limitation may occur, however, when the sale actually is made in a subsequent tax year.

Case 119
Depletion When Property Is Subject to a Reservoir Pressure Maintenance Program

> **C Company owns an undivided interest in a unitized tract on which a gas-injection pressure maintenance program has been initiated. The program permits recovery of heavy liquid hydrocarbons that may otherwise be lost. In connection with the program, gas is purchased from a nearby field (in which C Company has no interest) and injected into the reservoir. A small amount of native gas produced from the unitized tract, left over from operations, also is injected into the reservoir. No sales of gas are expected for 20 years. C Company wants to know the ultimate effect of the future production and sale of the purchased gas on its depletion allowance and tax treatment of the sale proceeds of its undivided interest in the unitized property, before the commencement of gas sales.**

The economic and operational facts of a pressure maintenance program differ substantially from the miscible-drive program discussed in Case 120. In a typical pressure maintenance program, nearly constant pressure must be maintained for continued production. If significant pressure is lost, it may not be economical to restore the reservoir to production.

The questions presented in a pressure maintenance program have been studied extensively for several years by the Internal Revenue Service (IRS) and oil and gas industry groups. The questions have not been brought before a court; however, the

718. Rev. Rul. 76-533, 1976-2 C.B. 189.
719. I.R.C. Sec. 4986(a); Reg. Sec. 51.4996-1(d); IRS Letter Ruling 8142116.
720. I.R.C. Sec. 4988(b).

IRS has ruled[721] that if a portion of the injected gas cannot be recovered in subsequent production, the cost of the unrecoverable portion is deductible in the tax year of injection or in a subsequent year in which the taxpayer sustains such a loss. Losses so claimed must be supported by sound engineering studies and data reflecting the amount of the loss. So-called "economic losses" will not be recognized. Costs not deductible under the above provisions must be capitalized and offset against the proceeds realized from the sale of the gas when it is produced and sold. The excess of the sales price over the cost of the injected gas is reported as ordinary income not subject to depletion. The IRS ruled that the portion of the unrecoverable material injected in a "miscible slug" that provides a continuing benefit during the life of the project should be capitalized and depreciated over the life of the project.[722]

Under such a procedure, C Company treats the proportion of the cost of the injected gas estimated to be unrecoverable as a current operating expense and will include it with all other deductible expenses of the unit to determine the net income limitation on percentage depletion. C Company will capitalize and offset the costs not deducted currently against the proceeds received when the gas is recovered and sold. Proceeds realized in excess of the cost of the injected gas due to price fluctuations will be reported as ordinary income not subject to depletion and will not be included in the net income limitation on percentage depletion. If the mineral interest is sold prior to recovery of the capitalized cost of the injected gas, the cost should be reported as the tax cost basis of the property interest sold to determine gain or loss from the sale of the property interest.

Another method that is reasonable (if followed consistently) excludes from gross depletable income, and treats as a credit to operating expenses, the proceeds from the sales of a volume of gas equal to that volume purchased and injected. If C Company can reasonably show that all the purchased gas will not be recovered, it should be allowed to adjust the excluded amount by the appropriate unrecoverable volumes. This exclusion may be made on the assumption that the purchased gas is produced first. Alternatively, some native gas may be considered produced first, thereby requiring exclusion of only a portion of the first gas sales as nondepletable income.

Regardless of the method employed, C Company should maintain complete records of costs and volumes of purchased gas injected into the reservoir and of future sales of gas to demonstrate to the IRS the reasonableness of the method used. If the project conducted by C Company had been considered a tertiary recovery method and if C Company had used nonhydrocarbon injectants, it would be entitled to a current deduction for the costs of these injectants, whether or not the injectant is recoverable.[723] *(See Case 120.)*

If C Company sells its undivided interest in the unitized property prior to recovery of all injected gas and if it has claimed the cost of the purchased gas as a current tax deduction, it may be required to report the sales price of any purchased gas remaining in the reservoir as ordinary income not subject to depletion. *(See Case 131.)* The purchaser of any property, with injected gas in its reservoir, may be required to allocate to that recoverable injected gas an amount equal to its fair market value in place. The purchaser may treat the sales proceeds of those recoverable volumes of gas as ordinary income not subject to depletion. *(See Case 95 for a discussion of the availability of percentage depletion for gas production.)*

---

721. Rev. Rul. 70-354, 1970-2 C.B. 50.
722. Rev. Rul. 73-469, 1973-2 C.B. 85.
723. I.R.C. Sec. 193(a).

Case 120
Depletion When Property Is Subject to a Miscible-Drive Program

> C Company owns an undivided interest in a unitized tract in which a miscible-drive program has been initiated to recover oil reserves unrecoverable by primary means. During 1987, the program's first year, $500,000 of carbon dioxide (CO_2) attributable to C Company's interest is purchased and injected into the reservoir. C Company wants to know the tax treatment of the current CO_2 expenditures and the tax treatment of the proceeds of the sale of its undivided interest in the unitized property with recoverable purchased CO_2 in the reservoir. C Company anticipates that as the CO_2 is recovered it will be reinjected into the reservoir. C Company also anticipates that, at the end of the life of the field, the recovered CO_2 could be sold.

Standard miscible-drive operations require the initial injection of miscible material to be followed by an injection of gas or water to maintain displacement of the miscible material in the reservoir. The following factors are unknown at the time C Company injects its CO_2: (1) the degree of success of the project, (2) the portion of the CO_2, if any, that will be recovered and (3) the cost of extracting the CO_2 from the liquids. If the project is successful, the portion of the recoverable miscible material is usually recovered within a few years.

Because C Company's process qualifies as a tertiary recovery method, the cost of the CO_2 will be deductible in the year injected.[724] Accordingly, C Company will be required to consider this deduction in computing net income from the property.

If C Company sells any recycled CO_2, the proceeds will be taxable as ordinary income not subject to depletion. If C Company uses an injectant comprised of more than an insignificant amount of natural gas or crude oil and the injectant is recoverable, it will not be allowed a current deduction for the cost attributable to the recoverable hydrocarbon portion of the injectant.[725]

Accounting for a recoverable hydrocarbon injectant is a difficult problem. Taxpayers must maintain records that indicate clearly the volumes of material injected and produced and any unrecoverable volumes. If any injected material is recovered, the taxpayer must show the portion of the current production attributable to the purchased material. If the injected portion of the production cannot be identified, the first hydrocarbons produced will be considered purchased injected material and the net proceeds from the sale of the production, less the cost of the injected material, must be reported as ordinary income not subject to depletion.[726] The sale of native hydrocarbons is eligible for percentage depletion. *(See Case 103.)*

Assume C Company uses natural gas rather than CO_2 as a miscible injectant and determines that 75% of the injectant will be recovered and that 5% of the production is attributable to injected gas and 95% to native gas. Each year, C Company will report 95% of the production sales proceeds as depletable income. C Company apparently will be entitled to a deduction in 1987 equal to the cost, $125,000 ($500,000 × 25%), of the unrecoverable portion of the injected gas.[727] The remaining cost of the injected

724. I.R.C. Sec. 193(a).
725. I.R.C. Sec. 193(b)(2).
726. Rev. Rul. 70-354, 1970-2 C.B. 50.
727. *Ibid.*

gas, \$375,000 (\$500,000 - \$125,000), should be capitalized and recovered as the injected gas is produced and sold.[728] The proceeds from the sale of the injected gas (5% of gross production sales) should be reported as ordinary income not subject to depletion. The cost of the injected gas lost in the process should be treated as operating expenses of production to compute the net income limitation for percentage depletion purposes.

If C Company sells its undivided interest in the unitized property before the injected CO_2 has been fully recovered, it may be required to recapture all or a portion of the previously deducted portion of any recoverable CO_2 remaining in the reservoir.[729] The purchaser of the property probably will be required to allocate a portion of the purchase price to the injected material and account for it as though he had injected the material originally.

Case 121
Elimination of Percentage Depletion and Adjustment of Intangible Drilling and Development Costs Deductions in Computing Earnings and Profits

During 1987, C Company obtains \$1 million in gross income from the sale of primary production from a working interest. It incurs intangible drilling and development costs (IDC) on productive wells of \$100,000, which it expenses for tax purposes. These productive wells began production in July of 1987. Amortization of current and previous year IDC costs capitalized for accounting purposes is \$65,000. Depletion of \$75,000 is recorded on the books. Direct operating expenses, production and windfall profit taxes and general expenses (excluding cost recovery allowances) total \$350,000. The accelerated cost recovery allowance claimed on C Company's lease and well equipment (all 7-year recovery period property) placed in service in 1987 is \$25,714. For earnings and profits purposes, the alternative depreciation system recovery allowance on C Company's equipment, using the straight-line method over the 14-year class life of the equipment, is \$6,429. For book purposes, C Company depreciates that property, using the straight-line method over 12 years. The book depreciation deduction is \$15,000. Cost depletion for earnings and profits is \$16,000, and the adjusted tax basis of depletable property at the beginning of the year is \$80,000. Current-year additions to leasehold cost are \$5,000. C Company declares and pays a dividend of \$275,000 to its stockholders.

C Company's total production for the year does not exceed 1,000 barrels per day. It is not engaged in any refining or retailing activities. C Company did not acquire its working interest in a disqualifying transfer after December 31, 1974. The corporation is neither a member of a controlled group of corporations nor of a group of business entities under common control. C Company is not an S corporation, a personal holding company, or an integrated oil company.

728. Rev. Rul. 70-354, 1970-2 C.B. 50.
729. I.R.C. Sec. 1245(a)(3)(C); Senate Report No. 96-394, 1980-3 C.B. 216.

C Company determines its net income per books, taxable net income and current earnings and profits as follows:

For Book Purposes:		
Sale of oil, net of royalties and other interest		$1,000,000
Less:		
Operating expenses, production taxes and general expenses	$350,000	
Depletion	75,000	
Depreciation	15,000	
Amortization of IDC capitalized per books	65,000	(505,000)
Net income per books before provision for federal income taxes		$ 495,000

For Tax Purposes:		
Gross revenues		$1,000,000
Less:		
Operating expenses, production taxes and general expenses	$350,000	
Depletion (15% of $1,000,0000)	150,000	
Depreciation	25,714	
IDC incurred during the year	100,000	(625,714)
Net income for tax purposes		$ 374,286

Computation of Current Earnings and Profits:	
Net income for tax purposes, as computed above	$ 374,286
Add:	
Excess of percentage depletion over depletion based solely on cost ($150,000 - $16,000)	134,000
Excess of accelerated cost recovery for tax purposes over straight-line recovery over extended period ($25,714 - $6,429)	19,285
Excess of IDC incurred during the year over 60-month amortization ($100,000 - $10,000)	90,000
Less:	
Federal income taxes (40% of $374,286)	(149,714)*
Current earnings and profits	$ 467,857

* Alternative minimum tax does not apply.

Because the earnings and profits for the current year exceed the amount distributed, the $275,000 distribution to the shareholders represents dividend income taxable to the recipients as ordinary income.[730]

C Company has no alternative minimum tax liability for 1987. In 1987, corporations are subject to an alternative minimum tax equal to 20% of alternative minimum taxable income.[731] This new tax base includes new tax preference items and adjustments which did not apply to corporations under prior law. For example, new preference items and adjustments were added for depreciation, excess intangible drilling costs and excess book income.[732] *(See Case 176 for a discussion of the corporate alternative minimum tax.)* As under prior law, a tax preference item exists for the excess ($65,000) of the percentage depletion ($150,000) over the tax basis of the

730. Reg. Sec. 1.316-1(a)(1).
731. I.R.C. Sec. 55(b).
732. I.R.C. Sec. 56; I.R.C. Sec. 57.

depletable property at the end of the tax year, determined without regard to the depletion deduction for the tax year ($80,000 plus $5,000).[733]

In determining taxable income, C Company deducts percentage depletion of 15% of gross income ($150,000), which is less than 50% of the net income before depletion ($262,143) and is greater than cost depletion ($16,000).[734] However, the amount deducted in arriving at current earnings and profits to determine the taxability of distributions is the cost depletion for earnings and profits purposes ($16,000).[735] Cost depletion for earnings and profits purposes is computed strictly on cost. A taxpayer does not reduce the tax basis of the asset by previously claimed percentage depletion. This requires a separate cost depletion computation from that used in determining taxable income for a given year.

For income tax purposes, a taxpayer computes cost depletion on the cost or other basis of the property, reduced by the previously allowed or allowable depletion, whether computed on the basis of cost or percentage of income. Assuming C Company elects to deduct IDC for income tax purposes, it may deduct any such costs incurred in tax years beginning before October 1, 1984, from earnings and profits in the year paid or incurred, even though the corporation capitalizes and amortizes those costs for book purposes.[736] IDC paid or incurred in tax years beginning after September 30, 1984, (other than costs incurred in connection with a nonproductive well) are required to be capitalized and deducted ratably for earnings and profits over the 60-month period, beginning with the month in which production from the well begins.[737] Therefore, for earnings and profits purposes, C Company must capitalize the productive IDC incurred in 1987 ($100,000) and deduct amortization of $10,000 (100,000 × 6/60). If C Company is an integrated oil company, it will be required to capitalize and amortize over a 60-month period 30% of its expenditures for IDC for income tax purposes.[738] Amounts capitalized and deducted under this 60-month rule are not subject to the 60-month amortization rule for earnings and profits purposes because those amounts are not treated as IDC.[739] In addition, IDC on wells located outside the United States are not subject to the 60-month amortization rule for earnings and profits purposes since these costs are subject to a longer amortization period for income tax purposes.[740] The amount of allowable depreciation or amortization to be deducted in arriving at current earnings and profits generally is limited to the amount that will be allowable if the straight-line method has been used for each tax year beginning after June 30, 1972.[741] A corporation must depreciate recovery property for earnings and profits purposes over an extended period (the class life), using the straight-line method of depreciation.[742] In the case of 7-year recovery property, the recovery period for earnings and profits purposes is 14 years.

If C Company had depreciable property placed in service before January 1, 1987, a different earnings and profits depreciation adjustment would be required. Generally, for property placed in service before January 1, 1987, recovery property (like lease and well equipment) is depreciated for earnings and profits purposes over 12 years.[743] *(See Case 70 for a discussion on the transition rules applicable to certain assets placed in service after 1986.)* In addition, for assets placed in service before 1987, if the

733. I.R.C. Sec. 57(a)(1).
734. I.R.C. Sec. 613; I.R.C. Sec. 613A(c).
735. Reg. Sec. 1.312-6(c)(1).
736. Rev. Rul. 60-123, 1960-1 C.B. 145.
737. I.R.C. Sec. 312(n)(2)(A).
738. I.R.C. Sec. 291(b).
739. I.R.C. Sec. 291(b); I.R.C. Sec. 263(c); I.R.C. Sec. 312(n)(2)(A).
740. I.R.C. Sec. 312(n)(2)(A); I.R.C. Sec. 263(c); I.R.C. Sec. 263(i).
741. I.R.C. Sec. 312(k)(1).
742. I.R.C. Sec. 312(k)(3)(A); I.R.C. Sec. 168(g)(2)(A); I.R.C. Sec. 168(g)(2)(C)(i).
743. I.R.C. Sec. 312(k)(3)(A) *(prior to amendment by the Tax Reform Act of 1986).*

corporation elected a recovery percentage based on one of the alternative recovery periods that is longer than the applicable recovery period required for earnings and profits purposes, the longer period must be used for earnings and profits purposes as well.[744] In the case of a 5-year recovery property, a taxpayer could elect to use straight-line recovery over a period of 5, 12 or 25 years.[745] For example, if a taxpayer had elected to depreciate its 5-year recovery period property over 25 years for income tax purposes, it also must use the 25-year period in computing earnings and profits.

In this example, C Company uses accelerated cost recovery for income tax purposes. Thus, C Company computes current-year earnings and profits, using straight-line depreciation over 14 years for its 7-year recovery property.

A distribution by a corporation is taxable to a stockholder as ordinary dividend income to the extent of the corporation's earnings and profits for the year of the distribution, even though the corporation may have an accumulated deficit in earnings and profits as a result of losses in prior years. On the other hand, if there is a deficit in earnings and profits for the year in which a distribution is made, but there are accumulated earnings and profits attributable to operations subsequent to February 28, 1913, (after adjustment for the current year's decrease), the distribution will be deemed to have been made from accumulated earnings and profits and will, therefore, be taxable as a dividend.[746]

The effect of these earnings and profits rules is that if a corporation operates oil and gas properties, that portion of the corporate income that is, in effect, tax free to the corporation by virtue of percentage depletion is taxed to the stockholder when it is paid out as a dividend. Consequently, an individual stockholder in such a corporation effectively forgoes the benefits of percentage depletion that would be available to him if the properties were operated through a partnership, individual or in joint ownership. *(See Section VI for a discussion of the various forms of organization for conducting oil and gas operations.)*

Case 122
Royalty Impounded During Title Dispute

> **Lessor R owns certain land on which he grants an oil and gas lease to Operator A in 1985, reserving a one-eighth royalty interest. A title dispute arises between Lessor R and another claimant and is settled in Lessor R's favor in 1987. Pending the outcome of the title litigation, Lessor R's share of the income from the property is placed in escrow by Operator A. Lessor R is uncertain how the income should be reported and seeks advice on whether to file amended returns for prior years to reflect the royalty income in the years in which the oil was actually produced (1985 and 1986) or to report that income in the year in which he received the funds from escrow (1987).**

If Lessor R files his tax returns on the cash basis, he must report the entire amount of the royalty in the year in which he receives payment from the escrow agent. If Lessor R files his tax return on the accrual basis, he should report the entire amount in the

744. I.R.C. Sec. 312(k)(3)(C) *(prior to amendment by the Tax Reform Act of 1986).*
745. I.R.C. Sec. 168(b)(3)(A) *(prior to amendment by the Tax Reform Act of 1986).*
746. I.R.C. Sec. 312(a); Reg. Sec. 1.316-2.

year in which the litigation is concluded or the payment is received, whichever is earlier.[747]

It should be noted that in this case the royalties are withheld because of a genuine dispute over ownership of the properties. The mere delay or refusal by a lessor to sign a division order will not permit him to defer the inclusion of the royalties in income.

With respect to production for 1985 and 1986, it appears to be proper for Lessor R to claim an allowance for percentage depletion (if higher than cost depletion) on the impounded royalty income for the year in which he reports the income.[748] However, if the production related to earlier years when depletion rates were greater than 15%, the IRS will likely contend that a depletion rate of 15% should be used.[749] Arguably, the depletion rate in effect for the year the oil is produced should be used since this rate is generally correlated to production.[750]

The costs incurred by Lessor R to define or perfect title to his property are not considered ordinary and necessary business expenses and, consequently, are not deductible. Costs of this nature are considered to be capital expenditures.[751] It has been held that the costs of defending or perfecting title to oil and gas royalty interests are capital expenditures under the regulations.[752] However, it also has been held that legal expenses are deductible when litigation was purely for conservation of property held for the production of income.[753]

Operator A has received the royalty owner's share of production and sold it for the owner, turning over the proceeds to an escrow agent. The amounts received for the royalty owner's share of production do not belong to Operator A and, therefore, are not income to him. The royalty owner's share of production is not Operator A's income under the "sharing arrangement" theory,[754] and it appears that the royalty owner's share is not taxable to Operator A, even if he merely retains the funds in suspense, instead of turning them over to an escrow agent, because he has no right to the proceeds.[755] Operator A is acting merely as an agent or conduit for the royalty owner.[756]

Case 123
Income from Working Interest During Litigation

Lessor R owns certain oil lands on which he has granted an oil and gas lease to Operator A. In 1985, Lessor R claims the lease is cancelled because of Operator A's failure to drill offset wells or otherwise properly develop the property. Lessor R then leases the property to Operator B, who develops and obtains production from the property. Operator A contests the validity of Operator B's lease. During the litigation, Operator B continues to operate the property and retains the earnings. In 1987, Operator A is held to be the lessee. During 1988, Operator B pays Operator A the equivalent of the income he received from the property,

747. Rev. Rul. 70-66, 1970-1 C.B. 114; North American Oil Consol. v. Burnet, 286 U.S. 417 (1932), 11 AFTR 16, 3 USTC 943; Macpherson v. U.S., 614 F. Supp 589 (C.D. Cal. 1985), 56 AFTR2d 85-6607, 85-1 USTC 9414; Mel Dar Corp., T.C. Memo Dec. (Mar. 30, 1960); IRS Letter Ruling 8410065 (Technical Advice Memorandum).
748. Reg. Sec. 1.613-3; Rev. Rul. 76-533, 1976-2 C.B. 189; Rev. Rul. 81-168, 1981-1 C.B. 384.
749. IRS Letter Ruling 8637124; IRS Letter Ruling 8439002 (Technical Advice Memorandum).
750. Rev. Rul. 81-168, 1981-1 C.B. 384.
751. I.R.C. Sec. 263(a); Reg. Sec. 1.263(a)-2(c); Porter Royalty Pool, Inc., 7 T.C. 685 (1946).
752. Burton-Sutton Oil Co. v. Comm'r, 150 F.2d 621 (5th Cir. 1945), 34 AFTR 68, 45-2 USTC 9359.
753. Ramsey v. White (S.D. Ill., 1955), 51 AFTR 1762, 56-1 USTC 9190.
754. Palmer v. Bender, 287 U.S. 551 (1933), 11 AFTR 1106, 3 USTC 1026.
755. North American Oil Consol.
756. 122 West 59th Street Corp. v. Helvering, 68 F.2d 397 (D.C. Cir. 1933), 13 AFTR 513, 3 USTC 1181.

and Operator B is reimbursed for his expenditures in connection with the development and operation of the property.

The income Operator B receives prior to settlement of the litigation is income to him, and he is entitled to the deduction for depletion.[757] Earnings received under a claim of right, without restriction as to their disposition, constitute income required to be reported for tax purposes, even though it may later be proved that Operator B is not entitled to it.[758] If Operator B files his tax returns on the cash basis, he will be entitled to a deduction for a loss in 1988, the year in which he is required to make payments to Operator A for income from prior sales. If he is an accrual-basis taxpayer, a deduction is claimed in 1987, the year in which litigation is concluded. Operator B's deductible loss must be reduced by the depletion previously allowed.[759] *(See Case 9 for a discussion of restrictions on using the cash method of accounting after the Tax Reform Act of 1986.)* If Operator B finds that his effective income tax rate has decreased in the year he claims the deduction, it may be possible for Operator B to avail himself of a relief provision in the Internal Revenue Code.[760] In general, when this provision applies, the tax benefits resulting from the loss will at least equal the tax paid on the income when it was received and reported for tax purposes. In that case, Operator B would compute his tax for the year in which the deduction is allowable by either: (1) claiming the deduction in that year or (2) computing the reduction in tax for prior years, excluding the income reported in those years that was later paid to Operator A and subtracting this prior-year tax reduction from the current year's tax.

If Operator A was the owner or holder of a capital investment in oil and gas in place in which ownership vested or capital investment was made prior to any litigation, he should be entitled to claim depletion on the gross income restored as a result of the litigation.[761] However, if Operator A had no interest in the oil and gas until the outcome of the litigation was determined, the Internal Revenue Service (IRS) may deny depletion on the amount received from Operator B.[762] Also, even where depletion is allowed, the IRS will allow a percentage depletion rate of only 15% even if the gross income restored was attributable to production prior to 1984 when the depletion rates were higher.[763] Operator A must report all the income in the year of receipt if he files his tax returns on the cash basis, or in the year litigation is concluded if he is an accrual-basis taxpayer.[764] Regardless of his accounting method, Operator A should not report the income in the disputed years prior to the year of settlement.[765]

If Operator B had been required to turn over the proceeds from production to an escrow agent or if the purchaser of the production had withheld payment, the results would probably be different. In this situation, Operator B's income should not include amounts paid to the escrow agent or funds held by the purchaser of production until he becomes entitled to such amounts.[766] In addition, Operator A would report the entire amount of the income in the year the litigation is concluded (1987) or in the

757. Parr v. Scofield, 185 F.2d 535 (5th Cir. 1950), 39 AFTR 1306, 50-2 USTC 9250.
758. North American Oil Consol. v. Burnet, 286 U.S. 417 (1932), 11 AFTR 16, 3 USTC 943; William T. Egolf, 87 T.C. 34 (1986).
759. U.S. v. Skelly Oil, 394 U.S. 678 (1969), 23 AFTR2d 69-1186, 69-1 USTC 9343.
760. I.R.C. Sec. 1341.
761. Thomas E. Arnett, 31 T.C. 320 (1958).
762. Parr.
763. IRS Letter Ruling 8637124.
764. Thomas W. Blake, Jr., 20 T.C. 721 (1953).
765. North American Oil Consol.; Parr; Mel Dar Corp., T.C. Memo Dec. (Mar. 30, 1960); Donald R. MacPherson v. U.S., 614 F. Supp. 589 (C.D. Cal. 1985) 56 AFTR2d 85-6607, 85-1 USTC 9414; Rev. Rul. 70-66, 1970-1 C.B. 114.
766. North American Oil Consol.; Donald R. MacPherson; Rev. Rul. 70-66, 1970-1 C.B. 114.

year it is received, depending on his method of accounting.[767] He then will be entitled to the deduction for depletion.[768]

In a situation where two co-owners participated in an oil and gas joint venture that later was denounced by one of them, the court held that the income of the joint venture was taxable to the co-owners in the years in which it was realized, whether or not it was distributed to them.[769]

If Operator B receives the income from the property, he should claim the operating expenses as deductions in the years in which they are incurred. However, the IRS may question Operator B's right to deduct these expenses if the income is placed in escrow or otherwise is not actually received by him.

The reimbursement of operating expenses to Operator B will be ordinary income or a reduction of his loss if he is permitted to deduct the expenses as incurred. If Operator B is not permitted to deduct the expenses, he should report no income from the reimbursement.

Operator A should be allowed a deduction for operating expenses reimbursed to B and should capitalize equipment costs to be returned through depreciation. Operator A also should be allowed a deduction for intangible drilling and development costs on the grounds that Operator B drilled the wells as Operator A's agent.[770] However, the IRS may require Operator A to capitalize the development costs to be returned through depletion because he acquired completed wells.

If Operator A has no interest in the oil and gas until the outcome of the litigation is determined, his receipt of an interest may constitute the transfer of a proven property so that percentage depletion on that property will not be allowable. *(See Case 108.)*

767. Rev. Rul. 70-66, 1970-1 C.B. 114.
768. National Petroleum and Ref. Co., 28 B.T.A. 569 (1933); Crews v. Comm'r, 89 F.2d 412 (10th Cir. 1937), 19 AFTR 365, 37-1 USTC 9196.
769. U.S. v. Baker, 233 F.2d 195 (10th Cir. 1956), 49 AFTR 1195, 56-1 USTC 9521.
770. Thomas E. Arnett.

Section V
Disposition of Properties

The principal problem arising from most grants or assignments of oil and gas interests is the determination of whether the transaction constitutes: (1) a sale or exchange or (2) a lease or sublease. This classification is necessary to determine the federal income tax treatment of the immediate and subsequent considerations passing between the parties to the transaction.

For federal income tax purposes, an assignment of a working interest or operating right usually is classified as a leasing arrangement if the assignor retains a nonoperating economic interest that continues over the life of the assigned property. A retained interest usually takes the form of a royalty, an overriding royalty or a net profits interest. If no such interest is retained, the assignment usually is classified as a sale or exchange.

An assignment free of development and operating obligations usually is treated as a sale or exchange. If the assignment of an oil and gas property is in consideration for the development of the property, the assignor realizes no taxable gain or loss but merely an enhancement in the value of the interest retained.

Whoever holds an economic interest in the oil or gas in place has a depletable interest. After an economic interest is assigned, percentage depletion is allowed to both the assignor and the assignee according to their respective shares of gross income from the property. *(However, see Section IV for a discussion of the disallowance of percentage depletion subsequent to the transfer of a proven property.)*

Tax treatment of the most common types of property disposition transactions may be summarized as follows.

Sales

The seller computes gain or loss only on the portion of the oil and gas interest transferred. The purchaser has a capital investment equal to the cash or its equivalent paid for the acquisition of the interest. A production payment retained by the seller is treated as a purchase money mortgage loan and not as an economic interest in the property. Disposition of an oil or gas property that was placed in service before January 1, 1987, may result in the recapture as ordinary income of intangible drilling and development costs (IDC) (less adjustment) paid or incurred after 1975. For properties placed in service after December 31, 1986, the full amount of IDC (without adjustments) plus depletion deductions (to the extent of basis) must be recaptured as ordinary income on the disposition of an oil or gas property. Equipment depreciation also may be subject to recapture as ordinary income. Any gain in excess of recaptured IDC, depletion and depreciation is treated as gain from the sale of a property used in a trade or business, eligible for long-term capital-gain treatment, assuming the requisite holding period is met.

Leases

The initial consideration for a lease or sublease is called a *bonus*. The lessor or sublessor reports the bonus as ordinary income and is taxable on the sale of production attributable to the interest retained. *(See Section IV for a discussion of percentage depletion on lease bonuses received or accrued before August 17, 1987, and on income from oil and gas production.)* The lessee or sublessee has a capital investment to the extent of any bonus paid but excludes from his income the share of production attributable to the lessor's or sublessor's retained interest.

Assignments in Consideration of Drilling

An assignor's cash payment for the drilling and equipping of a well should be allocated between tangible and intangible costs, and the intangible costs should be treated in accordance with his election for those intangibles. The cash received is income to the assignee (driller). If an interest in the lease is also assigned, subsequent production revenue attributable to the assignee (driller) is depletable income to the assignee and excludable from the assignor's income.

The sale, exchange, lease or sublease of an oil and gas property in the development or producing stage may take several forms, depending almost entirely on the creativity of the parties involved. The seller should seek a transaction that will provide the greatest economic benefit after payment of tax on his gain. This benefit usually comes from a nontaxable exchange or a sale that will produce potentially more favorable long-term capital gain. The buyer, on the other hand, should attempt to keep all depletable capital costs to a minimum. He should have reliable data to support any allocation of his purchase cost between depreciable equipment and depletable leasehold cost. *(See Section IV for a discussion of the disallowance of percentage depletion subsequent to the transfer of a proven property.)*

When transfers involve both depletable and depreciable properties, the buyer and the seller may have conflicting interests. An allocation of the consideration favoring one party to the transaction can create adverse tax effects for the other. Careful planning is required on the disposition of these types of oil and gas interests.

Exchanges

The general rules for determining the tax status of exchanges apply as much to oil and gas properties as to other classes of property. For an exchange to be nontaxable, property held for productive use in a business or for investment must be exchanged solely for property of like kind, also to be held for productive use in a business or for investment. If cash or other property is received in a transaction that otherwise would be nontaxable, gain is recognized but only to the extent of the cash or the value of the other property. If property subject to depreciation, depletion or IDC recapture is exchanged, gain also may be recognized to the extent of the fair market value of any property received that is not subject to that recapture.

Generally, oil and gas properties are interests in real estate that are considered to be of like kind if the interests continue for the depletable life of the properties. In nontaxable exchanges, the combined depreciable and depletable basis of the property transferred is assigned to the acquired property based on relative fair market values. If a producing property is exchanged for another producing property, the tax consequences can be adverse to both taxpayers. Because IDC typically is deducted, the taxpayer may have little basis in his leasehold interest and a high basis in his depreciable equipment. A like-kind exchange may result in an allocation of depreciable basis to leasehold cost because of the proportionately high value of the acquired leasehold interest compared to the value of the equipment received. In addition, percentage depletion may not be available on the acquisition of a proven property. *(See Section IV.)* Due to these problems, all exchanges should be analyzed carefully.

Unitizations present many tax problems relating to determining gains on exchanges of the properties, the proper tax treatment of equalization payments, the tax basis of interests in the unit and possible restrictions on percentage depletion. Unitizations require careful planning to avoid undesirable tax consequences for the parties concerned.

Case 124
Sales of Oil and Gas Rights for Cash With Retention of Surface and Treatment of Surface Damages

> **Landowner R owns the fee interest in land that has the potential for future production of oil or gas. In 1987, Landowner R conveys to Operator A for cash all his interests in the oil and gas under the land, and Landowner R retains the surface rights. The lease agreement between Landowner R and Operator A provides for a cash payment to be made by Operator A to Landowner R in connection with anticipated specified damages to the surface that may be caused by Operator A's operations.**

Landowner R has made an outright sale of all the oil and gas in place because he has not retained a continuing interest in the oil and gas.[1] Unless Landowner R is a dealer in mineral properties, the oil and gas rights probably represent a capital asset to him. Accordingly, gain or loss will be treated as a capital gain or loss for tax purposes.

Under the laws of some states, all minerals revert to the surface owner after a period of years unless production is obtained or operations are being conducted on the property. Whether this reversion is by contract or by state law does not appear to affect the conclusion that the assignment of all or an undivided interest in the mineral rights constitutes a sale. *(See Case 128 for a discussion on sales of a fraction of the minerals.)*

To determine basis in the mineral rights, Landowner R should apportion his total cost between the mineral rights and the surface rights in accordance with circumstances surrounding his acquisition of the property.[2] For example, when land is acquired before any prospects for oil or gas are known to exist in the area, often all (or substantially all) the cost is allocable to the surface rights.[3]

Operator A must capitalize the entire amount paid for the oil and gas rights as the cost of minerals acquired. His tax basis subsequently may be deducted from income if the

1. McLean v. Comm'r, 120 F.2d 942 (5th Cir. 1941), 27 AFTR 544, 41-2 USTC 9553; Cullen v. Comm'r, 118 F.2d 651 (5th Cir. 1941), 26 AFTR 887, 41-1 USTC 9364; U.S. v. Morgan, 321 F.2d 781 (5th Cir. 1963), 12 AFTR2d 5404, 63-2 USTC 9653.
2. Perkins v. Thomas, 86 F.2d 954 (5th Cir. 1936), 18 AFTR 699, 37-1 USTC 9012.
3. Plow Realty, 4 T.C. 600 (1945).

mineral interest is determined to be worthless,[4] through deductions for depletion if the interest is productive[5] or as a basis for gain or loss in the event of a sale.

Damage payments representing reimbursement for lost profits (i.e., damaged crops and interruption of surface operations) generally are taxed as ordinary income. Payments for damage to land or property rights generally are characterized as a return of capital and gain to the extent the payments exceed adjusted basis.[6] Proper treatment requires careful examination of the facts and circumstances surrounding the nature of the payment.

Payments for anticipated surface damages must be distinguished from payments for loss of income or surface use, which are taxable as ordinary rental income.[7] Evidence of actual damages suffered must be demonstrated to provide return-of-capital and capital-gain treatment.[8] Federal and local law limits on a surface owner's rights to damage payments also may affect the federal tax characterization of such payments. For example, if a federal land act limits claims to these damages due to negligent, unreasonable or excessive operations, the taxpayer must demonstrate that such damages occurred to sustain return-of-capital and capital-gain treatment.[9]

Case 125
Grant of Lease for Cash With Royalty Retained

Lessor R, a cash-basis taxpayer, owns the fee interest in certain land on which he grants in 1987 a standard-form oil and gas lease to Operator A in consideration of an initial payment of $5,000 and annual delay rentals of $5 per acre. Lessor R retains one-eighth of all the minerals produced and saved, free of all development and operating costs. No development or production takes place during the year in which the lease is granted.

Lessor R has made a lease in its simplest and most common form.[10] An assignment of a working interest or of operating rights in a transaction where the assignor retains an economic interest in the property assigned that continues over the life of the property usually is classified as a leasing arrangement.[11] An economic interest is the interest that results when a taxpayer acquires, by investment, a right to share in the proceeds derived from the production of oil and gas. He must look solely to this interest for return of his investment.[12] The cash receipt is regarded as a bonus or advance royalty to Lessor R and is subject to cost depletion, even though no production has occurred in the year of receipt.[13] Bonuses received or accrued before August 17, 1986, also qualify for percentage depletion. *(See Case 98 for a discussion of depletion on income from a lease bonus and advance royalty.)* Lessor R must report the $5,000 as ordinary income in the year received. If the lease is reassigned to Lessor R before any income is received from the sale of production, Lessor R will be required to restore to income in

4. Harvey A. Heller, 1 T.C. 222 (1942).
5. Reg. Sec. 1.611-1.
6. Rev. Rul. 73-161, 1973-1 C.B. 366; Inaja Land Co., Ltd., 9 T.C. 727 (1947); Raytheon Production Corp. v. Comm'r, 144 F.2d 110 (1st Cir. 1944), 32 AFTR 1155, 44-2 USTC 9424.
7. Vest v. Comm'r, 481 F.2d 238 (5th Cir. 1973), 32 AFTR2d 73-5209, 73-2 USTC 9513; Gilbertz v. U.S., 574 F. Supp. 177 (D.C. Wyo. 1983), 53 AFTR2d 84-1489, 84-1 USTC 9138; Rev. Rul. 73-161, 1973-1 C.B. 366.
8. IRS Letter Ruling 8728007 (Technical Advice Memorandum).
9. Gilbertz v. U.S., 808 F.2d 1374 (10th Cir. 1987), 59 AFTR2d 87-424, 87-1 USTC 9116.
10. Berg v. Comm'r, 33 F.2d 641 (D.C. Cir. 1929), 7 AFTR 9195, 1929 CCH D-9256.
11. Burton-Sutton Oil Co. v. Comm'r, 328 U.S. 25 (1946), 34 AFTR 1017, 46-1 USTC 9243; Rev. Rul. 69-352, 1969-1 C.B. 34; Rev. Rul. 69-466, 1969-2 C.B. 140.
12. Palmer v. Bender, 287 U.S. 551 (1933), 11 AFTR 1106, 3 USTC 1026; Reg. Sec. 1.611-1(b)(1); U.S. v. Swank, 101 U.S. 1931 (1981), 47 AFTR2d 81-1493, 81-1 USTC 9426.
13. Herring v. Comm'r, 293 U.S. 322 (1934), 14 AFTR 717, 35-1 USTC 9012.

the year of reassignment depletion previously claimed with respect to the lease bonus. *(See Case 127.)*

At the time Lessor R consummates the leasing of the minerals, his tax basis in the fee minerals becomes his unadjusted tax basis in the retained royalty. The tax basis of the royalty must be adjusted by the amount of allowable depletion on the bonus.[14]

Operator A must capitalize the $5,000 bonus as lease cost. If the property becomes productive, royalty payments to Lessor R are excludable from Operator A's taxable income[15] and are depletable income to Lessor R.[16] Operator A, in calculating the percentage depletion allowance with respect to his share of production, must exclude a pro-rata part of the lease bonus from depletable gross income (but not from taxable income) as production occurs.[17] *(See Cases 2 and 87.)*

Commissions and other expenses, such as engineering fees, etc., incurred in the assignment of a lease in which a nonoperating interest is retained, must be capitalized as cost of the retained nonoperating interest.[18]

The $5-per-acre rental receipts are taxable to Lessor R as ordinary income not subject to depletion.[19] Operator A may deduct rental payments, subject to the economic performance rules, if applicable.[20] *(See Case 9.)*

Case 126
Options To Acquire Government Oil and Gas Leases

> Operator B wishes to acquire from Operator A certain oil and gas leases covering 4,000 acres on government lands, with Operator A retaining a 5% overriding royalty. Because of the long delay expected in processing and transferring the leases through the government land offices, Operator A in 1987 grants Operator B options to acquire the leases at any time during the primary term for an initial cash consideration of $40,000 and an additional cash consideration of $1 per acre at the time an option is exercised. Operator A will retain a 5% overriding royalty on all acreage for which the option is exercised. Operator A is required to keep the leases in force, and Operator B will reimburse Operator A for the annual rentals.

It is common practice in dealing with government oil and gas leases to grant options rather than enter into a conventional sale or sublease. The option agreement frequently provides for the following:

- ☐ The optionee may perform exploratory operations on the property and may, at any time during the option period, request an assignment of the lease or the execution of an operating agreement.
- ☐ During the option period, the lease will be maintained in force by payment of any rentals that may become due. These rental payments usually are paid by the optionor and are reimbursed to him by the optionee.

14. I.R.C. Sec. 1016.
15. Reg. Sec. 1.613-2(c)(5)(i).
16. Burnet v. Harmel, 287 U.S. 103 (1932), 11 AFTR 1085, 3 USTC 990; Murphy Oil Co. v. Burnet, 287 U.S. 299 (1932), 11 AFTR 1095, 3 USTC 1002.
17. Reg. Sec. 1.613-2(c)(5)(ii).
18. Dorothy Cockburn, 16 T.C. 775 (1951).
19. Reg. Sec. 1.612-3(c)(2).
20. I.R.C. Sec. 461(h); I.R.C. Sec. 461(i).

- ☐ Substantially all the consideration required to be paid passes at the time the option is granted. There may be no additional consideration (or perhaps only nominal consideration) to be paid upon exercise of the option.

Federal law imposes certain acreage restrictions on federal lands taken under lease or option. Special rules and restrictions apply to lands in Alaska and in certain of the possessions. However, other than acreage limitations on the ownership of leases and options, the option arrangement cannot be distinguished for tax purposes from a sublease.

Generally, taxation of payments received pursuant to an option will be deferred until the option is exercised or expires.[21] Deferral is permitted because option expiration typicallv results in ordinary income, while option exercise may result in capital-gain treatment. *(See Case 1.)* It has been held,[22] however, that payments received for an option to lease oil and gas reserves are taxable in the year of receipt since the exercise of the option, as well as the expiration, will result in ordinary income. Although not relevant to the outcome in one of the cited cases,[23] the payments received upon the grant of the option constituted the predominant amount of consideration to be received, even if the option had been exercised. In a subsequent technical advice memorandum, the Internal Revenue Service ruled that taxation of option payments must be deferred because the characterization of the income as depletable (option exercised) or nondepletable (option expired) cannot be determined at the time of payment.[24] The facts of the ruling do not indicate whether the payments received under the agreements constituted the predominant amount of the total consideration that might be received by the optionor. If substantially all of the rights of a lessee pass upon the grant of the option and substantially all of the lease consideration is paid at that time, it may be appropriate to view the option as a lease. Accordingly, the option payment may be treated as a lease bonus (eligible for cost depletion) at the time of receipt. *(See Case 98.)* Otherwise, based on the rationale of the technical advice memorandum, taxation should be deferred until the option is exercised or expires. *(See Case 127 concerning restoration of depletion if the lease or option expires or is abandoned prior to the receipt of production income.)*

If the option arrangement is viewed as a sublease, the delay rentals paid by Operator A and reimbursed to him by Operator B are considered to be delay rentals paid or incurred on behalf of Operator B. *(See Case 9.)* However, if the option arrangement is not viewed as a sublease, Operator B probably will be required to capitalize as leasehold acquisition cost any amounts paid to Operator A to reimburse him for delay rentals coming due during the option period.

Case 127
Restoration of Depletion Claimed on Lease Bonus

In 1987, Lessor R, who owns the fee minerals in a single 2,000-acre tract, grants an oil and gas lease to Lessee E for a cash consideration of $20,000 and retains a one-eighth royalty. The lease is for a primary term of five years and provides for annual rental payments of $5 per acre; however, if production is obtained, rentals will not be payable on any 320-acre tract surrounding a producing well. Lessor R claimed a cost

21. Comm'r v. The Dill Company, 294 F.2d 291 (3d Cir. 1961), 8 AFTR2d 5265, 61-2 USTC 9611; Rev. Rul. 69-166, 1969-1 C.B. 37.
22. Comm'r v. Pickard, 401 F.2d 615 (10th Cir. 1968), 23 AFTR2d 69-318, 68-2 USTC 9607; Westates Petroleum Co., 21 T.C. 35 (1953).
23. Pickard.
24. IRS Letter Ruling 7949013 (Technical Advice Memorandum).

depletion deduction in 1987 on the $20,000. He now wants to know if he will be required to restore the bonus depletion to taxable income if the lease or any portion of the lease expires, terminates or is reassigned by Lessee E before any income is received from sale of production from the leased premises.

The regulations provide that if any grant of an economic interest in a mineral deposit for which a bonus was received expires, terminates or is abandoned before there has been any income from the extraction of the minerals, the grantor must restore to his tax basis in the property (and report as income in the tax year of the forfeiture of the interest) the depletion that was allowable on the lease bonus.[25] This provision commonly is referred to as the "depletion restoration" rule. Subsequently, the lessor may be entitled to an abandonment loss in the amount of the restored basis. *(See Cases 159 and 160.)*

If the original lessor has divested himself of his entire retained interest by sale, gift, devise, inheritance or other means while the lease is in force but before production is obtained, he will not be required to restore the bonus depletion to income in the year of expiration or termination of the lease,[26] or at the time of transfer.[27] The Internal Revenue Service (IRS) probably will contend that the entire bonus depletion must be restored if the original lessor still has any portion of his retained interest at the time the lease is terminated or expires without production. If community property laws apply to a bonus received by the community and one member of the community dies before the expiration of the lease, the surviving spouse may be required to restore only one half the bonus depletion in the tax year the lease is forfeited without production.[28]

It is not clear what constitutes income from the extraction of minerals sufficient to avoid restoration of depletion upon the forfeiture or expiration of the lease. A literal reading of the regulation[29] indicates that income from marketed production, regardless of the amount, would avoid restoration of the bonus depletion upon the expiration or termination of the lease. A lessor was not required to restore depletion previously claimed on a lease bonus when only a nominal amount of production was marketed.[30] However, the IRS indicates it will not follow this case.[31] Depletion was not allowed on a lease bonus in a case where the lessor received a nominal royalty payment from the lessee for the production of a nominal amount of oil not sold or used on the premises in the drilling operations.[32] In that case, a dry hole was drilled and the lease was terminated in the year of production, and the court stated that "there has been no production of oil in the ordinary sense."

Restoration of depletion is required only if the entire "property," as defined for purposes of the depletion computation,[33] is forfeited before there has been income from production.[34] The lessor will not be required to restore depletion if the lessee releases only a part of the acreage covered by a single lease, with no production having been sold from the released acreage.[35] The IRS has ruled that, when a portion of the

25. Reg. Sec. 1.612-3(a)(2).
26. Comm'r v. Seeligson, 141 F.2d 358 (5th Cir. 1944), 32 AFTR 390, 44-1 USTC 9238; Rev. Rul. 60-336, 1960-2 C.B. 195; Estate of Robert Driscoll, T.C. Memo Dec. (June 28, 1943).
27. Mary F. Waggoner, 47 B.T.A. 699 (1942).
28. Rev. Rul. 60-336, 1960-2 C.B. 195.
29. Reg. Sec. 1.612-3(a)(2).
30. Dolores Crabb, 41 B.T.A. 686 (1940), (NA) 1968-1 C.B. 3.
31. *Ibid.*
32. Seth Campbell, 4 T.C. 91 (1963).
33. Reg. Sec. 1.614-1.
34. Norman and Ernestine H. Freeman, 48 T.C. 96 (1967).
35. Driscoll v. Comm'r, 147 F.2d 493 (5th Cir. 1945), 33 AFTR 704, 45-1 USTC 9184; Houston Farms Dev. Co. v. Comm'r, 194 F.2d 520 (5th Cir. 1952), 41 AFTR 725, 52-1 USTC 9175.

property is unitized and the acreage outside the productive unit boundaries is relinquished, the lessor is not required to restore any of the depletion allowance taken on the lease bonus.[36] The unit-of-property concept also was accepted in a situation in which the taxpayers had received permission to aggregate nonoperating mineral interests and in which a portion of the acreage leased to one lessee expired at a time when oil was being produced from the other acreage included in the aggregated unit but leased to a different lessee.[37]

Frequently, the lessor will receive a lump-sum bonus covering more than one lease and more than one unit of "property." If a complete "property" is forfeited, thus requiring the restoration of depletion, it may be difficult to determine the amount of the depletion applicable to the released property. One court has held that depletion cannot be measured on an acreage basis.[38] However, another court, in holding that the entire bonus could not be allocated solely to the productive properties, allocated the bonus ratably over the bonus acres because the taxpayer could not show that a greater or lesser portion of the bonus had been paid for different acres.[39]

In the present case, Lessor R should not be required to restore any of the bonus depletion until the entire tract is forfeited by Lessee E, and then only if no income from production has been received from any portion of the 2,000-acre tract.

Case 128
Assignment by Deed of a Fraction of the Minerals

Landowner R, who is not a dealer in mineral properties, owns the fee interest in land on which he executes in 1987 a mineral deed conveying seven-eighths of the minerals to Operator A for a cash consideration of $10,000. Landowner R retains the surface rights and one-eighth of the minerals, free of development obligations and operating costs.

This case differs from an outright sale of all the minerals (*see Case 124*) because, in this instance, Landowner R retains a continuing interest in the minerals, free of development and operating charges. It differs from the ordinary leasing arrangement (*see Case 125*) in that a mineral deed does not include the rental payment and forfeiture and development clauses usually contained in the ordinary oil and gas lease.

The classification of a transaction as a lease or a sale depends on all the facts and circumstances surrounding the transaction. Generally, a transaction will be treated as a sale if the interest transferred is identical to the interest retained (except quantity) and if there is no shift of the burdens of development and operations. The shift of only the development obligation will not classify a transaction as a lease. *(See Case 38.)*

The courts have held[40] that a transaction, although styled as a sale, will be treated as a leasing transaction when the transferee is obligated to develop and operate the properties free of cost to the transferor. The courts and the Internal Revenue Service (IRS) have ruled[41] that, irrespective of the presence or absence of a dominant purpose of the parties to secure development and operation of the property, the lump-sum payment received by the transferor for the simple title to all minerals owned under

36. Rev. Rul. 68-78, 1968-1 C.B. 294.
37. Miller v. U.S., (E.D. Okla. 1969), 24 AFTR2d 69-5363, 69-2 USTC 9578.
38. Driscoll.
39. Freeman.
40. West v. Comm'r, 150 F.2d 723 (5th Cir. 1945), 34 AFTR 81, 45-2 USTC 9382.
41. U.S. v. White, 401 F.2d 610 (10th Cir. 1968), 22 AFTR2d 5641, 68-2 USTC 9605; Comm'r v. Pickard, 401 F.2d 615 (10th Cir. 1968), 23 AFTR2d 69-318, 68-2 USTC 9607; Rev. Rul. 69-352, 1969-1 C.B. 34.

certain lands (but in conjunction with which a royalty interest in any minerals produced is retained) will be treated as a leasing transaction. One Circuit Court[42] has held that instruments conveying fractional mineral interests in properties to other parties who agree to develop and operate the properties (with the transferor agreeing to pay a specified amount applicable to the interest retained) constitute mineral leases. The consideration received by the grantor was treated as ordinary income.

In a technical advice memorandum, the IRS ruled that an exchange of a producing mineral fee for an unspecified real property interest, followed by a separate conveyance reserving a royalty interest in the same mineral fee, constituted a leasing transaction and not a like-kind exchange.[43] The IRS determined that, in substance, the taxpayer entered into a leasing transaction, even though separate conveyances were used to execute the several steps.

In the instant case, the IRS will consider Landowner R to have entered into a leasing transaction, and the $10,000 will be treated as depletable lease bonus income. *(See Case 98.)*

Case 129
Sale by Landowner of a Fraction of Royalty Interest

> **Landowner R, who is not a dealer in mineral properties, acquired for investment the fee interest in a tract of land for $10,000 cash, of which three-fourths ($7,500) is properly attributable to the oil and gas rights. Operator A wants to lease the land from Landowner R but desires to pay only a minimum cash bonus. Therefore, Landowner R grants to Operator A in 1987 an oil and gas lease in consideration of a $500 cash payment with the retention of a three-sixteenths royalty interest. Landowner R subsequently assigns a one-sixteenth fee royalty to Operator B for $6,000 cash.**

The $500 cash receipt is a lease bonus on which depletion is allowable. Landowner R may claim cost depletion, but not percentage depletion, with respect to the $500 lease bonus. *(See Case 98 for a discussion of lease bonus depletion.)*

A bona fide assignment of the one-sixteenth royalty to a third party for $6,000 is a sale of a capital asset by Landowner R.[44] Landowner R's tax basis in the one-sixteenth royalty sold to Operator B is one-third of the $7,500 allocable to the oil and gas rights, reduced by any depletion allowable on the $500 bonus. Landowner R generally must recapture, as ordinary income, any depletion deductions (to the extent of basis) previously claimed with respect to the property if the property was placed in service after December 31, 1986.[45] *(See Case 131.)* Landowner R's holding period runs from the date of acquisition of the fee, not from the date of the lease.[46]

If, pursuant to a prior agreement, Landowner R assigns the one-sixteenth royalty to Operator A (the lessee) rather than to Operator B shortly after granting Operator A the lease, the Internal Revenue Service probably will contend that the $6,000 constitutes additional bonus in the hands of Landowner R, not proceeds from the sale of an economic interest.[47]

42. Campbell v. Fasken, 267 F.2d 792 (5th Cir. 1959), 3 AFTR2d 1602, 59-2 USTC 9515.
43. IRS Letter Ruling 8501004 (Technical Advice Memorandum).
44. Rev. Rul. 73-428, 1973-2 C.B. 303.
45. I.R.C. Sec. 1254(a)(1)(A)(ii).
46. Alice G. K. Kleberg, 2 T.C. 1024 (1943).
47. IRS Letter Ruling 8501004 (Technical Advice Memorandum).

Operator A must capitalize the $500 cash payment as his depletable leasehold cost. *(See Case 2.)* Any royalty payments to Landowner R and Operator B are excludable from Operator A's taxable income and are depletable income to Landowner R and Operator B, respectively. If the sale to Operator B represents the transfer of a proven property, he will be denied percentage depletion on that income.[48] *(See Case 108.)*

Case 130
Sale of a Purchased Royalty

During 1987, Operator A purchases a nonproducing royalty for $5,000 to augment his holdings in other oil and gas properties. Operator A is not a dealer in oil and gas properties, nor does he hold those properties primarily for sale to customers in the ordinary course of his trade or business. Seven months later, Operator A sells the royalty for $3,000.

The Internal Revenue Service has held that an oil and gas royalty constitutes an interest in real property for tax purposes.[49]

If the nature of Operator A's activities is such that the royalty is used in his trade or business, as opposed to its being merely an investment-type asset, the gain or loss realized on its sale will be subject to the special rules relating to sales of real and depreciable property used in a trade or business (Section 1231 property).[50] As such, the $2,000 loss will be deductible from ordinary income to the extent it is not offset by gains on other Section 1231 property. If gain is realized, it will be subject to capital-gains treatment to the extent it is not:

- ☐ Recharacterized as ordinary income due to the depletion recapture rules applicable to property placed in service after December 31, 1986.[51] (*See Case 131.*)
- ☐ Offset by losses on sales of Section 1231 property[52] or
- ☐ Recharacterized as ordinary income due to unrecaptured prior-year Section 1231 losses.

This latter recharacterization is limited to the excess of the aggregate amount of losses (net of gains) attributable to Section 1231 property for the five most recent preceding years beginning after 1981 over the portion of the losses for those preceding years that were previously recaptured.[53]

When a royalty interest is an investment-type asset, it will be a capital asset and any loss realized on its sale will be subject to the capital-loss limitations.[54] Any gain will be capital gain except to the extent of depletion recapture for property placed in service after December 31, 1986.

The holding period for Section 1231 property treatment and long-term capital-gain purposes is more than six months for property acquired after June 22, 1984, and before January 1, 1988, and more than one year for property acquired after December 31, 1987.[55]

48. I.R.C. Sec. 613A(c)(9)(A).
49. Rev. Rul. 73-428, 1973-2 C.B. 303.
50. I.R.C. Sec. 1231; Spragins v. U.S., (D.C. Tex. 1978), 42 AFTR2d 78-5389, 1978-1 USTC 9475; Robert H. Miller, T.C. Memo Dec. (Feb. 23, 1961).
51. I.R.C. Sec. 1254(a)(1).
52. I.R.C. Sec. 1231(a).
53. I.R.C. Sec. 1231(c).
54. I.R.C. Sec. 1211.
55. I.R.C. Sec. 1231(b); I.R.C. Sec. 1222.

Case 131
Calculation of Gain or Loss on Sale of Producing Oil and Gas Properties — Recapture of Intangible Drilling Costs and Depletion

Operator A acquired and drilled a producing well on Lease B during January 1987. Selected 1987 costs and operating results are as follows:

Leasehold cost	$ 15,000
Intangible drilling and development costs (IDC)	$550,000
Lease and well equipment	$150,000
Depreciation—1987	$ 20,000
Percentage of reserves recovered during 1987	5%
Percentage depletion deduction for 1987	$ 20,000

On January 1, 1988, Operator A sold his entire interest to an unrelated party (Operator C) for $2 million in cash. At the time of sale, the fair market values of the leasehold interest and equipment are $1,860,000 and $140,000, respectively.

The transaction between Operator A and Operator C is treated as a sale for income tax purposes because Operator A has not retained a continuing interest in the working interest conveyed to Operator C.[56] Unless Operator A is a dealer in oil and gas properties, Lease B will be treated as property used in a trade or business (Section 1231 property). As such, Operator A will recognize long term-capital gain (since the requisite holding period is met) to the extent the gain is not offset by losses on dispositions of Section 1231 property.[57] However, a portion of such gain may be recharacterized as ordinary income due to the IDC, depletion and depreciation recapture provisions.[58] Gain otherwise eligible for long-term capital-gain treatment may be recharacterized as ordinary income to the extent of the excess of the aggregate amount of losses (net of gains) attributable to Section 1231 property for the five most recent preceding years beginning after 1981 over the portion of those preceding years' losses not previously recaptured.[59]

Recapture Provisions for Properties Placed in Service After December 31, 1986

Gain on the sale of an oil or gas property placed in service after December 31, 1986, must be treated as ordinary income to the extent of previously deducted IDC and depletion (to the extent such depletion deductions reduced basis).[60] Different rules (discussed below) apply to a disposition of property placed in service: (1) before January 1, 1987, or (2) after December 31, 1986, if such property was acquired pursuant to a written binding contract entered into before September 26, 1985.[61] For

56. McLean v. Comm'r, 120 F.2d 942 (5th Cir. 1941), 27 AFTR 544, 41-2 USTC 9553; Cullen v. Comm'r, 118 F.2d 651 (5th Cir. 1941), 26 AFTR 887, 41-1 USTC 9364; U.S. v. Morgan, 321 F.2d 781 (5th Cir. 1963), 12 AFTR2d 5404, 63-2 USTC 9653.
57. I.R.C. Sec. 1231.
58. I.R.C. Sec. 1254; I.R.C. Sec. 1245.
59. I.R.C. Sec. 1231(c).
60. I.R.C. Sec. 1254.
61. P.L. 99-514 (Tax Reform Act of 1986), Sec. 413(c).

this purpose, the meaning of the term *placed in service* is unclear, and further guidance is needed. A post-1986 transfer of a property placed in service before January 1, 1987, between members of a consolidated group and a subsequent disposition of the property generally will continue to be subject to the rules applicable to disposition of a property placed in service before January 1, 1987.[62]

Recapture Provisions for Properties Placed in Service Before January 1, 1987

The calculation of recapture upon the disposition of an oil or gas property placed in service before January 1, 1987, (or subject to the binding contract exception) is more complicated. Depletion deductions are not required to be recaptured. The amount of IDC required to be recaptured as ordinary income is reduced by the amount, if any, by which depletion would have been increased if the IDC had been capitalized.[63] According to proposed regulations, the hypothetical increased depletion is the excess of the recomputed allowable percentage or cost depletion over the original allowable depletion.[64]

Capitalizing IDC may increase recomputed percentage depletion in the years in which those costs are incurred due to the favorable impact on the 50% of net income limitation. However, the proposed regulations often result in minimal or no reduction of recapture because, in years not subject to the 50% limitation, the increased cost depletion (due to capitalizing IDC) frequently is less than original percentage depletion.

Based on language contained in the Committee Reports and in the explanation by the Staff of the Joint Committee on Taxation, it appears that the intent of the law is to provide for a cost-depletion type reduction of the amount to be recaptured without regard to the effect of any percentage depletion actually allowed as a deduction.[65] The statutory construction does not appear to accomplish this intent.

According to the proposed regulations, costs that would have been capitalized as lease and well equipment (absent an election to expense IDC) are not taken into account in determining the recomputed depletion except to the extent they affect percentage depletion (due to the potential impact of "additional" accelerated cost recovery deductions or depreciation on the percentage depletion net income limitation).[66] Capitalizing IDC attributable to lease and well equipment (i.e., installation, etc.) as basis in the equipment eliminates those costs from the reduction provision, thereby reducing the overall benefit of the provision. To the contrary, a recent technical advice memorandum held that, since such costs are subject to recapture, they may be included as leasehold cost subject to the recapture adjustment provision.[67]

The following example demonstrates the effect of the recapture provisions. The second column represents the results based on the facts of this case. The first column

62. General Explanation of the Tax Reform Act of 1986, prepared by the Staff of the Joint Committee on Taxation, p. 203, Footnote 24.
63. I.R.C. Sec. 1254(a)(4) *(prior to amendment by the Tax Reform Act of 1986).*
64. Prop. Reg. Sec. 1.1254-1(a)(2)(ii).
65. Senate Report No. 94-1236, 1976-3 C.B. Vol. 3 818; General Explanation of the Tax Reform Act of 1976, prepared by the Staff of the Joint Committee on Taxation, 1976-3 C.B. Vol. 2 77.
66. Prop. Reg. Sec. 1.1254-1(a)(2)(ii).
67. IRS Letter Ruling 8622005 (Technical Advice Memorandum).

demonstates the results using similar facts, but assumes the property is subject to the rules pertaining to properties placed in service before January 1, 1987.

	Property Placed in Service	
	Before 1/1/87	**After 12/31/86**
Sales proceeds	$2,000,000	$2,000,000
Adjusted basis:		
Leasehold (fully depleted)	(-0-)	(-0-)
Equipment ($150,000 cost - $20,000 depreciation)	(130,000)	(130,000)
Gain recognized	$1,870,000	$1,870,000
Character of Gain		
Ordinary income due to:		
Depreciation recapture (Note 1)	$ 10,000	$ 10,000
Depletion recapture (Note 2)	N/A	15,000
IDC recapture (Note 3)	470,000	550,000
Total ordinary income	$ 480,000	$ 575,000
Section 1231 gain	1,390,000	1,295,000
Total gain recognized	$1,870,000	$1,870,000

Notes: 1. Depreciation recapture is limited to gain recognized.

Fair market value		$140,000
Cost	$150,000	
Less: Depreciation	(20,000)	
Adjusted basis		(130,000)
Net gain		$ 10,000

2. Depletion recapture is not applicable to properties placed in service before January 1, 1987. For properties placed in service after December 31, 1986, all depletion is recaptured, but only to the extent depletion deductions reduced basis.

3. IDC recapture for a property placed in service after December 31, 1986, equals the aggregate amount deducted, limited to the gain recognized on disposition. See below for recapture computations relating to property placed in service before January 1, 1987.

IDC recapture for the pre-January 1, 1987, disposition is calculated below. It is assumed that the hypothetical capitalization of IDC increases allowable percentage depletion to $100,000 (due to favorable impact on the 50% of net income limitation) and that $10,000 would be capitalized as tangible equipment in the absence of the election to deduct IDC.

Calculation of IDC Recapture	
Cost Depletion Approach (Note A)	
Leasehold cost	$ 15,000
Capitalized IDC	550,000
Less: Portion of IDC capitalized to tangible equipment (Note C)	(10,000)
Recomputed basis	$555,000
Cost depletion rate	× 5%
Recomputed cost depletion	$ 27,750
Original cost depletion ($15,000 × 5%)	(750)
Hypothetical increased cost depletion	$ 27,000(A)
Statutory Approach (Note B)	
Greater of recomputed percentage depletion ($100,000) or recomputed cost depletion ($27,750)	$100,000
Less: Original allowable depletion (greater of cost or percentage)	(20,000)
Hypothetical increased allowable depletion	$ 80,000(B)
IDC incurred	$550,000
Less: IDC recapture adjustment	(80,000)
Required IDC recapture	$470,000

Notes: A This calculation of the IDC recapture adjustment is consistent with apparent Congressional intent.

B This calculation of the IDC recapture adjustment is consistent with the statutory construction and proposed regulations.

C The proposed regulations require this reduction. However, the above-mentioned technical advice memorandum does not require it and would increase recomputed cost depletion by $500 ($10,000 × 5%).

The IDC recapture provisions apply to all taxpayers, including regular corporations. IDC recapture may be triggered by dispositions of partnership interests and S corporation stock to the extent the partnership or S corporation holds oil and gas properties otherwise subject to IDC recapture.[68]

The proposed regulations define the term *disposition* by reference to the definition in the depreciation recapture provisions.[69] The proposed regulations also state that the term *disposition* does not include abandonments, unitization and pooling arrangements, the creation of operating interests which shift by contractual terms, or the lease or sublease of an oil or gas property.[70] In the event of a lease or sublease of an operating interest subject to potential IDC recapture, the lessor or sublessor apparently retains the "taint" of recapture in the retained nonoperating interest (but see the discussion below).

The statute provides for exceptions to recapture that are similar to those for the recapture of depreciation as ordinary income on the disposition of depreciable personal property.[71] Accordingly, the recapture rules do not apply to:

☐ A disposition by gift.[72]

☐ A transfer at death.[73]

68. I.R.C. Sec. 751(c); I.R.C. Sec. 1254(b)(2).
69. Prop. Reg. Sec. 1.1254-1(a)(4).
70. *Ibid.*
71. I.R.C. Sec. 1254(b)(1).
72. I.R.C. Sec. 1245(b)(1); Prop. Reg. Sec. 1.1254-2(a).
73. I.R.C. Sec. 1245(b)(2); Prop. Reg. Sec. 1.1254-2(b).

☐ Common tax-free transfers to corporations, partnerships, etc.[74]

☐ The usual tax-free exchanges of like-kind property, except to the extent gain is recognized.[75]

☐ Transactions involving Sections 1071 and 1081 (sales to effectuate policies of the Federal Communications Commission or in obedience to orders of the Securities and Exchange Commission), except to the extent gain is recognized.[76]

In the case of a disposition of a divided interest in an oil or gas property, all IDC and depletion deductions (to the extent of basis) allocable to the property generally must be recaptured as ordinary income to the extent of the gain.[77] Any remaining amount not recaptured will be allocated to the interest retained.[78] However, if a divided interest is transferred under one of the exceptions noted above, potential IDC and depletion recapture is allocated based on the relative rights to income attributable to the retained and transferred interests.[79]

In the case of the disposition of an undivided interest in an oil or gas property, a proportionate amount of IDC and depletion deductions (to the extent of basis) attributable to the disposed interest must be recaptured to the extent of the gain.[80] IDC and depletion deductions may be allocated differently between the disposed and retained portions (whether divided or undivided interests) if supported by a statement in the tax return and if the taxpayer can establish to the satisfaction of the Internal Revenue Service (IRS) that the IDC and prior depletion deductions do not relate to the disposed portion.[81]

Other Issues

Although the Internal Revenue Code does not differentiate between IDC incurred on producing wells from those incurred on nonproductive wells for recapture purposes, the legislative history indicates that only productive-well intangibles were intended to be subject to recapture.[82] The proposed regulations specifically subject to recapture any IDC attributable to nonproductive wells.[83] However, the IRS has ruled that IDC attributable to dry holes is subject to recapture only in connection with the foreclosure of nonrecourse debt, the proceeds of which were used to finance the IDC.[84] Presumably, the purpose of the recapture provisions is to prevent favorable capital-gains treatment when the tax law permits deductions: (1) such as depreciation, which is not necessarily tied to an economic decline in the value of the related asset or (2) for expenditures such as IDC, which actually may enhance the value of the related asset. Since dry-hole costs typically do not contribute to or enhance the value of a lease and, in fact, typically detract from that value, it seems inappropriate to require their recapture. The uncertainty of treatment of IDC of nonproductive wells will have to be resolved by future developments.

74. I.R.C. Sec. 1245(b)(3); Prop. Reg. Sec. 1.1254-2(c).
75. I.R.C. Sec. 1245(b)(4); Prop. Reg. Sec. 1.1254-2(d).
76. I.R.C. Sec. 1245(b)(5); Prop. Reg. Sec. 1.1254-2(e).
77. I.R.C. Sec. 1254(a)(2)(A); Prop. Reg. Sec. 1.1254-1(b)(1)(i).
78. Prop. Reg. Sec. 1.1254-1(b)(1)(i).
79. Prop. Reg. Sec. 1.1254-1(b)(1)(ii).
80. I.R.C. Sec. 1254(a)(2)(B); Prop. Reg. Sec. 1.1254-1(b)(2).
81. I.R.C. Sec. 1254(a)(2); Prop. Reg. Sec. 1.1254-1(b)(3).
82. Senate Report No. 94-1236, 1976-3 C.B. Vol. 3 817; Summary of the Tax Reform Act of 1976, prepared by the Staff of the Joint Committee on Taxation, 1976-3 C.B. Vol. 1 429.
83. Prop. Reg. Sec. 1.1254-1(a)(2)(ii).
84. IRS Letter Ruling 8622005 (Technical Advice Memorandum).

Effective for tax years beginning after December 31, 1986, taxpayers may elect to capitalize IDC and amortize such costs over a 10-year period.[85] *(See Case 181.)* These capitalized costs and amortization deductions will not be treated as tax preference items. However, the amortization deductions allowed under these provisions are subject to the recapture rules discussed in this case.[86] In prior years, individuals could elect to capitalize IDC and amortize those costs over a 10-year period (with respect to limited business interest costs) or a 5-year period with respect to nonlimited business interest costs, and avoid tax preference treatment.[87] Similarly, such amounts were subject to the recapture rules.[88]

Integrated oil companies are required to capitalize a portion of IDC and amortize them over subsequent periods.[89] *(See Case 24.)* Amounts subject to amortization under these provisions also are subject to the recapture rules discussed in this case.[90]

Foreign IDC paid or incurred after December 31, 1986, is subject to a 10-year straight-line amortization period or cost depletion. *(See Cases 23 and 206.)* Amounts deducted under these provisions also are subject to the recapture rules discussed in this case.[91] In revising the IDC recapture rules, it appears that a drafting oversight exempts from recapture IDC paid or incurred after 1986 attributable to foreign properties placed in service before 1987. Presumably, this issue will be addressed in future technical corrections legislation.

In a highly controversial ruling,[92] the IRS determined that a corporation's transfer of a carved-out 75% net overriding royalty interest to a royalty trust, followed by a distribution of trust units to its shareholders, constituted a disposition for purposes of the recapture provisions. According to the IRS, the transaction caused recapture of 75% of the corporation's previously deducted adjusted IDC. *(See Case 173.)* The IRS reasoned that the IDC was "properly chargeable" to the net overriding royalty interests carved from the corporation's retained working interests. The IRS also ruled that overhead attributed to the previously deducted IDC under Council of Petroleum Accountants Societies of North America (COPAS) guidelines and any other item of overhead related to drilling and development activity must be treated as IDC for purposes of the IDC recapture provisions. *(See Case 90 concerning overhead allocations.)*

In 1951, a Court of Appeals ruled that the holding period of an oil or gas lease dates from the discovery of production and not from the date of acquisition of the lease.[93] This decision is contrary to a long-established practice in the oil and gas industry, and it is not followed by the IRS. Throughout this manual, it is assumed that the holding period is not affected by the discovery of production.

---

85. I.R.C. Sec. 59(e).
86. I.R.C. Sec. 59(e)(5)(A).
87. I.R.C. Sec. 58(i) *(prior to amendment by the Tax Reform Act of 1986)*; I.R.C. Sec. 58(i)(4) *(prior to amendment by the Tax Reform Act of 1986).*
88. I.R.C. Sec. 58(i)(6)(A) *(prior to amendment by the Tax Reform Act of 1986).*
89. I.R.C. Sec. 291(b).
90. I.R.C. Sec. 291(b)(3).
91. I.R.C. Sec. 1254(a)(1)(A).
92. IRS Letter Ruling 8622005 (Technical Advice Memorandum).
93. Petroleum Exploration Co. v. Comm'r, 193 F.2d 59 (4th Cir. 1951), 41 AFTR 453, 52-1 USTC 66,028.

Case 132
Sale of Working Interest With Reversion After Payout

Operator S owns 100% of the working interest in a partially developed property. Infill wells are needed to develop fully the underlying producing geological formation.

Operator S agrees to sell his entire working interest to Operator T for $100,000, subject to a 25% reversionary interest. At the time Operator T recovers from the net proceeds of production an amount equal to the sum of: (1) $100,000, (2) the cost to drill, equip and operate the infill wells and (3) an amount computed like interest on the unrecovered balances of items (1) and (2), a 25% working interest reverts to Operator S. Operator T has full operating rights, responsibilities and economic risk during the recoupment period. Proceeds (if any) from equipment dispositions during the recoupment period are credited to Operator T's payout account. Operator T has a legal right to sell the property, free of Operator S's reversionary working interest, with sales proceeds applied to the payout account.

At closing of the transaction, engineering and reserve reports indicate that the reversion may be expected to occur before the end of the productive life of the property.

The transaction between Operators S and T has some of the characteristics of several types of oil and gas exploration and development arrangements, including sales, carried interests, production payments, etc. Consequently, based on the limited facts, it is not clear what tax consequences should be accorded to the transaction. According to the rationale included in a private letter ruling[94] and technical advice memorandum[95] discussed more fully below, it appears that the portion of the property (75%) to which Operator S does not retain any reversionary interest should be accorded sale treatment. However, whether the remainder of the transaction should be controlled by the treatment generally accorded to sales, carried-interest arrangements, production payments (i.e., loans) or some type of mixed sharing arrangement depends on the substance and economic realities of the transaction.

Because Operator S has not retained a royalty or other nonoperating interest in the portion of the property treated as a sale, the excess of the proceeds attributable to that portion over its basis represents gain or loss from the sale of property used in a trade or business.[96] A portion of this gain may be taxable as ordinary income due to intangible drilling and development costs (IDC), depletion and depreciation recapture. *(See Case 131.)* The treatment of the proceeds (if any) and basis (if any) attributable to the remainder of the property will depend on the tax treatment ultimately accorded that portion of the transaction.

The transaction in the facts of this case bears a strong resemblance to a "carried-interest" arrangement *(see Cases 39, 42, 43 and 45)* except for the initial cash consideration received by Operator S. In a carried-interest arrangement, it is well settled that an assignment of an operating interest subject to partial reversion after the assignee recoups his cost of drilling, equipping and operating the property constitutes

94. IRS Letter Ruling 8049078.
95. IRS Letter Ruling 7709013250D (Technical Advice Memorandum).
96. I.R.C. Sec. 1231.

a transfer of an economic interest in the property.[97] The burdens of development and operation are the indicia of ownership of a working interest, and the owner of a working interest does not satisfy the debts of another when he incurs expenses attributable to that interest.[98] No part of the costs incurred by the assignee is treated as a loan to the assignor. Before payout, the assignee is considered the owner of the entire property interest and is entitled to deduct the IDC and other costs attributable to the property.[99] The production income before payout is reportable by the assignee, who is entitled to depletion with respect to those amounts.[100]

In a common carried-interest arrangement, the "pool-of-capital" doctrine provides that the assignor does not realize gain or loss because the successful development of the lease merely enhances the value of his residual interest.[101] However, the "pool-of-capital" doctrine does not apply to the payment of cash to the assignor.

In a 1977 technical advice memorandum,[102] the Internal Revenue Service (IRS) applied a carried-interest and sale rationale to facts similar to those of this case. In the memorandum, the buyer (H) acquired 100% of the working interest in certain producing and nonproducing properties. After Buyer H recovered: (1) 150% of its "purchase price" and the costs to drill, test, complete and equip certain wells and (2) 100% of its operating costs, a 50% working interest reverted to the seller (M). By agreement, Buyer H and Seller M allocated the purchase price between the permanent interest and the value of a "production payment" (loan) attributable to the reversionary interest. The IRS, relying in large part on two landmark carried-interest decisions,[103] concluded that Buyer H acquired a perpetual 50% working interest and that no part of the purchase proceeds was to be treated as a carved-out production payment (loan). Rather, the remainder of the transaction was to be accounted for under the rules for carried-interest arrangements. The National Office of the IRS noted that Congress did not intend to include carried-interest arrangements within the purview of the production payment rules. It is noteworthy that, in one of the cited cases,[104] the carried-interest arrangement provided interest on the "advance" made by the carrying party to the carried party.

In a 1980 private letter ruling (which was subsequently revoked as discussed below) involving circumstances similar to those in the memorandum and in this case, the IRS ruled[105] that a "loan" occurs to the extent that the cash consideration is properly allocable to the seller's reversionary working interest. The balance of the consideration received by the seller represents the sales proceeds of the portion of the working interest that never reverts to the seller. In the facts of the private letter ruling, the seller (A) "sold" working interests in certain developed and undeveloped properties to the buyer (F). Essentially, Seller A assigned its full working interest in the properties to Buyer F until the time Buyer F recovered its initial "purchase price" and the costs to drill, equip and operate the wells, plus an interest factor under a complex payout formula. Seller A retained a reversionary working interest in the properties. During the payout period, Buyer F agreed to bear all costs and expenses to develop and operate the properties as well as to assume all the attendant economic risk as the full working interest owner of the properties. Buyer F could sell the properties free and

97. Weinert v. Comm'r, 294 F.2d 750 (5th Cir. 1961), 8 AFTR2d 5417, 61-2 USTC 9644; U.S. v. Cocke, 399 F.2d 433 (5th Cir. 1968), 22 AFTR2d 5267, 68-2 USTC 9502. *See also* Husky Oil Company, 83 T.C. 717 (1984).
98. Brooks v. Comm'r, 424 F.2d 116 (5th Cir. 1970), 25 AFTR2d 70-1006, 70-1 USTC 9326.
99. Rev. Rul. 69-332, 1969-1 C.B. 87; Rev. Rul. 71-207, 1971-1 C.B. 160; Rev. Rul. 75-446, 1975-2 C.B. 95.
100. Weinert; Manahan Oil Co., 8 T.C. 1159 (1947).
101. G.C.M. 22730, 1941-1 C.B. 214; E. C. Laster, 43 B.T.A. 159 (1940).
102. IRS Letter Ruling 7709013250D (Technical Advice Memorandum).
103. Weinert; Cocke.
104. Weinert.
105. IRS Letter Ruling 8049078.

clear of Seller A's residual interest, although sales proceeds were to be credited to the payout account.

In concluding that a "part sale" and "part loan" transaction had occurred, the IRS noted that an "annual return" on the payout amount before the reversion was indicative of a charge for the use of funds (i.e., a "loan") to the extent of Seller A's reversionary working interest. The IRS did not address the resemblance to a carried-interest arrangement or the conclusion of an earlier published ruling,[106] which accorded carried-interest treatment to an arrangement providing for a payout computation in which the carrying party could recoup from net production revenues 200% of the costs to drill, equip and operate a well. Based on this ruling, it is clear that a carried-interest arrangement need not revert at payout and the parties are allowed discretion to determine a point in time subsequent to payout when that reversion will occur. Rather than specify that point by reference to a multiple recoupment of costs, the parties involved in the private letter ruling specified a recoupment of costs, plus an additional amount determined by formula, specifically, an interest factor.

According to the IRS in the private letter ruling, Seller A recognized gain equal to the excess of the consideration received (cash, notes and assumed liabilities exclusive of any portion of that consideration allocable to the retained interest and treated as a loan) over its adjusted basis. Adjusted basis is to be allocated between the transferred and retained interests in proportion to the respective fair market values of each. The IRS specifically declined to determine what portion of the initial consideration was allocable to the retained interest and treated as a loan. It further ruled that Seller A will realize ordinary income upon repayment of the principal and interest of the amounts loaned from Buyer F to Seller A, subject to Seller A's right to ordinary deduction for his interest payment. Furthermore, the IRS expressed no opinion on the deductibility by either party of exploration, development and operation expenditures.

Several years later, the 1980 private letter ruling was resubmitted to the IRS for reconsideration of the "part sale" and "part loan" conclusion. The IRS revoked the 1980 ruling and concluded that the transaction should be viewed as a complete sale of the properties in the tax year of the transfer, subject to a condition subsequent.[107] This treatment does not comport with the historical treatment of carried-interest arrangements previously established by the IRS and the courts *(see Cases 39 through 48)*.

The arrangements discussed in this case represent complicated business transactions. The appropriate tax treatment can be determined only after a careful review of the many facts of each arrangement relating to the substance and realities of the transaction.

Case 133
Sale of Working Interest With Capped Obligation for Future Operating Costs

> **Operator A acquired 100% of the working interest in Lease X in January 1987 for $35,000. Operator A then began development of the lease and incurred $250,000 of intangible drilling and development costs (IDC) and $45,000 of lease and well equipment costs. On August 15, 1987, Operator A sold 75% of his working interest in Lease X to Operator C for $500,000. Assume that Operator A may claim $5,000 of depletion based on his**

106. Rev. Rul. 75-446, 1975-2 C.B. 95.

107. IRS Letter Ruling 8714009 (Technical Advice Memorandum). *See also* IRS Letter Ruling 8642010 (Technical Advice Memorandum).

ownership of Lease X. Under an agreement with Operator C, Operator A's liability for subsequent operating costs with respect to the operation of Lease X may not exceed $2 per barrel for any given month (his 25% working interest share of $8 per barrel). Operator A seeks advice on how to report this transaction for tax purposes.

The purpose of this transaction is to limit Operator A's proportionate responsibility for subsequent operating costs in the event they become excessive, thereby shifting a greater portion of the economic risk inherent in operating Lease X to Operator C. To correctly reflect the tax consequences to Operator A, it is necessary to determine the nature of Operator A's retained interest.

An operating mineral interest (i.e., a working interest) includes "only an interest in respect of which the costs of production of the mineral" are required to be taken into account for purposes of the 50% of taxable income limitation in calculating percentage depletion.[108] *(See Case 87.)* Since Operator A would not be liable for his full share of operating costs if such costs exceeded $8 per barrel, the 25% interest retained by Operator A will probably be treated as a net profits interest for tax purposes.[109] The entire retained interest is considered a net profits interest, notwithstanding the fact that Operator A is fully liable for his share of operating costs up to $8 per barrel.

The retention of a net profits interest in connection with the disposition of mineral in place is treated as a sublease for tax purposes.[110] *(See Case 144.)* The impact of this special sharing of operating expenses effectively converts the transaction from a sale of an undivided 75% working interest (eligible for capital-gain treatment) to the retention of a nonoperating interest plus a cash bonus (a leasing transaction wherein cash payments are taxed as ordinary income). *(See Case 125.)*

Operator A, based on his business arrangement with Operator C, may have legally retained ownership of an undivided 25% in the lease and well equipment. However, notwithstanding retention of legal title, Operator A's economic stake in his legal interest in the equipment essentially may be limited to a proportionate share of salvage proceeds in the event the equipment is sold. Even so, Operator A should be careful when structuring his right to receive such proceeds to ensure economic interest status for his retained interest.

Prior to the Tax Reform of 1986 (the Act) it was well settled that when cash consideration exceeded the unrecovered tax basis of depreciable equipment in a leasing transaction, for tax purposes the transaction was considered a sale of the equipment at its adjusted tax basis, with cash consideration in excess of such basis treated as a lease bonus.[111] *(See Case 144.)* However, as discussed below it is unclear whether Operator A can follow this treatment under the current law. *(See Case 154.)*

In this case it appears that proceeds equal to the net tax basis of the equipment at the date of sale (adjusted for 1987 depreciation) are treated as proceeds from the sale of equipment. The balance of the $500,000 is treated as a lease bonus, subject to cost depletion. *(See Case 98.)* Operator A should estimate future recoverable reserves from Lease X to determine his cost depletion deduction in connection with the subleasing transaction to Operator C. *(See Case 98.)* Operator A's adjusted basis in his depletable investment that must be used in connection with the determination of his

108. I.R.C. Sec. 614(d); Reg. Sec. 1.614-2(b).
109. Beach Petroleum Corp., Ltd., T.C. Memo Dec. (July 26, 1946); Rev. Rul. 73-541, 1973-2 C.B. 206; U.S. v. Thomas, 329 F.2d 119 (9th Cir. 1964), 13 AFTR2d 949, 64-1 USTC 9332. *See also* IRS Letter Ruling 8415006.
110. Kirby Petroleum Co. v. Comm'r, 326 U.S. 599 (1946), 34 AFTR 526, 46-1 USTC 9149; Burton-Sutton Oil Co. v. Comm'r, 328 U.S. 25 (1946), 34 AFTR 1017, 46-1 USTC 9243.
111. Louisiana Land and Exploration Co., 6 T.C. 172 (1946).

cost depletion deduction is $30,000 ($35,000 cost basis less $5,000 depletion). Operator A should not have to recapture any IDC or depletion in connection with the sublease of Lease X to Operator C.[112] A subsequent disposition of Operator A's retained interest, however, may result in recapture.[113] *(See Case 131.)*

Operator C must allocate his $500,000 investment in Lease X between the lease and well equipment costs and the depletable leasehold cost. Operator C should make this allocation on some reasonable basis, but would not be required to follow the same allocation made by Operator A.

The Act requires special purchase price allocations in certain asset acquisitions.[114] The intent of these new provisions is to require consistency between the buyer and seller in the allocation of the purchase price among classes of assets. Consistency probably cannot be attained if the allocation for Operator C must be determined under the current law and the allocation for Operator A is determined under prior law. In this case, the allocation issue may be a moot point since only one property has been sold. Many situations may not be this simple. *(See Case 154 for a discussion of the implications of current law for allocations of lump-sum purchase price.)*

Operator A's retained net profits interest represents an economic interest in mineral in place,[115] but it will not be eligible for the lower windfall profit tax independent-producer rates *(see Cases 102 and 217)*.

Operator C will not be entitled to percentage depletion with respect to his interest in Lease X because of the transfer-of-proven-property rules *(see Case 108)*.

Case 134
Taxability of Income from Oil and Gas Lease Between Effective Date and Closing Date

> **Operator A is the owner of a producing oil and gas lease. On March 1, 1987, Operator A concludes negotiations with Operator B for the sale of the lease, to be effective as of March 31, 1987. On this date, both parties are obligated to complete the transaction as soon as the requisite legal documents are completed. Operator B is given possession of the property on March 31 and assumes responsibility for the operations on that date. The documents are completed, title is approved, and the closing date of the sale is September 1, 1987, when title actually passes. The net income from the lease during the period from March 31 to September 1 is $25,000.**

The Internal Revenue Service (IRS) probably will hold that the net income from the operation of the lease for the period from March 31 to September 1 should be reported by Operator B, the purchaser. Operator B will treat the transaction as though he acquired legal title to the property on March 31, the effective date of sale.

If the contract had provided that Operator A was to retain the net income from March 31 to September 1, the IRS probably would take the position that Operator B still should report the income for the period for tax purposes because he had all the aspects of ownership except bare legal title. The $25,000 received by Operator A

112. Prop. Reg. Sec. 1.1254-1(a)(4).
113. Prop. Reg. Sec. 1.1254-1(a)(3).
114. I.R.C. Sec. 1060.
115. Gray v. Comm'r, 183 F.2d 329 (5th Cir. 1950), 39 AFTR 750, 50-2 USTC 9386; Weinert v. Comm'r, 294 F.2d 750 (5th Cir. 1961), 8 AFTR2d 5417, 61-2 USTC 9644.

would be treated as an addition to the purchase price, resulting in additional basis in the lease for Operator B and additional gain for Operator A.

The IRS treatment is similar to that prescribed in the past for transactions of this nature.[116] The courts have held that income is taxable to the person who earns it and that the holding period generally commences on the date the acquiring party begins to exercise all rights of ownership, including possession of the property.[117] The date of sale for tax purposes is not always determined conclusively by the date of the passage of legal title because it also is influenced by the assumption of the benefits and burdens of ownership. The transfer of the obligation to bear all expenses and mortgage payments with respect to the property, without the legal ability to convey title initially, has been held not to transfer the benefits and burdens of ownership where the sale was subject to approval by the shareholders or board of directors of the taxpayer.[118]

The principal considerations of the IRS in determining that the net income for the period between the effective date and the closing date of a sale is taxable to the purchaser are that: (1) both parties are committed to close the transaction upon completion of the necessary documents and (2) all other aspects of the transaction are consistent with the fact that the agreement is binding on the purchaser and seller. The fact that the closing of a multiple oil and gas property sale is subject to the title being satisfactory to the purchaser and provision is made to adjust the purchase price for any property where the title is unacceptable to the purchaser should not, in and of itself, operate to shift the point of the passage of the benefits and burdens of ownership.

Assume that Operator A and B obtained a reserve valuation on January 1, 1987, that the agreed price was based on that valuation and that Operator B was entitled to net proceeds from the sale of production from that date forward. However, neither party was committed to complete the transaction until March 31, 1987, and closing occurred September 1, 1987. Based on the above discussion, Operator A probably will be required to report the income and expenses from January 1 to March 31. During that period, Operator A possessed the risks and rewards of ownership because negotiations could have failed and the sale may not have occurred. The proceeds of production, net of expenses, during that period probably will be treated as an adjustment to the sales price, reducing Operator A's potential gain (or increasing his loss) and reducing Operator B's basis in the property.

In a recent technical advice memorandum,[119] the IRS addressed the point in time that the benefits and burdens of ownership shifted to the purchasers of oil and gas properties. The buyer was credited with the net revenues (gross revenues less operating expenses) between the effective date and the closing date. The seller remained responsible for nonoperating and capital expenditures between the effective date and the closing date. If title to the oil and gas properties was unacceptable (for any reason) or if the personal property was in unacceptable condition, the buyer could terminate the agreement in its entirety before the closing. The seller bore the economic risk of casualty to the oil and gas properties between the effective date and the closing date. The National Office of the Internal Revenue Service found that the greater "bundle of rights" remained with the seller until the closing date, such that the net revenues between the effective date and closing date were treated as a purchase price adjustment. Although the buyer was responsible for the operating expenses between the

116. Rev. Rul. 54-607, 1954-2 C.B. 177; Rev. Rul. 71-265, 1971-1 C.B. 223; Rev. Rul. 83-59, 1983-1 C.B. 103.
117. Peavey v. U.S., 214 F. Supp. 934 (D.C. Kan. 1963), 11 AFTR2d 654, 63-1 USTC 9236; Merrill v. Comm'r, 336 F.2d 771 (9th Cir. 1964), 14 AFTR2d 5703, 64-2 USTC 9771.
118. Bryce's Mountain Resort, Inc., T.C. Memo Dec. (June 19, 1985).
119. IRS Letter Ruling 8718003 (Technical Advice Memorandum).

effective date and the closing date, the National Office found that ultimate economic burden remained with the seller until the closing since the buyer had extremely broad powers to terminate the agreement.

Case 135
Sale of a Carved-Out Production Payment

> **In October 1987, Operator A, the owner of two producing oil and gas Leases (X and Y), assigns to Operator B, in consideration for a cash payment of $400,000, a production payment in the amount of $500,000 payable out of one-half the production from Leases X and Y. The proceeds received by Operator A upon the assignment are not pledged for the exploration or development of the properties. Operators A and B reasonably expect production of oil and gas from Leases X and Y to satisfy the $500,000 production payment prior to exhaustion of the oil and gas reserves underlying Leases X and Y.**

In general, a production payment is a right to a specified share of production from mineral in place, or the proceeds from such production (if, as and when produced).[120] A production payment must constitute an economic interest in mineral in place and must have an expected economic life (at the time of its creation) of shorter duration than the economic life of one or more of the mineral properties burdened thereby.[121] A right to mineral in place, however, that can be required to be satisfied by other than production from the burdened mineral property is not an "economic interest" and, thus, cannot constitute a production payment.[122] A production payment may be limited by a dollar amount, a quantum of mineral or a period of time.[123] A right to mineral in place has an economic life of shorter duration than the life of the mineral property burdened thereby only if the right may not reasonably be expected to extend in substantial amounts over the entire productive life of the mineral property.[124]

A right that is in substance economically equivalent to a production payment is treated as a production payment irrespective of the language used to describe the right, the method of creation of such right or the form in which the right is cast (even though such form is that of an operating mineral interest).[125] Thus, production payments include certain sliding scale royalties (*see Case 145*) and the interest of a partner who provides capital for the partnership if such partnership interest is subject to acquisition or termination by another person under terms that merely provide for a recovery of the partner's capital and a reasonable return thereon.[126]

The regulations specifically provide that a production payment may burden more than one mineral property.[127] Notwithstanding the literal language of the regulations, the Internal Revenue Service (IRS), for many years, was apparently of the opinion based on a case[128] before the Tax Reform Act of 1969 that production payments "cross-collateralized" by several properties (i.e., production of several properties could satisfy a single production payment) did not qualify as production payments since the holder,

---

120. Reg. Sec. 1.636-3(a)(1).
121. *Ibid.*
122. *Ibid.*
123. *Ibid.*
124. Reg. Sec. 1.636-3(a)(1); U.S. v. Foster, 324 F.2d 702 (5th Cir. 1963), 12 AFTR2d 5945, 63-2 USTC 9822; U.S. v. Morgan, 321 F.2d 781 (5th Cir. 1963), 12 AFTR2d 5404, 63-2 USTC 9653; Rev. Rul. 86-119, 1986-41 I.R.B. 8.
125. Reg. Sec. 1.636-3(a)(2).
126. Reg. Sec. 1.636-3(a)(2); IRS Letter Ruling 8507037.
127. Reg. Sec. 1.636-3(a)(1).
128. Lehigh Portland Cement Company v. U.S., 433 F. Supp. 639 (E.D. Pa. 1977), 40 AFTR2d 77-5293, 77-2 USTC 9553; G.C.M. 33584.

in effect, could look to "alternative sources" (i.e., production from other mineral properties) for a return of capital invested. However, when a "blanket" production payment is created such that the holder does not have a definable or distinct interest in any specific property subject to the blanket production payment, the IRS has viewed the holder as owning a single economic interest in all of the burdened properties.[129] The rationale is similar to that employed by the IRS in a series of private letter rulings whereby "blanket" net profit interests carved out of properties in connection with the establishment of royalty trusts are treated as a single depletable economic interest. *(See Case 173.)* As a practical matter, it is often difficult to distinguish economically a blanket production payment burdening multiple properties from a production payment burdening a single property that is cross-collateralized by production from other mineral properties.

Although it is somewhat difficult to distinguish between "blanket" and "cross-collateralized" production payments, the IRS, for ruling purposes, generally has treated blanket arrangements as qualifying production payments, but considered transactions involving cross-collateralization to violate the requirements for production payment qualification.[130] In spite of the fact that there are some legal distinctions between the two production payment arrangements referred to above, both essentially involve multiple properties from which the production payment must be satisfied. Consequently, it is not entirely clear, based on the general regulatory authority allowing production payments to burden multiple properties, that it is appropriate to accord production payment status to one arrangement and not to the other. Additionally, the regulations provide that arrangements which are in substance economically equivalent to a production payment will be treated as a production payment.

It should be noted that the current view of the IRS is that neither "blanket" nor "cross-collateralized" production payments can qualify as production payments carved out for exploration or development.[131] *(See Case 150.)*

In some instances, however, the parties can attain the desired tax consequences associated with their transaction if "loan" treatment (i.e., an obligation is created where there is reasonable certainty that the obligation will be repaid) is sustained, notwithstanding that the transaction may not be viewed as a qualifying production payment.[132] In other instances, however, classification as a true production payment is necessary to accomplish properly the taxpayer's tax objective. *(See Cases 99 and 143.)*

The production payment assigned to Operator B should be treated as a loan on the X and Y mineral properties rather than as a sale of an economic interest in the mineral property.[133] The proceeds received by Operator A at the time of the assignment of the production payment to Operator B are not taxable at the time of receipt.[134] Operator A, however, must report proceeds applied in satisfaction of the production payment as gross income from the property.[135] Operator B also should report the transaction as a loan and not as an economic interest in the mineral in place. The proceeds Operator B receives in satisfaction of the production payment will be reported as repayment of the principal and interest on a loan.[136] Because Operators A and B are required to treat this assignment as the creation of a mortgage loan on the

129. G.C.M. 32478; G.C.M. 33347. *See also* G.C.M. 39181; IRS Letter Ruling 7008177040C (Technical Advice Memorandum).
130. G.C.M. 32478; IRS Letter Ruling 8302016 (Technical Advice Memorandum); IRS Letter Ruling 8312019; G.C.M. 33584.
131. IRS Letter Ruling 8125001; IRS Letter Ruling 7401280010A.
132. IRS Letter Ruling 8614033.
133. Reg. Sec. 1.636-3(a)(2).
134. Reg. Sec. 1.636-1(a)(1)(ii).
135. *Ibid.*
136. *Ibid.*

property, it should not be considered a transfer of a proven property for determining any limitation on percentage depletion. *(See Case 108.)*

The IRS has ruled that a payment made to the owner of an operating interest in a nonproducing lease did not qualify as a production payment because favorable geological and geophysical data, in the absence of actual production, could not provide reasonable expectation for payout.[137]

Production payments often contain a so-called "savings clause" which provides that, in all events, the production payment will terminate when, for example, 85% of the oil and gas reserves are recovered even if the stipulated dollar amount or quantum of mineral (oil or gas) has not yet been produced. Since the regulations[138] expressly require that the production payment must, at the time of creation, have an expected economic life of shorter duration than the economic life of one or more of the mineral properties burdened thereby, taxpayers have used savings clauses to ensure that the production payment will, in all events, terminate before economic exhaustion of the mineral property(ies). The current position of the IRS is that a savings clause, standing alone, does not satisfy the economic life requirement of a production payment.[139] The IRS interprets the regulations as requiring that the production payment must (at the time of its creation) be expressly limited by a specific dollar amount, a specific quantum of quantifiable mineral reserves or a fixed time period. A savings clause applied to a production payment covering a mineral property (such as a nonproducing property) with no "quantifiable" reserves that terminates the production payment at a point of ultimate reserve recovery (say 90%) apparently would not, according to the IRS, meet the requirement of the regulations.[140] This represents a significant change in previous administrative policy.[141]

The IRS's view that a specified dollar amount or quantum of mineral must be reasonably believed to exist at the time of the creation of the production payment creates uncertainty as to production payment classification in the case of subsequent development of a producing property where a savings clause using reserves as periodically redetermined is used as a basis for calculating the termination point. The regulations do not suggest that a production payment *must* be limited by a specific dollar amount, a specific quantum of mineral or a specified period of time. A properly drafted savings clause determines, in all events, that a production payment will not extend over the entire productive life of the mineral properties and, thus, satisfies the requirements of the regulations. Accordingly, a properly drafted savings clause should enable a production payment on partially developed or nonproducing properties to qualify under the regulations.

There are two exceptions to the general rule that production payments constitute mortgage loans for tax purposes. The exceptions pertain to production payments that are pledged for the future exploration or development of the property (*see Case 150*) or that are retained in a leasing transaction (*see Case 141*).

The excess of the production payment amount over the cash received at date of creation potentially is subject to the original-issue discount (OID) rules,[142] and the interest income (expense) of the parties to the production payment presumably must be accounted for on an economic accrual basis.[143] Under the contingent payment rules

137. Rev. Rul. 86-119, 1986-41 I.R.B. 8.
138. Reg. Sec. 1.636-3(a)(1).
139. G.C.M. 39488.
140. Rev. Rul. 86-119, 1986-41 I.R.B. 8.
141. IRS Letter Ruling 7952161; IRS Letter Ruling 6902287070C (Technical Advice Memorandum). *See also* G.C.M. 36749.
142. I.R.C. Sec. 1271-1275.
143. I.R.C. Sec. 163(e); I.R.C. Sec. 1272.

(discussed below), the actual amount of interest under the OID rules will be a function of the timing of the discharge of the production payment through oil and gas production. The proposed OID regulations do not expressly deal with production payment transactions, but it appears that the IRS intends such principles to apply, notwithstanding the production payment regulations' reference to Section 483.[144] The fact that principal payments under a production payment agreement are dependent on production leads to difficult mechanical and administrative calculations for the timing of the realization of deemed interest income (expense) treated as OID.

The proposed regulations likely would characterize a production payment as a debt instrument that provides for contingent payments since typically the holder must look solely to production for repayment.[145] The contingent payment rules applicable to debt instruments issued for cash, in effect, treat each payment as: (1) a payment of interest to the extent of interest deemed accrued for the current and all prior accrual periods (to the extent not previously paid) and (2) a payment of principal to the extent such payment exceeds the amount treated as interest.[146] The amount treated as principal, however, cannot exceed the excess of the issue price of the debt instrument over the sum of all noncontingent payments.[147] Any additional payments shall be treated as consisting entirely of interest.[148] The deemed interest accrual for each period is calculated by multiplying the adjusted issue price (original issue price (as subsequently adjusted for accrued but unpaid interest from prior periods) less prior payments) by the applicable federal rate (AFR).[149] It is unclear which AFR[150] must be used in making the interest calculations since typically the time period over which the production payment will be paid cannot be determined. Presumably, the expected duration of the production payment at the point of its creation can be used to determine the appropriate AFR. The amount of interest calculated for each period must be included in income in the year the payment becomes fixed. For production payments this would, presumably, mean when the oil is produced.

Assuming that the following payments are due to Operator B attributable to the 1987 production, the interest deemed accrued for 1987, assuming an AFR compounded monthly of 8%, is as follows:

Month of Production	Beginning Adjusted Issue Price	Interest Accrual*	Production Payment Due	Ending Adjusted Issue Price
October	$400,000	$2,667	$(4,000)	$398,667
November	398,667	2,658	(2,500)	398,825
December	398,825	2,659	(2,000)	399,484
Totals		$7,984	$(8,500)	

* Applying an 8% AFR × 1/12 = 0.6667% monthly interest rate applied to the monthly accrual periods (i.e., payments in oil and gas industry traditionally made on a monthly basis).

Operator A would report $7,984 of interest expense, and Operator B would report $7,984 of interest income for 1987 under the contingent payment rules. Presumably, Operators A and B must calculate the interest accrued for 1987 based on production in

144. Reg. Sec. 1.636-1(a)(1)(ii); Reg. Sec. 1.483-1(e)(1).
145. Prop. Reg. Sec. 1.1275-4(b)(2); Prop. Reg. Sec. 1.1275-4(f).
146. Prop. Reg. Sec. 1.1275-4(f)(2)(ii).
147. *Ibid.*
148. *Ibid.*
149. Prop. Reg. Sec. 1.1275-4(f)(2)(iii); Prop. Reg. Sec. 1.1275-4(f)(2)(iv).
150. Prop. Reg. Sec. 1.1274-6.

1987, notwithstanding a month or two lag in receiving cash from production, which is typical in the oil and gas industry.

The monthly portions of the payments that constitute interest and principal, respectively, on the production payment will depend on the future amounts of the monthly payment and the applicable required AFR. The proposed regulations effectively adjust for any over- or under-accruals of interest and payments toward principal at the final payment at maturity.[151] For example, assume that before making the final payment of $1,000 at maturity, Operator A has made payments allocable to interest and principal to Operator B in the following respective amounts:

Interest	$150,000
Principal	349,000
Total	$499,000

Since the outstanding principal balance of $51,000 (issue price ($400,000) less $349,000 (principal payments)) exceeds the total amount of the final payment ($1,000), the entire $1,000 is treated as principal and the debt instrument is treated as retired for that amount. The tax consequences associated with the recharacterization of principal and interest are unclear. Economically, Operator B should be entitled to an ordinary deduction to compensate for the fact that too much interest income was accrued in prior years. On the other hand, Operator A has deducted more interest than has economically accrued under the production payment. Recognition of the excess deduction as income by Operator A all in one year defeats the economic accrual concept of the OID rules. The final regulations should expressly address these issues and provide much needed guidance.

The proposed regulations provide that the IRS may reallocate interest under the debt instrument among the parties if the obligation is "reasonably expected" to produce front-loading or back-loading of interest, a principal purpose of which is the avoidance of federal income tax.[152] Among the various factors that may be applied in determining whether such a purpose exists, the proposed regulations[153] include the following:

- Whether one of the parties is exempt from federal income tax; and
- Where both parties are subject to tax, the relative tax brackets of the parties.

If the production payment in this case provided for front-loading or back-loading of interest, the rules discussed above would still be applicable due to the contingent nature of a production payment.

Case 136
Sale of a Carved-Out Net Profits Interest

Operator A owns the full working interest in several producing oil and gas properties (X, Y and Z) with substantial net operating cash flows. In 1987, to raise cash to pay on debt and support ongoing exploration and development activity, Operator A sold a 15% blanket net profits interest, burdening Properties X, Y and Z, to Institution F for $8 million. Operator A's adjusted basis in the leaseholds and production equipment is $4

151. Prop. Reg. Sec. 1.1274-4(f)(3).
152. Prop. Reg. Sec. 1.1274-4(g).
153. *Ibid.*

million and $5 million, respectively. Operator A requests information about how to account for the sale of the net profits interest to Institution F.

Operator A has made an outright sale of an interest in oil and gas in place since he has not retained a continuing interest in the portion of the oil and gas in place transferred to Institution F.[154] The transaction should be treated as a sale of real property used in a trade or business provided the oil and gas properties have been held for more than six months (one year for property acquired after December 31, 1987).[155] The sale by Operator A of the net profits interest to Institution F may be treated as a disposition for purposes of recapture of intangible drilling and development costs (IDC) and depletion deductions *(see Case 131)*. Operator A's gain in excess of any recapture required will be subject to capital-gains treatment to the extent it is not offset by losses from sales of other similar property or recapture of prior-year losses.[156] The recapture of prior-year losses is limited to the aggregate losses (net of gains) attributable to Section 1231 property for the five preceding years, reduced for any losses previously recaptured.

Operator A may not write off any unrecovered depreciable basis in the lease and well equipment in connection with the sale of the net profits interest to Institution F since he retains the working interest in Properties X, Y and Z.[157] Operator A must "equitably apportion" his remaining depletable investment in the oil and gas properties between the amount of in-place oil and gas retained and the amount sold.[158] The adjusted basis of the interest sold should be determined by apportioning the total adjusted basis between the working interest and the net profits interest based on the relative fair market values of each interest as of the date of sale. This is a logical approach and one embraced by the regulations[159] in other circumstances where less than the full interest in a property is sold.

In assessing the relative values, consideration must be given to the fact that a working interest is an inherently more risky interest than a net profits interest since the working interest bears the real economic risks that operating costs may exceed oil and gas revenues. Further, the working interest bears the economic burden of tort liability with respect to oil and gas drilling and production operations. The key economic point to consider is that a 15% net profits interest is more valuable than a 15% working interest and such difference in relative values should permit a greater proportional allocation of depletable basis to the net profits interest. In valuing the interests, Operator A should consider at least all of the following items:

- ☐ Future projected net cash flows (revenues less costs properly chargeable to the net profits interest such as operating costs, taxes and development costs).
- ☐ Appropriate interest rates for discounting working interest and net profits interest net cash flows.
- ☐ Any costs not chargeable to net profits interest.
- ☐ Estimated salvage value of equipment.
- ☐ Estimated plugging and abandonment costs.

154. Burton-Sutton Oil Co. v. Comm'r, 328 U.S. 25 (1946), 34 AFTR 1017, 46-1 USTC 9243; Rev. Rul. 69-352, 1969-1 C.B. 34; Rev. Rul. 69-466, 1969-2 C.B. 140.
155. I.R.C. Sec. 1231.
156. I.R.C. Sec. 1231(c).
157. Choate v. Comm'r, 324 U.S. 1 (1945), 33 AFTR 297, 45-1 USTC 9153.
158. Reg. Sec. 1.61-6(a); Columbia Oil & Gas Company v. Comm'r, 118 F.2d 459 (5th Cir. 1942), 26 AFTR 715, 41-1 USTC 9333.
159. Reg. Sec. 1.614-6(a)(2).

☐ Relative geological, developmental and operational risks.

☐ Relative size of the net profits interest.

☐ Stage of property development, etc.

To illustrate the basis allocation, assume that after considering all the items above, Operator A determines that the relative values of the working interest and net profits interests are $36,500,000 and $9,125,000 respectively.

Working interest	$36,500,000 / ($9,125,000 + $36,500,000)	= 80%
Net profits interest	$ 9,125,000 / ($9,125,000 + $36,500,000)	= 20%

Under this analysis, Operator A's gain on the transaction would be calculated as follows:

Gain Calculation	
Proceeds	$8,000,000
Basis (20% × $4,000,000)*	(800,000)
Gain	$7,200,000

* Operator A's net leasehold investment.

For illustrative purposes only, an aggregate calculation has been shown. Actually, Operator A would have a separate calculation of gain (loss) for Property X, Property Y and Property Z. An allocation of proceeds and basis among Properties X, Y and Z would be required. Additionally, it should be noted that Operator A's assessment of the relative value of the net profits interest exceeds the price that Institution F was willing to pay. It is important that Operator A use the same factors to determine the relative value of the interest sold and the interest retained. That relative value may or may not agree with the sales price. Institution F has determined a different value and Operator A, for whatever reasons, has accepted a lower price.

It is very important that the determination of the relative values of the net profits interest sold and the working interest retained in transactions of this nature be made on a case-by-case basis, with all the attendant facts and circumstances analyzed carefully. The determination of the various factors to apply in calculating the relative fair market values will vary with each particular case. There needs to be a determination of relative values, not just an allocation of estimated recoverable reserves. Taxpayers should carefully document their approach in allocating basis in these transactions.

As discussed, Operator A would not be entitled to write off any portion of his net investment in lease and well equipment in connection with the transaction. Thus, any previously claimed investment tax credits (ITC) are not subject to recapture.[160]

Institution F, according to present Internal Revenue Service ruling policy, will treat its net profits interest as a single depletable interest *(see Case 173)*. It is unclear what methodology Operator A must use to allocate the net profits payment to Institution F for making the 50% of taxable income calculation for percentage depletion *(see Case*

160. I.R.C. Sec. 47.

87) and the windfall profit tax net income limitation calculation *(see Case 221)* since Operator A is viewed as having three units of property *(see Case 58)*.

Case 137
Debt Instrument With Contingent Interest Obligation Measured by Share of Net Operating Cash Flow

> **Operator A, an individual, owns a 20% undivided working interest in several partially developed oil and gas properties. On January 1, 1987, Operator A arranges to borrow $5 million on a full recourse basis from Institution X (a tax-exempt entity) to finance his share of remaining development costs. The terms of the financing between Operator A and Institution X provide for a 10-year loan with interest payable monthly at a rate of 15% per annum. Principal payments of $500,000 are to be made at each January 1, through January 1, 1997. The agreement also provides that after Operator A recovers $5 million ("payout") from net revenues attributable to his 20% working interest, Institution X is entitled to additional monthly payments throughout the term of the loan. These are to be measured by reference to 5% of Operator A's monthly net cash revenues (as defined) throughout the remaining term of the loan. The net fair market value of Operator A's assets on January 1, 1987, is $30 million. Operator A and Institution X seek assistance in determining the tax consequences associated with their lending arrangement.**

The financial arrangement between Operator A and Institution X is designed such that Institution X receives a current premium interest rate on the loan made to Operator A and the opportunity to participate in a limited fashion with respect to future economic profits associated with the successful development of the oil and gas properties by Operator A. Based on the facts in this case, the business arrangement between Operator A and Institution X should be respected as a loan for tax purposes. The fixed interest of 15% per annum, plus the "contingent interest" measured by reference to 5% of the monthly net cash revenues after payout, should be treated as interest for tax purposes, notwithstanding that the contingent interest is not fixed and is dependent on Operator A's successful development of the oil and gas properties. The courts have viewed lending arrangements where "interest" is measured in whole or in part and based on cash flow or net profits of the borrower as reflecting a negotiated arm's-length charge for the use of capital provided the relationship between the parties is truly that of debtor-creditor.[161] The relationship between Operator A and Institution X, based on the facts of this case, is that of debtor-creditor.

The proposed regulations under the original-issue discount (OID) rules on debt instruments involving contingent payments support treating the "contingent interest" measured by 5% of monthly net cash revenues as interest for tax purposes.[162] These provisions, in effect, divide the debt instrument into noncontingent and contingent components.[163] In the case of lending transactions not involving the sale or exchange of property, the portion of the contingent payment treated as interest is includible in income by the holder and deductible from income by the issuer in their respective years in which the amount of the payment becomes fixed.[164] Thus, Operator A and

161. Comm'r v. Williams, 256 F.2d 152 (5th Cir. 1958), 1 AFTR2d 2032, 58-2 USTC 9614; Kena, Inc., 44 B.T.A. 217 (1941); Dorzback v. Collison, 195 F.2d 69 (3d Cir. 1952), 41 AFTR 878, 52-1 USTC 9263; Erwin De Reitzes-Marienwert, 21 T.C. 846 (1954).
162. I.R.C. Sec. 1275(d); Prop. Reg. Sec. 1.1275-4(e)(3).
163. Prop. Reg. Sec. 1.1275-4(e)(1).
164. Prop. Reg. Sec. 1.1275-4(e)(3)(i).

Institution X would report the contingent interest (i.e., 5% of monthly net cash revenues after payout) as a deduction and as income, respectively, only if and as it is payable under the terms of their lending agreement.

If Institution X's right to 5% of the additional monthly net revenues after payout survives the term of the loan, there is uncertainty as to the tax aspects of the economic arrangement between Operator A and Institution X.[165] Institution X may be viewed as acquiring some form of an equity interest in the oil and gas properties in addition to making a loan to Operator A. Thus, the transaction could be viewed as an acquisition by Institution X of a contractual right to future profits from the properties, coupled with a loan to Operator A. Under this approach, Institution X's contractual right is probably in the nature of a personal covenant to receive future payments that would not rise to the level of an economic interest in the minerals in place since Institution X does not have an assignable property interest evidencing an interest in real property (i.e., the oil and gas in place).[166] Accordingly, Operator A would be entitled to the depletion deduction attributable to the oil and gas revenues used to discharge Institution X's contractual right. The receipt of payments by Institution X attributable to the contractual right should not give rise to unrelated business income.[167]

Under the characterization outlined in the above paragraph, the OID rules applicable to the issuance of debt instruments and other property as an investment unit would apply.[168] These rules require that the issue price of the debt instrument be determined by discounting all payments under the debt instrument at a rate agreed to by the issuer and holder, based on the original yields of similar debt instruments with maturities and security issued in the last six months.[169] The contingent payments during the term of the loan would not be considered in making this calculation. In no event may the yield agreed to by the issuer and holder be less than the applicable federal rate (AFR) on the issue date of investment unit.[170] The excess (if any) of the $5 million over the issue price of the debt instrument, determined above, would be allocable to the contractual right. The amount allocated to the contractual right would be amortizable over the expected life of such right as payments to the holder commence in the future.[171] In this case, only nonpublicly traded property rights and debt instruments are issued; therefore, the calculation above should result in *zero basis allocable to the property right* since the stated interest rate is greater than the AFR. Payments made by Operator A to Institution X in satisfaction of the contractual right should be deductible by Operator A as an ordinary and necessary business expense.[172] In a somewhat related context, however, a court has held similar payments as capitalizable on the theory that they were payments in liquidation of an equity interest in property.[173]

If Institution X's right to 5% of the additional monthly net revenues after payout survives the term of the loan and Institution X's equity interest is structured as an economic interest in the mineral in place (such as a net profits interest), the tax consequences will be substantially different. If the consideration attributed to the net profits interest were pledged for the exploration or development of Operator A's properties, Operator A would treat the consideration similar to the proceeds received

165. Farley Realty Corp. v. Comm'r, 279 F.2d 701 (2d Cir. 1960), 5 AFTR2d 1646, 60-2 USTC 9525.
166. Helvering v. O'Donnell, 303 U.S. 370 (1938), 20 AFTR 785, 38-1 USTC 9156; Tuttle v. U.S., 101 F. Supp. 532 (Ct. Cl. 1951), 41 AFTR 549, 52-1 USTC 9102; Haynes v. U.S., 50 F. Supp. 238 (Ct. Cl. 1943), 31 AFTR 281, 43-1 USTC 9479.
167. I.R.C. Sec. 512.
168. I.R.C. Sec. 1273(c)(2).
169. Prop. Reg. Sec. 1.1273-2(d)(iv).
170. *Ibid.*
171. I.R.C. Sec. 167(a); Reg. Sec. 1.167(a)-3.
172. I.R.C. Sec. 162.
173. Farley Realty Corp.

for a production payment pledged for development (*see Case 150*). Institution X would treat the consideration paid as its depletable investment in the net profits interest.

If the consideration attributed to the net profits interest were not pledged for development, Operator A would be considered to have sold a net profits interest carved out of his working interest (*see Case 136*).

Institution X's holding of a net profits interest will not give rise to unrelated business income since it is in the nature of a royalty.[174]

Alternatively, if Institution X's right to 5% of the additional monthly net revenues is treated as an economic interest, the Internal Revenue Service may argue that Operator A and Institution X have formed a partnership for tax purposes. Then Institution X's $5 million payment to Operator A might be allocated between an acquisition of a partnership interest and a loan.

However, based on the facts of this case, it does not appear that the relationship between Operator A and Institution X will be treated as a partnership due to the lack of the following partnership characteristics: (1) intention to form a partnership;[175] (2) an agreement to share losses (in an equity sense)[176] and (3) some form of joint management and control of operations.[177]

It is very important for the parties to these types of financing arrangements to document properly the terms and nature of their relationships. Since the tax law in this area is not well developed, proper attention to the substantive nature of the terms of the transaction and the parties' rights and obligations under the agreement will, in many cases, be necessary to achieve the desired business and tax objectives.

Case 138
Installment Sale of Working Interest in Oil and Gas Properties

Operator A owns a working interest in an oil and gas property. On April 1, 1987, he sells the working interest to Operator B for $11 million, payable $1 million in cash and a note in the face amount of $10 million. The note is payable in 10 equal annual installments of $1 million, plus 6% simple interest on the unpaid balance. At the time of sale, Operator A's adjusted basis in the lease is $500,000. Operator A has no outstanding indebtedness at December 31, 1987, and does not sell personal or real property in the ordinary course of business.

Operator A has made an outright sale of his mineral interest because he has not retained a continuing interest in the oil and gas in place.[178] Assuming Operator A is not a dealer in mineral properties, his gain is subject to the special rules relating to sales of property used in a trade or business.[179] Any gain realized on the sale of the equipment is subject to the accelerated cost recovery (depreciation) recapture provisions,[180] and any gain realized on the sale of the working interest is subject to the

174. I.R.C. Sec. 512(b)(2); U.S. v. Welch Foundation, 334 F.2d 774 (5th Cir. 1964), 14 AFTR2d 5232, 64-2 USTC 9648.
175. Comm'r v. Culbertson, 337 U.S. 733 (1949), 37 AFTR 1391, 49-1 USTC 9323.
176. Estate of Smith v. Comm'r, 313 F.2d 724 (8th Cir. 1963) 11 AFTR2d 878, 63-1 USTC 9268; Rev. Rul. 75-43, 1975-1 C.B. 383.
177. Hubert M. Luna, 42 T.C. 1067 (1964).
178. McLean v. Comm'r, 120 F.2d 942 (5th Cir. 1941), 27 AFTR 544, 41-2 USTC 9553; Cullen v. Comm'r, 118 F.2d 651 (5th Cir. 1941), 26 AFTR 887, 41-1 USTC 9364; U.S. v. Morgan, 321 F.2d 781 (5th Cir. 1963), 12 AFTR2d 5404, 63-2 USTC 9653.
179. I.R.C. Sec. 1231.
180. I.R.C. Sec. 1245.

intangible drilling and development costs (IDC) and depletion recapture provisions.[181] *(See Case 131.)*

Assuming Operator A reports the transaction as an installment sale, his gain generally will be recognized as he collects the proceeds of sale[182] or is deemed to collect proceeds as a result of outstanding indebtedness (as discussed below).[183] However, all accelerated cost recovery (depreciation) recapture amounts must be recognized in the year of sale.[184]

Under the installment method, the amount of any payment treated as income is that portion of the payment (or deemed payment) received that the gross profit realized bears to the total contract price ("the gross profit ratio").[185] Gross profit equals the selling price less adjusted basis.[186] Any accelerated cost recovery (depreciation) recapture amount is added to adjusted basis for this purpose.[187] Contract price equals the selling price reduced by certain indebtedness assumed by the buyer.[188]

Applying these concepts to Operator A's leasehold sale and ignoring the impact of the imputed interest rules discussed below, the gross profit ratio would be 95.455% ($10.5 million ÷ $11 million). However, in this case, the gross profit percentage must be adjusted to reflect imputed interest. Any amount recharacterized as interest pursuant to the original-issue discount (OID) rules reduces the total sales price and contract price for gain calculation purposes.

The OID rules apply to debt obligations issued in exchange for property. OID is the excess of the stated redemption price at maturity over the issue price.

For debt instruments given in consideration for sales or exchanges after December 31, 1984, the OID rules generally apply if the stated redemption price exceeds the stated principal amount or the imputed principal amount (if appropriate) and some or all of the payments are due more than six months after the date of the sale or exchange.[189] In making the determination, the stated principal amount should be used if there is adequate stated interest associated with the debt instrument. If not, the imputed principal amount is used. If the OID rules apply, the amount of OID will be recognized as income by the holder[190] and as a deduction by the issuer[191] on the basis of a constant interest rate (defined below) over the term of the instrument.

To determine whether the OID rules are applicable, the items defined below must be determined.

Stated Redemption Price

The stated redemption price is the amount payable at maturity, including interest payable at that time. This interest does not include interest (qualified periodic interest) based on a fixed rate that is payable unconditionally at fixed periodic intervals of one year or less during the entire term of the instrument.[192] If the

181. I.R.C. Sec. 1254.
182. I.R.C. Sec. 453.
183. I.R.C. Sec. 453C.
184. I.R.C. Sec. 453(i).
185. Temp. Reg. Sec. 15a.453-1(b)(2).
186. Temp. Reg. Sec. 15a.453-1(b)(2)(v).
187. House Report No. 98-861, 1984-3 C.B. Vol. 2 262.
188. Temp. Reg. Sec. 15a.453-1(b)(2)(iii).
189. I.R.C. Sec. 1274(c)(1); Prop. Reg. Sec. 1.1274-1(a)(1).
190. I.R.C. Sec. 1272(a); Prop. Reg. Sec. 1.1272-1(a)(1).
191. I.R.C. Sec. 163(e); Prop. Reg. Sec. 1.163-7(b).
192. I.R.C. Sec. 1273(a)(2); Prop. Reg. Sec. 1.1273-1(b).

obligation provides for periodic reductions of principal, the proposed regulations treat such payments as part of the stated redemption price at maturity.[193]

Stated Principal Amount

The stated principal amount is the aggregate amount of all payments under the debt instrument, excluding any amount of interest provided for in the debt instrument.[194]

Imputed Principal Amount

The imputed principal amount is the sum of the present values of all payments (including interest) due under the debt instrument.[195] The payments are to be present valued to the date of the sale or exchange at a discount rate generally equal to 100% of the applicable federal rate (AFR) (defined below).[196]

Applicable Federal Rate

AFR for a particular debt instrument is determined as follows:[197]

In the Case of a Debt Instrument With a Term of	The Applicable Federal Rate Is
Not over 3 years	The federal short-term rate
Over 3 years but not over 9 years	The federal mid-term rate
Over 9 years	The federal long-term rate

The Imputed Interest Simplification Act of 1985 modified the application and determination of the AFR. For transactions occurring after June 30, 1985, the AFR is the lowest AFR (determined by the Treasury based on average market yields) in effect for any month in the three-calendar-month period ending with the first calendar month in which there is a binding contract in writing for the sale or exchange of property.[198] For transactions occurring before June 30, 1985, the AFR is the interest rate in effect for the six-month periods beginning January 1 and July 1, determined by the Treasury for the preceding six-month periods ending September 30 and March 31, respectively.[199]

Adequate Stated Interest

An obligation will be considered as having adequate stated interest if the stated principal amount of the debt instrument is less than or equal to the imputed principal amount of the obligation.[200]

193. Prop. Reg. Sec. 1.1273-1(b)(2)(ii).
194. Prop. Reg. Sec. 1.1274-2(b)(1).
195. I.R.C. Sec. 1274(b); Prop. Reg. Sec. 1.1274-4(a)(1).
196. I.R.C. Sec. 1274(b)(2)(B).
197. I.R.C. Sec. 1274(d); Prop. Reg. Sec. 1.1274-6.
198. I.R.C. Sec. 1274(d)(2)(B).
199. I.R.C. Sec. 1274(d)(1)(B) *(prior to amendment by the Tax Reform Act of 1986)*; I.R.C. Sec. 1274(d)(1)(C) *(prior to amendment by the Tax Reform Act of 1986)*; I.R.C. Sec. 1274(d)(1)(D) *(prior to amendment by the Tax Reform Act of 1986)*.
200. I.R.C. Sec. 1274(c)(2).

Issue Price

For property transactions, the issue price is determined based on whether there is adequate stated interest associated with the debt instrument. If there is, the issue price is the stated principal amount. If not, the issue price is the imputed principal amount.[201]

Various property transactions are excluded from the application of the OID rules for debt instruments issued for property.[202] These are:

☐ Sales of farms for less than $1 million by individuals or small businesses.

☐ Sales of principal residences—Any debt instrument arising from the sale or exchange by an individual of his principal residence (within the meaning of Section 1034).

☐ Sales involving total payments (principal, interest and other consideration) of $250,000 or less.

☐ Debt instruments that are publicly traded or issued for publicly traded property—Any debt instrument to which Section 1273(b)(3) applies.

☐ Certain sales of patents—In the case of any transfer described in Section 1235(a) (relating to a sale or exchange of patents), any amount contingent on the productivity, use or disposition of the property transferred.

☐ Transactions involving personal-use property.

☐ Transactions involving certain demand loans subject to the below-market interest loan provisions *(see Case 55)*.

☐ Transactions involving transfers of property between spouses or incident to divorce.

☐ Sales or exchanges to which Section 483(e) applies—Any debt instrument to the extent Section 483(e) (relating to certain land transfers between related persons) applies to that instrument.

Special rules apply in connection with the sale or exchange of property where debt is assumed or where property is acquired subject to debt.[203]

---

201. I.R.C. Sec. 1274(a); Prop. Reg. Sec. 1.1274-2.
202. I.R.C. Sec. 1274(c)(4); Prop. Reg. Sec. 1.1274-1(b).
203. I.R.C. Sec. 1274(c)(4); Prop. Reg. Sec. 1.1274-7.

In the present case, there is not adequate stated interest because the stated principal amount ($10 million) exceeds the imputed principal amount ($9,416,669), computed as follows:

Year	Principal Payments	Interest Payments	Total Payments	Present* Value
1	$1,000,000	$ 600,000	$1,600,000	$1,489,897
2	1,000,000	540,000	1,540,000	1,335,344
3	1,000,000	480,000	1,480,000	1,195,006
4	1,000,000	420,000	1,420,000	1,067,660
5	1,000,000	360,000	1,360,000	952,181
6	1,000,000	300,000	1,300,000	847,540
7	1,000,000	240,000	1,240,000	752,792
8	1,000,000	180,000	1,180,000	667,070
9	1,000,000	120,000	1,120,000	589,581
10	1,000,000	60,000	1,060,000	519,598
Totals		$3,300,000		$9,416,669

* Discounted at 7.39%, the lowest applicable federal long-term rate (February 1987) in the three-calendar-month period ending with the month of the transaction (April 1987).[204]

Thus, as discussed above, the imputed principal amount ($9,416,669) is treated as the issue price.

Because the stated redemption price at maturity ($10 million) exceeds the issue price ($9,416,669), the OID rules apply. The OID is $583,331, the difference between $10 million and $9,416,669. The OID de minimus rule does not apply since the amount of OID in this case ($583,331) is greater than the statutory de minimus amount of $137,500 (.0025 × $10,000,000 × 5½ years).[205]

As a result of these new provisions, the sales proceeds for purposes of determining gain or loss is now $10,416,669 ($9,416,669 imputed principal amount plus $1 million down payment) instead of $11 million. Additionally, Operator A's interest income is $3,883,331 instead of $3,300,000, as it would have been without regard to the OID provisions.

The amount of OID as determined above is recognized as interest income by Operator A over the life of the note.[206] The amount attributable to each year is the sum of the daily portions of OID for each day of each tax year. The daily portion is each day's ratable portion of the increase in the adjusted issue price during the accrual period.[207] This increase is the excess of the adjusted issue price at the beginning of the accrual period (as adjusted for prior accrual periods) multiplied by the yield to maturity (based on compounding consistent with the accrual period) over the sum of amounts payable as interest during the accrual period.[208] The accrual period is the one-year period commencing April 1, 1987, and each April 1 thereafter through April 1, 1997, based on the regulatory authority given Treasury to specify accrual periods greater than six months.[209]

204. Rev. Rul. 87-11, 1987-5 I.R.B. 5.
205. I.R.C. Sec. 1274(a)(3); Prop. Reg. Sec. 1.1273-1(a)(3)(ii).
206. I.R.C. Sec. 1272(a); Prop. Reg. Sec. 1.1272-1.
207. I.R.C. Sec. 1272(a)(3); Prop. Reg. Sec. 1.1272-1(c).
208. I.R.C. Sec. 1272(a)(3); Prop. Reg. Sec. 1.1272-1(c)(2).
209. I.R.C. Sec. 1272(a)(5); Prop. Reg. Sec. 1.1272-1(d)(1).

In the present case, Operator A will include in income, and Operator B will be allowed a deduction for, the following amounts in each year, assuming both use the cash method of accounting:

Year	OID*	Interest	Total
1987	$ 71,919	$ —	$ 71,919
1988	90,782	600,000	690,782
1989	83,590	540,000	623,590
1990	75,868	480,000	555,868
1991	67,574	420,000	487,574
1992	58,668	360,000	418,668
1993	49,104	300,000	349,104
1994	38,832	240,000	278,832
1995	27,802	180,000	207,802
1996	15,957	120,000	135,957
1997	3,235	60,000	63,235
Totals	$583,331	$3,300,000	$3,883,331

* Using the approximate method (as opposed to the exact method) for the short first accrual period.[210]

The amount of OID recognized each year is determined by the following formula:

(Adjusted issue price at beginning of accrual period × Yield to maturity) − Interest payable during accrual period

In this case, because there is a stated interest payment and principal reduction each year, the computation of the adjusted issue price must take into account the interest paid and the principal reduction. The following will illustrate how the computations for the first and second years are made:

Year 1:

Adjusted issue price at beginning of first accrual period = $9,416,669		
Yield to maturity for accrual period = 7.39%		
Calculated interest:	$9,416,669 × 7.39% =	$695,892
Interest payable (at April 1, 1988)		(600,000)
OID		$ 95,892
OID attributable to 1987 (¾ × $95,892)		$ 71,919

Year 2:

Adjusted issue price at beginning of second accrual period = $8,512,561*		
Yield to maturity for accrual period = 7.39%		
Calculated interest:	$8,512,561 × 7.39% =	$629,078
Interest payable (at April 1, 1989)		(540,000)
OID		$ 89,078
OID attributable to 1988 (¼ × $95,892 + (¾ × $89,078))		$ 90,782

* $9,416,669 + $695,892 − $600,000 − $1,000,000 (principal payment)

210. Prop. Reg. Sec. 1.1274-3(b)(2).

Special rules apply for determining the discount rate used in connection with certain sales or exchanges of property (other than new Section 38 property). Debt instruments issued in connection with the sale or exchange of property where the stated principal amount of the instrument does not exceed $2.8 million (subject to inflation adjustments after 1989) are subject to a maximum discount rate of 9%.[211] The law also provides for a special elective provision for sales or exchanges of property involving debt instruments that do not exceed $2 million. This provision permits, subject to certain conditions, both the borrower and lender to report the interest on the debt instrument under the cash receipts and disbursements method of accounting.[212]

The Tax Reform Act of 1986 (the Act) provides for complex provisions that trigger recognition of deemed payments attributable to outstanding installment obligations where a taxpayer has outstanding indebtedness during the year.[213] These provisions are effective for tax years ending after December 31, 1986, with respect to sales of property after February 28, 1986. This provision allocates outstanding indebtedness of the taxpayer to applicable installment obligations outstanding at yearend based on the ratio of the face amount of such installment obligations at yearend to the aggregate adjusted basis of all assets (other than installment obligations), plus the face amount of the installment obligations.[214] The amount of debt allocated to the installment obligations arising in the tax year (reduced by amounts included through this calculation for installment obligations (if any) that arose in prior years) is treated as a deemed payment of a portion of the face amount of the obligation.[215] Adjustments are made for actual cash payments and for allocable installment indebtedness that exceeds the face amount of installment obligations arising in the current tax year and outstanding at yearend.[216]

The indebtedness used to make this calculation is based on average quarterly indebtedness outstanding through the year, unless the taxpayer's only applicable installment obligations at any time during the tax year relate to sales of real property used in the taxpayer's trade or business or property held for the production of rental income for a sales price that exceeds $150,000.[217] If such is the case, installment indebtedness at the end of the tax year is used in lieu of the average quarterly amount. Generally, all indebtedness of the taxpayer, including accounts payable and accrued expenses existing at the end of each quarter (or yearend), is considered for this purpose.[218] Where any indebtedness or any installment obligation of the taxpayer is subject to the OID provisions, any restated principal amounts must be used for this purpose.[219]

Assume, for example, that Operator A had the following amounts of adjusted basis of assets and levels of indebtedness at the end of 1987 and 1988, respectively:

	Adjusted Basis of Assets	Outstanding Indebtedness
1987	$50,000,000	$5,000,000
1988	$45,000,000	$4,000,000

211. I.R.C. Sec. 1274A(a); Prop. Reg. Sec. 1.1274A-1.
212. I.R.C. Sec. 1274A(c); Prop. Reg. Sec. 1.1274A-1(c).
213. I.R.C. Sec. 453C.
214. I.R.C. Sec. 453C(b)(2).
215. I.R.C. Sec. 453C(a)(2).
216. I.R.C. Sec. 453C(c); I.R.C. Sec. 453C(d)(2).
217. I.R.C. Sec. 453C(b)(4).
218. General Explanation of the Tax Reform Act of 1986, prepared by the Staff of the Joint Committee on Taxation, p. 493.
219. *Ibid.*

Assuming that Operator A makes no installment sales in 1988, the following calculations must be made in 1987 and 1988 provided that Operator A does not elect out of installment sale reporting in 1987:

1987

$$\$5{,}000{,}000 \times \frac{\$9{,}416{,}669}{\$50{,}000{,}000 + \$9{,}416{,}669} = \$792{,}427$$

Operator A would treat $792,427 as a payment on the installment obligation from Operator B in 1987, recognizing gain of $754,391 (in addition to the gain on the $1 million down payment) after applying the gross profit ratio for the sale, calculated as follows:

Proceeds	$792,427
Gross profit ratio*	× 95.2%
Gain	$754,391

$$^{*}\ \frac{\$\ 9{,}916{,}669}{\$10{,}416{,}669} = 95.2\%$$

The gain reportable by Operator A in 1987 will be treated as ordinary income up to the amount (if any) of IDC recapture. *(See Case 131.)*[220] Any depreciation recapture is recognized as income in the year of sale, irrespective of the amount (if any) of proceeds received (or deemed received).[221]

1988

$$\$4{,}000{,}000 \times \frac{\$8{,}416{,}669}{\$45{,}000{,}000 + \$8{,}416{,}669} = \$630{,}265$$

The $1 million payment received on April 1, 1988, is not treated as a payment in 1988 to the extent of the deemed payment of $792,427 in 1987. The excess amount of $207,573 ($1,000,000 - $792,427) plus $630,265, the allocable installment indebtedness of 1988 which, in this case, is applied to the 1987 sale, is treated as a payment in 1988. This results in a 1988 gain of $797,622, calculated as follows:

Proceeds	$837,838
Gross profit ratio*	× 95.2%
Gain	$797,622

$$^{*}\ \frac{\$\ 9{,}916{,}669}{\$10{,}416{,}669} = 95.2\%$$

It appears that deemed payments of installment obligations under these provisions should not constitute payments for purposes of the modified debt instrument provisions in the proposed OID regulations[222] since a "payment" occurs for only one party to the transaction. Thus, the recognition of interest income and expense by the seller and buyer, respectively, under the OID rules should occur without regard to the new installment-sale provisions.

220. Prop. Reg. Sec. 1.1254-1(d).
221. I.R.C. Sec. 1245; I.R.C. Sec. 453(i).
222. Prop. Reg. Sec. 1.1274-1(c)(1).

The regulations provide special rules for calculating gain recognition in the event of a contingent selling price,[223] for example, an adjustment to the sales price based on actual production occurring after the sale. If the agreement provides neither a maximum selling price nor a fixed period for payment, the installment note may be recharacterized as a royalty.[224] *(See Case 144 for tax treatment if a royalty interest is retained upon the disposition of a working interest.)*

With limited exceptions, the sale or other disposition of an installment note triggers recognition of any remaining gain not previously recognized.[225]

Operator A may elect not to use the installment sale rules.[226] This election must be made on or before the due date (including extensions) of the return of the year of sale and may be revoked only with the consent of the Secretary of the Treasury.[227] If Operator A makes the election, he will report the entire gain in 1987, subject to the recapture rules.

Case 139
Disposition of Oil and Gas Properties Owned by a Corporation

> Operator A owns all the stock of C Company. C Company owns various producing oil and gas leases. During 1987, X Company offers to purchase the stock or assets of C Company for a price of $50 million, subject to adjustment for negotiated liabilities. If assets are sold, Operator A plans to liquidate C Company after the sale. The transaction is completed on June 30, 1987. C Company is neither a collapsible corporation (as defined by Section 341) nor an S corporation.

The Tax Reform Act of 1986 (the Act) repealed the so called *General Utilities Doctrine* which generally permitted corporations to escape taxation of certain sales and property distributions upon liquidation.[228] Prior law generally required taxation only of intangible drilling and development costs (IDC) and depreciation recapture, and certain other items. Subject to certain "binding contract" exceptions and transition rules, the changes made by the Act apply to:

- ☐ Liquidating distributions and sales after July 31, 1986, unless the corporation is completely liquidated before January 1, 1987.
- ☐ Transactions described in Section 338 (see discussion below) for which the acquisition date occurs after December 31, 1986.
- ☐ Nonliquidating distributions made after December 31, 1986.[229]

The Act provides special transition rules[230] for certain closely held corporations that liquidate before January 1, 1989. If the value of a corporation's stock is less than $10

223. Temp. Reg. Sec. 15a.453-1(c).
224. Temp. Reg. Sec. 15a.453-1(c)(4).
225. I.R.C. Sec. 453B.
226. I.R.C. Sec. 453(d).
227. I.R.C. Sec. 453(d)(2); I.R.C. Sec. 453(d)(3).
228. I.R.C. Sec. 336 *(prior to amendment by the Tax Reform Act of 1986);* I.R.C. Sec. 311 *(prior to amendment by the Tax Reform Act of 1986);* I.R.C. Sec. 337 *(prior to amendment by the Tax Reform Act of 1986).*
229. P.L. 99-514 (Tax Reform Act of 1986), Sec. 633(a).
230. P.L. 99-514 (Tax Reform Act of 1986), Sec. 633(d).

million, the corporation may avoid taxation of a percentage of gains or losses excluded under prior law other than:

- ☐ Ordinary gains and losses,
- ☐ Gains or losses on capital assets held for not more than six months and
- ☐ Gains attributable to certain installment-sale obligations.[231]

If X Company purchases assets, the tax consequences are essentially the same whether: (1) C Company sells its assets, pays tax and liquidates or (2) C Company distributes its assets to Operator A, who then sells the assets to X Company. Either approach to the sale of assets results in full recognition of gain or loss at the corporate level. *(See Case 131 for characterization of gain or loss on sales of oil and gas properties.)*

Special limitations apply to losses recognized for certain distributions to related persons and sales or exchanges of property in connection with liquidating distributions where the property was received by the corporation in certain Section 351 transactions.[232] In addition, investment tax credit (ITC) may be recaptured.

Provided Operator A has held his stock for more than 12 months (six months for stock acquired after June 22, 1984, and before January 1, 1988),[233] he will recognize long-term capital gain or loss equal to the difference between the cash and assets (net of any liabilities) received in liquidation and his basis in the stock. X Company's basis in the purchased properties will be equal to its cost, plus any liabilities it assumes.[234] *(See Case 157 for a discussion of reporting requirements relative to purchase price allocation.)* X Company will not be entitled to percentage depletion with respect to any proven properties so acquired.[235] *(See Case 108 concerning the loss of percentage depletion upon the transfer of proven properties.)*

If X Company purchases the C Company stock, Operator A will recognize capital gain or loss equal to the difference between the sales proceeds and his stock basis. For federal income tax purposes, X Company may elect under Section 338 to treat the stock acquisition as an asset purchase.[236] Generally, this election is irrevocable and must be made no later than the 15th day of the ninth month beginning after the month of acquisition.[237] X Company makes the election by filing a statement of election (Form 8023) with the Internal Revenue Service Center with which it files its annual income tax return.[238] X Company may be deemed to elect to treat a stock acquisition as an asset acquisition if C Company liquidates into X Company or certain other transactions occur during the acquisition period or one year before or after such period.[239]

If the stock acquisition is treated as an asset purchase, C Company ("old C Company") will be treated as having sold all its assets at the close of the acquisition date.[240] Old C Company will recognize gain or loss as though it sold its assets at fair market value.[241] Furthermore, C Company will be treated as a new corporation ("New C Company"), which purchased all the assets as of the beginning of the day

231. P.L. 99-514 (Tax Reform Act of 1986), Sec. 633(d)(2).
232. I.R.C. Sec. 336(d).
233. I.R.C. Sec. 1222.
234. I.R.C. Sec. 1012.
235. I.R.C. Sec. 613A(c)(9).
236. I.R.C. Sec. 338.
237. I.R.C. Sec. 338(g).
238. Temp. Reg. Sec. 1.338-1T.
239. I.R.C. Sec. 338(e).
240. I.R.C. Sec. 338(a)(1).
241. *Ibid.*

after the acquisition date.[242] New C Company will have a basis in the "acquired assets" equal to X Company's basis in the C Company stock, adjusted for C Company's liabilities.[243] New C Company will not be entitled to percentage depletion with respect to any oil and gas properties that are proven as of the date of the acquisition.[244] *(See Case 108 concerning the loss of percentage depletion upon the transfer of proven properties.)*

Old C Company must file a final return for the tax period ending with the acquisition date, and any tax liability resulting from the deemed sale of its assets must be included in that return.[245] Any net operating loss, percentage depletion and ITC carryovers of Old C Company will not be available to New C Company or to X Company. However, any such carryovers generally are available for use in the final tax return of Old C Company.

The use of a Section 338 election has been substantially diminished by the repeal of the *General Utilities Doctrine.* Many buyers will not be willing to pay a tax on the target company's asset appreciation to achieve a basis step-up that will provide tax benefits over a longer period of time. However, a Section 338 election may be beneficial if the target company's net operating loss and tax credits shelter the gain on the constructive sale of its assets.

Following the acquisition of its stock, New C Company may continue in existence as a subsidiary of X Company. If the stock purchase is not treated as an asset acquisition (either by an actual or a deemed election), C Company recognizes no gain or loss or recapture items as a result of the transaction. Assuming C Company was not required to share its depletable oil quantity with Operator A[246] *(see Case 110)* and its properties were not transferred to it by any business entities under common control *(see Cases 106 and 107)*,[247] it should continue to qualify for percentage depletion with respect to properties that were proven as of the date of its acquisition but subject to depletable quantity and other limitations applicable to X Company. *(See Cases 96, 106, 113 and 114.)* C Company's net operating loss (NOL), ITC carryovers and certain other tax attributes may carry over in whole or in part.[248] However, the yearly NOL use (and certain other tax attributes) is limited to the value of C Company's stock (at the date of purchase), multiplied by a published rate.[249] This rule's purpose is to limit the use of a NOL and certain other items after an ownership change or equity structure shift to the amount that could have been used by the C Company if it had sold its assets and invested the proceeds in long-term bonds.

Case 140
Charitable Contribution of a Mineral Property Interest

In 1983, Operator A (an individual) acquired for $5,000 a 50% working interest in an undeveloped property. To develop the property, he incurred intangible drilling and development costs (IDC) of $100,000 and equipment costs of $25,000. By appraisal, Operator A has determined that the fair market value of his share of the leasehold interest is $250,000 and the fair market value of his share of the equipment is $10,000. He has fully

242. I.R.C. Sec. 338(a)(2).
243. I.R.C. Sec. 338(b).
244. I.R.C. Sec. 613A(c)(9).
245. Temp. Reg. Sec. 1.338-1T(f)(2).
246. I.R.C. Sec. 613A(c)(10).
247. I.R.C. Sec. 613A(c)(9)(B)(v).
248. I.R.C. Sec. 381; I.R.C. Sec. 382.
249. I.R.C. Sec. 382(b).

depleted his basis in the leasehold, and his adjusted basis in the equipment is $6,000. Operator A wants to know the income tax consequences of a contribution of his entire interest in the property to a public charity in 1987. He plans no other contributions during the year.

Generally, the amount of a contribution is the fair market value of the property at the time of the contribution,[250] reduced by the amount of the gain that would not have been long-term capital gain if the property had been sold at its fair market value.[251] Fair market value is the price at which the property would change hands between a willing buyer and a willing seller, neither being under any compulsion to buy or sell and both having a reasonable knowledge of relevant facts.[252]

An individual's total charitable contribution deduction for any year generally is limited to 50%[253] of his adjusted gross income (AGI), without regard to any net operating loss carryback to the year.[254] However, more stringent percentage limitations apply to contributions to or for the use of certain types of charities and foundations.[255] Furthermore, certain types of property contributions are subject to additional limitations[256] and reduction in amount.[257] For example, contributions of capital-gain type property (including property used in a trade or business)[258] are subject to a deduction limitation of 30% of AGI.[259] Generally, an allowable contribution in excess of the applicable percentage limitation may be carried forward for five years and deducted subject to similar limitations.[260] *(See Case 117 for a discussion of the 65% of taxable income limitation on depletion and charitable contribution deduction interplay.)* Due to the complexities of the charitable contribution provisions, professional advice should be obtained to determine the timing and amount of any allowable deduction.

The portion of a charitable contribution of appreciated property that would give rise to capital gain if the property were sold at fair market value is an item of tax preference for alternative minimum tax (AMT) purposes.[261] Tax preference treatment generally applies to contributions in tax years beginning after December 31, 1986, although a contribution carryover from the preceding year may be affected. A tax preference item is not generated, however, to the extent an individual taxpayer elects[262] to claim a deduction for capital-gain property in an amount equal to the property's adjusted basis such that the contribution of property would be subject to the 50% of AGI limitation as opposed to 30% of AGI limitation.[263]

Operator A is entitled to a charitable contribution deduction equal to the fair market value of the contributed property, reduced by any depreciation, depletion and IDC recapture amounts.[264] If Operator A sells the property at fair market value, he would report $4,000 of depreciation recapture ($10,000 value minus $6,000 adjusted basis).[265] Assuming no allowable reduction of the IDC, Operator A would report

250. I.R.C. Sec. 170; Reg. Sec. 1.170A-1(c).
251. I.R.C. Sec. 170(e); Reg. Sec. 1.170A-4(a).
252. Reg. Sec. 1.170A-1(c)(2).
253. I.R.C. Sec. 170(b)(1)(A); Reg. Sec. 1.170A-8(b).
254. I.R.C. Sec. 170(b)(1)(F).
255. I.R.C. Sec. 170(b)(1)(B); Reg. Sec. 1.170A-8(c).
256. I.R.C. Sec. 170(b)(1)(C).
257. I.R.C. Sec. 170(e)(1)(B); I.R.C. Sec. 170(e)(3).
258. I.R.C. Sec. 170(b)(1)(C)(iv).
259. I.R.C. Sec. 170(b)(1)(C); Reg. Sec. 1.170A-8(d).
260. I.R.C. Sec. 170(b)(1)(B); I.R.C. Sec. 170(b)(1)(C)(ii); I.R.C. Sec. 170(d)(1).
261. I.R.C. Sec. 57(a)(6)(A).
262. I.R.C. Sec. 170(b)(1)(C)(iii).
263. I.R.C. Sec. 57(a)(6)(B).
264. I.R.C. Sec. 170(e)(1).
265. I.R.C. Sec. 1245.

$100,000 of IDC recapture.[266] *(See Case 131 for calculation of IDC recapture on the sale of an oil and gas property.)* Since the property was placed in service before December 31, 1986, Operator A would not report depletion recapture. *(See Case 131.)* Consequently, his contribution amount is $156,000, calculated as $260,000 ($250,000 fair market value of the leasehold plus $10,000 fair market value of equipment) minus $104,000 ($4,000 depreciation recapture plus $100,000 IDC recapture). Operator A may deduct this amount, limited to 30% of his adjusted gross income.[267] Operator A has an item of tax preference in the amount of $150,000 ($260,000 - $6,000 (adjusted basis) - $104,000 (ordinary income amount)).

Alternatively, Operator A may elect to reduce the allowable deduction by the amount of gain that would have been long-term capital gain and deduct the reduced amount, limited to 50% of his adjusted gross income.[268] The amount of deduction under this elective provision essentially is reduced to the donor's basis in the property.[269] If this election is made, the contribution deduction will not give rise to a tax preference item.

If Operator A's property is held by a partnership in which he owns a 50% interest, the contribution of the partnership interest will result in the same charitable deduction because he will recognize the same amount of ordinary income upon the sale of his partnership interest.[270] Operator A may be required to recapture investment tax credit attributable to the equipment.[271]

Generally, no deduction is allowed for a contribution of a partial interest, other than an undivided interest, in property.[272] The Internal Revenue Service (IRS) has ruled[273] that an owner of a working interest may contribute a carved-out royalty or net profits interest and deduct the fair market value of that interest. The IRS viewed the carved-out net profits interest as a "property" separate from the underlying working interest. *(See Case 65.)* However, the IRS has ruled that no deduction is allowed for a contribution of land if the taxpayer retains the mineral rights.[274] A deduction was allowed for a contribution of land and related royalty interest even though the working interest owned by a related entity was not contributed.[275] These rulings do not address whether state law considers mineral interests to be property interests separate and distinct from the surface interests.

Individuals and certain corporations generally must obtain a qualified written appraisal of the fair market value of any property contributed if the claimed value exceeds $5,000.[276] Failure to meet the appraisal and related documentation rules may result in a complete disallowance of the deduction. Substantial penalties also may be assessed for valuation overstatements.[277]

Case 141
Production Payment Retained in a Leasing Transaction

Operator A owns the entire working interest in a lease acquired in 1980 for $50,000. On June 30, 1987, Operator A assigns the property to

266. I.R.C. Sec. 1254.
267. I.R.C. Sec. 170(b)(1)(C)(i).
268. I.R.C. Sec. 170(b)(1)(C)(iii); Reg. Sec. 1.170A-8(d)(2).
269. General Explanation of the Tax Reform Act of 1986, prepared by the Staff of the Joint Committee on Taxation, p. 179.
270. I.R.C. Sec. 751; I.R.C. Sec. 170(e)(1).
271. Reg. Sec. 1.47-2(a).
272. I.R.C. Sec. 170(f)(3).
273. IRS Letter Ruling 8417058; I.R.C. Sec. 170(f)(3); Reg. Sec. 1.170A-7(b)(1)(i).
274. Rev. Rul. 76-331, 1976-2 C.B. 52; IRS Letter Ruling 8429021.
275. IRS Letter Ruling 8430014.
276. Temp. Reg. Sec. 1.170A-13T(c).
277. I.R.C. Sec. 6659.

Operator B, retaining a one-sixteenth overriding royalty, in consideration for $75,000 plus an additional $100,000 payable solely from 50% of the first production from the property. The $100,000 amount is to be increased by an interest-like calculation, computed by reference to a designated bank's prime interest rate.

A production payment retained in a leasing or subleasing transaction constitutes an economic interest in the property to the lessor, and subsequent payments thereon are treated as an installment bonus paid by the lessee.[278]

In the year of receipt, Operator A will treat the $75,000 lease bonus paid by Operator B as ordinary income subject to cost depletion. *(See Case 98.)* If production is not realized, any depletion may be required to be restored to income. *(See Case 127.)* Operator A is not required to report the fair market value of the retained production payment as income in 1987, even though he may be required to do so for other types of installment bonuses.[279]

When mineral production is realized, Operator B will include in his gross income the proceeds from the sale of produced minerals paid to Operator A in satisfaction of the production payment (including interest).[280] However, Operator B must exclude from gross income from the property for purposes of calculating percentage depletion an allocable portion of the production payment.[281] *(See Cases 87 and 88.)* Operator B will increase his tax basis in the property as those payments are made to Operator A.[282] A contrary position may be available to Operator B. The retention of a production payment in a leasing transaction is similar to an indebtedness secured only by the property and, in accordance with a Supreme Court decision,[283] it appears that Operator B may include the total amount of the production payment as basis for computing cost depletion. *(See Case 83.)* However, if the value of the property securing the indebtedness is not sufficient to pay off the production payment, the courts may view the production payment as too speculative to characterize it as a "true" loan for this purpose.[284]

Because a production payment retained in a leasing transaction is treated as an economic interest, amounts received by Operator A in satisfaction of the production payment will constitute ordinary income subject to depletion.[285]

Operator A should not be considered to have made a "disposition" of the property and will not be required to recapture any intangible drilling and development costs or depletion incurred before the assignment. *(See Case 131.)*

Although not considered in this factual situation, the effect of windfall profit tax on production payment transactions is uncertain. *(See Cases 86, 88 and 230 for a further discussion of this issue.)*

The provisions of the production payment should be drafted carefully to meet the qualification in the regulations[286] requiring the expected economic life (at the time of

---

278. I.R.C. Sec. 636(c); Reg. Sec. 1.636-2(b).
279. Cowden v. Comm'r, 289 F.2d 20 (5th Cir. 1961), 7 AFTR2d 1160, 61-1 USTC 9382; Alice G. K. Kleberg, 43 B.T.A. 277 (1941).
280. Reg. Sec. 1.636-2(a).
281. Reg. Sec. 1.613-2(c)(5)(ii).
282. Reg. Sec. 1.636-2(a).
283. Crane v. Comm'r, 331 U.S. 1 (1947), 35 AFTR 776, 47-1 USTC 9217.
284. Gibson Products Co. v. U.S., 637 F.2d 1041 (5th Cir. 1981), 47 AFTR2d 81-863, 81-1 USTC 9213; Brountas v. Comm'r, 692 F.2d 152 (1st Cir. 1982), 50 AFTR2d 82-5900, 82-2 USTC 9626; CRC Corp. v. Comm'r, 693 F.2d 281 (3d Cir. 1982), 50 AFTR2d 82-6105, 82-2 USTC 9677.
285. Reg. Sec. 1.636-2(b).
286. Reg. Sec. 1.636-3.

its creation) of the production payment to be shorter than the economic life of the burdened mineral property. If it is reasonable to expect, based on the facts known at the time of the assignment, that the retained production payment will not pay out, the production payment retained by Operator A is tantamount to an overriding royalty.[287] *(See Case 144.)* If the retained production payment is treated as an overriding royalty, Operator A will realize ordinary income subject to depletion on amounts received from Operator B in satisfaction of the production payment only when those amounts actually are received. Operator B will not include in gross income the amount received from the sale of the mineral production attributable to Operator A's overriding royalty and, accordingly, will not be required to capitalize those payments as leasehold cost. *(See Case 135 concerning the use of a "savings" clause to assure qualification as a production payment.)*

Case 142
Sale of a Retained Production Payment

> **Operator A owns and has developed an oil and gas lease. He has an adjusted tax basis of $75,000 for depreciable property and $40,000 for depletable property. On June 1, 1987, Operator A transfers the lease to Operator B for $150,000, retaining a production payment of $850,000 payable out of 80% of gross revenue applicable to the interest in the property assigned. Operator A subsequently sells the retained production payment to Investor L for $750,000, the unpaid balance at that time.**

The retained production payment is considered a purchase money mortgage loan and, therefore, is not treated as an economic interest in the property.[288] *(See Case 143.)* Thus, Operator A realizes income of $885,000 on the original transfer, the sum of the cash received ($150,000) and the amount of the production payment ($850,000) minus his basis in the property ($115,000). A portion of the income will be recharacterized as interest income under the original-issue discount (OID) rules discussed below. A portion of the income may be characterized as ordinary income due to depreciation, depletion or intangible drilling and development costs (IDC) recapture. *(See Case 131.)* Operator A may treat the disposition as qualifying for installment reporting. *(See Case 138.)* Accelerated cost recovery (depreciation) recapture must be reported as taxable income in the year of sale regardless of the timing of the receipt of installment payments.[289] Even if the amount of the production payment is based on units produced rather than on a fixed-dollar amount, the transaction still will qualify for installment reporting.[290]

Generally, the OID rules apply to obligations issued in exchange for property.[291] These complex rules divide the total amount payable on a debt obligation into principal and interest components based on compound-interest concepts,[292] using interest rates defined by the statute.[293] In this case, the rate used to compute imputed interest cannot exceed 9% since the debt instrument (i.e., the production payment) does not exceed $2.8 million. *(See Case 143 for a discussion of how the OID rules apply to production payments retained on the sale of a developed oil and gas lease.)*

287. U.S. v. Morgan, 321 F.2d 781 (5th Cir. 1963), 12 AFTR2d 5404, 63-2 USTC 9653; U.S. v. Foster, 324 F.2d 702 (5th Cir. 1963), 12 AFTR2d 5945, 63-2 USTC 9822; Castle v. Comm'r (D.C. Tex. 1971), 28 AFTR2d 71-6138, 72-1 USTC 9123; IRS Letter Ruling 8322003 (Technical Advice Memorandum).
288. I.R.C. Sec. 636(b).
289. I.R.C. Sec. 453(i).
290. Temp. Reg. Sec. 15a.453-1(c).
291. I.R.C. Sec. 1274.
292. I.R.C. Sec. 1274(b).
293. I.R.C. Sec. 1274(d); I.R.C. Sec. 1274A(a); Prop. Reg. Sec. 1.1274-3(e)(1)(ii).

If Operator A elects to report the sale of the property on the installment basis, the sale of the production payment to Investor L will constitute the disposition of an installment obligation by Operator A, and the remainder of the deferred gain must be reported in the year of disposition of the production payment.[294]

If Operator A reports all the gain in the year the property was sold by having elected not to report on the installment method, gain or loss will be reported on the disposition of the production payment to the extent there is a difference between the amount realized ($750,000) and the basis of the production payment when it is sold. Any amount previously recognized as income under the OID rules should increase the basis of the production payment for these purposes.[295]

As discussed in Section IV, Operator B will not be entitled to percentage depletion on production from the lease because the transaction constitutes a disqualifying transfer. *(See Case 108.)*

Case 143
Developed Lease Assigned for Cash With Production Payment Retained

> **Operator A owns an oil and gas lease that he developed and in which he has an adjusted tax basis of $50,000 for depreciable property and $40,000 for depletable property. On October 1, 1987, Operator A transfers the lease to Operator B for $75,000 cash, retaining a production payment of $975,000, payable out of 75% of the first oil or gas produced. It is estimated that the production payment will pay out in four to five years and that its fair market value is $785,000. At the time of the sale, the fair market values are $50,000 for the depreciable property and $810,000 for the leasehold interests.**

Operator A is considered to have made a sale of the depreciable property and all the oil and gas rights because he has not retained a continuing interest in the oil and gas lease. The retained production payment is treated as a purchase money mortgage loan and does not qualify as an economic interest in the property.[296] Production proceeds applied to Operator A's production payment are considered payments on the loan by Operator B and are depletable income to B, subject to the limitations on percentage depletion (such as the transfer of proven property rules) set forth in Section IV. The costs attributable to producing the minerals used to satisfy the production payment are deductible by Operator B in the year paid or accrued.[297] The excess of payments to Operator A over the principal portion (determined under the original-issue discount (OID) rules discussed below) of the production payment will be treated as interest income to Operator A and interest expense to Operator B.

Original-Issue Discount Considerations

Since a production payment issued for property is subject to the OID rules,[298] the interest expense (income) of the parties must be accounted for on an economic accrual basis.[299] Under the contingent payment rules (discussed below), the actual amount of

294. I.R.C. Sec. 453B(a).
295. Prop. Reg. Sec. 1.1271-1(c); I.R.C. Sec. 1271(d); I.R.C. Sec. 453B(b).
296. I.R.C. Sec. 636(b).
297. Reg. Sec. 1.636-1(a)(3), Example 1.
298. I.R.C. Sec. 1275(d); Prop. Reg. Sec. 1.1275-4(a); I.R.C. Sec. 1274; Prop. Reg. Sec. 1.1275-4(c).
299. I.R.C. Sec. 163(e); I.R.C. Sec. 1272.

interest under the OID rules will be a function of the timing of the discharge of the production payment through oil and gas production. The proposed OID regulations do not expressly deal with production payment transactions, but it appears that the Internal Revenue Service (IRS) intends such principles to apply, notwithstanding the production payment regulations' reference to Section 483.[300] The fact that payments under the production payment agreement are dependent on production from the property leads to difficult mechanical and administrative calculations on the timing of the realization of deemed interest income (expense) treated as OID.

The proposed regulations likely will characterize a production payment as a debt instrument that provides for contingent payments since typically the holder must look solely to production for repayment.[301] The contingent payment rules applicable to property transactions divide each payment into principal and interest. Each payment is treated as: (1) a payment of principal to the extent of the present value of the payment, determined by discounting the payment from the date it becomes fixed to the date the debt is issued and (2) a payment of interest to the extent such payment exceeds the amount treated as principal.[302] The amount treated as principal, however, cannot exceed the fixed issue price of the debt instrument. Any additional payments will be treated as consisting entirely of interest.[303] The present value of each payment is discounted, using a test rate defined in the regulations. The test rate for debt instruments of $2.8 million or less is the lower of: (1) the applicable federal rate (AFR)[304] or (2) 9% compounded semiannually.[305] The AFR to be used is the rate in effect on the date of sale based on a term beginning on the date the overall debt instrument is issued and ending on the date the contingent payment is due.[306] The amount of interest calculated for each period must be included in income by Operator A and deducted by Operator B in the year the payment becomes fixed. For production payments, the year the payment becomes fixed would presumably mean the year the oil is produced.

Assuming that the following payments are due to Operator A attributable to the 1987 production and an AFR using monthly compounding of 8%, the interest deemed accrued for 1987 is as follows:

Month of Production	Total Payment Due to Operator A	Present Value of Payment (Principal)*	Interest Portion
October	$25,000	$24,834	$166
November	25,000	24,670	330
December	25,000	24,507	493
Totals	$75,000	$74,011	$989

* Applying an 8% AFR × 1/12 = a .6667% monthly interest rate applied to the monthly accrual periods (i.e., payments in oil and gas industry traditionally made on a monthly basis).

Operator A would report $989 of interest income, and Operator B would report $989 of interest expense for 1987 under the contingent payment rules. Presumably, Operators A and B must calculate the interest accrued for 1987 based on production in

300. Reg. Sec. 1.636-1(a)(1)(ii); Reg. Sec. 1.483-1(e)(1).
301. Prop. Reg. Sec. 1.1275-4(b): Prop. Reg. Sec. 1.1275-4(c).
302. Prop. Reg. Sec. 1.1275-4(c)(3)(ii).
303. *Ibid.*
304. Prop. Reg. Sec. 1.1274-6(a).
305. Prop. Reg. Sec. 1.1274-3(e)(1)(ii).
306. Prop. Reg. Sec. 1.1275-4(c)(3)(iii)(B).

1987, notwithstanding the month or two lag in receiving cash from production, which is typical in the oil and gas industry.

The monthly portions of the payments that constitute interest and principal, respectively, on the production payment will depend on the future amounts of the monthly payment and the applicable required AFR.

Operator A's Gain Computation

If Operator A does not elect to use the installment method, the regulations provide complex rules on how to determine the amount realized for computing gain on the sale of the property.[307] If Operator A uses the cash method of accounting, then the amount realized in the year of sale includes the fair market value of the installment obligation (i.e. the production payment) and gain would be computed as shown below. Operator A should allocate the sales price based on relative fair market values. Therefore, $50,000 of the sales price is allocated to depreciable property, and the remaining $810,000 is allocated to the leasehold interest. *(See Case 154 for a discussion of possible additional rules concerning sale proceeds allocation.)*

Cash received	$ 75,000
Production payment	785,000
Total sales price	$860,000

	Depreciable Property	Lease-hold Interest
Sales price	$ 50,000	$810,000
Basis	$(50,000)	(40,000)
Gain taxable to Operator A	$ —	$770,000

In contrast, if Operator A does not elect to use the installment method and uses the accrual method of accounting, then the amount realized in the year of sale includes the total amount payable under the production payment excluding amounts treated as interest under the OID rules discussed above. However, since under these rules the amount of interest cannot be determined until each payment under the production payment becomes fixed, an approximation of the amount of internal interest implicit in the transaction may have to be used to determine the gain in the year of the sale. The gain would then be adjusted in later years when the actual amount of interest under the OID rules was determined. By discounting the production payment in this manner, the amount realized should approximate the fair market value of the production payment. However, based on the rate required by the OID rules, this may not be the case. Clarification of the interaction of the regulations dealing with electing not to use the installment method and the OID rules must await further guidance from future regulations or other pronouncements.

If Operator A had realized a gain on the equipment, any recapture of prior accelerated cost recovery or depreciation deduction would have been reported in the year of sale regardless of whether any cash had been received. *(See Case 138.)*

307. Temp. Reg. Sec. 15a.453-1(d)(2)(ii).

A portion of the gain on the leasehold may be taxed as ordinary income as a result of the recapture of intangible drilling and development costs and depletion. *(See Case 131.)*

Operator A may report the gain on the sale of the lease on the installment basis because the production payment is treated as if it were a purchase money mortgage loan.[308] The regulations provide special rules for calculation of gain recognition in the event of a contingent selling price,[309] for example, an adjustment to the sales price based on actual production after the sale. If the agreement provides for neither a maximum selling price nor a fixed period for payment, the installment note may be recharacterized as a royalty.[310] In this case, a maximum selling price does exist since the production payment is limited to $975,000.[311] The regulations provide that where a stated maximum selling price does exist, the maximum amount is used as the selling price in performing the necessary computations under the installment method.[312] The stated maximum selling price in this case is $1,050,000 ($75,000 plus $975,000). However, since a portion of each payment on the production payment will be recharacterized as interest income under the OID rules,[313] the maximum selling price will have to be redetermined each time a payment on the production payment becomes fixed. The regulations provide that when a payment is recharacterized as interest, the maximum selling price (and thus selling price, contract price and gross profit ratio under the installment method) must be recomputed.[314] Therefore, in applying the installment method to a production payment the gain computation must be adjusted each tax year to consider amounts treated as interest under the OID rules. Operator A also may be required to restore a part of any investment credit previously claimed on the equipment.

Operator B's Basis Computations

Operator B should divide his $1,050,000 purchase price ($75,000 cash plus $975,000 production payment) between depreciable equipment and depletable leasehold cost in the ratio of their respective fair market values.[315] However, since the production payment is potentially subject to the OID rules, a portion of the amount paid by Operator B will be characterized as interest expense.[316] Since under the OID rules it is not possible to determine the amount of interest expense and principal until each payment on the production payment becomes fixed, the proposed regulations dealing with contingent payments due within a fixed period of time will not allow Operator B to include any amount in depletable basis attributable to payments on the production payment until a principal payment is deemed to be made under the OID rules.[317] Arguably, Operator B should be allowed to include an amount in basis when the production payment is created. The resolution of the computation problem must be clarified in final regulations. *(See Case 154 for a discussion of possible additional rules concerning allocation of purchase price.)* The property will be proven, so Operator B wil not be entitled to percentage depletion. *(See Case 108.)*

308. Reg. Sec. 1.636-1(c)(4).
309. Temp. Reg. Sec. 15a.453-1(c).
310. Temp. Reg. Sec. 15a.453-1(c)(4).
311. Temp. Reg. Sec. 15a.453-1(c)(2).
312. Temp. Reg. Sec. 15a.453-1(c)(2)(i)(A).
313. Prop. Reg. Sec. 1.1275-4(c)(3)(ii).
314. Temp. Reg. Sec. 15a.453-1(c)(2)(ii).
315. Clifford Hemphill, 25 B.T.A. 1351 (1932); C.D. Johnson Lumber Corp., 12 T.C. 348 (1949); Estate of O. W. Killam, 33 T.C. 345 (1959).
316. Prop. Reg. Sec. 1.1275-4(c)(3)(ii)(B); I.R.C. Sec. 1275(d).
317. Prop. Reg. Sec. 1.1275-4(d)(2)(ii)(B).

The Supreme Court has held[318] that the outstanding balance of a nonrecourse note must be included as an amount realized upon disposition of the mortgaged property. Consequently, if Operator B subsequently sells the working interest, the unpaid balance of the production payment must be included as part of his sales proceeds for purposes of determining gain or loss.

Sublease Considerations

If, based on the facts known at the time of the assignment, it is reasonable to expect that the retained production payment will not pay out and the payments will continue for the entire term of the lease or the productive life of the field, the interest retained is tantamount to an overriding royalty.[319] The transaction then will be treated as a sublease rather than as a sale, and the tax consequences will be significantly different from those discussed here. *(See Cases 125, 141 and 144.)* However, when it was shown that estimated reserves produced under existing operations were insufficient to pay out the retained production payment, but sufficient reserves could be recovered by a successful program of pressure maintenance through water injection so that the production payment would be satisfied before the exhaustion of the property, the Tax Court found that a production payment, rather than a royalty, had been retained. Payout of the production payment need be only reasonably capable of determination and need not be certain.[320] *(See Case 135 for a further discussion of production payment definition issues.)*

If Operator A leases rather than sells the property to Operator B by retaining an overriding royalty interest in lieu of the $75,000 cash payment,[321] Operator B will treat the payments on Operator A's retained production payment as payments on an installment lease bonus. *(See Case 141.)*

Other Production Payment Considerations

Production payments that do not commence until the working interest owner recovers a specified sum or until the primary production payment pays out are termed *deferred* or *secondary* production payments. Production payments that are payable out of a *variable* percentage of production are called variable production payments. The hybrid nature of these production payments does not change the tax consequences of the transaction by which they are created. They are treated as purchase money mortgage loans when they are retained on the sale of a mineral property.

An exception to the general rule of mortgage loan treatment exists for a production payment carved out for exploration or development of the mineral property.[322] *(See Case 150.)*

---

318. Comm'r v. Tufts, 103 S. Ct. 1826 (1983), 51 AFTR2d 83-1132, 83-1 USTC 9328.
319. U.S. v. Morgan, 321 F.2d 781 (5th Cir. 1963), 12 AFTR2d 5404, 63-2 USTC 9653; U.S. v. Foster, 324 F.2d 702 (5th Cir. 1963), 12 AFTR2d 5945, 63-2 USTC 9822; Castle v. Comm'r (D.C. Tex. 1971), 28 AFTR2d 71-6138, 72-1 USTC 9123; IRS Letter Ruling 8322003 (Technical Advice Memorandum).
320. Howard Glenn, 39 T.C. 427 (1962).
321. Reg. Sec. 1.636-2(b).
322. I.R.C. Sec. 636(a).

Case 144
Producing and Nonproducing Leases Assigned for Cash With Overriding Royalty Retained

> Operator A owns the full working interest in three oil and gas leases. He has drilled one productive well on one of the leases; the other leases have not been drilled. Operator A has a tax basis of $50,000 in the equipment, $3,000 of depletable tax basis in the producing lease and $10,000 of tax basis ($5,000 each) in the two nonproducing leases. Operator A assigns the three leases, subject to a one-eighth overriding royalty, to C Company for $250,000 cash.

Operator A has made a sublease by retaining a continuing economic interest in the minerals free of the burdens of development and operation.[323] The retention of a net profits interest instead of a royalty payable out of gross production also will be treated as a sublease.[324]

In leasing transactions, the courts[325] have held that cash consideration in excess of the unrecovered tax basis of the depreciable equipment is tantamount to a sale of the equipment at its tax basis, with the excess of cash consideration over the tax basis of the equipment representing a lease bonus or advance royalty. The Internal Revenue Service (IRS) has ruled that no loss is allowable in a subleasing transaction when the cash received is less than the unrecovered tax basis of the equipment assigned.[326] The ruling states that the excess of the unrecovered tax basis of the equipment over the cash received represents additional cost of the retained royalty and is returnable to the sublessor only as depletion. However, this ruling has been declared obsolete, and, therefore, it is not clear what position the IRS now will take. Some courts have held that depletion allowances are not applicable to depreciable costs and that a deduction is allowable for the excess of the unrecovered tax basis of the equipment over the cash consideration received.[327] Although those cases involved a cash consideration of less than the unrecovered tax basis of the equipment, they also involved the seller's reservation of a production payment before enactment of the Tax Reform Act of 1969. *(See Case 133 for a discussion of potential conflict with the purchase price allocation rules of the Tax Reform Act of 1986.)*

In 1983, the IRS held in a private letter ruling[328] that, even though no cash may be received, the transferor of a working interest must allocate the fair market value of a retained net profits interest between the transferred working interest and tangible equipment. The transferor must recognize taxable gain to the extent the portion of the fair market value of the net profits interest allocable to the equipment exceeds the transferor's basis in the equipment. This ruling does not mention, and clearly is in conflict with, court decisions dealing specifically with similar transactions[329] as well as longstanding principles applicable to the taxation of leasing transactions.

Assuming the $250,000 consideration is allocable (based on relative fair market values) equally among the three leases, Operator A recognizes ordinary income equal

323. Palmer v. Bender, 287 U.S. 551 (1933), 11 AFTR 1106, 3 USTC 1026; Rev. Rul. 69-352, 1969-1 C.B. 34.
324. Gray v. Comm'r, 183 F.2d 329 (5th Cir. 1950), 39 AFTR 750, 50-2 USTC 9386; Weinert v. Comm'r, 294 F.2d 750 (5th Cir. 1961), 8 AFTR2d 5417, 61-2 USTC 9644.
325. Louisiana Land and Exploration Co., 6 T.C. 172 (1946).
326. Rev. Rul. 53-35, 1955-1 C.B. 286.
327. Choate v. Comm'r, 324 U.S. 1 (1945), 33 AFTR 297, 45-1 USTC 9153; Kline v. Comm'r, 268 F.2d 854 (9th Cir. 1959), 4 AFTR2d 5211, 59-2 USTC 9563; Megert v. Campbell (N.D. Tex. 1963), 12 AFTR2d 5913, 63-2 USTC 9800.
328. IRS Letter Ruling 8317043.
329. Louisiana Land and Exploration Co.; Kline; Palmer; Thomas v. Perkins, 301 U.S. 655 (1937), 19 AFTR 538, 37-2 USTC 9315.

to the $200,000 sublease income received, representing the excess of cash consideration ($250,000) over his tax basis ($50,000) in the equipment. He may be entitled to cost depletion.[330] *(See Case 98.)*

C Company will not be entitled to percentage depletion on the lease that was productive at the time of transfer nor on the two undrilled leases if they are considered proven properties. *(See Cases 108 and 109.)*

Although a subleasing transaction does not result in the recapture of intangible drilling and development costs,[331] a subsequent disposition of the retained overriding royalty may result in recapture.[332] Additionally, depletion recapture may result if the property was placed in service after 1986.[333] *(See Case 131.)*

Case 145
Lease Assigned for Development With Limited-Variable Overriding Royalty and Deferred Working Interest Retained

> **Operator A owns an oil and gas lease on which he has drilled and partially equipped two shut-in wells. He estimates that an additional $1 million of expenditures will be necessary to complete the two shut-in wells and fully develop the lease; however, he does not have sufficient capital to undertake the project. Operator A also wants to participate in the income from the lease as soon as production is established. Operator B agrees to complete the two shut-in wells and develop the lease for an interest equivalent to one-half the future net revenue from the property. Pursuant to their agreement, Operator A conveys the lease to Operator B, subject to a limited overriding royalty payable out of 50% of gross income from the lease during the period Operator B is developing the lease. As soon as the development work is completed or when Operator B has expended $1 million, the royalty then is payable out of 45% of the net income from the lease. When Operator B has recouped all his costs of completing the two shut-in wells and development expenditures from the net income from the lease, for a 30-day period Operator A has an option to convert the royalty to an undivided 50% of the working interest. The agreement provides that an election will be made to be excluded from the partnership provisions of the Internal Revenue Code.**

The purpose of this rather complex arrangement is to provide Operator A with a share of the income when production is established, to encourage Operator B to develop the properties as expeditiously as possible and to allow Operator B to acquire a 50% interest in the lease without incurring a substantial leasehold cost that may have only limited tax benefit to him.

An operator may deduct intangible drilling and development costs (IDC) only to the extent of his operating interest on any drilling or development project undertaken for the grant or assignment of a fraction of the operating rights.[334] Operator B will own all the working interest during the time he is recouping his costs, will receive all the working (operating) interest income and should be entitled to all the working interest deductions, including IDC and depletion, during the payout period.

330. Collums v. U.S., 480 F. Supp. 864 (D.C. Wyo. 1979), 45 AFTR2d 80-751, 80-1 USTC 9203.
331. Prop. Reg. Sec. 1.1254-1(a)(4).
332. Prop. Reg. Sec. 1.1254-1(a)(3).
333. I.R.C. Sec. 1254(a)(1).
334. Reg. Sec. 1.612-4(a)(3); Rev. Rul. 70-336, 1970-1 C.B. 145.

The Internal Revenue Service (IRS) has ruled that payout computations must be made on a property-by-property basis.[335] The agreement between Operators A and B should define payout accordingly. The payout period of the new wells may be shortened due to the production from the two previously drilled wells. As long as the wells are located on a single unit of property, it appears that Operator B's deduction will not be jeopardized. *(See Case 46.)*

A portion of the royalty retained by Operator A may be a production payment even though the transaction is a sublease by Operator A. The production payment portion of the royalty is that portion attributable to the rate of the royalty that exceeds the lowest possible rate at any later time.[336] The IRS has ruled that no part of a variable royalty based on prior production levels is a production payment.[337] In this case, the excess of the royalty rate of 50% of gross income from the lease over 45% of net income from the lease during the period Operator B is developing the lease will be treated as a production payment. Because Operator A, the lessor, has retained a production payment in a leasing transaction, the production payment will be treated as an economic interest in the mineral in place and the receipts in discharge of the production payment will constitute ordinary income subject to depletion.[338] Therefore, Operator A will report as ordinary income, subject to depletion, all proceeds from the limited-variable overriding royalty.[339] Percentage depletion may not be allowable to Operator B if the property is proven. *(See Case 108.)* Operator B will be allowed to exclude from gross income only the amount of the variable royalty applicable to the amount of 45% of net income from the lease. The excess of 50% of gross income from the lease over 45% of net income from the lease during the period the royalty is payable at the rate of 50% of gross income must be reported as working interest income by Operator B.

Operator B's payments of these excess amounts to Operator A are treated as installment bonus payments that Operator B must capitalize as leasehold cost.[340] Because Operator B treats the payments as lease bonus payments, he should exclude a pro-rata portion of those payments from his depletable gross income each year for purposes of calculating his percentage depletion. *(See Cases 83 and 141.)*

Case 146
Exchange of Working Interest for Working Interest

Operator A exchanges in 1987 the working interest in a nonproductive oil and gas lease, in which he has a tax basis of $25,000, for the working interest in a productive oil and gas lease owned by Operator B. Operator B has an adjusted tax basis of $20,000 for cost recovery (depreciable) property and $10,000 for depletable property in the lease he gives up in the exchange.

The exchange of a working interest for another working interest generally is an exchange of properties of like kind. The equipment on an oil and gas lease, although not permanently affixed, generally is considered under local law to be an improvement of real estate and like property to the working interest.

335. Rev. Rul. 80-109, 1980-1 C.B. 129.
336. Reg. Sec. 1.636-3(a)(2).
337. Rev. Rul. 76-34, 1976-1 C.B. 177.
338. Reg. Sec. 1.636-2(b).
339. Reg. Sec. 1.636-2(c).
340. Reg. Sec. 1.636-2(a);Reg. Sec. 1.636-2(c).

The exchange in this case involves property of like kind, and Operator A recognizes no gain or loss.[341] Operator A's $25,000 tax basis in the property given up should be allocated between the working interest and the equipment on the property acquired in proportion to their relative fair market values.

Although Operator B also has exchanged property of a like kind, he may be subject to ordinary income recapture because he has exchanged equipment (a cost recovery or depreciable asset) for an interest in a nonproductive lease (not a cost recovery or depreciable asset).[342] Operator B must allocate the value of the nonproductive lease received between the equipment and the leasehold interest given up in proportion to their respective values. If the amount allocated to the equipment given up is in excess of Operator B's adjusted tax basis, the excess is taxable as ordinary income to the extent of cost recovery deductions or depreciation allowed or allowable on the equipment.[343]

Operator B's tax basis in the nonproductive lease received in the exchange is equal to the sum of his tax basis in the lease and the equipment given up, plus any gain recognized.[344]

The production from the property transferred by Operator B will not qualify after the exchange for percentage depletion because Operator B has transferred a proven property. (*See Case 108.*)

Exchanges also may result in recognition of ordinary income because of the recapture of intangible drilling and development costs (IDC) and depletion (*see Case 131*). Although possibly not consistent with Congressional intent, the proposed regulations provide that the amount of IDC recapture is limited to the amount of gain recognized by reference to Sections 1031 and 1033 determined without regard to the IDC recapture provisions.[345]

According to proposed regulations, the transferee of an oil or gas property succeeds to any potential recapture of IDC incurred by the transferor, to the extent not reported as ordinary income by the transferor, as a result of the exchange.[346] Consequently, Operator A should consider this potential "taint" in his negotiation of the exchange. In the absence of regulations, the treatment of depletion recapture on properties placed in service after 1986 is unclear.

If Operators A and B both exchange only nonproductive leases, no gain or loss will be recognized by either party.

However, if both exchange productive leases with equipment, either Operator A or B may recognize ordinary income from accelerated cost recovery or depreciation recapture to the extent the value of equipment given up exceeds the value of equipment received and the difference is made up by the value of the leasehold interest received,[347] limited to the cost recovery or depreciation previously allowed or allowable on the equipment given up in the exchange.[348]

In exchanges of productive leases, the leasehold interests and the interests in equipment sometimes are exchanged separately. When this occurs, gain is recognized on each exchange only to the extent of other property or money received. The tax basis of

341. I.R.C. Sec. 1031(a).
342. I.R.C. Sec. 1245(a)(3); I.R.C. Sec. 1245(a)(5).
343. I.R.C. Sec. 1245(b)(4); Reg. Sec. 1.1245-4(d).
344. I.R.C. Sec. 1245(c); Reg. Sec. 1.1245-5; I.R.C. Sec. 1031(d).
345. Prop. Reg. Sec. 1.1254-2(d).
346. Prop. Reg. Sec. 1.1254-4(d)(1).
347. Reg. Sec. 1.1245-4(d)(4); Reg. Sec. 1.1245-4(d)(1).
348. I.R.C. Sec. 1245(a)(1).

each type of property received is equivalent to the tax basis of the corresponding type of property given up, increased by any gain recognized and decreased by any money or the value of any nonqualifying property received.[349]

If any exchange of oil and gas properties involves tangible property on which an investment credit was allowable, all or a part of that credit may be subject to recapture if the exchange occurs before the end of the holding period anticipated in the determination of that investment credit.[350]

The like-kind exchange provisions generally do not apply to exchanges of partnership interests.[351] The provisions prohibiting like-kind exchange treatment for partnership interests do not specifically address potential application to exchanges of interests in ventures for which the participants elect[352] not to be subject to the partnership provisions. However, in comments introducing the Tax Reform Act of 1984, a senator specifically stated[353] that the prohibition is not intended to apply to exchanges of those interests. These comments were intended to clarify Congressional intent. Regulations may be necessary to clarify this issue.

Case 147
Exchange of Royalty for Production Payment

During 1987, Lessor R exchanges a producing royalty interest with Operator L for a production payment that Operator L had retained upon a prior sale of his property during 1980.

A production payment retained on the sale of a mineral property is treated as a purchase money mortgage loan on the property and not as an economic interest.[354] Notes and other evidences of indebtedness are excluded specifically from the type of property that can be exchanged without the recognition of gain or loss.[355] Accordingly, the exchange of the royalty interest for the retained production payment is a taxable transaction on which gain or loss will be recognized for both parties.

The gain or loss to Operator L is the difference between his adjusted tax basis in the production payment and the fair market value of the royalty at the time of the exchange. If Operator L's 1980 sale was an installment sale, Operator L will be treated as having disposed of the installment obligation (production payment), and the deferred gain will be triggered.[356] Lessor R's gain or loss is the difference between his adjusted tax basis in the royalty and the fair market value of the production payment at the time of the exchange.

The prohibition against characterizing production payments as economic interests in property is significant in determining the proper tax treatment of the receipts. Subsequent receipts by Lessor R under the production payment are not ordinary income subject to depletion. Instead, they represent a return of principal and interest income to Lessor R as they did to Operator L when he owned the production payment. *(See Case 142 for a discussion of original-issue discount implications.)* Amounts applied to the production payment constitute ordinary income subject to

349. E. C. Laster, 43 B.T.A. 159 (1940); I.R.C Sec. 1033(d).
350. I.R.C. Sec. 47.
351. I.R.C. Sec. 1031(a).
352. I.R.C. Sec. 761(a).
353. Comments of Senator Dole contained in *Congressional Record*, Volume 130, No. 90 p.S 8410, June 27, 1984.
354. I.R.C. Sec. 636(b).
355. I.R.C. Sec. 1031(a); Reg. Sec. 1.1031(a)-1(a).
356. I.R.C. Sec. 453B(a).

depletion to the owner of the property from whose interest the production payment was retained.

Subsequent receipts by Operator L under the royalty will be ordinary income subject to cost depletion. He will compute the cost depletion by reference to the value of the royalty interest established at the time of the exchange. The income from the royalty production will not qualify for percentage depletion because the royalty was a proven property when transferred. *(See Case 108.)*

The exchange of royalty interests, working interests, fee interests, unlimited surface rights, suburban real estate, etc., that are rights extending over the life of the property for any type of real estate rights extending over the life of a property is considered to be tax free if the properties involved either are held for investment or used in a trade or business.[357] *(However, see Case 131.)* The exchange of a personal residence for a royalty or working interest is a taxable exchange because a residence is neither held for investment nor used in a trade or business. It should be noted, however, that one district court[358] has stated that an exchange of a lease for an overriding royalty probably will be a taxable transaction.

With several judges dissenting, the Tax Court[359] ruled that tax-free treatment is allowed even though property received in a like-kind exchange is contributed immediately to a partnership for a general partnership interest. The like-kind exchange provision generally does not apply to exchanges of partnership interests.[360] *(See Case 146.)*

Case 148
Voluntary Unitization of Leases

> In 1980, Operator A acquired a 300-acre oil and gas lease on which are several producing wells. The lease is located in a 1,500-acre field. Operator A has spent $400,000 for intangible drilling and development costs (IDC) and $175,000 for tangible equipment in developing his lease. Operator A has an adjusted basis of $10,000 in the lease and $60,000 in the equipment on the lease. The equipment has a fair market value of $71,000, and the leasehold has a fair market value of $639,000. Owners of the leases on the remaining 1,200 acres in the field have expended $950,000 for intangibles and $250,000 for equipment. The fair market value of the entire field is $3,250,000, of which $325,000 is attributable to equipment. Operator A and the other owners agree to a unitization of the field.
>
> Operator A's interest in the unit is 20%. Because Operator A's lease is more developed than the other leases, he is entitled to receive cash of $54,000 for his drilling expenditures and $6,000 for his equipment expenditures.

If the parties to the unitization agreement elect to be excluded from the partnership provisions of the Internal Revenue Code, Operator A has exchanged property held for productive use in his trade or business for property of like kind to be similarly held,

357. Rev. Rul. 68-331, 1968-1 C.B. 352.
358. Badgett v. U.S., 17 F. Supp. 120 (W.D. Ky. 1959), 3 AFTR2d 973, 59-1 USTC 9336.
359. Norman J. Magneson, 81 T.C. 47 (1983).
360. I.R.C. Sec. 1031(a).

plus the receipt of $60,000 ($54,000 for drilling expenditures plus $6,000 for equipment expenditures) in cash.[361] An interest received in a unitization transaction will be treated as a single unit of property for depletion purposes.[362]

Because Operator A has held the property for more than 12 months, any gain recognized will be gain from the disposition of real property used in a trade or business or of depreciable property used in a trade or business.[363] Except for the amounts attributable to depreciation recapture (discussed below) and IDC recapture *(see Case 131)*, that gain will be treated as long-term gain to the extent it is not offset by losses on sales of property used in a trade or business. For property acquired after June 22, 1984, and before January 1, 1988, a holding period of more than six months is required to qualify for this treatment.[364] The net gain from sales of property used in a trade or business may be recharacterized as ordinary income. The recharacterization is limited to the excess of the aggregate amount of losses from the sale of such property for the five most recent preceding years beginning after 1981 over the portion of such preceding years' losses previously recaptured.[365] Also, for property placed in service after 1986, cost and percentage depletion are subject to recapture to the extent of basis reduction.[366]

In computing that portion of the gain subject to ordinary income treatment as depreciation recapture, Operator A first must allocate the consideration received to leasehold value and equipment value in accordance with the respective fair market values of those items at the date of exchange. In this case, the total fair market value of Operator A's interest is $710,000 ($650,000 fair market value plus $60,000 in cash), of which $71,000 is attributable to the equipment and $639,000 to the reserves in place. Accordingly, Operator A will allocate 10% of the amounts received, or $71,000, to equipment and 90%, or $639,000, to the reserves. The gain recognizable with respect to the exchange of the equipment is limited to the portion of the cash received that relates to the equipment ($6,000). Thus, even though the realized gain is $11,000 ($71,000 minus $60,000), the maximum amount subject to depreciation recapture is $6,000.[367] The gain recognizable with respect to the exchange of the leasehold interest also is limited to the cash received relating to that interest ($54,000). This gain will be subject to rules relating to the recapture of IDC.[368] *(See Case 131.)*

Restoration of investment credit will not be required if Operator A retains a substantial interest in the "trade or business," though in a different form.[369] However, the Internal Revenue Service may contend that here the interest retained is not substantial.

Operator A's basis in the property received in the exchange will be the same as that of the property given up, decreased by the amount of any money received and increased by the amount of gain recognized.[370] In this case, Operator A's basis in the equipment will be $60,000, the basis of the equipment given up ($60,000) minus the cash received attributable to the equipment ($6,000), plus the gain recognized ($6,000). This result appears to follow from certain provisions of the regulations[371] that require that exchanges of property subject to depreciation recapture together with other

361. Rev. Rul. 68-186, 1968-1 C.B. 354.
362. I.R.C. Sec. 614(b)(3).
363. I.R.C. Sec. 1231; Rev. Rul. 68-186, 1968-1 C.B. 354.
364. I.R.C. Sec. 1231(b).
365. I.R.C. Sec. 1231(c).
366. I.R.C. Sec. 1254(a)(1).
367. I.R.C. Sec. 1245(b)(4); Reg. Sec. 1.1245-1(a)(5); Reg. Sec. 1.1245-4(d)(4)(ii).
368. I.R.C. Sec. 1254.
369. I.R.C. Sec. 47; Reg. Sec. 1.47-3(f)(2).
370. I.R.C. Sec. 1031(d); Rev. Rul. 68-186, 1968-1 C.B 354.
371. Reg. Sec. 1.1245-4(d)(4)(ii).

property are to be treated as first applying to the exchange of property subject to depreciation recapture. For the same reason, the basis for the leasehold will be $10,000. *(See Case 146 for the rules governing depreciation recapture when no cash is received in the like-kind exchange.)*

For unitizations covered by a single conveyance, it still may be necessary to reallocate basis between depreciable and depletable properties in proportion to the relative fair market values of the assets received.[372] Present regulations do not deal directly with the basis allocation problem.

To avoid this concern, it is suggested that taxpayers complete unitization transactions by making separate exchanges of the equipment and of the leaseholds.

The like-kind exchange provisions generally do not apply to exchanges of partnership interests.[373] The provisions prohibiting like-kind exchange treatment for partnership interests do not specifically address potential application to exchanges of interests in ventures for which the participants elect[374] not to be subject to the partnership provisions. However, in comments introducing the Tax Reform Act of 1984, a senator specifically stated[375] that the prohibition is not intended to apply to exchanges of those interests. These comments were intended to clarify Congressional intent. Regulations may be necessary to further clarify this issue. *(See Case 146 for other considerations involving like-kind exchanges.)*

If the parties to this unitization do not elect to be excluded from the partnership provisions of the Internal Revenue Code, the result to Operator A could be different.

If Operator A transfers his entire interest in the properties for a 20% interest in the "partnership" as constituted after the transactions, he still will receive $60,000 cash as an equalization payment. Under regulations to be prescribed by the Secretary of Treasury, if property is transferred to a partnership and there is a direct or indirect transfer of money or property to that partner and the transfers (when viewed together) properly are characterized as a sale, the transaction generally will not be treated under the partnership rules.[376] Presumably, this will result in the treatment discussed above.[377] Substance will govern rather than form.[378]

Operator A's basis in his partnership interest will be $10,000 ($70,000 basis before the exchange less $60,000 cash received). However, Operator A probably will be required to restore any investment credit previously claimed because he will not be considered merely to have changed the form of doing business.[379] If no gain is recognized, the tax basis to the partnership after the exchange will be the same as the tax basis to Operator A preceding the exchange, the partnership will inherit the potential "recapture," and Operator A will not be required to report any amount as ordinary income from recapture.[380]

A similar result as outlined in the preceding two paragraphs will follow if the parties were to transfer separately equipment and reserves in exchange for partnership interests.

---

372. E. C. Laster, 43 B.T.A. 159 (1940).
373. I.R.C. Sec. 1031(a).
374. I.R.C. Sec. 761(a).
375. Comments of Senator Dole contained in *Congressional Record*, Volume 130, No. 90 p.S 8410, June 27, 1984.
376. I.R.C. Sec. 707(a).
377. *Ibid.*
378. Reg. Sec. 1.721-1(a); Reg. Sec. 1.731-1(c)(3); I.R.C. Sec. 707(a).
379. I.R.C. Sec. 47; Reg. Sec. 1.47-3(f)(2).
380. Reg. Sec. 1.1245-4(c)(4); Prop. Reg. Sec. 1.1254-5.

Income, gain, loss and deductions with respect to property contributed to a partnership generally must be shared among the partners so as to take into account the variation between the basis of the property to the partnership and its fair market value at the time of contribution.[381] *(See Case 166.)*

A unitization is not considered a transfer of a proven property for purposes of computing percentage depletion under the independent-producer and royalty-owner exemption. *(See Cases 108 and 109.)*

Case 149
Holding Period of Aggregated Properties

In one lease, Operator A owns separately acquired, undivided operating mineral Interests X, Y and Z. The same producing horizon underlies the entire lease. Operator A has elected to treat his three interests in the lease as a single unit of property. Operator A decides to sell one-half his interest in the lease. On the date of sale (July 1, 1987), Interest X and Interest Y had been held more than six months, while Interest Z had been held less than six months. The sales price is $80,000, of which $30,000 is attributable to the portion of Interest Z sold. The adjusted tax basis of the combined property at the date of sale is $20,000, and its fair market value (FMV) at the date of sale is $160,000.

The sales price and tax basis attributable to the interest sold must be allocated in proportion to the relative fair market values of all the interests as of the date of sale to determine the amount of income represented by the sale of property held for six months or less.

Operator A has sold a part of the combined property that includes part of an operating mineral interest that was held for six months or less.[382]

The basis applicable to the interest sold is computed as follows:

Basis applicable to one-half the combined property:

$$\frac{\text{\$80,000 (FMV of portion sold)}}{\text{\$160,000 (FMV of combined property)}} \times \text{\$20,000} = \text{\$10,000 (basis of half sold)}$$

Basis applicable to portion of Interest Z that is sold:

$$\frac{\text{\$30,000 (FMV of portion of Interest Z being sold)}}{\text{\$80,000 (FMV of portion sold)}} \times \text{\$10,000 (basis of half sold)} = \text{\$3,750}$$

The gain attributable to the sale of portions of Interests X and Y is $43,750 ($50,000 proceeds less $6,250 basis), and the gain attributable to the sale of a portion of Interest Z is $26,250 ($30,000 proceeds less $3,750 basis).

If Operator A is not a dealer, the properties will constitute "real property used in the trade or business."[383] The gain from the sale of portions of Interests X and Y generally will be treated as long-term capital gain (except for depreciation, depletion and intangible drilling and development costs recapture) if it is not offset by losses from disposition of other assets used in a trade or business. The gain on the sale of a portion of Interest Z will

381. I.R.C. Sec. 704(c).
382. Reg. Sec. 1.614-8(b)(5); Reg. Sec. 1.614-6(a)(2); Reg. Sec. 1.614-6(b).
383. I.R.C. Sec. 1231.

be treated as gain from the sale of other than a capital asset because Interest Z was held for less than six months. Recapture of investment credit also will be required. The purchaser will be prohibited from claiming percentage depletion on his share of production if the property was proven at the time of transfer. *(See Case 108.)*

Gain on the sale of property used in a trade or business may be recharacterized as ordinary income. The recharacterization is limited to the excess of the aggregate amount of those losses from the five most recent preceding years beginning after 1981 over the portion of those preceding years' losses previously recaptured.[384]

Case 150
Production Payment Pledged for Development

> Operator A, an individual, has completed a discovery well on a prospect and desires to obtain financing to drill several more development wells on four leases. He estimates that his share of the costs to drill and equip these wells will be $400,000 in 1987. He enters into negotiations with a lending institution and makes arrangements to obtain the necessary funds in consideration of a production payment of $400,000 plus an interest factor of 10%, payable out of 60% of his share of the production. The funds are to be used solely for the purpose of drilling and equipping the wells and, if the amount required to develop the leases is less than $400,000, the excess is to be returned and the production payment will be reduced. The production payment amount and payout are to be computed separately for each lease. Operator A wants to know the income tax effect of the use of a production payment pledge for development under these circumstances.

A production payment pledge for development is an exception to the general rule that a carved-out production payment is to be treated as a nonrecourse mortgage loan.[385] When a production payment pledged for development is used to obtain funds to drill and equip an oil or gas well, the operator is not taxed on the proceeds from the sale of the production payment, is not entitled to any tax basis or tax deductions for the amount spent to drill and equip the well (to the extent of the production payment) and is not taxed on that portion of the gross income from the sale of oil and gas applied to discharge the production payment.

To qualify under this exception,[386] the following conditions must be met:

- ☐ The production payment must not be given to satisfy a liability previously incurred.
- ☐ The production payment must be carved out of the unit of property on which the development is to occur.
- ☐ The assignee of the production payment must look solely to production of oil or gas for the recovery of his capital investment.
- ☐ The assignor must either return to the assignee any excess funds not used for the development of the property or treat the excess proceeds as a mortgage loan on the mineral property.

In connection with the requirement that the assignee of the production payment must look solely to production of oil or gas for the recovery of his investment, a Circuit

384. I.R.C. Sec. 1231(c).
385. I.R.C. Sec. 636(a).
386. Reg. Sec. 1.636-1(b).

Court held that, even when the added security (consisting of the leases out of which the production payments were carved and the equipment thereon) had only nominal value, the interests did not qualify as production payments.[387]

Operator A will not have to pay tax on the receipt of the $400,000 pledged for development, nor may he claim a deduction for that part of the $400,000 he spends for intangible drilling and development costs (IDC). Therefore, any such costs he incurs on a producing well will not be an item of tax preference for purposes of computing the alternative minimum tax.[388] In addition, Operator A will not have to recapture any IDC he pays out of the $400,000 production payment as ordinary income on subsequent disposition of the property.[389]

Similarly, Operator A will have no tax basis in any equipment purchased with the $400,000. Therefore, he will not be entitled to the accelerated cost recovery deductions (depreciation) attributable to that equipment.[390] In addition, he should not be required to recapture any accelerated cost recovery deductions (depreciation) as ordinary income on disposition of the property (on equipment acquired with the $400,000 production payment).[391]

Operator A will not be taxed on the income used to satisfy the production payment. Assume the total amount paid to retire the production payment, including the interest element, is $500,000. Operator A must exclude the entire $500,000 from his taxable income, and he will not be entitled to any percentage depletion on that $500,000 because this income belongs to the holder of the production payment. Accordingly, the loss of the tax benefits of percentage depletion should be considered in determining whether to use a production payment pledged for development to finance the drilling of oil and gas wells.

In planning these transactions, an operator should consider that the basis of equipment may be retained by either paying for or financing the equipment costs with a regular loan and limiting the pledged production payment to the IDC.

Although not considered in this factual situation, the effect of the windfall profit tax on production payment transactions is uncertain. *(See Cases 86, 88 and 230 for a further discussion of this issue.)*

It is common for lending institutions to request cross-collateralization of the leases as additional security for each loan. If the leases represent separate units of property and are jointly pledged under each production payment, the Internal Revenue Service (IRS) may assert that[392] because no specific property is burdened by a specific production payment, the advance payment made to Operator A does not qualify as a production payment carved out for exploration or development. The regulations specifically provide that a production payment can cover multiple properties.[393] Additionally, the IRS has accorded economic interest status to net profits interest in separate tracts or parcels of land conveyed in a single conveyance when the calculation of net profits is made on an aggregate basis instead of separately for each unit of property.[394] In spite of the above rationale and regulatory guidance, it is understood that the IRS, for ruling purposes, continues to accord economic interest status to

387. Gibson Products Co. v. U.S., 637 F.2d 1041 (5th Cir. 1981), 47 AFTR2d 81-863, 81-1 USTC 9213. *See also* Standard Oil Co. (Indiana) v. Comm'r, 465 F.2d 246 (7th Cir. 1972), 30 AFTR2d 72-5157, 72-2 USTC 9549.

388. I.R.C. Sec. 57(a)(2).

389. I.R.C. Sec. 1254.

390. I.R.C. Sec. 168.

391. I.R.C. Sec. 1245.

392. IRS Letter Ruling 8125001.

393. Reg. Sec. 1.636-1(a).

394. IRS Letter Ruling 8302016 (Technical Advice Memorandum); IRS Letter Ruling 8312019; IRS Letter Ruling 8611002 (Technical Advice Memorandum).

production payments pledged for exploration or development only where the production payment burdens one tract of land. Essentially, the IRS interprets the requirements for qualification very narrowly, requiring the funds invested to be recouped solely out of the oil and gas property in which the investment is made. Given the IRS's treatment of a "blanket" production payment as an economic interest and the express language in the regulations allowing production payments to burden multiple properties, it is not clear that economic interest status should be withheld from production payments pledged for exploration or development that burden multiple leases under circumstances similar to a "blanket" production payment. *(See Case 135.)*

The tax effects of using pledged production payments for IDC are important to determine the overall economic effect of this type of arrangement. Due to the complexities and interrelationships of various tax provisions, a thorough comparison of all factors (tax and nontax) should be made.

(See Case 151 for a discussion of the circumstances in which proceeds from a production payment may be used to purchase tangible equipment.)

Case 151
Production Payment Pledged for Development With Proceeds Specifically for Tangible Equipment

> Operator A, an individual, has completed a discovery well on a prospect and desires to drill several more development wells on four leases. He estimates that his share of the costs to drill these wells in 1987 will be $400,000. He estimates that his share to equip these wells will be $100,000. He enters into negotiations with a lending institution and makes arrangements to obtain the necessary funds for the purchase of the tangible equipment to equip the wells, in consideration of a production payment of $100,000 plus an interest factor of 10%, payable out of 60% of his share of the production. The funds are to be used solely for the purpose of equipping the wells and, if the amount required to equip the wells is less than $100,000, the excess is to be returned and the production payment will be reduced. The production payment amount and payout are to be computed separately for each lease. Operator A wants to know the income tax effect of the use of a production payment pledged for development under these circumstances.

For a carved-out production payment to meet the "pledged for exploration or development" exception discussed in Case 150, the cash received must be used for the exploration or development of property. The regulations[395] state:

> For purposes of section 636(a) and this paragraph, an expenditure is for exploration or development to the extent that it is necessary for ascertaining the existence, location, extent or quality of any deposit of mineral or is incident to and necessary for the preparation of a deposit for the production of mineral. However, an expenditure which relates primarily to the production of mineral (as, for example, in the case of a pilot water flood program with respect to the secondary recovery of oil) is not for exploration or development as those terms are used in section 636(a) and this paragraph. Whether or not a production payment is carved out for exploration or

395. Reg. Sec. 1.636-1(b)(1).

> development shall be determined in light of all relevant facts and circumstances, including any prior production of mineral from the mineral deposit burdened by the production payment.

In this case, it seems the equipment can be considered incident to and necessary for the preparation of a mineral deposit for production. However, it must not relate primarily to the production of the mineral. The regulations consider a pilot water-flood program for secondary recovery of oil to relate primarily to production rather than to exploration or development, but they provide no other guidance. In addition, the Internal Revenue Service has ruled that mining equipment does not qualify as a development expenditure.[396] Therefore, it is unclear whether the expenditure for the equipment necessary to produce the mineral initially can qualify as a production payment pledged for exploration or development.

There are no judicial interpretations to clarify the requirements for qualification as a production payment pledged for exploration or development. Consequently, caution should be exercised in using such a production payment to finance equipment.

If the subject production payment is considered to be pledged for development, Operator A will not be entitled to cost recovery deductions (depreciation) with respect to the equipment purchased with the production payment proceeds. He also will not be taxed on the income used to satisfy the production payment. *(See Case 150 for tax considerations of a production payment pledged for development.)*

If the subject production payment is not considered to be pledged for development, it will be treated as a nonrecourse mortgage loan. Operator A will be entitled to cost recovery deductions (depreciation) with respect to the purchased equipment, potentially subject to the "at-risk" limitations. Income from the sale of production used to satisfy the production payment will be taxable to Operator A and will qualify for percentage depletion. Operator A will be entitled to an interest deduction for payments made with respect to the 10% interest factor. *(See Case 135 concerning the tax consequences of a production payment treated as a loan.)*

Although not considered in this factual situation, the effect of windfall profit tax on production payment transactions is uncertain. *(See Cases 86, 88 and 230 for a further discussion of this issue.)*

Case 152
Basis After Transfer to Corporation When Debt Exceeds Basis of Transferor

> Operator A, an individual, acquires an oil and gas lease for $20,000. He drills and completes two productive oil wells on the property for a total expenditure of $160,000, of which $80,000 represents intangible drilling and development costs (IDC) and $80,000, equipment costs. Development is financed by borrowing $160,000 from a bank. Operator A transfers the lease and equipment, which are valued at $420,000 and $80,000, respectively, to a newly organized corporation in exchange for all its stock and for its assumption of the indebtedness. The transfer to the corporation is supported by a bona fide business purpose.

396. Rev. Rul. 74-549, 1974-2 C.B. 186.

The transfer of property to a controlled corporation generally is tax free.[397] However, some or all of the gain is recognized by the transferor when: (1) money or property other than stock or securities of the transferee corporation is received or (2) the transferee corporation assumes liabilities or receives properties subject to liabilities that are in excess of the transferor's total adjusted tax basis of the properties transferred.[398]

After deducting all IDC, following completion of the wells, Operator A has tax basis in the lease of $100,000 ($20,000 lease cost plus $80,000 equipment costs). Upon transfer of the lease and equipment to the corporation in exchange for stock and the assumption of debt, Operator A must recognize a gain of $60,000 which is equal to the excess of the indebtedness ($160,000) over his tax basis in the property transferred ($100,000). A portion of the gain will be attributable to the sale of property held for use in a trade or business, potentially subject to long-term capital-gain treatment provided Operator A has held title to the property for more than 12 months (six months for property acquired after June 22, 1984 and before January 1, 1988)[399] and is not a dealer in oil or gas properties. Another portion of the gain will be treated as ordinary income to the extent of the IDC (less adjustment if the property was placed in service before 1987) paid or incurred after 1975. *(See Case 131.)* In addition, a portion of the gain on depreciable assets and the gain on assets that are not capital will be taxed at ordinary income rates.[400] Also for properties placed in service after 1986, depletion must be recaptured to the extent of basis reduction.[401]

The regulations provide that the character of the recognized gain is determined by allocating that gain among the transferred assets by reference to their relative fair market values.[402] In the instant case, 84% ($420,000 ÷ $500,000) of the $60,000 gain ($50,400) is allocated to the leasehold and 16% ($80,000 ÷ $500,000) of the $60,000 gain ($9,600) is allocated to the equipment. Assuming the potential recapture of IDC exceeds $50,400, Operator A will report the $50,400 as ordinary income. The $9,600 gain allocable to equipment will be treated as ordinary income to the extent of accelerated cost recovery deductions and depreciation allowed or allowable.[403] The remaining gain attributable to the equipment will be subject to taxation as gain from the sale of property used in a trade or business. *(See Case 131 for a discussion of the possible recharacterization as ordinary income of long-term capital gain from the sale or exchange of property used in a trade or business and held for the requisite holding period.)*

Operator A's tax basis in the stock received in exchange for the property is zero. This is determined by taking the sum of the tax basis of the assets transferred ($100,000) and the gain recognized by Operator A on the transfer ($60,000) and reducing that amount by the indebtedness assumed by the corporation ($160,000).[404]

Following the transfer of the properties, the corporation's basis in the assets received will be $160,000, determined by taking Operator A's basis in the property ($100,000) and adding the gain recognized by Operator A ($60,000).[405]

When more than one asset is transferred to a corporation and the transferor is unable to determine accurately his cost basis in the separate assets transferred but is able to

397. I.R.C. Sec. 351.
398. I.R.C. Sec. 357(c).
399. I.R.C. Sec. 1231. *But see* I.R.C. Sec. 1231(c).
400. I.R.C. Sec. 1231; I.R.C. Sec. 1239; Rev. Rul. 60-302, 1960-2 C.B. 223.
401. I.R.C. Sec. 1254(a)(1).
402. Reg. Sec. 1.357-2. *See also* David Rosen, 62 T.C. 11 (1974).
403. I.R.C. Sec. 1245.
404. I.R.C. Sec. 358(a)(1); Reg. Sec. 1.358-3.
405. I.R.C. Sec. 362(b).

determine accurately his basis in the entire group, the transferor should allocate his total basis in the assets to the separate items in the ratio of their relative fair market values. This allocation of basis to separate assets will carry through to the transferee corporation.[406] Applying this rule to the present situation, the corporation will allocate its basis in all the properties acquired from Operator A ($160,000) between tangible equipment (depreciable) and leasehold cost (depletable), based on their relative fair market values.

The determination of basis following a tax-free, or partially tax-free, transfer or exchange is an extensive subject. However, in general, the basis to the transferor of the stock and securities received is his tax basis in the property given in exchange, increased by the amount of gain recognized and decreased by the amount of money and the fair market value of other property received.

Generally, percentage depletion is not available to a transferee following the transfer of a proven property. However, certain transfers to qualified transferee corporations of qualified properties are excepted from this rule.[407] *(See Cases 108, 109 and 110 for a discussion of the allowance for percentage depletion subsequent to the transfer of proven properties.)* In addition, transfers to S corporations are exceptions to this rule and receive essentially the same treatment as transfers to a partnership.[408] *(See Case 111.)*

Case 153
Valuation of Properties and Selected Tax Issues in Corporate Liquidations

> Individuals A and B each own 50% of the outstanding stock of C Company. C Company owns cash, accounts receivable and numerous producing and nonproducing working interests and associated lease and well equipment. C Company is not an S corporation or a collapsible corporation. The shareholders wish to know the tax consequences of liquidating the corporation and methods for valuing the working interests.

Generally, gain or loss will be recognized by a liquidating corporation on the distribution of property to its shareholders as if such property was sold to the shareholders at its fair market value.[409] Each shareholder recognizes gain or loss on the liquidation equal to the difference between the fair market value of assets received (net of liabilities) and his adjusted basis in his stock.[410] Assuming Individuals A and B are not dealers in their stock, they will recognize long-term capital gain or loss if the requisite holding period is met.[411] Under certain circumstances, a shareholder's loss on liquidation may be characterized as an ordinary loss.[412]

Different tax rules apply at the corporate level for: (1) liquidations completed before January 1, 1987, (2) sales and distributions pursuant to a plan of liquidation adopted before August 1, 1986, if the liquidation is completed before January 1, 1988, and (3) sales and distributions in liquidation pursuant to certain binding contracts.[413]

406. North Carolina Feldspar Corp., B.T.A. Memo Dec. (Dec. 29, 1939).
407. I.R.C. Sec. 613A(c)(10).
408. I.R.C. Sec. 613A(c)(13)(C).
409. I.R.C. Sec. 336(a).
410. I.R.C. Sec. 331(a); I.R.C. Sec. 1001.
411. I.R.C. Sec. 1221; I.R.C. Sec. 1222.
412. I.R.C. Sec. 1244.
413. P.L. 99-514 (Tax Reform Act of 1986), Sec. 633(c).

Under the so-called *General Utilities Doctrine* applicable to such situations, a corporation generally recognizes no gain or loss on sales (within 12 months of liquidation and other than in the ordinary course of business) or distributions of assets in liquidation.[414] Despite this general rule, the corporation recognizes gain on assets distributed or sold (other than in the ordinary course of business) within 12 months of liquidation to the extent of depreciation recapture, intangible drilling and development costs (IDC) and depletion recapture *(see Case 131)*, the LIFO (last-in, first-out) recapture amount, certain deferred installment-sale gain and certain other items.[415] Unearned investment tax credit must be recaptured.

A special transition rule continues the availability of the *General Utilities Doctrine* to a "qualified corporation" completely liquidated before January 1, 1989.[416] However, in addition to the above-mentioned items, such corporations must recognize all ordinary gain or loss, any gain or loss on capital assets held not more than six months and deferred installment-sale gain (other than long-term capital and Section 1231 gain).[417]

According to the statute, as explained by statements of Congressional intent and as potentially modified by proposed technical corrections legislation, a "qualified corporation" is any corporation if:

- ☐ On August 1, 1986, and at all times thereafter, more than 50% (by value) of its stock is owned directly or indirectly by the same 10 or fewer individuals, estates or certain trusts that at all times during the five-year period ending on the date of adoption of the plan of liquidation owned more than 50% (by value) of the stock and
- ☐ The fair market value of all of the stock of the corporation on the date of adoption of the plan of liquidation, or if greater, on August 1, 1986, (the "applicable value") does not exceed $10 million.[418]

The relief provided by this provision is phased out if the "applicable value" exceeds $5 million.

Regardless of which provision applies to the determination of gain or loss at the corporate level, fair market value of the corporation's assets must be determined. The fair market value is the price that could be agreed upon between a willing seller and a willing buyer as of the date of the transaction.[419] Assets such as cash and accounts receivable normally are easily valued and present no difficult problem. However, the valuation of producing and nonproducing leases often is quite difficult, especially if there are no recent sales or transfers of similar properties in the locality.

If data can be obtained regarding sales of oil and gas properties in the general area, certain yardsticks, or formulas, based on those sales may be used.[420] For example, sales prices for comparable properties may be expressed in terms of a year's payout (price divided by one year's income) or an amount per unit of reserves (barrels or MCF). When those methods are not considered reliable or those sales data are not available, analytical appraisal methods, such as the present value method, may be used. Under

414. I.R.C. Sec. 336 *(prior to amendment by the Tax Reform Act of 1986)*; I.R.C. Sec. 337 *(prior to amendment by the Tax Reform Act of 1986)*.
415. I.R.C. Sec. 337 *(prior to amendment by the Tax Reform Act of 1986)*; I.R.C. Sec. 1245; I.R.C. Sec. 1254.
416. P.L. 99-514 (Tax Reform Act of 1986), Sec. 633(d)(1).
417. P.L. 99-514 (Tax Reform Act of 1986), Sec. 633(d)(2); General Explanation of the Tax Reform Act of 1986, prepared by the Staff of the Joint Committee on Taxation, p. 353.
418. P.L. 99-514 (Tax Reform Act of 1986), Sec. 633(d); General Explanation of the Tax Reform Act of 1986, prepared by the Staff of the Joint Committee on Taxation, p. 353; Technical Corrections Bill of 1987, Sec. 106(g)(6); Description of the Technical Corrections Bill of 1987, prepared by the Staff of the Joint Committee on Taxation, p. 50.
419. Reg. Sec. 1.611-1(d)(2); Reg. Sec. 20.2031-1(b).
420. Reg. Sec. 1.611-2(d).

this method, the fair market value of the properties is the present value of the expected future net cash flow to be derived from the properties, giving recognition to a risk factor.[421]

To determine expected future net cash flow, it first is necessary to arrive at the anticipated income by years over the life of the property. Future production is based on reliable estimates of recoverable reserves.[422] The estimated annual production for future years takes into account the expected decline in rate of production. Estimates of annual production costs; general and administrative expenses allocable to the property; additional development costs and capital expenditures required to recover the oil and gas; and windfall profit, severance and ad valorem taxes are deducted from the annual gross income from the property. The resulting expected annual net cash flow then is discounted to present value, using the prevailing rate of interest. The fair market value is determined by discounting the present value by a risk factor that takes into account the hazardous nature of oil and gas operations.[423] In some cases, the risk factor may be combined with the present value discount factor. The objective is to determine the present market value, taking into account what a prospective purchaser could expect to earn on his investment, considering all pertinent factors.

Individuals A and B will have basis in the distributed assets equal to fair market value at the time of distribution. *(See Cases 108 and 109 concerning percentage depletion on the transferred proven properties.)*

(See Case 155 concerning a possible alternative liquidation rule.)

Case 154
Allocation of Lump-Sum Purchase Price

In 1987, C Company acquires substantially all the assets of another corporation for a total cash consideration of $600,000. The various classes of property included in the purchase are valued by independent appraisers as follows:

Accounts receivable	$ 90,000
Materials and supplies	10,000
Drilling tools and equipment	200,000
Lease and well equipment	150,000
Producing leaseholds	300,000
Total	$750,000

Generally for "applicable asset acquisitions" after May 6, 1986, the buyer and seller are required to allocate the consideration under the residual method. The allocation controls the seller's calculation of gain or loss attributable to each asset sold and the purchaser's basis in each acquired asset.[424]

An "applicable asset acquisition" is any transfer (whether directly or indirectly) of assets that constitute a trade or business if the transferee's basis in the assets is determined wholly by reference to the consideration paid.[425] Although the statutory

421. Reg. Sec. 1.611-2(e)(4).
422. J. B. Cage, T.C. Memo Dec. (Sept. 28, 1950); Reg. Sec. 1.611-2(e).
423. Reg. Sec. 1.611-2(e)(1).
424. I.R.C. Sec. 1060(a).
425. I.R.C. Sec. 1060(c).

provision does not define the term *trade or business,* the Committee Reports appear to restrict the provision by stating that a group of assets will constitute a business for this purpose if their character is such that goodwill or going-concern value could, under any circumstances, attach to such assets. Businesses will be subject to the allocation rules even though they may not constitute "active" businesses under the corporate reorganization provisions.[426]

Although one or more working interests typically are treated as trade or business assets (as opposed to passive assets held for investment), goodwill or going-concern value is not considered to attach to them. However, if the acquisition of working interests is accompanied by the acquisition of an operating organization, goodwill or going-concern value could exist. Although the statutory language does not appear to differentiate between these situations, the Committee interpretations discussed above may require the application of the allocation provisions only in the latter acquisition.

The residual allocation rules are intended to apply to indirect applicable asset acquisitions, including a sale of a partnership interest in which the basis of the purchasing partner's proportionate share of the partnership's assets is adjusted to reflect the purchase price.[427] Technical correction legislation has been proposed to clarify that the applicable asset acquisition rules will apply to a distribution of partnership property or a transfer of a partnership interest requiring an adjustment to partnership property basis,[428] but only for purposes of determining the value of goodwill or going-concern value.[429]

The residual allocation method requires assets to be divided into four classes as follows:

Class I: Cash, demand deposits and similar accounts in banks, savings and loan associations, and similar depository institutions.

Class II: Certificates of deposit, U.S. Government securities, readily marketable stock and securities, and foreign currencies.

Class III: All assets (other than Class I, II and IV assets), both tangible and intangible (whether or not depreciable, depletable or amortizable).

Class IV: Intangible assets in the nature of goodwill and going-concern value.[430]

The purchase consideration is allocated first to Class I assets to the extent of the amount of such assets. The remaining consideration then is allocated among Class II assets in proportion to their fair market values, among Class III assets in such proportion, and, finally, to Class IV assets in such proportion. In no event may the purchase price allocated to an asset (other than a Class IV asset) exceed its fair market value.[431]

Under regulations to be issued, the transferor and transferee in an applicable asset acquisition must furnish certain information to the Internal Revenue Service.[432]

If the acquisition is not treated as an applicable asset acquisition (or if the acquisition occurred before May 7, 1986, or was subject to a binding contract in effect on and at

426. Senate Report No. 99-313, 1986-3 C.B. Vol. 3 255; General Explanation of the Tax Reform Act of 1986, prepared by the Staff of the Joint Committee on Taxation, p. 359; Reg. Sec. 1.355-1(c); I.R.C. Sec. 355(b).
427. Senate Report No. 99-313, 1986-3 C.B. Vol. 3 255; General Explanation of the Tax Reform Act of 1986, prepared by the Staff of the Joint Committee on Taxation, p. 359.
428. I.R.C. Sec. 755.
429. Technical Corrections Bill of 1987, Sec. 106(h).
430. Temp. Reg. Sec. 1.338(b)-2T(b).
431. Temp. Reg. Sec. 1.338(b)-2T(c).
432. I.R.C. Sec. 1060(b).

all times after May 6, 1986), different rules apply. The amount properly allocable to each asset is that portion of the total consideration that the appraised value of that asset bears to the total appraised values of all assets acquired.[433] In asset sales and purchase contracts, the buyer and seller may bargain separately for a particular asset, such as accounts receivable. In these situations, the costs allocated to these items should be the separately bargained for amounts, with the remainder allocated to the assets not separately bargained for, based on their relative fair market values.[434]

Assuming the acquisition is an "applicable asset acquisition," all of the acquired assets are characterized as Class III assets. Since the consideration equals 80% ($600,000 ÷ $750,000 = 80%) of the aggregate fair market value of the acquired assets, each asset is allocated consideration equal to 80% of its individually appraised fair market value. This allocated amount is used by C Company as its basis in each asset and by the seller to determine its gain or loss on the sale of each asset.

If the acquisition is not an "applicable asset acquisition," C Company and the seller could bargain separately for each asset or selected assets. For example, consistent with the typical expectations of the parties to this type of transaction, C Company and the seller could agree that the accounts receivable should be valued at $90,000 and permit the remaining consideration of $510,000 ($600,000 - $90,000) to be allocated among the other assets in proportion to their relative fair market values.

If the consideration exceeded $750,000 and there were no other identifiable assets, the excess portion would be treated as goodwill or going-concern value.

(See Case 153 concerning valuation of oil and gas properties, Case 131 concerning recapture of depletion and intangible drilling and development costs, and Cases 108 and 109 concerning percentage depletion upon the transfer of a proven property.)

Case 155
Liquidation of Corporation Under Section 333

C Corporation's tax balance sheet at June 30, 1987, is as follows:

Assets	
Cash	$100,000
Lease and well equipment (at cost less reserve)	200,000
Producing leaseholds (at cost less reserve)	75,000
Total	$375,000
Liabilities and Capital	
Capital stock—at par	$300,000
Retained earnings (earnings and profits)	75,000
Total	$375,000

Operator A (an individual) owns all the capital stock, which he acquired from Operator B for $200,000 several years ago. At the balance-sheet date above, the producing leases are worth $800,000, and the lease and well equipment have a fair market value of $200,000. Operator A wants to

433. Rev. Rul. 69-539, 1969-2 C.B. 141.
434. Maysteel Products Corp. v. U.S., 341 F. Supp. 485 (E.D. Wis. 1972), 29 AFTR2d 72-860, 72-1 USTC 9322.

know what the tax consequences will be to him if C Corporation is liquidated under the provisions of Section 333. The corporation is not a collapsible corporation as defined in Section 341 of the Internal Revenue Code.

The Tax Reform Act of 1986 repealed the *General Utilities Doctrine,* thereby generally eliminating favorable tax treatment of corporate liquidations after December 31, 1986. However, for certain small corporations, the repeal of general utilities is not effective in the case of complete liquidations made before January 1, 1989. To qualify for this transition rule relief, the corporation must have been in existence on August 1, 1986, its value must not exceed $10 million and more than 50% (by value) of the stock in such corporation must be owned by 10 or fewer individuals (or estates and certain trusts) who have held such stock for five years or longer (or the life of the corporation if less than five years). Full relief is available under this rule only if the corporation's value does not exceed $5 million. If the fair market value exceeds $5 million (but is less than $10 million), a pro-rata percentage of the gain must be reported. For purposes of this rule, a corporation's value will be the higher of the value on August 1, 1986, or the date of adoption of a plan of liquidation. Aggregation rules are applied to determine the value of the corporation at the applicable date. The corporation must recognize all ordinary gain (recapture items, including inventory), gain on capital assets held for six months or less and unrecognized gain on certain installment obligations.[435] Therefore, the provisions of Section 333 may still apply to the facts in this case if the liquidating corporation qualifies for transition rule relief as described above.

Section 333 sometimes is referred to as the one-month liquidation provision. If the shareholders of a corporation make a proper election,[436] the corporation is completely liquidated and the assets are distributed to the shareholders during one calendar month, the regular rules requiring shareholder recognition of gain *(see Case 153)* do not apply. In lieu of the tax treatment of an ordinary corporate liquidation, an electing noncorporate shareholder must treat his share of the corporation's accumulated earnings and profits as a dividend. Additionally, the shareholder must treat the amount by which cash and the value of stock or securities (acquired by the corporation after December 31, 1953) received in the liquidation exceed those earnings and profits as a capital gain.[437] The remainder of the realized gain is not recognized for tax purposes. Different rules apply for corporate shareholders and certain personal holding company liquidations.[438] It should also be noted that although the provisions of Section 333 apply, additional shareholder gain may result from an increase in corporate earnings and profits resulting from the corporate level phaseout of the *General Utilities Doctrine.*

This one-month liquidation procedure frequently is beneficial when a corporation's properties are worth considerably more than their tax bases and accumulated earnings and profits are relatively low. Computations always should be made to determine whether a regular liquidation or a one-month liquidation will result in a lower amount of tax liability to the shareholders. Proven properties transferred pursuant to a one-month liquidation do not qualify for percentage depletion to the transferee-shareholder. *(See Cases 108 and 109.)*

---

435. P.L. 99-514 (Tax Reform Act of 1986), Sec. 633(d).
436. Reg. Sec. 1.333-3.
437. I.R.C. Sec. 333(e) (*prior to amendment by the Tax Reform Act of 1986*); Reg. Sec. 1.333-4(c)(1).
438. I.R.C. Sec. 333(f) (*prior to amendment by the Tax Reform Act of 1986*); I.R.C. Sec. 333(e) (*prior to amendment by the Tax Reform Act of 1986*); Reg. Sec. 1.333-4(c)(1).

Operator A will be required to treat $75,000 as dividend income and $25,000 as long-term capital gain. Operator A's tax basis in the assets other than cash received in the liquidation will be his basis in the stock ($200,000) reduced by the cash received ($100,000) and increased by the gain recognized ($100,000), or a total of $200,000.[439] If Operator A assumes liabilities or takes assets subject to any liabilities of the corporation, he should also add the amount of the liabilities to his tax basis in the various assets received in the liquidation.[440] His total basis should be allocated between the producing leases and the lease and well equipment, based on their relative net fair market values.[441] If any assets are pledged to secure specific indebtedness, the amount of the debt is subtracted to determine net fair market value of those assets for allocation purposes. The basis determined by this allocation is added to the amount of the specific indebtedness to determine the total tax basis of these pledged assets. In this case, the amount that should be allocated to producing leases is $160,000 (80% of $200,000), and the amount that should be allocated to lease and well equipment is $40,000 (20% of $200,000).

As in the case of a regular liquidation, C Corporation will be required to recognize as ordinary income the lesser of accelerated cost recovery deductions (or depreciation) claimed after December 31, 1961, or the excess of the fair market value of the lease and well equipment distributed over the adjusted tax basis of that equipment to C Corporation as of the date of liquidation. In addition, C Corporation will be required to restore any unearned investment tax credit as of the liquidation date.

Intangible drilling and development costs (IDC) (less adjustment) also are subject to recapture as ordinary income by C Corporation upon liquidation.[442] For properties placed in service after 1986, all IDC deductions and depletion deductions (to the extent basis has been reduced) are subject to recapture as ordinary income by C Corporation upon liquidation.[443]

If C Corporation must recognize ordinary income on the liquidation, its earnings and profits are generally increased by that income, less related income taxes, thus increasing the amount of potential dividend income Operator A recognizes on the liquidation. As discussed below, the computation of earnings and profits is complex. The increase in earnings and profits as a result of recapture items is adjusted downward to the extent those items have not previously decreased earnings and profits. The Treasury has clarified recently its position for adjustments to a corporation's earnings and profits with respect to a liquidating distribution for purposes of certain liquidations.[444]

Great care should be exercised in computing the earnings and profits of an oil and gas company. For example, depletion is allowed only on the basis of cost; therefore, the excess of percentage depletion over cost depletion is not deductible in computing earnings and profits.[445] *(See Case 121.)* This factor alone has caused serious tax consequences to many unwary shareholders. Earnings and profits are adjusted for accelerated cost recovery allowances by recomputing the allowable deduction using the straight-line method over longer recovery periods.[446] Earnings and profits with respect to productive-well IDC are calculated by capitalizing and amortizing those costs ratably over the 60-month period, beginning with the month in which production

439. I.R.C. Sec. 334(c) (*prior to amendment by the Tax Reform Act of 1986*); Reg. Sec. 1.334-2.
440. Reg. Sec. 1.334-2.
441. *Ibid.*
442. I.R.C. Sec. 1254.
443. I.R.C. Sec. 1254(a)(1).
444. Rev. Rul. 87-1, 1987-2 I.R.B. 4; Rev. Rul. 87-4, 1987-2 I.R.B. 6.
445. Reg. Sec. 1.312-6(c)(1).
446. I.R.C. Sec. 312(k)(3).

begins.[447] If oil and gas properties are ultimately determined to be subject to the uniform capitalization rules, further adjustments to earnings and profits may be necessary.[448]

Case 156
Determination of Basis After Partnership Dissolution

> Operators A and B are partners engaged in the development of oil and gas properties. Each owns a one-half interest in their partnership. They dissolve the partnership and distribute its assets in kind. Each partner originally invested $150,000 in cash. Net taxable income (after deducting intangible drilling and development costs (IDC) and percentage depletion) reported by each partner amounts to $30,000. The depletion allowable totals $100,000, while the unadjusted tax basis of the properties subject to depletion is $10,000. Total withdrawals by each partner are $140,000. At the date of the partnership liquidation, the tax bases of its assets are: cash—$90,000; depletable assets—$20,000; and depreciable assets—$60,000. Operators A and B want to know how to determine tax basis in the depletable and depreciable assets received in liquidation.

If a partnership distributes its assets in kind, the partners generally realize no gain or loss until a subsequent disposition of the property received in liquidation. The basis of a partner's interest in the partnership first is allocated to any cash received, and the balance is allocated among the other assets received in liquidation.[449]

Operators A and B each have an $85,000 basis in their partnership interest, determined as follows:[450]

Original investment	$ 150,000
Net taxable income from partnership	30,000
Excess of allowable depletion over unadjusted tax basis of properties subject to depletion	45,000
Total	$ 225,000
Less: Withdrawals	(140,000)
Tax basis in partnership interest immediately before liquidation	$ 85,000

From this amount ($85,000), each partner must deduct cash received in liquidation ($45,000), leaving each a tax basis of $40,000 to be allocated to the depletable and depreciable assets received in the liquidation in the ratio of their relative tax bases to the partnership.[451] This results in an allocation of $10,000 to depletable assets and $30,000 to depreciable assets to each partner.

A distribution of producing properties from a partnership to its partners in proportion to their ownership in the property does not constitute a transfer of proven properties which would result in the disallowance of percentage depletion. Therefore, Operators A and B should continue to claim percentage depletion on income from the properties received upon dissolution of the partnership. *(See Cases 108 and 109 for a discussion of transfers of proven properties.)*

447. I.R.C. Sec. 312(n)(2).
448. I.R.C. Sec. 312(n)(1).
449. I.R.C. Sec. 732(b).
450. I.R.C. Sec. 705(a).
451. I.R.C. Sec. 732(c)(2).

In this case, because Operators A and B each own one-half the partnership and each receives his half of each asset, there has been no disposition by either partner of his interest in the partnership's unrealized receivables or substantially appreciated inventory items.[452] However, the partnership's obligation to recapture depreciation,[453] depletion and IDC[454] attaches to the properties and will have to be reported by each partner on subsequent dispositions of those properties. *(See Case 78 concerning potential recapture of investment credit.)*

Case 157
Allocation of Basis When Only Part of a Unit of Property Is Sold

> C Company is the owner of a 4,000-acre oil and gas lease for which it paid $420,000 in January 1987. It has conducted extensive drilling operations on a 400-acre section of the lease. The remaining 3,600 acres are undeveloped.
>
> C Company sells outright the producing portion of the lease (400 acres) for $1,120,000 and subleases the remaining 3,600 acres for $40,000 cash, retaining a 1/32 overriding royalty which has a value of $160,000 in September 1987.
>
> The extensive drilling activities by C Company on the 400-acre section of the lease result in four producing wells. A total of $400,000 in drilling costs was paid to prepare the wells for commercial production. At the date of sale, only 5% of estimated reserves has been produced. Depletion totaling $50,000 has been claimed thereon.
>
> Further, the equipment on all four wells has a cost basis of $120,000 and accumulated depreciation of $12,000 on the date of sale. C Company wants to know the amount and nature of its gain from the sale of the 400 acres. The sales agreement allocates $120,000 of the total purchase price to tangible equipment.

C Company should apportion its $370,000 adjusted basis in the 4,000-acre tract between the 400 acres sold outright and the 3,600 acres subleased.[455] Some argue for an allocation on an acreage basis or, as an alternative, on the basis of relative fair market values at the date of purchase. However, it appears that an allocation of cost on the basis of relative fair market values of the two areas at the date of sale may be appropriate based on the discussion below.

As to the $40,000 cash received, the courts consistently have held that a lease bonus is a prepayment for oil and gas in place.[456] As such, it follows that the bonus attaches to the oil or gas, wherever it is found under the lease.

A lease bonus frequently is stated initially in terms of a specified amount per acre. This usually is a mere measure of the bonus and bears no reasonable relationship to the actualities that exist at the time of purchase when the exact location of the mineral deposit is unknown.

452. I.R.C. Sec. 751.
453. I.R.C. Sec. 1245(b)(6).
454. I.R.C. Sec. 1254(b)(1).
455. Reg. Sec. 1.612-1(a).
456. Houston Farms Dev. Co. v. U.S., 132 F.2d 861 (5th Cir. 1943), 30 AFTR 698, 43-1 USTC 9254.

This situation is analogous to one in which a portion of an aggregated property is transferred. In that situation, the regulations require an allocation of total costs between the portion disposed of and the portion retained on the basis of their relative fair market values at the date of disposition.[457] Thus, there is no requirement that a determination be made of the actual costs incurred with respect to the acreage transferred.

Furthermore, whenever a part of a lease is unitized, it is the Internal Revenue Service's policy to require an allocation of cost between the portion of the lease included in the unit and the portion excluded, in accordance with their relative fair market values.

Assuming the sales price received by C Company represents fair market value at the date of sale, C Company should allocate its $370,000 adjusted basis in the lease as follows:

To the 400-acre tract sold	$\frac{\$1,000,000}{\$1,200,000^*} \times \$370,000 =$	$308,333
To the 3,600-acre tract subleased	$\frac{\$\ 200,000}{\$1,200,000^*} \times \$370,000 =$	61,667
Total		$370,000

*$1,120,000 - $120,000 + $40,000 + $160,000

The allocation is based on a total fair market value of $1,200,000 attributable to the lease (excluding the $120,000 allocated to the equipment).

The basis to be allocated ($370,000 in the example) is calculated by subtracting the $50,000 of depletion allowable before the sale from the original cost of $420,000. Also, the adjusted basis of $61,667 attributable to the subleased tract of 3,600 acres will be reduced by cost depletion allowable (if any) with respect to the $40,000 lease bonus in determining the tax basis of the retained 1/32 overriding royalty *(see Case 98)*. Lease bonus income no longer qualifies for percentage depletion.[458] Production from transferred proven properties does not qualify for percentage depletion by the transferee. *(See Cases 108 and 109 for a further discussion.)*

For properties placed in service after 1986, deductions for intangible drilling and development costs (IDC) and depletion deductions not in excess of basis are subject to recapture as ordinary income on disposition of the property.[459] *(See Case 131.)*

457. Reg. Sec. 1.614-6(a)(2).
458. I.R.C. Sec. 613A(d)(5).
459. I.R.C. Sec. 1254(a)(1).

Under the principles discussed above, C Company recognizes the following gain on the sale of the 400 acres.

Sales price		$1,120,000
Allocated basis:		
Leasehold cost	$308,333	
Lease and well equipment costs	120,000	
Less: depreciation	(12,000)	(416,333)
Gain		$ 703,667
Character of gain:		
Ordinary		
Depletion recapture		$ 50,000
Recapture of IDC		400,000
Recapture of depreciation (limited to realized gain)		12,000
Long-term capital gain (Section 1231)		241,667
Total gain		$ 703,667

Case 158
Tax Basis After Termination of Unitization

In 1981, Operator A acquired three operating mineral interests in noncontiguous tracts, designated Nos. 1, 2 and 3. The properties were included in a compulsory unitization from January 1, 1982, to December 31, 1986. The adjusted bases of the properties at January 1, 1982, were $50,000, $10,000 and $40,000, respectively. Total depletion for the unit during the five-year period is $50,000, $24,000 of which is allocable to property No. 1, $16,800 to No. 2 and $9,200 to No. 3. Operator A wants to know his depletable tax basis in the properties on December 31, 1986, when the unitization is terminated.

Without the unitization, each interest constitutes a separate property. However, since the properties are unitized, the depletion deduction is computed for the group as a single property, and the adjustments to basis are not required to be allocated to the separate properties included in the unit.[460]

When the unitization is terminated, the treatment of all properties as a single property ceases and the adjusted basis of the separate properties must be determined.[461] The actual depletion allowed during unitization is allocated to the separate properties on a reasonable basis considering such matters as production records, reasonable cost allocations, etc.[462] If the aggregate of the adjusted bases of the separate properties thus determined exceeds the adjusted basis of the unitized property when the unitization

460. I.R.C. Sec. 614(b)(3); Reg. Sec. 1.614-8(b)(1).
461. Reg. Sec. 1.614-8(b)(5); Reg. Sec. 1.614-6(a)(2)(ii)(b).
462. Reg. Sec. 1.614-6(a)(2)(ii)(b).

terminated, the adjusted bases of the separate properties are reduced proportionately to an amount equal to the adjusted basis of the unitized property, as follows.

Property	Adjusted Basis at Beginning of Unitization	Depletion Adjustments During Unitization	Tentative Adjusted Basis Upon Termination of Unitization	Allocation of Remaining Adjustment (Rounded)	Adjusted Basis of Separate Properties (Rounded)
No. 1	$ 50,000	$24,000	$26,000	$3,100	$22,900
No. 2	10,000	16,800	—	—	—
No. 3	40,000	9,200	30,800	3,700	27,100
	$100,000	$50,000	$56,800	$6,800	$50,000

Transfers pursuant to a unitization (including termination) should not be considered a transfer of proven properties; therefore, the transferee may claim percentage depletion on subsequent production from the property, assuming he was entitled to percentage depletion before the unitization. *(See Cases 108 and 109 for a discussion of transfers of proven properties and the disallowance of percentage depletion subsequent thereto.)*

Case 159
Mineral Interest Claimed as Worthless

> **Lessor R owns certain nonproducing mineral interests (both operating and nonoperating) which he acquired in prior years. He does not own the surface rights. Because he considers the mineral interests to be worthless, he wants to know the rules governing the deduction of his acquisition costs.**

There is no fixed rule for determining the year in which worthless mineral interests may be claimed as deductions. Generally, a deduction is allowable for worthless property if the loss actually is sustained during the tax year, is evidenced by closed and completed transactions and is fixed by identifiable events.[463] The year of deduction is not necessarily the year in which an overt act of abandonment of the property or loss of title occurs.[464]

Loss deductions are allowable in the tax year in which an event occurs that demonstrates the improbability of oil and gas production in commercial quantities and that destroys any value for the interests in the ordinary channels of trade.[465] The establishment of an identifiable event depends on the facts in each particular case. Negative geological and geophysical information alone usually is not sufficient proof to sustain a tax deduction. However, negative information followed by the lessee's dropping the lease should be sufficient to claim a deduction for worthlessness because the lease may not be renewed and the dropping of the lease may be the only identifiable event that occurs.[466]

463. Reg. Sec. 1.165-1(b).
464. Rev. Rul. 54-581, 1954-2 C.B. 112.
465. Arthur Finston, T.C. Memo Dec. (Aug. 29, 1956); James Petroleum Corp. v. Comm'r, 238 F.2d 678 (2d Cir. 1956), 50 AFTR 771, 56-2 USTC 10,041; C. C. Harmon, 1 T.C. 40 (1942).
466. Richard B. Lack, T.C. Memo Dec. (Sept. 28, 1956).

The abandonment of a well as a dry hole on or near a small property usually will be sufficient reason for condemning a property,[467] but additional evidence may be necessary for a larger property because the entire interest in a property unit must be condemned before a loss deduction will be allowed.[468] For example, if one of Lessor R's mineral interests consists of a tract of 5,000 acres, the drilling of one or two dry holes in a corner of the tract probably will not provide proof of worthlessness sufficient to sustain a loss on the entire tract. No loss will be allowable in the year a dry hole is drilled if further activity takes place in a subsequent year.[469]

In the absence of other factors that would establish conclusively the worthlessness of a lease in another year, a loss is deductible in the year in which the lease terminates by its own terms or lapses by the lessee's failure to pay delay rentals.[470] The same general rule as to the year in which an abandonment loss is allowable applies for both leases and royalties. With regard to leases, the usual practice of paying annual delay rentals until production is obtained or the lease is forfeited gives the lessee an identifiable event on which to base the deduction for loss. In these instances, it also may be necessary to prove that the lease had some value at the beginning of the tax year in which the deduction is claimed.[471]

It has been held that an abandonment loss is allowable for the year in which the abandonment itself occurs, even though the lease actually does not terminate until the following year. There must, however, be evidence of an intention to abandon, supported by physical withdrawal or abandonment of the property.[472] Neither the intention to abandon[473] nor the physical abandonment[474] alone will be sufficient to support the deduction. A loss will be allowed only when it can be related to some identifiable event.[475] If lease rentals are paid in the year subsequent to an event that may otherwise prove the worthlessness of the lease (i.e., a dry hole on or near the lease), the abandonment loss probably will not be allowed in the earlier year.[476] This rule applies even in cases in which several dry holes have been drilled on the lease.[477] The Tax Court ruled that no abandonment deduction was allowed where the taxpayer's only support for its intention to abandon the separate strata was internal records supporting the decision to abandon.[478] The court was influenced by the fact that the taxpayer paid delay rentals on the lease and retained the right to drill and explore on all portions of the lease. Additionally, since the court reached its conclusion primarily based on what it viewed as inadequate support for an abandonment loss, it did not specifically address the validity of the taxpayer's treatment of separate horizontal strata as separate properties.

Proof of abandonment or worthlessness before the year of the lease termination is difficult and often involves disputes with the Internal Revenue Service (IRS). The taxpayer should, if possible, take steps before the end of the year to assure his right to the deduction for the year in which he considers the lease to have become worthless. When the taxpayer wishes to claim an abandonment loss in the current year for a

467. L. S. Randolph, T.C. Memo Dec. (Dec. 21, 1942); James Petroleum Corp.
468. Davis v. Comm'r, 241 F.2d 701 (7th Cir. 1957), 50 AFTR 1721, 57-1 USTC 9441.
469. L. M. Fischer, 14 T.C. 792 (1950).
470. C. H. Goodwin, 9 B.T.A. 1209 (1928); A. T. Jergins Trust, 22 B.T.A. 551 (1931).
471. Davis.
472. Cotton v. Helvering, 68 F.2d 436 (D.C. Cir. 1933), 13 AFTR 534, 1934 CCH 9006; A. H. Fell, 7 B.T.A. 263 (1927); Davis.
473. A. L. Huey, 4 B.T.A. 370, (1926); Goodwin.
474. Helvering v. Canisteo Mining Co., 76 F.2d 378 (8th Cir. 1935), 15 AFTR 1120, 35-1 USTC 9180; Boggs Oil Corp., 19 B.T.A. 940 (1930).
475. Reg. Sec. 1.165-1(b); Rev. Rul. 54-581,1954-2 C.B. 112; U.S. v. White Dental Mfg., 274 U.S. 398 (1927), 6 AFTR 6750, 1 USTC 235.
476. Huey; A. T. Jergins Trust; S. W. Forrester, 23 B.T.A. 942 (1931); Macon Oil and Gas Co., 23 B.T.A. 54 (1931); Goodwin.
477. A. T. Jergins Trust.
478. Gulf Oil Corp., 87 T.C. 135 (1986).

lease that may be held until the following year by delay rentals already paid, the taxpayer may ensure the allowance of the loss in the current year if he reassigns all the lease rights to the grantor, assignor or some other unrelated third party. This procedure precludes possible disputes with regard to the proper year in which the loss otherwise may be allowed, provided the worthlessness of the lease and the desire to fix the year of the tax deduction are the only considerations of the reassignment.

The IRS often disallows deductions claimed for the worthlessness of mineral interests on the grounds that the events occurring within the year were insufficient or were too far removed geographically from the property to establish worthlessness in that year. The amounts disallowed may and should be claimed again as tax deductions, without prejudice, in a subsequent year in which additional indications of worthlessness occur or in the year the lease expires. A deduction for worthlessness should be handled carefully because the taxpayer is faced with the possibility that the IRS will establish a property's worthlessness in a prior year barred by the statute of limitations.[479] If, however, the taxpayer claims a deduction for the worthlessness of a mineral interest and the IRS contends that worthlessness occurred in an earlier year for which the statute of limitations had not expired at the time the deduction originally was claimed, the IRS may not disallow the tax deduction for the earlier year.[480]

No deduction is allowable for the partial worthlessness of an oil or gas lease.[481] The entire lease must be proven worthless for any part of the cost to qualify for a tax deduction. There must be a closed and completed transaction fixed by an identifiable event.[482] When several contiguous leases are acquired in a single transaction for a lump sum, the cost applicable to each lease must be deducted in the year it is dropped if leases are dropped in different years.[483] However, to sustain these deductions, the contiguous leases must constitute individual units of property as separate leases that retain their separate identities in the group conveyance.[484] The amount of the deduction will be the portion of the total tax basis of the leases allocable to the surrendered leases. The allocation of lease bonus to the separate leases acquired in this manner usually is made on a net acreage basis at the date of acquisition, unless other factors indicate that some of the acreage is more valuable than the remainder.

The owner of an oil and gas lease probably will be held to be conducting a business if he engages in any exploration or development activity, although he may not be engaged primarily in oil and gas operations. He probably should deduct losses on account of the worthlessness of mineral properties in computing his adjusted gross income. Apparently, this is in conformity with a Supreme Court decision[485] holding that co-owners of a working interest carried on a trade or business.

When the lease has expired under its own terms or when the lessee has relinquished the lease prior to production, the lessor must restore to his tax basis in the property (and report as income in the tax year of forfeiture of the interest) any depletion that was allowable on the lease bonus. (*See Case 127.*)

479. James Petroleum Corp.
480. I.R.C. Sec. 1311(b)(2)(B); Reg. Sec. 1.1311(b)-2(b).
481. Paul P. Brountas, 73 T.C. 491 (1979); Brountas v. Comm'r, 692 F.2d 152 (1st Cir. 1982), 50 AFTR2d 82-5900, 82-2 USTC 9626.
482. Reg. Sec. 1.165-1(b); Rev. Rul. 54-581, 1954-2 C.B. 112; Driscoll v. Comm'r, 147 F.2d 493 (5th Cir. 1945), 33 AFTR 704, 45-1 USTC 9184; Houston Farms Dev. Co. v. Comm'r, 194 F.2d 520 (5th Cir. 1952), 41 AFTR 725, 52-1 USTC 9175.
483. L. B. Maytag, 32 T.C. 270 (1959); American Smelting and Ref. Co.-Consol. v. U.S., 423 F.2d 277 (Ct. Cl. 1970), 25 AFTR2d 853, 70-1 USTC 9287.
484. L. B. Maytag; Rev. Rul. 68-566, 1968-2 C.B. 281; American Smelting. (*See* Rev. Rul. 77-187, 1977-1 C.B. 50 for the treatment to be afforded non-oil and gas minerals by the IRS under similar circumstances.)
485. Helvering v. Combs, 296 U.S. 365 (1935), 16 AFTR 1272, 36-1 USTC 9023.

A producing lease does not become worthless until the year in which commercial production ceases, even though the production for the prior years may have been small and the well may have been operating at a loss.[486] Any remaining basis in unsalvageable equipment generally should be claimed as a loss in the year that equipment is abandoned[487] (typically, when the well is plugged). Any remaining leasehold cost generally should be claimed as cost depletion for the last year in which production was obtained from the lease.

Case 160
Worthlessness of Mineral Fee When All Mineral and Surface Rights Are Owned

> **Lessor R owns all the mineral and surface rights in a 320-acre tract of land. In a prior year, Lessor R granted an oil and gas lease to Operator A, retaining a one-eighth landowner's royalty. During the current year, Operator A drilled two dry holes on the tract of land, abandoned the property and reassigned the lease to Lessor R. Lessor R wants to know if he can claim a deduction for the worthlessness of the mineral right because the two wells effectively condemned the property for any possible production of oil or gas.**

Lessor R is required to allocate his basis in the entire fee between surface rights and minerals for the purpose of computing depletion. Lessor R also will be required to make such an allocation if he sells the mineral rights instead of leasing them. It follows that Lessor R should be allowed a deduction for the worthlessness of the mineral fee based on that allocation. However, under present practice, Lessor R probably will not be allowed to claim a deduction on account of the worthlessness of the oil and gas rights, even though he may be able to prove that worthlessness.[488] Lessor R may not be allowed such a deduction because of the argument that a loss cannot be determined until the entire property is sold (including the surface rights and rights to any other minerals) resulting in a closed transaction. Under these circumstances, a deduction is not allowed for partial worthlessness because presumably there is some value remaining in the surface and other mineral rights.

If a fee owner acquires his interest in the surface and minerals at different times by separate instruments or conveyances, there is some question whether he will be allowed a deduction for the cost of the mineral interest in the year in which it can be proved to be worthless.[489] However, in one situation, the underlying minerals were valued separately from the surface rights on a federal estate tax return at a time when the minerals were under lease. When the minerals later were determined to be worthless, a deduction was allowed to the estate for the loss on that worthlessness for the year in which the lease on the minerals was allowed to expire.[490]

---

486. Macon Oil and Gas Co., 23 B.T.A. 54 (1931).
487. Prop. Reg. Sec. 1.168-6; Reg. Sec. 1.167(a)-8.
488. Louisiana Land and Exploration Co. v. Comm'r, 161 F.2d 842 (5th Cir. 1947), 35 AFTR 1388, 47-1 USTC 9266; Coalinga-Mohawk Oil Co. v. Comm'r, 64 F.2d 262 (9th Cir. 1933), 12 AFTR 389, 3 USTC 1084.
489. Henley v. U.S., 396 F.2d 956 (Ct. Cl. 1968), 21 AFTR2d 1535, 68-1 USTC 9427.
490. Pool v. U.S., 119 F. Supp. 202 (Ct. Cl. 1954), 45 AFTR 706, 54-1 USTC 9263.

Section VI
Forms of Organization for Conducting Oil and Gas Operations

Oil and gas operations historically have been conducted under many forms of organization. Sole proprietorship continues to be a common form. Although the sole proprietor conducts his operations as an individual, he often acts as a co-owner with other parties in the joint conduct of exploration, drilling, development and production. Many of the tax problems involved in selecting the form of organization relate to these joint operations.

The customary joint operating agreement used by co-owners in the oil and gas industry establishes relationships that are classified as partnerships for tax purposes. However, the regulations allow the parties to these agreements to elect to be excluded from application of the partnership provisions of the Internal Revenue Code under certain circumstances. By electing not to be taxed as a partnership, each co-owner is required to report his proportionate share of each item of income, expense or other item of tax significance in his own tax return. Taxpayers who plan to report their joint oil and gas operations as co-owners should be certain their agreement is drafted properly and the organization correctly makes the election not to be treated as a partnership. Failure to make this election properly can invalidate various other elections because of improper methods of tax reporting.

Joint operations may be conducted as a partnership (either general or limited) to achieve certain tax advantages that cannot be achieved solely through co-ownership. A legal partnership or a joint venture taxed as a partnership is a common form of business organization for oil and gas operations. The partnership agreement and tax provisions must be drafted carefully if taxable income, deductions and the like are not shared proportionately by the partners. These provisions can affect materially the partners' economic sharing arrangements.

The operations also may be conducted in corporate form, but there are significant disadvantages when that form is used in the conduct of oil and gas operations. A so-called "S corporation," however, may be considered an acceptable form of organization in some instances. The requirements for the initial qualification of a corporation to be treated as an S corporation are somewhat restrictive. Therefore, before a decision is made to conduct operations in this form, it should be determined that all requirements can be met now and in the future. Perhaps the greatest disadvantages to operating in corporate form (other than as an S corporation) are the potential for double taxation and the loss of percentage depletion benefits.

When joint operations are conducted by two or more co-owners, or as a partnership or trust, extreme care should be exercised to avoid treatment as an association taxable as a corporation. This classification usually has disastrous tax consequences to the owners who expect to include the entity income and deductions in their own returns.

Individuals, closely held corporations and certain other entities may be subject to limitations on deductions and credits attributable to passive activities. *Passive activity* generally means a trade or business in which the taxpayer does not materially participate in operations on a regular, continuous and substantial basis. Aggregate passive-activity losses (net of income) and aggregate credits (net of any passive-activity tax liability) generally are disallowed and must be carried forward. Working interests owned directly or through an entity that does not limit the liability of the taxpayer are not subject to the passive-activity rules. S corporation shareholders who do not materially participate and generally all limited partners will be subject to these rules.

Certain investment organizers may be required to register offerings with the Internal Revenue Service if the investment is considered a tax shelter. The statute defines *tax shelter* broadly to include any investment: (1) in which it could be reasonably inferred from representations made that the tax shelter ratio (the ratio that the cumulative aggregate gross deductions plus 350% of the credits bears to the investment base) for any investor at the end of any of the first five years exceeds 2 to 1 and (2) that is required to be registered under federal or state securities laws or sold pursuant to an exemption from registration requiring notification, or in which the aggregate investment offered for sale exceeds $250,000 and five or more investors participate. Investors are required to include the tax-shelter registration number on their own tax returns.

Case 161
Co-Owned Oil and Gas Properties

Co-owner-Operators A, B and C each own an undivided one-third interest in a block of leases. The three co-owners enter into an operating agreement covering the joint development and operation of the properties, but each retains title to his undivided interest in the leases. Operator A is designated "operator" of the properties and is given the usual authority with respect to the drilling, developing and producing operations on the properties. Operators B and C are designated as "nonoperators."

Operator A obligates himself to consult with the nonoperators on all substantive matters and to keep them informed at all times of his actions and the progress of the development of the properties. Operators B and C, however, reserve the right, upon written notice to Operator A, to take in kind or to dispose separately of their respective shares of the production obtained from the leases. If the nonoperators (B and C) do not exercise these rights, Operator A is given the express revocable authority to enter into contracts to dispose of the entire production from the properties currently at a price not less than the posted field price for similar production in the area and to have the purchasers of the production pay the co-owners directly in accordance with properly executed division orders. Operator A's authority to contract is limited to his contracting for the sale of production for periods of time that are not in excess of the minimum needs of the industry and that do not, in any event, exceed one year. This authority is revocable at the will of any co-owner.

The Internal Revenue Code (the Code) broadly defines the term *partnership* to include a syndicate, group, pool, joint venture or other unincorporated organization through which any business, financial operation or venture is conducted.[1]

It often is difficult to determine when a partnership exists and who its partners are. Reviewing appropriate documentation and intent of the parties is necessary to determine the proper characterization of the arrangement. The Internal Revenue Service (IRS) has issued a technical advice memorandum involving a mining exploration farmout arrangement in which the farmee earned an interest in the property by assuming all development obligations and the farmor reserved an overriding royalty interest convertible into a working interest at payout. The IRS concluded that there was no intent by the parties to form a partnership, no present sharing of profits and losses, no business conducted in the joint names of the parties and no mutual control over the operations; accordingly, the arrangement was not a partnership.[2]

Participants in the joint production, extraction or use of property may elect to be excluded from the application of the partnership tax provisions (Subchapter K) if they:

- □ Own the property as co-owners, either in fee or under a lease or another form of contract granting exclusive operating rights;
- □ Reserve the right separately to take in kind or dispose of their shares of any property produced, extracted or used; and
- □ Do not jointly sell the property produced or extracted, although each participant may delegate authority to sell his share for a period of time not in excess of the minimum needs of the industry and for no more than one year.[3]

The arrangement among Operators A, B and C will be treated as a partnership for federal income tax purposes, even though it may not constitute a partnership under the state law where operations are conducted.[4] However, if Operators A, B and C consent and a proper election is made, the organization may be excluded from the partnership provisions of the Code.[5]

This election, which must be made in the first year in which the organization wants to be excluded from the partnership provisions, is filed in a statement attached to the customary partnership return of income (Form 1065).[6] Although the regulations require that an election be filed, the unincorporated group may be deemed to have made an election to be excluded from the partnership provisions if all the surrounding facts and circumstances clearly indicate that all the members of the group intended from inception of their arrangement to be so excluded.[7] (*See Case 25.*)

The right of participants to elect out of the partnership provisions is subject to certain requirements, one of which is that the parties "reserve the right separately to take in kind or dispose of their shares of any property produced, extracted or used . . . ." The IRS has issued a technical advice memorandum that addresses a factual situation in which a right of first refusal or call on production existed.[8] It provides that the existence of such a call is inconsistent with the right to take in kind and separately

1. I.R.C. Sec. 761(a); I.R.C. Sec. 7701(a)(2).
2. IRS Letter Ruling 8302002 (Technical Advice Memorandum).
3. Reg. Sec. 1.761-2(a)(3).
4. Reg. Sec. 1.761-1(a).
5. Reg. Sec. 1.761-2(a).
6. Reg. Sec. 1.761-2(b)(2).
7. Reg. Sec. 1.761-2(b)(2)(ii).
8. IRS Letter Ruling 8226014 (Technical Advice Memorandum).

dispose of production. This position is an indication that the IRS may narrowly construe the requirements for electing out of Subchapter K.

The determination of partnership status and the validity of any election to be excluded from Subchapter K is particularly important since partnerships, not their partners, make most tax elections including the election to deduct intangible drilling and development costs (IDC).[9] Therefore, absent clear statutory, regulatory or judicial authority determining status, consideration should be given to filing a partnership return of income to protect the validity of these elections.

Legal or record title to oil and gas properties sometimes is held by a nominee for the benefit of several interest owners.[10] The nominee may receive oil and gas sales proceeds and periodically distribute the proceeds to the actual owners. In some instances, owners may instruct the nominee to pay monthly lease operating expenses as billed by the operator to the extent cash is available from current sales of the production.

Taxpayers should exercise extreme caution in establishing a nominee entity. If such entity is characterized as the true owner of the properties, it will be taxable on the production sales proceeds and will be entitled to deductions for operating and other expenses incurred. The Supreme Court set forth guidelines in determining whether an actual agency relationship is established between the nominee and its principal. These guidelines include determinations as to whether the agent:

- ☐ Operates in the name and for the account of the principal.
- ☐ Binds the principal by its actions.
- ☐ Transmits money received to the principal.
- ☐ Receives income that is attributable to the services of the principal's employees and assets.
- ☐ Carries on the normal duties of an agent as its business purpose.

In addition, if the nominee is a true agent, its relations with its principal must not be dependent on the fact that it is owned by the principal if such is the case.[11]

In numerous real estate cases, the lower courts disagree as to the proper interpretation of this latter requirement and its application under varying factual situations. Using a literal interpretation, some courts require the taxpayer to establish that the agency relationship is, in fact, an arm's-length arrangement.[12] Other courts believe the requirement is satisfied if the nominee acts no differently than an independent agent would act if it had bargained with its principal for its services at arm's length.[13] The Supreme Court has agreed to resolve this judicial dispute.[14] The IRS will not issue an advance ruling whether a nominee arrangement will be recognized for tax purposes.[15]

---

9. I.R.C. Sec. 703(b).
10. Prairie Center Oil Dev. Co., T.C. Memo Dec. (Sept. 25, 1958); K-C Land Co., T.C. Memo Dec. (Feb. 29, 1960).
11. Moline Properties v. Comm'r, 319 U.S. 436 (1943), 30 AFTR 1291, 43-1 USTC 9464; National Carbide Corp. v. Comm'r, 336 U.S. 422 (1949), 37 AFTR 834, 49-1 USTC 9223.
12. Jones v. Comm'r, 640 F.2d 745 (5th Cir. 1981), 47 AFTR2d 81-1145, 81-1 USTC 9284; Roccaforte v. Comm'r, 708 F.2d 986 (5th Cir. 1983), 52 AFTR2d 83-5332, 83-2 USTC 9452; George Sarkisian, T.C. Memo Dec. (Apr. 14, 1982); Vaughn v. U.S., 740 F.2d 941 (Fed. Cir. 1984), 54 AFTR2d 84-5664, 84-2 USTC 9706; Ourisman v. Comm'r, 760 F.2d 541 (4th Cir. 1985), 55 AFTR2d 85-1428, 85-1 USTC 9357.
13. Raphan v. U.S., 759 F.2d 879 (Fed. Cir. 1985), 55 AFTR2d 85-1154, 85-1 USTC 9297, *cert. den.* 106 S. Ct. 129; Moncrief v. U.S., 730 F.2d 276 (5th Cir. 1984), 53 AFTR2d 84-1479, 84-1 USTC 9417; Bollinger, Jr. v. Comm'r, 807 F.2d 65 (6th Cir. 1986), 58 AFTR2d 86-6277, 86-2 USTC 9821, *cert. granted* June 8, 1987.
14. Bollinger.
15. Rev. Proc. 87-3, 1987-1 I.R.B. 27 (Sec. 4.3).

A person holding a partnership interest as nominee for another person must furnish certain information to the partnership and such other person.[16] The nominee must notify the partnership of its name, address and identification number; the name, address and identification number of the beneficial owner; and a description of the interest held during the year. This information must be provided by the last day of the first month following the end of the partnership's tax year.[17] The nominee also must furnish to the beneficial owner the partnership's taxable income and deduction information.[18]

The IRS has published two rulings dealing at length with the circumstances under which the operation of a co-owned producing oil and gas property may constitute an association taxable as a corporation.[19] These rulings were issued before enactment of the present Code and pertinent regulations, but they still appear to apply directly to situations in which the co-owners have elected to be excluded from the partnership provisions of the Code. In the rulings, the IRS discusses the various phases of the operation of a co-owned oil and gas property and states there can be no association taxable as a corporation when there is no possibility of joint profit. This statement also is contained in the regulations[20] and in at least one Tax Court case[21] pertaining to this same issue. (*See Case 162 regarding the classification of an organization as an association taxable as a corporation.*)

The IRS also has ruled that the regulations under the Natural Gas Act governing the filing of rate schedules and applications for certificates do not affect the way these rulings apply to joint operating agreements among co-owners of producing gas properties.[22]

Losses and credits attributable to the leases should not be subject to the passive-activity limitations[23] since Operators A, B and C will own the working interests directly or through a tax partnership that does not limit their liability.[24] (*See Case 185 for further discussion of the passive-activity rules.*)

Case 162
Association Taxable as a Corporation

Operator A, Operator B and C Company are co-owners of oil and gas leases on adjoining tracts of land that overlie a common gas distillate reservoir. Operators A and B and C Company, together with the royalty owners, execute a unitization agreement covering the joint development and operation of the property. The unitization agreement provides for the appointment of an operating committee to manage and control the development and operation of the property. The committee is given the authority to dispose of all production and to divide the proceeds according to a formula based on gas reserves. The agreement is binding on the co-owners and their heirs and assignees. The committee contracts with a nearby natural gas plant to process the gas, sell the products and remit 60% of the proceeds to the committee. The residue gas is sold by the committee to a gas transmission line under a 20-year contract.

16. I.R.C. Sec. 6031(c).
17. IRS Notice 87-10, 1987-3 I.R.B. 13.
18. I.R.C. Sec. 6031(b).
19. I.T. 3930, 1948-2 C.B. 126; I.T. 3948, 1949-1 C.B. 161.
20. Reg. Sec. 301.7701-2(a)(2).
21. Bush #1 c/o Stonestreet Lands Co., 48 T.C. 218 (1967).
22. Rev. Rul. 56-630, 1956-2 C.B. 964.
23. I.R.C. Sec. 469.
24. I.R.C. Sec. 469(c)(3).

The Supreme Court[25] and the Internal Revenue Service (IRS)[26] have set forth certain salient features that, if present in an unincorporated business enterprise, make it analogous to a corporate organization. These characteristics are: (1) associates, (2) an objective to carry on business and divide the gains therefrom (joint profit motive), (3) continuity of life, (4) centralization of management, (5) liability for corporate debts limited to corporate property and (6) free transferability of interests. The regulations provide that an unincorporated organization may not be classified as an association unless such an organization has more corporate characteristics than noncorporate characteristics, disregarding the characteristics common to both types of organizations.

The regulations further provide that, unless there are both associates and a joint profit motive, there cannot be an association taxable as a corporation.[27] The IRS reasons that profits arise not from the mere extraction or processing of minerals but from their sale. Accordingly, a joint profit motive may be avoided by leaving the property ownership and the control of the sale of production in the hands of the respective co-owners, usually in the form of an agreement providing that each co-owner will have the right to take his share of the production in kind and to dispose of that production separately.

When, as here, the group permits a committee or an operator to act in an irrevocable representative capacity for marketing, the joint venture will be treated as an association.[28] The association includes only those individuals owning undivided interests in the working and operating rights who have granted to a co-owner or third party irrevocable control over the sale of production or the right to grant options to purchase that production. Holders of royalties, overriding royalties, production payments or net profits interests are considered to have interests that are substantially adverse to a lessee interest, and those parties are not included in the association.

The IRS probably will hold that an association is present as a result of any agreement by which: (1) two or more of the co-owners jointly grant irrevocable marketing authority to the same agent or (2) one co-owner irrevocably grants to another co-owner the right to sell the production from the jointly owned property.[29] The maximum sales contract that an agent acting under a revocable power may have the authority to make, without creating an association, is one that is considered necessary to meet the minimum needs of the industry but that does not exceed a period of one year from the effective date of that contract.

Mineral fee interests sometimes are included in the corpus of an investment trust, with the trustee having limited powers with respect to leasing the minerals. If the trustee has no right to exploit the minerals and must obtain permission of the trust's beneficial owners to execute an oil and gas lease, the trust probably will not be treated as an association taxable as a corporation.[30] *(See Case 173.)* Testamentary and intervivos trusts generally must lack associates or a joint profit motive to avoid association status.[31]

The courts have had occasion to rule on the validity of the regulations in setting out the six tests and in requiring that more than one half of the corporate characteristics

25. Morrissey v. Comm'r, 296 U.S. 344 (1935), 16 AFTR 1274, 36-1 USTC 9020.
26. Reg. Sec. 301.7701-2(a)(1).
27. Reg. Sec. 301.7701-2(a)(2); I.T. 3930, 1948-2 C.B. 126; I.T. 3948, 1949-1 C.B. 161; Bush #1 c/o Stonestreet Lands Co., 48 T.C. 218 (1967).
28. U.S. v. Stierwalt, 287 F.2d 855 (10th Cir. 1961), 7 AFTR2d 1013, 61-1 USTC 9330; John Provence #1 Well v. Comm'r, 321 F.2d 840 (3d Cir. 1963), 12 AFTR2d 5059, 63-2 USTC 9582.
29. I.T. 3948, 1949-1 C.B. 161.
30. Rev. Rul. 57-112, 1957-1 C.B. 494.
31. Reg. Sec. 301.7701-4(a); Elm Street Realty Trust, 76 T.C. 803 (1981), (A) 1981-2 C.B. 1; Harry M. Bedell, Jr., 86 T.C. 1207 (1986); Rev. Rul. 80-75, 1980-1 C.B. 314; Rev. Rul. 78-371, 1978-2 C.B. 344; IRS Letter Ruling 8552010 (Technical Advice Memorandum).

be present for an organization to be held to be a corporation. The Court of Claims[32] found a limited partnership to be a partnership and not an association taxable as a corporation on the basis that it did not have more corporate than noncorporate characteristics by applying the regulations. In holding that two limited partnerships were not associations taxable as corporations, the Tax Court observed that the IRS should consider changing its regulations if it intended to attack the status of limited partnerships. Shortly after this decision, in the *Larson* case,[33] the IRS proposed restrictive regulations that would have made it more difficult for limited partnerships to avoid taxation as corporations. These regulations were withdrawn, and the IRS then acquiesced in the *Larson* decision. Later, the IRS further expressed its willingness to follow the *Larson* case by a published ruling[34] in which it listed the following factors that will not be considered "other factors" that are significant in determining whether a limited partnership will be taxed as a corporation *(see Case 167 for a discussion of requirements for obtaining an advance ruling regarding partnership status)*:

☐ The division of limited partnership interests into units or shares, and the promotion and marketing of those interests in a manner similar to corporate securities.

☐ Whether the managing partner has the discretionary right to retain or distribute profits according to the needs of the business.

☐ Whether the limited partner has the right to vote on the removal and election of general partners, and on the sale of all or substantially all the assets of the partnership.

☐ Whether the limited partnership interests are represented by certificates.

☐ Whether the limited partnership observes corporate formalities and procedures.

☐ Whether the limited partners are required to sign the partnership agreement.

☐ Whether the limited partnership provides a means of pooling investments while limiting the liability of some of the participants.

When an association is determined to exist, the income and deductions attributable to the jointly owned property are considered to be the income and deductions of the association rather than of the individual co-owners. Amounts advanced by the co-owners are treated as investments in stock, and any repayments to the co-owners are considered to be corporate dividends, taxable to the extent considered to be distributed out of earnings and profits. The association or corporate relationship applies throughout the life of the organization; upon liquidation, the provisions of the law applicable to corporate liquidations will control.

If it is held that a co-ownership is taxable as a corporation, a transfer of a proven property to that "corporation" can result in the denial of percentage depletion to the transferee. *(See Case 108 for a discussion of percentage depletion subsequent to the transfer of a proven property.)*

32. Zuckman v. U.S., 524 F.2d 729 (Ct. Cl. 1975), 36 AFTR2d 75-6193, 75-2 USTC 9778.
33. Phillip G. Larson, 66 T.C. 159 (1976), (A) 1979-1 C.B. 1.
34. Rev. Rul. 79-106, 1979-1 C.B. 448.

Case 163
Co-Ownership Treated as a Tax Partnership and General and Limited Partnerships

Operators A, B and C each own an undivided interest in a block of leases. They decide to develop and operate the properties. They do not wish to incorporate because of the double taxation associated with a corporation.

Operators A, B and C have several alternatives to consider in reaching a decision as to the type of unincorporated organization they should choose:

1. Form a general partnership under local law.
2. Form a limited partnership under local law, permitting the general partner to conduct all the business operations of the partnership.
3. Execute a joint operating agreement that will provide, among other things, for the following:
   a. One of the co-owners will be designated as operator of the properties.
   b. Each co-owner will retain individually his respective interest in the block of leases and the right to receive his share of the production in kind or dispose of his share of production separately.
   c. The operator will incur development and operation costs on behalf of the co-owners, with periodic billings to the co-owners for their shares of the actual costs plus an agreed operating or overhead fee. Each co-owner will have the right to review the propriety of the joint account charges and credits.

If Operators, A, B and C choose the third alternative, they may elect to be excluded from the partnership provisions of the Internal Revenue Code (the Code).[35] If they so elect, their pro-rata shares of the income and deductions attributable to the properties will be treated as the income and deductions of the individual co-owners. *(See Cases 25 and 161 for a discussion of this election.)*

Assume, however, that Operators A, B and C do not so elect and want to be treated as a partnership for tax purposes. If the joint operations are to be treated as a partnership for tax purposes, all provisions of Subchapter K of the Code will apply. For example, a partner may deduct his share of losses only to the extent of his adjusted basis in his partnership interest.[36]

The tax results under all three alternatives generally are the same because each will be treated as a partnership for tax purposes. There is no distinction at the organizational level between a general or limited partnership and a co-ownership treated as a partnership for tax purposes.[37] However, limited partners generally are subject to the passive-activity limitations on losses and credits attributable to their interests.[38] *(See Case 182 for discussion of the passive-activity limitations.)*

In each case, the partnership, as the owner of the operating rights, will have a separate election for expensing intangible drilling and development costs (IDC). Even though a partnership is not a taxpayer, it is an entity for which net income must be

35. I.R.C. Sec. 761(a); Reg. Sec. 1.761-2(a).
36. Rev. Rul. 58-465, 1958-2 C.B. 376.
37. I.R.C. Sec. 761(a).
38. I.R.C. Sec. 469.

computed separately; therefore, the partnership rather than the individual partners must make the election.[39] This election will have no effect on the treatment of similar costs incurred by the partners on other separately owned properties. Even though the election with respect to intangibles is available to the partnership, IDC attributable to each partner must be set out separately in the partnership income return.[40] *(See Case 181 regarding the election to capitalize IDC.)*

In addition to the IDC election, the partnership also must make all other elections affecting the computation of taxable income that ordinarily are available to individual taxpayers on their personal tax returns, except those that must be made specifically by the partners. Elections made by each partner with respect to partnership items include the treatment of foreign taxes as a deduction or as a credit, special elections regarding capitalization of IDC *(see Case 181)* and certain miscellaneous elections that generally do not apply to operating oil and gas partnerships.[41]

A partnership with a corporate partner (other than an S corporation) may not use the cash receipts and disbursements accounting method unless it and certain related entities had combined average annual gross receipts of $5 million or less for all prior tax years beginning after December 31, 1985 (based on a three-year moving average).[42] Tax shelters may not use the cash receipts and disbursements accounting method regardless of the amount of gross receipts.[43]

Assuming the subject venture is not a tax shelter, Operators A, B and C may use their individual methods of accounting with respect to the venture if they elect not to be subject to partnership treatment. However, the venture will be required to use the accrual method of accounting if any of its partners are corporations, if it is treated as a partnership for tax purposes and if it has average annual gross receipts in excess of $5 million. Under certain circumstances, the gross receipts of a partner are included in the latter determination.[44]

Income, gain, loss and deductions attributable to contributed property must be shared among partners to take into account the variation, if any, between the basis of the property to the partnership and its fair market value at the time of contribution.[45] *(See Case 166.)*

If a partner renders services in lieu of making a capital contribution to the partnership, consideration must be given to determining whether the partner has income from the receipt of a partnership interest or an interest in the partnership profits in return for those services. *(See Case 18.)*

Although a partnership generally provides tax results that are as good as, or better than, those available to individual co-owners, it sometimes limits the flexibility of the co-owners with respect to tax planning. For example, the partners may find that it is more difficult to divide their interests among members of the family group or to plan their income and deductions because the tax needs of all partners may not be the same.

A partnership agreement must be drafted carefully to avoid the characteristics that cause an organization to be classified as an association taxable as a corporation. *(See Case 162 for further discussion of an association taxable as a corporation and Case 167*

39. I.R.C. Sec. 703(b); Reg. Sec. 1.703-1(b); Bentex Oil Corp., 20 T.C. 565 (1953).
40. Reg. Sec. 1.702-1(a)(8)(i); Reg. Sec. 1.703-1(a)(1).
41. I.R.C. Sec. 703(b); Reg. Sec. 1.703-1(b).
42. I.R.C. Sec. 448.
43. I.R.C. Sec. 448(b)(3).
44. I.R.C. Sec. 448(c)(2).
45. I.R.C. Sec. 704(c).

for a discussion of the requirements for obtaining an advance ruling regarding partnership status.)

Case 164
Treatment of Various Partnership Expenditures and Losses

X Corporation is the general partner of a limited partnership engaged in oil and gas operations. In 1987, the partnership had the following expenditures:

Management fee	$400,000
Offering costs (brokerage commissions and printing costs of prospectus)	300,000
Organization expenses (legal fees incurred in connection with preparing partnership agreement and state filing fees)	10,000
Total	$710,000

The prospectus describes the $400,000 management fee as "remuneration to the general partner for overseeing partnership operations during the initial year of drilling activity." The partnership agreement provides that Corporation X is to receive a $200,000 management fee in 1988 for "overseeing the completion and early producing operations of initial wells and supervising the drilling and completion of any development wells." The partnership agreement does not provide for assessment of the limited partners, and no drilling activity is scheduled to take place after 1988. After 1988, Corporation X is to receive a monthly "per-well" charge for services provided in connection with the operation of producing oil and gas properties.

The partnership began operations on January 1, 1987. On July 1, 1987, 10 additional partners were admitted, and upon their admittance they collectively received a 40% interest in the profits and capital of the partnership. The taxable loss for 1987 is $1 million. If the books of the partnership had been closed on June 30, 1987, the partnership's tax loss on an accrual basis would have been $600,000.

The partners share all items of income, deductions, losses, credits, etc., of the partnership according to their general interests in the profits and capital of the partnership.

The controller of X Corporation wants to know the income tax treatment of the above items.

Because the management fee is determined without regard to the income of the partnership, it constitutes a "guaranteed payment" that can be deducted to the extent it is an ordinary and necessary business expense of the partnership.[46] If the management fee relates to the acquisition of an asset having a useful life in excess of one year, the fee is a capital expenditure of the partnership and not deductible. To the extent

46. I.R.C. Sec. 707(c); Cagle v. Comm'r, 539 F.2d 409 (5th Cir. 1976), 38 AFTR2d 76-5834, 76-2 USTC 9672; Sidney Kimmelman, 72 T.C. 294 (1979); Estate of Boyd, 76 T.C. 646 (1981); Keller v. Comm'r, 725 F.2d 1173 (8th Cir. 1984), 53 AFTR2d 84-663, 84-1 USTC 9194, *aff'g* 79 T.C. 7 (1982); Blitzer v. U.S., 684 F.2d 874 (Ct. Cl. 1982), 50 AFTR2d 82-5293, 82-2 USTC 9465; Paul P. Brountas, 73 T.C. 491 (1979).

the management fee relates to services to be performed in later years, the fee may not be deductible until the year the services are performed.

If a management fee qualifies as a startup expenditure of the partnership and is paid to a partner, it also must be capitalized and amortized.[47] The partnership should maintain records and other documentary evidence such as time reports, internal cost allocations and invoices evidencing payment to outside vendors that support the propriety of the management fee in relation to actual services performed by Corporation X personnel or outside contractors for the years to which the payments relate (i.e., 1987 and 1988). The burden of proof is on the partnership to sustain the deductibility of the management fee.

In several private letter rulings, the Internal Revenue Service (IRS) has discussed the possible treatment of management fees paid by a limited partnership engaged in the exploration for and production of oil and gas. A portion of the management fee may be allocable to the acquisition of leases and recovered through depletion or a loss upon the abandonment of the property, and a portion may be allocable to the drilling of wells.[48]

In some instances, the partnership agreement will provide for the charging of an overhead fee that represents reimbursement to the general partner for general and administrative costs incurred by the general partner on behalf of the limited partnership. The rules for determining the deductibility of such a fee are the same as for determining the deductibility of a management fee. Again, the burden of proof is on the partnership to sustain the appropriate tax treatment of the overhead fee.

The monthly per-well fee payable after 1988 appears to be an ordinary and necessary business expense and should be deductible.

Amounts paid or incurred to organize a partnership must be capitalized and, at the election of the partnership, may be amortized ratably over a period of not less than 60 months beginning in the month in which the partnership begins business.[49] If the partnership is liquidated before the end of the 60-month period, the unamortized portion of those expenditures may be deducted in the final partnership tax return.[50] Organization expenses are limited to those incident to the creation of the partnership, chargeable to capital account and of a character that, if the partnership had an ascertainable life, would be amortized over that life.[51]

The regulations indicate that legal fees for organizing the partnership (including negotiation and preparation of the partnership agreement), the accounting fees for establishing a partnership accounting system and filing fees are examples of organization costs subject to amortization.[52] Costs or expenses relating to the acquisition or transfer of assets to the partnership, expenses connected with a contract relating to the operation of the partnership trade or business and syndication fees are not organization costs.[53]

The election to amortize organization expenses is made by attaching a statement to the partnership's return of income for the tax year in which the partnership begins business. The statement should include a description of each organization expense incurred (whether or not paid), the amount of the expense, the date the expense was

47. Rev. Rul. 81-150, 1981-1 C.B. 119.
48. IRS Letter Ruling 7804037; IRS Letter Ruling 7804038; IRS Letter Ruling 7806068.
49. I.R.C. Sec. 709(b)(1); Reg. Sec. 1.709-1(b)(1).
50. I.R.C. Sec. 709(b)(1); Reg. Sec. 1.709-1(b)(2).
51. I.R.C. Sec. 709(b)(2); Reg. Sec. 1.709-2(a).
52. Reg. Sec. 1.709-2(a).
53. *Ibid.*

incurred, the month in which the partnership began business, and the number of months (not less than 60) over which the expenses will be amortized. The regulations provide that a partnership using the cash receipts and disbursements method of accounting also should indicate the amount paid before the end of the tax year with respect to each expense.[54] The election must be made with the original timely filed return (including extensions) for the year in which business begins, although once an election has been made, amended returns and statements may be filed to include any organization expenses not originally included.[55]

The partnership should amortize the $10,000 of organization expenses over a 60-month period beginning in January 1987. Accordingly, the partnership should claim a $2,000 deduction (12/60 × $10,000) in 1987.

Syndication fees that represent amounts paid to promote the sale of an interest in a partnership are not deductible by the partnership or by any partner.[56] Any expenses connected with the issuing and marketing of an interest in the partnership, such as brokerage fees and registration fees, constitute syndication fees. Other examples of syndication fees include legal fees of the underwriter, placement agent, general partner or the partnership for securities advice and for advice pertaining to the adequacy of tax disclosures in the prospectus or placement memorandum for security law purposes; accounting fees for preparation of representations to be included in the offering materials; and the printing costs of the prospectus, placement memorandum and other selling and promotional material.[57]

Accordingly, offering costs of $300,000 are not amortizable or deductible by the partnership or the partners. Additionally, upon the winding up or liquidation of the partnership, the partnership will not be allowed a deduction for the syndication costs.[58] However, although it is not clear, it appears that the partners will be permitted to deduct such costs as a loss when they are of no more benefit to the partnership.

Although the following arrangement is not included in the facts of this case, some partnerships have attempted to circumvent the capitalization rules for organization and syndication costs by providing for special allocations of income and corresponding distributions to a partner in place of direct payments for reimbursement of those costs. The special allocations have the intended effect of a deduction for the remaining partners by reducing the amount of taxable income that otherwise would be allocated to them. However, when a partner provides services to a partnership and allocations of income are provided for as discussed above, the transactions will be viewed as between the partnership and a partner acting outside his capacity as a partner, which normally will require the partnership to capitalize the organization and syndication costs.[59]

If other costs are incurred that qualify as startup expenditures, the taxpayer must capitalize those costs unless he elects to amortize them equally over a period of not less than 60 months.[60]

When a change in partners occurs during a tax year, items of partnership income, gain, loss, deduction and credit must be allocated properly among the partners. A change in partners may occur when a partner sells or exchanges all or a portion of his interest or from a number of other events including the entry of a new partner.

---

54. Reg. Sec. 1.709-1(c).
55. *Ibid.*
56. I.R.C. Sec. 709(a); Reg. Sec. 1.709-1(a).
57. Reg. Sec. 1.709-2(b).
58. Reg. Sec. 1.709-1(b)(2).
59. I.R.C. Sec. 707(a)(2).
60. I.R.C. Sec. 195.

If a partner disposes of his entire interest, the partnership's taxable year shall be closed to determine that partner's share of any item of income, gain, loss, deduction or credit. In the case of a disposition of less than an entire interest, the Internal Revenue Code (the Code) provides for the Treasury to promulgate regulations to determine each partner's distributable share of any item of income, gain, loss, deduction or credit when partners' interests in the partnership vary during the year.[61]

For cash-basis partnerships, interest, taxes, payments for services or for the use of property or any other item specified by the Treasury in regulations shall be allocated by assigning the appropriate portion of each item to each day in the period to which it is attributable.[62] The amounts so assigned then are apportioned among the partners in proportion to their interests in the partnership at the close of the day. This rule effectively requires that certain items be allocated on a basis similar to the accrual method of accounting.

If any portion of a cash-basis item is properly attributable to a period before the beginning of the tax year in which it is paid, that amount must be assigned to the first day of that tax year and allocated to the partners during the period to which that portion is attributable in proportion to their varying interests in the partnership on those days. If the allocation results in an amount attributable to a person who is not a partner on the first day, that amount must be capitalized by the partnership and allocated to the basis of partnership assets in a manner required by the Code.[63]

If any portion of an item is attributable to periods after the tax year in which it is paid, that item will be assigned to the partners owning an interest on the last day of the year.[64]

The Treasury will promulgate regulations to allow a monthly convention. That is, partners entering after the 15th day of a month will be treated as entering on the first day of the following month, and partners entering during the first 15 days of a month will be treated as entering on the first day of the month. The Treasury may provide for other methods and may deny the use of any method that could result in significant tax avoidance.[65]

It is unclear whether regulations to be promulgated will apply to normal oil and gas revenue and expenditures. If these provisions do apply, the daily apportionment rules could affect the partner allocation of these items because of the normal delay between the time an item is incurred versus the actual date of payment or receipt.

In this fact situation, the $600,000 of accrual-basis tax loss for the period January 1 through June 30, 1987, will be allocated to the original partners according to their original sharing ratios. The $400,000 of accrual-basis loss incurred after June 30, 1987, will be allocated among the partners according to their post-June 30, 1987, sharing ratios.

Tax shelters and certain partnerships with corporate partners may not use the cash receipts and disbursements method of accounting.[66] *(See Case 163 for further discussion.)* In the instant case, assume the partnership properly may use the cash method of accounting and incurs expenditures resulting in a $600,000 tax loss through June 30, 1987, and a $1 million tax loss for the year. To the extent the expenditures comprising the $400,000 loss paid after June 30, 1987, were incurred before that date and applied

61. I.R.C. Sec. 706(c).
62. I.R.C. Sec. 706(d)(2)(A).
63. I.R.C. Sec. 706(d)(2)(D)(ii).
64. I.R.C. Sec. 706(d)(2)(C)(ii).
65. House Report No. 98-861, 1984-3 C.B. Vol. 2 112.
66. I.R.C. Sec. 448.

to taxes, interest, payment for services or any other item the Secretary includes in regulations to be promulgated, it may be necessary for the partnership to allocate the expense to the original partners.[67] Conversely, expenditures for such items made before July 1, 1987, attributable to later periods may be allocable to the partners according to their post-June 30, 1987, sharing ratios.

Limited partners will be subject to the passive-activity limitations on losses and credits attributable to their interests.[68] *(See Case 182 for a discussion of the passive-activity limitations.)*

Case 165
Partnership With Special Allocations — General Principles

A, an independent producer, and B, a retailer, form a partnership on January 1, 1987, to explore for oil and gas on a property (tax basis and fair market value of $150,000) owned by Retailer B. The partnership agreement provides for the following sharing ratios:

	Partner	
Item	**A (Producer)**	**B (Retailer)**
Leasehold cost	0%	100%
Drilling and completion costs	100%	0%
Production income	80%	20%
Operating expenses	80%	20%
All other items, including any gains or losses from disposition of assets (except as noted below)	80%	20%

The partnership agreement provides that a capital account will be established for each partner, to be credited with the amount of cash and the fair market value of property (adjusted for certain liabilities) contributed to the partnership and with his share of income or profits and charged with his share of expenses, losses, distributions and withdrawals. The partners' capital accounts will be further adjusted for actual cost-depletion allowances (computed based on the partnership's recorded book value for the property) in the sharing ratio used to allocate the adjusted basis of the property giving rise to that allowance. Upon the taxable disposition of an oil or gas property, proceeds representing a recovery of adjusted basis maintained solely for capital account purposes shall be allocated to the partners in the same manner that the adjusted basis of the property was allocated previously. The balance of the proceeds (and the associated gain) shall be allocated 80% to Producer A and 20% to Retailer B. Any loss on the disposition of an oil or gas property shall be allocated in the same manner as proceeds, which represent a recovery of adjusted basis maintained solely for capital account purposes.

Deductions for depreciation (or cost recovery deductions), credits, etc., shall be allocated to the partners in the same proportion as the partners contributed to the cost of the asset giving rise to the deductions, credit, etc. Upon the taxable disposition of a depreciable asset, proceeds to the extent of adjusted basis shall be allocated to the partners in the same

67. I.R.C. Sec. 706(d)(1).
68. I.R.C. Sec. 469.

ratio as the partners contributed to the cost of the asset. The balance of the proceeds (and associated gain) shall be allocated 80% to Producer A and 20% to Retailer B. Any loss on the disposition of a depreciable asset shall be allocated in the same manner as proceeds, which represents a recovery of basis.

Upon liquidation of the partnership, the agreement provides that all remaining partnership property be valued and the capital accounts be adjusted as if the property had been sold at its fair market value. After this adjustment, the property is to be distributed to the partners in accordance with their positive adjusted capital account balances. To the extent there is a deficit in a partner's adjusted capital account following the distribution of the liquidation proceeds, that partner must restore the deficit by making a corresponding cash contribution to the partnership.

A partner's share of income, gain, loss, deduction or credit is determined by the partnership agreement,[69] unless that allocation does not have substantial economic effect.[70] If the partnership agreement is silent with respect to an item of income, gain, loss, deduction or credit or if the allocation provided for by the partnership agreement does not have substantial economic effect, that item shall be allocated according to the partners' interests in the partnership (determined by taking into account all facts and circumstances relating to the economic arrangements of the partners).[71]

Since the "substantial economic effect" concept was enacted in 1976,[72] numerous technical and practical problems have arisen in determining if an allocation of income, gain, loss, deduction or credit has substantial economic effect. The uncertainty has been magnified by the policy of the Internal Revenue Service (IRS) not to issue advance rulings with respect to the validity of such allocations.[73] Although the judicial interpretations of substantial economic effect primarily relate to real estate arrangements, investments in which the economic and business considerations are substantially different from investments in oil and gas,[74] there have been both judicial[75] and administrative[76] interpretations involving oil and gas partnerships.

In December 1985, the Treasury adopted complex regulations[77] concerning allocations and substantial economic effect, which provide some much needed guidance. These regulations generally are effective for tax years beginning after December 31, 1975. However, an allocation in years beginning before May 1, 1986, and not respected under these regulations will be respected if it has substantial economic effect under relevant case law, legislative history and previous regulations.[78]

The regulations provide three distinct ways in which allocations will be respected. The allocation must:

☐ Have substantial economic effect,

---

69. I.R.C. Sec. 704(a).
70. I.R.C. Sec. 704(b)(2).
71. I.R.C. Sec. 704(b)(1).
72. I.R.C. Sec. 704(b); P.L. 94-455 (Tax Reform Act of 1976), Sec. 213(d).
73. Rev. Proc. 87-3, 1987-1 I.R.B. 27.
74. Leon A. Harris Jr., 61 T.C. 770 (1974); Stanley Orrisch, 55 T.C. 395 (1970); Martin Magaziner, T.C. Memo Dec. (June 5, 1978); Holladay v. Comm'r, 649 F.2d 1176 (5th Cir. 1981), 48 AFTR2d 81-5501, 81-2 USTC 9559; Sellers v. U.S. 617 F.2d 1042 (4th Cir. 1980), 45 AFTR2d 80-945, 80-1 USTC 9285; Ogden v. Comm'r, 788 F.2d 252 (5th Cir. 1986), 57 AFTR2d 86-1333, 86-1 USTC 9368.
75. Allison v. U.S. (Ct. Cl. 1982), 49 AFTR2d 82-614, 82-1 USTC 9163. The United States Court of Appeals for the Federal Circuit has reversed this decision. *See also* Allison v. U.S., 701 F.2d 933 (Fed. Cir. 1983), 51 AFTR2d 83-1209, 83-1 USTC 9241; Hamilton v. U.S., 687 F.2d 408 (Ct. Cl. 1982), 50 AFTR2d 82-5599, 82-2 USTC 9546.
76. IRS Letter Ruling 8133021; IRS Letter Ruling 8133028.
77. Reg. Sec. 1.704-1(b).
78. Reg. Sec. 1.704-1(b)(1)(ii).

☐ Be in accordance with the partners' interests in the partnership, *or*

☐ Be deemed to be in accordance with the partners' interests in the partnership.[79]

To the extent an allocation of an item of income, gain, loss, deduction or credit does not comply with any of the above requirements, it will be ignored and reallocated in accordance with the partners' interests in the partnership.

Substantial Economic Effect

To determine whether an allocation has substantial economic effect, the regulations adopt a two-pronged test.[80] First, the allocation must have "economic effect" and, second, the economic effect must be "substantial."

Economic Effect

The regulations provide that an allocation has economic effect if it is consistent with the underlying economic arrangement of the partners. This "consistency" requirement is met only if, throughout the full term of the partnership, the partnership agreement provides:

☐ For the maintenance of capital accounts in accordance with the regulations,

☐ Upon liquidation, distributions are required to be made in accordance with positive capital account balances, *and*

☐ Upon liquidation, deficit capital account balances must be restored through corresponding capital contributions.[81]

Each partner's capital account must be maintained on a cumulative basis throughout the term of the partnership. The following items reflect the additions to and subtractions from the capital accounts:[82]

+	Partner contributions (money and fair market value of property, net of liabilities)
+	Allocated share of partnership income and gain
−	Partner distributions (money and fair market value of property, net of liabilities)
−	Allocated share of loss and deduction
=	Partner's capital account balance

The fair market value for purposes of property contributions and distributions will be respected if it is reasonably agreed to among the partners in arm's-length negotiations and the partners have sufficiently adverse interests.[83] If property is recorded in the capital accounts in an amount different from adjusted tax basis, the partnership income, deduction, gain and loss *for capital account purposes* must be calculated by reference to the amount recorded in the capital account rather than tax basis. The allocation of *taxable* income, deduction, gain and loss with respect to such property is rather complex *(see discussion below under "Partners' Interests in the Partnership")*, particularly with respect to property contributed to the partnership *(see Case 166)*. When property is distributed to a partner, it is treated as sold for fair market value, and any unrealized gain or loss must be allocated to the partners and reflected in the

79. Reg. Sec. 1.704-1(b)(1)(i).
80. Reg. Sec. 1.704-1(b)(2).
81. Reg. Sec. 1.704-1(b)(2)(ii).
82. Reg. Sec. 1.704-1(b)(2)(iv)(b).
83. Reg. Sec. 1.704-1(b)(2)(iv)(h).

capital accounts to the extent not previously reflected[84] (i.e., upon an earlier contribution of such property to the partnership). Recording property and calculating income, deduction, gain and loss by reference to fair market value add considerable complexity and effectively require partnerships to maintain separate sets of books and records for capital account and tax purposes.

A partnership allocates the adjusted basis of an oil and gas property to each partner at the time the property is acquired. This allocation is made in accordance with the partners' shares of partnership income or capital and is used in the partners' depletion calculations.[85] Despite this rule, such basis must be reflected in the capital accounts. A basis allocation will be recognized as in accordance with the partners' interests in partnership capital if depletable property is recorded in the capital accounts *(see below)* and the economic effect of all other material allocations is substantial.[86] *(See Case 166 for special rules relating to contributions to a partnership of an oil and gas property having a tax basis different from fair market value.)*

Depletion of oil and gas properties must be reflected in the capital accounts. The partnership may reduce capital accounts by each partner's actual depletion.[87] However, if the capital accounts reflect a book value different from the adjusted tax basis (e.g., due to the requirement that contributed property must be reflected at fair market value), that book value must be used in the calculation of the capital account depletion adjustment.[88]

The regulations recognize that the partnership may not have information as to each partner's depletion calculations. Accordingly, the regulations permit capital accounts to be adjusted for "simulated" depletion. The partnership must make a binding, property-by-property election to use either simulated cost depletion or simulated percentage depletion, computed under the normal depletion rules, but without regard to any limitations theoretically applicable to any partner.[89] Simulated depletion must be calculated by reference to the book values of properties reflected in the capital accounts.

Each partner's aggregate depletion adjustments may not exceed his allocable share of each property's tax basis or, if applicable, book value reflected in his capital account. *(See Case 166 for a discussion of allocations of book value and the impact on capital accounts.)*

Each partner individually computes taxable gain or loss on the sale of a partnership oil or gas property by reference to his share of adjusted tax basis and proceeds of sale.[90] However, special rules govern the partners' sharing of proceeds and gain or loss for capital account purposes. Proceeds must be allocated first to the partners to the extent of their aggregate adjusted tax basis (or adjusted simulated basis if simulated cost or percentage depletion was used by the partnership). Amounts realized in excess of these amounts may be allocated in any manner provided all other allocations have substantial economic effect.[91] The capital accounts are adjusted for each partner's simulated gain or loss computed as the difference between allocated proceeds of sale and adjusted actual basis for capital account purposes (or simulated basis if simulated

84. Reg. Sec. 1.704-1(b)(2)(iv)(e)(1).
85. I.R.C. Sec. 613A(c)(7)(D).
86. Reg. Sec. 1.704-1(b)(4)(v).
87. Reg. Sec. 1.704-1(b)(2)(iv)(k)(3).
88. Reg. Sec. 1.704-1(b)(2)(iv)(k)(4).
89. Reg. Sec. 1.704-1(b)(2)(iv)(k)(2).
90. I.R.C. Sec. 613A(c)(7)(D).
91. Reg. Sec. 1.704-1(b)(4)(v).

depletion is used).[92] *(See Case 166 for special rules governing allocations with respect to contributed property with a basis different from fair market value.)*

Upon liquidation, distributions must be made in accordance with positive capital account balances and any partners' deficit balances must be restored through contributions to be used for payment of creditors or distribution to other partners in accordance with their positive capital account balances.[93]

A deficit make-up provision need not be unlimited, and allocations of losses to a partner may be respected so long as the deficit balance does not exceed the dollar amount such partner is unconditionally obligated to restore and the partnership agreement contains a "qualified income offset."[94] To determine whether a deficit exceeds the restoration obligation, the amount of the deficit must be adjusted to reflect depletion and other deductions reasonably expected (as of the end of the year) to be made to the partner's capital account and distributions reasonably expected (as of the end of the year) to be made to the partner. The partners' unconditional obligation to restore deficit balances may be expressed in the partnership agreement or, under certain circumstances, local law or a promissory note.[95] A "qualified income offset" allocates income or gain to offset an unexpected deficit capital account balance in excess of the restoration obligation.[96]

Under certain circumstances, a partnership may increase ("book up") or decrease ("book down") the capital accounts to reflect a revaluation to fair market value of property on the partnership's books. These circumstances include the admission of a new partner or a distribution to a retiring partner as consideration for the relinquishment of his partnership interest. Subsequently, for capital account purposes, depreciation, depletion, gain and loss adjustments must be computed by reference to book value. The related tax items must be allocated to take into account the variation between adjusted tax basis and book value in the same manner as required for contributions of property with a value different from tax basis.[97] *(See Case 166.)*

To illustrate the purpose of the revaluation provision, assume Partners A and B each own 50% income and capital interests. The partnership owns property with a fair market value of \$10,000, but such property is recorded in the capital accounts at \$5,000. Partner C contributes \$5,000 cash for a one-third interest. The following chart demonstrates the revaluation provision:

	Without Revaluation		**With Revaluation**	
Partner	**Capital Account**	**Percentage Ownership of Capital**	**Capital Account**	**Percentage Ownership of Capital**
A	\$ 2,500	25%	\$ 5,000	33⅓%
B	2,500	25	5,000	33⅓
C	5,000	50	5,000	33⅓
Total	\$10,000	100%	\$15,000	100 %

92. Reg. Sec. 1.704-1(b)(2)(iv)(k).
93. Reg. Sec. 1.704-1(b)(2)(ii)(b)(3).
94. Reg. Sec. 1.704-1(b)(2)(ii)(d).
95. Reg. Sec. 1.704-1(b)(2)(ii)(c).
96. Reg. Sec. 1.704-1(b)(2)(ii)(d).
97. Reg. Sec. 1.704-1(b)(2)(iv)(f); Reg. Sec. 1.704-1(b)(4)(i).

Failure to revalue the property and adjust capital accounts effectively shifts capital ownership among the partners and could have substantial detrimental tax consequences.[98]

According to the allocation regulations, a revaluation of an oil or gas property may give rise to a reallocation of the adjusted tax basis of the property or a change in the partners' relative shares of simulated depletion.[99] However, the proposed depletion regulations do not provide for such a reallocation.[100] Further guidance is needed in this regard.

Substantiality

For an allocation to be respected, its economic effect must be substantial. Economic effect is substantial if there is a reasonable possibility that the allocation will affect substantially the dollar amounts to be received by the partners, independent of the tax consequences. The regulations provide three situations in which the economic effect of an allocation may lack substantiality.

First, the regulations state that economic effect is not substantial if at the date the allocation enters the partnership agreement:

- The after-tax economic consequences, on a present-value basis, of at least one partner may be enhanced compared to such consequences absent such allocation and
- There is "strong likelihood" that the present-value after-tax economic consequences of no partner will be substantially diminished compared to such consequences absent such allocation.

The partners' tax attributes unrelated to the partnership (e.g., net operating losses, tax-exempt status, etc.) are taken into account for this purpose.[101] Based on the "strong likelihood" test, it is unlikely that typical oil and gas arrangements will violate this rule due to the inherent substantial uncertainties of exploration and development, production risks, price volatility and other factors.

Second, an allocation's economic effect lacks substantiality if it merely shifts tax consequences. Specifically, economic effect is not substantial if at the time the allocation enters the agreement there is a "strong likelihood" that:

- The net capital account adjustments for a year will not differ substantially from the adjustments that would have occurred absent the allocation and
- The partners' overall tax liabilities will decrease compared to the liabilities absent the allocation, determined by taking into account the partners' tax attributes unrelated to the partnership.[102]

For example, assume a partnership in which A, an independent producer eligible for percentage depletion, and B, a retailer not eligible for percentage depletion, are equal partners. The partnership agreement allocates all production revenue from transferred Property T (i.e., one not eligible for percentage depletion) to Retailer B and an equal amount of production revenue from Property U (i.e., one eligible for percentage depletion) to Independent Producer A. Any additional revenue is divided equally. Also, assume the agreement provides an annual balancing provision which reallocates revenue from either property to the extent necessary to ensure that both partners will

98. Reg. Sec. 1.704-1(b)(2)(iv)(f).
99. Reg. Sec. 1.704-1(b)(2)(iv)(k)(4).
100. Prop. Reg. Sec. 1.613A-3(e).
101. Reg. Sec. 1.704-1(b)(2)(iii)(a).
102. Reg. Sec. 1.704-1(b)(2)(iii)(b).

be allocated identical amounts of revenue in total. This allocation merely shifts tax consequences and is not substantial. However, absent the balancing provision, Partners A and B are subject to production risks (i.e., revenue from Property U may differ from the revenue from Property T), and the economic effect may be substantial.

Finally, the economic effect of a "transitory allocation" is not substantial. Transitory allocations exist if one or more allocations may be largely offset by other allocations and, at the time such allocations enter the agreement, there is a "strong likelihood" that:

- The capital account balances, including the offsetting allocations, will not differ substantially from the balances absent the allocations and
- The partners' total tax liability is reduced by the allocations, taking into account each partner's unrelated tax attributes.

The regulations provide for a facts-and-circumstances determination; however, it is presumed that a transitory allocation does not exist if there is a "strong likelihood" that the original allocation will not be offset within five years.[103]

For example, a typical carried-interest arrangement specially allocates intangible drilling and development costs to one partner and provides another special allocation of production revenue until such partner recoups his invested capital. However, due to drilling and production risks, price volatility and other factors, this arrangement should not be considered a transitory allocation since there cannot be a "strong likelihood" that production revenue will be sufficient to offset the drilling cost allocation. If production from existing producing wells also may be allocated as an offset to the drilling cost, these risks still may be sufficient to rebut the "strong likelihood" standard.

Partners' Interests in the Partnership

The second way for an allocation to be respected under these regulations is for the allocation to be in accordance with the partners' interests in the partnership. This concept requires a determination of the manner in which the partners have agreed to share the economic benefit or burden corresponding to the income, gain, loss, deduction or credit that is allocated. The method is subjective and considers such factors as:

- The partners' relative contributions to the partnership.
- The interests of the partners in economic profits and losses.
- The interests of the partners in cash flow and other nonliquidating distributions.
- The rights of the partners to distributions of capital upon liquidation.[104]

The regulations present an example in which Partner DG contributes an oil lease with a fair market value (FMV) and adjusted basis of $100,000 and Partner JC contributes a stated dollar amount ($100,000) to finance drilling activities. The agreement further provides that all additional cash requirements will be borne equally.

Deductions attributable to the property (including money) contributed by each partner will be allocated to such partner. All income, cash flow and proceeds at liquidation

103. Reg. Sec. 1.704-1(b)(2)(iii)(c).
104. Reg. Sec. 1.704-1(b)(3).

will be distributed equally irrespective of capital account balances. The regulations conclude that:

- ☐ The allocations of income, gain, loss and deduction provided in the agreement do not have economic effect because capital accounts do not govern sharing of proceeds in liquidation. Accordingly, such items must be reallocated in accordance with the partners' interests in the partnership.
- ☐ The partners' interests in the partnership are equal and all partnership income, gain, loss and deduction must be allocated equally.[105]

Assume the facts are changed such that Partner JC agrees to contribute all cash necessary for drilling operations. Although not addressed by the regulations, this alteration in sharing of economic burden presumably may dramatically change the partners' interests in the partnership as it relates to deduction allocations. Partner JC now assumes all the risk and burdens of drilling operations including errors in cost estimate, uninsured risk of loss due to casualty, cost overruns due to drilling and completion difficulties and the like. Additionally, Partner JC will benefit if drilling ultimately costs less than the estimated amount. Accordingly, although the regulations provide no direct guidance, a careful examination of the true economic sharing of drilling burden given the inherent risks of oil and gas exploration and development may lead to a different determination of the partners' interests in the partnership and require a greater portion of the drilling cost deductions to be allocated to Partner JC.

Deemed Partners' Interests in the Partnership

Certain allocations may be deemed to be in accordance with the partners' interests in the partnership. Such allocations include tax items that differ in amount from the corresponding book items. For example, if the fair market value of partnership property reflected in the capital accounts differs from the tax basis, book depreciation, depletion and gain or loss calculated for capital account purposes by reference to such values will differ from the corresponding item calculated by reference to adjusted tax basis. Since the tax items are not reflected in the capital accounts, their allocation cannot have economic effect and must be made in accordance with the partners' interests in the partnership. Accordingly, such tax items generally must be allocated to the partners based on principles similar to those applicable to a contribution of property having a tax basis different from fair market value.[106] *(See Case 166).*

Application of Allocation Regulations

Assume the following activity for 1987:

Intangible drilling and development costs (IDC)	$500,000
Lease and well equipment cost	105,000
Production income	200,000
Operating expense	80,000
Depletion (actual cost)	7,500
Cash distribution	120,000

105. Reg. Sec. 1.701-1(b)(5), Example 19(iii).
106. Reg. Sec. 1.704-1(b)(4)(i).

Based on these assumptions, the partners' capital accounts will be maintained as follows:

	Partner A (Producer)	Partner B (Retailer)	Total
Contributions*:			
Property (FMV)	$ —	$150,000	$ 150,000
Cash	605,000	—	605,000
Allocations:			
Production income	160,000	40,000	200,000
Operating expense	(64,000)	(16,000)	(80,000)
IDC	(500,000)	—	(500,000)
Depreciation	(15,000)	—	(15,000)
Depletion (actual cost)	—	(7,500)	(7,500)
Cash distribution	(96,000)	(24,000)	(120,000)
Capital account balances	$ 90,000	$142,500	$ 232,500

* In this type of cost-sharing arrangement, it is common for the actual relative contributions to differ (sometimes materially) from the agreed sharing of revenues. This disparity may be caused by the relative bargaining power of the participants (particularly as to the assumption of risk), differences between estimated and actual costs and other factors.

The allocation of leasehold cost adjusted basis to Partner B is in accordance with the partners' interests in the partnership because the capital account depletion adjustments comply with the requirements of the regulations and all other allocations have substantial economic effect.[107]

Assume that on January 1, 1988, the partnership liquidates at a time when the total value of the property is $890,000 (including lease and well equipment with a value of $90,000). The following capital account adjustments reflect the effect of the deemed sale of the partnership's assets:

			Partner A (Producer)	Partner B (Retailer)	Total
Capital account balance before deemed sale			$ 90,000	$142,500	$232,500
Allocation of simulated gain from deemed sale of:					
Leasehold:	Proceeds	$ 800,000			
	Basis	(142,500)			
	Gain (allocated 80%/20%)		526,000	131,500	657,500
Equipment:	Proceeds	$ 90,000			
	Basis	(90,000)	—	—	—
Capital account balance before distribution			$616,000	$274,000	$890,000
Percent of total			69.2%	30.8%	

Upon liquidation, property must be distributed based on relative capital account balances. Therefore, Producer A will be entitled to 69.2% of the partnership property, while Retailer B will receive 30.8% even though Producer A and Retailer B, under a

107. Reg. Sec. 1.704-1(b)(5), Example 19(i).

typical industry arrangement similar to this case, contemplated an 80%/20% sharing of the net production income and the total proceeds on the disposition of the property.

This distortion could have been eliminated in this situation if the partnership agreement had provided for a different special allocation of gains from the disposition of assets. Specifically, simulated gain (and the related cash proceeds in the event of actual sale) could have been allocated to the extent possible in a way that would result in a sharing of the total value of partnership property consistent with the general income-sharing ratio (i.e., 80%/20%). This allocation can be illustrated as follows:

		Allocation per Agreement		Alternative Allocation	
		Partner A	Partner B	Partner A	Partner B
Capital account balance before deemed sale		$ 90,000	$142,500	$ 90,000	$142,500
Allocation of simulated gain from deemed sale of:					
Leasehold: Proceeds	$ 800,000				
Basis	(142,500)				
Gain	$ 657,500				
Special allocation		N/A	N/A	480,000	—
Regular allocation (80%/20%)		526,000	131,500	142,000	35,500
Equipment:					
Proceeds	$ 90,000				
Basis	(90,000)				
Gain	$ —	—	—	—	—
Capital account balance before distribution		$616,000	$274,000	$712,000	$178,000
Percent of total		69.2%	30.8%	80%	20%

Under these alternative allocation provisions, the partners will share the value of the assets in the desired ratios. However, in some situations, the gain (or appreciation in the value of the assets in excess of the value on date of contribution) may not be sufficient to allow for the desired sharing of the value (a "balancing" of the capital accounts). It should be noted that in this case the simulated gain necessary to "balance" the capital accounts is $480,000.

The use of simulated percentage depletion also may more rapidly reduce the property contributor's capital account, thereby further reducing the amount of gain necessary to "balance" the capital accounts.

Case 166
Partnership With Special Allocations — Property Contributions

A, an independent producer, and B, a retailer, form a partnership on January 1, 1987, to explore for oil and gas on a property (tax basis of

$100,000 and fair market value of $1 million) owned by Retailer B. The partnership agreement provides for the following sharing ratios:

Item	Partner A (Producer)	Partner B (Retailer)
Leasehold cost	0%	100%
Drilling and completion costs	100%	0%
Production income	50%	50%
Operating expenses	50%	50%
All other items, including any gains or losses from disposition of assets (except as noted below)	50%	50%

The partnership agreement provides that a capital account will be established for each partner, to be credited with the amount of cash and the fair market value of property (adjusted for certain liabilities) contributed to the partnership and with his share of income or profits and charged with his share of expenses, losses, distributions and withdrawals. The partners' capital accounts will be further adjusted for simulated cost depletion allowances (computed based on the partnership's recorded book value for the property) in the sharing ratio used to allocate the adjusted basis of the property giving rise to that allowance. Upon the taxable disposition of an oil or gas property, proceeds representing a recovery of adjusted basis maintained solely for capital account purposes shall be allocated to the partners in the same manner that the adjusted basis of the property was allocated previously. The balance of the proceeds (and the associated gain) shall be allocated 50% to Producer A and 50% to Retailer B. Any loss on the disposition of an oil or gas property shall be allocated in the same manner as proceeds, which represent a recovery of adjusted basis maintained solely for capital account purposes.

Deductions for depreciation (or cost recovery deductions), credits, etc., shall be allocated to the partners in the same proportion as the partners contributed to the cost of the asset giving rise to the deductions, credit, etc. Upon the taxable disposition of a depreciable asset, proceeds to the extent of adjusted basis shall be allocated to the partners in the same ratio as the partners contributed to the cost of the asset. The balance of the proceeds (and associated gain) shall be allocated 50% to Producer A and 50% to Retailer B. Any loss on the disposition of a depreciable asset shall be allocated in the same manner as proceeds, which represents a recovery of basis.

Upon liquidation of the partnership, the agreement provides that all remaining partnership property be valued and the capital accounts be adjusted as if the property had been sold at its fair market value. After this adjustment, the property is to be distributed to the partners in accordance with their positive adjusted capital account balances. To the extent there is a deficit in a partner's adjusted capital account following the distribution of the liquidation proceeds, that partner must restore the deficit by making a corresponding cash contribution to the partnership.

Income, gain, loss and deduction with respect to property contributed to a partnership must be shared among the partners, taking into account the variation between tax basis and fair market value at the time of contribution.[108] This provision is intended to prevent an artificial shifting of tax consequences between the partners for "built-in" gains or losses from contributed property. Congress directed Treasury to issue regulations describing how the "built-in" gains or losses will be shared among the partners. Until new regulations are proposed, the Conference Committee Report on the law allows partnerships to rely on current regulations[109] issued under prior law, under which this provision was elective, for guidance.

By way of example, assume Partners C and D each own 50% interests in partnership income and capital. Partner C contributes depreciable property with a fair market value of $10,000 and a basis of $4,000, and Partner D contributes $10,000 cash. If the contributed property is sold for $10,000, the law contemplates that the $6,000 gain must be allocated to Partner C in recognition of the built-in gain at contribution.[110]

In addition to gains and losses, the statute requires regulations to prescribe allocations of income and deduction to take into account the difference between fair market value and tax basis at the time of contribution. Apparently, Congress intended for regulations to require this difference to be eliminated by allocations of depreciation and depletion, not operating income or loss.[111] Continuing the preceding example, assume that the property is not sold and that the first-year depreciation deduction is 10%. Applying the prior-law elective provision, Partner D is entitled to a depreciation deduction of up to $500 (10% of $5,000) since he has, in effect, purchased an undivided one-half interest in the property for $5,000. However, the so-called "ceiling rule" limits the total depreciation or depletion deduction to $400 (10% of the actual adjusted tax basis of $4,000). No depreciation or depletion is allocated to Partner C, the contributor of the property.[112] If the property then is sold for $9,200, the entire gain of $5,600 ($9,200 sales proceeds less $3,600 adjusted tax basis) apparently must be allocated to Partner C. Any additional taxable gain due to sales proceeds in excess of $9,200 will be shared equally.[113] In effect, Partner C has recognized his entire built-in gain of $6,000 by foregoing depreciation deductions ($400) and recognizing the first portion of gain on sale ($5,600).

Congress apparently intends for the regulations to provide flexibility in nontax avoidance situations by permitting the disparity between the value and adjusted basis of contributed property to be eliminated more rapidly by substituting allocations of items not subject to this provision. Additionally, regulations may require allocation only of built-in gain or loss and permit allocations of depreciation and depletion to be governed by the partnership allocation provisions *(see Case 165)*, but only in situations that do not have the effect of permitting the contributing partner to avoid the allocation of built-in gain or loss. This avoidance could occur when the property is expected to be held until it has little or no fair market value.[114]

Partners individually compute depletion allowances and gain or loss on oil and gas property dispositions by reference to allocated adjusted basis and amount realized.[115] Congress directed Treasury to issue regulations allocating adjusted basis and amount realized to account for any built-in gain or loss on contributed oil and gas properties

108. I.R.C. Sec. 704(c).
109. Reg. Sec. 1.704-1(c)(2).
110. Reg. Sec. 1.704-1(c)(2)(i), Example 2.
111. House Report No. 98-861, 1984-3 C.B. Vol. 2 110.
112. Reg. Sec. 1.704-1(c)(2)(i), Example 1.
113. Reg. Sec. 1.704-1(c)(2)(i), Example 2 *as amended by* House Report No. 98-432, Tax Reform Act of 1984, Sec. 71, Footnote 3; General Explanation of the Tax Reform Act of 1984, prepared by the Staff of the Joint Committee on Taxation, p. 213, Footnote 4.
114. House Report No. 98-861, 1984-3 C.B. Vol. 2 111; General Explanation of the Tax Reform Act of 1984, prepared by the Staff of the Joint Committee on Taxation, p. 213.
115. I.R.C. Sec. 613A(c)(7)(D).

and to permit flexibility in allocating adjusted basis in nonabusive situations.[116] Absent such regulations, it is unclear how the Internal Revenue Service may apply these concepts and to what extent, if any, basis and depletion must be shifted to the noncontributing partner.

The built-in gain rule interacts with the partnership allocation provisions. *(See Case 165 for a general discussion of the allocation provisions.)* The allocation provisions respect allocations only if they have substantial economic effect or if they are (or are deemed to be) in accordance with the partners' interests in the partnership. Assuming the partnership intends allocations to have substantial economic effect, the capital account maintenance provisions require certain adjustments and provide some guidance concerning contributed property with a basis different from fair market value. Although the allocation provisions do not directly determine distributive shares of *tax* items attributable to such contributed property, the regulations provide that such shares must be determined with reference to distributive shares of corresponding *book* items under the allocation provisions.[117] Conversely, in determining whether the economic effect of an allocation of *book* items is substantial (for allocation purposes), consideration must be given to the effect of the book allocation on the distributive share of corresponding *tax* items under the built-in gain rule.[118]

It appears that the intent of the allocation regulations is that special allocations of book items (i.e., the capital account adjustments) will determine the allocation of tax items subject to the built-in gain rule, but only if the book item allocation has substantial economic effect. As noted in the above brief example, the built-in gain rules normally will allocate all or part of the tax depreciation (attributable to built-in gain property) to the partners other than the contributor of the property. However, the regulations indicate that, if book depreciation attributable to an item subject to the built-in gain provision is allocated to the contributor of the built-in gain property and if such allocation has substantial economic effect, then the tax depreciation also may be allocated to that partner.[119] *(See Case 165 concerning the determination of substantiality.)*

Although not entirely clear, it appears that this interaction may be extrapolated to apply to the allocation of tax basis in contributed oil and gas properties subject to the built-in gain rules. If: (1) the fair market value of an oil and gas property is properly recorded in the contributing partner's capital account, (2) book depletion is properly calculated by reference to that value and allocated to the contributing partner's capital account and (3) such allocations have substantial economic effect, then it follows that the tax basis may be allocated to the contributing partner for his use in calculating the tax depletion deduction with respect to that property. This extrapolation is consistent with the regulations' view that the partner bearing the economic cost of depletion (through allocations to his capital account) also should receive the tax consequences of the depletion tax deduction.

---

116. House Report No. 98-861, 1984-3 C.B. Vol. 2 111.
117. Reg. Sec. 1.704-1(b)(1)(vi).
118. Reg. Sec. 1.704-1(b)(2)(iv)(g)(1).
119. Reg. Sec. 1.704-1(b)(5), Example 17; Reg. Sec. 1.704-1(b)(5), Example 18.

Although subsequent regulations may require a different approach, the following example demonstrates the apparent effect of these provisions. Assume the following activity for 1987:

Intangible drilling and development costs (IDC)	$800,000
Lease and well equipment cost	200,000
Production income	200,000
Operating expense	80,000
Simulated depletion (cost)	50,000
Cash distribution	120,000

In accordance with the partnership agreement, the partners' capital accounts are maintained as follows:

	Partner A (Producer)	Partner B (Retailer)	Total
Contribution:			
Property Fair Market Value	$ —	$1,000,000	$1,000,000
Cash	1,000,000	—	1,000,000
Allocations:			
Production income	100,000	100,000	200,000
Operating expense	(40,000)	(40,000)	(80,000)
IDC	(800,000)	—	(800,000)
Depreciation	(30,000)	—	(30,000)
Simulated depletion (cost)	—	(50,000)	(50,000)
Cash distribution	(60,000)	(60,000)	(120,000)
Capital account balances	$ 170,000	$ 950,000	$1,120,000

This partnership's special allocation provisions appear to prevent the potentially abusive shifting of tax consequences which normally are within the purview of the built-in gain rules. The above capital account analysis demonstrates that, upon contribution, Partner B retains his interest in the initial value of the property and no economic shifting of built-in gain occurs. For example, if the property is sold for $1 million before production commences, the entire proceeds must be allocated to Partner B and he will recognize the full amount of the built-in gain ($1,000,000 proceeds − $100,000 tax basis = $900,000 gain recognized.) As production depletes the value of the property, Partner B suffers the economic effect as demonstrated by the depletion charges to his capital account. There is no economic shifting to Partner A of the value decline since his capital account is unaffected by depletion. Since there is no economic shifting of the value to which the built-in gain relates, it appears that the potentially abusive shifting of tax consequences contemplated by the built-in gain rules does not exist. Accordingly, the allocation regulations appear to permit special allocations of book items attributable to contributed property to determine the allocation of the related tax items.

Although not entirely clear, it appears that the tax basis of the contributed property may be allocated to Partner B under the allocation provisions since the allocations to Partner B of the book basis (i.e., fair market value), simulated depletion and sales proceeds to the extent of adjusted book basis have economic effect. This economic effect is substantial because there is not a "strong likelihood" that: (1) the present-value after-tax economic consequences of any partner will not be substantially diminished compared to such consequences absent the allocation, (2) the allocation merely shifts tax consequences or (3) the allocation is merely transitory. *(See Case 165 concerning economic effect of allocations pertaining to oil and gas properties and substantiality.)*

Assume that on January 1, 1988, the partnership sells the property for $2 million (including lease and well equipment with a value of $170,000). The following capital account adjustments reflect the sale of the partnership's assets:

		Partner A (Producer)	Partner B (Retailer)	Total
Capital account balance before sale		$170,000	$ 950,000	$1,120,000
Allocation of simulated gain:				
Sales proceeds	$2,000,000			
Less simulated basis for capital account purposes:				
Leasehold cost	(950,000)			
Equipment cost	(170,000)			
Simulated gain	$ 880,000	440,000	440,000	880,000
Capital account balance before distribution		$610,000	$1,390,000	$2,000,000
Percent of total		30.5%	69.5%	

Thus, Producer A will be entitled to 30.5% of the partnership property, while Retailer B will receive 69.5% even though both partners, under a typical industry arrangement similar to this case, contemplated an equal sharing of the net production income and the total proceeds on the disposition of the property.

The partners calculate taxable gain as follows:

	Partner A (Producer)	Partner B (Retailer)	Total
Allocation of sales proceeds:			
Equipment	$170,000	$ —	$ 170,000
Leasehold:			
To extent of book capital account adjusted basis*	—	950,000	950,000
Excess	440,000	440,000	880,000
Total allocation of proceeds	$610,000	$1,390,000	$2,000,000
Less adjusted tax basis:			
Equipment	(170,000)		(170,000)
Leasehold		(95,000)	(95,000)
Taxable gain	$440,000	$1,295,000	$1,735,000

* This allocation is required by Reg. Sec. 1.704-1(b)(4)(v).

Note that Partner B's recognized gain exceeds Partner A's recognized gain by $855,000. This excess equals the difference between book and tax basis at the date of sale and may be calculated as follows:

Fair market value at time of contribution		$1,000,000
Less tax basis at contribution		(100,000)
Built-in gain at contribution		$ 900,000
Less: Depletion for capital account purposes	$50,000	
Depletion for tax purposes	(5,000)	
		(45,000)
Net built-in gain recognized at sale		$ 855,000

The distortion of economic sharing of proceeds could have been eliminated in this situation if the partnership agreement had provided for a different special allocation of gains from the disposition of property. Specifically, simulated gain (and the related cash proceeds) could have been allocated to the extent possible in a way that would result in a sharing of the total proceeds from the sale of the property consistent with the general income-sharing ratio (i.e., 50/50). In this example, the amount of simulated gain available for equalizing capital accounts is $880,000. The built-in gain cannot be used for this purpose because the recognition of built-in gain does not impact the capital accounts (i.e., the gain element is credited to the capital accounts as part of the fair market value of the property upon contribution). *(See Case 165 for an example of a special allocation of gain to "balance" the capital accounts.)*

If an existing partnership is deemed terminated due to a sale or exchange of 50% or more of the partnership interest in profits and capital within 12 consecutive months,[120] the capital accounts must be adjusted to reflect unrealized gains and losses as if the partnership property had been distributed to the partners. The constructive reformation of the partnership requires the capital accounts to be adjusted as if the partners formed a new partnership by contribution of the deemed terminated partnership's assets and liabilities.[121]

Due to the significance to the industry of the issues discussed above, guidance from Treasury is needed.

Case 167
Requirements for Obtaining an Advance Ruling Regarding Limited Partnership Status

C Company, an operating oil company with a net worth of $500,000 (net fair market value of assets in excess of liabilities), organized Drilling Fund A as a Texas limited partnership and offered partnership units to various investors. C Company is the sole general partner. The partnership is expected to sell investment units to limited partners. Total contributions to the partnership will be $5 million. Included among the investors subscribing to the offering are shareholders of C Company who own, in the aggregate, 15% of the outstanding stock.

The partnership agreement provides that C Company has a 5% interest in all items of partnership income, deduction and credits. It is estimated that

120. I.R.C. Sec. 708(b).

121. Reg. Sec. 1.704-1(b)(2)(ii)(g); Reg. Sec. 1.704-1(b)(2)(iv)(l).

the aggregate losses to be allocated to all the partners during the first two years will not exceed the partners' equity capital contributed to the partnership. Any partnership borrowings are expected to be on a recourse basis. No stock or other security of the corporate general partner or an affiliate is offered to the limited partners as a part of the offering of units of the limited partnership.

C Company has requested assistance in determining whether the drilling fund may obtain a ruling that it will be considered a partnership for federal income tax purposes.

The Internal Revenue Service (IRS) has issued two sets of guidelines that set forth the conditions that must exist for a limited partnership to obtain an advance ruling that it is a partnership for federal income tax purposes.

The first set of guidelines is applicable to all limited partnerships.[122] To obtain an advance ruling that the entity will be recognized as a limited partnership, the general partners, as a group, must share in at least 1% of each material item of partnership income, deduction and credit at all times during the existence of the partnership. In making this determination, the general partner's interest, if any, as a limited partner is not considered. In addition, the aggregate deductions allocated to all partners during the first two years of operation cannot exceed the equity capital contributed to the partnership. A third condition is that any creditor that makes a nonrecourse loan to the partnership may not have or acquire, as a result of making the loan, any direct or indirect interest in the profits, capital or property of the partnership except as a secured creditor. Drilling Fund A meets all the general conditions for obtaining an advance ruling that are applicable to all limited partnerships.

The second set of guidelines applies only to a limited partnership with a sole corporate general partner.[123] The first requirement is that the limited partners must not own, directly or indirectly, more than 20% of the stock of the corporate general partner. In addition, the corporate general partner must meet a minimum net worth requirement at all times during the existence of the partnership. If the total contributions to the partnership are less than $2.5 million, the net worth of the corporate general partner must be at least 15% of those total contributions, or $250,000, whichever is less. If total contributions exceed $2.5 million, the net worth of the corporate general partner must be at least 10% of those contributions. Although these conditions appear to relate to the corporate characteristics of continuity of life and limited liability, they are general tests that must be satisfied to obtain an advance ruling, in addition to satisfying the specific requirements stated in the regulations. *(See Case 162.)*

Another condition that must be met if a sole corporate general partner exists is that the purchase of a limited partnership interest by a limited partner cannot entail either a mandatory or discretionary purchase or option to purchase any type of security of the corporate general partner or one of its affiliates. In addition, the organization and operation of the limited partnership must be in accordance with the applicable state statute relating to limited partnerships.

Drilling Fund A meets the ownership test in that only 15% of C Company's stock is owned by limited partners and the net worth requirement is fulfilled. C Company also must maintain the net worth requirement throughout the life of the partnership to continue to rely on a private ruling from the IRS. In addition, the limited partnership is formed in Texas and presumably will be operated in accordance with state law.

---

122. Rev. Proc. 74-17, 1974-1 C.B. 438.
123. Rev. Proc. 72-13, 1972-1 C.B. 735.

Also, no limited partner is required or given an option or right to purchase stock of C Company in connection with the offering of the limited partnership units. Accordingly, all the requirements for obtaining an advance ruling are met.

The rules relating to stock ownership in the corporate general partner also apply to the ownership of certain related corporations. For this purpose, the rules defining an affiliated group of corporations entitled to file a consolidated income tax return are used.[124] Generally, these rules require an ownership of at least 80% of the total voting stock and 80% of the total value of all stock of the corporation. In addition to the direct ownership of stock, the ownership of stock by parties related to a limited partner must be considered in determining if the limited partners own more than 20% of the stock of the corporate general partner or an affiliated corporation. The attribution rules provide that a limited partner is deemed to own stock owned by members of the family, partnerships of which he is a partner, an estate or trust of which he is a beneficiary and a corporation of which he owns, directly or indirectly, 50% or more of the value of the stock.[125] These rules are complex, and a thorough understanding is mandatory to ascertain that the advance ruling requirements are fulfilled.

In determining the net worth of the corporate general partner, the value of its interest in the limited partnership cannot be considered. In addition, accounts and notes receivable from and payable to the limited partnership are excluded. The current fair market value of corporate assets, not the book value, is used in determining the corporate net worth.

When the corporate general partner acts in that capacity for more than one limited partnership, the IRS requires that the minimum net worth requirements be applied on an aggregate basis.[126] The corporate general partner's net worth must equal at all times at least the sum of the amounts of net worth required with respect to each partnership. For example, if, in addition to acting as general partner of Drilling Fund A, C Company were also to act as general partner of Drilling Fund B, which has received contributions of $2 million from its partners, C Company's minimum net worth requirement would be computed as follows:

Minimum net worth with respect to—	
Drilling Fund A (10% x $5,000,000)	$500,000
Drilling Fund B (lesser of $250,000 or 15% X $2,000,000)	250,000
Minimum net worth of C Company	$750,000

The requirements applicable to a partnership with a sole corporate general partner do not apply if there is an individual general partner in addition to a corporate general partner.

Taxpayers desiring an advance IRS ruling that an entity be treated as a limited partnership for tax purposes should submit sufficient information and documents to allow for a complete review. The IRS has listed the items that must be submitted.[127] The IRS issues rulings on limited partnership status in situations involving publicly held limited partner interests promoted and marketed in a manner similar to corporate securities.[128] *(See Case 172.)* However, the IRS will not rule as to the nonrecognition of gain on contribution of widely held oil and gas properties.[129]

124. I.R.C. Sec. 1504(a).
125. I.R.C. Sec. 318.
126. Rev. Proc. 72-13, 1972-1 C.B. 735.
127. Rev. Proc. 75-16, 1975-1 C.B. 676; Rev. Proc. 87-1, 1987-1 I.R.B. 7.
128. IRS Letter Ruling 8602062; IRS Letter Ruling 8520105.
129. Rev. Proc. 87-3, 1987-1 I.R.B. 27 (Sec. 5.23).

It should be understood that it is not necessary to obtain an advance ruling on the association question or any other tax question relating to the partnership. Also, the above criteria are not statutory but apply solely for ruling purposes. A partnership may be treated as such, and not as an association taxable as a corporation, even though it does not specifically meet all the ruling criteria and no advance ruling is obtained.

Case 168
Regular Corporation Chosen for Conducting Oil and Gas Operations

> **Operator A has been conducting oil and gas operations as an individual proprietor and as a general partner for several years. Recently, he has become concerned that his liability insurance may not protect adequately against damages that could result from an accident such as a blowout. Legal counsel has recommended the formation of a new corporation for conducting his oil and gas operations. Operator A is receptive to the proposal to incorporate but wants to know the principal income tax advantages and disadvantages of the plan, assuming the corporation is taxed as a regular corporation (i.e., does not elect S corporation status).**

For tax years beginning in 1987, graduated income tax rates of up to 38.5% apply to individuals doing business as an individual proprietor, as a partner or as a stockholder in an S corporation.[130] For subsequent years, the maximum individual income tax rate is 28%, although the phaseout of the 15% tax bracket and personal exemptions of higher-income taxpayers may result in a somewhat higher marginal tax rate at certain income levels.[131] Additionally, individuals may be subject to the alternative minimum tax (AMT) provisions[132] *(see Case 175)* and the "at-risk" limitations.[133] *(See Cases 32 and 33.)*

In the case of a regular corporation, for tax years beginning after June 30, 1987, the tax rates range from 15% to 25% on the first $75,000 of taxable income, with the excess taxed at 34%. However, corporations with taxable incomes in excess of $100,000 are subject to a surcharge which has the effect of phasing out the lower tax brackets. This surcharge equals the lesser of 5% of taxable income in excess of $100,000 or $11,750.[134] For tax years that include July 1, 1987, these tax rates are blended with the old tax rates of up to 46%, based on the proportion of days in the fiscal year preceding July 1, 1987, and subsequent to June 30, 1987.[135]

Corporations are subject to a complex AMT.[136] *(See Case 176.)* Preference items for AMT purposes include percentage depletion in excess of adjusted basis[137] *(see Case 87)*, excess intangible drilling and development costs (IDC) reduced by 65% of net oil and gas income[138] *(see Case 174)* and 50% of the excess of adjusted net book income over alternative minimum taxable income (AMTI).[139] In addition, certain closely held corporations may be subject to the "at-risk" rules.[140] *(See Case 32.)*

---

130. I.R.C. Sec. 1(h).
131. I.R.C. Sec. 1(g).
132. I.R.C. Sec. 55.
133. I.R.C. Sec. 465.
134. I.R.C. Sec. 11(b).
135. I.R.C. Sec. 11(b)(2); I.R.C. Sec. 15(a).
136. I.R.C. Sec. 55.
137. I.R.C. Sec. 57(a)(1).
138. I.R.C. Sec. 57(a)(2).
139. I.R.C. Sec. 56(f).
140. I.R.C. Sec. 465.

There are three principal tax disadvantages in using a regular corporation. First, after 1987, the maximum 34% corporate income tax rate exceeds the maximum individual rate of 28%. Although the marginal rates may be higher due to the phaseout of lower brackets and exemptions, there is a distinct potential for corporate tax rates to exceed individual rates.

The second disadvantage of using a regular corporation is the double taxation of the earnings, first through the tax paid by the corporation on its taxable income and second when the corporate earnings and profits are distributed either as a dividend or as gain on liquidation. In the case of a corporation engaged in oil and gas operations, the computation of earnings and profits disallows the tax benefits of the excess of percentage depletion over cost depletion[141] and includes the following adjustments *(see Case 121)*:

- ☐ The excess of accelerated depreciation over straight-line depreciation (generally using extended lives) must be computed, with the computation depending upon varying laws in effect since 1971[142] and
- ☐ IDC (other than costs incurred in connection with nonproductive wells) paid or incurred in tax years beginning after September 30, 1984, must be capitalized and deducted ratably over the 60-month period beginning with the month in which the well begins production.[143]

A regular corporation can avoid double taxation by continuing to reinvest its earnings into the active business rather than distribute those earnings to the shareholders. However, it must be prepared to demonstrate that the accumulation is for the reasonable needs of the business to avoid an accumulated earnings tax of up to 38½% (28% for tax years beginning after December 31, 1987) of accumulated taxable income net of regular income taxes and certain credits.[144]

The third principal disadvantage of using a regular corporation is the potential for double taxation of asset appreciation. Before the Tax Reform Act of 1986 (the Act), corporations generally escaped taxation of gains realized upon distribution of appreciated assets in certain stock redemptions and on sales and distributions in liquidation.[145] However, IDC, depreciation and certain other recapture rules applied at the corporate level. Subject to numerous transition rules from 1986 through 1988,[146] corporations will be taxable on all gain attributable to appreciated property distributed to shareholders in stock redemptions[147] or in liquidation.[148] In addition, the Act eliminates the nonrecognition of gain and loss provisions relating to asset sales within 12 months of liquidation.[149]

The passive-activity loss and credit limitations differ for corporations and individuals. Closely held corporations (other than personal-service corporations) may deduct passive-activity losses and credits against working interest income and taxes attributable thereto.[150] An individual may not deduct passive-activity losses and credits against working interest income and related taxes unless the working interest is held

141. Reg. Sec. 1.312-6(c).
142. I.R.C. Sec. 312(k); Reg. Sec. 1.312-15.
143. I.R.C. Sec. 312(n)(2).
144. I.R.C. Sec. 531; Technical Corrections Bill of 1987, Sec. 101(a)(2), *amending* I.R.C. Sec. 531.
145. I.R.C. Sec. 311(d) *(prior to amendment by the Tax Reform Act of 1986)*; I.R.C. Sec. 336 *(prior to amendment by the Tax Reform Act of 1986)*; I.R.C. Sec. 337 *(prior to amendment by the Tax Reform Act of 1986)*.
146. P.L. 99-514 (Tax Reform Act of 1986), Sec. 633.
147. I.R.C. Sec. 311(b).
148. I.R.C. Sec. 336.
149. I.R.C. Sec. 337 *(prior to amendment by the Tax Reform Act of 1986)*.
150. I.R.C. Sec. 469(e)(2).

in a manner that limits the individual's liability.[151] An individual may deduct working interest losses and related credits against active income (i.e., compensation and business income if the individual materially participates in the business) and portfolio income (i.e., dividends, interest and royalties) and related taxes only if the working interest is held in a manner that does not limit his liability[152] or if the individual materially participates in the oil and gas activity.[153] Generally, a closely held corporation (other than a personal-service corporation) may deduct working interest losses and credits against all types of income and related taxes. However, losses and taxes attributable to a working interest held in a manner that limits the corporation's liability may not be deducted against portfolio income and related taxes.[154] *(See Case 182 for a further discussion of the passive-activity rules.)*

Unlike individuals, a corporation (other than an S corporation) generally may not use the cash receipts and disbursements method of accounting unless it and certain related entities had combined average annual gross receipts of $5 million or less for all prior tax years beginning after December 31, 1985 (based on a three-year moving average).[155]

Despite the inherent tax disadvantages of using a corporate form, long-range tax strategy may be accommodated by doing so. Gifts to family members are made more easily in the form of stock. The use of multiple classes of stock to freeze the value for estate tax purposes while allowing control to remain with the older generation is beneficial. If an operation is conducted in corporate form, a tax-free exchange with a publicly held corporation can provide liquidity and solve the problem of who will manage the business after the owner's death.

Operator A will realize no taxable income if he transfers his interests in the leases to the new corporation solely for stock and securities of the corporation.[156] If, however, the new corporation assumes any indebtedness on the leases or if the leases are transferred subject to any indebtedness, whether or not it is assumed by the corporation, there will be a taxable gain to Operator A if the indebtedness exceeds the tax basis in the leases. If there is more than one transferor, gain is computed separately for each without regard to the adjusted basis and liabilities of any other transferor.[157] *(See Case 152.)* Also, if other property, such as indebtedness that does not qualify as a "security" for tax purposes, or money is received by a transferor in addition to the stock, that other property or money will constitute "boot" and gain will be recognized to the extent of the fair market value of the "boot."[158] The gain recognized will be reported as ordinary income to the extent of depreciation, depletion or IDC recapture.[159] *(See Case 131 for a discussion of the possible recharacterization as ordinary income of long-term capital gain from the sale or exchange of property used in a trade or business and held for the requisite holding period.)*

Generally, in a tax-free exchange of leases to a new corporation solely for stock, no investment tax credit will be recaptured, assuming the exchange qualifies as a mere change in the form of conducting the trade or business.[160]

---

151. I.R.C. Sec. 469(a)(1); I.R.C. Sec. 469(c)(3)(A).
152. *Ibid.*
153. I.R.C. Sec. 469(c)(1).
154. I.R.C. Sec. 469(e)(2)(B)(ii); I.R.C. Sec. 469(c)(3)(A).
155. I.R.C. Sec. 448.
156. I.R.C. Sec. 351(a).
157. I.R.C. Sec. 357(c); Rev. Rul. 66-142, 1966-1 C.B. 66; George F. Smith, Jr., 84 T.C. 889 (1985).
158. I.R.C. Sec. 351(b).
159. I.R.C. Sec. 1245; I.R.C. Sec. 1254.
160. I.R.C. Sec. 47(b); Reg. Sec. 1.47-3(f).

For assets transferred by Operator A, the new corporation generally must use the same depreciation system as was used before the transfer.[161]

If the transfer of the leases to the new corporation is nontaxable, the tax basis of the properties in the hands of the new corporation will be the same as the tax basis of the properties in the hands of Operator A before the conveyance. If the transfer is partially taxable, the corporation's basis is increased by the amount of any gain recognized by Operator A on the transfer.[162]

Nonresident alien individuals and foreign corporations may not be eligible for tax-free transfers similar to that described above.[163]

If Operator A decides to conduct his oil and gas operations in corporate form, he must consider whether to transfer all his oil and gas properties or just his nonproducing properties to the new corporation. Generally, the contribution of proven properties to a corporation by a noncorporate transferor will eliminate the benefit of percentage depletion on the subsequent production under the independent-producer and royalty-owner exemption. However, a very limited exception is provided for certain transfers of qualified property by individuals to a qualified transferee corporation solely in exchange for stock in that corporation.[164] Assuming the transfer qualifies under this exception, Operator A must reduce his depletable oil quantity for the corporation's depletable oil quantity deemed attributable to the transferred properties. In addition, if Operator A disposes of the corporation's stock, the corporation's depletable oil quantity may be reduced or eliminated. *Qualified property* means: (1) an oil or gas property that has not been transferred previously; (2) cash up to a maximum of $1,000 and (3) necessary production equipment in place on the property at the time of transfer for which the transferor has elected these provisions to apply.[165] A *qualified transferee corporation* means a corporation, all the outstanding stock of which has been issued to individuals solely in exchange for qualified property. *(See Case 110.)*

If an individual oil operator has production in excess of his depletable oil quantity, he should determine if his percentage depletion deduction under the independent-producer exemption can be increased by transferring certain of his marginal properties to a controlled corporation in a tax-free transfer or by a taxable sale to the corporation. Properties that should be considered are those subject to the 50% of net income limitation on the percentage depletion deduction or those for which the oil or gas sales prices are relatively low compared with the sales price of production from other properties. Such a disposition may be advantageous, even if the corporation will not be allowed to claim percentage depletion in the future. This result can occur because the limitation resulting from production in excess of the depletable oil quantity is applied pro rata to the percentage depletion otherwise allowable on all properties subject to the independent-producer exemption.

Careful attention should be given to the capital structure of the corporation. If the amount of capital contributed to the corporation in exchange for stock or as paid-in-surplus is too low in relation to the amount of debt, some or all of the debt may be treated for tax purposes as if it were preferred stock. Debt also may be reclassified as stock because of its terms or for other reasons. This reclassification will cause interest payments to be treated as nondeductible dividends. Repayment of principal also can be taxed as a dividend.

---

161. I.R.C. Sec. 168(e)(4)(C) *(prior to amendment by the Tax Reform Act of 1986)*; I.R.C. Sec. 168(f)(5).
162. I.R.C. Sec. 362(a).
163. I.R.C. Sec. 897(e).
164. I.R.C. Sec. 613A(c)(10).
165. I.R.C. Sec. 613A(c)(10)(E).

Case 169
Corporation Electing Under Subchapter S of the Internal Revenue Code

Operators A and B each own 50% of the stock of C Company. The assets of C Company consist of producing and nonproducing oil and gas properties. The corporation historically has been in a tax loss position or has had taxable net income of less than $100,000 per year, due primarily to deductions for intangible drilling and development costs (IDC) and percentage depletion. Operators A and B are considering whether an election should be made under Subchapter S of the Internal Revenue Code (the Code) and ask how the election would affect the corporation and its shareholders.

The election under Subchapter S of the Code (hereinafter referred to as an S corporation election) permits the use of the corporate form of organization without double taxation of earnings. Because an S corporation is a conduit entity,[166] the character of every item of income, gain, deduction, credit, etc., passes through to the shareholders and is taxed/utilized as such in the shareholders' returns.[167]

Eligibility Rules

A regular corporation (hereinafter referred to as a C corporation) is eligible to make an S corporation election only if it is a domestic corporation with no more than 35 shareholders. No shareholder may be a nonresident alien, and all shareholders must be individuals, estates or certain types of trusts. The corporation can have only one class of stock outstanding, although there may be differences in voting rights among the shares of stock. It cannot be a member of an affiliated group eligible to file a consolidated return.[168] All qualifications must be met on the earlier of the date of the S corporation election or the first day of the first S corporation tax year, and continuously thereafter.

An S corporation can own 80% or more of an inactive corporation, but its S corporation election will terminate on the day the inactive corporation begins business and has gross income.[169] An S corporation must adopt a "permitted" year as its tax year.[170] A permitted year is a calendar year unless the corporation establishes a business purpose and the Internal Revenue Service approves a fiscal year.[171] The S corporation election must be made on or before the 15th day of the third month of the tax year for which the election is to apply or at anytime during the preceding tax year.[172]

Income and Deduction Considerations

Each shareholder of an S corporation must include in income for the tax year in which or with which the tax year of the corporation ends his pro-rata share of:

- ☐ Any item of income, loss, deduction or credit that may affect the tax liability of any shareholder if stated separately and

---

166. I.R.C. Sec. 1366(a).
167. I.R.C. Sec. 1366(b).
168. I.R.C. Sec. 1361(b); I.R.C. Sec. 1361(c)(4).
169. I.R.C. Sec. 1361(c)(6).
170. I.R.C. Sec. 1378(a).
171. I.R.C. Sec. 1378(b); Rev. Proc. 87-32, 1987-28 I.R.B. 14.
172. I.R.C. Sec. 1362(b).

□ Nonseparately computed income or loss.[173]

To determine nonseparately computed income or loss, all items other than the separately stated items (i.e., capital gains and losses, charitable contributions, tax-exempt income, foreign items, intangible drilling costs, etc.) are combined.[174] As mentioned above, the character of each item for each shareholder is determined as if the item was realized directly by the shareholder instead of by the corporation.

Depletion is computed at the shareholder level rather than at the corporate level, which is similar to the computation of depletion by partners in a partnership.[175] Thus, the shareholders receive the direct benefits (both tax and cash) of percentage depletion. An S corporation election by a C corporation is treated as a transfer of proven properties, resulting in a loss of percentage depletion subsequent to the effective date of the election.[176] *(See Case 111 for a discussion of the determination of percentage depletion and the effects of the transfer rule.)*

Tax preference items, such as the excess of percentage depletion over the adjusted basis of the property and excess IDC, are calculated at the shareholder level. By computing excess IDC at the shareholder level, net income from oil and gas properties unrelated to the S corporation can be utilized to reduce the preference amount. Shareholders of an S corporation also can reduce the excess IDC preference by electing to capitalize and amortize IDC over a 10-year period.[177] *(See Case 181 for a discussion of capitalizing IDC.)*

Corporate tax benefit reduction rules applicable to tax preference items (e.g., the reduced deduction of IDC for integrated oil companies) apply to any S corporation (or its predecessor) that was a C corporation for any of the three immediately preceding tax years. This rule prevents C corporations from avoiding corporate preference rules by making an S corporation election.[178]

The "at-risk" provisions are applied only at the S corporation shareholder level.[179] *(See Case 33 for a discussion regarding the application of the "at-risk" rules.)* S corporation shareholders must consider the implications of the passive-activity loss and credit rules.[180] *(See Case 182 for a discussion regarding the application of the passive-activity rules.)*

A corporate-level tax is imposed on any *net built-in gain* that arose prior to the S corporation election and that is recognized by the S corporation within 10 years after the effective date of the election. This provision does not apply to corporations which filed S corporation elections prior to January 1, 1987, and is subject to certain transitional rules. The term *net built-in gain* means the excess of the fair market value of assets over adjusted bases as of the effective date of the election. This built-in gain is taxed at the highest C corporation rate in the years in which built-in gain is recognized through sale, distribution or other income-recognition event. Any C corporation net operating loss, tax credit and other carryovers are allowed as a deduction or credit against the built-in gain and related tax.[181] In determining the

173. I.R.C. Sec. 1366(a).
174. I.R.C. Sec. 1366(a)(2).
175. I.R.C. Sec. 613A(c)(13)(A).
176. I.R.C. Sec. 613A(c)(13)(C).
177. I.R.C. Sec. 59(e).
178. I.R.C. Sec. 1363(b)(4).
179. I.R.C. Sec. 465(a)(1).
180. I.R.C. Sec. 469.
181. I.R.C. Sec. 1374; I.R.C. Sec. 1374(b); Conference Committee Report No. 99-841, 1986-3 C.B. Vol. 4 203; General Explanation of the Tax Reform Act of 1986, prepared by the Staff of the Joint Committee on Taxation, p. 344.

shareholder's income, the recognized built-in gain is reduced by any tax imposed on the S corporation.[182]

All gains recognized during the 10-year period are subject to the built-in gains tax except to the extent the S corporation establishes that: (1) the asset was not held by it as of the beginning of its first S corporation year or (2) the recognized gain exceeds the built-in gain.[183] Therefore, C company should consider obtaining an appraisal of the fair market values of its assets as of the first day of its first S corporation year and should establish appropriate recordkeeping procedures. While these rules will apply to dispositions of oil and gas property interests, they should not apply to revenue generated from production subsequent to conversion to S corporation status. Congress intended the built-in gain tax to apply to post-conversion dispositions of assets and to income realized prior to conversion that is recognized for tax purposes subsequent to conversion (e.g., collection of accounts receivable by a cash method of accounting taxpayer and completion of a long-term contract by a taxpayer using the completed contract method of accounting).[184] Congress did not intend the tax to apply to post-conversion operating income. The Treasury should promulgate regulations implementing this apparent Congressional intent.

Gain on the sale or exchange of S corporation stock may be recharacterized as ordinary income due to IDC and depletion recapture.[185] Although not equitable in result, it appears that the recapture rules also apply to IDC and depletion deductions attributable to pre-S Corporation years.

Distributions and Basis Considerations

The treatment of S corporation distributions is similar, with certain exceptions, to the tax treatment of partnership distributions. The most significant difference is that a distribution of property by an S corporation to a shareholder is measured by fair market value rather than adjusted basis as is the case in measuring a partnership distribution. To the extent the fair market value of the property distributed exceeds the S corporation's adjusted basis in the property, gain will be recognized by the S corporation and passed through to the shareholders.[186] This gain could be subject to tax at the corporate level. Accordingly, the shareholder's basis in the distributed property will be the property's fair market value. The distribution of an oil or gas property with a fair market value in excess of the S corporation's adjusted basis will trigger gain including potential IDC, depletion and depreciation recapture.[187] Therefore, if it is anticipated that appreciated property will be distributed, the partnership vehicle presumably will be desirable because a distribution by a partnership generally will not trigger gain including recapture items (as long as the distribution is pro rata).

If an S corporation does not have accumulated earnings and profits (i.e., from earlier C corporation years or, possibly, S corporation years before 1983), distributions first will reduce a shareholder's basis in his stock. Any excess will be treated as gain by the shareholder from the sale or exchange of stock[188] (generally as capital gain unless the corporation is collapsible).

182. I.R.C. Sec. 1366(f)(2).
183. I.R.C. Sec. 1374(d)(2).
184. General Explanation of the Tax Reform Act of 1986, prepared by the Staff of the Joint Committee on Taxation, p. 344.
185. I.R.C. Sec. 1254(b)(2).
186. I.R.C. Sec. 1363(d).
187. I.R.C. Sec. 1254(a)(1)(B); I.R.C. Sec. 1245(a)(1)(B).
188. I.R.C. Sec. 1368(b).

If an S corporation has accumulated earnings and profits, the tax treatment of distributions is more complex. These distributions first will reduce the accumulated adjustments account (AAA). The AAA, determined at the end of the S corporation's tax year, is an account maintained by the S corporation and defined as the sum of the adjustments to basis discussed below other than tax-exempt income and related expenses. The AAA is calculated on a cumulative basis for all S corporation years beginning after 1982. The AAA balance can be reduced below zero.[189] Thus, loss years may generate a negative AAA, and income in a later year can cause the AAA account to be positive only after the negative balance has been restored. Distributions in excess of the AAA first will be considered as ordinary dividends from accumulated earnings and profits, then as reduction of stock basis and finally will be treated as gain from the sale or exchange of stock.[190]

Special rules are provided for distributions of taxable income accumulated in S corporation years beginning before 1983.[191]

If an S corporation has accumulated earnings and profits, the corporation may elect to treat distributions in a tax year as coming first from accumulated earnings and profits rather than from the AAA.[192] The election is applicable only for the tax year for which it is made and is not binding for future years. The election may prevent an unintended termination of the S corporation election due to the passive-investment income rules applicable to S corporations with C corporation earnings and profits.[193]

The amount of losses a shareholder can deduct is limited to his adjusted basis in the stock and the adjusted basis of any indebtedness of the corporation to him as of the end of the corporation's tax year.[194] Corporate indebtedness other than to the shareholder does not increase the shareholder's basis in his stock. If losses are to be generated by nonshareholder debt, a partnership vehicle should be considered to avoid this S corporation restriction. The shareholder's portion of the corporation's net loss first reduces his basis in the stock, but not below zero. If the loss exceeds his basis in the stock, it then reduces his adjusted basis in any indebtedness from the corporation to him, but not below zero.[195] Any loss in excess of basis in stock and indebtedness is allowed as a loss in succeeding tax years, but only to the same shareholder, subject to the same basis limitation rules applied to that year. These excess losses can be carried over as long as the S corporation election still is in effect.[196] Subsequent items that increase basis first increase basis in indebtedness before increasing basis in stock.[197]

189. I.R.C. Sec. 1368(e)(1)(A).
190. I.R.C. Sec. 1368(c).
191. I.R.C. Sec. 1379(c).
192. I.R.C. Sec. 1368(e)(3).
193. I.R.C. Sec. 1362(d)(3).
194. I.R.C. Sec. 1366(d)(1).
195. I.R.C. Sec. 1367(b)(2)(A).
196. I.R.C. Sec. 1366(d)(2).
197. I.R.C. Sec. 1367(b)(2)(B).

A shareholder's basis in his stock is computed similarly to the computation of a partner's basis in his partnership interest. The initial basis is adjusted as follows:[198]

Increased by:

- ☐ All income items (separately or nonseparately computed) but only to the extent actually reported by the shareholder.
- ☐ Depletion in excess of basis of non-oil and gas properties.
- ☐ Contributions to capital.

Decreased by (but not below zero):

- ☐ Distributions not includable in income.
- ☐ Loss items (separately or nonseparately computed).
- ☐ Nondeductible expenses not charged to capital.
- ☐ Depletion deduction with respect to an oil and gas property to the extent of the adjusted basis of that property.

In cases in which a corporation repays an indebtedness, the basis of which has been reduced, the shareholder will realize taxable income equal to the excess of the amount received over his remaining basis in the indebtedness. This income generally will be treated as capital gain if the indebtedness is evidenced by a written note, bond, certificate, etc.,[199] and as ordinary income in other circumstances.[200]

S Corporation Termination Provisions

The S corporation election may be terminated by a revocation,[201] which must be consented to by shareholders owning more than 50% of the outstanding stock. The revocation must be filed by the 15th day of the third month of the tax year to which it is to be effective. A new shareholder cannot terminate an existing election simply by refusing to consent to the election. If the shareholders elect, the revocation may be effective on a prospective basis at a future, specified date during the tax year.

The election automatically terminates[202] if: (1) the number of shareholders exceeds 35; (2) an ineligible shareholder acquires stock; (3) the corporation becomes a member of an affiliated group or (4) the corporation has C corporation earnings and profits and its passive investment income exceeds 25% of total gross receipts for each of three consecutive S corporation years.[203]

If an S corporation election is terminated, the effective date of termination depends on the nature of the disqualification. Generally, the termination will be effective on the date of the disqualifying event.[204] If the termination is caused by failure of the passive-investment income test, it will be effective on the first day of the fourth tax year.[205] S corporation status will be deemed to continue if the Secretary of the Treasury determines the termination was inadvertent, the problem is corrected quickly and the

198. I.R.C. Sec. 1367.
199. Rev. Rul. 68-537, 1968-2 C.B. 372.
200. Joe M. Smith, 48 T.C. 872 (1967).
201. I.R.C. Sec. 1362(d)(1).
202. I.R.C. Sec. 1362(d)(2).
203. I.R.C. Sec. 1362(d)(3).
204. I.R.C. Sec. 1362(d)(2)(B).
205. I.R.C. Sec. 1362(d)(3)(A)(ii).

shareholders agree to any adjustments specified by the Secretary of the Treasury.[206] Otherwise, once an election is terminated, a corporation must wait five years before it can make a new S corporation election unless consent to a new election is granted.[207]

Generally, all cash distributions made within one year following the termination of the S corporation election will apply to reduce a shareholder's basis to the extent of the AAA balance.[208] An S corporation may elect not to apply all distributions to reduce stock basis during the post-termination transition period, but to treat those distributions as dividends that could reduce any potential accumulated earnings tax or personal holding company tax problems. All shareholders of the S corporation receiving distributions during the post-termination transition period must consent to the election.[209]

If an S corporation election terminates during the year, the "S termination year" is generally divided into an S corporation short year ending on the day before the terminating event occurs and a C corporation short year beginning on the date of the terminating event and ending on the normal S corporation's yearend. Generally, all income, gain, loss, etc., are allocated pro rata between the two years.[210] However, an election to allocate these items according to normal accounting rules may be made if all persons who are shareholders at any time during the S corporation's short year and persons who are shareholders of the C corporation on the first day of the C corporation's short year consent.[211] Normal accounting rules must be used, however, if 50% or more of the corporation's stock is sold or exchanged in the S corporation's termination year, or for any items to which I.R.C. Section 338 applies.[212]

The S corporation election can be a useful method to minimize taxes, but each situation must be analyzed carefully. In the case of C Company, it may not be advisable to make the election because the shareholders can lose the benefit of any net operating losses and percentage depletion on properties that would be considered proven at the date of election.

Case 170
Personal Holding Company

Individuals A and B each own 50% of the capital stock of C Company. C Company's 1987 income consists of $140,000 of oil and gas royalties and a $60,000 lease bonus. C Company purchased a production payment several years ago and receives $124,000 of proceeds in 1987 in retirement of the oil and gas production payment, with $100,000 of the amount constituting principal reduction. The production payment qualifies as a mortgage loan for income tax purposes. C Company incurs property and severance taxes of $12,000 attributable to the royalties. Percentage depletion is allowable with respect to the royalties.

C Company pays $40,000 in administrative expenses that were unrelated to the income from oil and gas operations. This amount does not include any payment for personal services to either Individual A or B. C Company

206. I.R.C. Sec. 1362(f).
207. I.R.C. Sec. 1362(g).
208. I.R.C. Sec. 1371(e)(1); I.R.C. Sec. 1377.
209. I.R.C. Sec. 1371(e)(2); I.R.C. Sec. 1377(b).
210. I.R.C. Sec. 1362(e)(2).
211. I.R.C. Sec. 1362(e)(3).
212. I.R.C. Sec. 1362(e)(6)(C); I.R.C. Section 1362(e)(6)(D).

also paid $15,000 of interest expense on a loan obtained to acquire the production payment. The company paid no dividends during the tax year.

A personal holding company is defined as any domestic corporation of which more than 50% in value of the outstanding stock is owned directly or indirectly by five or fewer individuals at any time during the last half of the tax year and at least 60% of the adjusted ordinary gross income for the tax year is personal holding company income.[213] Most passive investment income such as interest and dividends constitutes personal holding company income.[214] Special rules exist to determine when rents and certain other types of income are considered personal holding company income.[215]

Personal holding company income includes mineral, oil and gas royalties unless: (1) the "adjusted ordinary gross income" from those royalties constitutes 50% or more of the total "adjusted ordinary gross income"; (2) the personal holding company income for the tax year without regard to that royalty income is not more than 10% of the "ordinary gross income" and (3) the sum of the trade or business expenses allowable as deductions under Section 162 (other than deductions for compensation for services rendered by shareholders) constitutes 15% or more of the "adjusted ordinary gross income." Any deductions specifically allowable under sections of the Internal Revenue Code other than Section 162 are not to be taken into account.[216] The Internal Revenue Service (IRS) characterizes delay rentals as rents, not royalties.[217]

Ordinary gross income generally is the same as *gross income*, except that gains from the disposition of capital assets and certain property used in the trade or business are excluded.[218] Adjusted ordinary gross income from oil and gas production is the gross production income less the following deductions:[219]

☐ Exhaustion, wear and tear, obsolescence, amortization and depletion.

☐ Property and severance taxes.

☐ Interest.

☐ Rent.

Adjusted ordinary gross income should be computed separately for mineral, oil and gas royalties that may constitute personal holding company income and other types of production income, such as working interest income, that never will be personal holding company income. Certain adjustments also are made to rent income, and some types of interest income are excluded in determining adjusted ordinary gross income.[220]

Gross income from mineral, oil and gas royalties includes production income from royalty, overriding royalty, and net profits interests and production payments that constitute an economic interest in the property. The courts have held that lease bonus income constitutes personal holding company income.[221] The Supreme Court consistently has held that lease bonus income represents royalties received in advance

213. I.R.C. Sec. 542(a).
214. I.R.C. Sec. 543(a).
215. I.R.C. Sec. 543(a)(2).
216. I.R.C. Sec. 543(a)(3).
217. Rev. Rul. 70-153, 1970-1 C.B. 139.
218. I.R.C. Sec. 543(b)(1).
219. I.R.C. Sec. 543(b)(2)(B).
220. I.R.C. Sec. 543(b)(2)(A); I.R.C. Sec. 543(b)(2)(C).
221. Comm'r v. Clarion Oil Co., 148 F.2d 671 (D.C. Cir. 1945), 33 AFTR 1141, 45-1 USTC 9218; Bayou Verret Land Co. v. Comm'r, 450 F.2d 850 (5th Cir. 1971), 28 AFTR2d 71-5961, 71-2 USTC 9713.

of production.[222] This characterization also should be valid for purposes of the personal holding company provisions. However, a circuit court ruled that lease bonus income is not passive income for the purposes of qualifying as a Subchapter S corporation.[223] Although an analogy may be made to this case for purposes of the personal holding company provisions, the IRS probably will continue to view lease bonus income as personal holding company income.

When a production payment is carved out for exploration or development or retained by a lessor in a leasing transaction, it is treated as an economic interest in property.[224] As such, the proceeds of the production payment are included in mineral, oil and gas royalties in computing adjusted ordinary gross income.[225]

In this case, the production payment is treated as a loan. The only income reported is the proceeds in excess of the principal payment ($24,000), which is interest income.

In this case, the total adjusted ordinary income for the tax year is $191,000, computed as follows:

	Total	Royalties	Lease Bonus	Production Payment Interest Income
Ordinary gross income	$224,000	$140,000	$60,000	$24,000
Deductions				
Depletion	$ 21,000	$ 21,000	$ —	$ —
Property and severance taxes	12,000	12,000	—	$ —
Total deductions	$ 33,000	$ 33,000	$ —	$ —
Adjusted ordinary gross income	$191,000	$107,000	$60,000	$24,000

Applying the three-part test, C Company's royalties and lease bonus must be included in personal holding company income. The first part is passed because the adjusted ordinary gross income of $167,000 from mineral, oil or gas royalties is more than 50% of the company's total adjusted ordinary gross income of $191,000. The second test is failed because interest income of $24,000 is personal holding company income and exceeds 10% of the company's ordinary gross income of $224,000. Assuming that the administrative expenses of $40,000 constitute deductions only under Section 162, those deductions exceed 15% of the company's adjusted ordinary gross income and, therefore, the third test is passed.

Since at least 60% of C Company's adjusted ordinary gross income is personal holding company income and C Company has five or fewer shareholders, it is a personal holding company in 1987.

As previously noted, for the purpose of determining the total adjusted ordinary gross income from all sources, gross income from working interests (gross receipts less lifting costs)[226] is reduced by the same deductions applicable to mineral, oil and gas royalties.

222. Burnet v. Harmel, 287 U.S. 103 (1932), 11 AFTR 1085, 3 USTC 990; Murphy Oil Co. v. Burnet, 287 U.S. 299 (1932), 11 AFTR 1095, 3 USTC 1002; Herring v. Comm'r, 293 U.S. 322 (1934), 14 AFTR 717, 35-1 USTC 9012; Comm'r v. Engle, 82 U.S. 599 (1984), 54 AFTR2d 84-415, 84-1 USTC 9134.
223. Swank & Son, Inc. v. U.S., 522 F.2d 981 (9th Cir. 1975), 36 AFTR2d 75-5610, 75-2 USTC 9675.
224. I.R.C. Sec. 636(a); I.R.C. Sec. 636(c).
225. Reg. Sec. 1.543-1(b)(11)(ii).
226. Laguna Royalty Co. v. Comm'r, 406 F.2d 703 (5th Cir. 1969), 23 AFTR2d 69-544, 69-1 USTC 9206; Rev. Rul. 60-344, 1960-2 C.B. 186.

However, the amounts subtracted from royalties or working interests may not exceed the taxpayer's respective amounts of gross income from those interests.[227]

Working interest income received by a corporation is not personal holding company income.[228] Working interest income received by a limited partnership in which a corporation is a partner retains its character in the hands of the corporation and, therefore, is not personal holding company income.[229]

The personal holding company tax equals 28% (38.5% for the tax year beginning in 1987) of the undistributed personal holding company income.[230] Undistributed personal holding company income is taxable income with certain adjustments and reduced by federal income taxes.[231] For this purpose, only the immediately preceding year's net operating loss may be deducted in arriving at taxable income.[232] Undistributed personal holding company income also is reduced by dividends during the year or on or before the 15th day of the third month of the following year.[233] In addition, certain shareholders may consent to treat as a dividend an amount specified in the corporation's income tax return.[234]

Since the personal holding company tax rate exceeds the individual tax rate applicable to a dividend, C Company should consider payment of a dividend no later than the 15th day of the third month following its yearend. If that deadline has passed, the consent dividend procedure should be considered. However, a consent dividend is considered as distributed in money to the shareholders and contributed to the capital of the corporation.[235] The shareholders will incur a tax liability without actually receiving funds from the corporation. A later withdrawal of cash from the corporation to obtain funds for tax payment also may be taxable as a dividend to the extent of the corporation's current or accumulated earnings and profits.

Case 171
Exchange of Partnership Interests of Drilling Fund Partnerships and Co-Owned Properties for Stock in a New Corporation

In the past, Corporation G has sponsored public oil and gas drilling programs. Some of its earlier programs were conducted as co-owned properties for which the election to be excluded from the partnership provisions of Subchapter K of the Internal Revenue Code has been made. In more recent years, the drilling programs have been organized as limited partnerships in which Corporation G is the general partner. At the end of 1986, 23 limited partnerships were in existence, in which 165 partners had invested.

Corporation G is considering consolidation of ownership of the limited partnerships and the co-owned oil and gas properties into a publicly owned corporation which will result in a larger and more diversified investment base. The consolidation, or "rollup," is expected to permit the investors to benefit from administrative and operational efficiencies, to

227. I.R.C. Sec. 543(b)(2)(B).
228. Rev. Rul. 77-127, 1977-1 C.B. 158.
229. IRS Letter Ruling 8043098.
230. I.R.C. Sec. 541; P.L. 99-514 (Tax Reform Act of 1986), Sec. 104(b)(8).
231. I.R.C. Sec. 545.
232. I.R.C. Sec. 545(b)(4).
233. I.R.C. Sec. 545(a); I.R.C. Sec. 561; I.R.C. Sec. 563.
234. I.R.C. Sec. 565.
235. I.R.C. Sec. 565(c).

provide greater capacity to finance continuing exploration and development activities and to provide greater liquidity. In furtherance of these objectives, new Corporation N is created. Corporation N offers to exchange shares of its common stock for limited partnership interests and co-owned oil and gas properties that presently are owned by investors. The exchange will be on the basis of one share of stock for $10 of exchange value.

After the exchange, stockholders who provided the initial capitalization of Corporation N will own approximately 10% of Corporation N's outstanding stock. Corporation N will not be an investment company.

The exchange offer by Corporation N is intended to qualify as a tax-free transfer to a controlled corporation. With certain exceptions, no gain or loss will be recognized upon the transfer of partnership interests or working interests to Corporation N if immediately after the exchange the transferors as a group own at least 80% of the total combined voting power of all classes of voting stock and at least 80% of the total shares of all other classes of stock.[236] Gain will be recognized to the extent that money or other property ("boot") is received by the transferors in addition to stock and permitted securities.[237] If a transferor is relieved of liabilities in excess of basis, he will be treated as receiving money to the extent of that excess.[238] Also, a transferor who is relieved of liabilities may be treated as having received money, even though the liabilities do not exceed basis, when the assumption of or the taking subject to a liability is to avoid federal income tax or does not have a business purpose.[239]

The tax-free transfer provision does not apply to a transfer of property to an "investment company"; however, these rules will not be reviewed because it is assumed that Corporation N will not be an investment company.[240]

Certain offerees who are nonresident alien individuals or foreign corporations may not be eligible for the tax-free transfer provisions if rules apply that require the recognition of gain from the disposition of certain U.S. real property.[241]

Any gain recognized by a working interest transferor under these rules will be reported as ordinary income to the extent of depreciation, depletion and intangible drilling and development costs (IDC) recapture.[242] Any gain recognized by a transferor of a partnership interest must be reported as ordinary income to the extent of his share of the partnership's depreciation, depletion and IDC recapture as well as his share of any other "unrealized receivables" or "substantially appreciated inventory."[243] Any gain in excess of the ordinary income portion generally will be treated as a long-term capital gain if the partnership interest has been held by the transferor for more than six months (12 months if acquired after 1987) and the transferor is not a dealer.[244]

Certain reporting requirements exist with respect to a sale or an exchange of a partnership interest that potentially results in ordinary income due to various recapture provisions, unrealized receivables or substantially appreciated inventory items.[245] *(See Case 172 for discussion of these reporting requirements.)*

236. I.R.C. Sec. 351(a); IRS Letter Ruling 8107136; IRS Letter Ruling 8220096; IRS Letter Ruling 8220109.
237. I.R.C. Sec. 351(b).
238. I.R.C. Sec. 357(c).
239. I.R.C. Sec. 357(b).
240. I.R.C. Sec. 351(e)(1).
241. I.R.C. Sec. 897.
242. I.R.C. Sec. 1245; I.R.C. Sec. 1254.
243. I.R.C. Sec. 751.
244. I.R.C. Sec. 1222.
245. I.R.C. Sec. 6050K.

The "at-risk" provisions may have prevented a partner or co-owner from deducting his entire share of prior-year losses.[246] His basis in his partnership or co-ownership interest, nevertheless, is reduced by his full share of such losses.[247] These disallowed losses (hereinafter referred to as "suspended losses") should be deductible by a transferor to the extent he recognizes any gain as a result of the exchange.[248] When a partner's or co-owner's suspended losses exceed the amount of gain recognized by him in the exchange, those excess suspended losses will not be deductible after the exchange[249] and will not increase his basis in his stock.[250] *(See Case 33 for further discussion of the "at-risk" rules.)*

Partners also may have "suspended losses" that have not been deducted because of lack of basis in their partnership interests.[251] *(See Case 172.)* Finally, limited partners may have suspended losses under the passive-activity rules.[252] *(See Case 182 for a discussion of the passive-activity rules.)*

Exchanges of partnership interests or working interests may result in investment tax credit recapture, depending on the portion of the useful life of the property that has elapsed before the exchange[253] or whether the transaction results in a mere change in the form of doing business.[254] *(See Case 78.)*

A partner who exchanges his partnership interest for stock in Corporation N will be required to report his distributive share of income, losses, deductions and credits of the partnership for that portion of the partnership's tax year preceding the exchange.[255]

If 50% or more of the interest in profits and capital in a partnership is exchanged within a consecutive 12-month period, the partnership will be terminated for federal income tax purposes.[256] This termination will be treated as a constructive distribution of all the partnership's assets to the new partner (Corporation N) and the nonexchanging partners, followed by a constructive contribution of the assets to a new partnership.[257] The tax results of this termination may include, among other things: (1) gain to a partner if his share of partnership cash constructively distributed exceeds his adjusted tax basis in the partnership; (2) permanent loss of partnership deductions not utilized because of the "at-risk" limitations; (3) inability of the new partnership to use accelerated depreciation on existing assets; (4) closing of the partnership's tax year with possible bunching of income and (5) possible recapture of investment tax credit by nonexchanging partners. The deemed termination also may alter the partners' economic sharing of capital due to the impact of the capital account provisions of the partnership agreement.[258] Additionally, certain rules relating to contributions of appreciated property and allocations with respect to that property may apply to the newly constituted partnership.[259] *(See Case 166 concerning these latter two issues.)*

Corporation N's basis in assets transferred to it in the exchange will be the same as the transferor's basis immediately before the exchange, increased by any gain recognized by the transferor.[260] Proposed regulations indicate that Corporation N's

---

246. I.R.C. Sec. 465.
247. Prop. Reg. Sec. 1.465-1(e).
248. Prop. Reg. Sec. 1.465-66.
249. Prop. Reg. Sec. 1.465-67(b).
250. Prop. Reg. Sec. 1.465-1(e); Prop. Reg. Sec. 1.465-67(b).
251. I.R.C. Sec. 704(d).
252. I.R.C. Sec. 469.
253. I.R.C. Sec. 47(a)(1); Reg. Sec. 1.47-6(a).
254. I.R.C. Sec. 47(b); Reg. Sec. 1.47-3(f).
255. I.R.C. Sec. 706(c)(2).
256. I.R.C. Sec. 708(b)(1)(B).
257. IRS Letter Ruling 8220085.
258. Reg. Sec. 1.704-1(b)(2)(ii); Reg. Sec. 1.704-1(b)(2)(ii)(g).
259. I.R.C. Sec. 704(c).
260. I.R.C. Sec. 362(a).

basis in assets transferred to it may be increased by the amount by which losses of partners or co-owners not deducted by virtue of the "at-risk" limitations exceed the gain recognized.[261]

The basis of Corporation N stock in the hands of a transferor of a partnership interest or of oil and gas properties also will be the same as his basis in the assets transferred, increased by any gain recognized in the exchange and decreased by the amount of money or fair market value of other property received by the transferor.[262] The "taint" of potential depreciation, depletion and IDC recapture will carry over to the transferee.[263]

The holding period of the assets received by Corporation N will include the time they were held by the transferor.[264] The holding period of the Corporation N stock received by a transferor will include the period during which the assets transferred to Corporation N in exchange were held provided they were held as capital assets or assets used in a trade or business on the date of the exchange.[265]

Corporation N will not be entitled to percentage depletion on production from properties that were proven at the date of the exchange.[266] If percentage depletion has been disallowed to any transferor by reason of the 65% of taxable income limitation, the amount of the transferor's depletion carryover must be reduced by the lesser of: (1) the adjusted basis of the property at the time of disposition or (2) the difference between that basis and the adjusted basis the transferor would have had in the property in the absence of the 65% of taxable income limitation.[267]

Generally, reduced windfall profit tax rates apply to certain independent producers for 1,000 barrels per day of tier-1 and tier-2 working interest production.[268] *(See Case 217.)* However, following the transfer, the reduced rates will apply to each separate property interest only if it can be established that that property has not been held by a person who is not an independent producer or a person whose tier-1 and tier-2 working interest production exceeded the 1,000-barrel independent-producer amount for any calendar quarter ending after September 30, 1979.[269] Property held by a partnership is considered owned proportionately by the partners.[270] Consequently, Corporation N will need to establish that the tier-1 and tier-2 properties it received qualify for the independent-producer rates after the exchange offer. *(See Case 219 for a discussion of the transfer rules related to windfall profit tax and exceptions thereto.)*

This discussion is limited to some of the more general business and tax considerations associated with exchange offers. Because of the complexity of the legal, tax and accounting issues associated with these exchanges, taxpayers are urged to consult with their professional advisers before undertaking these transactions.

---

261. Prop. Reg. Sec. 1.465-67(b).
262. I.R.C. Sec. 358(a)(1); I.R.C. Sec. 358(d).
263. Reg. Sec. 1.1245-2(c)(2); Prop. Reg. Sec. 1.1254-4(b).
264. I.R.C. Sec. 1223(2).
265. I.R.C. Sec. 1223(1).
266. I.R.C. Sec. 613A(c)(9).
267. Prop. Reg. Sec. 1.613A-4(a).
268. I.R.C. Sec. 4992(a); I.R.C. Sec. 4987(b)(2).
269. I.R.C. Sec. 4992(d)(3)(A); I.R.C. Sec. 4992(d)(3)(B).
270. I.R.C. Sec. 4992(d)(3)(B)(iii)(1).

Case 172
Exchange of Partnership Interests in Drilling Fund Partnerships for a Partnership Interest in a Publicly Held Partnership

For several years, Corporation B has sponsored public oil and gas drilling programs, all of which have been organized as limited partnerships of which Corporation A is the general partner. There are several hundred limited partners in the 16 partnerships that Corporation B has sponsored.

Corporation B intends to consolidate the 16 partnerships into a new limited partnership known as Partnership Z. Partnership Z units will be publicly traded. The "rollup" will allow participation by limited partners in a larger business enterprise (commonly referred to as a "master limited partnership") with more diverse oil and gas reserves and will result in operating advantages, including administrative efficiencies as well as a dependable source of cash flow for ongoing oil and gas exploration and development.

Partnership Z's partnership agreement requires distribution of at least 50% of its annual adjusted cash flow. Annual adjusted cash flow is equal to cash revenues less cash expenses and less reserves for business needs exclusive of exploration and development activities. The undistributed portion of adjusted cash flow will be used for development of Partnership Z's properties and for participation in exploration activities with Corporation B.

In furtherance of the plan of consolidation, Partnership Z offers to exchange units of limited partnership interest for partnership interests in the drilling partnerships. Partners who accept the exchange offer will receive one unit of limited partnership interest in Partnership Z for each $10 of exchange value attributable to their drilling partnership interests. The drilling partnerships will be valued by reference to the estimated fair market value of their underlying assets, the most significant of which will be the estimated present value of future net revenues from proved reserves. In addition, Partnership Z offers to purchase interests in the drilling partnerships for cash and for notes that bear interest at 10%. Partnership Z will not be an investment company.

Generally, no gain or loss is recognized to a partnership or to any of its partners upon a contribution of property to the partnership in exchange for an interest in the partnership. If a partner is relieved of more liabilities than he assumes in new Partnership Z, the excess is treated as a cash distribution to the partner, possibly triggering a taxable gain.[271]

The nonrecognition of gain provisions do not apply to transfers to a partnership that would be treated as an investment company if the partnership were incorporated.[272] However, these rules will not be reviewed because it is assumed that Partnership Z will not be an investment company.

271. I.R.C. Sec. 752(b); I.R.C. Sec. 731(a)(1); Arthur E. Long, 77 T.C. 1045 (1981).
272. I.R.C. Sec. 721(b).

Certain partners who are nonresident alien individuals or foreign corporations may not be eligible for the nonrecognition of gain provisions because of a provision that requires recognition of gain from the disposition of certain U.S. real property.[273]

The sale by a partner of an interest in a drilling partnership for cash and notes will be a taxable transaction. Gain, other than depreciation recapture, will be reported on the installment basis, unless an election is made to recognize the entire gain in the year of sale.[274] If the transferor is not a "dealer," the gain recognized should be capital gain, except that the transfer of "unrealized receivables" (which include any accounts receivable not previously included in income and depreciation, depletion and intangible drilling and development costs (IDC) recapture) or substantially appreciated inventory items will result in ordinary income.[275] *(See Case 138 for a discussion of the original-issue discount rules as they apply to installment sales.)* Partners who exchange their partnership interests for units in Partnership Z, but who recognize gain because of the treatment of liabilities (discussed above), must determine the nature of the gain in a similar manner.

When a change of partners occurs during a tax year, items of partnership income, deduction, etc., must be properly allocated among the partners.[276] These rules may apply to the drilling partnerships, when interests are acquired by the publicly held partnership, and to the publicly held partnership, when units are traded in the market. *(See Case 164 for further discussion.)*

Certain of the partners who tender their partnership interests may have been prevented from deducting all their share of prior-year partnership losses due to either the "at-risk" provisions or the provisions limiting the allowance of losses to the adjusted basis of the partners' interests in the partnership. *(See Case 171 for a further discussion of the "at-risk" limitations as they may apply to a "rollup.")* Partnership losses suspended by the basis limitation may be lost forever unless used during the year in which the exchange occurs. Partners who have suspended losses due to lack of basis may want to contribute additional cash to the drilling partnership involved to create additional basis and with the expectation of receiving more units in the exchange. It appears that a contribution of additional cash in this manner shortly before the exchange will permit deduction of the loss; however, the position of the Internal Revenue Service (IRS) with regard to this matter is uncertain.

Limited partners also may have losses suspended under the passive-activity loss rules. *(See Case 182 for a discussion of these rules.)*

Partners who sell their partnership interests to Partnership Z may be required to recapture investment tax credit previously claimed by them, depending on the portion of the useful life of the property that has elapsed before the sale.[277] Partners who exchange their partnership interests for units in Partnership Z also may be required to recapture investment tax credit.[278]

Partners in a drilling partnership who elect not to exchange or sell their partnership interests (the "continuing partners") may find that the drilling partnership is deemed terminated and reconstituted into a new partnership.[279] This event occurs if 50% or more of the total interests in the capital and profits of that drilling partnership is

273. I.R.C. Sec. 897.
274. I.R.C. Sec. 453(a).
275. I.R.C. Sec. 751.
276. I.R.C. Sec. 706(d).
277. Reg. Sec. 1.47-6(a)(2).
278. Reg. Sec. 1.47-3(f).
279. I.R.C. Sec. 708(b)(1)(B).

transferred during any consecutive 12-month period.[280] *(See Case 171 for a discussion of the possible adverse tax results of such a termination.)* The technical termination does not disqualify percentage depletion for the continuing partners if their interests in the reconstituted partnership are identical to their interests in the deemed terminated partnership.[281] An unexpected technical termination and reconstitution of Partnership Z may occur under the same rules. A system must be developed to monitor this potential event as units are traded on the market.

When drilling partnership interests are contributed to Partnership Z, the basis of those interests will be the same as the basis to the contributing partner.[282] The basis of units received in the exchange will be equal to the basis of the drilling partnership interests transferred to Partnership Z.[283] No basis adjustment is permitted for property contributed to a partnership or for a contributing partner's interest due to gain recognized by the contributing partner, except in rare situations where the partnership would be treated as an investment company if that partnership were incorporated.[284] However, a basis adjustment still may be available to the partner if the partnership makes a special election to adjust the basis of partnership property.[285] The "taint" of potential depreciation, depletion and IDC recapture will carry over to the transferee.[286] The holding period of assets received by Partnership Z in the exchange and the holding period of units in Partnership Z will include the period the drilling partnership interests were held as either capital assets or property used in a trade or business.[287]

Income, gain, loss and deductions with respect to property contributed to a partnership must be shared among the partners so as to take into account the variation between the tax basis and fair market value at the time of contribution.[288] *(See Case 166 for further discussion of contributions of appreciated property.)*

After the exchange, partners in Partnership Z who acquired their interests by exchange of drilling partnership interests no longer will be able to deduct percentage depletion on proven properties owned by the drilling partnerships at the time of the exchange except to the extent of their continuing interest in those properties. A drilling partner's continuing interest in the proven properties will be reduced significantly in the exchange because there will be many more partners in Partnership Z than previously in any one drilling partnership. Numerous changes in partners' interests in proven properties owned directly or indirectly by Partnership Z will occur because the units will be actively traded on a stock exchange. This situation will create many complexities in supplying data needed to compute percentage depletion.

Partnership Z may make an election that will require all subsequent purchasers of units to have their share of the tax basis of Partnership Z's assets adjusted to reflect the price paid for the units.[289] Active trading in units will make the basis calculations very complex. Additional cost depletion and depreciation that will result probably will make the election worthwhile.

If a partner acquires additional units in the market and subsequently disposes of a portion of his interest in the partnership, the IRS has ruled that the basis of the

---

280. I.R.C. Sec. 708(b)(1)(B); IRS Letter Ruling 8220085.
281. IRS Letter Ruling 8026071.
282. I.R.C. Sec. 723.
283. I.R.C. Sec. 722.
284. I.R.C. Sec. 722; I.R.C. Sec. 723; Rev. Rul. 84-15, 1984-1 C.B. 158.
285. I.R.C. Sec. 754.
286. Reg. Sec. 1.1245-2(c)(2); Prop. Reg. Sec. 1.1254-4(b).
287. I.R.C. Sec. 1223(1).
288. I.R.C. Sec. 704(c).
289. I.R.C. Sec. 754.

interest sold equals an amount that bears the same relation to the partner's basis in the partner's entire partnership interest as the fair market value of the interest sold bears to the fair market value of the entire partnership interest.[290]

Partnerships and transferors of partnership interests must comply with certain reporting requirements[291] if the partnership holds unrealized receivables, substantially appreciated inventory items or assets potentially subject to depreciation, depletion, IDC or other ordinary income recapture.[292] The transferor of a partnership interest must notify the partnership in writing within 30 days of the sale or exchange (or, if earlier, January 15 of the following calendar year). This information must include the names, addresses and taxpayer identification numbers of the transferor and transferee and the date of exchange.[293] The partnership must furnish to the transferor and transferee a written statement indicating that certain information has been supplied to the IRS and that the transferor must comply with certain reporting requirements in connection with its income tax return. This notification generally is provided to the transferor and transferee on Form 8308 on or before January 31 of the calendar year following the calendar year of transfer or, if later, 30 days after the partnership receives notice or obtains knowledge of the transfer. The partnership must include a copy of the Form 8308 with its annual return of income (Form 1065).[294]

Publicly traded partnerships receive some relief from these reporting requirements. No return is required for a sale or exchange for which a broker must file a return (Form 1099-B).[295] However, since brokers are not required to file information returns with respect to sales by corporations, tax-exempt organizations and certain other entities,[296] publicly traded partnerships still may be required to report these transfers. Composite document and magnetic media filings are permitted.[297]

A person holding partnership interests as a nominee for another person must furnish certain information to the partnership and such other person.[298] *(See Case 161 for a further discussion of this requirement.)*

An investment organizer must register "tax-shelter" investments. A *tax shelter* generally is an investment: (1) where it could be reasonably inferred from representations made that the tax-shelter ratio (the ratio that the cumulative aggregate gross deductions plus 350% of the credits bears to the investment base) for any investor at the end of any of the first five years exceeds 2 to 1 and (2) that is required to be registered under federal or state securities laws or is subject to an exemption from the registration requiring notification, or where the aggregate investment offered for sale exceeds $250,000 and five or more investors participate.[299]

By ignoring gross income in computing the 2 to 1 tax-shelter ratio, it appears likely that many ordinary operating businesses, such as Partnership Z, will be required to register. The investment organizer generally is responsible for registering the investment. The IRS will issue a tax-shelter registration number, which must be furnished to each investor. Each investor is required to include the registration number on a form in his own income tax return. There are penalties for failure to comply with these provisions.

290. Rev. Rul. 84-53, 1984-1 C.B. 159.
291. I.R.C. Sec. 6050K.
292. I.R.C. Sec. 751.
293. Reg. Sec. 1.6050K-1(d).
294. Reg. Sec. 1.6050K-1(c); Reg. Sec. 1.6050K-1(e); Reg. Sec. 1.6050K-1(f).
295. Reg. Sec. 1.6050K-1(a)(2); I.R.C. Sec. 6045.
296. Temp. Reg. Sec. 5f.6045-1(c)(3).
297. Reg. Sec. 1.6050K-1(a)(3).
298. I.R.C. Sec. 6031(c).
299. I.R.C. Sec. 6111(c).

It is extremely important that Partnership Z not be classified as an association taxable as a corporation. Although it apparently will possess the corporate characteristic of free transferability of interest, it should be able to avoid at least two and possibly three of the other three major characteristics pertinent to corporations (i.e., continuity of life, limited liability and centralization of management). *(See Case 162 for a further discussion of the association issue.)* The IRS has ruled that partnership arrangements similar to that in the instant case will be classified as a partnership and not as an association taxable as a corporation.[300] Although the IRS will issue advance rulings with respect to certain partnership exchange offers, it will not rule as to the nonrecognition of gain upon contribution of widely held real property or oil and gas interests.[301]

This discussion is limited to some of the general business and tax considerations associated with a partnership exchange offer. Because of the complexity of the legal, tax and accounting issues associated with these exchanges, taxpayers are urged to consult with their professional advisers before undertaking these transactions.

Case 173
Oil and Gas Royalty Trust Arrangements

Corporation R proposes to transfer net profits interests in several producing fields to the X Royalty Trust in exchange for Units of Beneficial Interest (units). Corporation R then will declare a dividend of the Units to its shareholders during 1987. Corporation R expects to have no current or accumulated earnings and profits as of the date of the distribution or December 31, 1987. The units subsequently will be traded separately from Corporation R's stock.

A conveyance of property in trust to an independent trustee by a corporation for the benefit of its shareholders, which is followed by a distribution by the corporation of certificates of ownership in the trust to its shareholders, is considered by the Internal Revenue Service (IRS) as a distribution of the property by the corporation to its shareholders, followed by a transfer in trust of the property by the shareholders.[302]

If a corporation distributes appreciated property, it must recognize gain (with certain exceptions) in an amount equal to the excess of the property's fair market value over its adjusted basis as if the property had been sold at the time of distribution.[303]

The distribution of the units is treated as a dividend taxable as ordinary income to the extent of the corporation's current and accumulated earnings and profits. Earnings and profits are increased by the amount of any gain recognized upon the distribution of appreciated property. The amount of the distribution in excess of current and accumulated earnings and profits is treated as a return of capital to the extent of each shareholder's basis in his stock. Any excess should be capital gain.[304] Therefore, Corporation R should calculate the earnings and profits effects of the distribution to determine the potential impact on the taxation of its shareholders.

The basis of each unit in the hands of noncorporate holders will be equal to the fair market value on the date of distribution. The basis of each unit for each corporate

300. IRS Letter Ruling 8116041; IRS Letter Ruling 8143069; IRS Letter Ruling 8229034; IRS Letter Ruling 8247108.
301. Rev. Proc. 87-3, 1987-1 I.R.B. 27.
302. Rev. Rul. 72-137, 1972-1 C.B. 101; IRS Letter Ruling 8223015 (Technical Advice Memorandum); IRS Letter Ruling 8351101; IRS Letter Ruling 8412003 (Technical Advice Memorandum).
303. I.R.C. Sec. 311(b).
304. I.R.C. Sec. 301(c); IRS Letter Ruling 8104176.

holder will be the lesser of the fair market value of the property on the date of distribution or the adjusted basis immediately before the distribution increased by gain recognized to the distributing corporation due to distribution.[305]

The royalty trust should be structured as a fixed investment trust to avoid being classified as an association taxable as a corporation; accordingly, the trustee should be prohibited from varying the investments of the trust or engaging in business.[306] The trustee may be given the power to sell trust assets and to place in bank accounts or certificates of deposit cash held by the trust between distribution dates. Neither of these powers should constitute a power to vary the investments of the trust.[307]

The trust is treated as a grantor trust, and each beneficiary (unit holder) includes in computing his taxable income his pro-rata share of the trust's income, deductions and credits.[308] Because the trust is a grantor trust, each beneficiary is treated as the owner of a proportionate part of each asset in trust and his basis in those assets is determined by allocating his basis in his unit of interest among the assets based on their relative fair market values.[309] Therefore, each unit holder is entitled to deduct cost depletion with respect to his pro-rata share of the trust's oil and gas properties. This depletion is determined with reference to the unit holder's allocated basis.[310]

The transfer of a net profits interest in a number of separate tracts or parcels of land to a trust in a single conveyance, when the calculation of net profits is made on an aggregate basis instead of separately for each unit of property, originally was challenged by the IRS as an anticipatory assignment of income.[311] When there was a separate conveyance of a net profits interest in a single unit of property and when the calculation of net profits was made separately for the unit of property, the IRS agreed with the taxpayer that this net profits interest was an economic interest in the property.[312] However, the IRS later issued another technical advice memorandum revoking the original, stating it "now believes that a multiproperty net profits interest is an economic interest and that the transfer of such interest by a corporation to its shareholders is not an assignment of income."[313] Additionally, the IRS has ruled that multiproperty nonoperating interests should be aggregated and treated as a single unit of property for tax purposes.[314] *(See Case 60.)*

This conclusion is appropriate because the regulations provide that "an economic interest is possessed in every case in which the taxpayer has acquired by investment any interest in mineral in place . . . and secures by any form of legal relationship income derived from the extraction of the mineral . . . to which he must look for a return on his capital."[315] The Supreme Court has held that a net profits interest is an economic interest because it is a right to a share of the gross production from a mineral property, measured by net profits.[316] It is common practice to measure the net profits interest's share of production by a formula approach, including direct costs associated with the mineral property as well as other costs in accordance with the net profits

---

305. I.R.C. Sec. 301(d).
306. Reg. Sec. 301.7701-4(c); Rev. Rul. 78-149, 1978-1 C.B. 448; IRS Letter Ruling 8351101; IRS Letter Ruling 8412003 (Technical Advice Memorandum); IRS Letter Ruling 8632025.
307. Rev. Rul. 75-192, 1975-1 C.B. 384; IRS Letter Ruling 8223015; IRS Letter Ruling 8512061; IRS Letter Ruling 8626030.
308. Reg. Sec. 1.671-2(c); IRS Letter Ruling 8223015; IRS Letter Ruling 8351101; IRS Letter Ruling 8412003 (Technical Advice Memorandum).
309. I.R.C. Sec. 301(d); IRS Letter Ruling 8223015; IRS Letter Ruling 8412003 (Technical Advice Memorandum).
310. IRS Letter Ruling 8543030.
311. IRS Letter Ruling 8223016 (Technical Advice Memorandum).
312. IRS Letter Ruling 8223016 (Technical Advice Memorandum); IRS Letter Ruling 8337019; IRS Letter Ruling 8351101; IRS Letter Ruling 8411017; IRS Letter Ruling 8412002 (Technical Advice Memorandum).
313. IRS Letter Ruling 8302016 (Technical Advice Memorandum).
314. IRS Letter Ruling 8312019; IRS Letter Ruling 8531059.
315. Reg. Sec. 1.611-1(b)(1).
316. Kirby Petroleum Co. v. Comm'r, 326 U.S. 599 (1946), 34 AFTR 526, 46-1 USTC 9149; Burton-Sutton Oil Co. v. Comm'r, 328 U.S. 25 (1946) 34 AFTR 1017, 46-1 USTC 9243.

agreement.[317] The net profits interest should not lose its economic interest status as long as the holder of that interest has a right only to a share of the gross proceeds from production of the property to which he must look for a return of his capital. This status should apply even if a formula used to determine the extent of the right to a share of the gross production includes costs not directly attributable to the particular property.

Because the net profits interests constitute economic interests, depletable income will be recognized by the unit holders. Cost depletion, but not percentage depletion, will apply to units of property that were proven at the time of transfer to the trust.[318]

If a royalty interest is carved out from a working interest and sold, the resulting gain should qualify for capital-gain treatment. The working interest owner should be allowed to allocate a portion of its basis in the working interest to the nonproducing interest sold.[319] Because the working interest owner will retain ownership of the lease and well equipment, none of the gain on sale of the nonoperating interest should result in investment tax credit recapture or depreciation recapture.[320] In addition, because the working interest owner retains 100% of the working interest (the interest with respect to which the intangible drilling and development costs (IDC) were incurred), it appears that none of the gain on the sale of the carved-out nonoperating interest should be treated as ordinary income because of the recapture of IDC. The proposed regulations do not address this particular situation. However, in a private letter ruling, the IRS took a contrary position and required recapture of 75% of previously incurred IDC upon the carve-out of a 75% net profits interest.[321] *(See Case 131.)*

The receipt of a royalty trust unit as a taxable dividend by a corporate shareholder generally has no effect on the corporate shareholder's basis in the stock of the distributing corporation, and the dividend generally qualifies for the 80% dividend-received deduction. However, a corporate shareholder must reduce its basis in the distributing corporation's stock held less than two years for nonliquidating, extraordinary dividends to the extent of the nontaxed portion of that dividend.[322] Extraordinary dividends generally are any dividends that equal or exceed 5% of the corporate shareholder's adjusted tax basis in preferred stock or 10% for all other stock.[323] There also are certain aggregation rules for dividends received that can result in those dividends being treated as extraordinary dividends.[324] The nontaxed portion of a dividend is the amount of the dividend reduced by the taxable portion (after including the dividend-received deduction).[325] There is a reduction of the benefits of the 80% dividend-received deduction to the extent the distributing corporation's stock is acquired directly through debt financing.[326] The holding period for qualifying for the dividend-received deduction for nonpreferred stock is 46 days.[327]

---

317. William D. Gray, 13 T.C. 265 (1949), *aff'd* 183 F.2d 329 (5th Cir. 1950), 39 AFTR 750, 50-2 USTC 9386.
318. I.R.C. Sec. 613A(c)(9).
319. IRS Letter Ruling 8113044.
320. IRS Letter Ruling 8115094.
321. IRS Letter Ruling 8622005 (Technical Advice Memorandum).
322. I.R.C. Sec. 1059(a).
323. I.R.C. Sec. 1059(c)(2).
324. I.R.C. Sec. 1059(c)(3).
325. I.R.C. Sec. 1059(b).
326. I.R.C. Sec. 246A.
327. I.R.C. Sec. 246(c)(1)(A).

Section VII
The Alternative Minimum Tax, Passive-Activity Limitations and Other Special Accounting Provisions

The Tax Reform Act of 1986 (the Act) made significant changes to the alternative minimum tax (AMT) provisions as well as adding significant new provisions which will limit the ability for taxpayers to shelter income (passive-activity limitations) and defer timing of other deductions (uniform cost-capitalization rules). In addition, with the increasing importance of the oil futures market, taxpayers must use care in determining the tax consequences of such transactions.

Alternative Minimum Tax

In an effort to ensure that taxpayers with substantial economic income pay tax currently, the Act amends and broadens the application of the AMT. Under the Act, corporate and noncorporate taxpayers are subject to AMT. Generally, the AMT computation is the same as under prior law, however, the Act does provide for a credit (subject to limitations) against future regular tax for previously paid AMT. Additionally, for corporate taxpayers, the Act adds a controversial adjustment based on book income that increases the amount of income subject to AMT. It is likely this change will result in a re-examination by certain corporate taxpayers of the differences between their tax and financial methods of accounting in an effort to lower their potential AMT liability.

The new AMT is extremely complex and will result in additional difficulty for tax planning.

Passive-Activity Limitations

In an effort to thwart tax-shelter investments, the Act provides for significant limitations on the deductibility of losses from passive activities. Generally, under the Act, losses from passive activities may be deducted only to the extent of income from passive activities. A passive activity generally is any trade or business activity of the taxpayer in which the taxpayer does not materially participate and any rental activity. Generally, limited partnership interests will be treated as passive activities. The Act provides an exception to the material participation requirement for an oil and gas working interest that is not owned through an entity that limits liability (e.g., an S Corporation). These limitations may have a significant effect on the future form of investment in oil and gas.

Other

The Act contains sweeping changes to the rules of capitalization of indirect costs for all activities that involve production of property or acquisition of property for resale. The Act generally broadens the range of costs to be capitalized. While the Act specifically excepts oil and gas intangible drilling and development costs from these rules, the Committee Reports make it clear that drilling an oil or gas well is considered production of an asset. Therefore, the capitalization rules apply to overhead and interest expense allocable to the drilling period.

Case 174
Intangible Drilling and Development Costs on Productive Wells as a Tax Preference Item

Operator A, an accrual-basis taxpayer, incurred $300,000 in intangible drilling and development costs (IDC) during 1987 in drilling the following wells:

Well	Date of First Production	Date Initial Revenues Received	Status of Well at December 31, 1987	Net Income Before IDC Deductions	IDC Incurred	Cost Depletion Rate
A	10/87	12/87	Producer	$(10,000)	$ 50,000	2%
B	—	—	Dry	(4,000)	70,000	N/A
C	12/87	2/88	Producer	(5,000)	40,000	1%
D	—	—	Drilling (Dry-5/88)	(2,000)	40,000	N/A
E	—	—	Prepaid (Producer-3/88)	(1,000)	20,000	N/A
F	6/87	8/87	Producer	60,000	60,000	15%
G	10/87	12/87	Producer (Aban.-3/88)	(5,000)	20,000	40%
				$ 33,000	$300,000	

Operator A wants to know how to calculate his tax preference intangible drilling costs so that he can file his income tax return on April 1, 1988. Operator A has no other oil and gas activity and did not incur any leasehold cost for the acreage.

For tax years beginning after December 31, 1986, domestic IDC incurred in drilling a *productive well* are a tax preference item for all taxpayers.[1] For integrated oil companies, the amortization of the amount required to be capitalized must also be treated as IDC subject to preference treatment only in the year the costs are incurred. Thus, future amortization of amounts incurred and capitalized in prior years should be disregarded in the preference calculation.[2] *(See Case 24 for a discussion of integrated oil company IDC.)* The IDC preference amount and other preference items the taxpayer may have, such as percentage depletion in excess of tax basis *(see Case 87)*, are included in the computation of the taxpayer's alternative minimum tax (AMT). *(See Cases 175, 176 and 177.)*

1. I.R.C. Sec. 57(a)(2).
2. I.R.C. Sec. 57(a)(2)(B)(i); General Explanation of the Tax Reform Act of 1986, prepared by the Staff of the Joint Committee on Taxation, pp. 442-443.

A *productive well* is not defined in the law, but the Committee Reports define a *nonproductive well* as one that is plugged and abandoned without producing oil and gas in commercial quantities for any substantial period. The Committee Reports further provide that a well that has been plugged and abandoned may have produced some relatively small amount of oil or gas and still be considered a nonproductive well, depending on the amount of oil or gas produced in relation to the costs of drilling.[3] There are no definitive guidelines available for determining how much production is required before a property is to be considered "productive" for tax preference purposes. Pending the issuance of Treasury regulations, it is unclear whether the well can be considered nonproductive for tax preference purposes if available reserve information (at the time the taxpayer's return is filed) indicates that future net revenue will not equal or exceed the cost of developing the property (i.e., the well will not pay out). For purposes of the windfall profit tax (WPT) net income limitation *(see Case 221)*, the regulations define a *nonproductive well* as "any well that has been abandoned or is reasonably expected never to produce oil and gas in *commercial quantities*."[4] The WPT regulations also define the term *commercial quantities*.[5] However, it is unclear whether the Internal Revenue Service (IRS) will apply this definition of a nonproductive well for tax preference purposes.

As discussed in Case 20, it is necessary to determine whether workover costs constitute IDC. Any workover costs that result in the deepening of an existing well, or in the fracturing of a zone that has not produced oil or gas, should be considered IDC. Other workover costs (e.g., those incurred to stimulate a producing zone) should be treated as lease operating expenses.[6]

It also may be necessary to determine if amounts of overhead expense allocated to a property for percentage depletion purposes should be treated as an amount of IDC that constitutes a tax preference item. The IRS has taken the position that an allocable portion of overhead must be included in the amount of IDC that constitutes a tax preference item.[7] This recharacterization also would have the effect of increasing the amount of potential IDC recapture. Specifically, the IRS's position is that overhead expenses that have been apportioned to a property on the basis of direct expenses (pursuant to the percentage depletion regulations) further should be apportioned between direct drilling expenses and other direct expenses with the amount apportioned to drilling being treated as IDC. This position is consistent with a similar position the IRS has taken in connection with a recent field examination with respect to treating overhead expenses as IDC for purposes of computing the WPT net income limitation.[8] *(See Case 187 for a discussion of the effect of the uniform capitalization rules on oil and gas operations.)*

A well must be treated as a producing well and the IDC classified as a tax preference item if the well's status is not known when the return is due (including extensions). If the well subsequently is determined to be nonproductive, the taxpayer may file for refund of any incremental taxes resulting from the initial treatment of the IDC as a tax preference item.[9] This "pay-first" rule often proves troublesome for taxpayers, especially for partnerships with many partners, because it frequently is not possible to

3. Senate Report No. 94-938, 1976-3 C.B. Vol. 3 426.
4. Reg. Sec. 51.4988-2(b)(3)(iii). *See also* IRS Letter Ruling 8245006 (Technical Advice Memorandum); Rev. Rul. 83-5, 1983-1 C.B. 298.
5. Prop. Reg. Sec. 51.4996-1(n).
6. Internal Revenue Manual—Audit Sec. 4232.8-12, Para. 620 (April 18, 1985).
7. Internal Revenue Manual—Audit Sec. 4232.8-12, Para. 620(1)(b)(5) (April 18, 1985).
8. IRS Letter Ruling 8406006 (Technical Advice Memorandum); IRS Letter Ruling 8622005 (Technical Advice Memorandum); IRS Letter Ruling 8640006 (Technical Advice Memorandum).
9. Senate Report No. 94-938, 1976-3 C.B. Vol. 3 426.

determine whether a well will be commercially productive before the tax return must be filed.

The computation of IDC subject to the preference tax is somewhat complex. First, the amount of the productive IDC is reduced by an amount of amortization.[10] The amount is computed by ratably amortizing the intangibles over a 120-month period, beginning with the month production from the well begins, or, by election, the current-year cost depletion rate may be used.[11] The amortization is computed on a well-by-well basis and only with respect to the costs incurred in the year the computation is made.[12]

The "excess" IDC remaining after the reduction for the amortization discussed above is further reduced by 65% of the taxpayer's aggregate net income, if any, from oil and gas properties for the tax year to arrive at the taxpayer's IDC preference amount.[13]

Net income from oil and gas properties is the excess of the aggregate amount of depletable gross income from all the taxpayer's oil and gas properties over the amount of any deductions allocable to the properties (including cost or percentage depletion), except for excess IDC.[14] In making this computation, deductions attributable to properties with no gross income for the tax year are not taken into account.[15] Net income from oil and gas properties generally can be computed most easily by first aggregating net income as computed for percentage depletion purposes for all properties (with depletable gross income), then reducing total net income by any allowable cost or percentage depletion and, finally, by adding back the amount of excess IDC attributable to those same properties. In a technical advice memorandum,[16] the IRS has taken a position substantially consistent with this concept. However, the conclusion drawn in the memorandum seems to have the effect of reducing net income from oil properties by a portion of IDC attributable to productive wells equal to the amortization allowed thereon for determining the preference amount. To the extent this amortization is attributable to properties with no gross income, the result seems contrary to this concept and to Congressional intent indicated by quotations from the Conference Committee Report contained in the memorandum.

The IRS also has taken a position contrary to Congressional intent by stating that deductions attributable to shut-in wells must be included as deductions for purposes of computing the net income offset.[17] The IRS has apparently misinterpreted the Conference Report[18] and considers properties with no gross income only to mean nonproductive properties.

The costs incurred in drilling a dry hole do not represent a tax preference item, even if the dry hole is located on a producing property. However, dry-hole costs on producing properties do reduce the taxpayer's net income from oil and gas properties. Thus, if the taxpayer has net income from oil and gas properties (discussed above), a portion of the dry-hole costs will essentially be treated as a preference item since the net income offset is reduced. Similar results occur when drilling is done through a productive zone

10. I.R.C. Sec. 57(a)(2)(B)(ii).
11. I.R.C. Sec. 57(b); Temp. Reg. Sec. 7.57(d)-1(b).
12. Temp. Reg. Sec. 7.57(d)-1(c).
13. I.R.C. Sec. 57(a)(2)(A).
14. I.R.C. Sec. 57(a)(2)(C).
15. Conference Committee Report No. 95-1800, 1978-3 C.B. Vol. 1 602; IRS Letter Ruling 8002016 (Technical Advice Memorandum).
16. IRS Letter Ruling 8239005 (Technical Advice Memorandum).
17. Rev. Rul. 84-128, 1984-2 C.B. 15 *as corrected by* IRS Announcement, 84-127, 1984-53 I.R.B. 27.
18. Conference Committee Report No. 95-1800, 1978-3 C.B. Vol. 1 602.

to a greater depth, resulting in noncommercial production at the greater depth. In this situation, the well is plugged back and completed in the shallower productive zone.[19]

In many situations, a taxpayer can eliminate the negative effect of dry-hole costs attributable to producing properties by making appropriate separate property elections if possible. *(See Case 58.)* Dry-hole costs then will be attributable to a separate property unit (which will not have any gross income) and will not affect the calculation of the taxpayer's net income from oil and gas properties. Before a decision is made to make a separate property election, the total impact of the election should be considered. For example, an election to treat a dry hole as a separate property to impact favorably the taxpayer's AMT calculation can have the effect of significantly reducing, or even eliminating, a potential refund of WPT under the 90% of net income limitation.[20]

The Secretary of the Treasury or his delegate is required to provide regulations to allow an adjustment to the amount of preferences taxed when the preference item does not actually result in a regular tax benefit (as opposed to an alternative minimum tax benefit) to the taxpayer.[21] To date, no such regulations have been proposed. *(See Case 179 for a discussion of the minimum tax credit.)*

The calculation of Operator A's tax preference IDC as of April 1, 1988, can be summarized as follows:

Excess IDC

Well	Productive IDC	Amortization Percentage	Excess IDC
A	$ 50,000	2.50%	$ 48,750
B	N/A	—	—
C	40,000	1.00%	39,600
D	40,000	—	40,000
E	20,000	—	20,000
F	60,000	15.00%	51,000
G	N/A	—	—
			$199,350

Net Income from Oil and Gas Properties with Current-Year Gross Income

Well	Net Income (Loss) Before Deductions for IDC	Amortization (Including Nonproductive IDC)	Net Income (Loss)
A	$(10,000)	$ 1,250	$ (11,250)
C	(5,000)	400	(5,400)
F	60,000	9,000	51,000
G	(5,000)	20,000	(25,000)
Total			$ 9,350
Tax Preference Amount ($199,350 - ($9,350 x 65%))			$ 193,273

19. Conference Committee Report No. 95-1800, 1978-3 C.B. Vol. 1 602; IRS Letter Ruling 7925011 (Technical Advice Memorandum).
20. Rev. Rul. 77-136, 1977-1 C.B. 167; Rev. Rul. 82-71, 1982-1 C.B. 185; IRS Letter Ruling 7925011 (Technical Advice Memorandum).
21. I.R.C. Sec. 59(g).

The $40,000 of IDC incurred for Well D must be reported as a preference item because the well was not determined to be nonproductive until after Operator A filed his 1987 income tax return. Operator A must file an amended 1987 tax return to recover the related tax. Alternatively, Operator A could have extended his return until after the productive status of Well D was determined, avoiding the need to file an amended return. Wells B, D and E are not included in the net income from oil and gas properties calculation because they did not produce gross income during 1987. Well C is included but would not have been if Operator A was a cash-basis taxpayer. Well G was excluded from the excess IDC calculation because it did not produce in commercial quantities. However, Well G is included in the net income from oil and gas properties calculation because it produced gross income during 1987. Amortization using the cost depletion rates is most beneficial for Wells C and F; however, three-month ratable amortization (over 120 months) is most beneficial for Well A.

Taxpayers may elect to capitalize IDC and amortize those amounts over 10 years.To the extent capitalized, those amounts are not included as a tax preference item. *(See Cases 175, 176 and 181.)*

Case 175
Intangible Drilling and Development Costs as a Tax Preference Item in the Alternative Minimum Tax Computation for Individuals

During 1987, General Partner A, an individual, paid $200,000 as his share of intangible drilling and development costs (IDC) of an exploratory program. Of the total amount, $120,000 was for IDC on producing wells and $80,000 on dry holes. The wells began to produce in December 1987, but Partner A received no income until 1988. Partner A has salary and other income of $300,000. Partner A's 1987 taxable income is computed below:

Salary and other income		$300,000
IDC from partnership		(200,000)
Adjusted gross income (AGI)		$100,000
Itemized deductions:		
Medical expenses	$6,000	
Less: 7.5% of AGI	(7,500)	—
Real estate taxes		(6,000)
Home mortgage interest		(28,000)
Charitable contributions		(3,000)
Miscellaneous deductions	$4,000	
Less: 2% of AGI	(2,000)	(2,000)
Exemptions		(9,500)
Taxable income		$ 51,500

Partner A is married and files a joint return on a cash basis. He has a tax preference item of $36,000, representing the excess of fair market value at exercise over the option price of an incentive stock option.

Partner A wants to know the effect of the alternative minimum tax (AMT) on his IDC deductions from oil and gas operations for the year.

For tax years beginning after December 31, 1986, all taxpayers, including corporations, are subject to the AMT. *(See Case 176 for a discussion of corporate AMT.)*

The AMT is based on alternative minimum taxable income (AMTI) for the year. AMTI is a taxpayer's taxable income adjusted by certain defined adjustments and increased by any tax preference items.[22] The resulting amount is reduced further by an exemption ($40,000 on joint and surviving spouse returns; $20,000 for married taxpayers filing separately and for estates and trusts; $30,000 for other noncorporate taxpayers).[23] The amount of the allowable exemption decreases as a taxpayer's AMTI increases. The decrease is 25% of the excess of AMTI over $150,000 for joint and surviving spouse returns; $75,000 for married taxpayers filing separately and for estates and trusts; and $112,500 for other noncorporate taxpayers. AMTI reduced by any allowable exemption is taxed at a 21% rate.[24] If the resulting AMT (reduced by allowable foreign tax credits)[25] exceeds the regular tax liability (net of all allowable credits and excluding investment credit recapture),[26] the excess plus the net regular tax liability becomes the tax liability for the year. A credit is provided for future years to the extent the AMT is attributable to other than exclusion preferences and adjustments.[27] *(See Case 179 for a complete discussion of the minimum tax credit.)*

As mentioned above, to arrive at AMTI, a taxpayer starts with taxable income and makes certain adjustments to it before increasing it further by items of tax preference. The adjustments that must be made by all taxpayers relate to depreciation methods *(see Case 70)*, mining exploration and development costs, treatment of certain long-term contracts, amount of net operating loss deductions, amortization deduction for pollution-control facilities, installment sales and basis computations.[28]

Additionally, individuals must do the following to adjust their taxable income:[29]

- ☐ Eliminate deductions for miscellaneous itemized deductions.
- ☐ Eliminate deductions for real estate taxes, personal property taxes and state income taxes.
- ☐ Apply a 10% AGI limitation on medical expenses versus the 7.5% AGI limitation for regular tax.
- ☐ Apply narrower restrictions on the amount of interest expense that is deductible.
- ☐ Eliminate tax refunds related to real estate, personal property or state income taxes from income.
- ☐ Eliminate the standard deduction and deduction for personal exemption.[30]
- ☐ Capitalize and amortize circulation and research and experimental expenditures.

In addition to the above adjustments, certain farm losses and passive-activity losses are denied in computing AMTI.[31] *(See Case 178 for a discussion of the impact of passive-activity limitations on AMTI.)*

---

22. I.R.C. Sec. 55(b).
23. I.R.C. Sec. 55(d)(1).
24. I.R.C. Sec. 55(b)(1)(A).
25. I.R.C. Sec. 55(b)(1)(B).
26. I.R.C. Sec. 55(c)(2).
27. I.R.C. Sec. 53.
28. I.R.C. Sec. 56(a).
29. I.R.C. Sec. 56(b).
30. Technical Corrections Bill of 1987, Sec. 107, *amending* I.R.C. Sec. 56(b)(1)(E).
31. I.R.C. Sec. 58.

Once taxable income is adjusted as discussed above, the taxpayer must add any tax preferences to arrive at AMTI. Tax preferences include:[32]

- ☐ Depletion in excess of basis in a property. *(See Case 87.)*
- ☐ Amount by which excess intangible drilling costs exceed 65% of net income from oil and gas properties. *(See Case 174.)*
- ☐ Excess of fair market value of stock over option price on exercise of an incentive stock option.
- ☐ Certain tax-exempt interest.
- ☐ Appreciated property charitable deduction.
- ☐ Accelerated depreciation or amortization on certain pre-1987 property.

Individuals, like corporations, are allowed to utilize AMT net operating loss (NOL) deductions only to the extent of 90% of AMTI.[33] Thus, a taxpayer cannot avoid AMT unless the taxpayer incurs a current year AMT NOL. As with other items, the AMT NOL is computed differently than the regular tax NOL. To compute the AMT NOL the regular tax NOL must be recomputed, considering any of the AMTI adjustments and items of tax preference discussed above.[34]

Unlike corporate taxpayers, however, individuals may not offset AMT with investment tax credit (ITC) carryover or any transition-property ITC. *(See Case 76 for a discussion of the repeal of ITC and transition rules.)*

---

32. I.R.C. Sec. 57(a).
33. I.R.C. Sec. 56(d)(1)(A).
34. I.R.C. Sec. 56(d)(2).

Applying these rules to this case results in the following:

Regular Tax—1987		
Salary and other income		$300,000
IDC from partnership		(200,000)
Adjusted gross income (AGI)		$100,000
Deductions:		
Medical expenses—gross	$6,000	
Less: 7.5% of AGI	(7,500)	—
Home mortgage interest		(28,000)
Charitable contributions		(3,000)
Real estate taxes		(6,000)
Miscellaneous deductions	$4,000	
Less: 2% of AGI	(2,000)	(2,000)
Exemptions		(9,500)
Taxable income		$ 51,500
Regular tax		$ 11,115

Alternative Minimum Tax—1987	
Taxable income	$ 51,500
Adjustments: increase (decrease)	
Real estate taxes	6,000
Miscellaneous itemized deductions	2,000
Personal exemptions	9,500
Preferences:	
Excess IDC over 65% of net income from oil and gas properties	119,000
Incentive stock option preference	36,000
AMTI	$224,000
Exemption ($40,000 - [($224,000 - $150,000) × 25%])	(21,500)
AMTI after exemption	$202,500
AMT	$ 42,525

Tax Payable for 1987	
Regular tax ($11,115) + excess of AMT over regular tax ($42,525 - $11,115 = $31,410)	$ 42,525

Partner A, in effect, received only a 22.5% tax benefit from his IDC deduction for 1987 due to the AMT. Partner A will be entitled, however, to a credit against future regular tax for the AMT ($31,410) paid in 1987 since the AMT is not attributable solely to exclusion preferences. *(See Case 179 for a discussion of the minimum tax credit.)*

(See Case 181 for a discussion of annual IDC elections that are available to reduce or eliminate the adverse impact of the AMT.)

Case 176
Intangible Drilling and Development Costs as a Tax Preference Item in the Alternative Minimum Tax Computation for Corporations

During 1987, Corporation C, a publicly held company, engaged in the exploration, development and production of oil and gas, incurred $5 million of intangible drilling and development costs (IDC). Of the total amount, $4 million was attributable to producing properties with the remaining $1 million attributable to dry holes. The producing wells began production in October 1987.

A summary of Corporation C's 1987 financial statement and taxable income is as follows:

	Financial Statement Income	Taxable Income
Oil and gas revenues (net of lease operating expenses)	$ 200,000	$ 200,000
Other income	2,000,000	2,000,000
General and administrative expenses	(1,000,000)	(1,000,000)
Depreciation, depletion and amortization	(220,000)	
Cost depletion		(20,000)
IDC and dry-hole costs	—	(5,000,000)
Net income before tax	$ 980,000	
Taxable income (loss) before net operating loss (NOL)		$(3,820,000)

Corporation C's net income from oil and gas properties for purposes of calculating its IDC preference is $100,000. Corporation C also has an NOL carryover from 1986 of $50,000 and wants to know the effect of the alternative minimum tax (AMT) on its 1987 tax liability.

Corporation C is not an integrated oil company.

Effective for tax years beginning after December 31, 1986, all corporate taxpayers are now subject to the AMT.[35] The computation of the corporate AMT is essentially the same as that for individuals discussed in Case 175 except for differences in adjustments that are required in calculating alternative minimum taxable income (AMTI) and a tax rate differential of 20% for corporations compared to 21% for individuals.

In addition to the adjustments applicable to all taxpayers discussed in Case 175, the following adjustments must be made by corporate taxpayers in arriving at AMTI:[36]

- Adjustment for book income or adjusted earnings and profits. For tax years beginning in 1987, 1988 and 1989, this adjustment is for 50% of book income in excess of AMTI before this adjustment and before the AMT NOL. For years beginning after 1989, the adjustment is for 75% of the excess of adjusted current earnings (ACE) over AMTI before this adjustment and before the AMT NOL. If ACE is less than AMTI, a negative adjustment will be permitted (for 75% of this

35. I.R.C. Sec. 55(a).
36. I.R.C. Sec. 56(c).

difference) provided it does not exceed the comulative net positive adjustments made in prior years. *(See Case 180 for a discussion of this adjustment and for special rules relating to its calculation.)*

- Treatment of merchant marine capital construction funds.

- Disallowance of special deductions for certain insurance companies.

Corporations must consider the same tax preference items as noncorporate taxpayers discussed in Case 175 in computing AMTI.[37] For tax years beginning before January 1, 1987, IDC were not a tax preference item for most corporate taxpayers.

Corporate taxpayers, like individuals, are allowed to use AMT NOL deductions only to the extent of 90% of AMTI.[38] Thus, the AMT cannot be avoided unless a taxpayer incurs a current-year AMT NOL. As with other items, the AMT NOL is computed differently than the regular tax NOL. The AMT NOL is computed by recomputating the regular tax NOL, considering any of the AMTI adjustments and items of tax preference discussed above. No adjustment is required, however, for NOL carryovers from years beginning before January 1, 1987, other than a reduction for the effect of any deferred add-on minimum tax.[39] An election to forego the carryback of an NOL applies for both regular tax and AMT purposes. If a regular tax NOL is carried back to a year prior to 1987, the AMT NOL is reduced by the amount of taxable income in those years even though AMT was not applicable for those years.[40]

Corporations are allowed an exemption of $40,000.[41] The allowable exemption is decreased by 25% of the excess of AMTI over $150,000. Thus, the exemption is fully phased out at $310,000 of AMTI.

Like individuals, corporations are allowed to offset AMT with allowable foreign tax credits (FTC).[42] The amount of offset is limited to 90% of AMT before credits.[43] The allowable AMT FTC is computed differently than allowable regular tax FTC. It requires a calculation of foreign AMTI and worldwide AMTI.[44] *(See Case 195 for a discussion of foreign tax credits.)*

AMT after reduction for any allowable AMT FTC can be further reduced by investment tax credit (ITC) carryovers and transition property ITC. *(See Case 76 for a discussion of the repeal of ITC and applicable transition rules.)* However, the ITC may offset only 25% of AMT (after reduction for the allowable AMT FTC).[45]

In addition to the separate limitations on NOLs and credits discussed above, there is an overall limitation that provides that the combination of AMT NOLs, AMT FTC and ITC cannot reduce AMT liability to less than 10% of AMT before NOLs and credits.[46] Consistent with Congressional intent, this additional limitation ensures that all profitable corporations will pay tax.

---

37. I.R.C. Sec. 57(a).
38. I.R.C. Sec. 56(d)(1)(A).
39. I.R.C. Sec. 56(d)(2)(B).
40. General Explanation of the Tax Reform Act of 1986, prepared by the Staff of the Joint Committee on Taxation, p.469.
41. I.R.C. Sec. 55(d)(2).
42. I.R.C. Sec. 55(b)(1)(B).
43. I.R.C. Sec. 59(a)(2).
44. I.R.C. Sec. 59(a)(1).
45. I.R.C. Sec. 38(c)(3).
46. I.R.C. Sec. 38(c).

Applying these rules to this case results in the following:

Alternative Minimum Tax—1987	
Taxable income (loss) before NOL	$(3,820,000)
Adjustments other than book income adjustment	—
Preferences:	
IDC preference [$4,000,000 - ($100,000 × 65%) - (($4,000,000 ÷ 120) × 3)]	3,835,000
AMTI before book income adjustment	$ 15,000
Book income adjustment (see below)	482,500
AMTI	$ 497,500
AMTI NOL	(50,000)
AMTI before exemption	$ 447,500
Exemption (fully phased out)	—
AMTI	$ 447,500
AMT (20% of AMTI)	$ 89,500

Book Income Adjustment	
Pre-tax financial statement income	$ 980,000
AMTI before book income adjustment	(15,000)
Excess	$ 965,000
50% of excess	$ 482,500

Tax Payable—1987	
Regular tax	$ — *
AMT	89,500
Total	$89,500

* Due to current-year regular NOL of $3,820,000.

As shown above, even though Corporation C has a regular tax NOL for 1987 of $3,820,000, a tax payment of $89,500 must be made for 1987. Corporation C will be allowed, however, a credit of $89,500 against future regular taxes since the entire AMT liability is attributable to other than exclusion preferences. *(See Case 179 for a discussion of the minimum tax credit.)*

As shown below, Corporation C could have reduced the $89,500 tax liability to $66,000 by electing to capitalize all $4 million of its productive IDC for 1987. *(See Case 181 for a discussion of the annual election to capitalize otherwise deductible IDC.)*

Revised Alternative Minimum Tax—1987	
Taxable income (loss) before NOL per above	$(3,820,000)
Add: Productive IDC capitalized	4,000,000
Less: Amortization of capitalized IDC	(400,000)
Revised taxable income (loss) before NOL	$ (220,000)
IDC preference	—
AMTI before book income adjustment	$ (220,000)
Book income adjustment (see below)	600,000
AMTI	380,000
AMTI NOL	(50,000)
AMTI before exemption	$ 330,000
Exemption (fully phased out)	—
AMTI	$ 330,000
AMT (20% of AMTI)	$ 66,000

Book Income Adjustment	
Pre-tax financial statement income	$ 980,000
AMTI loss before book income adjustment	220,000
Excess	$ 1,200,000
50% of excess	$ 600,000

Revised Tax Payable	
Regular Tax	$ — *
AMT	66,000
	$66,000

* Due to revised current-year regular NOL of $220,000.

Corporation C has a credit of $66,000 against future regular taxes since the entire AMT liability is attributable to other than exclusion preferences.

It is very important to note that the capitalized amount of IDC in 1987 must be recovered ratably over a 10-year period for both regular tax and AMT purposes. Therefore, before the election to capitalize is made, taxpayers must consider the multiple-year impact of such an election. For example, assume that in 1988 Corporation C has the following:

	Financial Statement Income	Taxable Income
Oil and gas revenues (net of lease operating expenses)	$ 3,000,000	$ 3,000,000
Other income	2,000,000	2,000,000
General and administrative expenses	(1,000,000)	(1,000,000)
Depreciation, depletion and amortization	(800,000)	
Cost depletion		(40,000)

Corporation C's 1988 tax, assuming an election to capitalize the 1987 productive IDC compared to not capitalizing the 1987 IDC, would be as follows:

Regular Tax—1988	1987 Productive IDC Capitalized	No Capitalization of 1987 IDC
Oil and gas revenues (net of lease operating expenses)	$ 3,000,000	$ 3,000,000
Other income	2,000,000	2,000,000
General and administrative expenses	(1,000,000)	(1,000,000)
Cost depletion	(40,000)	(40,000)
Amortization of capitalized IDC	(400,000)	N/A
Taxable income (loss) before NOL	$ 3,560,000	$ 3,960,000
1987 NOL carryover	(270,000)	(3,870,000)
Taxable income (loss)	$ 3,290,000	$ 90,000
Regular tax	$ 1,118,600	$ 18,850
AMT credit	(66,000)	—
Net regular tax	$ 1,052,600	$ 18,850
Alternative Minimum Tax—1988		
Taxable income (loss) before NOL	$ 3,560,000	$ 3,960,000
Adjustments other than book income adjustment	—	—
AMTI before book income adjustment	$ 3,560,000	$ 3,960,000
Book income adjustment (see below)	—	—
AMTI before exemption	$ 3,560,000	$ 3,960,000
Exemption	—	—
AMTI	$ 3,560,000	$ 3,960,000
AMT	$ 712,000	$ 792,000
Book Income Adjustment		
Pre-tax financial statement income	$ 3,200,000	$ 3,200,000
AMTI before book income adjustment	3,560,000	3,960,000
Excess	$ —	$ —
50% of excess	$ —	$ —
Tax Payable—1988		
Regular tax	$ 1,052,600	$ 18,850
AMT	—	773,150
Total	$ 1,052,600	$ 792,000

Had Corporation C capitalized all of the productive IDC in 1987, its two-year tax liability would have increased by $237,100. As demonstated above, any decision to capitalize should be carefully evaluated due to the complexities of the AMT.

Case 177
Impact of Percentage Depletion Preference on Calculation of Intangible Drilling Cost Preference

A, an individual, has taxable income before depletion and intangible drilling and development costs (IDC) deductions of $300,000 for 1987. A's 1987 depletion deduction is $40,000 and of that amount $30,000 is considered preference depletion. A also has IDC in 1987 of $160,000. All IDC is attributable to producing properties. A's net income from oil and gas before considering depletion is $40,000. A is married and files a joint return.

Operator A asks if he must consider preference depletion in the calculation of his IDC preference amount.

As discussed in Case 174, a taxpayer is allowed to reduce excess IDC by 65% of net income from oil and gas properties.[47] Net income from oil and gas properties must be reduced by the taxpayer's depletion deduction for the year.[48] Thus, the depletion deduction (percentage or cost) can increase the IDC preference amount. Since percentage depletion in excess of the basis in a property is itself a preference item *(see Case 87)*, the result is that one preference item can increase another and, therefore, result in a portion of the preference item being taxed twice. In addition, the interaction can accelerate the phaseout of the exemption allowed in computing alternative minimum tax (AMT). *(See Cases 175 and 176 for a discussion of the exemption and its phaseout.)*

The above concepts are illustrated below. Revised AMT is AMT computed without consideration of the interaction discussed above.

	Regular Tax	AMT	Revised AMT
Taxable income	$100,000	$100,000	$100,000
Depletion preference		30,000	30,000
IDC preference		160,000	140,500
Personal exemption		3,800	3,800
AMT exemption		(4,050)	(8,925)
Taxable base	$100,000	$289,750	$265,375
Tax	$ 28,440	$ 60,848	$ 55,729

As illustrated, the effective AMT tax rate on depletion is 38%: 21% tax on the depletion preference plus an increase of approximately 17% (($60,848 – $55,729) ÷ $30,000) resulting from the interaction of the depletion preference with the IDC preference calculation and the exemption phaseout.

Under prior law, the statute provided that an item of tax preference would not be treated as a preference if it did not result in a tax benefit (regular or alternative minimum tax).[49] The Tax Reform Act of 1986 amended prior law to provide that items of tax preference will be adjusted only if no regular tax benefit is received.[50] Although, as discussed in Case 179, Congress provided for a minimum tax credit

47. I.R.C. Sec. 57(a)(2)(A).
48. I.R.C. Sec. 57(a)(2)(C).
49. I.R.C. Sec. 58(h) *(prior to amendment by the Tax Reform Act of 1986)*.
50. I.R.C. Sec. 59(g).

which can offset regular tax, there is no indication that it intended an effective AMT rate of this magnitude. It is hoped that a technical correction will be made or regulations promulgated to eliminate the inequitable result that by claiming a deduction (i.e., depletion), a taxpayer's tax liability increases. The Committee Reports indicate that as particular circumstances are identified, Treasury may, at its discretion, apply the tax benefit rule to prevent adverse impacts from switching from one system to the other (e.g., AMT to regular or vice versa).[51] Since the adverse impact is not a result of switching from AMT in one year to regular tax in another year, which Congress believes will be remedied through the minimum tax credit, Treasury should exercise its discretion to prevent such inequitable results.

In this case, had Operator A not claimed a deduction for percentage depletion in excess of cost basis, Operator A's overall tax liability would have been $55,729 instead of $60,848.

A similar result may occur for the interaction of AMT depreciation on the calculation of the net income offset for IDC preference purposes. It is not clear whether Congress intended that the net income offset be recomputed for AMT purposes. *(See Case 70 for a discussion of AMT depreciation.)*

Case 178
Impact of Passive-Activity Limitations on Alternative Minimum Tax Calculation

B, an individual, invested in oil and gas drilling fund limited partnerships in 1981 and 1982. In January 1986, B invested in an oil and gas joint venture, which elected out of the partnership provisions, and a limited partnership which purchased producing properties which the partnership will further develop. For 1987, Individual B projects the following taxable amounts:

Salary	$200,000
1981 limited partnership	5,000
1982 limited partnership	10,000
1986 limited partnership	(165,000)
1986 joint venture	(10,000)
Interest income	5,000
Home interest expense	(20,000)
Net income from oil and gas properties	-0-
IDC preference from 1986 limited partnership (included in above loss)	90,000

Individual B is contemplating making another investment in a limited partnership which will purchase producing properties. This proposed investment is expected to generate taxable income for all future years. In 1987, the investment is expected to generate taxable income (and net income from oil and gas) of $50,000. Individual B may, at his option, purchase the investment and participate as a general partner rather than a limited partner. Individual B has determined through legal counsel that he is willing to invest as a general partner if there is a tax advantage. Individual B is single.

51. General Explanation of the Tax Reform Act of 1986, prepared by the Staff of the Joint Committee on Taxation, p. 472.

Generally for tax years beginning after December 31, 1986, a taxpayer will be allowed a deduction for a loss from a passive activity only to the extent of income from passive activities.[52] For passive activities owned on the date of enactment (October 22, 1986) of the Tax Reform Act of 1986, special phasein rules apply.[53] *(See Case 182 for a complete discussion of the passive-activity limitations.)*

In addition to being applied for computing taxable income, the passive-activity limitations also must be applied for computing alternative minimum taxable income (AMTI). The application, however, is modified.[54] For purposes of computing AMTI, income and losses from passive activities must be computed, taking into account the adjustments to taxable income specified for computing AMTI in general, and any deduction that is a tax preference item will not be allowed. It is possible, therefore, for a taxpayer to have a regular tax net passive loss and alternative minimum tax (AMT) net passive income. In addition, the phasein rules for pre-enactment losses do not apply for AMT purposes. Thus, as with other calculations for the AMT, taxpayers must essentially make two separate passive-activity limitation calculations, one for regular tax and one for AMT.

The amount of passive loss disallowed for AMT purposes will be reduced if the taxpayer is insolvent.[55] The amount of reduction is limited to the amount of insolvency.[56]

Before consideration of the contemplated investment, Individual B's 1987 estimated tax liability is as follows:

	Regular Tax	AMT
Salary	$ 200,000	$200,000
Interest income	5,000	5,000
1986 joint venture	(10,000)	(10,000)
Interest expense	(20,000)	(20,000)
Personal exemption	(1,900)	— *
Taxable income before passive activities	$ 173,100	$175,000
Passive-activity income (loss) before limitation	(150,000)	(60,000)
Passive loss disallowance	52,500	60,000
AMT exemption	N/A	(14,375)
Taxable base	$ 75,600	$160,625
Tax	$ 23,070	$ 33,731

* Assumes proposed technical correction is effective.

As shown above, the passive-activity loss for AMTI is different from that for regular tax due to the IDC preference ($90,000) not being deducted for purposes of computing the AMT net passive loss. Thus, for 1988 B will have a regular tax passive loss carryover of $52,500 and an AMT passive loss carryover of $60,000.

52. I.R.C. Sec. 469(a).
53. I.R.C. Sec. 469(l).
54. I.R.C. Sec. 58(b).
55. I.R.C. Sec. 58(c)(1).
56. *Ibid.*

The impact of the contemplated investment can be illustrated as follows:

	Investment as a General Partner		Investment as a Limited Partner	
	Regular Tax	AMT	Regular Tax	AMT
Taxable income before passive activities	$223,100	$225,000	$ 173,100	$175,000
Passive-activity income (loss) before limitation	(150,000)	(60,000)	(100,000)	(42,500)*
Passive loss disallowance	52,500	60,000	35,000	42,500
AMT exemption	N/A	(1,875)	N/A	(14,375)
Taxable base	$125,600	$223,125	$ 108,100	$160,625
Tax	$ 42,320	$ 46,856	$ 35,583	$ 33,731

*Regular tax passive loss	($ 100,000)
Add: Preference IDC ($90,000 less 65% of $50,000 net income from oil and gas properties)	57,500
AMT passive loss	($ 42,500)

As illustrated above, it is better for Individual B to invest in the 1987 investment as a limited partner. B's effective tax rate on $50,000 of income is 26.25% if he invests as a general partner versus 3.7% if he invests as a limited partner. Because Individual B expects the investment to generate taxable income, it is much more beneficial for him to invest as a limited partner since Individual B can partially offset the income with otherwise limited passive losses.

Before business considerations, it is generally advisable from a tax standpoint to invest as a general partner in oil and gas activities that are expected to generate losses and as a limited partner in those that are expected to generate income. *(See Case 185 for a discussion of passive activities and the exception for working interest investments.)*

Case 179
Minimum Tax Credit

C Corporation's financial statement and taxable income for calendar year 1989 are as follows:

	Financial Statement Income	Taxable Income
Oil and gas revenue (net of lease operating costs)	$2,000,000	$ 2,000,000
Other income	1,000,000	1,000,000
General and administrative expenses	(1,500,000)	(1,500,000)
Depreciation, depletion and amortization	(400,000)	
Cost depletion		—
Percentage depletion (all preference)	—	(320,000)
Net income before tax	$1,100,000	
Taxable income (loss)		$ 1,180,000

The management of C Corporation asks how the credit for previously paid alternative minimum tax (AMT) is computed and when it can be used. They provide the information below relating to 1987 and 1988.

	1987		1988	
	Financial Statement Income	Taxable Income	Financial Statement Income	Taxable Income
Pre-tax net income	$980,000		$1,700,000	
Taxable income (loss)		$(8,820,000)		$850,000
Preference depletion		—		610,000
Intangible drilling and development costs (IDC) preference		$ 8,645,000		190,000
Regular tax		—		$289,000
AMT		80,500		46,000
Total		$ 80,500		$335,000

The net operating loss (NOL) for 1987 was carried back to a previous year, and no unused NOL remains for carryover from 1987.

For tax years beginning after December 31, 1986, all taxpayers are subject to the alternative minimum tax (AMT). *(See Cases 175 and 176.)* The AMT essentially represents a prepayment of a taxpayer's tax liability. Consistent with this concept, taxpayers are allowed a credit against regular tax for AMT previously paid, if applicable.[57] This credit is designed to account for switches between years from the AMT system of taxation to the regular tax. The credit does not, however, remedy certain situations where within one year the interplay between preference items causes adverse impacts on a taxpayer's tax liability. *(See Case 177 for a discussion of one such interplay between preference depletion and the calculation of IDC preference.)*

The minimum tax credit represents the excess, if any, of the adjusted net minimum tax imposed for all prior tax years beginning after 1986 over the amount of minimum tax credit allowed for those prior years.[58] The use of the minimum tax credit is limited to an amount equal to the excess of the taxpayer's regular tax liability (after credits but before recapture taxes) over the tentative minimum tax for the tax year.[59] Any unused minimum tax credit can be carried forward indefinitely.

The net minimum tax for any tax year is the amount by which the alternative minimum tax exceeds the regular tax for the year. To determine the adjusted net minimum tax, the net minimum tax is reduced by the net minimum tax attributable to the adjustments for itemized deductions, for special deductions for certain insurance companies, preference depletion, tax-exempt interest preference and the preference for appreciated property charitable contributions.[60] Thus, for taxpayers involved in oil and gas, any AMT related to preference depletion will not be allowed as a credit against future regular tax. As discussed above, to determine AMT attributable to preference depletion, the AMT must be recomputed considering only exclusion

57. I.R.C. Sec. 53(a).
58. I.R.C. Sec. 53(b).
59. I.R.C. Sec. 53(c).
60. I.R.C. Sec. 53(d)(1)(B)(i).

preferences since generally it is not possible to shortcut the computation. AMT related to the IDC preference, on the other hand, will be allowed as a future credit.

C Corporation's minimum tax credit carryover to 1989 can be computed as follows:

1987 Minimum Tax Credit	
Net minimum tax	$80,500
Less: Recomputed net minimum tax*	—
Adjusted 1987 net minimum tax	$80,500

* Computation not necessary since C Corporation had no exclusion preferences in 1987.

1988 Minimum Tax Credit	
Net minimum tax	$46,000
Less: Recomputed net minimum tax (see below)	3,000
Adjusted 1988 net minimum tax	$43,000

Recomputed Net Minimum Tax—1988	
Taxable income before NOL	$ 850,000
Preference depletion	610,000
AMTI before exemption	$1,460,000
Exemption (fully phased out)	—
AMTI	$1,460,000
AMT	$ 292,000
Regular tax	(289,000)
Recomputed net minimum tax	$ 3,000

For 1989, C Corporation has a minimum tax credit carryover from prior years of $123,500. C Corporation's allowable minimum tax credit for 1989 is computed below:

Regular Tax—1989	
Taxable income	$1,180,000
Regular tax	$ 401,200

Alternative Minimum Tax—1989	
Taxable income	$1,180,000
Preference depletion	320,000
AMTI before exemption	$1,500,000
Exemption (fully phased out)	—
AMTI	$1,500,000
AMT	$ 300,000

Tax Payable—1989	
Regular tax	$ 401,200
Less: AMT credit	(101,200)
Total payable	$ 300,000

Even though C Corporation had $123,500 of AMT credit available, it could use only $101,200 since the minimum tax credit can be used only to reduce regular tax as opposed to AMT. As discussed above, the unused credit of $22,300, in this case, can be carried forward to future years.

Case 180
Alternative Minimum Tax Book Income Adjustment for Corporations

Corporation B, a publicly held company, presently uses the full cost method of accounting for its oil and gas operations. Corporation B's management is considering changing to the successful efforts method of accounting and wants to know the impact of such a change on its tax liability. Corporation B is contemplating changing on January 1, 1988, and projects 1988 activity to be as follows:

	Financial Statements		Tax Return (Regular Tax Liability)
	Full Cost Method	Successful Efforts Method	
Oil and gas revenues	$16,000,000	$16,000,000	$16,000,000
Lease operating expense	(2,000,000)	(2,000,000)	(2,000,000)
Depreciation, depletion and amortization	(6,000,000)	(5,000,000)	(1,200,000)
Intangible drilling and development costs (IDC) for successful wells	—	—	(8,500,000)
Exploratory dry-hole costs	—	(500,000)	(500,000)
Development dry-hole costs	—	—	(1,500,000)
Geological and geophysical costs	—	(400,000)	(100,000)
Abandoned leasehold costs	—	—	(1,000,000)
Impairment provision for unproved properties	—	(2,000,000)	
Depreciation of support facilities of other equipment	(700,000)	(700,000)	(900,000)
Net income before income taxes and extraordinary items	$ 7,300,000	$ 5,400,000	$ 300,000
Federal income taxes**	(2,404,750)	(1,758,750)	
Net income before extraordinary items	$ 4,895,250	$ 3,641,250	$
Extraordinary items (net of taxes)	500,000*	500,000*	(100,000)
Net income	$ 5,395,250	$ 4,141,250	$ 200,000

* Net of federal income taxes ($257,576).

** The financial provision for income taxes varies from the maximum corporate tax rate (of 34%) due to exclusion preferences that create alternative minimum tax not allowed as a credit in future years.

Other pertinent projected tax information for 1988 follows:

- ☐ Amortization rate for IDC on producing properties drilled during the year—5%.
- ☐ Net income from oil and gas (NIOG) properties—$11,800,000.
- ☐ Tax preference depletion—$400,000.
- ☐ Depreciation preference for lease and well and support equipment acquired during the year—$45,000.
- ☐ No credits.

As discussed in Case 176, all corporate taxpayers are subject to the alternative minimum tax (AMT) in years beginning after December 31, 1986. In computing a corporation's alternative minimum taxable income (AMTI), an adjustment is required (among others) for tax years beginning in 1987, 1988 and 1989 for 50% of the excess of adjusted net book income over AMTI before the book income adjustment and before the AMT net operating loss (NOL) deduction.[61] As discussed below, for tax years beginning after 1989, an adjustment is required for 75% of the excess of adjusted current earnings (ACE) over AMTI before the ACE adjustment and the AMT NOL deduction.[62]

For tax years beginning in 1987, 1988 and 1989, it is necessary to determine *adjusted net book* income so that the so-called book income adjustment can be computed. The statute defines adjusted net book income as the net income or loss from the taxpayer's applicable financial statement adjusted by certain defined amounts.[63] A priority list is provided to determine which financial statements are to be used for this purpose.[64] In order of priority, the list includes financial statements that are:

- ☐ Required to be filed with the Securities and Exchange Commission.
- ☐ Certified audited income statements used for credit purposes, reports to shareholders or for any substantial nontax purpose.
- ☐ Income statements required to be filed with federal, state or local governments or agencies.
- ☐ Income statements prepared for credit purposes, reports to shareholders or for a substantial nontax purpose.

If no statement is prepared, or if the only statement is one that falls in the last category listed and an irrevocable election is made, the taxpayers must use earnings and profits (without a deduction for distributions or federal taxes) as a reference point for computing the book income adjustment.[65]

Once the applicable financial statement has been selected, the net income or loss must be adjusted.[66]

- ☐ No deduction is allowed for federal income taxes. Therefore, the effect of any deductions for or recoveries of federal income taxes must be eliminated from book income. Foreign taxes are treated the same as federal income tax unless the taxpayer has elected to expense foreign taxes rather than claim them as a credit.[67]
- ☐ Any income included in the financial statement that relates to another taxpayer or a corporation not included in the taxpayer's consolidated return must be eliminated (e.g., income from foreign subsidiaries consolidated for financial statement purposes). Book income should include the full amount of actual and deemed distributions (as measured for tax purposes). If another method (e.g., the equity method) is used for recording income of companies that are not part of the taxpayer's consolidated tax return, this method should be reversed.[68]

---

61. I.R.C. Sec. 56(c)(1)(A); I.R.C. Sec 56(f)(1).
62. I.R.C. Sec. 56(c)(1)(B); I.R.C. Sec. 56(g)(1).
63. I.R.C. Sec. 56(f)(2).
64. I.R.C. Sec. 56(f)(3).
65. I.R.C. Sec. 56(f)(3)(B); Senate Report No. 99-313, 1986-3 C.B. Vol. 3 532-534; General Explanation of the Tax Reform Act of 1986, prepared by the Staff of the Joint Committee on Taxation, p. 451; Temp. Reg. Sec. 1.56-IT(d).
66. I.R.C. Sec. 56(f)(2).
67. I.R.C. Sec. 56(f)(2)(B).
68. I.R.C. Sec. 56(f)(2)(C).

☐ Income must be conformed to the tax year if the financial statement period is different.[69] Generally, this should be done on a pro-rata basis.[70]

☐ Generally, book income includes all items on the income statement, including extraordinary items, unless they are a tax benefit or expense (e.g., use of a NOL carryover). Extraordinary items stated net of tax must be adjusted to remove the tax benefit or expense.[71]

Treasury has the authority to promulgate regulations to require additional adjustments to prevent double counting and omissions.

Once the above adjustments are made, the adjusted book income is compared to the taxpayer's alternative minimum taxable income (AMTI) before the book income adjustment is made and before consideration of any AMT NOL. To the extent adjusted book income exceeds AMTI, 50% of the excess represents the book income adjustment.[72] The Committee Reports make it clear that a book income adjustment can result even in a situation where there is a pre-tax financial statement loss if such loss is less than the AMT loss before the book income adjustment.[73] Applying the above to the facts of this case yields the following:

Calculation of AMT

	Full Cost Method	Successful Efforts Method
Regular taxable income	$ 200,000	$ 200,000
Adjustments:		
Depreciation	45,000	45,000
Book income adjustment (See below)	3,503,788	2,553,788
Preferences:		
IDC (See below)	405,000	405,000
Depletion	400,000	400,000
AMTI	$4,553,788	$3,603,788
AMT rate	× 20%	× 20%
Tentative AMT	$ 910,758	$ 720,758
Regular tax	(61,250)	(61,250)
AMT	$ 849,508	$ 659,508

Note: This taxpayer is not allowed an AMT exemption because it is fully phased out *(see Case 176)*.

69. I.R.C. Sec. 56(f)(2)(D).
70. Senate Report No. 99-313, 1986-3 C.B. Vol. 3 533; General Explanation of the Tax Reform Act of 1986, prepared by the Staff of the Joint Committee on Taxation, p.454; Temp. Reg. Sec. 1.56-IT(b)(4).
71. Senate Report No. 99-313, 1986-3 C.B. Vol. 3 533; General Explanation of the Tax Reform Act of 1986, prepared by the Staff of the Joint Committee on Taxation, p.454; Temp. Reg. Sec. 1.56-IT(b)(4).
72. I.R.C. Sec. 56(f)(1).
73. Senate Report No. 99-313, 1986-3 C.B. Vol. 3 535; General Explanation of the Tax Reform Act of 1986, prepared by the Staff of the Joint Committee on Taxation, p. 449; Temp. Reg. Sec. 1.56-IT(a)(4), Example 3.

Calculation of Book Income Adjustment		Full Cost Method	Successful Efforts Method
Net income per financial statements		$5,395,250	$4,141,250
Tax on extraordinary items		257,576	257,576
Federal tax provision		2,404,750	1,758,750
Book income restated for AMT	(1)	$8,057,576	$6,157,576
AMTI before book income adjustment			
Regular taxable income		$ 200,000	$ 200,000
Adjustments:			
Depreciation		45,000	45,000
Preferences:			
IDC (See below)		405,000	405,000
Depletion		400,000	400,000
	(2)	1,050,000	1,050,000
Excess (1) − (2)		$7,007,576	$5,107,576
Book income adjustment factor		× 50%	× 50%
Book income adjustment		$3,503,788	$2,553,788

Calculation of IDC Preference	
IDC on producing properties (successful wells)	$8,500,000
Amortization allowance ($8,500,000 × 5%)	(425,000)
Excess IDC	8,075,000
Less: NIOG ($11,800,000 × 65%)	(7,670,000)
IDC preference	$ 405,000

As discussed in Case 179, a minimum tax credit can be used to offset regular tax in future years. In this case, the minimum tax credit is computed as follows:

Minimum Tax Credit Calculation	Full Cost Method	Successful Efforts Method
AMT as originally computed	$849,508	$659,508
Less: Recomputed AMT, considering only exclusion preferences	(58,750)	(58,750)
AMT credit	$790,758	$600,758

As illustrated above, the AMT and, more specifically, the book income adjustment impact must be carefully considered to determine tax consequences of decisions that will impact financial statement income. Multiple-year analyses should be performed where possible to determine the full impact.

As discussed above, beginning in 1990, the AMT adjustment that is based on book income will be replaced by the use of ACE.[74] ACE is not the same as the corporation's earnings and profits (E&P), although some of the same concepts used in determining E&P are also applied in calculating ACE. ACE is determined by taking AMTI, as already computed, and making further specified adjustments.[75] If ACE exceeds

74. I.R.C. Sec. 56(c)(1)(B); I.R.C. Sec. 56(g).
75. I.R.C. Sec. 56(g)(4).

AMTI, 75% of the excess is added to AMTI before proceeding to compute AMT liability. If ACE is less than AMTI, a negative adjustment will be permitted (for 75% of this difference) provided it does not exceed the cumulative net positive adjustments made in prior years.[76]

Congress has instructed the Treasury to study and report on refinements that should be made to the calculations of ACE,[77] and, therefore, it is likely that changes will be made before the ACE provisions become effective in 1990.

Case 181
Annual Intangible Drilling and Development Cost Election and Its Impact on Alternative Minimum Tax and Regular Tax

During 1987, Individual A, who has previously elected to expense intangible drilling and development costs (IDC), invests in three new oil and gas ventures. All three ventures (X, Y and Z) have drilling activity but no production during 1987. The following is a summary of taxable loss and IDC tax preference for each of the three ventures:

	Taxable Losses	Excess IDC Preference Amounts
Venture X	$100,000	$ 50,000
Venture Y	150,000	100,000
Venture Z	80,000	70,000
	$330,000	$220,000

X is a limited partnership. Y is a joint venture that has not elected to be excluded from the partnership provisions, and Z is a joint venture that has elected to be excluded from the partnership provisions. X and Y elect to expense intangible drilling costs for tax purposes.

Individual A is married and files a joint return on a cash basis. Individual A has tax preference depletion of $60,000 and net income before depletion of $50,000, all from oil and gas activities other than the three new ventures. A recap of Individual A's 1987 taxable income follows:

Salary	$ 490,000
Loss from 1987 oil and gas ventures	(330,000)
Net income from other oil and gas activities	50,000
Percentage depletion in excess of cost basis	(60,000)
Itemized deductions:	
Real estate taxes	(6,000)
Home mortgage interest	(30,000)
Charitable contributions	(20,000)
Exemptions	(9,500)

76. I.R.C. Sec. 56(g)(2).

77. Conference Committee Report No. 99-841, 1986-3 C.B. Vol. 4 278; General Explanation of the Tax Reform Act of 1986, prepared by the Staff of the Joint Committee on Taxation, pp. 461-462.

Individual A requests information concerning his 1987 tax liability and any appropriate steps to minimize the impact of the alternative minimum tax (AMT).

Taxpayers may elect to capitalize otherwise deductible intangible drilling and development costs on an annual basis.[78] These annual election provisions give taxpayers an opportunity to avoid alternative minimum tax (AMT) by electing to defer certain deductions,[79] including IDC. *(See Cases 175 and 176 for a discussion of the alternative minimum tax computations.)* The election provisions apply to any portion of IDC incurred,[80] either directly to a working interest owner or indirectly to a partner in a partnership or to a shareholder in an S corporation.[81] Additionally, the election can presumably be made for nonproductive IDC as well as productive IDC.[82] The election to capitalize applies for the computation of the regular tax and the AMT.[83]

A taxpayer may deduct the capitalized IDC ratably over a 10-year period, beginning with the tax year in which the taxpayer paid or incurred the IDC.[84] The IDC a taxpayer elects to capitalize is not a tax preference item to be taken into account in computing the AMT.[85]

For integrated oil companies, however, the election discussed above applies only to the portion of IDC that is currently deductible. Thus, a portion of the amortization deducted on amounts required to be capitalized and amortized over a 60-month period will be treated as a preference item. This presumably unintended result should be remedied through technical correction to allow an integrated oil company the same option as other taxpayers. *(See Case 24 for a discussion of IDC of integrated companies.)*

If Individual A computes the 1987 tax liability by taking an immediate deduction for all IDC paid during 1987, he would have an AMT liability *(see Alternative I below)*. If an election is made to capitalize $79,804 of the productive IDC (and, therefore, preference IDC in this case) paid or incurred in 1987 from Ventures Y and Z, Individual A's AMT liability will be eliminated *(see Alternative II below)*.

For passive-activity investments, such as Venture X in this case, the election to capitalize any IDC attributable to that investment would make no difference since the entire passive loss is disallowed *(see Case 182 for a discussion of the passive-activity limitations)*. Additionally, an election would be ineffective for AMT purposes since passive income (losses) must be computed, ignoring deductions for preference items. *(See Case 178 for a discussion of the impact of passive-activity limitations on the alternative minimum tax.)*

---

78. I.R.C. Sec. 59(e).
79. I.R.C. Sec. 59(e)(2).
80. I.R.C. Sec. 59(e)(4)(A).
81. I.R.C. Sec. 59(e)(4)(C).
82. I.R.C. Sec. 59(e)(2); I.R.C. Sec. 263(c).
83. I.R.C. Sec. 59(e)(1).
84. *Ibid.*
85. I.R.C. Sec. 59(e)(6).

Regular Tax—1987

	Alternative I	Alternative II
Salary	$ 490,000	$ 490,000
Loss from 1987 oil and gas ventures*	(230,000)	(150,196)
Amortization of capitalized IDC	—	(7,980)
Net income from other oil and gas activities	50,000	50,000
Percentage depletion in excess of cost basis	(60,000)	(60,000)
Adjusted gross income	$ 250,000	$ 321,824
Deductions:		
Real estate taxes	(6,000)	(6,000)
Home mortgage interest	(30,000)	(30,000)
Charitable contributions	(20,000)	(20,000)
Personal exemptions	(9,500)	(9,500)
Taxable income	$ 184,500	$ 256,324
Regular tax	$ 60,973	$ 88,625

* Due to passive-activity limitation, no deduction is allowed for loss from Venture X investment.

Alternative Minimum Tax—1987

	Alternative I	Alternative II
Taxable Income	$ 184,500	$ 256,324
Percentage depletion preference	60,000	60,000
IDC preference	170,000	90,196
Personal exemptions	9,500	9,500
Real estate taxes	6,000	6,000
AMTI	$ 430,000	$ 422,020
AMT exemption (fully phased out)	-0-	-0-
AMT taxable base	$ 430,000	$ 422,020
AMT @ 21%	$ 90,300	$ 88,625

Tax Payable for 1987

Higher of regular tax or AMT	$ 90,300	$ 88,625

As shown above, taxable income increases by the amount of IDC capitalized under the annual IDC elections, less the current year's amortization of those costs. The IDC tax preference amount decreases by the amount of IDC capitalized.

Since the capitalized portion of IDC must be recovered ratably over a 10-year period, taxpayers should consider the multiple-year impact of making the election.

Upon the disposition of a property, the amount of amortization previously deducted is considered IDC subject to recapture.[86] *(See Case 131.)* Additionally, any unamortized IDC should constitute basis for purposes of determining gain or loss from sale, exchange or abandonment.[87]

86. I.R.C. Sec. 59(e)(5)(A).
87. I.R.C. Sec. 1016(a)(23).

The election to capitalize is available even if the taxpayer does not have an AMT liability. This offers an opportunity to preserve net operating loss carryovers that would otherwise expire.

Case 182
Application of the Passive-Activity Limitations

A, an individual, has invested in various oil and gas ventures for the past three years. Individual A is contemplating making a $100,000 investment in an oil and gas limited partnership in 1987. The proposed venture will acquire a working interest in a lease and drill the initial test well on the lease. Individual A expects a net loss from the 1987 limited partnership (87LP) of $84,000, computed as follows:

Interest income	$ 1,000
Intangible drilling and development costs (IDC)	(85,000)
Net loss	$ (84,000)

Individual A wants to know how the passive-activity limitations will affect him in 1987. His estimated income and deductions before considering the 1987 investment are shown below:

Salary	$300,000
Dividends	50,000
Interest income	20,000
1984 limited partnership (84LP)	10,000
1985 working interest	(10,000)
1986 limited partnership (86LP)*	(20,000)

* Interest acquired on October 1, 1986.

Generally, for tax years beginning after December 31, 1986, noncorporate taxpayers and personal-service corporations must apply the passive-activity limitations in computing taxable income.[88] These limitations are imposed to prohibit taxpayers from using net losses from passive activities to offset other taxable income. To accomplish this goal a taxpayer's income is separated into three categories: (1) passive-activity income (losses), (2) portfolio income (e.g., interest, dividends, etc.) and (3) active income (e.g. salary). Once categorized, net passive-activity losses cannot be used to offset either portfolio or active income. Any passive-activity loss disallowed may be carried over and used to offset future passive-activity income.[89] Suspended passive losses are used before a taxpayer's nonpassive net operating loss (NOL) carryforward.[90] This allows a taxpayer to obtain the full benefit of suspended passive losses before using nonpassive NOLs. Generally, upon the taxable disposition of a taxpayer's entire interest in a passive activity any suspended loss attributable to that activity can be used without limitation. *(See Case 186 for a discussion of passive-activity dispositions.)*

88. I.R.C. Sec. 469.
89. I.R.C. Sec. 469(b).
90. Senate Report No. 99-313, 1986-3 C.B. Vol. 3 723; General Explanation of the Tax Reform Act of 1986, prepared by the Staff of the Joint Committee on Taxation, p. 222.

The passive-activity limitations also apply to certain closely held C corporations.[91] However, the application is modified only to prohibit such a corporation from using passive-activity losses to offset portfolio income. Thus, net passive losses of a closely held C corporation may be used to offset its active income.[92] Additionally, in the case of affiliated groups of corporations filing consolidated returns, these rules will be applied on a consolidated basis.[93]

As mentioned above, to apply the passive-activity limitations a taxpayer must categorize income as either passive, portfolio or active. To so categorize the taxpayer must first determine the separate activities involved. An activity generally consists of all economically interrelated endeavors.[94] Multiple or single activities may be found in any business enterprise. Alternatively, business endeavors conducted in two different business forms (e.g., two different partnerships) may constitute a single activity.[95] The determination of the number of activities a taxpayer is engaged in is made on the basis of the facts and circumstances surrounding each situation.[96] *(See Case 183 for a discussion of considerations in determining activities.)*

Once the activities of the taxpayer have been defined, it must then be determined which activities are passive. In general, a *passive activity* is defined as any trade or business wherein the taxpayer does not materially participate. *Material participation* is defined as active involvement in the operations of the business on a regular, continuous and substantial basis.[97] The material participation test is also made on the basis of the facts and circumstances surrounding each situation.[98] *(See Case 184 for a detailed discussion of the material participation test.)*

Limited partnership interests are always treated as passive activities unless otherwise provided in regulations to be promulgated by Treasury.[99] Working interests in oil and gas properties are not treated as passive activities as long as the working interest is not owned through an entity that limits liability (e.g., S corporation). Material participation is not necessary as long as this requirement is met.[100] *(See Case 185 for a discussion of the working interest exception.)*

State and local property taxes incurred with respect to passive activities are subject to the passive-activity limitations whether they are claimed as "above-the-line" deductions or as itemized deductions.[101] Interest expense attributable to a passive activity is not subject to the investment interest limitation, but is considered in computing the taxpayer's passive-activity income or loss.[102]

Special rules apply to interest expense incurred in connection with the acquisition of or the operation of an oil and gas working interest. In general, the new investment interest limitation rules apply to limit the deduction of any interest paid on debt incurred to acquire or operate an oil and gas working interest where the interest is not

91. I.R.C. Sec. 469(a)(2).
92. I.R.C. Sec. 469(e)(2).
93. Conference Committee Report No. 99-841, 1986-3 C.B. Vol. 4 140; Technical Corrections Bill of 1987, Sec. 105(a)(9), *amending* I.R.C. Sec. 469(j)(11).
94. Senate Report No. 99-313, 1986-3 C.B. Vol. 3 739; General Explanation of the Tax Reform Act of 1986, prepared by the Staff of the Joint Committee on Taxation, p. 245.
95. Senate Report No. 99-313, 1986-3 C.B. Vol. 3 740; General Explanation of the Tax Reform Act of 1986, prepared by the Staff of the Joint Committee on Taxation, p. 247.
96. Senate Report No. 99-313, 1986-3 C.B. Vol. 3 741; General Explanation of the Tax Reform Act of 1986, prepared by the Staff of the Joint Committee on Taxation, p. 247.
97. I.R.C. Sec. 469(h).
98. Senate Report No. 99-313, 1983-3 C.B. Vol. 3 732-733; General Explanation of the Tax Reform Act of 1986, prepared by the Staff of the Joint Committee on Taxation, p. 237.
99. I.R.C. Sec. 469(h)(2).
100. I.R.C. Sec. 469(c)(3); I.R.C. Sec. 469(c)(4).
101. Conference Committee Report No. 99-841, 1986-3 C.B. Vol. 4 139; General Explanation of the Tax Reform Act of 1986, prepared by the Staff of the Joint Committee on Taxation, p. 218.
102. *Ibid.*

treated as a passive activity and where the owner of the interest is not a material participant in the activity.[103] *Material participation* for this purpose is defined using the same criteria as discussed above. *(See Case 184.)* The phasein rules discussed below for using passive losses also apply to limit investment interest, subject to certain ceilings.[104] This phasein provision, however, applies without regard to when the obligation was incurred.

As discussed above, the statute requires that interest expense attributable to a working interest in which the taxpayer does not materially participate be treated as investment interest expense. The statute, however, fails to include income from such working interest as investment income. This apparent drafting error will be corrected by the Technical Corrections Bill of 1987 if passed in its present form.

As discussed above, the passive-activity limitation rules apply generally to tax years beginning after December 31, 1986.[105] A five-year phasein exists for losses and credits from passive activities held on or before October 22, 1986 (the date of enactment of the Tax Reform Act of 1986).[106] Disallowance of losses and credits from pre-enactment interests is phased in at the rate of 35% for 1987, 60% for 1988, 80% for 1989 and 90% for 1990. For 1991 and later years, passive-activity losses and credits generated from pre-enactment interests are subject to the same treatment as other passive activities. To qualify for the special five-year phasein provisions, the activity must have commenced as of October 22, 1986, unless the property used in the activity was acquired under a written contract in effect on August 16, 1986, or construction of the property used in the activity began by August 16, 1986.[107] The phasein provisions are applicable only for purposes of determining the taxpayers regular tax liability and are not considered for the alternative minimum tax computation. *(See Case 175.)*

Applying the passive-activity limitations to 1987 results in the following for Individual A:

Active Income:		
Salary	$300,000	
1985 working interest	(10,000)	$290,000
Portfolio Income:		
Dividends	50,000	
Interest ($20,000 + $1,000 from 87 LP)	21,000	71,000
Passive-Activity Income:		
84 LP	10,000	
86 LP	(20,000)	
87 LP	(85,000)	
	($ 95,000)	
Disallowance ($85,000 + (35% × $10,000))	88,500	
Allowable Passive-Activity Loss	($ 6,500)	(6,500)
Adjusted Gross Income		$354,500

As shown above, Individual A received no current tax benefit from the 1987 LP loss. The $88,500 disallowed loss will be available for carryover to future years.

103. I.R.C. Sec. 163(d)(5).
104. I.R.C. Sec. 163(d)(6).
105. I.R.C. Sec. 469; P.L. 99-514 (Tax Reform Act of 1986), Sec. 501(a).
106. I.R.C. Sec. 469(l).
107. I.R.C. Sec. 469(l)(3)(B).

Since Individual A had invested in a working interest, the 1985 working interest loss is considered active rather than passive. Prior to the application of the passive-activity limitations, Individual A would have received a current deduction of the full loss from the 87 LP. Accordingly, it is very important to consider the effect of these provisions on future investments expected to generate losses.

Case 183
Definition of Activity Under Passive-Activity Limitations

> **Limited Partnership P owns a 25% working interest in three producing oil and gas wells (S, T and U) on Lease D covered by a single operating agreement. Partnership P purchased its interest in S, T and U from Operator A. Partnership P also owns a 50% and 30% working interest, respectively, in two producing oil and gas wells (V and W) covered by separate operating agreements. Partnership P purchased its interest in the V and W properties from Operator B. Partnership P participated in the drilling of three wells during 1987 under a single farmout agreement from Operator C. Two of the wells were dry holes (X and Y), and one well was completed as a producing oil and gas well (Z). Partnership P seeks advice in determining the number of its activities for purposes of applying the passive-activity limitations.**

As discussed in Case 182, the definition of activity is critical in applying the passive-activity limitations since the material participation test is applied with respect to each separate activity (*see Case 184*), and to apply the special rules relating to the disposition of an activity, a determination must be made that the taxpayer has disposed of the entire interest in the activity (*see Case 186*).

The statute does not expressly define the term *activity*.[108] The Committee Reports indicate that the determination of what constitutes a separate activity is to be made in a realistic economic sense.[109] According to the Committee Reports, an *activity* is an undertaking consisting of an integrated and interrelated economic unit, conducted in coordination or reliance upon each other, that constitutes an appropriate unit for the measurement of gain or loss.[110] The Committee Reports[111] indicate that the definition of *activity* for purposes of the hobby loss rules is relevant for purposes of determining the scope of an activity for purposes of applying the passive-activity limitations. Regulations interpreting the definition of *activity* for purposes of the hobby loss rules[112] indicate that the most significant facts and circumstances in defining what constitutes any activity are:

- □ The degree of organizational and economic interrelationship of various undertakings.
- □ The business purpose which is (or might be) served by carrying on the various undertakings separately or together in a trade or business setting.
- □ The similarity of various undertakings.

---

108. I.R.C. Sec. 469(c).
109. Senate Report No. 99-313, 1986-3 C.B. Vol. 3 739; General Explanation of the Tax Reform Act of 1986, prepared by the Staff of the Joint Committee on Taxation, p. 245.
110. *Ibid.*
111. Senate Report No. 99-313, 1986-3 C.B. Vol. 3 739; General Explanation of the Tax Reform Act of 1986, prepared by the Staff of the Joint Committee on Taxation, p. 246.
112. Reg. Sec. 1.183-1(d)(1).

The hobby loss regulations[113] indicate that the characterization by the taxpayer of several undertakings either as a single activity or as separate activities will normally be accepted by the Internal Revenue Service (IRS).The Committee Reports, however, expressly indicate that there is no presumption that the taxpayer's characterization of undertakings as single or separate activities is correct for purposes of the passive-activity limitations.[114] The Committee Reports indicate that the "at-risk" rules' definition of the term *activity* (*see Case 32*) has a different context and purpose than for purposes of the passive-activity limitations.[115] Thus, the strict property concept that controls for the purposes of applying the "at-risk" rules does not necessarily apply for the passive-activity limitations.[116]

In addition to the guidance provided by reference to the hobby loss regulations discussed above, the Committee Reports provide the following additional guidance:

☐ The providing of two or more substantially different products or services constitutes engaging in more than one activity.[117]

☐ Different stages in the production and sale of a particular product not carried on in an integrated fashion generally are not part of the same activity (e.g., oil and gas drilling and operating a retail gas station).[118]

☐ Separate real estate rental projects built and managed in different locations by a real estate operator will each generally constitute a separate activity.[119] Similarly, in the case of farming, each farm generally will constitute a separate activity.[120]

The Committee Reports expressly provide that normal commercial practices are very important in determining whether two or more undertakings are or may be part of a single activity.[121]

Integration of management responsibilities or financing sources is not sufficient, in and of itself, to establish that undertakings are part of the same activity.[122] The fact that two undertakings are conducted by the same entity does not establish that they are part of the same activity; conversely, the fact that two undertakings are conducted by different entities does not establish that they are different activities.[123] The activity concept for purposes of applying the passive-activity limitations is generally applied by disregarding the existence of passthrough entities such as partnerships and S corporations.[124]

The Committee Reports do not indicate precisely how the term *activity* will be applied in the context of the fact situation presented in this case. Because of the variety of transactions in the oil and gas industry, it is likely that no standard rule can be used to define *activity*. As noted previously, the Committee Reports indicate that normal

113. Reg. Sec. 1.183-1(d)(1).
114. Senate Report No. 99-313, 1986-3 C.B. Vol. 3 739, Footnote 29; General Explanation of the Tax Reform Act of 1986, prepared by the Staff of the Joint Committee on Taxation, p. 246, Footnote 41.
115. Senate Report No. 99-313, 1986-3 C.B. Vol. 3 739, Footnote 28; General Explanation of the Tax Reform Act of 1986, prepared by the Staff of the Joint Committee on Taxation, p. 246, Footnote 40.
116. I.R.C. Sec. 465(c)(2)(A)(iv).
117. Senate Report No. 99-313, 1986-3 C.B. Vol. 3 739; General Explanation of the Tax Reform Act of 1986, prepared by the Staff of the Joint Committee on Taxation, p. 246.
118. Senate Report No. 99-313, 1986-3 C.B. Vol. 3 740; General Explanation of the Tax Reform Act of 1986, prepared by the Staff of the Joint Committee on Taxation, p. 246.
119. *Ibid.*
120. *Ibid.*
121. *Ibid.*
122. Senate Report No. 99-313, 1986-3 C.B. Vol. 3 740; General Explanation of the Tax Reform Act of 1986, prepared by the Staff of the Joint Committee on Taxation, p. 247.
123. *Ibid.*
124. *Ibid.*

commercial practices are very important in determining the confines of the activity concept for purposes of applying the passive-activity limitations.[125]

To define *activity* for purposes of oil and gas investments, operations, etc., the primary focus should be the economic interrelated relationships of those investments, operations, etc. For example, the return on investment and the overall economics of an investment in currently producing properties may be sufficiently different from the risk and potential rewards associated with exploration so that the exploration activity may be viewed as a separate activity from the producing-property activity in the case of a taxpayer that has those two types of investments. On the other hand, the producing activity of a taxpayer may be essentially funding part or all of the exploration investments made by a taxpayer so that the taxpayer may have only one activity. The nature of a taxpayer's oil and gas investments will be critical to the activity determination. For example, an isolated intermittent investment may appropriately be viewed as a single activity, whereas a taxpayer involved in the oil and gas business on a continuous, ongoing basis may have only a single activity. Pending the issuance of regulations by Treasury, it is unclear how the determination of the number of activities Partnership P is engaged in should be made. If oil and gas investments are analogous to real estate projects, the Committee Reports' example dealing with real estate projects built and managed by the same operator might mean that each unit of property, as that term is defined for depletion purposes, represents a separate activity. It may not be appropriate, however, to draw the analogy to the real estate project since the economic relationships, risks and rewards of oil and gas investments generally are significantly different from those of real estate projects and, accordingly, must be viewed differently.

Applying these concepts to the facts of this case, it may be possible to view Partnership P as being involved in a single activity, two activities or perhaps multiple activities. If Partnership P's limited partners essentially look to the pool of income generated by Partnership P's investments for a return of their capital and there are no distinguishing factors between any of Partnership P's investments relative to the partner, then the proper determination could be that Partnership P is involved in a single activity. On the other hand, because of the nature of Partnership P's investment, it may be more appropriate to view Partnership P as being involved in two activities: producing activity and exploration activity. If this view were appropriate, wells S, T, U, V and W would be aggregated and would comprise the producing activity whereas wells X, Y and Z would be aggregated to comprise the exploration activity.

The fact that the S, T and U wells on lease D are covered by a single operating agreement when purchased by Partnership P from Operator A could be indicative that Partnership P was viewing the three wells as an integrated economic investment. This may be particularly relevant when the wells are in the producing stage and there is little or no substantial rework requirement or development drilling opportunity whereby Partnership P might exercise its rights (i.e., under the nonconsent provisions) under the operating agreement in any economically significant fashion. The existence of significant rework or development drilling opportunities, thus necessitating the exertion of an affirmative decision by Partnership P to spend additional funds with respect to existing wells or prospective new wells, might, depending on all the facts and circumstances, lead to a determination that the wells S, T and U are not economically interrelated or interdependent, thus creating multiple activities. Alternatively, the wells could become part of a broader defined activity for purposes of

125. Senate Report No. 99-313, 1986-3 C.B. Vol. 3 740; General Explanation of the Tax Reform Act of 1986, prepared by the Staff of the Joint Committee on Taxation, p. 246.

passive-activity provisions. The fact, however, that the wells S, T and U are covered by the same operating agreement should not, in and of itself, be determinative.

Partnership P's interest in V and W acquired from Operator B might also be viewed as separate activities if no economic interrelationships exist.

If the farmout agreement for wells X, Y and Z required Partnership P to participate in the drilling of all three wells, the X, Y and Z wells might be viewed as a single activity. In that case, the dry-hole costs attributable to X and Y wells would not be considered a disposition of an activity, and, therefore, the losses could not be currently used by the limited partners of Partnership P (*see Case 186*). If the farmout agreement from Operator C did not require Partnership P to participate in the drilling of all three wells, but instead gave Partnership P the option to continue participating on a well-by-well basis, each well may constitute a separate activity.

As discussed and demonstrated above, due to the uniqueness of oil and gas investments, no standard rule can be applied. From a practical administrative standpoint, the Treasury needs to develop workable regulations to apply the activity concept for the passive-activity limitations so taxpayers may plan and document their transactions with certainty.

Case 184
Passive-Activity Limitations — Material Participation Test

> Company A, an S corporation, was formed on January 1, 1987, and is owned equally by individuals Y and Z. The corporation's day-to-day operations are directly supervised by Individual Y, who also makes all decisions regarding drilling activities conducted by Company A. Individual Z participates in Company A's activities only to a limited extent. Individuals Y and Z each contributed cash upon formation of Company A.
>
> Company A operates exclusively in the oil and gas exploration and production business. In 1987, Company A incurred losses from its oil and gas activities as follows:
>
> ☐ Working interests owned directly,
>
> ☐ Working interests owned through a limited partnership and
>
> ☐ Working interests owned through a general partnership.

As discussed in Case 182, passive-activity losses are subject to limitations for tax years beginning after December 31, 1986. In general, losses and credits that arise from passive activities may no longer be used to offset income generated from other sources.[126]

A *passive activity* is generally defined as a trade or business in which the taxpayer does not materially participate.[127] Absent regulations to the contrary, a limited partnership interest will always be considered a passive activity.[128] The material participation test must be applied on a year-by-year basis with respect to each activity of a taxpayer.[129] *(See Case 183 for a discussion of considerations in defining activities.)* The statute provides that a taxpayer shall be treated as materially participating in an

126. I.R.C. Sec. 469(a).
127. I.R.C. Sec. 469(c)(1).
128. I.R.C. Sec. 469(h)(2).
129. Senate Report No. 99-313, 1986-3 C.B. Vol. 3 731; General Explanation of the Tax Reform Act of 1986, prepared by the Staff of the Joint Committee on Taxation, p. 236.

activity only if the taxpayer is involved in the operations of the activity on a basis that is regular, continuous and substantial.[130] The statute provides no further guidance in defining material participation other than to indicate that regulations shall be issued which will further specify the types of involvement by the taxpayer that will be deemed to constitute material participation.[131] The Committee Reports indicate that a facts-and-circumstances test for material participation will apply in making the determination.[132] In the absence of further regulatory guidance, criteria[133] to be considered in making the material participation determination should include:

☐ Whether the activity is the taxpayer's principal business;

☐ Whether the taxpayer's involvement in the activity relates to and makes significant contributions to the activity;

☐ Whether the taxpayer is present, and how regularly, at the place of business;

☐ Whether or not the taxpayer performs substantive management functions and

☐ The extent of the taxpayer's involvement in decisions critical to the success of the activity.

Taxpayers that satisfy most or all of these criteria should meet the material participation test. The Committee Report clarifies that an individual who works full time in a business which consists of one or more activities is likely to be considered to be a material participant even if the individual's role is in management rather than in operations.[134] The Committee Report recognizes the substantial likelihood that, despite the difficulty in many circumstances of ascertaining whether the management services rendered by an individual are substantial and bona fide, such services are likely to be so when an individual is rendering them on a full-time basis and the success of the activity depends in large part upon his exercise of business judgment.[135] The actual amount of work performed by the individual is not determinative in meeting the test if he does everything required to conduct the activity.[136]

Generally, a working interest will not be considered a passive activity regardless of whether the taxpayer materially participates. This so-called working interest exception does not apply, however, if the working interest is held in an entity that limits liability (e.g., an S corporation).[137] *(See Case 185 for a discussion of the working interest exception.)*

In the case of an S corporation, the material participation test is applied at the shareholder level. Therefore, it is possible for one shareholder to pass the material participation test and for another shareholder to fail.

As mentioned above, material participation must exist with respect to each activity. Therefore, S corporation shareholders must demonstrate material participation in each activity of the S corporation.[138] The statute does not define the term *activity,* but does provide that regulations are to be issued which will specify which endeavors

130. I.R.C. Sec. 469(h)(1).
131. I.R.C. Sec. 469(k)(1).
132. Senate Report No. 99-313, 1986-3 C.B. Vol. 3 732. *See also* General Explanation of the Tax Reform Act of 1986, prepared by the Staff of the Joint Committee on Taxation, p. 237.
133. General Explanation of the Tax Reform Act of 1986, prepared by the Staff of the Joint Committee on Taxation, p. 237.
134. Conference Committee Report No. 99-841, 1986-3 C.B. Vol. 4 147. *See also* General Explanation of the Tax Reform Act of 1986, prepared by the Staff of the Joint Committee on Taxation, p. 239.
135. Conference Committee Report No. 99-841, 1986-3 C.B. Vol. 4 148. *See also* General Explanation of the Tax Reform Act of 1986, prepared by the Staff of the Joint Committee on Taxation, p. 240.
136. *Ibid.*
137. I.R.C. Sec. 469(c)(3)(A).
138. Senate Report No. 99-313, 1986-3 C.B. Vol. 3 740; General Explanation of the Tax Reform Act of 1986, prepared by the Staff of the Joint Committee on Taxation, p. 247.

constitute an activity.[139] *(See Case 183 for a discussion of defining activities.)* In classifying each economic endeavor as a single activity or as a component of a larger activity, it is important to remember that the classification impacts not only whether current income is deemed passive or active but also the application of various other passive-activity rules, such as the phasein provisions and the deductibility of suspended losses on the disposition of an interest.

The facts in this case and the discussion above indicate that it is unlikely that Individual Z materially participates in the operations of Company A. Individual Z's allocable share of Company A's losses should, therefore, constitute passive losses to Individual Z. If Company A's activities constitute two activities (i.e., limited partnership interest as one and working interest investment as the other), Individual Y's involvement in Company A's day-to-day operations and his responsibility for drilling decisions critical to the success of Company A's endeavors should be sufficient to enable him to be considered as materially participating in the working interest activity of Company A. If it is determined that Company A has more than two activities, Individual Y must look to his involvement on each of these to determine whether he can be considered to be materially participating with respect to each activity. The fact that Company A is the operator of a property should clearly constitute material participation. However, the fact that Individual Y is not the operator of a property does not mean that he does not materially participate since the overall level of participation in Company A's activities must be considered in determining material participation. Under the general rule contained in the statute, the limited partnership losses of Company A will flow through to Individual Y as passive losses.

Concepts similar to those discussed above also apply to limit losses for regular corporations where five or fewer individuals directly or indirectly own more than 50% of the stock of the corporation.[140] Such closely held corporations, other than personal-service corporations, may offset passive losses and credits against active income but not against portfolio income.[141] *(See Case 182 for a discussion of active versus portfolio income.)*

A closely held C corporation will be considered as materially participating in an activity if:

- ☐ One or more shareholders, owning in the aggregate more than 50% in value of the outstanding stock of the corporation, materially participate in the activity[142] or

- ☐ The corporation meets the following requirements:[143]

  - ☐ For the 12-month period ending on the last day of the tax year the corporation had at least one full-time employee who provided sufficient services in active management of the activity;

  - ☐ During the same period, at least three full-time nonowner employees provided sufficient services directly related to the activity and

  - ☐ The amount of the taxpayer's business deductions attributable to the activity exceeds 15% of gross income from the activity for the year.

---

139. I.R.C. Sec. 469(k)(1).
140. I.R.C. Sec. 469(a)(2); I.R.C. Sec. 469(j)(1); I.R.C. Sec. 465(a)(1)(B); I.R.C. Sec. 542(a)(2).
141. I.R.C. Sec. 469(e)(2).
142. I.R.C. Sec. 469(h)(4)(A).
143. I.R.C. Sec. 469(h)(4)(B); I.R.C. Sec. 465(c)(7)(C).

For closely held corporations that are members of consolidated groups, the material participation test discussed above is applied on a consolidated basis.[144]

Unfortunately, many of the complex technical issues involved with determining consolidated profit and loss items, carryovers of tax attributes, etc., are not discussed in the statute or the Committee Reports. Clarification of these issues must await regulations.

Case 185
Passive-Activity Limitations — Working Interest Exception

A, an individual, is expecting to receive a large bonus from his employer in 1987. Individual A has been advised that it is possible to reduce his 1987 tax liability by participating in an oil and gas drilling activity. Individual A and his attorney have preliminarily decided that Individual A's participation in the oil and gas drilling activity could be structured in any of the following manners:

- ☐ **As a direct working interest owner with industry partners under a standard form joint operating agreement (JOA).**
- ☐ **As a general partner in a general partnership.**
- ☐ **As a general partner in a general partnership with optional or mandatory conversion feature to a limited partner in a limited partnership.**

Individual A seeks assistance in planning the structuring of his investment in oil and gas drilling to minimize his 1987 tax liability.

As discussed in Case 182, the passive-activity rules do not apply to a working interest in an oil and gas property which a taxpayer holds directly or through an entity that does not limit the liability of the taxpayer.[145] This is true regardless of whether the taxpayer materially participates in the activity. *(See Case 184.)*[146] If the taxpayer's working interest is held by an entity that limits the liability of the taxpayer (e.g., an S corporation), the working interest exception does not apply and the taxpayer must, therefore, demonstrate material participation.[147] A limited partner's interest in a limited partnership is passive by definition unless otherwise provided by regulations yet to be issued.[148] For purposes of determining ownership of the working interest tiered entities are ignored.[149] The Committee Reports provide that for purposes of applying the working interest exception any form of ownership that is "substantially equivalent" to limited liability, even if not in corporate or limited partnership form, will result in disqualification of the working interest for this exception.[150]

The statute does not define what constitutes a *working interest* for purposes of the working interest exception. The Committee Reports define *working interest* as an interest in an oil and gas property that is burdened with the cost of development and

144. Conference Committee Report No. 99-841, 1986-3 C.B. Vol. 4 140; Technical Corrections Bill of 1987, Sec. 105(a)(9), *amending* I.R.C. Sec. 469(j)(11); General Explanation of the Tax Reform Act of 1986, prepared by the Staff of the Joint Committee on Taxation, p. 221.
145. I.R.C. Sec. 469(c)(3)(A).
146. I.R.C. Sec. 469(c)(4).
147. General Explanation of the Tax Reform Act of 1986, prepared by the Staff of the Joint Committee on Taxation, pp. 251-252.
148. I.R.C. Sec. 469(h)(2); I.R.C. Sec. 469(k)(3).
149. Senate Report No. 99-313, 1986-3 C.B. Vol. 3 745; General Explanation of the Tax Reform Act of 1986, prepared by the Staff of the Joint Committee on Taxation, p. 252.
150. Senate Report No. 99-313, 1986-3 C.B. Vol. 3 745; General Explanation of the Tax Reform Act of 1986, prepared by the Staff of the Joint Committee on Taxation, p. 251.

operation of the property.[151] Overriding royalty interests, production payments and similar nonoperating interests that are not burdened with the responsibility to share expenses of drilling, completing or operating an oil and gas property do not constitute a working interest.[152] The Committee Reports[153] indicate that a working interest generally has the following characteristics:

- □ Responsibility for signing authorizations for expenditures with respect to the activity.
- □ Receiving periodic drilling and completion reports.
- □ Receiving periodic reports regarding the amount of oil extracted.
- □ Possession of voting rights proportionate to the percentage of the working interest possessed by the taxpayer.
- □ The right to continue activities if the present operator decides to discontinue operations.
- □ A proportionate share of tort liability with respect to the property.
- □ Responsibility to share in further costs with respect to the property in the event a decision is made to spend more than amounts already contributed.

These rights and responsibilities are present in the typical industry JOA. The Committee Reports also indicate that the existence of a nonconsent provision in a JOA does not contradict the existence of a working interest.[154] Further, the fact that tort liability may be insured against does not invalidate the existence of a working interest.[155] Although not expressly dealt with in the legislative history, it appears that free-well or carried-interest arrangements *(see Cases 38 and 39)*, where the economic burden of drilling expenditures is shifted among the co-owners, will not alter the existence of a working interest for the co-owner(s) whose share of drilling costs are borne by other co-owners during the development period. Similarly, for example, a conversion of an overriding royalty interest to a working interest at payout should enable the working interest created thereby to qualify for the working interest exception provided all other requirements for the exception are satisfied. It is hoped that regulations to be promulgated by Treasury will expressly cover these situations.

If the working interest exception applies and the taxpayer claims a loss from the working interest, subsequent net income from the working interest is treated as income that is not from a passive activity.[156] Thus, future income is essentially "tainted" as active income. The statute, however, does not provide for continued active treatment of any losses incurred if, for example, the working interest is subsequently transferred to an S corporation. *(See Case 184 for a discussion of S corporations and material participation rules.)* Thus, it is not clear whether losses would be treated as passive losses if material participation cannot be demonstrated. Arguably, the losses should be treated as active losses to the extent of any income treated as active income. Several unanswered questions exist concerning the application of this rule. The statute does not define the term *property* or *loss* for this purpose. Presumably, the application of the property concept and taxable income concept for depletion purposes[157] will control for this purpose *(see Case 87)*. The

151. Senate Report No. 99-313, 1986-3 C.B. Vol. 3 744; General Explanation of the Tax Reform Act of 1986, prepared by the Staff of the Joint Committee on Taxation, p. 251.
152. *Ibid.*
153. *Ibid.*
154. Senate Report No. 99-313, 1986-3 C.B. Vol. 3 745; General Explanation of the Tax Reform Act of 1986, prepared by the Staff of the Joint Committee on Taxation, p. 251.
155. *Ibid.*
156. I.R.C. Sec. 469(c)(3)(B).
157. I.R.C. Sec. 614; I.R.C. Sec. 613.

statute and related Committee Reports also provide that the active income "taint" will apply to any property received by a taxpayer, the basis of which is determined in whole or in part by reference to the former active "tainted" working interest (e.g., property received in a like-kind exchange).[158]

Based on the effective date of the statute,[159] working interests that created losses in tax years beginning before January 1, 1987, (which would have qualified for the working interest exception provided such law was in effect in such prior years) that are contributed to an entity that limits the liability of the taxpayer (e.g., a limited partnership) should not be "tainted" (i.e., should be treated as passive) provided no losses are incurred in tax years beginning after December 31, 1986, or prior to contribution to the entity that limits the liability of the taxpayer. Regulatory authority extended to the Treasury to carry out the passive-activity limitations should not be applied to alter this result.[160]

Even though a working interest in which a taxpayer does not materially participate may not be subject to the passive-activity limitations, the working interest is, nevertheless, considered property held for investment for purposes of applying the investment interest limitations.[161] Any interest expense allocable to acquiring or otherwise funding the development or operation of the working interest is subject to the investment interest limitations. Any loss from the working interest (other than interest expense) reduces any investment income of the taxpayer.[162] Income from the working interest, assuming the statute is modified based on the proposed Technical Corrections Bill of 1987, will increase the investment income of the taxpayer.[163]

Individual A can participate in the oil and gas drilling activity under any one of the structures described in the facts of this case and offset his bonus income with deductions generated by the drilling activity. Individual A will qualify for the working interest exception under each structure. The fact that Individual A is protected by insurance provided in standard industry deals should not affect his qualifications. As mentioned above, subsequent income from the working interest will be considered active, regardless of the form in which Individual A ultimately decides to hold the interest. For example, if Individual A invests as a direct working interest owner and later decides to contribute the working interest to an S corporation or if Individual A invests as a general partner and contributes the interest to a limited partnership or S corporation, the income from the working interest will, nevertheless, be active instead of passive. The same result will apply for the conversion of Individual A's general partnership interest to a limited partnership interest if Individual A decides to invest in the partnership with the conversion feature.

Because of the complicated economic, business and tax considerations associated with the working interest provision in the passive-activity rules, careful planning with professional legal and tax advisers is critical to the successful evaluation and structuring of the investment.

---

158. I.R.C. Sec. 469(c)(3)(B); Senate Report No. 99-313, 1986-3 C.B. Vol. 3 745; General Explanation of the Tax Reform Act of 1986, prepared by the Staff of the Joint Committee on Taxation, p. 252.
159. I.R.C. Sec. 469(c)(3)(B).
160. I.R.C. Sec. 469(k)(3).
161. I.R.C. Sec. 163(d)(5)(A)(ii).
162. I.R.C. Sec. 163(d)(4)(C).
163. Technical Corrections Bill of 1987, Sec. 105(c)(2), *amending* I.R.C. Sec. 163(d)(4).

Case 186
Disposition of Interest in Passive Activity Under Passive-Activity Provisions

Limited Partnership P, a calendar-year partnership formed in January 1987, owns two oil and gas investments (A and B). A is an investment in a limited partnership interest, and B is an investment in a working interest. Investor X, a limited partner, owns 90% of Partnership P. Operator Y, a general partner owns 10% of Partnership P. The partnership agreement provides for no special allocations of income or loss.

Partnership P incurred the following expenditures relating to investments A and B in 1987:

	A	B
Intangible drilling and development costs (IDC)	$100,000	$150,000
Tangible lease and well equipment costs	20,000	30,000

Partnership P realized the following revenues and incurred the following expenses during 1987:

	A	B
Oil and gas revenues	$ 0*	$ 5,000**
Lease operating expenses (including depreciation)	5,000	5,000

* Began production 1/1/88.
** Began production 12/1/87.

Operator Z has offered to buy Partnership P's limited partnership interest in investment A on January 1, 1988, for $175,000. Investor X asks for assistance in applying the passive loss limitations. Investor X has no other sources of passive-activity income (loss) and has sufficient partnership and "at-risk" basis to otherwise absorb any losses from Partnership P.

The passive-activity limitation provisions *(see Case 182)* provide that upon a fully taxable disposition of the entire interest in a passive activity any suspended losses of the activity are no longer subject to the passive-activity limitations.[164] Thus, any suspended loss in excess of the gain on disposition and in excess of other net passive income may be used to offset active or portfolio income.[165] For these rules to apply, the disposition must be to an unrelated party.[166]

If a disposition is made to a related party, suspended losses are not triggered, but remain with the taxpayer; such suspended losses may offset income from other passive activities owned by the taxpayer.[167] The basis of the property in the hands of the transferee in such cases is reduced by the amount of suspended losses in the hands of the transferor. If a taxpayer holds an interest in the same activity through multiple entities, the taxpayer must dispose of each interest in all the entities (or each entity must dispose of the activity) for a disposition of the taxpayer's entire interest to

164. I.R.C. Sec. 469(g).
165. Senate Report No. 99-313, 1986-3 C.B. Vol. 3 725; General Explanation of the Tax Reform Act of 1986, prepared by the Staff of the Joint Committee on Taxation, p. 227.
166. I.R.C. Sec. 469(g)(1)(B).
167. Technical Corrections Bill of 1987, Sec. 105(a), *amending* I.R.C. Sec. 469(g)(1)(A).

occur.[168] The disposition of an activity by a limited partnership will give rise to the allowance of suspended losses from the activity that flows through to the limited partners.[169]

The statute does not define *disposition* for purposes of the passive-activity limitation provisions. It is clear, however, that an abandonment deductible as a loss under general tax principles constitutes a disposition for this purpose.[170] The fact that the nature of an activity changes in the course of its development (e.g., as from construction of a real estate project to a rental activity upon completion of construction) does not constitute a disposition for purposes of the passive-activity provisions.[171] It appears that a lease or sublease (or any assignment with any form of reversionary interest) of an oil or gas property or the carve-out of a production payment (pledged for development of the property or treated as a mortgage loan *(see Cases 135 and 150)*) will not constitute a disposition for purposes of the passive loss provisions since such a transaction does not result in a disposition of the entire interest. Transactions designed in form to represent a sale (or other taxable disposition) will not give rise to the allowance of suspended losses if such transactions are deemed to be a sham or a wash sale or involve transfers involving put or call rights or similar rights to repurchase the property.[172]

Special rules are applicable in applying the passive-activity disposition provisions in the case of death, gifts and transactions involving the nonrecognition of gain or loss. These rules are discussed briefly below:

□ *Death*—A transfer of property at death constitutes a disposition, triggering suspended losses to the extent any suspended losses exceed the amount (if any) by which the basis of the interest in the activity is increased at death.[173] Suspended losses to the extent of the basis increases are eliminated. The allowed suspended losses (if any) are reportable on the final return of the deceased taxpayer.[174]

□ *Gift*—A gift of all or part of the taxpayer's interest in a passive activity does not trigger suspended losses. Suspended losses allocable to the portion of the activity gifted are added to the basis of the property (i.e., the interest in the activity) immediately before the gift.[175]

□ *Nonrecognition Transactions*—An exchange of a taxpayer's interest in a nonrecognition transaction (such as an exchange governed by Section 351, 721 or 1031) in which no gain or loss is recognized does not trigger suspended losses. However, if the taxpayer recognizes any gain on the transaction (e.g., "boot"), it is treated as passive income, thus permitting a deduction of suspended losses. Suspended losses not triggered in the nonrecognition transaction that are not absorbed by passive income in the future are deductible when the taxpayer disposes of the property received in the tax-free exchange.[176]

---

168. Senate Report No. 99-313, 1986-3 C.B. Vol. 3 725; General Explanation of the Tax Reform Act of 1986, prepared by the Staff of the Joint Committee on Taxation, p. 226.
169. Conference Committee Report No. 99-841, 1986-3 C.B. Vol. 4 145; General Explanation of the Tax Reform Act of 1986, prepared by the Staff of the Joint Committee on Taxation, p. 228.
170. Conference Committee Report No. 99-841, 1986-3 C.B. Vol. 4 143; General Explanation of the Tax Reform Act of 1986, prepared by the Staff of the Joint Committee on Taxation p. 227.
171. Conference Committee Report No. 99-841, 1986-3 C.B. Vol. 4 145; General Explanation of the Tax Reform Act of 1986, prepared by the Staff of the Joint Committee on Taxation p. 229.
172. Conference Committee Report No. 99-841, 1986-3 C.B. Vol. 4 143; General Explanation of the Tax Reform Act of 1986, prepared by the Staff of the Joint Committee on Taxation p. 227.
173. I.R.C. Sec. 469(g)(2).
174. Senate Report No. 99-313, 1986-3 C.B. Vol. 3 726; General Explanation of the Tax Reform Act of 1986, prepared by the Staff of the Joint Committee on Taxation, p. 226.
175. *Ibid.*
176. Senate Report No. 99-313, 1986-3 C.B. Vol. 3 726-727; General Explanation of the Tax Reform Act of 1986, prepared by the Staff of the Joint Committee on Taxation, p. 229.

If a taxpayer disposes of his entire interest in an activity in an installment sale, the disposition provisions apply in such a way as to trigger suspended losses as the gain is included in income over the term of the installment note.[177] The Technical Corrections Bill of 1987, if enacted, will clarify that gains recognized on the installment method in years beginning after December 31, 1986, attributable to the sale or exchange of an interest in a passive activity that occurred in a tax year beginning before January 1, 1987, is treated as gain from a passive activity.[178]

The statute provides for special rules where credits have been suspended because of the passive-activity rules. The taxpayer may elect to increase the basis of property immediately before the disposition by an amount equal to the portion of the credit which required a prior basis adjustment.[179]

Investor X has suspended losses for regular tax and alternative minimum tax (AMT) purposes at December 31, 1987, as follows:

Investment	Regular Tax	AMT
A	$ 94,500[1]	$4,500[3]
B	135,000[2]	0[4]
Total	$229,500	$4,500

1 ($100,000 + $5,000) × 90% = $94,500
2 ($5,000 - $5,000 - $150,000) × 90% =($135,000)
3 ($5,000 × 90% = $4,500) For AMT purposes IDC preference is excluded from the passive loss calculation.
4 For AMT purposes IDC preference is excluded from the passive loss calculation.

Assume that investment A is sold on January 1, 1988, for the $175,000 offered by Operator Z and that investment B generates the following income and deductions during 1988:

Oil and gas revenues	$50,000
Lease operating expenses	(10,000)
Depreciation (units of production)	(5,000)
Net	$35,000[1]

1 Investor X's share is $31,500 (90% × $35,000).

Partnership P has a $139,500 gain on the sale of property A, calculated as follows:

	Equipment[1]	Leasehold
Proceeds	$ 20,000	$155,000
Basis	(20,000)	0
Gain[2]	$ 0	$155,000

1 Assume equipment is sold for net book value.
2 Investor X's share is $139,500 (90% x $155,000).

177. I.R.C. Sec. 469(g)(3).
178. Technical Corrections Bill of 1987, Sec. 105(a)(4), *amending* I.R.C. Sec. 469(g)(3).
179. I.R.C. Sec. 469(j)(9).

Investor X will report the following from Partnership P in 1988:

	Regular Tax		AMT	
Passive income before dispositions and passive loss carryovers		$ 31,500		$ 31,500
Gain on sale of A	$139,500		$139,500	
Less: Passive loss carryover attributable to A	(94,500)		(4,500)	
Net gain	$ 45,000	45,000	$135,000	135,000
Passive loss carryover attributable to B		(135,000)		0
Net passive income (loss)		$ (58,500)		$166,500

As shown above, Investor X will have a passive loss carryover for regular tax purposes of $58,500. On the other hand, Investor X will have net passive income of $166,500 for AMT purposes. *(See Case 178 for a discussion of the passive-activity limitations application for AMT purposes.)*

Assume, for illustrative purposes only, that Partnership P incurred a $20,000 loss on the sale of A (Investor X's share is $18,000). In this case, Investor X's regular tax suspended loss for 1987 from investment A ($94,500) is combined with Investor X's share of the loss on disposition ($18,000), producing a total loss of $112,500. Since the loss of $112,500 on investment A cannot be offset by any income from investment B (since investment B has a cumulative net suspended loss of $103,500), Investor X is permitted to use the $112,500 cumulative loss on investment A to offset income that is not from a passive activity (e.g., salary or portfolio income).

In light of the considerable complexity and interaction of the passive loss disposition provisions, careful planning is necessary to evaluate properly the tax implications of dispositions of investments that constitute passive activities.

Case 187
Application of the Uniform Cost-Capitalization Provisions to the Oil and Gas Industry

> Company A, an independent oil and gas producer, engages exclusively in the oil and gas business. Many of the wells drilled by Company A are the result of extensive planning, research and development by its personnel. Company A also engages in oil and gas exploration by investment in prospects generated by other oil and gas companies. In each case, Company A may act as operator for the property or invest in a fractional working interest as a nonoperating participant. Company A is concerned about the tax consequences of the uniform cost-capitalization provisions on its activities.

Under prior law, numerous different provisions existed that required taxpayers to capitalize various costs associated with different types of activities. In general, however, these capitalization provisions did not have broad application to the independent oil and gas producer. The Tax Reform Act of 1986 (the Act) introduces a single, uniform and comprehensive set of cost-capitalization criteria. Unlike the old rules, the new uniform cost-capitalization rules apply to all taxpayers. The rules generally are effective for costs paid or incurred after December 31, 1986, but special phasein rules exist with respect to certain self-constructed assets.[180]

The rules generally apply to all real and tangible personal property produced by a taxpayer and to all real or personal property acquired by a taxpayer for resale to customers.[181] The rules, therefore, apply to the taxpayer's inventory and to assets, such as equipment and buildings, which are constructed by the taxpayer for use in his trade or business. The uniform cost-capitalization rules do not apply to property that is used for personal purposes. Nor do they apply to any costs allowable as a deduction as intangible drilling and development costs (IDC).

The uniform cost-capitalization rules are very complex and provide numerous pitfalls for the independent oil and gas producer. In the absence of final regulations which specifically address the oil and gas industry, the resolution of many issues will remain uncertain. In general, the rules require that costs attributable to inventory be added to the cost of producing the inventory and that the costs attributable to producing or acquiring other property be capitalized. The discussion in this case will focus on the uniform cost-capitalization rules as they apply to the production of assets.

Essentially, three types of expenditures incurred by a typical oil and gas producer will be subject to the new uniform cost-capitalization rules. These costs include direct costs associated with real and tangible personal property produced by the taxpayer, indirect costs associated with real and tangible personal property produced by the taxpayer and interest expense incurred with respect to property produced by the taxpayer.[182] In each case, these costs are required to be capitalized during the production period of the asset.

One of the initial concerns presented by the new uniform cost-capitalization rules involves the determination of an asset's "production period." The statute states that a taxpayer produces tangible property if he constructs, builds, installs, manufacturers, develops or improves the property.[183] Where a taxpayer makes progress or advance payments to a contractor, the taxpayer is treated as producing any property that the contractor produces for the taxpayer under the contract.[184]

Unfortunately, neither the statute nor the regulations expand on the definition of the *period* covered by the terms *construction, build, install, manufacture, develop* or *improve.* This apparent shortcoming provides a difficult, practical problem in that the costs discussed above are to be capitalized only during the period of this activity. With respect to interest, the Committee Reports indicate that the production period for property begins when construction or production is commenced and ends when the property is ready to be placed in service.[185] The Committee Reports further indicate that activities such as planning or design generally will not cause the production period to begin.[186] With respect to interest, it seems reasonable that capitalization should not be required until some overt activity at the drill site commences such as staking, spudding, etc. It also appears reasonable that the production period would cease when the well is completed and capable of production. Unfortunately, the Committee Reports do not address the term *production period* with respect to direct and indirect costs. Absent clarification of the issue, it appears reasonable for taxpayers

180. I.R.C. Sec. 263A.
181. I.R.C. Sec. 263A(b)(1); I.R.C. Sec. 263A(b)(2).
182. Senate Report No. 99-313, 1986-3 C.B. Vol. 3 141-143; General Explanation of the Tax Reform Act of 1986, prepared by the Staff of the Joint Committee on Taxation, pp. 509-511.
183. I.R.C. Sec. 263A(g)(1).
184. I.R.C. Sec. 263A(g)(2).
185. House Report No. 99-426, 1986-3 C.B. Vol. 2 627; Senate Report No. 99-313, 1986-3 C.B. Vol. 3 145; General Explanation of the Tax Reform Act of 1986, prepared by the Staff of the Joint Committee on Taxation, p. 511.
186. *Ibid.*

to consider the term *production period* for interest capitalization and for direct and indirect cost capitalization as synonymous.

Certain interest incurred by a taxpayer with respect to produced property is capitalized to the extent paid or incurred during the production period. Interest subject to the cost-capitalization rules includes interest incurred with respect to real property, property with a class life of 20 years or more as determined under I.R.C. Section 168, property with an estimated production period exceeding two years and property with an estimated production period exceeding one year and a cost exceeding $1 million.[187] Given the nature of oil and gas drilling, it appears unlikely that interest will be required to be capitalized in many situations.

In situations where the interest capitalization is required, the temporary regulations contain general rules relating to the allocation of interest with respect to development activities. In general, the amount of interest capitalized is determined, using the "avoided cost concept," wherein the determination of the amount deemed incurred to finance the development activity is based on the amount of interest expense that would have been avoided if development activity expenditures had not been made and the amount of such expenditures had been used to repay other indebtedness of the company.[188] This concept provides that debt that can be specifically traced to a production activity must first be allocated to that activity. If the development activity expenditures exceed the amount of debt specifically traceable to that development activity, other debt of the taxpayer is to be treated as allocable to that activity. The interest rate applied to the allocable debt is the weighted average of interest rates on the taxpayer's outstanding debt during the development period, excluding the debts specifically traced to the development activity.[189] As a practical matter, these rules create an exceptionally burdensome framework for cost capitalization for large companies. Taxpayers that drill multiple wells during any tax year will be faced with the possibility of having to capitalize a moving average of interest with respect to each well drilled in the tax year.

The statute and temporary regulations provide that direct and indirect costs allocable to the production period also must be capitalized by the taxpayer. The costs required to be capitalized by the taxpayer are first identified and then allocated among the various activities of the taxpayer.[190] Once allocated, the costs are recovered in the same manner as the asset to which they pertain.[191] For example, costs allocable to depreciable equipment are recovered through the allowance for depreciation. The regulations set forth numerous examples of both direct costs and allocable indirect costs that are required to be capitalized by the taxpayer.[192] They also set forth various direct and indirect costs that are not required to be considered in the uniform cost-capitalization determination.[193] The table below summarizes the types of expenditures covered in the temporary regulations.

187. I.R.C. Sec. 263A(f)(1).
188. Temp. Reg. Sec. 1.263A-1T(b)(2)(iv).
189. *Ibid.*
190. Temp. Reg. Sec. 1.263A-1T(a)(5).
191. *Ibid.*
192. Temp. Reg. Sec. 1.263A-1T(b).
193. *Ibid.*

Direct Costs Requiring Capitalization[194]	Indirect Costs Requiring Capitalization[195]	Costs Not Requiring Capitalization G[196]
Direct material costs	Repair of equipment or facilities	Marketing, selling, advertising and distribution expenses
Labor costs associated with the activity including:	Maintenance of equipment or facilities	Unsuccessful bidding expenses
Basic compensation	Utilities	General administrative expenses not directly benefiting a particular production activity
Overtime pay	Rental of equipment, facilities or land	
Vacation pay		
Holiday pay		
Sick leave pay		
Payroll taxes	Indirect labor	Research and experimental activities
	Indirect material and supplies	Section 165 losses
	Tool and equipment costs not otherwise capitalized	Depreciation and amortization on temporarily idle equipment
	Quality control and inspection	Income taxes
	Certain taxes	Contributions paid to employee benefit plans
	Depreciation and amortization	Repair expenses not relating to production of property
	Depletion	Costs and strikes
	Administrative costs	
	Direct and indirect costs incurred by any administrative, service or support function	
	Compensation paid to officers attributable to services performed in connection with particular activities	
	Insurance	
	Contributions to employee benefit plans	
	Rework labor scrap and spoilage	
	Successful bidding expenses	
	Engineering and design expenses	

Although this table is not an all inclusive list of potential costs, the regulations are clear that Treasury contemplates an exhaustive review of all costs incurred by the taxpayer for purposes of complying with the uniform cost-capitalization rules. Given the number of wells the typical oil and gas company drills, the various drilling or production periods and the types of costs typically incurred by oil and gas producers, the practical problems of complying with these rules appear endless.

Costs attributable to more than one activity of the taxpayer should be allocated among all activities benefited by the expenditure. In addition, costs incurred by departments responsible for overall management or policy-setting and costs incurred for chief executive, financial, accounting and legal officers, including their immediate staff, generally would not be required to be allocated to a particular activity unless one

194. Temp. Reg. Sec. 1.263A-1T(b)(8)(2)(i).
195. Temp. Reg. Sec. 1.263A-1T(b)(8)(2)(ii); Temp. Reg. Sec. 1.263A-1T(b)(8)(2)(iii).
196. Temp. Reg. Sec. 1.263A-1T(b)(8)(2)(v).

particular activity directly benefits from the expenditure of funds in one of these areas.[197] Similar rationale would apply to costs incurred for financial accounting, general financial planning, internal audit, shareholder and public relations, tax department and other expenditures.

The statute provides that the uniform cost-capitalization rules do not apply with respect to IDC.[198] The exact implications of this exclusion are unclear. In two recent private letter rulings, the Internal Revenue Service held that a portion of overhead expenses should be allocated to IDC and treated as such for tax preference and recapture purposes.[199] Presumably, overhead expenses would continue to be allocated to IDC as one of the activities to which such costs are allocable under the general rules.

Case 188
Using Futures Contracts To Hedge Against Petroleum Price Fluctuations

> Company A, an independent producer, normally sells 10,000 barrels of crude oil each month. In January, Company A is concerned that current crude oil posted prices of $20/bbl. will drop in the next several months. To reduce the risk of falling prices by midyear, Company A executes in January a futures contract to sell ten 1,000-barrel crude oil contracts in the futures market beginning in July at a current futures contract price of $20.50/bbl. and designates the futures contracts as a hedging transaction. During June, Company A sells his current production at an average posted price of $18/bbl., and before the end of June, Company A buys back the July futures contract for the contract's current trading price of $18.50/bbl.

For decades, futures contracts have been used to reduce business risks in a diverse range of industries. In the late 1970s, the first energy futures contract, number two heating oil, was introduced in the New York Mercantile Exchange. Crude oil contracts began trading in 1983, and now there are several types of energy products being traded. The petroleum futures market provides the energy industry with an alternative method for managing business operations, risks and profit margins during periods of volatile price changes.

Petroleum futures contracts are commitments to purchase or sell a specific quantity (usually 1,000 barrels) of a standardized petroleum commodity on a specified future date at an agreed price. Contracts may be traded for delivery of the commodity many months after the month the contract is executed. Futures contract commitments may be fulfilled either by the physical delivery of the commodity or by offsetting the commitment by buying or selling the futures contract on the exchange before the expiration date of the contract.

Virtually every sector of the energy industry including oil traders, integrated oil and gas companies, refiners and independent producers can use futures contracts as a means of profiting from price fluctuations.

197. Temp. Reg. Sec. 1.263A-1T(b)(4).
198. I.R.C. Sec. 263A(c)(3).
199. IRS Letter Ruling 8622005 (Technical Advice Memorandum); IRS Letter Ruling 8640006 (Technical Advice Memorandum).

Hedging is the buying or selling of futures contracts to lock in profit margins, protect cash market sales of products or inventory against future price fluctuations and enhance credit ratings.

For tax purposes, a transaction is treated as a hedging transaction if the following three conditions are satisfied: (1) the transaction occurs in the normal course of business, primarily to reduce the risk of price change for assets held by the taxpayer, (2) the property, when sold, will produce ordinary income or loss and (3) the taxpayer identifies the transaction as a hedge before the close of the day the transaction takes place.[200]

In this situation, Company A has used the futures market to hedge against the risk of falling prices and avoid a $2/bbl. ($20/bbl.-$18/bbl.) loss from the cash market drop in crude oil. Company A actually recovered $18/bbl. cash price plus a $2/bbl. ($20.50/bbl.-$18.50/bbl.) gain (before commissions and other costs) on the sale of the futures contracts.

Company A would recognize a $2-per-barrel hedging gain as ordinary income.[201] Once a contract is designated as a hedging transaction, gain or loss will be treated as ordinary even if the taxpayer chooses, after executing the contract, to hold the position for investment purposes.

An integral part of any hedging program is the relationship between prices in the cash market with those in the futures market. While hedging may reduce price risk caused by fluctuations in the cash markets, there still remains a basis risk. The difference between the cash and futures market price of a commodity is called basis.

In this case, Company A was successful in exactly offsetting the $2/bbl. loss because the cash market price drop equaled the $2/bbl. gain in the futures market. This exact offsetting is generally referred to as a perfect hedge because the basis remained constant ($2/bbl. in this case). Had Company A bought back the futures contracts at a trading price of $19/bbl. rather than $18.50/bbl., as stated in the case, the $2/bbl. loss in the cash market would have been offset by only $1.50/bbl. gain ($20.50/bbl.-$19/bbl.) in the futures market, resulting in a 50 cents/bbl. basis risk. Although hedging can provide protection against an adverse price movement in the cash markets, it does not eliminate all price risk because basis risk remains.

200. I.R.C. Sec. 1256(e)(2).
201. I.R.C. Sec. 1256(f)(3)(B).

Section VIII
Foreign Operations

U.S. taxpayers have significant investments in oil and gas operations in different countries in many areas of the world, including the North Sea, Southeast Asia, South America, the Middle East and the African Coast. This section discusses the rules that control the U.S. income tax consequences of these operations. A discussion of the income tax rules of foreign countries is beyond the scope of this manual.

Significant investments in U.S. oil and gas operations also have been made by citizens of other countries or by corporations organized outside the United States. This section also discusses general rules of U.S. taxation relating to these investments.

U.S. taxpayers who intend to conduct foreign oil and gas operations should consider numerous business factors before commencing actual operations. In doing so, competent local advisers in the specific countries should be consulted to determine that the proposed organization and plan of operation comply with local law and are acceptable to the government of the country. Management also should consider U.S. and foreign income tax matters relating to any proposed foreign oil and gas operations. Of primary concern in planning these matters is the choice of business organization.

As with most foreign business activities, foreign oil and gas operations may be conducted directly by a U.S. taxpayer through branch operations or indirectly through a domestic or foreign corporation formed for that purpose. *(See Case 207.)* Other types of organizations, such as a U.S. or foreign partnership or joint venture, also may be considered if complex sharing arrangements or certain concession licensing is contemplated.

U.S. citizens, including domestic corporations, are subject to taxation in the United States on all income, from whatever source derived. Accordingly, taxable income or loss realized from foreign oil and gas operations conducted directly by a U.S. individual, through a branch of an existing domestic corporation or through a domestic subsidiary included in a consolidated group of affiliated corporations, must be included in determining total taxable income for U.S. income tax purposes. If the operations are transferred to a foreign subsidiary, the income from future operations generally will be taxable in the United States only when repatriated. However, such a transfer can result in the current recognition of U.S. taxable income. *(See Case 208.)* It is generally prudent to examine the impact of the entity's legal structure on domestic and foreign taxes before engaging in international business.

Provisions relating to claiming income tax payments made to foreign countries as a foreign tax credit apply to individuals and domestic corporations. There are many restrictions on the use of foreign taxes as a credit against U.S. income tax, some of which apply only to oil and gas activities. First, the payments made to foreign governments must constitute creditable taxes. *(See Case 197.)* In addition, the foreign taxes may be used against only U.S. tax imposed on foreign-source income. *(See Case 199.)* A special limitation requires that a net extraction loss from one country offset extraction income from other countries for computing the amount of creditable oil and gas extraction taxes. *(See Case 201.)* In addition, if a taxpayer incurs an overall foreign loss in one year, the loss is subject to recapture in later years through a possible reduction in the foreign tax credit. *(See Case 203.)*

As an alternative to conducting foreign oil and gas operations either directly or through a domestic subsidiary, the operations may be conducted through a foreign corporation. Generally, a foreign corporation is not subject to U.S. income tax unless it has income effectively connected with the conduct of a trade or business in the United States. A U.S. stockholder of such a corporation generally is subject to U.S. tax only when the corporate earnings are distributed. There are, however, exceptions to these general rules. For example, U.S. shareholders are taxable on certain undistributed earnings of a foreign personal holding company. *(See Case 190.)* In addition, U.S. shareholders of a controlled foreign corporation are taxed on certain passive income (foreign personal holding company income), on certain income from oil-related activities (foreign base company oil-related income) and on certain income resulting from transactions with related parties (foreign base company income) even though that income is not distributed to the U.S. shareholders. *(See Cases 191, 192 and 193.)* If a controlled foreign corporation increases its investment in U.S. property, U.S. income tax may be imposed on its shareholders. *(See Case 194.)* The Tax Reform Act of 1986 enlarges the scope of taxation on unremitted earnings of a foreign company by subjecting the U.S. owners to tax on certain income of a foreign company that is not controlled by U.S. persons. *(See Case 189.)*

Foreign income tax payments made directly by foreign corporations may be treated as made indirectly by certain U.S. corporate stockholders. In effect, dividends received from foreign corporations may be "grossed up" to include these foreign income tax payments, which, in turn, may be used by the domestic corporate shareholders to offset U.S. income taxes. *(See Case 200.)*

Gain realized from the sale of stock in foreign corporations may be treated as ordinary income rather than as capital gain. *(See Case 195.)* Without this provision, foreign corporations owned by U.S. shareholders that accumulate earnings in lieu of making dividend distributions effectively could reduce U.S. taxation on foreign business profits. Obviously, this technique is valid only when a tax rate differential exists between ordinary income and capital gain.

A taxpayer must determine taxable income attributable to specific activities to apply various foreign tax credit provisions. For example, to determine the limitation on foreign oil and gas extraction taxes, a taxpayer must determine taxable income (loss) from foreign countries in which it conducts oil and gas extraction activities. Further, the regulations provide complex and detailed rules for the allocation and apportionment of deductions to foreign-source income for purposes of computing the foreign tax credit limitation. These allocation and apportionment rules apply to many computations necessary for the determination of the amount of foreign tax credit that can be used currently. *(See Case 205.)*

Case 189
Passive Foreign Investment Company Provisions

On December 31, 1985, Corporation X, a U.S. company, bought a 15% common stock ownership in Corporation F, a foreign corporation, for

$100,000. The remaining stock was owned by unrelated foreign entities. Corporation F owns oil and gas royalty interests and unimproved land. Corporation F reports for tax purposes on a calendar year. Corporation F makes no distributions to its shareholders. On December 31, 1990, Corporation X sells its interest in Corporation F for $200,000.

Although Corporation F is not a controlled foreign corporation (CFC), the Tax Reform Act of 1986 (the Act) added new provisions that will have a U.S. tax impact on Corporation X's ownership of Corporation F. Through enactment of the passive foreign investment company (PFIC) provisions, Congress intended to remove the economic benefit of tax deferral and the ability to convert ordinary earnings into capital gains for U.S. persons owning interests in foreign corporations generating passive income.[1] Before enactment of the PFIC provisions, the income of a foreign corporation that was not a CFC or a foreign personal holding company (FPHC) generally escaped current U.S. taxation, even though the corporation was owned by U.S. persons.

The Act defines a *PFIC* as any foreign corporation if: (1) 75% or more of the gross income of such corporation is "passive income" or (2) if at least 50% of the average percentage of assets (by value) produces passive income or is held for the production of passive income.[2] Value is not defined by the Act. It is not certain whether gross or net value, after consideration of liabilities, should be taken into account. The Technical Corrections Bill of 1987 does not address this question. Subject to certain enumerated exceptions, *passive income* generally is defined by reference to the definition of the term for purposes of the separate foreign tax credit limitations.[3] Under this section, *passive income* is any income that would be Subpart F foreign personal holding company income.[4] Examples of passive income for PFIC purposes include: (1) interest, dividends, rents, royalties and annuities; (2) gains from the sale or exchange of property that give rise to income under (1) or from property that does not give rise to any income; (3) gains over losses from commodities transactions (exceptions are provided for active business gains); (4) foreign currency gains over losses not directly related to the business needs of the foreign entity and (5) income equivalent to interest, including commitment fees. Passive income does not include rents and royalties derived from the active conduct of a business and received from an unrelated person.[5] *(See Case 192.)*

Corporation F would be considered to be a PFIC under either test since it is generating only passive royalty income and owns only passive assets—oil and gas royalty interests and unimproved land. It is unclear whether undeveloped land could lose its "taint" as a passive asset if purchased with the intent to develop into active trade or business property. It should be noted Corporation F is not a CFC nor an FPHC. Therefore, neither the Subpart F nor FPHC provision applies, even though Corporation F is generating passive income. Under the PFIC provisions, Corporation X will now lose the economic benefit of U.S. tax deferral, have certain elections to consider and face potential current U.S. tax consequences.

The PFIC rules require all U.S. shareholders of a foreign corporation that is a PFIC without having elected status as a qualified electing fund, (discussed more fully below), to pay U.S. tax and an interest charge, based on the value of tax deferral at the time the shareholder disposes of stock in a PFIC or upon receipt of an excess

1. House Report No. 99-426, 1986-3 C.B. Vol. 2 411; Senate Report No. 99-313, 1986-3 C.B. Vol. 3 394.
2. I.R.C. Sec. 1296(a).
3. I.R.C. Sec. 1296(b)(1); I.R.C. Sec. 904(d)(2)(A).
4. I.R.C. Sec. 954(c)(1).
5. I.R.C. Sec. 1296(b)(2); I.R.C. Sec. 954(c)(2); I.R.C. Sec. 954(c)(3).

distribution.[6] It is uncertain whether interest charged under the PFIC provisions is a tax or true interest for other purposes of the Internal Revenue Code (the Code) (since it is defined as part of the deferred tax amount), and, therefore, deductible by a U.S. corporation. For individual U.S. shareholders, PFIC interest would be personal interest and, subject to the phasein rules, nondeductible.[7] Dispositions of PFIC stock include the pledge of PFIC stock as security for a loan, and, if regulations later provide, can also include a disposition of PFIC stock in an otherwise nonrecognition transaction.[8] The Technical Corrections Bill of 1987 would grant the Internal Revenue Service authority to include as dispositions otherwise nonrecognition transfers such as gifts or transfers at death.[9] *Excess distributions* are defined as actual distributions from a PFIC that exceed 125% of the average amount of distributions in respect of the stock received during the preceding three years (or if shorter, during the shareholder's holding period). Under the Technical Corrections Bill of 1987, provisions are made so that actual distributions of previously taxed income from FPHC, Subpart F or qualified electing fund inclusions are not taxed as excess distributions.[10] The term *excess distribution* does not require that the PFIC have earnings and profits. Thus, any distribution from a PFIC, including a return of capital distribution, is subject to this rule.

The PFIC provisions do not affect other Code provisions governing distributions that are not excess distributions with respect to a foreign corporation's stock (for example, I.R.C. Section 316 defines a *dividend* as any distribution to shareholders of a corporation with current or accumulated earnings and profits).

Gain from a disposition of PFIC stock or receipt of an excess distribution with respect to PFIC stock is deemed to have been earned pro rata over the U.S. shareholder's holding period in the stock.[11] Once the gain or excess distribution is allocated over the shareholder's holding period, the U.S. income tax due is the sum of: (1) the tax computed, using the highest statutory rate for ordinary income for each year (without regard to other unrelated income, expenses or attributes of the U.S. shareholder) to which amounts are allocated in the shareholder's holding period (other than the current year and years before the foreign corporation was a PFIC); plus (2) interest on the tax from amounts allocated to prior PFIC years; plus (3) tax on the income (treated as ordinary income) attributable to the year of disposition or receipt and to the years the foreign corporation was not a PFIC that precede the year of disposition (for which no interest is due). The additional U.S. tax and interest, computed from the gain or distribution allocable to PFIC years before the year of disposition, is called the deferred tax amount.[12] It should be noted that the interest portion of the deferred tax amount should be personal interest for individual U.S. shareholders and, therefore, nondeductible, after the phasein period. In addition, such interest may be offset by direct foreign tax credits, if any.[13]

To compute the deferred tax amount, several steps must be taken. First, excess distributions or gain from the sale of the stock is allocated ratably over each day in the shareholder's holding period of the stock, including years before the foreign corporation was a PFIC, or if earlier, the effective date of the PFIC provisions (tax years of a foreign corporation beginning after December 31, 1986). Amounts allocated to the year of disposition and amounts allocated to years beginning before 1987 (referred to

6. I.R.C. Sec. 1295(a); I.R.C. Sec. 1291(a).
7. I.R.C. Sec. 163(h).
8. I.R.C. Sec. 1291(f).
9. Technical Corrections Bill of 1987, Sec. 112(n)(6).
10. Technical Corrections Bill of 1987, Sec. 112(n)(3).
11. I.R.C. Sec. 1291(a)(1)(A).
12. I.R.C. Sec. 1291(c).
13. General Explanation of the Tax Reform Act of 1986, prepared by the Staff of the Joint Committee on Taxation, p. 1027.

as the "current portion") are reported as ordinary income and subject to U.S. taxation along with the shareholder's other income and deductions.[14] Amounts allocated to prior PFIC years, "noncurrent portions," are taxed at the highest ordinary income tax rate in effect during that tax year, as an additional tax (the deferred amount).[15] Thus, the current portion can be offset by a U.S. shareholder's other deductions or losses, whereas the noncurrent portion cannot. Also, since the deferred tax amount is calculated at the highest ordinary income tax rate in effect for each applicable year, PFIC taxation presumes that the U.S. shareholder would have been taxed at that rate had actual distributions or gains occurred in that year. Finally, the deferred tax amount includes an interest charge, which runs for the period from the due date of the tax return for the tax year to which the noncurrent portion of income is allocated and ends on the due date for the return of the tax year of the disposition or excess distribution. The interest rate and method of calculating interest are the same as that for underpayments of estimated taxes.[16]

Corporation X's 1990 gain from the sale of its Corporation F stock is $100,000. Corporation F became a PFIC on January 1, 1987.[17] The $100,000 gain would be deemed to be attributable to each of the years Corporation X held its Corporation F stock (i.e., $20,000 per year). Thus, the tax Corporation X will have to pay in 1990 will be the sum of: (1) $20,000 for 1986 × 34%, or $6,800 tax; (2) $20,000 for 1987 × 40%, or $8,000 tax, plus interest for three years; (3) $20,000 for 1988 × 34%, or $6,800 tax, plus interest for two years; (4) $6,800 tax for 1989, plus interest for one year and (5) $6,800 of tax allocated to 1990. Assuming an interest rate of 10% compounded daily, the total interest would be $5,018 ($0 + $2,798 + $1,505 + $715 + $0) on the additional tax of $35,200, or a total of $40,218 added to Corporation X's U.S. tax liability for 1990. Although the PFIC provisions currently disallow an indirect foreign tax credit unless the foreign corporation makes a qualified electing fund election, the Technical Corrections Bill of 1987 allows for the credit in either situation.[18] Also, the PFIC provisions allow the noncurrent portion of income to be considered gross income in the year of receipt for purposes of calculating the foreign tax credit limitation.[19]

If Corporation F were to make a qualified electing fund election, some of the harsher effects of the PFIC provisions to Corporation X could be mitigated. If Corporation F makes the election, the U.S. shareholder avoids: (1) the requirement that earnings of the foreign corporation are deemed earned ratably over the holding period of the stock; (2) taxation at the highest statutory tax rate when the U.S. shareholder's effective tax rate for the applicable year is lower and (3) the requirement that the unrealized appreciation of the foreign corporation's assets be deemed to be earned ratably over the shareholder's holding period.

If Corporation F makes a qualified electing fund election, Corporation X must include in its income the pro-rata share of Corporation F's current earnings and long-term capital-gain income each year, whether or not such income is distributed.[20] It should be noted that Corporation F, the foreign corporation, makes the election, not its U.S. shareholders. However, once the election is made, it is binding on all U.S. share-

14. I.R.C. Sec. 1291(a)(1)(B).
15. I.R.C. Sec. 1291(c)(1); I.R.C. Sec. 1291(c)(2).
16. I.R.C. Sec. 1291(c)(3); I.R.C. Sec. 6621(b)(2).
17. I.R.C. Sec. 1297(h).
18. Technical Corrections Bill of 1987, Sec. 112(n)(7).
19. I.R.C. Sec. 1291(a)(4).
20. I.R.C. Sec. 1293(a).

holders until the foreign corporation ceases to be a PFIC or the election is revoked with consent of the Commissioner of Internal Revenue.[21]

If Corporation F makes the qualified electing fund election for 1987, Corporation X must include 15% of Corporation F's ordinary earnings and long-term capital-gain income in its taxable income each year thereafter, until Corporation X disposes of its Corporation F stock or Corporation F ceases to be a PFIC.[22] For U.S. shareholders subject to the Subpart F or FPHC rules, any qualified electing fund inclusions are taken into account after Subpart F or FPHC.[23] As a U.S. corporation owning more than 10% of the foreign corporation, Corporation X would be allowed a pro-rata share of any indirect foreign tax credits for any foreign taxes paid or accrued by Corporation F.[24] As Corporation X includes Corporation F's earnings in its taxable income, Corporation X receives an increase in its basis in its Corporation F stock, and as actual distributions are made from Corporation F to Corporation X, Corporation X's basis in the Corporation F stock is reduced.[25] If distributions are made in later tax years by a qualified electing fund, the U.S. shareholder is allowed to exclude the distribution from income under the qualified electing fund provisions provided such shareholder can demonstrate that the distribution was from the fund's earnings.[26]

If Corporation F elects to become a qualified electing fund and does not currently distribute earnings, there is a separate election whereby any U.S. shareholder can defer the tax amount related to any fund inclusion until the earlier of the year of an actual distribution, the disposition of the fund stock or the foreign corporation ceases to be a PFIC.[27] An election to defer the payment of tax is not available if any amounts are required to be currently included in income under the FPHC rules or the Subpart F rules.[28] If a U.S. shareholder makes this election, interest accrues until the actual payment of the tax.[29] As with a PFIC, any interest paid by an individual taxpayer would be personal interest and nondeductible after the phasein period.[30]

Case 190
Foreign Personal Holding Companies

F Corporation, a foreign corporation, is owned 30% by Individual A, 30% by Individual B and 40% by Y Corporation. Individuals A and B are U.S. citizens, and Y Corporation is a domestic corporation.

During 1987, F Corporation received sublease bonus income of $200,000 and royalty proceeds of $120,000 from oil and gas production. F Corporation also had expenses of $140,000 and paid $100,000 in foreign income taxes. The stockholders ask if the operations of F Corporation had any effect on their personal income tax liabilities for 1987.

21. Conference Report No. 99-841, 1986-3 C.B.Vol. 4 643; General Explanation of the Tax Reform Act of 1986, prepared by the Staff of the Joint Committee on Taxation, p. 1030.
22. I.R.C. Sec. 1293(a); I.R.C. Sec. 1293(b); I.R.C. Sec. 1295(b)(1).
23. I.R.C. Sec. 951(f); I.R.C. Sec. 551(g).
24. I.R.C. Sec. 1293(f).
25. I.R.C. Sec. 1293(d).
26. I.R.C. Sec. 1293(c).
27. I.R.C. Sec. 1294(a); I.R.C. Sec. 1295(b)(1).
28. I.R.C. Sec. 1294(a)(2).
29. Conference Report No. 99-841, 1986-3 C.B. Vol. 4 643; General Explanation of the Tax Reform Act of 1986, prepared by the Staff of the Joint Committee on Taxation, p. 1029. *See also* Technical Corrections Bill of 1987, Sec. 112(n)(8).
30. I.R.C. Sec. 6601(e); Technical Corrections Bill of 1987, Sec. 112(n)(8).

The enactment of statutory provisions concerning foreign personal holding companies in 1937 was the first attempt by Congress to tax U.S. shareholders on the income earned by their foreign corporations. Since 1937, various tax provisions have been steadily expanded to insure that U.S. shareholders of foreign corporations are taxed currently on certain types of worldwide income.

In general, a *foreign personal holding company* is defined as any foreign corporation of which at least 60% (50% for years after a company once attains foreign personal holding company status) of its gross income is foreign personal holding company income and of which more than 50% of its total combined voting power of all classes of voting stock or the total value of its stock is owned, directly or indirectly, by not more than five individuals who are citizens or residents of the United States.[31] If these two tests are met, a U.S. citizen or resident shareholder must include his portion of undistributed foreign personal holding company income in his gross income.[32] For purposes of the 60% test, foreign personal holding company income includes dividends, interest, rents and royalties, which generally are the same types of passive income included in the personal holding company income of domestic corporations.

Under current law, it is no longer possible to avoid the foreign personal holding company rules by, for example, imposing a foreign partnership or other foreign entity that was not a foreign personal holding company (because it had only U.S. gross income) between the U.S. shareholders and the foreign personal holding company.[33] The prior rule, which allowed the foreign personal holding company rules to control when both the foreign personal holding company rules and the Subpart F rules were applicable has been repealed. If a foreign corporation meets the definitions of both a foreign personal holding company and a controlled foreign corporation, generally the U.S. shareholders are subject to taxation under the rules applicable to Subpart F.[34]

In certain circumstances, the Subpart F provisions do not apply to royalties, from persons other than related persons, derived in the active conduct of a trade or business of the corporation. Also, the provisions do not apply to royalties received from a related person for the use of property in the country in which the controlled foreign corporation is organized. *(See Case 192.)* These exceptions do not apply to the foreign personal holding company definition of *royalty income.*

The foreign personal holding company rules require U.S. shareholders to include in their gross income the corporation's undistributed foreign personal holding company income.[35] The amount so included will reduce the foreign corporation's earnings and profits and increase its contributed capital; thus, it also will increase the U.S. shareholder's basis in the stock of the corporation.[36]

Undistributed foreign personal holding company income is defined in essentially the same way as undistributed personal holding company income of a domestic corporation. In general, it represents the taxable income of the foreign corporation after considering certain adjustments, including a deduction for dividends paid.[37] Since U.S. rules apply, the passive loss rules could prevent use of a limited partnership loss to reduce portfolio income and thereby increase the amount taxed currently in the United States. *(See Case 182.)* A deduction for percentage depletion is not allowed on foreign oil and gas production, but a deduction for cost depletion is available in

31. I.R.C. Sec. 552(a).
32. I.R.C. Sec. 556(a).
33. I.R.C. Sec. 552(c); I.R.C. Sec. 951(d).
34. I.R.C. Sec. 951(d).
35. I.R.C. Sec. 551(b).
36. I.R.C. Sec. 551(d); I.R.C. Sec. 551(e).
37. I.R.C. Sec. 556(a); I.R.C. Sec. 561.

computing the taxable income attributable to foreign oil or gas production.[38] In computing its taxable income and its undistributed personal holding company income, F Corporation can deduct income, war profits and excess profits taxes paid or accrued to foreign countries but cannot elect to take these taxes as a credit.[39]

F Corporation is a foreign personal holding company if the sublease bonus income is treated as royalty income for this purpose. The ownership test is met because Individuals A and B, both of whom are residents or citizens of the United States, own more than 50% in value of the stock of the corporation. Royalty income received from oil and gas production is personal holding company income without regard to the percentage of total gross income or the other mechanical tests used to define personal holding company income of a domestic corporation.[40]

Sublease bonus income generally is treated for income tax purposes as a royalty received in advance of actual production. *(See Case 4.)* This income also has been held to be personal holding company income for domestic personal holding company purposes.[41]

One case,[42] however, has held that lease bonus income is to be distinguished from royalty income to qualify a corporation as a Subchapter S corporation. *(See Case 169.)* The Internal Revenue Service (IRS) is likely to resist the application of this case to domestic personal holding companies, particularly because the statute itself prescribes rules under which royalties are not personal holding company income if certain conditions relating to active business expenses are present.[43] Similarly, the IRS probably will resist any distinction between sublease bonus income and royalties for foreign personal holding company purposes.

If sublease bonus income is treated as foreign personal holding company income, the undistributed foreign personal holding company income of F Corporation for 1987 is $80,000, computed as follows:

Gross income	$ 320,000
Expenses	(140,000)
Foreign income taxes	(100,000)
Taxable income of F Corporation	$ 80,000
Adjustments to arrive at undistributed foreign personal holding company income	—
Undistributed foreign personal holding company income	$ 80,000

The $80,000 of undistributed foreign personal holding company income must be included in the gross incomes of Individuals A and B and Y Corporation in proportion to their stock ownership determined at the end of 1987. The undistributed foreign personal holding company income is taxed to each U.S. shareholder as if a dividend of the undistributed personal holding company income had been made pro rata to all shareholders on the last day of the tax year of the foreign personal holding company.[44]

Generally, a corporate shareholder owning at least 10% of the voting stock of a foreign corporation from which it receives dividends paid out of accumulated profits is deemed

38. I.R.C. Sec. 611(a); I.R.C. Sec. 613A.
39. Reg. Sec. 1.556-2(a)(3).
40. I.R.C. Sec. 553(a)(1); Reg. Sec. 1.553-1(b)(1).
41. Bayou Verret Land Co. v. Comm'r, 450 F.2d 850 (5th Cir. 1971), 28 AFTR2d 71-5961, 71-2 USTC 9713.
42. Swank & Son, Inc. v. U.S., 552 F.2d 981 (9th Cir. 1975), 36 AFTR2d 75-5610, 75-2 USTC 9675, *aff'g* 362 F. Supp. 897 (D.C. Mont. 1973), 32 AFTR2d 73-5781, 73-2 USTC 9677.
43. I.R.C. Sec. 543(a)(3); Bayou Verret Land Co.
44. I.R.C. Sec. 551(b).

to have paid a certain portion of any creditable income tax paid by that foreign corporation.[45] The IRS takes the position, based on the 1937 Joint Committee Report, that a U.S. corporate shareholder of a foreign personal holding company that must include undistributed foreign personal holding company income in its taxable income is not entitled to any credit against its U.S. income tax for foreign income taxes paid by that corporation on undistributed earnings.[46] When a consent dividend is used by the corporate shareholder and the foreign personal holding company, it is treated as a cash dividend for the allowance of the foreign tax credit.[47] Y and F Corporations should consider following the consent dividend procedure in this instance so that Y Corporation can claim a credit for foreign taxes paid by F Corporation. The amount of the credit and the additional amount to be treated as dividend income will be determined by following the general rules relating to the credit for taxes deemed paid. *(See Case 200.)* In the future, F Corporation should consider paying a cash dividend equal to its foreign personal holding company income. Y Corporation will be able to claim a foreign tax credit for the foreign income taxes paid by F Corporation. The indirect or deemed paid credit does not apply to individuals.[48] Thus, Individuals A and B will not be entitled to a foreign tax credit even if a dividend is paid in cash or the consent dividend procedures are used. Because F Corporation is a controlled foreign corporation and assuming it does not qualify as a foreign personal holding company, Individuals A and B will be entitled to a foreign tax credit if they elect to be taxed as a corporation on that income.[49]

If F Corporation's gross income consists of 10% or more of U.S.-source income, a proportionate amount of the consent dividend will constitute U.S.-source, not foreign-source, income.[50] This characterization may limit the ability to use foreign tax credits currently. *(See Case 200.)*

Case 191
Controlled Foreign Corporations — In General

The president of Corporation X, a domestic corporation, wants to expand its business overseas by setting up a wholly owned subsidiary, Corporation F, which will be organized and operated in a foreign country. The president of Corporation X wants to know if the earnings of Corporation F will be subject to taxation in the United States in the year in which earned.

Complex provisions, commonly referred to as Subpart F, restrict the ability to defer U.S. taxation on earnings realized by controlled foreign corporations. These statutory provisions define the categories of a foreign corporation's income that are subject to taxation currently in the United States.

Subpart F generally provides that each U.S. shareholder owning stock on the last day on which the corporation is a controlled foreign corporation is taxed currently on certain earnings of a controlled foreign corporation whether or not those earnings are distributed to its shareholders. A corporation is a controlled foreign corporation if more than 50% of either the voting power or value of the stock of the corporation is

45. I.R.C. Sec. 902(a).
46. Rev. Rul. 74-59, 1974-1 C.B. 183; Conference Committee Report, 1937-2 C.B. 623.
47. Rev. Rul. 74-59, 1974-1 C.B. 183; Conference Committee Report, 1937-2 C.B. 623; IRS Letter Ruling 8244070; Rev. Proc. 82-55, 1982-2 C.B. 845.
48. I.R.C. Sec. 902(a).
49. I.R.C. Sec. 962.
50. I.R.C. Sec. 904(g).

owned by U.S. shareholders on any day during the tax year of that foreign corporation. However, the foreign corporation must be a controlled foreign corporation for an uninterrupted period of 30 days or more during a tax year before the U.S. shareholders are required to include in gross income the "tainted" earnings (if any) of the controlled foreign corporation.[51] A U.S. shareholder includes a U.S. citizen or resident, a domestic corporation, partnership, estate or trust that owns 10% or more of the voting stock of the foreign corporation.[52] Constructive ownership rules are used to determine if persons are U.S. shareholders.[53]

In general, the events that result in current taxation to a U.S. shareholder include, but are not limited to:

- □ The realization of Subpart F income of the controlled foreign corporation.
- □ An investment of the earnings of the controlled foreign corporation in U.S. property.[54]

Subpart F income includes, but is not limited to:

- □ Income derived from the insurance of U.S. risks.
- □ Foreign personal holding company income (certain passive income).
- □ Foreign base company sales income (certain sales transactions involving a related party).
- □ Foreign base company services income (certain services income realized in dealings with a related party).
- □ Foreign base company shipping income (certain income derived from the use of any aircraft or vessel in foreign commerce).
- □ Foreign base company oil-related income (other than income derived from extraction activity).[55]

Under prior law, income of the type described above, except for foreign base company oil-related income, was not taxable currently to the U.S. shareholders if the reduction of income tax was shown not to be a significant purpose for the creation or organization of the controlled foreign corporation and if the reduction of tax was not a significant purpose of the transaction that gave rise to the income. Prior law generally applied to tax years of foreign corporations beginning before January 1, 1987.

The Tax Reform Act of 1986 (the Act) replaces the subjective test of I.R.C. Section 954(b)(4) with an objective test. Foreign base company income does not include any item of income received by a controlled foreign corporation if the taxpayer establishes to the Internal Revenue Service's satisfaction that the income was subject to an effective rate of income tax imposed by a foreign country greater than 90% of the maximum U.S. corporate tax rate (30.6% in 1988). This calculation is to be made under U.S. tax concepts. As under prior law, this exception does *not* apply to foreign base company oil-related income.[56]

Under prior law, none of a controlled foreign corporation's income was treated as foreign base company income if less than 10% of the controlled foreign corporation's gross income was foreign base company income. The Act drastically reduced the de

51. I.R.C. Sec. 951(a)(1).
52. I.R.C. Sec. 951(b); I.R.C. Sec. 7701(a)(30); I.R.C. Sec. 957(d).
53. I.R.C. Sec. 958.
54. I.R.C. Sec. 951(a)(1)(B).
55. I.R.C. Sec. 952; I.R.C. Sec. 954(a).
56. I.R.C. Sec. 954(b)(4).

minimis rule so that a controlled foreign corporation has currently taxable Subpart F income if its foreign base company income exceeds the lesser of $1 million or 5% of gross income. This change could generate substantial amounts of currently taxable income for U.S. companies with numerous foreign subsidiaries.[57] If the ratio exceeds 70%, all the company's income is Subpart F income.

The amount of the constructive dividend taxable to U.S. shareholders is limited to the current earnings and profits of the controlled foreign corporation.[58] Earnings and profits are computed according to complex rules in the regulations that attempt to calculate the foreign corporation's taxable income, using U.S. income tax concepts.[59] The Technical Corrections Bill of 1987 provides that for purposes of determining the earnings and profits limitation for Subpart F income under I.R.C. Section 952(c), earnings and profits are to be computed without regard to the LIFO (last-in, first-out), installment sales or completed contract methods of accounting.[60]

A corporate shareholder that is required to include undistributed earnings and profits of a controlled foreign corporation in its U.S. taxable income is deemed to have paid a pro-rata share of the foreign taxes of the controlled foreign corporation.[61] If the corporate shareholder makes an appropriate increase in the amount of the dividend taxed, it is allowed to treat the foreign taxes deemed paid by it as a credit against its U.S. income tax, subject to certain limitations.[62] An individual shareholder may claim a foreign tax credit for foreign taxes paid by a controlled foreign corporation only if an election is made to compute the tax on income from the controlled foreign corporation at corporate income tax rates.[63]

If a controlled foreign corporation has income from U.S. sources, the nature of the income must be reviewed to determine if the income is "tainted". If the controlled foreign corporation is engaged in a trade or business in the United States, U.S.-source income effectively connected to the trade or business is not Subpart F income.[64] However, U.S.-source income that, pursuant to a treaty, is either exempt from U.S. tax or taxed at a reduced rate may constitute Subpart F income, depending on its nature.

If a controlled foreign corporation has Subpart F income and other income, deductions must be allocated or apportioned based on rules provided by the regulations to determine the taxable amount of Subpart F income.[65]

Corporation F is a controlled foreign corporation. Because its operations are to be conducted in a foreign country, it will not be subject to U.S. tax. A close review of its operations should be conducted, however, to determine if the activities will result in current U.S. income tax to its parent, Corporation X.

If Corporation F generates income from oil-related activities other than extraction, this income may constitute Subpart F income. *(See Case 193.)*

57. I.R.C. Sec. 954(b)(3).
58. I.R.C. Sec. 952(c).
59. I.R.C. Sec. 964(a).
60. Technical Corrections Bill of 1987, Sec. 112(h)(16).
61. I.R.C. Sec. 960(a).
62. I.R.C. Sec. 902.
63. I.R.C. Sec. 962.
64. I.R.C. Sec. 952(b).
65. I.R.C. Sec. 954(b)(5).

Case 192
Controlled Foreign Corporations — Foreign Personal Holding Company Income

> F Corporation, incorporated under the laws of Country B, was formed on January 1, 1987, and throughout the year is owned 30% by Individual A, 30% by X Corporation and 40% by Y Corporation. Individual A is a citizen of the United States, and both X Corporation and Y Corporation are domestic corporations that are public companies. No single shareholder of Corporation X or Y owns more than 1% of its outstanding stock.
>
> During 1987, F Corporation realizes from non-U.S. sources sublease bonus income of $200,000, and oil and gas production royalty income of $120,000. F Corporation also has expenses of $140,000 allocable to that income and pays foreign taxes in the amount of $100,000. Advice is requested as to the effect, if any, that the above transactions have on the U.S. taxable income of the shareholders of F Corporation.

F Corporation is not a foreign personal holding company because not more than 50% of either the voting power or value of F Corporation's outstanding stock is owned directly or indirectly by five or fewer individuals who are citizens of the United States. However, F Corporation does meet the definition of a controlled foreign corporation because more than 50% of both the voting power and value of its stock is owned by U.S. shareholders for the entire year.[66] Further, each of its shareholders owns at least 10% of the stock's voting power, and each must include in gross income the pro-rata share of the company's Subpart F income because F Corporation was a controlled foreign corporation for an uninterrupted period of at least 30 days during 1987.[67]

Subpart F income includes foreign personal holding company income.[68] Foreign personal holding company income generally includes interest, dividends, rents, royalties and annuities and gain from the sale of stock. The Tax Reform Act of 1986 expands the definition of foreign personal holding company income for Subpart F purposes to include net gains from the sale of property that does not generate active income. In addition, income from commodities transactions, other than bona fide hedging transactions, and foreign currency gains, other than those directly related to the company's business needs, are foreign personal holding company income.[69] If the corporation's foreign personal holding company income and certain other Subpart F income do not exceed the lesser of $1 million or 5% of gross income, no part of the company's income is taxed currently to the shareholders.[70]

Generally, income received from royalties on mineral or oil and gas properties is foreign personal holding company income that constitutes Subpart F income.[71] An exception to this rule exists for royalty income, including production royalties, derived in the active conduct of a trade or business and received from an unrelated person.[72] In addition, rents or royalties received from a related person for the use of property in the country in which the controlled foreign corporation is created or organized is not foreign personal holding company income.[73]

---

66. I.R.C. Sec. 957(a).
67. *Ibid.*
68. I.R.C. Sec. 954(a)(1).
69. I.R.C. Sec. 954(c).
70. I.R.C. Sec. 954(b)(3)(A).
71. I.R.C. Sec. 954(c).
72. I.R.C. Sec. 954(c)(3)(A).
73. *Ibid.*

The rules for determining whether rent or royalty income is personal holding company income for a domestic corporation provide an exception if either type of income constitutes a certain percentage of the company's income and other conditions are fulfilled. No similar exception exists for determining rents and royalties that constitute personal holding company income for purposes of Subpart F.[74]

Sublease bonus income generally is treated for U.S. purposes as royalty income received in advance of production. (*See Case 4.*) It also has been held to be domestic personal holding company income, but one court has held that it does not constitute passive income for Subchapter S purposes. (*See Case 170.*) The Internal Revenue Service probably will take the position that it is foreign personal holding company income and Subpart F income. The active business implications often found in connection with lease bonus income, however, may support the position that this income is not foreign personal holding company income that constitutes Subpart F income.

If F Corporation's income meets none of these exceptions, a pro-rata share of the sublease bonus income and oil and gas royalty income, reduced by any applicable expenses, will be included in the income of its U.S. shareholders. Individual A and X Corporation each are taxed on $24,000 and Y Corporation, on $32,000 of F Corporation's income, computed as follows:

	Individual A	X Corporation	Y Corporation
Gross Subpart F income	$ 96,000	$ 96,000	$128,000
Expenses	(42,000)	(42,000)	(56,000)
Foreign taxes	(30,000)	(30,000)	(40,000)
Net Subpart F income	$ 24,000	$ 24,000	$ 32,000

In computing the amount of income taxed to each of the shareholders, deductions are allowed for those expenses properly allocable to the gross Subpart F income.[75] A deduction for percentage depletion is not allowed on foreign oil and gas production, but a deduction for cost depletion may be allowed. (*See Case 94.*)

For foreign tax credit purposes, the corporate shareholders are deemed to have paid a portion of F Corporation's foreign taxes. X Corporation and Y Corporation are entitled to treat the foreign taxes paid to Country B as a credit against their U.S. income tax if they make appropriate increases to the amount of gross income they report as Subpart F income.[76] If Individual A elects to compute his tax on his income from the controlled foreign corporation at corporate income tax rates, he also is entitled to treat the foreign taxes paid to Country B as a credit against his U.S. income tax liabilities.[77] The foreign tax credit for both corporate and individual shareholders who elect to be taxed as corporations is subject to the limitations applicable to foreign tax credits in general and to the special limitations relating to foreign oil and gas income.[78] (*See Case 196.*)

---

74. I.R.C. Sec. 954(c).
75. I.R.C. Sec. 954(b)(5).
76. I.R.C. Sec. 960.
77. I.R.C. Sec. 962.
78. I.R.C. Sec. 904; I.R.C. Sec. 907.

Case 193
Controlled Foreign Corporations — Base Company Income

Corporation C, a domestic corporation, is engaged in numerous business activities in the United States and overseas.

It owns all the voting stock of Corporation F1, which is organized in Country Y. Corporation F1 is engaged only in the business of buying and reselling crude oil. Generally, Corporation F1 purchases crude oil that is extracted in countries other than foreign Country Y and sells the crude oil to unrelated parties outside the country from which the oil was extracted. Corporation F1 earned a net income of $100,000 from this activity, after deducting expenses of $20,000.

Corporation C owns all the voting stock of Corporation F2, which is organized in Country Z. Corporation F2 owns and operates working interests located in Country Z and sells its share of production from these wells to parties that are not directly or indirectly related to Corporation C or its affiliates. Corporation F2 realizes production income of $500,000, receives interest income of $10,000, incurs lease operating expenses of $200,000 and pays income taxes of $100,000 to Country Z. Corporation F2 also acts as an operator for unrelated parties on wells located outside Country Z and earns $50,000 for its services.

Corporation C also is engaged in the exploration for and production of oil and gas in several foreign countries. It has an average daily production in excess of 1,000 barrels from foreign sources.

Under pre-Subpart F law, some companies structured their foreign operations to shift income from a high-tax-bracket country to a low-tax-bracket country. A holding company or base company was formed in a tax haven country, and income from other foreign countries then was shifted to the base company. In addition to lowering the foreign tax rate, the earnings of the base company could be invested in other foreign activities without incurring U.S. tax. The Subpart F provisions were enacted to prevent this practice.

Subpart F provides that each U.S. shareholder is taxed currently on certain earnings of a controlled foreign corporation whether or not those earnings are distributed to its shareholders.[79] A corporation is a controlled foreign corporation if more than 50% of either its voting stock or the value of its stock is owned by U.S. shareholders that individually own at least 10% of the voting stock.[80] A U.S. shareholder includes a U.S. citizen or resident, a domestic corporation, partnership, estate or trust.[81] Constructive ownership rules are used to determine if persons are U.S. shareholders.[82]

Each U.S. shareholder is taxed currently on its pro-rata share of certain undistributed earnings of the controlled foreign corporation. The "tainted" earnings include, but are not limited to, Subpart F income. Categories of Subpart F income that may be pertinent in this case are foreign base company sales, services, oil-related income and foreign personal holding company income.

---

79. I.R.C. Sec. 951(a).
80. I.R.C. Sec. 957(a); I.R.C. Sec. 951(b).
81. I.R.C. Sec. 951(b); I.R.C. Sec. 957(d).
82. I.R.C. Sec. 958.

Foreign base company sales income is gross income resulting from the purchase of personal property from or on behalf of, or sale of personal property to or on behalf of, a related person if: (1) it is manufactured, produced, grown or extracted outside the country of incorporation of the controlled foreign corporation and (2) the property is sold or purchased for use, consumption or disposition outside the country of incorporation of the controlled foreign corporation.[83]

Foreign base company sales income is not limited to profits from the purchase or sale of personal property. It also includes commissions, fees and any other income recognized from purchases or sales of property, regardless of the characterization of the income.

For production income from working interests to constitute foreign base company sales income, two elements must be present: (1) the sale of the production must be to or on behalf of a related party and (2) the production must have been from outside the country of incorporation. In Corporation F1's situation, the crude oil is not sold to or on behalf of a related person. In Corporation F2's situation, neither element is present. The production is from properties located in Country Z, and the production is not sold to or on behalf of a related person; consequently, Corporation F2's production income of $500,000 does not constitute foreign base company sales income. If the production income of Corporation F2 were from properties located outside Country Z and the production were sold to a related person, the production income would constitute foreign base company sales income.

Foreign base company services income, another category of Subpart F income, is gross income from services performed by a controlled foreign corporation outside its country of incorporation for or on behalf of a related person.[84] The services of Corporation F2 as an operator are performed outside its country of incorporation and, thus, meet one of the criteria of foreign base company services income. However, because the services are performed for unrelated persons, the second criterion is not fulfilled and the $50,000 earned by Corporation F2 does not constitute foreign base company services income. Foreign base company services income also is realized when the services performed relate to the sale of property by a related person and the services are a material part of the sale. Finally, services income includes income for services (drilling companies, seismic operations, deep sea diving, etc.) that can be performed by the controlled foreign corporation only with substantial assistance from a related person. The Internal Revenue Service (IRS) has taken the position that the managerial skills (for negotiating contracts, preparing bids and arranging financing, etc.) of the joint officers of the U.S. parent and the controlled foreign corporation can be a principal element in producing the foreign corporation's income and, therefore, constitute substantial assistance.[85] The result of this classification is that all of the income of the controlled foreign corporation related to these services is Subpart F income. The IRS considers this participation to be the same as if the foreign subsidiary rendered the services on behalf of the parent (a related person).

If Corporation F2 received income for acting as operator of wells located outside Country Z for Corporation C, the income would constitute foreign base company services income.

Another category of Subpart F income is foreign base company oil-related income. It is generally income of a controlled foreign corporation derived from oil-related activities (other than extraction activities) and is Subpart F income if earned in

83. I.R.C. Sec. 954(d).
84. I.R.C. Sec. 954(e).
85. IRS Letter Ruling 8127017 (Technical Advice Memorandum).

countries other than the country in which the oil and gas is extracted or consumed.[86] Foreign base company oil-related income generally includes income from the processing, transportation, distribution and sale of oil and gas products derived therefrom,[87] as well as from the performance of any related service. The term also includes certain dividends, interest, deemed distributions under the Subpart F rules and partnership income.[88] The provision is applicable to tax years of U.S. shareholders in which, or with which, that tax year of the foreign corporation ends.

The foreign base company oil-related income category of Subpart F income applies only to a *large oil producer*, which is defined as a corporation that has or is deemed to have average daily production of foreign crude oil and natural gas of at least 1,000 barrels in the current tax year or any preceding tax year.[89] Average daily production of the corporation includes the actual foreign production of the foreign corporation and the foreign production of any related persons.[90] *Related persons* include a corporation that controls or is controlled by the controlled foreign corporation and a corporation that is controlled by the same person or persons that control the controlled foreign corporation. In addition, an individual partnership, trust or estate that controls the controlled foreign corporation is a related person. *Control* means the direct or indirect ownership of stock possessing 50% or more of the total combined voting power of all classes of stock, the holders of which are entitled to vote, or of the total value of stock of such corporation.[91] Constructive ownership rules apply in determining ownership.[92] The Technical Corrections Bill of 1987 provides that *control* means direct and indirect ownership of stock possessing more than 50% of the total combined voting power of all classes of stock, the holders of which are entitled to vote, or of the total value of stock.[93]

Only foreign production of the related group is considered in determining if a foreign corporation is a large oil producer. Crude oil produced from wells located inside the United States is not taken into account.[94] The production of natural gas is converted to barrels, using the ratio of 6,000 cubic feet to one barrel of crude oil. Generally, average daily production is determined, using the rules applicable for percentage depletion of domestic crude oil.[95] *(See Case 94.)*

Corporation F1 has foreign base company oil-related income because of its purchase and resale of crude oil. Because the crude oil is purchased in, but sold outside, the country of extraction, the income is foreign base company oil-related income.

Corporation F1 is considered a large oil producer because a related party, Corporation C, has average daily production of foreign crude oil of at least 1,000 barrels. Consequently, Corporation C must include in its U.S. taxable income the undistributed earnings of Corporation F1 attributable to its foreign base company oil-related income. Deductions properly allocable to the foreign base company oil-related income are taken into account in determining the amount of foreign base company oil-related income.[96]

---

86. I.R.C. Sec. 954(g).
87. I.R.C. Sec. 954(g); I.R.C. Sec. 907(c)(2).
88. I.R.C. Sec. 954(g); I.R.C. Sec. 907(c)(2); I.R.C. Sec. 907(c)(3).
89. I.R.C. Sec. 954(g)(2).
90. I.R.C. Sec. 954(g)(2)(C).
91. I.R.C. Sec. 954(g)(3).
92. I.R.C. Sec. 954(d)(3); I.R.C. Sec. 958.
93. Technical Corrections Bill of 1987, Sec. 112(h)(14)(A).
94. I.R.C. Sec. 954(g)(2)(B).
95. I.R.C. Sec. 954(g)(2)(D).
96. I.R.C. Sec. 954(b)(5).

A corporation's income that constitutes foreign base company oil-related income also could meet the definition of another type of Subpart F income, for example, foreign base company sales income. The Internal Revenue Code specifically provides that foreign base company oil-related income shall not be considered foreign base company income under another provision.[97] This exception does not apply to foreign base company shipping income.[98] By definition, only a large oil producer may realize foreign base company oil-related income. Thus, a controlled foreign corporation that is not a large oil producer still will have to determine if its oil-related income is included in another category of foreign base company income.

A fourth category of Subpart F income, foreign personal holding company income, consists of interests, dividends, rents, royalties and other passive income, with certain exceptions. *(See Case 192.)* The interest income of $10,000 constitutes foreign personal holding company income because none of the exceptions is met.

For purposes of these provisions, a related person includes an individual, corporation, partnership, trust or estate that controls the foreign corporation or is controlled by the foreign corporation.[99]

Deductions properly allocable to foreign personal holding company income and foreign base company sales and services income are taken into account to determine the Subpart F income that is taxable to a U.S. shareholder.[100] *(See Case 205.)*

A percentage limitation may prevent foreign base company income from being Subpart F income even if it otherwise qualifies. This de minimis rule provides that a controlled foreign corporation has currently taxable Subpart F income only if its foreign base company income exceeds the lesser of $1 million or 5% of gross income.[101]

Foreign base company income also can arise when the foreign branch of a controlled foreign corporation engages in activities that have substantially the same effect as if the branch itself were a controlled foreign corporation.[102]

The foreign base company incomes of Corporations F1 and F2 are computed as follows:

	Corporation F1	Corporation F2
Foreign base company sales income	$ —	$ —
Foreign base company services income	—	—
Foreign base company oil-related income	100,000	—
Foreign personal holding company income	—	10,000
Total foreign base company income	$100,000	$10,000

Because Corporation F1's foreign base company income of $100,000 is greater than 70% of its gross income of $120,000, the net income from crude sales of $100,000 is Subpart F income.

Because Corporation F2's foreign base company income of $10,000 is less than 5% of its gross income of $360,000, the interest income of $10,000 is not Subpart F income.

97. I.R.C. Sec. 954(b)(8).
98. I.R.C. Sec. 954(b)(6).
99. I.R.C. Sec. 954(d)(3).
100. I.R.C. Sec. 954(b)(5); Reg. Sec. 1.954-1(c).
101. I.R.C. Sec. 954(b)(3).
102. I.R.C. Sec. 954(d)(2).

Case 194
Controlled Foreign Corporations — Earnings Invested in U.S. Property

The voting stock of F Corporation, a controlled foreign corporation, is wholly owned by X Corporation, a domestic corporation. During 1987, F Corporation realized substantial income and paid foreign taxes at a rate of approximately 40%.

During 1987, F Corporation acquires an oil and gas lease in Oklahoma for $100,000, invests $50,000 in U.S. Treasury bills and purchases 2,000 shares of stock of Corporation Y, a domestic corporation, for $10,000. Corporation Y's stock is widely held and is listed on the New York Stock Exchange.

F Corporation also owns a semisubmersible oil drilling rig that is registered outside the United States. The rig is not self-propelled but must be towed to location and held in the drilling position by a number of large anchors and heavy chains. It is intended that the rig operate outside the territorial waters of the United States but within the Continental Shelf.

Corporation F seeks advice as to how these investments should be reported for U.S. tax purposes.

F Corporation is a controlled foreign corporation because all its voting stock is owned by a U.S. corporation. *(See Case 191.)* The statute defines circumstances when a U.S. shareholder must include its pro-rata share of the undistributed earnings of the controlled foreign corporation in its U.S. taxable income. One circumstance that may result in current U.S. taxation is when the controlled foreign corporation invests its undistributed earnings in "United States property."[103] The rationale of this provision is that earnings invested in property in the United States by a controlled foreign corporation are equivalent to a dividend.

"United States property" generally includes most tangible and intangible property acquired after the effective statutory date.[104] Tangible property includes both real and personal property. The definition of *United States property* is complex and includes numerous exceptions. Those exceptions pertinent to the present situation include:[105]

- ☐ Obligations of the United States, money and deposits with persons carrying on the banking business.
- ☐ Stock or obligations of a domestic corporation as long as the corporation is not related to the controlled foreign corporation. A corporation is related for this purpose if it is a U.S. shareholder of the controlled foreign corporation or if more than 25% of its stock is owned by those U.S. shareholders.
- ☐ Any movable property (other than a vessel) that is used for the purpose of exploring for, developing, removing or transporting resources from the Continental Shelf of the United States.

The lease purchased by F Corporation constitutes United States property. However, the U.S. Treasury bills do not constitute United States property because of the exception outlined above. Assuming that neither Corporation X nor its shareholders

103. I.R.C. Sec. 951(a).
104. I.R.C. Sec. 956(b)(1).
105. I.R.C. Sec. 956(b)(2).

own more than 25% of the stock of Corporation Y, the stock investment is not U.S. property for this purpose. The semisubmersible oil drilling rig is deemed to be movable (and not a vessel); therefore, as to the rig, F Corporation has not made an investment of earnings in U.S. property. In a private letter ruling, the Internal Revenue Service (IRS) determined that an offshore drilling rig that is not self-propelled and is not documented under the laws of the United States will not be considered to be an investment of earnings in U.S. property under certain facts.[106]

The rules are complex. Consequently, any investment in the United States by a controlled foreign corporation should be reviewed carefully to determine if the investment constitutes U.S. property. In addition, certain indirect investments, such as pledges and guaranties, may be treated as a direct investment in U.S. property.[107] The IRS takes the position that the pledge by a U.S. person of stock of a controlled foreign corporation is an indirect pledge or guaranty by the controlled foreign corporation.[108] In one case, decided before the issuance of the current regulations, the Tax Court disagreed with this position.[109] Further, the IRS takes the position that when a controlled foreign corporation facilitates a loan to its parent, there is an investment in U.S. property.[110]

The amount that is subject to current taxation to the U.S. shareholder is the increase in earnings invested in U.S. property. The amount of the investments in U.S. property at the end of a tax year is the adjusted tax basis of property less any liability to which the property is subject.[111] The amount so computed is limited to the amount that would be a dividend if distributed on that date. The excess of the amount invested in U.S. property at the end of the tax year over the amount at the end of the preceding tax year is a constructive dividend to the U.S. shareholder.[112]

The determination of the amount of the constructive dividend at the end of each year necessitates a computation of the earnings and profits of the foreign corporation just as if an actual distribution had been made. Rules are provided for computing the earnings and profits of a foreign corporation for this purpose. They are similar, although not identical, to the rules for computing earnings and profits of a domestic corporation.[113] Earnings and profits are reduced by: (1) undistributed amounts that have been previously taxed to the U.S. shareholders, such as the undistributed income of a foreign personal holding company; (2) amounts previously taxed as earnings invested in U.S. property and (3) Subpart F income that has been taxed previously to the shareholder.[114]

Although an increase in earnings invested in U.S. property and the realization of Subpart F income may result in the current taxation of undistributed earnings of a controlled foreign corporation, the two concepts should not be confused. The Subpart F income provisions are designed to discourage certain business transactions that, except for these provisions, would allow the avoidance of income tax on foreign-source income.

Consequently, foreign base company income does not include any item of income received by a controlled foreign corporation other than foreign base company oil-related income if the taxpayer establishes to the IRS's satisfaction that the income was

106. IRS Letter Ruling 8424027.
107. I.R.C. Sec. 956(c).
108. Reg. Sec. 1.956-2(c)(2); Rev. Rul. 76-125, 1976-1 C.B. 204.
109. Daniel K. Ludwig, 68 T.C. 979 (1978).
110. Rev. Rul. 76-192, 1976-1 C.B. 205.
111. I.R.C. Sec. 956(a)(3).
112. I.R.C. Sec. 956(a).
113. I.R.C. Sec. 964(a); Reg. Sec. 1.956-1(b)(1).
114. Reg. Sec. 1.956-1(b)(3).

subject to an effective rate of tax in the foreign country greater than 90% of the maximum U.S. corporate rate.[115] *(See Case 193.)* The provisions resulting in the current taxation of an increase in earnings invested in the United States are based on the theory that foreign earnings should be subject to U.S. tax when the earnings are repatriated to the United States, whether the repatriation is accomplished through a cash distribution or an investment in certain U.S. property. Consequently, the relief exception available for Subpart F income if income tax avoidance is not a primary purpose of the transaction is not available for the increase in earnings invested in U.S. property.

This case illustrates only the impact of I.R.C. Section 956 and does not consider the sourcing of income for purposes of foreign tax credit limitations. *(See also Case 200.)*

Case 195
Sale of Stock in a Foreign Corporation

> **F Corporation, a foreign corporation, is owned 30% by Individual A, 30% by X Corporation and 40% by Y Corporation. This ownership has remained constant since F Corporation was formed in 1970. Individual A is a U.S. citizen, and both corporations are domestic corporations. At the end of 1987, F Corporation had accumulated earnings and profits of $100,000 after deducting $120,000 of foreign income taxes paid. None of the accumulated earnings has been taxed in the United States at either the shareholder or corporate level.**
>
> **In 1987, Individual A and X Corporation sold their shares to Z Corporation and recognized a gain of $300,000 each.**

Although the F Corporation stock is otherwise a capital asset held for more than six months, the gain the shareholders recognize on the sale or exchange of that stock is taxed partially as dividend income based on a provision enacted in 1962.[116]

This provision applies to the sale or exchange of stock in a foreign corporation by U.S. persons who have owned, directly or indirectly, 10% or more of the total combined voting power of the foreign corporation at any time during the five-year period ending on the date of sale or exchange when that corporation was a controlled foreign corporation.[117] Citizens and residents of the United States and domestic partnerships and corporations, trusts and estates are considered U.S. persons for this purpose.[118] Because this provision applies to the sale of F Corporation stock, each shareholder must report as a dividend gain to the extent of the earnings and profits accumulated after December 31, 1962, attributable to his stock ownership. Gain in excess of the current and accumulated earnings and profits is a long-term capital gain.

Earnings and profits for these purposes are computed under rules substantially similar to those for domestic corporations.[119] Adjustments to be made to the earnings and profits include a reduction for amounts previously taxed to the shareholders.[120]

If a shareholder is a U.S. corporation, it may claim a credit for the foreign taxes paid by the foreign corporation as if the amount of gain taxed as ordinary income was, in

115. I.R.C. Sec. 954(b)(4).
116. I.R.C. Sec. 1248.
117. I.R.C. Sec. 1248(a); I.R.C. Sec. 957.
118. I.R.C. Sec. 957(c); I.R.C. Sec. 7701(a)(30).
119. I.R.C. Sec. 1248(c); Reg. Sec. 1.1248-2(d); I.R.C. Sec. 964.
120. I.R.C. Sec. 1248(d); I.R.C. Sec. 951; I.R.C. Sec. 959.

fact, a dividend.[121] To mitigate the distortion that may be caused by taxing all the prior accumulated earnings as ordinary income in one tax year, an individual shareholder's tax is limited by a formula intended to determine the tax burden that would have been imposed if the controlled foreign corporation had been a domestic corporation subject to full U.S. income tax and the individual had withdrawn his share of the after-tax earnings and profits of the corporation at capital-gains rates.[122] This treatment is intended to place the individual shareholder in the same after-tax position as if the foreign corporation had been a domestic corporation.

Individual A and X Corporation each must report $30,000 of gain as dividend income. X Corporation is entitled to treat its share of ordinary income as a dividend to compute its foreign tax credit for 1987, including the "deemed-paid" credit.[123] X Corporation must "gross up" its dividend income by its share of the foreign income taxes. Consequently, X Corporation's total dividend income is $66,000 ($30,000 gain plus $36,000 foreign taxes), and it may claim a foreign tax credit of $36,000, which may be used to offset U.S. income tax subject to the normal rules on use of the foreign tax credit. (*See Case 196.*)

This tax provision applies to a shareholder if he owned 10% or more of the voting power at any time during the five years preceding the sale or liquidation. Thus, the gain can be taxed as ordinary income even though only a minor amount of stock was held at the time of the sale. Taxpayers that previously have reduced their ownership to less than 10% also may find it advantageous to postpone selling their remaining stock to avoid the prescribed time period.[124]

In taxable sales, exchanges and liquidations, this provision recharacterizes the nature of the gain from capital gain to ordinary income; however, in certain transactions, it may result in the recognition of gain that otherwise would not be recognized.[125]

The deemed dividend may not be all foreign source if a portion of the controlled foreign corporation's earnings and profits was from sources in the United States.[126] This sourcing could limit the amount of U.S. tax liability that could be offset by the foreign tax credit.

To the extent earnings and profits are deemed distributed as ordinary income, the earnings and profits are reduced by this amount for any future transactions.[127]

In 1987, ordinary income and capital gains are taxed at different rates; however, when the rates are identical, whether earnings and profits are deemed distributed as ordinary income or as capital gains generally makes no difference before consideration of sourcing and foreign tax credits discussed below.

The excess of the gain recognized over the dividend amount, $270,000, would not be treated as foreign-source income for foreign tax credit purposes. The Tax Reform Act of 1986 provides that only a gain from an 80%-or-more owned foreign subsidiary that is engaged in the active conduct of a trade or business and the stock of which is sold in the country in which more than 50% of the gross income was generated would be treated as a foreign-source gain.[128] The Technical Corrections Bill of 1987 will

121. Reg. Sec. 1.1248-1(d).
122. I.R.C. Sec. 1248(b).
123. Reg. Sec. 1.1248-1(d).
124. Reg. Sec. 1.1248-1(a)(4), Example 2.
125. I.R.C. Sec. 1248(f).
126. I.R.C. Sec. 904(g)(4); I.R.C. Sec. 904(g)(7).
127. I.R.C. Sec. 1248(j).
128. I.R.C. Sec. 865(f).

require that the more-than-50% active trade or business test be met for the country of sale.[129] It also imposes strict requirements on the sale of a group of foreign companies.

Case 196
Foreign Tax Credit — In General

> Corporation C, which is engaged in the refining business in the United States, expanded its operations into foreign Country F in 1987 by purchasing a refinery. Corporation C conducts the refinery operations through a branch. An income tax rate of 50% on business profits from operations in Country F is imposed. The income tax statutes of Country F are similar in concept to the tax statutes of the United States.
>
> In 1987, Corporation C realizes taxable income of $500,000 from its Country F refinery operations and incurs foreign taxes of $250,000. Corporation C, which has no other foreign operations, realizes taxable income of $1 million from its domestic operations in 1987. Corporation C's U.S. tax is $600,000 without considering any deduction or credit for tax paid to Country F.

Corporation C has an option to claim the tax paid to Country F as a credit against its U.S. regular or alternative minimum income tax if the tax meets certain requirements or as a deduction in computing its U.S. taxable income.[130] Use of the credit is subject to certain limitations. Because Corporation C is taxable on its income from foreign sources, its foreign-source income would be subject to double taxation if a credit were not permitted for taxes paid to foreign countries. The foreign tax credit provisions originally were enacted to encourage international trade and expansion by preventing the double taxation of foreign-source income.

A foreign tax is creditable if it is an income, war profits or excess profits tax paid or accrued to a foreign country or a possession of the United States.[131] *(See Case 197.)* In addition, a tax in lieu of an income, war profits or excess profits tax is creditable.[132] Generally, a tax is creditable if the tax statutes of the foreign country are similar to the tax statutes of the United States; however, the regulations provide complex rules to determine whether a tax is creditable. *(See Cases 197 and 198.)*[133]

Generally, U.S. citizens, U.S. residents and domestic corporations may take advantage of the credit for foreign taxes imposed on their income.[134] A credit for these taxes is referred to as a "direct credit." The statute also permits foreign corporations and nonresident alien individuals to use the credit when the taxes are paid or accrued with respect to income effectively connected with the conduct of a U.S. trade or business.[135]

U.S. corporate taxpayers receiving dividends from foreign corporations generally may claim a foreign tax credit for taxes paid by the foreign corporation. This credit, referred to as the "deemed-paid" credit, also may apply when a U.S. taxpayer is required to include earnings of related foreign entities in U.S. taxable income because of the controlled foreign corporation rules.[136]

---

129. Technical Corrections Bill of 1987, Sec. 112(d)(4).
130. I.R.C. Sec. 901(a); I.R.C. Sec. 164(a)(3).
131. I.R.C. Sec. 901(b); I.R.C. Sec. 901(i).
132. I.R.C. Sec. 903.
133. Reg. Sec. 1.901-2; Reg. Sec. 1.903-1.
134. I.R.C. Sec. 901(b).
135. I.R.C. Sec. 901(b)(4); I.R.C. Sec. 906(a).
136. I.R.C. Sec. 902(a); I.R.C. Sec. 960(a).

Use of the credit as a direct reduction in U.S. tax is subject to several limitations and restrictions. The amount of the foreign tax that can be credited in any year is limited to the U.S. tax imposed on foreign-source income.[137] For this limitation, foreign-source income must be segregated and a separate foreign tax credit limitation computation made for each category.

The categories used for purposes of making the computation include:

- ☐ Domestic international sales corporation (DISC) dividend income.
- ☐ Taxable income of a foreign sales corporation attributable to foreign trade income.
- ☐ Foreign sales corporation distribution income.
- ☐ Passive income.
- ☐ Financial services income.
- ☐ Shipping income.
- ☐ High withholding tax interest income.
- ☐ Dividend income from each noncontrolled foreign corporation.
- ☐ Foreign oil-extraction income.
- ☐ All other income.

Before 1987, separate limitations were computed only for the passive interest income, DISC dividend income, foreign sales corporation dividend income, taxable income of a foreign sales corporation attributable to foreign trade income, foreign oil-extraction income and all other income categories.[138] *(See Case 198.)* Due to the existence of different limiting categories between years, complexities arise when carrying foreign tax credits forward and back. Additional complexities arise when one category has a loss while others have income. *(See Case 203.)*[139]

In addition, before calculating the foreign tax credit, taxable income from sources outside the United States must be determined by reducing the foreign-source gross income by any direct expenses related to earning that income. Indirect expenses then are allocated and apportioned between U.S.- and foreign-source income. *(See Case 205.)*

Because Corporation C has only one category of income, only one computation is made. The limitation is determined by multiplying the U.S. tax by the ratio of taxable income from sources outside the United States to taxable income from all sources. The credit that can be utilized in that year is the lesser of the foreign tax or the computed limit. Assuming the tax is creditable, Corporation C should compute its limitation as follows:

$$\frac{\text{Taxable income from foreign sources}}{\text{Taxable income from all sources}} \times \text{U.S. income tax} = \text{Foreign tax credit limitation}$$

$$\frac{\$500{,}000}{\$1{,}500{,}000} \times \$600{,}000 = \$200{,}000$$

137. I.R.C. Sec. 904(a).
138. I.R.C. Sec. 907; I.R.C. Sec. 904 *(prior to amendment by the Tax Reform Act of 1986)*.
139. I.R.C. Sec. 904(f).

Because the foreign tax of $250,000 exceeds the foreign tax credit limit, Corporation C may use only $200,000 of foreign tax in 1987 to reduce its U.S. tax liability. Corporation C's 1987 U.S. tax liability is $400,000, which is the U.S. tax of $600,000 reduced by the foreign tax credit of $200,000.

The foreign tax credit of $50,000 not currently used may be carried back for two years and carried forward for five years until fully used.[140] The ability to carry back foreign tax credits arising after 1986 is significantly limited. Post-1986 credits that are excess credits solely because of the rate reductions contained in the Tax Reform Act of 1986 cannot be carried back to higher tax rate years. For purposes of this provision, post-1986 foreign tax credit limitations are recomputed, using pre-1987 tax rates. Available post-1986 excess credits are then used to reduce the U.S. tax on pre-1987 overall limitation income, regardless of which post-1986 credit category limitation applies. In performing this computation, it is important to consider that excess credits from high withholding tax interest, however, may not be carried back to pre-1987 years.[141] *(See Case 199.)*

Except for limited instances for the financial services and shipping income categories, pre-1987 excess credits can be carried forward to post-1986 years only to reduce U.S. tax on the corresponding pre-1987 limitation category.

If Corporation C elects to deduct foreign taxes in a year to which the excess credit is carried, the amount carried over cannot be deducted. If the taxpayer deducts foreign taxes in the current year, however, a net operating loss containing such taxes apparently may be carried back to a year when the foreign tax credit was claimed without affecting the original election to claim the credit.[142] Further, a portion of the carryover may be lost in a deduction year to the extent that amount could have been used had Corporation C elected to take a credit.[143] The carryover amount can be used only after the credit incurred in the current year is used. In addition, the ordering rules provide that if carrybacks or carryovers from more than one year can be used in a particular year, amounts from the earlier years are used first.[144]

Generally, it is more favorable to use foreign taxes as a credit against U.S. income tax because a credit reduces U.S. tax dollar-for-dollar, while a deduction reduces only U.S. taxable income. However, there may be circumstances in which the deduction is more favorable because of the limitations and restrictions imposed on claiming the credit. For example, if the U.S. taxpayer has a net loss from foreign operations, no credit may be allowable in the current year because the credit can offset only U.S. tax imposed on foreign-source income. The taxpayer may wish to claim the foreign taxes as a deduction in this instance. The election may be changed at any time before the expiration of the time for making a claim for credit or refund of income taxes.[145] A taxpayer can amend one or several years' returns to take the greater benefit after analyzing all factors (e.g., carryovers, carrybacks, limitations). To permit the proper use of credits related to countries in which it may take several years to finalize the tax liability, there is a special 10-year statute of limitations to file a claim for refund or credit.[146] Further, a taxpayer must notify the Internal Revenue Service of any changes in the amount of foreign tax credits previously claimed due to exchange rate fluctuations and refunds.[147]

---

140. I.R.C. Sec. 904(c).
141. I.R.C. Sec. 904.
142. I.R.C. Sec. 905; I.R.C. Sec. 904(c); I.R.C. Sec. 904(e).
143. Reg. Sec. 1.904-2(d); Reg. Sec. 1.904-2(g), Example 3.
144. Reg. Sec. 1.904-2(g).
145. I.R.C. Sec. 901(a).
146. I.R.C. Sec. 6511(d)(3).
147. I.R.C. Sec. 905(c).

A taxpayer using the accrual method of accounting for federal income tax purposes should use that method to determine the amount of the foreign taxes available for the credit.[148] Under this method, a tax can be taken into account when all events have occurred to fix the amount of and liability for the tax. If the accrual method is used, the credit is translated into dollars at the rates in effect on the last date of the tax year used for foreign income tax purposes.[149] If the country's currency fluctuates, the U.S. dollar equivalent of the actual tax paid may vary from the credit. The taxpayer then should file an amended return to convert the accrued amount to the amount actually paid.[150]

A cash-basis taxpayer may determine the foreign tax credit on either the cash or accrual basis. If the accrual basis is selected, the taxpayer must follow that method for all subsequent years.[151] If the cash basis is adopted, a foreign tax is considered paid when there is actual payment of the tax liability and when foreign law requires withholding or estimated payments of legal and actual liability.[152]

A taxpayer incurring losses in its foreign operations may have to reduce the amount of the foreign tax credit used to offset U.S. tax in subsequent years because of the provisions requiring the recapture of foreign losses. *(See Case 203.)* The same loss recapture provisions can require the recognition of taxable income when assets are transferred to a foreign entity, even if the transaction otherwise would be tax free.[153]

For years beginning after December 31, 1986, U.S. taxpayers must also calculate the alternative minimum tax (AMT) foreign tax credit in computing alternative minimum tax.[154] Several differences exist in the calculation for this purpose. For example, preference items and other adjustments, such as depreciation for AMT purposes, would make alternative minimum taxable income (AMTI) and foreign-source AMTI differ from those amounts under regular tax in the calculation of the foreign tax credit limitation as described below:

$$\frac{\text{Foreign-source AMTI}}{\text{AMTI from all sources}} \times \text{U.S. tax} = \text{Foreign tax credit limitation for AMT purposes}$$

The U.S. tax in the formula above is equal to the applicable rate (20% or 21%) multiplied by AMTI, less any exemption.[155]

Taxpayers will have to make separate calculations and separate carryover schedules for this credit. Also, the book income adjustment will not affect the limitation formula.[156] The Committee Reports state that the taxpayer's election to deduct or credit foreign taxes for regular tax purposes is controlling for AMT purposes. Presumably, transition rules will be issued to describe the use of carryovers from post-effective date years and carrybacks to pre-effective date years. Finally, the credit is limited to the excess of the applicable rate (21% or 20%) times the AMTI over 10% of that derived amount determined without regard to the alternative tax net operating loss deduction.[157]

---

148. I.R.C. Sec. 905(a).
149. Rev. Rul. 73-491, 1973-2 C.B. 267.
150. I.R.C. Sec. 905(c).
151. I.R.C. Sec. 905(a).
152. Rev. Rul. 59-101, 1959-1 C.B. 189; Rev. Rul. 57-516, 1957-2 C.B. 435.
153. I.R.C. Sec. 904(f).
154. I.R.C. Sec. 55(b)(1)(B).
155. I.R.C. Sec. 59(a)(1)(A).
156. I.R.C. Sec. 59(a)(1)(C).
157. I.R.C. Sec. 59(a)(2).

Case 197
Foreign Tax Credit — Creditable Taxes

Corporation C is engaged in numerous oil and gas ventures in foreign countries. The president of Corporation C wants to know the criteria used to determine whether a foreign tax qualifies for the foreign tax credit.

The statutory provision giving the taxpayer the option to claim a credit for foreign taxes permits the credit for "income, war profits and excess profits taxes" paid or accrued to a foreign country or a U.S. possession.[158] The statute also provides that a payment to a foreign government that is in lieu of an income, war profits or excess profits tax may be considered a creditable tax.[159]

An income, war profits or excess profits tax is not a creditable tax, however, if the amount of such tax is used to provide a subsidy to the taxpayer and such subsidy is determined by reference to the amount of such tax.[160]

Because the statute does not provide rules for determining when a payment to a foreign government constitutes a creditable tax, the rules have been established over the years by regulations and judicial interpretation.

The Internal Revenue Service (IRS) believed that some of the payments of the international oil companies to foreign governments, which were designed to fulfill the technical requirements of creditable taxes, were abusive of the intent of the foreign tax provisions. Because of this and other perceived abuses, it issued a series of revenue rulings on the criteria that must be fulfilled for a payment to a foreign government to be a creditable tax.[161] Several of these rulings revoked prior revenue rulings dealing with oil- and gas-production sharing arrangements.[162] Next, proposed regulations applicable to all industries were issued. These regulations then were revised and issued as temporary regulations. The criteria established in the temporary regulations for determining the creditability of a tax are more stringent than criteria developed through judicial interpretation of the statute. However, the IRS issued final regulations, which provided a degree of relief from the harshness of the temporary regulations.

For companies involved in the exploration and development of oil and gas properties, foreign taxing authorities often impose a greater tax burden on the income of those companies than they impose on other industries. In this situation, the temporary regulations treated payments made to foreign countries as compensation for the business privileges and rights extended by the countries to the taxpayer rather than as income tax.[163] The most troublesome aspect of this treatment, from the creditability of tax paid to the foreign countries, was that it was imposed on an "all or nothing" basis. That is, if the burden imposed on the oil and gas company by the regulation was greater than the burden imposed by the general tax application, the entire payment, not just the excess burden, by the oil and gas company was treated as compensation for a business privilege or right (a royalty), and no part of the payment of tax was accorded creditability.

158. I.R.C. Sec. 901(b).
159. I.R.C. Sec. 903.
160. I.R.C. Sec. 901(i).
161. Rev. Rul. 78-61, 1978-1 C.B. 221; Rev. Rul. 78-62, 1978-1 C.B. 226; Rev. Rul. 78-63, 1978-1 C.B. 228; Rev. Rul. 76-215, 1976-1 C.B. 194.
162. Rev. Rul. 76-215, 1976-1 C.B. 194; Rev. Rul. 78-63, 1978-1 C.B. 288.
163. Temp. Reg. Sec. 4.901-2(b)(2)(ii).

Although the final regulations differ from the temporary regulations in many respects, the most important change is that a special industry taxpayer, known as a dual-capacity taxpayer such as an oil and gas company, can receive credit for a portion of its tax payment in all situations, even when the taxing country does not have a general tax law.[164] Thus, the final regulations recognize that a levy may be partly a tax and partly a payment in exchange for a specific economic benefit and give the taxpayer the opportunity to establish the creditable component.[165] When there is no general tax, the tax rate in the safe harbor formula is modified to use the lower of the rate of the qualifying levy or the rate of tax specified in I.R.C. Section 11(b)(5), which is 34% for 1988. The final regulations cover more than 45 pages, and a complete discussion is beyond the scope of this manual. A table highlighting important features of the regulations follows:

Subject	Final Regulations
☐ Character of tax	Predominant character of foreign tax must be income tax in U.S. sense.[166]
☐ Realization	Prerealization events qualify provided the consequence of those events is the recapture (in whole or part) of a tax deduction, tax credit or other tax allowance previously accorded the taxpayer.[167]
☐ Gross receipts	Alternate gross receipts method qualifies if "likely" to produce an amount not greater than fair market value.[168]
☐ Net income	Gross receipts must be reduced to permit recovery of significant costs and expenses (including significant capital expenditures).[169]
	Comments in the final regulations clarify several points regarding the net income requirement that are unique to the oil and gas industry: separate contract/concession areas constitute separate activities within a trade or business, and oil and gas extraction constitutes a separate trade or business from oil and gas refining and processing.[170]
☐ In lieu of income tax	Comparability not required.
☐ Soak-up tax	No credit available, but credit may be allowed when the tax is widely imposed on taxpayers not eligible for a credit.[171]
☐ Contested taxes	Regulations are silent; but longstanding IRS policy is that contested foreign taxes cannot be accrued.[172]

If a treaty between the United States and a foreign country exists, it should be reviewed to determine if it contains any provisions relating to whether the foreign taxes qualify as creditable taxes. If the treaty so provides, the tax will constitute a creditable tax even if the regulations are not satisfied. For example, the IRS ruled that the petroleum revenue tax (PRT) imposed on profits from oil extraction in the United

164. Reg. Sec. 1.901-2A(e)(5).
165. Reg. Sec. 1.901-2A(a); Reg. Sec. 1.901-2A(b).
166. Reg. Sec. 1.901-2(a)(1)(ii).
167. Reg. Sec. 1.901-2(b)(2)(i)(B).
168. Reg. Sec. 1.901-2(b)(3)(i)(B).
169. Reg. Sec. 1.901-2(b)(4)(I)(A).
170. Reg. Sec. 1.901-2(b)(4)(ii).
171. Reg. Sec. 1.901-2(c)(1).
172. Rev. Rul. 58-55, 1958-1 C.B. 266; Rev. Rul. 70-290, 1970-1 C.B. 160; Rev. Rul. 77-487, 1977-2 C.B. 479.

Kingdom is not a creditable tax.[173] However, the treaty between the United States and the United Kingdom provides that it is.[174] A taxpayer subject to the treaty provisions may consider the PRT in the computation of its foreign tax credit because, in this instance, the treaty provisions take precedence over the general U.S. tax laws.

Case 198
Foreign Tax Credit — Income Tax Based on Posted Price

Corporation C, a domestic corporation, is engaged in the production of oil and gas in Country F and pays an income tax based on the profits from the operation of its concession. Deductions similar to U.S. income tax deductions are permitted. Income from the concession is measured based on the gross receipts realized from the exporting of crude oil, except those receipts cannot be less than the income that would have been realized if the barrels of exported oil had been sold at the posted price applicable to those barrels. The posted price of a barrel of oil is fixed by an agency of the government of Country F and usually is based on 110% of the "spot price" of a barrel of crude oil of the same quality. Only oil and gas operations are subject to tax in Country F.

Subject to certain limitations, domestic corporations are entitled to claim a credit for income taxes paid or accrued to foreign countries. A foreign tax may qualify as a creditable tax under two separate provisions: the payment to a foreign government may qualify as an income, war profits or excess profits tax, or the payment may constitute a tax "in lieu of" an income tax.[175]

In no event, however, is a levy by a foreign government considered a tax if the consideration therefore is a specific economic benefit.[176] Examples cited in the regulations of specific economic benefits include: concession to extract government-owned minerals; right to use, acquire or extract resources; property; a service; a fee or other payment, etc.[177]

The statute adds that a tax used to provide the taxpayer with a subsidy where such subsidy is determined by reference to the amount of the tax is also not a creditable tax.[178]

Furthermore, the amount paid or accrued during a tax year to any foreign country in connection with the purchase and sale of oil and gas extracted in that foreign country is not a tax if the taxpayer does not own an economic interest and either the purchase or sale price is not at fair market value.[179]

A person who is subject to a foreign levy and who also receives specific economic benefit from the foreign country in exchange for payment pursuant to the levy is a dual-capacity taxpayer.[180] A dual-capacity taxpayer first must prove that the foreign levy satisfies all the criteria of I.R.C. Section 901 or 903 other than the determination

173. Rev. Rul. 78-424, 1978-2 C.B. 197.
174. Convention for the Avoidance of Double Taxation & Prevention of Fiscal Evasion, December 31, 1975, United States-United Kingdom-Northern Ireland, Art. 23, T.I.A.S. No. 9682.
175. I.R.C. Sec. 901(a); I.R.C. Sec. 903.
176. Reg. Sec. 1.901-2(a)(2)(ii)(B).
177. Reg. Sec. 1.901-2(a)(2)(ii)(B). *See also* Reg. Sec. 1.901-2(b).
178. I.R.C. Sec. 901(i).
179. I.R.C. Sec. 901(f).
180. Reg. Sec. 1.901-2(a)(1)(ii).

of the distinct element of the levy that is a tax ("qualifying levy") before determining the portion of the levy that is a tax.[181]

According to the rules established in the regulations, a tax paid to a foreign government is a creditable income tax as long as its predominant character is that of an income tax in the U.S. sense.[182] The predominant character of a foreign tax is that of an income tax in the U.S. sense if the foreign tax is likely to reach net gain under normal circumstances in which it applies, but only to the extent liability for the tax does not depend on the availability of a credit for the tax against the income tax liability of another country.[183] To reach net gain, the foreign tax must satisfy three tests: realization, gross receipts and net income.[184]

The realization test is satisfied if the foreign tax is imposed on: (1) the occurrence of events that would result in the realization of income under U.S. tax rules; (2) the occurrence of an earlier event provided the consequence of the earlier event is the recapture of a tax deduction, credit or allowance previously accorded the taxpayer or (3) the occurrence of a prerealization event provided the foreign country does not impose a second tax on the later event without credit or other relief for the initial event.[185]

The gross receipts test is satisfied provided the tax is imposed on gross receipts that are either: (1) actual gross receipts or (2) gross receipts derived under a method likely to produce an amount not greater than fair market value in the case of certain transactions.[186]

The net income test requires the base of foreign tax to be computed by reducing gross receipts to permit recovery of significant costs and expenditures under reasonable principles.[187]

The tax paid to Country F does not qualify as a creditable tax based on the tests provided by the regulations. The method of determining gross receipts is designed to provide an amount greater than fair market value; consequently, the gross receipts test is not satisfied.[188] Because the tax imposed by Country F is based on an arbitrarily determined value (the posted price), the base on which the tax is levied is artificial or fictitious. Therefore, the tax of Corporation C almost certainly will not reach net gain.

Even though the tax imposed by Country F is not equivalent to an income tax in the U.S. sense, if the tax qualifies as a tax in lieu of the income tax, it still may qualify as a creditable tax. *(See Case 197.)* For this purpose, a tax is in lieu of an income tax when it: (1) is not compensation for a specific economic benefit; (2) is a compulsory payment pursuant to the authority of a foreign country to levy taxes and (3) is intended and operates as a tax in substitution for and not in addition to an income tax otherwise generally imposed.[189] Because Country F has no general income tax law, the tax will not qualify as an "in lieu of" tax according to the criteria set forth in the regulations.[190] The Internal Revenue Service has ruled, in one instance, that if a country imposes no general income tax, a tax on petroleum companies will not qualify as a tax "in lieu of" income tax.[191]

---

181. Reg. Sec. 1.901-2A(c)(1).
182. Reg. Sec. 1.901-2(a)(1).
183. Reg. Sec. 1.901-2(a)(3)(i). *See also* Reg. Sec. 1.901-2(b)(3).
184. Reg. Sec. 1.901-2(b)(1). *See also* Reg. Sec. 1.901-2(b)(3)(i)(B).
185. Reg. Sec. 1.901-2(b)(2)(i). *See also* Reg. Sec. 1.901-2(b)(3)(i).
186. Reg. Sec. 1.901-2(b)(3)(i). *See also* Reg. Sec. 1.901-2(b)(3)(ii), Example 3.
187. Reg. Sec. 1.901-2(b)(4)(i).
188. Reg. Sec. 1.901-2(b)(3)(ii), Example 3.
189. Reg. Sec. 1.903-1(a).
190. Reg. Sec. 1.903-1. *See also* Reg. Sec. 1.901-2(c)(2)(ii), Example 1.
191. Rev. Rul. 78-63, 1978-1 C.B. 228. *See also* Reg. Sec. 1.901-2(b)(3)(ii), Example 3.

Therefore, the payment by Corporation C to Country F does not constitute, in whole or in part, a creditable foreign income tax.

Case 199
Foreign Tax Credit — General Limitations

Corporation C owns and operates refineries located in the United States and Country R that process crude oil into gasoline and other primary products. It also conducts rental activities overseas and in the United States.

Corporation C's taxable income for 1987 was attributable to the following activities:

	Income Taxable in the United States
Foreign rental income	$ 500,000
Foreign refining income	400,000
U.S.-source income	600,000
Taxable income from all sources	$1,500,000

In 1987, Corporation C incurred creditable foreign taxes of $290,000 with respect to passive foreign rental activities and $174,000 with respect to foreign refining activities. Corporation C's U.S. income tax, before considering the foreign tax credit, is $600,000.

The foreign tax credit provisions originally were enacted to avoid double taxation of income from foreign sources. For many years, the primary limitation on the use of foreign tax credits was to offset only U.S. tax imposed on foreign-source income. Under this approach, taxes imposed on operations in high-tax-bracket countries (such as some foreign oil-producing countries) could be used to offset the U.S. tax on foreign-source income from low-tax-bracket countries without limit.

Before the Tax Equity and Fiscal Responsibility Act of 1982 (TEFRA), the law provided that foreign-source income be grouped into the following four categories for purposes of computing the general limitation on the use of the foreign tax credit: (1) foreign oil-related income, (2) certain passive interest income, (3) certain dividends from domestic international sales corporations (DISCs) and (4) all other foreign-source income. TEFRA eliminated the requirement to segregate oil- and gas-related income for this purpose. Consequently, effective for years beginning after 1982 and ending before 1985, it generally is necessary to segregate foreign-source income into only the other three categories mentioned above to determine the respective general limitations on the use of foreign tax credits.[192]

For years ending after 1984, the Tax Reform Act of 1984 added two additional categories: foreign trade income and distributions from a foreign sales corporation.[193]

192. I.R.C. Sec. 904(a); I.R.C. Sec. 904(d) *(prior to amendment by the Tax Reform Act of 1984)*; P.L. 97-248 (Tax Equity and Fiscal Responsibility Act of 1982), Sec. 211(c).
193. I.R.C. Sec. 904(d)(1)(C) *(prior to amendment by the Tax Reform Act of 1986)*; I.R.C. Sec. 904(d)(1)(D) *(prior to amendment by the Tax Reform Act of 1986)*.

TEFRA provides transition rules for determining the amount of foreign tax credits that can be used when a tax is incurred in a year subject to one set of rules and is carried to a year subject to the other set of rules. When the transition rules apply, a taxpayer may have to continue to determine its foreign oil-related income (i.e., refineries) even though the year in question is after the effective date of TEFRA.[194]

Congress again addressed the use of separate income categories in the Tax Reform Act of 1986 (the Act). For years beginning after December 31, 1986, the passive interest income category was replaced by the passive income category, and the financial services income, shipping income, high withholding tax interest income and dividends from each noncontrolled foreign corporation income categories were added. Therefore, after 1986, there are nine basic categories and a separate computation of foreign oil-extraction income.

To illustrate the complexities of the multicategory approach, the limitation of the foreign tax that can be used as a credit in 1987 by Corporation C is computed as follows:

Passive Income Limitation

$$\frac{\text{Taxable income from passive foreign sources}}{\text{Taxable income from all sources}} \times \text{U.S. income tax} = \text{Passive foreign tax credit limitation}$$

$$\frac{\$500{,}000}{\$1{,}500{,}000} \times \$600{,}000 = \$200{,}000$$

Active Income Limitation

$$\frac{\text{Taxable income from active foreign sources}}{\text{Taxable income from all sources}} \times \text{U.S. income tax} = \text{Active foreign tax credit limitation}$$

$$\frac{\$400{,}000}{\$1{,}500{,}000} \times \$600{,}000 = \$160{,}000$$

Because there are two income categories, there are two separate foreign tax credit limitation calculations for 1987. Foreign tax credits available to reduce the U.S. tax liability from the passive income limitation equal $200,000, with $90,000 available for carryover or carryback. Foreign tax credits available to reduce the U.S. tax liability from the active income limitation equal $160,000, with $14,000 available for carryover or carryback. *(See Case 196.)* In addition, because the credits would be carried back to 1985, a year in which the use of this foreign tax credit was subject to the old rules, transition rules must be considered.

In general, post-1986 credits that are excess credits solely because of the rate reductions contained in the Act cannot be carried back to years with higher tax rates. For purposes of this provision, post-1986 foreign tax credit limitations are recomputed, using pre-1987 tax rates. Available post-1986 excess credits are then used to reduce the U.S. tax on pre-1987 overall limitation income, regardless of which post-1986 credit category limitation applies, except for excess credits from high

194. I.R.C. Sec. 907(e).

withholding taxes on interest, which may only be carried forward. In this case, credits available for carryback would be computed as follows:

U.S. taxable income	$1,500,000
Pre-1987 tax rate	×46%
Restated U.S. tax liability	$ 690,000
Foreign taxes paid	464,000
Credits available for carryback	$ 0*

* Only to the extent that foreign taxes paid exceed the restated U.S. tax liability.

In this case, no foreign tax credits may be carried back. The $90,000 and $14,000 excess credits must be carried forward to future years to offset U.S. taxes imposed on their respective categories.

At this point, it is also important to note that pre-1987 excess credits can be carried forward to offset post-1986 U.S. tax only on the corresponding pre-1987 limit category. For example, pre-1987 foreign taxes on portfolio dividend income are carried forward to offset post-1986 U.S. taxes only on income subject to the overall limitation, with limited exceptions available for the financial services and shipping income limitations.

Numerous problems arise for taxpayers that have carryovers of foreign tax credits subject to the pre-TEFRA rules. Such taxpayers must consider the transition rules of both the Tax Reform Act of 1986 and TEFRA in determining the proper carryforward.[195] For example, if Corporation C had a carryover of foreign taxes to 1987 that arose in a year governed by the pre-TEFRA rules, the amount of the carryover that could be used cannot exceed the amount that could have been used had the pre-TEFRA rules remained in effect.

In this case, if Corporation C had foreign oil-related income in 1982, a category eliminated by TEFRA and not contained in the Tax Reform Act of 1986, it will be necessary for Corporation C to determine its foreign oil-related income in 1983 under the TEFRA transition rules, even though the computation is not required under TEFRA.[196] The redetermined credit is then presumably available for carryforward to future years, subject again to the Tax Reform Act of 1986 transition rules discussed above.

In addition, under pre-TEFRA law, foreign oil-related income included foreign oil-extraction income. TEFRA modified the law by excluding extraction income from the definition of oil-related income.[197] However, when making hypothetical computations under the transition rules as if the old rules were in effect, the definition of oil-related income should be determined under the pre-TEFRA rules.

Management of Corporation C also should be cognizant of the provision that grants the Treasury regulatory authority to limit the amount of creditable foreign taxes with respect to foreign oil-related income if the foreign taxes are excessive in comparison to the taxes imposed on other industries. *(See Case 202.)*

The regulations provide detailed rules on how to allocate and apportion deductions to U.S.- and foreign-source gross income for purposes of determining taxable income and computing the foreign tax credit limitation. *(See Case 205.)*

195. I.R.C. Sec. 904.
196. *Ibid.*
197. I.R.C. Sec. 907(c)(2).

If Corporation C had incurred overall losses in its foreign operations in prior years, the rules concerning the recapture of these overall foreign losses will result in converting a portion of the foreign-source income to domestic-source income to limit the use of the foreign tax credit. *(See Case 203.)*

Case 200
Foreign Tax Credit — Credit for Stockholders of a Foreign Corporation

Y Corporation is a foreign corporation that is owned 100% by F Corporation. F Corporation, also a foreign corporation, is owned 10% by Individual A (a U.S. citizen) and 10% by X Corporation (a domestic corporation). The remaining stock is owned by unrelated foreign corporations. Accordingly, F Corporation is not a controlled foreign corporation because not more than 50% of the voting stock is owned by U.S. shareholders.

At the end of 1987, Y Corporation had non-U.S.-source post-1986 undistributed earnings of $50,000 after payment of $60,000 of creditable foreign income taxes. F Corporation has post-1986 undistributed earnings of $200,000 after payment of $100,000 of creditable foreign income taxes. The undistributed earnings of F Corporation have been computed without including Y Corporation's undistributed earnings.

During 1987, F Corporation paid a dividend of $50,000 to its shareholders. Advice is requested on the effect, if any, of the payment of this dividend on the U.S. income tax liabilities of Individual A and X Corporation.

In computing available foreign tax credit, a domestic corporation owning at least 10% of the voting stock of a foreign corporation (and receiving dividends from it) is deemed to have paid a portion of the foreign taxes paid by the foreign corporation. The amount of taxes deemed paid is determined by multiplying the amount of foreign income taxes paid by the foreign corporation by the amount of the dividends received before gross-up for foreign taxes paid, divided by the amount of the post-1986 undistributed earnings of the foreign corporation.[198] This rule may be expressed by the following formula.

$$\frac{\text{Dividend received (before gross-up)}}{\text{Post-1986 accumulated undistributed earnings (after foreign income taxes)}} \times \text{Post-1986 accumulated foreign income taxes} = \text{Foreign tax deemed paid}$$

For distributions attributable to years beginning before January, 1, 1987, the amount of undistributed earnings is computed according to rules substantially similar to those applicable for computing earnings and profits for domestic corporations. Several differences exist, however.[199] For distributions attributable to years beginning after December 31, 1986, the rules of Sections 964 and 986 apply.[200]

198. I.R.C. Sec. 902(a).
199. Reg. Sec. 1.902-1(g); I.R.C. Sec. 964.
200. I.R.C. Sec. 902(c)(1).

The foreign tax credit is available to a domestic corporation only if it elects to treat all foreign taxes paid (including those paid directly) as credits against its U.S. income tax liability. The "deemed-paid" provisions are not applicable if the domestic corporation elects to treat foreign taxes paid or accrued as deductions for calculating taxable income.[201]

If the domestic corporation elects to treat its foreign taxes as a credit, the credit it is entitled to because of the "deemed-paid" provisions is subject to the special credit limitation category for dividends from 50%- to 10%-owned subsidiaries.[202] Because a separate category is established for each first-tier subsidiary, the ability to average taxes imposed on various joint ventures that are eligible for the "deemed-paid" foreign tax credit is limited.[203] The amount of the foreign tax deemed paid by the domestic corporation must be reported as dividend income.[204]

The thrust of the mechanics of the formula above is twofold. First, pools of post-1986 accumulated foreign taxes and accumulated undistributed earnings are created. Although this approach may be beneficial in some cases, its overall impact will be to limit the taxpayer's ability to repatriate funds selectively with the highest effective tax rate. For distributions out of pre-1987 undistributed earnings, old rules continue to apply wherein the "deemed-paid" credit for foreign taxes related to a dividend is determined on an annual LIFO (last-in, first-out) basis by taking the percentage of foreign taxes for the applicable year, beginning with the most current year, multiplying it by the dividends received for the year, and then dividing it by earnings and profits for the year.[205] If the dividend is from earnings and profits attributed to several pre-1987 years, a separate "deemed-paid" credit is made for each year.

Dividends paid within 60 days of a taxpayer's yearend could be considered to be paid from the prior year's earnings and profits under old law. The 60-day rule no longer applies for dividends paid on or after January 1, 1987.

The "deemed-paid" provisions also can apply to dividends paid by second- and third-tier foreign subsidiaries to their foreign parent corporation (for example, a dividend from Y Corporation to F Corporation). Both the dividend and foreign tax credits thus allocated to the foreign parent corporation enter into the foreign parent's computations in determining the amount of dividend and credit available to the domestic corporate shareholder.[206]

Foreign income taxes paid by the second-tier or third-tier foreign corporation will be available to the domestic parent only if: (1) the foreign parent corporation owns 10% or more of the voting stock of the foreign subsidiary corporation and (2) the percentage of voting stock owned by the domestic corporation in the foreign parent corporation (when multiplied by the percentage of voting stock owned by the foreign parent corporation in the foreign subsidiary corporation) equals at least 5%.[207]

Because Y Corporation does not pay dividends to F Corporation during 1987, none of the foreign income taxes paid during 1987 is attributable to either F Corporation or X Corporation. However, a foreign tax credit will be available to X Corporation for

201. Reg. Sec. 1.902-1(b)(1)(iv); I.R.C. Sec. 275.
202. I.R.C. Sec. 904.
203. *Ibid.*
204. I.R.C. Sec. 78; Reg. Sec. 1.902-1(b)(1)(iii).
205. I.R.C. Sec. 902(c)(6).
206. I.R.C. Sec. 902(b).
207. I.R.C. Sec. 902(b)(1); I.R.C. Sec. 902(b)(3).

the dividends received from F Corporation. The amount of creditable tax available to X Corporation will be $2,500, computed as follows:

$$\frac{\$50,000}{\$200,000} \times \$100,000 = \$25,000 \times 10\% \text{ stock ownership} = \$2,500$$

X Corporation must report the $2,500 "deemed paid" credit as additional ordinary dividend income for 1987 because of the gross-up rules. Thus, X Corporation should report total dividend income from F Corporation of $7,500.

The amount of the credit that X Corporation may claim on its 1987 return also may be limited by the other provisions applicable to foreign tax credits. *(See Case 188.)* There is no dividends-received deduction available in the case of dividends from foreign corporations, except in certain limited situations.[208]

Individual A is not allowed to claim the indirect foreign tax credit because the "deemed paid" credit is not available to individual shareholders. The only exception is when the foreign corporation is a controlled foreign corporation and the individual shareholder elects to be taxed as a corporation on his share of Subpart F income from the controlled corporation.[209] *(See Case 183.)* If the foreign corporation is a controlled foreign corporation, the foreign taxes deemed to have been paid by the domestic corporation or individual shareholder (who elects to be taxed as a corporation) are computed under special rules applicable to controlled foreign corporations.[210]

Case 201
Foreign Tax Credit — Limitation of Foreign Tax Credit on Foreign Oil- and Gas-Extraction Income

Corporation C, a domestic corporation, is engaged in the exploration for and production of oil and gas in the United States and in foreign countries R, S and T. In 1987, Corporation C has U.S. taxable income, without claiming a deduction for foreign income taxes, of $1,200,000, as follows:

Location of Production Activities	**Taxable Income (Loss)**	**Foreign Tax Incurred**
U.S.	$ 800,000	$ —
Country R	500,000	300,000
Country S	(400,000)	50,000
Country T	300,000	160,000
Total	$1,200,000	$510,000

Corporation C's U.S. tax liability, before considering the foreign tax credit, is $480,000.

Foreign oil- and gas-extraction income generally is defined as taxable income from foreign sources from the extraction of minerals from oil and gas wells and the sale or

208. I.R.C. Sec. 245.
209. I.R.C. Sec. 962.
210. I.R.C. Sec. 960.

exchange of assets used in the business of extracting oil and gas.[211] In computing taxable income, a U.S. taxpayer must include its pro-rata share of a partnership's foreign oil- and gas-extraction income in addition to taxable income from its own activities. Foreign oil- and gas-extraction income also includes dividends from a foreign corporation when foreign taxes are deemed paid to the extent those dividends are attributable to that income. In addition, the undistributed earnings of a controlled foreign corporation included in a U.S. shareholder's taxable income will be treated as foreign oil- and gas-extraction income if so defined in the hands of the controlled foreign corporation.[212]

Corporation C has an economic interest in the minerals in place. Consequently, the amount of its foreign oil- and gas-extraction income is the gross income from the property less appropriate deductions, such as amortization of intangible drilling costs, cost depletion, lease operating expenses and other related expenses. Gross income from the property is determined by reference to the fair market value of the oil and gas in the immediate vicinity of the well.[213] A taxpayer also may have extraction or oil-related income from the performance of certain directly related services, the lease of related property or certain interest income directly related to the actual conduct of the activities in I.R.C. Sections 907(c)(1) and (2).[214] Extraction income from services can arise when the amount of income depends on the amount of minerals extracted or discovered. However, a taxpayer will not have extraction or oil-related income if one of two conditions exist:

- The taxpayer has no extraction or oil-related income from the active conduct of extraction, transportation or distribution with regard to the property or[215]
- Less than 50% of the taxpayer's gross income from sources outside the United States, exclusively related to the performance of services, is derived from related persons.[216]

Foreign oil- and gas-extraction income does not include income attributable to the marketing, distribution, processing or transportation of oil or gas or its primary products.[217]

When a taxpayer has expenses that cannot be attributed directly to any particular activity, they are allocated or apportioned between foreign oil- and gas-extraction income and other income according to rules provided in the regulations.[218] *(See Case 205.)*

The Tax Equity and Fiscal Responsibility Act of 1982 (TEFRA) modified the provision that limits the amount of foreign taxes imposed on the income from the extraction of oil and gas that can be used as a credit against U.S. tax. Under law before TEFRA's enactment, the amount of income taxes paid to a foreign government that could be used as a foreign tax credit was limited to the amount that would have been incurred if the foreign tax rate were equal to the maximum U.S. income tax rate. If the limitation applied, an amount not to exceed 2% of the foreign oil- and gas-extraction income could be carried over to other years, subject to the rules relating to

211. I.R.C. Sec. 907(c).
212. I.R.C. Sec. 907(c)(3).
213. Reg. Sec. 1.907(c)-1(b)(2).
214. Reg. Sec. 1.907(c)-1(b); Prop. Reg. Sec. 1.907(c)-1(f); Prop. Reg. Sec. 1.907(c)-1(e)(3); Prop. Reg. Sec. 1.907(c)-1(e)(4); Prop. Reg. Sec. 1.907(c)-1(e)(5); Prop. Reg. Sec. 1.907(c)-1(e)(6).
215. Prop. Reg. Sec. 1.907(c)-1(f)(1)(i).
216. Prop. Reg. Sec. 1.907(c)-1(f)(1)(ii).
217. Reg. Sec. 1.907(c)-1(b)(5).
218. Reg. Sec. 1.907(c)-1(e)(2).

carryovers. Extraction taxes in excess of the current limitation and the 2% carryover could not be deducted or claimed as a credit in any other tax year.

TEFRA modified the extraction limitation for tax years beginning after December 31, 1982, in several significant ways. First, if the actual extraction taxes exceed the limitation, the entire amount of the excess constitutes a carryover.[219] Second, under prior law, only the countries in which taxpayers had taxable income from oil- and gas-extraction activities were considered in computing foreign oil- and gas-extraction income. TEFRA, on the other hand, requires the taxpayer to base the limitation on the taxable income (loss) from all extraction activities. A taxable extraction loss incurred in one country must be offset against extraction income realized in other countries to determine the base for computing the limitation. Third, if a taxpayer incurs an overall loss from foreign extraction activities in one year, subsequent foreign extraction income of an equal amount cannot be treated as extraction income for purposes of computing this limitation.[220] Because TEFRA significantly changed the rules, complex carryover rules were developed to determine the amount of foreign taxes that can be carried over to another year when the credit arises in a year in which one set of rules applies and is carried to a year in which the other set of rules applies.[221]

The purpose of the provision is to limit the amount of foreign taxes imposed on the income from the extraction of oil and gas that can be used as a foreign tax credit in any tax year to the amount that would have been incurred if the foreign tax rate were equal to the maximum U.S. income tax rate. The limit for corporate taxpayers is based on the maximum corporate tax rate for the applicable year. The limit for an individual taxpayer is the taxpayer's effective tax rate, computed by dividing his actual U.S. tax (against which the foreign tax credit may be used) by his taxable income.[222]

The practical effect is to prevent foreign oil- and gas-extraction taxes from offsetting U.S. taxes on other types of foreign income. It is possible in some cases, however, to use excess foreign taxes on other types of foreign income to offset U.S. tax on foreign oil- and gas-extraction income.

The Tax Reform Act of 1986 further tightens the above limitations by creating nine basic foreign tax credit categories in addition to the foreign oil-extraction income category. *(See Case 199.)* In some cases, this interplay of categories under I.R.C. Section 904 and the Section 907 limitations is unclear as is the case for 10% to 50% U.S.-owned foreign corporations. It appears that the separate limitation for dividends from such entities is not intended to limit the application of Section 907. Instead, the credit limitation for dividends from 10% to 50% U.S.-owned foreign corporations and the lookthrough rules of I.R.C. Section 907(c)(3) are to operate in tandem. In essence, "deemed paid" credits attached to dividends of 10% to 50% U.S.-owned foreign corporations are limited by both the provisions of Section 904 and by the application of Section 907.[223]

Corporation C's foreign oil- and gas-extraction income for 1987 is $400,000, or the sum of the taxable income (loss) from extraction activities in Countries R, S and T. Corporation C must use the taxable loss from extraction activities in Country S to offset the extraction income realized in Countries R and T. The foreign extraction taxes that may be considered in computing the foreign tax credit are limited to

219. I.R.C. Sec. 907(f)(1).
220. I.R.C. Sec. 907(c)(4).
221. I.R.C. Sec. 907(e).
222. I.R.C. Sec. 907(a).
223. General Explanation of the Tax Reform Act of 1986, prepared by the Staff of the Joint Committee on Taxation, p. 888.

$160,000, or 40% of the foreign extraction income of $400,000. Of the total foreign extraction taxes of $510,000, only $160,000 may be considered in computing the 1987 foreign tax credit limitation.

The excess extraction taxes of $350,000 may be carried over to other years and considered in the computation of the available extraction taxes in that year.[224] The rules for determining the amount that can be carried to and used in another year differ depending on which set of transition rules is in effect for the carryover year.

Once the extraction limitation has been determined, the general limitation on the current use of the foreign tax credit must be computed. *(See Case 199.)* In this instance, the limitation is $160,000, computed as follows:

$$\frac{\text{Taxable income from foreign sources}}{\text{Taxable income from all sources}} \times \text{U.S. income tax} = \text{Foreign tax credit limitation}$$

$$\frac{\$400,000}{\$1,200,000} \times \$480,000 = \$160,000$$

Consequently, all $160,000 of the foreign taxes (after the extraction limitation) may be offset against U.S. tax in 1987.

Had any unused foreign taxes remained, they could have been carried back to 1985. Although regulations have not been issued on the mechanics of the carryback computation, two separate carryback items may exist: the overall excess foreign tax credit and the excess extraction tax, $350,000 in this case. Presumably, the overall foreign tax credit available for carryback would be computed under the transition rules of the Tax Reform Act of 1986 *(see Case 196)*, and both of the limited taxes would be carried back to 1985 where Sections 904 and 907 limits would again be computed, with any excess credits available for carryover to future years.

If Corporation C incurs an extraction loss from all its foreign extraction activities in any year after 1982, the extraction losses must be recaptured in later years. To accomplish the recapture, subsequent foreign income from extraction activities must be treated as income from nonextraction activities in determining the limitation on foreign taxes incurred with respect to foreign extraction activities. *(See Case 203.)*

The limitation relating to foreign extraction income is applicable only if the taxpayer elects to claim a credit for foreign taxes. No limitation applies to taxes incurred in a year in which the taxpayer elects to claim a deduction for foreign taxes.[225]

Case 202
Foreign Tax Credit — Limitation of Excessive Taxes on Foreign Oil-Related Income

Corporation C, a domestic corporation, is engaged in the refining of oil and gas in the United States and overseas. It operates one refinery in foreign Country F. Under the general tax laws applicable to industries other than certain oil-related industries in Country F, taxes are imposed at a rate of 40%. However, the taxable income from certain oil-related activities, including refining activities, is subject to a tax rate of 80%.

224. I.R.C. Sec. 907(f).
225. Reg. Sec. 1.907(a)-1(e)(2).

The Tax Equity and Fiscal Responsibility Act of 1982 (TEFRA) gave the Treasury the regulatory authority to determine that all or a portion of certain foreign taxes imposed on oil-related income will not qualify as creditable taxes if it is determined that the foreign law in effect places a greater tax burden on oil-related income than on income from other activities. In effect, foreign oil-related taxes are "split" into creditable and noncreditable taxes. The amount that will not qualify as a creditable tax will be treated as a deduction under the foreign tax law. Whether a greater tax burden is imposed on oil-related activities is not determined on an annual basis, but over a reasonable period.[226]

Before the enactment of TEFRA, foreign extraction income was considered as one type of foreign oil-related income. TEFRA modified the definition of foreign oil-related income to exclude extraction income. Consequently, foreign oil-related taxes include only taxes incurred on income from the processing or refining of oil or natural gas into their primary products; the transportation of crude oil, natural gas or products derived therefrom; the distribution or sale of those minerals or their primary products; the performance of any related service and the income derived from the sale or exchange of assets used in these trades or businesses.[227]

Congress apparently did not make this provision applicable to oil- and gas-extraction income because it believed the other provisions concerning extraction income imposed sufficient limitations on the use of foreign extraction taxes to offset U.S. income tax. *(See Case 201.)*

It appears that Treasury can apply this provision to the oil-related income earned in Country F because the tax imposed on refining activities in Country F will be materially greater than the tax imposed on other industries over a reasonable period. However, Corporation C must wait to determine, based on the particular facts and circumstances, whether it is appropriate to continue treating all taxes paid to Country F as a creditable tax until Treasury determines whether the new provision applies to Country F.

The statute does not provide any guidelines on the manner of determining the amount of the payments to a foreign government that will be treated as a deduction under foreign tax law. It is possible that a simultaneous equation must be used to determine the amount of the creditable tax because a reclassification of a portion of the tax to a deduction could be viewed as changing foreign taxable income, which in turn changes the foreign tax. Taxpayers will have little guidance on the application of this provision until regulations are issued.

Informal discussions with representatives of the Internal Revenue Service, however, indicate that the safe harbor formula used to compute the creditable portion of a foreign tax levy, as contained in the final regulations to I.R.C. Section 901, is essentially the same formula as that envisioned by Congress in TEFRA for determining the qualifying amount of tax for I.R.C. Section 907(b) purposes. Thus, if a taxpayer uses the safe harbor method to compute the creditable part of the tax, a separate calculation under I.R.C. Section 907(b) is not necessary. Alternatively, if the facts-and-circumstances method is used to determine creditable taxes, the taxpayer still must make an I.R.C. Section 907(b) computation.

226. I.R.C. Sec. 907(b).
227. I.R.C. Sec. 907(c)(2).

Case 203
Foreign Tax Credit — Recapture of Foreign Losses

Corporation C, a domestic corporation, is engaged in three separate businesses: the exploration for and the production of oil and gas, the refining of oil and gas and the manufacture of widgets. All businesses are conducted in the United States and in various foreign countries. Corporation C's activities for 1987 and 1988 are summarized below:

Foreign-source taxable income (loss)	**1987**	**1988**
Production	$ (100,000)	$200,000
Refining	(500,000)	600,000
Manufacturing	(200,000)	600,000
Foreign taxes		
Production	$ —	$100,000
Refining	—	400,000
Manufacturing	—	300,000

In each of the years, Corporation C's U.S. taxable income from all sources is $2,400,000, and the U.S. tax, before considering the foreign tax credit, is $960,000 in 1987 and $816,000 in 1988.

Corporation C is not a member of a consolidated group.

Another restriction on the use of foreign tax credit is embodied in the rules requiring the recapture of overall foreign losses. In certain instances, this provision requires that taxable losses from foreign operations be restored as U.S.-source income for foreign tax credit limitation purposes in future years. The recapture is accomplished through a reduction in the foreign tax credit otherwise allowable in future years when foreign operations are profitable.[228] Until this provision was enacted, it was possible to use losses relating to the exploration of oil and gas properties that generally occurred in the earlier years of operation to reduce taxable income from profitable domestic operations. If the tax rate of the foreign country was equal to the U.S. tax rate, U.S. income tax on the foreign-source taxable income could be avoided when the operations became profitable because the foreign tax credit would offset any U.S. tax otherwise payable on the foreign-source taxable income. The purpose of the recapture provision is to require taxpayers to "pay back" any U.S. tax benefit derived from foreign operations when taxable income is recognized from the foreign operations for foreign tax credit purposes. The mechanics of the provision operate by converting the source of subsequent income from foreign to domestic, thereby placing a limit on the foreign tax credit that can be used to offset U.S. taxes. Before 1987, significant excess losses were typically generated through expensed foreign intangible drilling and development costs (IDC). Although foreign IDC must now be capitalized and amortized, foreign losses may still be generated by taxpayers operating in the oil and gas industry by the amortization of foreign IDC and other expenses incurred by the taxpayers.

Before the enactment of the Tax Reform Act of 1986 (the Act), a foreign loss attributable to a separate foreign tax credit category limitation reduced U.S. taxable income before it reduced other foreign income of the taxpayer subject to another

228. I.R.C. Sec. 904(f).

separate category limitation. Under the Act, a foreign loss incurred in tax years beginning after December 31, 1986, in one category is required to reduce other foreign income categories proportionately before it can offset U.S.-source income. To the extent the foreign income that is offset by the loss has associated foreign tax credits, they are not creditable in the year of the loss if the taxpayer's foreign tax credit limitation for that category is reduced sufficiently. In a later year in which the taxpayer earns foreign income under the category that incurred the loss, the loss is recaptured by treating that income as foreign-source income subject to the category that was previously reduced.[229] If the aggregate of items from each foreign tax credit category results in a loss, the loss is then used to offset U.S.-source income.[230]

To recapture foreign losses used to offset U.S.-source income, foreign-source income is converted to domestic-source income before computing the allowable foreign tax credit. Generally, the amount of foreign-source taxable income that can be converted to domestic-source income in any tax year is the lesser of two amounts: the amount of the loss or 50% of the foreign-source taxable income. The taxpayer may elect to use a percentage higher than 50% in a tax year.[231]

The foreign loss is recaptured in each succeeding year in which foreign income is derived until fully recaptured, whether or not foreign taxes are credited or deducted by the taxpayer. The proposed regulations indicate that foreign losses cannot be recaptured in a succeeding year, unless the foreign tax credit is elected.[232] This position is apparently without authority and should be revised.

As stated above, the intent of recapturing foreign loss under I.R.C. Section 904(f)(1) was to insure that a taxpayer did not receive a double benefit by deducting a foreign loss against U.S.-source income and then claiming a foreign tax credit in a future year when foreign operations were profitable. This intent is fully achieved by recapturing foreign losses in years when foreign taxes are not claimed as credits and in years when there is no adverse impact on the foreign tax credit calculation as well as in years in which the use of the credit is elected.

Other pertinent provisions of the January 24, 1986, proposed regulations include:

☐ A tax-benefit rule requiring that only losses that offset U.S.-source income can be recaptured. Therefore, to the extent a foreign loss offsets foreign taxable income, there is no recapture.[233]

☐ Coordination between the overall foreign loss (OFL) rules and the net operating loss (NOL) rules so that double recapture does not occur. In general, the NOL rules apply before the OFL rules. To the extent a foreign NOL reduces foreign-source income in the year to which the loss is carried, the OFL amount is reduced.[234]

☐ A separate basket approach for determining and recapturing OFLs. As a result, there can be as many as seven different type of OFLs: one for each of the five separate items in I.R.C. Section 904(d)(1), one under I.R.C. Section 936 and another under I.R.C. Section 907 foreign oil-related loss (for years 1976 through 1982). If the taxpayer sustains a loss under one separate limitation (e.g., an overall "other foreign" loss under I.R.C. Section 904(d)(1)(E)), income from another separate limitation, such as domestic international sales corporation (DISC) dividend income under I.R.C. Section 904(d)(1)(B), cannot be used to eliminate this

229. I.R.C. Sec. 904(f)(5)(C).
230. I.R.C. Sec. 904(f)(5)(A).
231. I.R.C. Sec. 904(f)(1).
232. Prop. Reg. Sec. 1.904(f)-2(a); Prop. Reg. Sec. 1.904(f)-2(c)(3), Example 3.
233. Prop. Reg. Sec. 1.904(f)-2.
234. Prop. Reg. Sec. 1.904(f)-3.

loss. On the recapture side, only income from the basket that generated the loss can be used to recapture the loss. Thus, if the taxpayer in the above example has no "other foreign" income but generated DISC dividend income subject to the I.R.C. Section 904(d)(1)(B) limitation, such income cannot be used to recapture the I.R.C. Section 904(d)(1)(E) loss.[235]

- ☐ Ordering rules for recognizing gain when the taxpayer disposes of an asset used outside the United States in a trade or business. In general, I.R.C. Section 904(f)(3) does not override other I.R.C. provisions to the contrary until 100% of the gain that is to be recognized on the disposition, irrespective of I.R.C. Section 904(f)(3), is recaptured. If there is still an OFL, additional gain is deemed to be recognized on the disposition and any subsequent dispositions.[236]
- ☐ Special rules for recapturing the OFL of a trust and for recapturing amounts on accumulation distributions from foreign trusts.[237]
- ☐ Special consolidated rules. The rules for determining the OFL of a consolidated group provide that the substantive rules of I.R.C. Section 904(f) apply, using the following special rules:
  - ☐ There is no consolidated OFL unless the aggregate OFL of all members exceeds the aggregate foreign taxable income of all members. Thus, if one member of a group has a $100 OFL and the other members have aggregate foreign taxable income of $200, there is no group OFL and nothing to recapture.
  - ☐ The group's consolidated OFL is recaptured out of consolidated foreign taxable income regardless of which member generated the loss.
  - ☐ For purposes of the consolidated rules, each member is to keep a "notional" OFL account that reflects its pro-rata share of the group's OFL. When the group loss is recaptured, each member's notional OFL account is reduced.
  - ☐ When a member leaves the group, it takes with it the amount of the group's unrecaptured OFL in its notional account.
  - ☐ The rules provide for recapturing an OFL of a member that was incurred before the member joined in the filing of the consolidated return. If the member's OFL was incurred in a separate return year, such OFL is immediately added to the group's OFL account and is recaptured out of the group's foreign taxable income. If the loss was incurred in a separate return limitation year (SRLY), the loss stays initially in the member's separate OFL account. However, each year a portion of the loss is added to the group's OFL account to the extent of the members' foreign taxable income. Amounts so added to the group's account are recaptured out of the group's foreign taxable income.

The Tax Equity and Fiscal Responsibility Act of 1982 (TEFRA) changed the rules relating to the recapture of foreign losses. Before TEFRA was enacted, foreign loss recapture rules were applied separately with respect to foreign oil-related income and other foreign-source income. The recapture rules effective for losses incurred in tax years beginning after December 31, 1982, eliminate the separate limitations.

However, proposed regulations under I.R.C. Section 904 provide that pre-1983 overall foreign losses are to be recaptured in post-1982 years by keeping separate accounts for pre-1983 foreign oil-related income, pre-1983 overall foreign income and

235. Prop. Reg. Sec. 1-904(f)-3.
236. Prop. Reg. Sec. 1.904(f)-2(d).
237. Prop. Reg. Sec. 1.904(f)-4.

post-1982 overall foreign income. Recapture for each year is then computed under rules set forth in the proposed regulations. The transition rules indicate that if, by considering each account, the taxpayer's foreign oil-related and pre-1983 overall foreign losses are not fully recaptured by the taxpayer's eighth post-1982 tax year, the remaining losses are to be added to the post-1982 overall foreign loss account.[238]

In addition, TEFRA added a provision that requires a taxpayer incurring a loss from extraction activities to recapture those losses in subsequent years. The recapture is effected by reducing subsequent foreign extraction income for purposes of computing the limit on foreign extraction taxes.[239]

Because Corporation C has a loss from its foreign extraction activities and an overall foreign loss in 1987, the impact of both the overall foreign loss recapture provisions and the foreign oil- and gas-extraction loss recapture provisions must be considered. First, the loss of $100,000 from foreign oil- and gas-extraction activities in 1987 must be recaptured by treating extraction income of $100,000 realized in 1988 as income that is not from foreign oil- and gas-extraction activities for purposes of computing the limitation on foreign extraction taxes.

The foreign extraction tax limitation for 1988 is computed by multiplying the maximum corporate tax rate of 34% by the extraction income. Corporation C's 1988 extraction income is $100,000 (total extraction income of $200,000 reduced by 1987 extraction loss of $100,000). Consequently, extraction taxes of $34,000 (34% of $100,000) can be considered in the foreign tax credit computation. The excess of the actual extraction taxes of $100,000 over the $34,000 limitation can be carried over to other years, subject to the regular foreign tax credit carryover rules. In addition, if the tax is carried back to a year covered by the old rules relating to the extraction tax limitation, additional computations as required by the transition rules must be made to determine the amount that can be used. *(See Case 201.)*

Generally, foreign oil- and gas-extraction income for computing the foreign extraction tax limitation is defined as it is for computing the limitation of the foreign tax credit on foreign oil- and gas-extraction income. However, it is clear that no net operating loss deduction allowable for the tax year is taken into account.[240] In addition, expropriation and casualty losses are not taken into account in determining whether a loss from extraction activities exits.[241] Expenses allocable to extraction activities are deducted in determining the extraction losses.[242] The rules for determining such expenses were substantially changed by the Tax Reform Act of 1986. *(See Case 205.)*

After determining the limitation on the foreign extraction taxes that can be used currently as a credit, the general limitation on the use of the foreign tax credit must be computed. Corporation C must consider the impact of the overall foreign loss recapture provisions in computing this limitation in 1988.

Corporation C must treat foreign-source income of $700,000 as domestic-source income. This amount is the lesser of: (1) the loss of $800,000 to be recaptured or

---

238. Prop. Reg. Sec. 1.904(f)-6.
239. I.R.C. Sec. 907(c)(4).
240. I.R.C. Sec. 907(c)(4)(B)(ii).
241. I.R.C. Sec. 907(c)(4)(B)(iii).
242. I.R.C. Sec. 907(c)(4)(B)(i).

(2) 50% of the 1988 estimated foreign-source income of $1,400,000. The general limitation on the use of the foreign tax credit then is computed as follows:

$$\frac{\text{Taxable income from foreign sources}}{\text{Taxable income from all sources}} \times \text{U.S. income tax} = \text{Foreign tax credit limitation}$$

$$\frac{\$700{,}000}{\$2{,}400{,}000} \times \$816{,}000 = \$238{,}000$$

The foreign taxes available for credit are $734,000 computed as follows:

Activity	Amount
Production (after extraction limitation)	$ 34,000
Refining	400,000
Manufacturing	300,000
	$734,000

Only $238,000 of the available taxes may be used currently to offset U.S. income tax because the general limitation applies. The excess taxes of $496,000 may be carried over to other years and used, subject to the regular carryover rules. In addition, a carryover of extraction taxes of $66,000 is available. Special carryover rules apply if the tax is carried back to a year in which the provisions of the new law did not apply.

Only $700,000 of the foreign loss is recaptured in 1988; the remaining loss of $100,000 is subject to recapture in later years.

If C Corporation is engaged in the exploration for and production of oil and gas or another activity resulting in foreign oil- and gas-extraction income, the limitation on foreign taxes on oil- and gas-extraction income should be computed before computing the limitation due to the overall foreign loss recapture rules. *(See Case 201.)*

If property that has been used in a trade or business outside the United States is disposed of in a taxable transaction, the income is foreign-source income. For purposes of applying the overall foreign loss recapture rules, the entire gain (to the extent of the loss subject to recapture) is converted to domestic-source income to determine the amount of foreign tax that may be credited against U.S. tax. The 50% limit applicable to the conversion of ordinary foreign source income to domestic-source income is not available if the income is from the disposition of property.[243]

The overall foreign loss recapture rules also may result in the recognition of income in certain transactions that otherwise would be tax free. If property that has been used in a trade or business outside the United States is disposed of in certain nontaxable transactions, the taxpayer generally must recognize taxable income in an amount equal to the excess of the fair market value of that property over its adjusted basis. The gain that must be recognized is limited to the amount of foreign loss subject to recapture, and its character is the same as if the property had been sold.[244] A disposition for this purpose does not include a disposition of property that is not a material factor in the realization of income.[245]

243. I.R.C. Sec. 904(f)(3).
244. *Ibid.*
245. I.R.C. Sec. 904(f)(3)(C).

For purposes of the recapture rules, a sale, exchange, distribution or gift of property constitutes a disposition whether or not gain or loss otherwise would be recognized. A transfer of property to a foreign corporation in a reorganization that otherwise would be tax free constitutes a disposition. For example, the transfer of foreign assets to a wholly owned foreign subsidiary is a disposition.[246] A disposition does not include transfers of foreign property to a domestic corporation in certain nontaxable reorganizations; however, a taxable liquidation of a subsidiary into its parent and a stock-for-stock reorganization are dispositions that will trigger income.[247] Prior to a disposition of significant assets used in a foreign trade or business, a careful review of these complex rules should be made.

In a private letter ruling, the Internal Revenue Service (IRS) concluded that a farmout of an oil and gas mineral property by a domestic corporation to a foreign corporation (in which no cash consideration was received) was not a disposition of property for purposes of the recapture of foreign loss provisions. The domestic corporation assigned all the working interest in a foreign production license to the foreign corporation, retaining an overriding royalty interest. The foreign corporation assumed the obligation to develop and operate the property. The domestic corporation reserved the right to convert its overriding royalty to a working interest after the foreign corporation recouped its development expenditures. The IRS viewed the transaction as a sharing arrangement in which the U.S. corporation did not part with any capital interest in the property. Consequently, it ruled that the transaction was not a disposition for purposes of the recapture of foreign loss provisions. It also concluded that a subsequent conversion by the domestic corporation of the overriding royalty to a working interest will not constitute a disposition.[248]

No cash consideration was received in connection with the farmout in the transaction described in the private letter ruling. If a lease bonus is received in a leasing transaction, it should constitute foreign-source income for purposes of the recapture rules; however, the income should be from ordinary business operations and not from the disposition of property. Consequently, the amount of the lease bonus converted to domestic-source income should be subject to the 50% limitation applicable to income from ordinary operations.

If foreign operations conducted in a branch are incorporated, the transfer of assets can be treated as a disposition within the meaning of the overall foreign loss recapture provisions.[249] If a loss was incurred from all foreign operations in prior years, gain will be recognized on the transaction in an amount equal to the lesser of the loss, subject to recapture, or the unrealized gain. The transfer rules are applicable even if the transfer is to a domestic subsidiary. The transfer rules should not be applicable to a transfer from a U.S. parent to a U.S. subsidiary when a consolidated U.S. income tax return is filed. The consolidated return regulations provide that gain or loss is not recognized upon an intercompany transfer of assets until the assets are transferred outside the consolidated group.[250] *(See Case 208.)*

The foreign loss account is generated in any year in which an overall foreign loss exists. It does not matter whether the taxpayer elects to claim a foreign tax credit or to deduct foreign taxes in that year.[251] If foreign taxes are deducted, however, the deduction increases the amount of the foreign loss subject to recapture in later years.

---

246. I.R.C. Sec. 904(f)(3)(B).
247. I.R.C. Sec. 904(f)(3)(C).
248. IRS Letter Ruling 7931034.
249. I.R.C. Sec. 904(f)(3)(B).
250. Reg. Sec. 1.1502-13(c).
251. I.R.C. Sec. 904(f)(2).

An overall foreign loss exists when the gross income from sources outside the United States is exceeded by the deductions properly apportioned or allocated thereto. A net operating loss deduction, foreign expropriation loss and casualty loss are not considered in the computation.[252]

If Corporation C is a member of a group filing a consolidated U.S. income tax return, the computation of the overall foreign loss should be made on a consolidated basis. An overall foreign loss subject to recapture exists only if the group's foreign-source income was less than the group's deductions related to foreign operations. Similarly, the computation of the amount of foreign-source income that must be characterized as U.S.-source income for determining the limitation on the foreign tax is made on a consolidated basis.

Case 204
Currency Translation Gain/Loss Recognition

R is a domestic corporation with multinational operations. Although Corporation R has significant domestic operations, it also conducts business in Country N through its branch, A. Records for Branch A's operations in Country N are kept in U.S. dollars, and all transactions conducted by Branch A are based on the U.S. dollar.

Results of Branch A operations for the prior three years are as follows:

						Foreign	
Year	Income	Foreign Tax	Exchange Rate	Remittance	Gross U.S. Tax	Tax Credit	U.S. Net Tax
1	100N*/$50	23N/$11.50	2N:$1	0	$17.00	$11.50	$ 5.50
2	100N/$80	23N/$18.40	1.25N:$1	0	$27.20	$18.40	$ 8.80
3	100N/$100	23N/$23	1N:$1	231N/$231	$34.00	$23.00	$11.00

*N = The unit of currency of Country N.

Corporation R also conducts operations in Country Y through its wholly owned foreign subsidiary, D. D's books and records are kept in the foreign currency of Country Y, and all transactions are denominated in Country Y's currency.

Before the enactment of the Tax Reform Act of 1986 (the Act), the rules regarding recognition of foreign currency translation gains and losses were, at best, confusing. The rules were not consistent in approach to currency translation gain or loss recognition and often resulted in the accelerated recognition of unrealized gain or loss on currency transactions. In recognition of this problem, Congress created Subpart J, consisting of I.R.C. Sections 985 through 989. The thrust of Subpart J is to eliminate the recognition of translation gains or losses on all foreign currency transactions other than "nonfunctional currency" transactions.

A functional currency is that currency used by a qualified business unit for conducting a "significant" part of the unit's activities and in which the unit's books and records are kept.[253] A qualified business unit is any separate and clearly identified unit of a trade or business for which the taxpayer maintains a separate set of books and

252. I.R.C. Sec. 904(f)(2).
253. I.R.C. Sec. 985(b)(1)(B).

records.[254] The statute is somewhat unclear in its application to a qualified business unit where different functional currencies are used for different purposes. For example, the functional currency for keeping books and records may be the currency of the foreign country, while most transactions are conducted in the U.S. dollar. The statute provides that the functional currency shall be the U.S. dollar if the activities of the qualified business unit are "primarily" conducted in U.S. dollars.[255] The statute does not define, though, either the term *significantly* or *primarily*. The statute provides an option, however, for qualified business units that keep their books and records in U.S. dollars or that use a method of accounting that approximates a separate transactions method to elect to use the U.S. dollar as its functional currency.[256] Once made, the election is irrevocable without the consent of the Commissioner of Internal Revenue. If a new functional currency is adopted, a change in accounting methods occurs.[257]

The facts above indicate that the functional currency of Branch A is the U.S. dollar. Branch A's books and records are kept on the basis of the U.S. dollar, and the U.S. dollar is the currency used to generate revenues and expenses for the branch. The use of the U.S. dollar as the functional currency under Section 985 means that Corporation R will not be required to recognize foreign currency translation gains or losses as a result of conducting operations through Branch A in Country N for all functional currency transactions.

In many cases, selecting a functional currency will not be as clear-cut as the facts above indicate. Where it is uncertain whether the U.S. dollar is the functional currency but the taxpayer either keeps his books and records on the basis of the U.S. dollar or uses an accounting method that approximates the separate transactions method, the taxpayer may elect to use the U.S. dollar as its functional currency.[258] If the taxpayer is a U.S. entity, the election is placed in the first tax return where the qualified business unit exists. If the taxpayer is a foreign entity, the election is placed in the U.S. owner's tax return in the first year in which the U.S. owner owns a 10%-or-more interest in the foreign entity. It should be noted that the requirements for electing the U.S. dollar as a functional currency are relaxed for countries with hyperinflationary economies although the statute does not define *hyperinflationary economy*.[259] In such instances, the U.S. dollar may be adopted as the functional currency, even though the taxpayer does not keep his books and records on the basis of the U.S. dollar.

Based on the facts above, Foreign Subsidiary D's functional currency appears to be the currency of Country Y. Because the functional currency is not the U.S. dollar, Corporation R will be required to recognize exchange gains or losses on the repatriation of funds to the United States from Foreign Subsidiary D's operations. The Act repealed the net worth method of determining such transaction gains and losses. In general, the profit and loss method existing before 1987 was adopted. In determining translation gain or losses, the profit and loss method, as set forth in I.R.C. Section 986, provides first that the earnings and profits of Foreign Subsidiary D are to be calculated using its functional currency—in this case, the currency of Country Y. Next, the earnings and profits of Foreign Subsidiary D are translated at the exchange rate in effect when either actual or constructive dividends are included in Corporation R's income. This approach leads to the result that no currency translation exchange

254. I.R.C. Sec. 989(a).
255. I.R.C. Sec. 985(b)(2).
256. I.R.C. Sec. 985(b)(3)(B).
257. I.R.C. Sec. 481; I.R.C. Sec. 985(b)(4).
258. I.R.C. Sec. 985(b)(3).
259. I.R.C. Sec. 989(c)(3).

gains or losses are recognized on either actual or Section 1248 deemed distributions. However, for deemed distributions of Subpart F income, gain or loss is recognized for currency fluctuation between the deemed dividend income inclusion by Corporation R and the date that the dividend is actually paid to Corporation R. The dividend income will be recognized by Corporation R as ordinary income or loss and will be sourced by reference to the income that gave rise to the dividend.

If Branch A's functional currency were not the U.S. dollar, the calculation of exchange gain or loss is straightforward.

To calculate the exchange gain or loss to be recognized by Corporation R from Branch A in such situations, Branch A must first compute its taxable income in its functional currency. The taxable income of Branch A is then translated into U.S. dollars at the weighted average exchange rate for the tax year of the qualified business unit (Branch A).[260] Foreign taxes are translated at the rate when paid. Corporation R then recognizes gain or loss on the difference between the value of the currency when it is earned by Branch A and when the funds are remitted to Corporation R. In this case, the exchange gain recognized by Corporation R is $53.90 ($231.00 - $177.10), computed as follows:

Year 1	77N ÷ 2N	$ 38.50
Year 2	77N ÷ 1.25N	$ 61.60
Year 3	77N ÷ 1N	$ 77.00
	231N	$177.10

Because of the fluctuation in the value of currency N relative to the U.S. dollar, a $38.50 currency translation gain is recognized from Year 1, and an $15.40 gain is recognized from Year 2. For purposes of determining the exchange gain or loss, post-1986 remittances are treated as being made pro rata out of post-1986 accumulated earnings. The translation gain of $53.90 ($38.50 + $15.40) is treated as ordinary income sourced by reference to the source of income that gave rise to Branch A's post-1986 accumulated earnings. No foreign tax credits are available to offset the exchange gain.

Certain nonfunctional currency transactions will require the recognition of currency translation gains or losses before the actual remittance of funds to Corporation R. Such transactions, commonly called Section 988 transactions, include a foreign branch or subsidiary's acquisition of a debt instrument or becoming the obligor under a debt instrument; such entity's accrual of any item of expense or gross income that is to be paid or received after the accrual date; such entity's entering into any forward contract, futures contract option or similar financial instrument; or such entity's disposition of any nonfunctional currency.[261]

The statute leaves uncertain many of the problems associated with the use of the functional currency concept. The Secretary of the Treasury is directed by the statute to address many of these problems, including: (1) the change of accounting method issue associated with taxpayers currently using the net worth method of computing foreign currency translation gains and losses that switch to the functional currency concept set forth in I.R.C. Section 985; (2) limiting the recognition of foreign currency loss on remittances from qualified business units to the actual loss incurred by the

260. I.R.C. Sec. 989(b).
261. I.R.C. Sec. 988.

domestic parent and (3) recharacterizing interest and principal payments on obligations associated with hyperinflationary currency.

Case 205
Allocation and Apportionment of Deductions

> Corporation C, a domestic corporation, is engaged in the exploration for and production of oil and gas in the United States and foreign Country F. Operations in Country F are conducted through a branch. Corporation C's deductions include the typical deductions incurred by a company engaged in oil and gas operations, such as intangible drilling and development costs (IDC), depreciation on lease and well equipment, depletion and lease operating expenses.
>
> Corporation C maintains an office in Country F, and all activity of that office is devoted to the oil and gas operations there. Corporation C also maintains an office in the United States. In addition to incurring deductions directly related to its domestic oil and gas activities, certain supervisory functions are performed from the U.S. office relating to activities both in the United States and Country F.
>
> Corporation C has borrowed substantial sums of money to finance its exploration and development activities, and its interest expense deduction is significant.
>
> Corporation C has requested assistance in determining how the deductions should be allocated or apportioned among its various activities.

A U.S. taxpayer (individual, domestic corporation, etc.) may be required to determine taxable income by geographical source (United States or foreign) or by activity (foreign oil extraction or other) for various provisions of the Internal Revenue Code (the Code).[262] For example, a determination of taxable income from foreign oil- and gas-extraction activities is required to compute the foreign oil- and gas-extraction tax credit limitation *(see Case 201)*. The computation of taxable income is required for a number of other areas as well, including the determination of foreign base company income of controlled foreign corporations *(see Case 193)* and the determination of effectively connected income for foreign corporations and nonresident alien individuals *(see Cases 210 and 211)*.

Many of the deductions incurred in oil and gas exploration and production activities are definitely related to a class of gross income, i.e., production income, and can be easily related to foreign-source or U.S.-source income. For example, IDC, lease operating expenses, delay rentals, depletion and depreciation on lease and well equipment are clearly identifiable with a particular country. In addition, many general and administrative expenses are directly attributable to an activity and should be allocated to the gross income from that activity. For example, the deductions attributable to the maintenance of an office by Corporation C for conducting its oil and gas operations in Country F should be directly allocated to the corporation's oil and gas production income in Country F.

Although many items of income and expense can be directly associated with a particular country or a particular activity, items not bearing a direct relationship must

262. Reg. Sec. 1.861-8(f)(1).

be allocated among countries and among activities to reflect properly taxable income. The allocation of interest expense and other expenses not directly identifiable with specific income-producing activities is subject to complex rules.[263] Generally, these rules differ for expenses incurred after December 31, 1986, and are made even more complex by the transition rules of the Tax Reform Act of 1986 (the Act) for interest expense allocations related to debt outstanding before November 16, 1985.

Pre-Tax Reform Act of 1986

For general and administrative expenses incurred before December 31, 1986, and for interest expense subject to the transition rules of the Tax Reform Act of 1986, the basic premise of the allocation and apportionment rules is that all expenses are required to be allocated to a class of gross income.[264] For this purpose, gross income includes amounts excluded from taxable income, such as tax-exempt interest and intercompany dividends eliminated in a consolidated tax return.[265] In addition, even though no gross income is derived from an activity or property during a tax year, expenses still may be allocated to that activity.[266] Deductions first should be allocated to the activity or property to which they relate and then to the gross income derived or expected to be derived from the activity or property. Some deductions are not directly related to any activity or property but are related to all classes of gross income. These deductions are to be apportioned among all classes on some reasonable basis. Precise guidelines are provided for the method of allocating some deductions, such as interest expense and research and development costs. However, the rules relating to the allocation of general and administrative, stewardship and supportive expenses are not precise.

Corporation C has a significant deduction for interest expense, and careful consideration should be given to the manner in which the deduction is allocated. The regulations under prior law provide six methods for allocating and apportioning business interest expense.[267] These methods include an allocation based on assets, two optional gross income methods, specific tracing and special rules relating to indebtedness incurred before 1977. If the asset method is used, interest expense is allocated on the basis of either the tax basis or the fair market value of assets used in the business and then to the income derived or expected to be derived from that property.[268] An example of the asset method might be the following: If 75% of the tax basis of a corporation's assets is located in the United States, 75% of the total interest expense is apportioned to U.S.-source income and the remaining 25% to foreign-source income. Generally, the use of the fair market value or tax basis is acceptable; however, once the fair market value method is used, it must be used consistently unless the Internal Revenue Service grants permission to change.[269]

Corporation C may, at its election, apportion interest expense ratably on the basis of gross income provided the interest apportioned to foreign-source income and domestic-source income is at least 50% of the interest apportioned under the asset method. If the 50% test is not met, the second gross income method can be selected. Under this second method, if the 50% test for foreign-source income is not met, only one-half the interest expense apportioned to foreign-source income under the asset method is apportioned to foreign-source income. The remainder is apportioned to domestic-source income.

263. I.R.C. Sec. 864(e).
264. Reg. Sec. 1.861-8(a)(2).
265. Reg. Sec. 1.861-8(d)(2).
266. Reg. Sec. 1.861-8(d)(1).
267. Reg. Sec. 1.861-8(e)(2).
268. Reg. Sec. 1.861-8(e)(2)(v).
269. *Ibid.*

Likewise, if the 50% test is failed for domestic-source income, only one-half the interest expense apportioned to the domestic-source income under the asset method is apportioned to domestic-source income. The remainder is apportioned to foreign-source income.[270]

Direct tracing of indebtedness to specific properties may be used only in limited situations that meet certain facts and circumstances listed in the regulations. As a practical matter, this method will be available only in rare circumstances.[271]

The allocation and apportionment of general and administrative expenses, stewardship, overhead and supervisory expenses are governed by imprecise rules. Examples in the regulations indicate that supportive expenses can be allocated on a time factor when personnel maintain adequate records. These costs also can be allocated on the basis of gross income, units sold, profit contributions or other reasonable methods.[272] If Corporation C had several wholly owned subsidiaries, each corporation should apply the rules separately for allocating and apportioning deductions among its own activities, regardless of whether a consolidated tax return is filed. Members included in a consolidated return must exercise a degree of consistency in the method they use to allocate and apportion interest and certain other expenses.[273]

If Corporation C conducted its foreign operations in a domestic subsidiary, more flexibility may exist in the allocation of interest expense. For example, by having the foreign subsidiary financed primarily through capital rather than borrowings, the interest expense allocable to foreign operations may be minimized.

Post-Tax Reform Act of 1986

After December 31, 1986, the Act significantly decreased the flexibility taxpayers had in allocating expenses between domestic and foreign operations. However, transition rules provide for a phasein period with respect to interest expense over three, four or five tax years depending on when the related debt was acquired by the taxpayer.[274] The Technical Corrections Bill of 1987 substantially changes the transition rules.[275]

The Act repealed all methods for allocating expense between U.S.- and foreign-source income other than the two asset methods.[276] The capitalization of foreign IDC *(see Case 206)* will substantially increase foreign assets and the amount of interest expense apportioned to foreign sources under the tax book value method. In addition, the Act requires that members of an affiliated corporate group be treated as a single taxpayer rather than as separate taxpayers in determining the appropriate allocation of the group's interest expense to foreign-source income.[277] An affiliated group for this purpose is defined by I.R.C. Section 1504 (without regard to I.R.C. Section 1504(b)(4)).[278] The affiliated group provision prevents affiliate members from shifting interest expense to U.S. affiliates and thereby reducing U.S.-source income while still maintaining high foreign tax credit limitations. The affiliated group approach matches interest expense (which under prior law may have been shifted to an affiliate and deducted against U.S.-source income) with the affiliated group's foreign-source

270. Reg. Sec. 1.861-8(e)(2)(vi).
271. Reg. Sec. 1.861-8(e)(2)(iv).
272. Reg. Sec. 1.861-8(e)(4).
273. Reg. Sec. 1.861-8(e)(2)(vi); Reg. Sec. 1.1502-4(d)(1); Reg. Sec. 1.1502-12.
274. P.L. 99-514 (Tax Reform Act of 1986), Sec. 1215(c).
275. Technical Corrections Bill of 1987, Sec. 112(g)(7).
276. I.R.C. Sec. 864(e)(2).
277. I.R.C. Sec. 864(e)(1).
278. I.R.C. Sec. 864(e)(5).

income. Theoretically, this approach leads to a clearer association of the expense and the related income-generating activity.

The statute presents numerous technicalities for allocating interest expense under the asset method. For example, assets that produce tax-exempt U.S. income are not a factor in the apportionment. For this purpose, 80% of the stock basis (or value if the taxpayer uses the fair market value method) that produces dividends eligible for the dividends-received deduction is considered a tax-exempt asset.[279] In addition, stock of corporations included in the affiliated group and interaffiliate debt are disregarded.[280] Special rules also exist for stock of corporations that are not part of the affiliated group but in which members of the affiliated group own 10% or more of the voting stock. Under the tax book value method, the adjusted basis of the stock held is increased by the corporation's earnings attributable to that stock during the period held by the taxpayer or reduced (but not below zero) by the portion of the deficit earnings attributable to the stock.[281] It is unclear how the provision for the elimination of tax-exempt assets, (i.e., dividends that qualify for the dividends-received deduction) and the basis adjustment rules for 10%-or-more owned corporations are to interact. The statute also does not address the practical difficulties of obtaining earnings and profits information from corporations in which the taxpayer holds a minority interest.

The Technical Corrections Bill of 1987 provides that the earnings and profits of any lower-tier corporations owned by first-tier nonaffiliated 10%-owned corporations must be included in the earnings and profits adjustment to the tax book value amount.[282] In addition, it is made clear that the earnings and profits adjustment must be made for years before the Act.

As under prior law, interest expense arising from nonrecourse debt may be allocated to a specific class of gross income if the tests of Regulation Section 1.861-(8)(e)(2)(iv) are met. In addition, the Code authorizes the issuance of regulations allowing the specific allocation of interest expense for certain integrated financial transactions.[283]

Expenses other than interest not directly allocable or apportionable to a specific income-producing activity are allocated and apportioned as if all members of the affiliated group were a single corporation using the asset method.[284] Regulations are to be issued prescribing the method of apportioning interest and other expenses among members of an affiliated group to the categories of income described in the separate foreign tax credit limitation computations.[285]

To illustrate the application of the new rules, assume that Corporation C incurred \$500 of interest expense in 1987 on funds borrowed in 1987 and that Corporation C has no other debt. In addition, Corporation C owns one tax-exempt U.S. asset with a basis of \$500. Corporation C also owns domestic oil- and gas-related assets with a basis of \$1,500. Foreign assets used in branch operations have a basis of \$600. In addition, Corporation C owns 10% of the stock of a foreign corporation. This stock has a basis of \$300 and retained earnings associated with the stock of \$500.

To determine the amount of Corporation C's interest expense that must be deducted from foreign-source income, the \$500 of interest expense incurred in 1987 must be multiplied by the ratio of worldwide foreign assets to worldwide total assets. In this case, Corporation C has U.S. assets of \$1,500. Assets producing tax-exempt U.S.

279. I.R.C. Sec. 864(e)(3).
280. P.L. 99-514 (Tax Reform Act of 1986), Sec. 1215.
281. I.R.C. Sec. 864(e)(4).
282. Technical Corrections Bill of 1987, Sec. 112(g).
283. I.R.C. Sec. 864(e)(7).
284. I.R.C. Sec. 864(e)(6).
285. I.R.C. Sec. 864(e)(7).

income are not a factor in the expense apportionment. Corporation C's foreign assets are $1,400, which consists of the foreign assets of its branch operations, Corporation C's basis in its foreign stock and the stock's related retained earnings of $500. The amount of interest expense allocated to foreign sources is, therefore, $241 ($500 × $1,400 ÷ $2,900). The amount allocated to U.S.-source income is $259.

Case 206
Exploration for and Production of Oil and Gas on Foreign Concessions

Corporation C, a domestic corporation, enters into an arrangement for the exploration of oil and gas in foreign Country F. All oil and gas located within Country F is owned by the government. Corporation D, a corporation wholly owned by the government, has been granted the exclusive right to explore, develop and produce crude oil and natural gas within Country F. Corporation C enters into a production-sharing agreement with Corporation D, whereby Corporation C is granted an exclusive concession for the development of oil and gas in two noncontiguous areas. Corporation C does not obtain legal title to the minerals. The term of the agreement is for a period of 30 years.

Corporation C agrees to bear all the costs of exploration, development and production activities, and it must look solely to the production of oil and gas from the areas covered by the agreement to recover those costs. Corporation C is entitled to take 20% of all oil and gas produced each year to recover costs, and any production remaining after the recovery of costs is split 60% to Corporation D and 40% to Corporation C. If the costs to be recovered in a year are less than the 20% cost recovery oil, the excess is shared in the 60:40 ratio. The production-sharing agreement provides that lease operating costs are recoverable by Corporation C in the year incurred. Exploration and development costs are capitalized and amortized according to a specified number of years. Corporation C pays no income tax to Country F.

Corporation C pays a production bonus to Corporation D for a specified amount per acre in the year the agreement is consummated. The production bonus is consideration to Corporation D for the right to explore for and produce the minerals. Corporation C is obligated to expend $1 million on seismic costs in each area during the first year of the agreement. Corporation C must drill an exploratory well in each area in Year 2 to retain its interest in that area. If an exploratory well is successful, sufficient additional wells must be drilled to develop the property. Additional exploratory wells may be drilled in any year.

After the fifth anniversary of the agreement, Corporation C must relinquish its interest in one-third of the nonproductive acreage. Another one-half of the remaining nonproductive acreage must be relinquished after the eighth anniversary, and all remaining nonproductive acreage must be relinquished after the eleventh anniversary date.

Because the terms of the production-sharing arrangements differ from the agreements generally entered into for the exploration and development of domestic properties, the provisions must be reviewed carefully to determine the appropriate U.S. tax treatment. Generally, the same U.S. tax rules apply to the exploration, development and operation of an oil and gas property located in a foreign country as for property located in the United States; however, several significant differences exist.

The first significant difference in the treatment of domestic and foreign exploration and production operations is that percentage depletion is not allowable on foreign oil and gas production. Another important consideration is to determine whether any of the payments made to a foreign country constitute a creditable tax that can be used to offset U.S. tax.

To claim a deduction for cost depletion and amortization of foreign intangible drilling and development costs (IDC), Corporation C must have an economic interest in the minerals. This arrangement differs from most domestic arrangements in that Corporation C may never obtain legal title to the minerals. The Supreme Court has held that legal title to minerals is not necessary to have an economic interest in the minerals when the taxpayer acquires, by investment, an interest in minerals in place. The taxpayer must look to the income derived from the extraction of the mineral to recover his capital investment.[286] Because Corporation C is making a contribution essential to the extraction of minerals and it must look solely to the mineral extraction from the concession to recoup its investment, it should possess an economic interest in the minerals. In some countries, only corporations organized under the laws of that country may conduct oil and gas operations. It may be possible for a U.S. corporation to form a wholly owned foreign subsidiary to obtain the license and, if the laws of the foreign country permit, farm out the interest in the license to a U.S. corporation (or a domestic subsidiary). In a similar fact situation, the Internal Revenue Service (IRS) ruled that, because the U.S. company was to provide all funds for the development of the property and must look solely to production for a return of its investment, the U.S. company acquired an economic interest in the property.[287]

IDC associated with foreign (non-U.S.) properties are no longer currently deductible but must be amortized over a 10-year period[288] or capitalized as leasehold cost and recovered through the cost depletion allowance. Foreign property dry-hole costs are still currently deductible.[289] Corporation C is solely liable for the exploration and development of the property and for the payment of lease operating expenses once the property is placed in production. The interest retained by Corporation D is a nonoperating interest because it does not bear any of the burdens of developing and operating the property. Accordingly, Corporation C should be entitled to amortize all the foreign IDC because it owns all the operating rights in the property.[290]

The terms of foreign concessions differ significantly; consequently, a careful review of the manner in which the foreign country participates in production should be made. For example, in some cases, the foreign government or a company owned by the foreign government owns a portion of the operating rights or can elect to convert a nonoperating interest to an operating interest. If the U.S. company is paying a disproportionate amount of the IDC, it may have to capitalize as leasehold cost the portion that is not applicable to its operating interest. Presumably, the same rules regarding the recoupment of costs in carried-interest arrangements that are applicable to domestic operations also apply to foreign operations.[291] *(See Case 38.)*

286. Palmer v. Bender, 287 U.S. 551 (1933), 11 AFTR 1106, 3 USTC 1026; Comm'r v. Southwest Exploration Co., 350 U.S. 308 (1956), 48 AFTR 683, 56-1 USTC 9304.
287. Rev. Rul. 68-551, 1968-2 C.B. 261.
288. I.R.C. Sec. 263(i).
289. *Ibid.*
290. Reg. Sec. 1.612-4(a); I.R.C. Sec. 263(i).
291. I.R.C. Sec. 263(c); I.R.C. Sec. 263(i).

The production bonus paid to Corporation D is consideration for the assignment of the lease that should be capitalized by Corporation C as leasehold cost and recovered through cost depletion provided the property proves productive, or as a loss upon the worthlessness or abandonment on the property. *(See Case 2.)* The detailed provisions regarding any initial payments should be reviewed to see if any are in the nature of a delay rental that may be currently deductible.

Corporation C also is obligated to expend substantial sums of money for seismic costs. These costs should be capitalized as leasehold cost and recovered through cost depletion or through a loss upon the worthlessness or abandonment of the property. *(See Case 6.)*

Corporation C is not entitled to claim a foreign tax credit because no income tax is paid to Country F. The laws of many foreign countries impose an income tax on oil and gas operations, and a careful review of the concession agreement, the income tax statutes and the provisions of any tax treaties should be made to determine if the payments qualify as a creditable tax. *(See Cases 197 and 198.)*

To the extent Corporation C incurs an overall foreign loss from the concession operations, it is possible the losses will have to be recaptured in later years when operations become profitable. The mechanism for recapturing these losses is accomplished by limiting the amount of foreign tax credits that can be used. *(See Case 203.)*

In the agreement, Corporation C must relinquish its interest in a portion of the nonproductive acreage at specified times. There is a question whether a deduction may be claimed on the relinquishment of the property. Corporation C has at least two units of property because the two separate areas of interest are not contiguous.[292] It is clear a deduction will be allowed if all the acreage in one area is dropped because Corporation C will retain no further interest in that unit of property. The IRS probably will take the position that no deduction is allowable if only a portion of the interest in one of the areas is relinquished. The IRS holds that a deduction should be allowed when each separate unit of property is proven worthless.[293]

If the taxpayer has defined separate reservoirs or pools under each concession area, an election to treat the separate reservoirs as separate units of property should be considered. *(See Case 64.)* Because this election is valid for all purposes of the income tax provisions, if an interest in a complete pool or reservoir constituting a separate unit of property is relinquished, a loss can be claimed because all the interest in that reservoir or pool was relinquished.

Case 207
Vehicle for Conducting Foreign Operations

Corporation C, a domestic corporation, plans to explore for oil and gas in Country F. Corporation C is obligated to drill three exploratory wells in two years and, if any of the exploratory wells is successful, to drill a sufficient number of development wells to develop the properties.

For legal reasons, the president of Corporation C has been advised to conduct operations through a subsidiary. The company is considering the business and tax implications of operating either as a corporation incorporated in the foreign country or as a domestic corporation.

292. Reg. Sec. 1.614-1(a)(3).
293. Reg. Sec. 1.614-1(a)(1); I.R.C. Sec. 165; L. B. Maytag, 32 T.C. 270 (1959); Rev. Rul. 68-566, 1968-2 C.B. 281.

Corporation C has numerous subsidiaries and files a consolidated U.S. income tax return. Neither Corporation C nor any of its subsidiaries has foreign-source income.

Choosing the appropriate vehicle for conducting oil and gas operations in a foreign country generally involves many complex considerations. First, the company should determine if local laws permit operation of a corporation organized in the United States. In some countries, only a corporation organized in that country can conduct business. In addition, Corporation C should determine whether business reasons unrelated to tax considerations dictate a particular form of organization. Assuming there are no other business considerations, the most advantageous form of operation for Corporation C is the one that will result in the lowest combined U.S. and foreign tax over the life of the operations.

The following alternatives should be considered:

- ☐ Operation as a U.S. subsidiary throughout the life of the properties.
- ☐ Operation as a U.S. subsidiary until operations are profitable, with a subsequent transfer of assets to a corporation in the foreign country.
- ☐ Operation as a subsidiary organized in the foreign country.

If operations are conducted initially through a U.S. subsidiary, the Tax Reform Act of 1986 (the Act) mandates that foreign intangible drilling and development costs (IDC) be capitalized and deducted over 10 years or capitalized as leasehold cost and recovered through the cost depletion allowance. Although this requirement is clearly a detriment, the potentially lower U.S. tax rates make this form of organization attractive.

Deductions incurred in the foreign operations may result in no permanent reduction in U.S. tax if operations are conducted through a U.S. subsidiary. Although the deductions reduce U.S. taxable income, the foreign tax credit that can be used in later years may be reduced because of the provisions requiring the recapture of foreign losses.[294] If Corporation C incurs a loss from foreign activities subject to the rules requiring the recapture of foreign losses, the transfer of assets to a foreign subsidiary may result in the recognition of taxable income, even if the transaction will otherwise be nontaxable.[295] *(See Case 203.)* Even if the foreign loss recapture provisions apply, any current deduction for the amortization of IDC and other expenses incurred by the taxpayer may be beneficial since the decrease in U.S. tax enables the company to use the tax savings.

A transfer of property to a foreign corporation generally is a taxable transaction.[296] An exception is provided for the transfer of assets to be used in the active conduct of a trade or business.[297] *(See Case 208.)*

Because Corporation C has no other foreign activities, the decision is not as complex as it would be if other foreign activities were involved. In certain instances, a U.S. company may realize tax advantages through the use of a foreign corporation. If operations are conducted by a foreign subsidiary, an indirect benefit may be obtained by maximizing the available foreign tax credit through proper arrangement of the foreign subsidiary's dividend payments. For example, if Corporation C has a subsidiary operating in a high-tax-rate country and if the proposed foreign operations

294. I.R.C. Sec. 904(f)(1).
295. I.R.C. Sec. 904(f)(3).
296. I.R.C. Sec. 367(a)(1).
297. I.R.C. Sec. 367(a)(3)(A).

are to be conducted in a low-tax-rate country, proper planning of the timing of the dividends can result in averaging the tax rates to an amount equal to or below the U.S. tax rate. The rules limiting the amount of foreign taxes incurred for foreign oil- and gas-extraction income that may be used as a credit must be considered to determine the effectiveness of dividend timing. *(See Case 201.)* In addition, the benefits of this technique have been limited for post-1986 dividends because of the earnings and profits pooling computations introduced by the Act.

The earnings and profits of a foreign subsidiary must be computed to determine the amount of a dividend that is taxable and the amount, if any, of the foreign tax paid by the foreign subsidiary that will be deemed to have been paid by its U.S. parent. Under prior law, there were several different methods by which the earnings and profits of a foreign corporation could be computed.[298] One provided for elections similar to U.S. tax elections. The existence of these elections provided more flexibility to maximize the amount of the foreign tax credit, particularly if the taxpayer had numerous foreign activities. The Act limits the calculation to the rules under Sections 964 and 986 for tax years beginning after December 31, 1986.[299] For purposes of calculating earnings and profits, foreign IDC also must be amortized.[300]

If the exploration operations are conducted in a foreign subsidiary and the exploration activities are not successful, thus, proving that the oil and gas properties are worthless, a U.S. tax loss is achieved by establishing the worthlessness of the stock.[301] Because exploration operations entail great risk, it may be advisable to form a new foreign subsidiary for each major project rather than undertaking a new project in a foreign subsidiary that already has successful operations. If the new project is not successful, a U.S. tax benefit can be obtained by claiming a deduction for worthless stock, provided that the subsidiary has no other activity nor net assets. It may be difficult, however, to establish that a subsidiary is worthless and to sustain the deduction. If other operations are conducted by the subsidiary or if the subsidiary has assets in excess of liabilities, no deduction relating to the oil and gas activities may be claimed in the parent's U.S. tax return. If any U.S. tax benefit is obtained, it will be through a reduction in the taxable amount of dividends from the foreign subsidiary. The reason for this result is that the earnings and profits of the subsidiary will be reduced by the loss incurred on the worthlessness or abandonment of the property.

Another factor that should be considered in determining the most beneficial form of operation is the structure of the foreign country's withholding tax. Many foreign countries impose a withholding tax on actual dividends paid by a corporation operating in the foreign country. Such a withholding tax generally is a creditable tax; however, its payment may not result in a U.S. tax savings if the effective foreign tax rate, based on the total of the withholding tax and any foreign tax deemed paid by the U.S. corporation, exceeds the U.S. tax rate. If withholding taxes are not imposed on the profits of a branch operation, operation as a branch may result in a lower effective combined U.S. and foreign income tax. The laws for withholding taxes vary significantly from country to country. Thus, a careful review should be made to determine the manner in which these taxes are assessed. In addition, if the foreign country has a tax treaty with the United States, the treaty provisions should be reviewed to determine if a reduced rate applies to the withholding of tax on the payment of dividends.

298. I.R.C. Sec. 312; Reg. Sec. 1.964-1.
299. I.R.C. Sec. 902(c)(1).
300. I.R.C. Sec. 263(i).
301. I.R.C. Sec. 165(g)(3).

Case 208
Incorporation of a Branch

Corporation C, which is organized in the state of Delaware, is engaged in the exploration for and production of oil and gas in foreign Country F through a branch. For business reasons, management of Corporation C has decided to transfer the assets and operation of this business to a corporation organized in Country F in exchange for all the voting stock of the new corporation. The operations of the branch resulted in U.S. tax losses in 1985 and 1986 of approximately $300,000 and $400,000, respectively. The operations are expected to break even in 1987, and the company will complete the transfer on March 31, 1987.

Corporation C is engaged in the oil and gas exploration and production business in numerous foreign countries, and its combined activities have generated taxable income on a cumulative basis. Corporation C does not have any other types of foreign operations.

Before the Tax Reform Act of 1984, a U.S. person who transferred property to a foreign corporation in a transaction that otherwise would be accorded nonrecognition treatment was required to request an Internal Revenue Service (IRS) ruling within 183 days of the transfer.[302] The request had to demonstrate that the transfer was not part of a plan having as one of its principal purposes the avoidance of federal income taxes. If a ruling was not requested, the foreign corporation was not considered to be a corporation for U.S. tax purposes relating to the transaction. Because any applicable nonrecognition provision would require the transferee to be a corporation, the full amount of gain would be recognized and taxed. If a ruling was requested and the IRS determined that the transfer did not have tax avoidance as one of its principal purposes, generally no gain or loss would be recognized.

IRS guidelines published in 1968 focused on the use of the transferred property in determining whether a transfer qualified for nonrecognition.[303] If the transferee was going to use the property in the active conduct of its trade or business, a favorable ruling generally was granted. This rule did not apply to the transfer of certain assets, however, because the tax avoidance potential was considered too great. For these assets, called "tainted assets," the IRS required payment of a "toll charge" (i.e., a tax on the gain realized on the transfer of those assets), even if the assets were used in the foreign transferee's trade or business.[304] In the instance of the incorporation of a branch operation that incurred losses, the IRS took the position that these cumulative losses represented "tainted assets" and were subject to recapture to the extent the transferor had used the losses.[305]

In a similar fact situation, the Tax Court concluded that the transfer of foreign assets to a foreign corporation did not have tax avoidance as one of its principal purposes when there were valid business reasons for the transfer.[306] In that case, the IRS refused to issue a favorable ruling unless the taxpayer agreed to include in its U.S. taxable income an amount equal to the losses deducted in prior years. The IRS viewed the transfer of an unprofitable business to a foreign corporation as tax avoidance because future foreign-source income would not be subject to federal income tax. The Tax Court found this position to be unreasonable. Further, in situations where it was

---

302. I.R.C. Sec. 367 *(prior to amendment by Tax Reform Act of 1984).*
303. Rev. Proc. 68-23, 1968-1 C.B. 821; Rev. Proc. 80-14, 1980-1 C.B. 617.
304. *Ibid.*
305. Rev. Rul. 78-201, 1978-1 C.B. 91.
306. Hershey Foods Corp., 76 T.C. 312 (1981). *See also* Mars, Incorporated and Uncle Ben's, Inc., 88 T.C. No. 19 (1987).

demonstrated that there was no avoidance of federal income taxes, the Second Circuit Court of Appeals held that the recognition of income as a precedent to receiving a favorable ruling is not necessary or proper.[307]

This conflict was resolved by legislative action. The Tax Reform Act of 1984 provides that the incorporation of a foreign branch with excess losses that were deducted by the U.S. taxpayer may trigger recognition of gain. This occurs if the sum of the deducted branch losses exceeds the taxable income derived by the branch in years after the loss years and the amount of overall foreign losses recaptured on the transfer. The gain so recognized is treated as having the same character (capital gain or ordinary income) as the previous branch loss.[308] The Conference Report provides[309] that the recaptured branch losses to Corporation C are characterized as foreign oil-extraction income.

In addition, the Tax Reform Act of 1984 amended I.R.C. Section 367(a). The general rule is that all transfers of property to a foreign corporation are taxable, except the rule does not apply to property transferred to a foreign corporation for use in the active conduct of a trade or business outside the United States.[310] In a private letter ruling, the IRS reversed its earlier position that a nonoperated oil and gas working interest does not qualify for tax-free treatment because it is not used in the active conduct of a trade or business.[311] (*See Case 211.*) In addition, regulations issued in 1986 provide guidelines that should permit tax-free treatment for most such working interest transfers regardless of whether the transferor is the operator.[312]

Under prior IRS guidelines, it was clear that the gain recognized under the recapture rules for branch losses was reduced by any gain recognized on the transfer as a result of I.R.C. Section 904(f)(3).[313] However, due to the statutory construction of the Tax Reform Act of 1984, it is possible to recognize a gain on the incorporation of a loss branch that is greater than the gain realized as a result of the interplay between I.R.C. Section 367(a)(3)(C) and I.R.C. Section 904(f)(3).

For example, assume Corporation C wishes to convert Branch F to a corporation. Branch F has incurred $600 of losses which have been deducted by Corporation C. Branch F has never made a profit. Corporation C has a $200 overall foreign loss which has not been recaptured. Corporation C realizes a $300 gain on the incorporation of Branch F. The total gain recognized on the transfer is as follows:

Section 904(f)(3)	$200
Section 367(a)(3)(c)—lower of gain realized, $300, *or* loss incurred less Section 904(f)(3) recapture, ($600 - $200), $400	300
Total	$500

Thus, $500 of income would be recognized on the transfer, although only $300 of gain would be realized. Although Treasury officials are aware of this problem, it is understood there currently are no plans to correct the statute.

307. Gerli and Co. Inc. v. Comm'r, 668 F.2d 691 (2d Cir. 1982), 49 AFTR2d 82-569, 82-1 USTC 9167.
308. I.R.C. Sec. 367(a)(3)(C).
309. House Report No. 98-861, 1984-3 C.B. Vol. 2 956.
310. I.R.C. Sec. 367(a)(3)(A).
311. IRS Letter Ruling 8708053.
312. Temp. Reg. Sec. 1.367(a)-4T(e).
313. Rev. Rul. 80-246, 1980-2 C.B. 125.

Case 209
Conducting Oil and Gas Operations in the United States by Foreign Investors Through a U.S. Corporation

> Corporation B, a corporation organized in foreign Country F, plans to enter the oil and gas business in the United States. The corporation plans to open and staff an office in the United States, enter into leases of nonproducing acreage, develop the properties and operate any productive properties. Corporation B's attorneys advised, for legal reasons, that its operations be conducted through a subsidiary organized in the United States.
>
> The tax statutes of Country F generally tax the income from activities conducted within its boundaries. Income from operations conducted elsewhere is taxable in Country F only when repatriated.
>
> There is no tax treaty between the United States and Country F.

Deciding on the appropriate vehicle for a foreign entity to conduct operations in the United States involves complex business, legal and tax considerations. In some instances, business or legal reasons will dictate the vehicle to be used; in other cases, the primary goal will be to minimize the total tax burden imposed by the United States and the foreign country. The determination of the amount of the overall tax burden generally involves a review of the appropriate U.S. tax statutes, foreign tax statutes and the appropriate treaty provisions if an income tax treaty exists between the United States and the foreign country.

The U.S. taxation of the ownership of oil and gas working interests in the United States conducted by a foreign corporation is discussed in the next case. *(See Case 210.)* Due to changes pursuant to the Tax Reform Act of 1986 in this area (namely, lower U.S. corporate tax rates and the imposition of an additional branch tax on foreign corporations), reconsideration of the existing structure is often necessary.

The ownership of U.S. government leases is restricted to domestic corporations and U.S. citizens. If an investment in U.S. government leases is contemplated, additional consideration must be given to the appropriate form of organization.

The United States imposes a 30% withholding tax on dividends paid from a U.S. corporation to a foreign recipient.[314] *(However, see Case 210.)* Since Corporation B is conducting its U.S. activities through a U.S. subsidiary, the 30% withholding tax must be paid on dividends paid by the subsidiary to Corporation B.

A decision on the method of operation also should consider future needs for profits (and capital) anticipated from the U.S. operations. Will they be repatriated to Country F, or will there be a need for them in another country? Thus, some long-term planning is needed. Tax considerations related to the long-term use of the profits may be inconsistent with the ideal tax results that can be achieved while entering into and carrying on the U.S. oil and gas business. Generally, it is difficult to take U.S. profits and use them directly in another country without subjecting future profits in that country to U.S. tax.

---

314. I.R.C. Sec. 1442.

In addressing long-term structural needs, there is no single answer. Various factors need to be analyzed and evaluated, including:

- ☐ The countries in which Corporation B may like to use the profits and how their tax systems work.
- ☐ The amount of losses likely to be incurred and the countries in which Corporation B may have profits against which it would like to deduct these losses.
- ☐ The withholding tax rates that may apply on interest and dividends paid from the United States to a tax haven country.
- ☐ Whether a legal entity is available in a tax haven country that may be a corporation for U.S. tax purposes and a partnership for tax purposes in Country F.

Several alternative structures can be used, including a U.S. holding company, a foreign (tax haven) holding company, a branch of the U.S. company, etc.

Case 210
U.S. Taxation of a Foreign Corporation

> **Corporation B, a corporation organized under the laws of Country F, plans to invest substantial sums in oil and gas exploration in the United States. Although definite arrangements have not been finalized, Corporation B's management anticipates acquiring working interests in various oil and gas properties. Because of the tax laws of Country F, Corporation B will conduct these activities through a branch.**
>
> **There is no tax treaty between the United States and Country F.**

The manner in which a branch of a foreign corporation is taxed in the United States depends on whether it is engaged in a trade or business within the United States. If it is engaged in a trade or business, the income from the U.S. trade or business is first taxed at the regular corporate tax rates, and then the net earnings, to the extent not reinvested in the United States, are subject to the branch-profits tax (BPT) at 30%.[315] In addition, a 30% U.S. withholding tax is imposed on certain passive income from U.S. sources (including interest, dividends, rents and royalties) that is not effectively connected with the branch's trade or business.[316] On the other hand, if a foreign corporation is not engaged in a trade or business in the United States, it is taxed at a rate of 30% on passive income from sources within the United States.[317] The 30% withholding tax is imposed on gross income, while deductions for business expenses are allowed in determining the income from a trade or business. Consequently, it is important to understand the meaning of the term *engaged in a trade or business.* The Tax Reform Act of 1984 contains a repeal of the 30% withholding tax on interest paid on portfolio indebtedness by U.S. borrowers to nonresident aliens and foreign corporations not engaged in a U.S. trade or business;[318] however, neither the statute nor the regulations define a *U.S. trade or business.* The passive receipt of income is generally not a trade or business. However, when a corporation's activities in the United States are continuous and regular, the corporation generally is engaged in a trade or business.[319] For example, if a foreign corporation maintains an office in the United States that conducts manufacturing activities or purchases goods for resale in

---

315. I.R.C. Sec. 882(a); I.R.C. Sec. 884.
316. I.R.C. Sec. 881(a); I.R.C. Sec. 882(a).
317. I.R.C. Sec. 881(a).
318. I.R.C. Sec. 1441(c)(9); I.R.C. Sec. 871(h)(2); I.R.C. Sec. 881(c)(2).
319. Rev. Rul. 73-522, 1973-2 C.B. 226; Elizabeth Herbert, 30 T.C. 26 (1958); European Naval Stores; 11 T.C. 127 (1948).

the United States, it is engaged in a trade or business.[320] However, if it has an office located in the United States that merely fills orders for its home office located in its country of incorporation it generally is not engaged in a trade or business.[321]

If a foreign corporation owns an operating or working interest in oil and gas properties in the United States, it generally is considered to be engaged in a trade or business within the United States and, consequently, will be taxed on all its income effectively connected with the operation of the oil and gas properties.[322] Legislation enacted in 1980 governs taxation on dispositions of United States real property interests. *(See Case 211.)*

Detailed rules exist for determining whether rents, royalties, dividends, interest and other passive income derived from U.S. sources are effectively connected with a U.S. trade or business.[323] Similar rules exist to determine whether income from foreign sources is effectively connected with a U.S. trade or business.[324] A nonresident alien individual or a foreign corporation is considered to be engaged in a U.S. trade or business if a partnership of which it is a partner is so engaged.[325]

Another common type of mineral interest that may be owned in the U.S. is a royalty interest entitling the owner to a specified share of the gross production from an oil and gas well. A royalty interest owner usually does not participate in making decisions concerning the development and operation on the property and does not bear any portion of these costs. To determine how royalty income is taxed, a determination first must be made whether it is included with other business income. If it is not effectively connected with the conduct of a U.S. trade or business, U.S. tax at a rate of 30% of the gross royalty income is imposed. Generally, the payor of the royalty will be required to withhold the 30% U.S. tax.

The statute provides a special election under which royalty income not effectively connected with the trade or business may be treated by the taxpayer as if it were so connected.[326] Once an election is made, it is applicable for all subsequent tax years and applies to income from all royalty interests.

The Tax Reform Act of 1986 (the Act) imposes a branch-profits tax on a foreign corporation engaged in a U.S. trade or business. The BPT is in addition to the U.S. corporate tax and is imposed at the rate of 30% (or lower treaty rate) on the corporation's effectively connected "earnings and profits" without reduction for dividend distributions (i.e., the dividend equivalent amount or "DEA").[327] Prior years' deficits will not carry forward to reduce current-year effectively connected earnings and profits for purposes of determining the BPT. If the DEA is invested in U.S. assets (i.e., oil and gas properties and associated lease and well equipment effectively connected with the U.S. trade or business), the DEA can be decreased or eliminated for that year. However, where there is a decrease in the aggregate adjusted basis of plant, property or equipment, a branch-profits tax on the amounts previously reinvested is imposed, unless the decrease is due to a complete liquidation or termination of the foreign corporation's U.S. trade or business. The Technical Corrections Bill of 1987 clarifies the calculation of the DEA such that the DEA is

320. European Naval Stores; Continental Trading, Inc. v. Comm'r, 265 F.2d 40 (9th Cir. 1959), 3 AFTR2d 923, 59-1 USTC 9316.
321. I.R.C. Sec. 864(c)(4); I.R.C. Sec. 864(c)(5).
322. I.R.C. Sec. 882(a).
323. I.R.C. Sec. 864(c)(2).
324. I.R.C. Sec. 864(c)(4).
325. I.R.C. Sec. 875.
326. I.R.C. Sec. 882(d).
327. I.R.C. Sec. 884(a).

limited to the post-1986 accumulated effectively connected earnings and profits of the U.S. branch that have not been remitted to the branch's home office.[328]

Treaty provisions precluding a branch-profits tax are not overridden unless treaty shopping is involved. Treaty shopping is involved if: (1) the foreign corporation is at least 50% owned (directly or indirectly) by individuals who are not residents of the treaty country or who are not U.S. citizens or resident aliens or (2) 50% or more of its income is used to meet liabilities to persons who are not treaty country residents or who are not U.S. citizens or residents. Under the changes proposed by the Technical Corrections Bill of 1987, if a foreign corporation is treaty shopping, the BPT will be imposed, regardless of whether the treaty between the United States and the country in which the corporation is a resident allows the U.S. to impose its withholding tax on dividends.[329]

On December 12, 1986, the Internal Revenue Service (IRS) indicated[330] that regulations will be issued providing that a branch-profits tax will not generally be imposed: (1) when a foreign corporation completely terminates its U.S. business, (2) when a foreign corporation liquidates its U.S. business into a foreign parent under Section 332, (3) when a foreign corporation transfers its U.S. trade or business in a reorganization to another foreign corporation or (4) when a foreign corporation incorporates its U.S. branch under Section 351. Thus, a foreign corporation with no annual earnings and profits will not be subject to the BPT during the operating years or on its gain on the final disposal of its assets. Also, a foreign corporation that continually reinvests its earnings and profits to avoid an annual BPT will no longer be subject to the BPT on its gain when it finally disposes of its assets, nor will it have to recapture reinvested amounts for purposes of the BPT. As a result, depending on the nature of the operations, it may not be necessary for certain branches to be restructured to avoid the BPT. The IRS notice indicates that the rules contained in the notice may be relied on with respect to the transactions specified therein. Note that in situation (4) above (i.e., Section 351 incorporation of a U.S. branch), the IRS may provide regulations indicating that distributions from a U.S. subsidiary or gain from sale of stock in the subsidiary may be subject to a BPT or a withholding tax.

The Act also lowers the threshold for imposition of the U.S. secondary withholding tax on dividends to 25% of gross income instead of 50% under prior law. Thus, if more than 25% of a foreign corporation's gross income for the three preceding years is effectively connected with a U.S. trade or business, it can be subject to the secondary withholding tax on dividends. The Technical Corrections Bill of 1987 also clarifies that the withholding tax on dividends is not imposed for any tax year with respect to dividends paid out of earnings and profits of the corporation for that year if the BPT may be imposed for that year (even if no BPT may be due in that year).[331] Thus, the withholding tax on dividends paid by a foreign corporation may be imposed in two cases. First, the withholding tax may be imposed on dividends that are attributable to pre-1987 earnings and profits. Second, the withholding tax may be imposed on dividends that are attributable to any earnings and profits when the BPT is prohibited by an operable treaty with the United States, regardless of when the dividends are distributed.

The threshold is eliminated entirely for interest. Thus, a secondary withholding tax is imposed, regardless of the percentage of the foreign corporation's gross income that is effectively connected with its U.S. trade or business. The branch-level interest tax is

328. Technical Corrections Bill of 1987, Sec. 112(o)(1).
329. Technical Corrections Bill of 1987, Sec. 112(o)(2).
330. IRS Notice 86-17, 1986-52 I.R.B. 19.
331. Technical Corrections Bill of 1987, Sec. 112(o)(2)(B).

imposed on: (1) interest paid directly by the U.S. branch and (2) the interest expense allocated to the branch under Regulation Section 1.882-5 in excess of the interest actually paid by it. The rate of withholding tax on the amount of excess interest expense allocable to the U.S. branch is 30% or the lower treaty rate for the foreign corporation. (In effect, the branch is treated as if it were a separate U.S. subsidiary of the foreign corporation.) Interest paid by the branch to third parties is subject to the withholding tax applicable between the United States and the third party. Rules similar to the treaty overrides applicable to the BPT are also applicable to the branch-level interest tax. The Technical Corrections Bill of 1987 clarifies that the prohibition against treaty shopping of recipients of interest paid or deducted by a U.S. trade or business of a foreign corporation applies to any person attempting to claim benefits under the interest articles of the treaty of the country in which the foreign corporation is resident.[332] The bill specifically allows the recipient to claim benefits under the treaty in the country in which the recipient is resident, unless the recipient is treaty shopping as well.

The U.S. tax laws have certain unique provisions for the exploration and development of minerals. The two most significant provisions in oil and gas taxation concern the option to deduct domestic intangible drilling and development costs (IDC) and the allowance for depletion.

If a taxpayer makes a proper election, IDC (which may include a substantial portion of the cost of drilling and preparing a well for the production of oil and gas) are deductible in the year paid or incurred. The election is binding on future years and must be made in the U.S. income tax return for the year in which the costs first were paid or incurred. *(See Case 23.)*

A taxpayer may not be able to deduct all IDC. In some drilling arrangements, a participant is responsible for paying a percentage of the costs of drilling a well that is greater than the profits attributable to his share of the working interest in the well. In these arrangements, the excess portion may not be deducted but must be capitalized as leasehold cost. The structure of the arrangement sometimes can be changed to avoid this capitalization. The rules governing the capitalization of IDC in these arrangements are very complex. *(See Section II.)*

The costs of lease and well equipment and other tangible assets are recovered by claiming a deduction for depreciation. *(See Section IV.)* The deduction may be based on rules provided for in the statute or, in the case of lease and well equipment, based on the percentage of reserves produced in the tax year. Once a method of depreciation has been adopted, depreciation must be claimed. In contrast to the practice allowable in many countries where the taxpayer has an option on the amount of capital costs to be recovered in a tax year, for U.S. tax purposes, a taxpayer must deduct the amount of depreciation computed under one of the available methods. The U.S. income tax law provides that the cost of acquiring an oil and gas property can be recovered through the allowance for depletion. This deduction is the greater of cost depletion or percentage depletion, if available, computed on a property-by-property basis. Cost depletion is computed by amortizing the cost of the property over the life of the oil and gas reserves, with the deduction each year being based on the percentage of reserves produced during that year. Percentage depletion is based on a percentage of gross income from each property, subject to many restrictions and limitations. Generally, the depletion allowance is 15% of gross income. In addition, percentage depletion may be claimed only with respect to a limited amount of production. Certain taxpayers

332. Technical Corrections Bill of 1987, Sec. 112(o)(2)(C).

who are engaged in the refining or retailing of oil and gas products may not claim percentage depletion, except for certain production of natural gas. *(See Section IV.)*

The United States and Country F have not entered into an income tax treaty. If a treaty exists, U.S. taxation generally will be governed by the treaty provisions rather than by the U.S. tax statutes because the provisions of an income tax treaty generally take precedence in case of a conflict.[333] However, a section of the Internal Revenue Code enacted subsequent to a treaty, which manifests a specific intent by Congress to override an earlier treaty provision, will take precedence over the treaty.[334]

Generally, a treaty exempts certain types of income from U.S. or foreign tax and provides for the types of activities taxable in each country. Because each treaty is negotiated with representatives of that particular country, provisions of the treaties vary. Even the definitions of terms vary from treaty to treaty. Accordingly, each treaty in question must be analyzed to determine its impact on a particular fact situation. An income tax treaty also may contain provisions defining exactly when a taxpayer is engaged in a U.S. trade or business. For example, many treaties provide two criteria. First, the foreign company must be engaged in a trade or business. Second, the trade or business must be carried on through a permanent establishment located in the United States. A permanent establishment may include a branch, an office, a factory, a workshop, a place of management, a mine, or an oil or gas well or other place of extraction. Under many treaties, an oil or gas well is a permanent establishment in the U.S., and the owner of a working interest in the well usually is considered to be engaged in a U.S. trade or business.

If Corporation B were to invest in a U.S. partnership engaged wholly in U.S. oil and gas operations, the partnership would have to withhold 20% of any cash distributed to Corporation B.[335] If less than 80% of the partnership's gross income is effectively connected with a U.S. trade or business, then only the effectively connected percentage of any distribution would be subject to this withholding.[336]

Case 211
U.S. Taxation of Nonresident Individuals Who Are Not Citizens of the United States

> Individual A, a citizen and resident of Country F, invested substantial sums in the exploration for oil and gas in the United States in 1987. Because of Country F's tax laws, Individual A conducts these operations as an individual rather than in corporate form.
>
> There is no tax treaty between the United States and Country F.

The U.S. taxation of individuals who are not citizens of the United States depends on whether the individual is a resident of the United States.[337] A resident who is not a U.S. citizen is, nevertheless, subject to U.S. tax on his income from U.S. and foreign sources. However, an individual who is neither a citizen nor resident of the United States generally is taxed on U.S.-source income effectively connected with a U.S. trade or business and on passive income from U.S. sources, such as dividends, rents, interest, etc., that is not effectively connected with a U.S. trade or business. Income effectively

333. I.R.C. Sec. 7852(d).
334. Cook v. U.S., 288 U.S. 102 (1933).
335. I.R.C. Sec. 1446(a).
336. I.R.C. Sec. 1446(b).
337. I.R.C. Sec. 871. *See also* I.R.C. Sec. 7701(b).

connected with a U.S. trade or business is taxed at regular, graduated U.S. individual tax rates, while passive income not effectively connected with a U.S. trade or business is subject to U.S. tax at a rate of 30%.[338] Under certain specific exceptions, passive income satisfying the definition of portfolio interest is not subject to U.S. tax.[339]

Neither the Internal Revenue Code nor regulations define the term *trade or business* for this purpose. Ownership of an oil and gas working interest constitutes a trade or business for purposes of the income tax, estate tax and self-employment tax.[340] However, in denying two private letter rulings[341] seeking a determination under I.R.C. Section 367, the Internal Revenue Service (IRS) stated that activity from nonoperator working interests does not constitute the conduct of an active trade or business. The technical arguments advanced in denying the rulings disregard the longstanding principle that a working interest constitutes a trade or business. *(See Case 208.)* Recently, the IRS reversed its previous position in earlier private letter rulings finding that, indeed, nonoperator working interests (as well as royalty interests, convertible into working interests) do constitute an active trade or business.[342] The reversal is welcomed and follows other IRS policy; e.g., it is the position of the IRS that a nonresident owner of rental real estate is engaged in a U.S. trade or business when activities are more than mere receipt of income and payment of expenses and are considerable, continuous and regular.[343] Also, when a partnership is engaged in a U.S. trade or business, its partners who are nonresident aliens or a foreign corporation also are so engaged.[344]

Individual A is engaged in a trade or business in the United States by virtue of his ownership of working interests located in the United States, and the net income attributable to his U.S. oil and gas operations (including any income from U.S. and certain foreign sources that is effectively connected with the conduct of his oil and gas business) is subject to U.S. tax. Correspondingly, Individual A is allowed a deduction for all U.S.-source and certain foreign-source ordinary and necessary business expenses relating to his oil and gas operations.[345] Interestingly, the U.S. Court of Claims held[346] that income received by a nonresident alien from trusts holding oil and gas leases is not effectively connected with a U.S. trade or business. The trust had assigned extensive operating rights under its leases to a management company. Further, the trust had no interest in or control over the management company. This case specifically conflicts with the IRS's general position that a working interest owner is engaged in a trade or business.[347]

I.R.C. Section 897 provides that gain or loss of a nonresident alien or foreign corporation from disposition of a U.S. real property interest shall be treated as if the taxpayer were engaged in a U.S. trade or business and as if the gain or loss were effectively connected with that trade or business.[348] Included in the definition of *U.S. real property interests* are interests in a mine, well or other natural deposit located in the United States, interests in personal property associated with the use of the real property and certain interests in U.S. corporations.[349] The regulations, however, point out that personal property, such as a contracted drilling rig, will be included in the

338. I.R.C. Sec. 871(a); I.R.C. Sec. 871(b).
339. I.R.C. Sec. 871(h).
340. Rev. Rul. 68-226, 1968-1 C.B. 362; Rev. Rul. 61-55, 1961-1 C.B. 713; Rev. Rul. 58-166, 1958-1 C.B. 324.
341. IRS Letter Ruling 8406059; IRS Letter Ruling 8415037.
342. IRS Letter Ruling 8708053.
343. Rev. Rul. 73-522, 1973-2 C.B. 226.
344. I.R.C. Sec. 875(1).
345. I.R.C. Sec. 873.
346. Di Portanova v. U.S., 690 F.2d 169 (Ct. Cl. 1982), 50 AFTR2d 82-5839, 82-2 USTC 9598.
347. Rev. Rul. 68-226, 1968-1 C.B. 362; Rev. Rul. 61-55, 1961-1 C.B. 713; Rev. Rul. 58-166, 1958-1 C.B. 324.
348. I.R.C. Sec. 897(a); I.R.C. Sec. 871(b)(1); I.R.C. Sec. 882(a)(1).
349. I.R.C. Sec. 897(c)(1); I.R.C. Sec. 897(c)(6).

definition of U.S. real property interests only where both the rig and the oil interest (U.S. real property) is held by the same (or related) person.[350] Thus, lease and well equipment is normally U.S. real property. The definition of *real property* includes improvements to the land (e.g., oil derricks, oil and gas pipelines and storage tanks).[351] Individual foreign investors who hold real property directly have tax reporting requirements.[352]

Unique U.S. tax provisions exist for entities engaged in the exploration and production of oil and gas. Of primary importance is the election to deduct intangible drilling and development costs and the allowance of a deduction for depletion. *(See Cases 23 and 79.)* Individual A may take advantage of these provisions in determining the taxable income attributable to his U.S. oil and gas operations.

Individual A also could be subject to the alternative minimum tax, a tax in lieu of the regular tax.[353] *(See Case 175.)*

If Individual A were a resident of a country with which the United States has entered into a tax treaty, the provisions of the tax treaty should be reviewed because the treaty provisions generally take precedence over federal tax law. The purpose of the treaties is to alleviate double taxation of income from transactions that cross national boundaries, and often the tax treaty may contain more favorable tax treatment than the regular federal income tax rules. *(See Case 209.)*

If Individual A were to invest in a U.S. partnership engaged wholly in U.S. oil and gas operations, the partnership would have to withhold 20% of any cash distributed to him.[354] If less than 80% of the partnership's gross income is effectively connected with a U.S. trade or business, then only the effectively connected percentage of any distribution would be subject to this withholding.[355]

350. Reg. Sec. 1.897-1(b)(4).
351. Reg. Sec. 1.897-1(b)(3).
352. I.R.C. Sec. 6039C.
353. I.R.C. Sec. 55.
354. I.R.C. Sec. 1446(a).
355. I.R.C. Sec. 1446(b).

Section IX
The Crude Oil Windfall Profit Tax

The windfall profit tax (WPT) was coupled with the phased decontrol of domestically produced crude oil prices, which began on June 1, 1979, and was scheduled to be completed on September 30, 1981, to " . . . prevent unearned, excessive profits which the oil companies would receive as a result of decontrol and possible future OPEC increases." The decontrol program then was accelerated with the removal of all government price controls on January 28, 1981, eight months earlier than scheduled under the phased decontrol program.

The Crude Oil Windfall Profit Tax Act of 1980 imposes an excise tax on the windfall profit (as defined) derived from the sale of crude oil produced from domestic wells. The rate of tax depends on the classification of the oil and the status of the producer. The WPT is imposed on the producer (generally, any economic interest owner) and, based on information the producer provides, it generally is calculated initially, withheld and paid by the first purchaser of the oil. The amount subject to the tax, i.e., the windfall profit, cannot exceed 90% of the net income (as defined) from the property attributable to the production of crude oil. The WPT, which is withheld initially by the first purchaser and paid on behalf of the producer, may be excessive and later may become the subject of a claim for refund or credit.

The WPT generally is imposed on each barrel of domestic crude oil removed from the premises after February 29, 1980; however, certain domestic crude oil production is exempt from the WPT. Generally, exempt oil is restricted to certain new discoveries in Alaska, qualifying front-end tertiary oil, certain stripper well oil and limited amounts of royalty oil.

The WPT is imposed on the "windfall profit," which is the excess of the removal price of each barrel of crude oil over the sum of a defined base price (adjusted for inflation since June 1979) and a severance tax adjustment. The applicable base price depends on the classification of the oil. The depressed prices of oil recently have resulted essentially in the elimination of the windfall profit and, thus, the tax because the removal price has been less than the defined base price.

Oil is classified according to June 1979 Department of Energy regulations, even though those regulations no longer are effective for their original purpose of price control. Taxable crude oil production is divided into three tiers:

Tier 1. Taxable crude oil other than tier-2 and -3 oil, i.e., generally, oil produced from a property that had production in 1978 and oil produced from Outer Continental Shelf leases entered into before January 1, 1979.

Tier 2. Oil from a stripper well property and oil produced from an economic interest in a Naval Petroleum Reserve held by the United States.

Tier 3. Newly discovered oil (as defined in the June 1979 Department of Energy regulations), heavy oil and incremental tertiary oil.

The various WPT rates by tier and nonexempt producer status are:

Classification of Oil	Rates of Tax (Percent) Independent Producer[1]	Other Nonexempt Producer
Tier 1—Working Interest	50	70
Nonoperating interest	70	70
Tier 2—Working Interest	30[2]	60
Nonoperating interest	60	60
Tier 3—Newly discovered	22½[2,3]	22½[3]
Heavy and incremental tertiary oil	30	30

1. Rates apply to the first 1,000 barrels per day of combined tier-1 and -2 working interest production (not including exempt stripper well production or production from certain transferred properties)—excess is subject to the same rates as other nonexempt producers.
2. Production from a stripper well property attributable to an independent producer's working interest in the property generally is exempt from WPT, effective for oil removed after December 31, 1982.
3. This rate is effective for tax periods (calendar quarters) beginning in 1984 through 1987. The rates are scheduled to be reduced to 20% in 1988 and 15% in 1989 and thereafter.

Independent-producer status for WPT purposes generally is determined under the same criteria used to determine eligibility for percentage depletion under federal income tax regulations. Thus, an independent producer is any producer except one considered to be a retailer or refiner. A refiner is a producer with refinery throughput of more than 50,000 barrels on any day during a calendar year. A retailer is a producer with sales of oil, natural gas or products derived therefrom, through retail outlets, exceeding $5 million for a calendar year.

Generally, the first purchaser of the oil is required to withhold the WPT from the sales proceeds payable to the producer. Deposits of the withheld taxes are required of first purchasers, other than integrated oil companies and certain independent refiners, no later than 45 days following the end of the month during which the oil is removed from the premises. Quarterly excise tax returns also are required to be filed by the first purchaser. In addition, the first purchaser must furnish a report annually to the producer, with a copy to the Internal Revenue Service, showing the WPT withheld from remittances for oil removed during the year and certain other information.

To carry out the reporting and withholding responsibilities, the first purchaser must have a great deal of data and information regarding the property and the status of the producer(s) that hold economic interests in the property. The operator of the property must provide this data and this information to the first purchaser.

The WPT withheld and deposited by the first purchaser is treated as WPT paid by the purchaser on the last day of the first February following the end of the calendar year during which the oil is removed from the premises. The producer is not required to file an annual WPT return unless his liability for WPT is more than the tax withheld by the first purchaser.

In certain situations, the first purchaser is relieved of his responsibilities for withholding and depositing WPT and for filing quarterly returns. The most notable of these situations are as follows:

- ☐ The oil is removed from the premises before it is sold, or manufacture or conversion of the oil into refined products begins before the oil is removed from the premises.
- ☐ The producer is an integrated oil company that has furnished a certificate that states that, as the producer, the company will deposit its own WPT.
- ☐ The first purchaser has received a qualified disburser certificate.

☐ The purchaser and the operator have elected jointly to have the operator assume the purchaser's duties of withholding and depositing the WPT.

☐ The producer has filed an exemption certificate with the first purchaser (or operator).

If not relieved of the responsibility to withhold, the first purchaser is liable for the payment of the amount of tax required to be withheld.

Integrated oil companies are required to deposit both the WPT withheld by them as first purchasers and WPT on oil for which withholding is not required on the ninth day of the semimonthly period after the period during which the oil is removed from the premises. Thus, integrated oil companies are subject to more stringent deposit requirements than are other first purchasers.

Producers cannot file claims for refund or credit of overpaid WPT due to withholding errors until after the WPT is deemed paid by them on the last day of the first February following the end of the calendar year during which the oil is removed from the premises. Thus, calendar-year taxpayers need not delay filing their claims for refund of overpaid WPT, whether due to withholding errors or the application of the 90% net income limitation, beyond the due date of their income tax returns. Fiscal-year taxpayers, on the other hand, must delay filing their 90% net income limitation claims until the end of their tax year. In most cases, this delay will necessitate the filing of two claims if fiscal-year taxpayers want to obtain the WPT refunds as soon as possible.

Case 212
Computation of Windfall Profit Tax

Operator A, an independent producer, and Company C, an integrated oil company, each have production for 1987 from Property X (tier-1 oil), Property Y (tier-2 oil, Naval Petroleum Reserve) and Property Z (tier-3, newly discovered oil). Both Operator A and Company C use calendar years for income tax reporting purposes. Following is an example of the computation of the windfall profit tax (WPT) for the month of June 1987, using various assumed amounts:

	Operator A (Per Barrel)			Company C (Per Barrel)		
	Property X	Property Y	Property Z	Property X	Property Y	Property Z
Removal price*	$30.00	$30.00	$30.00	$30.00	$30.00	$30.00
Less:						
Adjusted base price	18.51	22.51	28.46	18.51	22.51	28.46
Severance tax adjustment	.57	.37	.08	.57	.37	.08
Windfall profit	$10.92	$ 7.12	$ 1.46	$10.92	$ 7.12	$ 1.46
90% net income limitation for 1987 (separately computed)	$ 8.00	$10.00	$11.00	$ 8.00	$10.00	$11.00
Amount subject to WPT	$ 8.00	$ 7.12	$ 1.46	$ 8.00	$ 7.12	$ 1.46
WPT rate	50%	30%	22.5%	70%	60%	22.5%
WPT	$ 4.00	$ 2.14	$ .33	$ 5.60	$ 4.27	$ .33

*Assumed for illustration purposes only.

The excess of the removal price (generally, the selling price) of the taxable crude oil over the sum of a defined base is the *windfall profit.*[1] This windfall profit amount then is compared to a separately computed 90% net income limitation amount for the year. The lesser of the two amounts is multiplied by the applicable tax rate to determine the windfall profit tax.[2]

For tax periods (calendar quarters) beginning after 1983, the WPT rate for newly discovered oil is as follows:

For Tax Periods Beginning in	Applicable Percentage[3]
1984-1987	22.5
1988	20
1989 and thereafter	15

These scheduled rate reductions do not apply to heavy and incremental tertiary oil, which will remain subject to tax at the 30% rate.

The currently proposed definition of *newly discovered* oil for purposes of the WPT is that it must be taxable crude oil: (1) from a lease on the Outer Continental Shelf entered into on or after January 1, 1979, (2) from a property (not on the Outer Continental Shelf) that did not produce crude oil in commercial quantities in calendar year 1978 or (3) from any unitized property made up entirely of leases from (1) or (2).[4]

Crude oil is considered to have been produced in commercial quantities if any of the crude oil produced is sold, exchanged or retained for the beneficial economic use of the operator or producer of that production.[5] However, production *incidental* to the drilling of an exploratory well need not be considered when determining whether there has been commercial production.[6] (It has been held that production from a well shut-in during November 1978 would qualify as newly discovered tier-3 oil. The well was started in September 1978, and well casing was perforated during November 1978. The well was then shut-in, and the test oil that had been flowed into a pit was burned. Apparently, there was no other production during 1978.)[7] Whether production can be considered incidental depends on facts and circumstances, but production after the installation of the Christmas tree is not to be considered incidental.[8]

Unfortunately, in many cases, a certain amount of testing to determine if a well is productive actually occurs after the installation of the Christmas tree. If the date of that testing was during 1978, the proposed regulation would treat such well as a commercial producer as of the date of that test production even though the well may be abandoned after the testing has been completed. Production from other wells drilled and completed on that same WPT property after 1978 would never be considered newly discovered oil and, thus, eligible for the lower WPT rates. This arbitrary definition seemed overly restrictive. The Tax Reform Act of 1986 provides some relief. If the aggregate amount of oil produced from the property during 1978 did not exceed 2,200 barrels (whether or not the oil was sold) and no well on the property was in

1. I.R.C. Sec. 4988(a); Reg. Sec. 51.4988-1(a).
2. I.R.C. Sec. 4988(b).
3. I.R.C. Sec. 4987(b)(3).
4. Prop. Reg. Sec. 51.4996-1(m).
5. Prop. Reg. Sec. 51.4996-1(n).
6. *Ibid.*
7. IRS Letter Ruling 8324010 (Technical Advice Memorandum).
8. Prop. Reg. Sec. 51.4996-1(n).

production for more than 72 total hours, the property will not be considered to have produced oil in commercial quantities.[9]

An independent producer's production attributable to his working interest in a stripper well property will generally be exempt from WPT for oil removed after December 31, 1982.[10] (*See Case 228.*)

The Internal Revenue Service (IRS) has published its amended rules regarding appeals of WPT issues.[11] Generally, the IRS will now provide a single, consolidated appeals conference to determine all "oil items" arising in connection with a property or lease if such a conference would be more effective for administration of the WPT. An item is an *oil item* if it is more readily determined at the property level rather than the producer level. Tax tier, adjusted base price and removal price are examples of oil items. These amendments will not affect a producer's administrative appeal rights with respect to "producer items" (items more readily determined at the producer level, such as exemptions and independent-producer status). If the IRS elects to review a property, it will contact the operator of the property. If an adjustment is proposed, the IRS will notify each producer of the proposed change in a letter that also invites written comments and indicates where the appeals conference will be held. The operator must provide a current list of the producers with an interest in the property. Any producer wishing to attend the consolidated appeals conference must provide a written statement of his intention to attend. *(See Cases 225 and 226 for a discussion of partnership WPT rules.)*

Case 213
Property Unit for Windfall Profit Tax Purposes

In December 1971, Landowner A granted a single oil and gas lease covering a 640-acre tract of land to Producer B. The term of the lease was 20 years.

In March 1973, Producer B subleased the 160-acre northeast quarter of the 640-acre tract to Producer C. Simultaneously, Producer B subleased the 160-acre southeast quarter of the 640-acre tract to Producer D.

In 1974, Producer C drilled a commercially productive oil well on his tract, and, in 1976, Producer D drilled a commercially productive oil well on his tract.

In March 1987, Producer B farmed out an undivided 50% interest in the 320-acre west half of the 640-acre tract to Corporation E, an integrated producer that, together with Producer B, drills a commercially productive oil well on the southern half of the 320-acre tract.

Production from the wells drilled by Producers C and D continuously has averaged 30 barrels per day from 1974 and 1976, respectively. Corporation E seeks advice whether production from the well he drilled in 1987 is eligible for the tier-3 windfall profit tax rate on newly discovered oil.

In this situation, the first determination of the property unit for windfall profit tax (WPT) purposes is made in 1974 when production begins, by reference to the

9. I.R.C. Sec. 4991(e)(2).
10. I.R.C. Sec. 4991(b)(6).
11. Procedural Rules, 1983-2 C.B. 618.

geographical boundaries of Producer C's sublease from Producer B. A second property for WPT purposes is established in 1976 when production begins, by reference to the geographical boundaries of Producer D's sublease from Producer B. The 320-acre tract farmed out to Corporation E is not a property for WPT purposes in March 1987 because there has not been commercial production on that tract. The 320-acre tract becomes a property for WPT purposes as of the date of first commercial production in 1987. Accordingly, because Corporation E's property did not produce crude oil in commercial quantities in 1978, the production is eligible for tier-3 WPT rates as newly discovered oil.[12]

If Corporation E had acquired an undivided interest from Producers C or D in 1987 and participated in the drilling of a second well (to the same producing reservoir) on either of the 160-acre tracts (which had established property status for WPT purposes in 1974 and 1976, respectively), the production from the second well would be classified as tier 1 because of the commercial production on the properties in 1978.[13] Production from the second well will not be eligible immediately for tier-2 classification because of the failure of Producers C's and D's initial wells on the properties to meet the stripper well property definition.[14] *(See Case 228.)*

The boundaries of the property must be identified before the appropriate WPT rate can be determined. *(See Case 212.)* The WPT property is defined by reference in part to the June 1979 Department of Energy (DOE) regulations, even though government price controls on crude oil production were removed on January 28, 1981.[15] Also, the Treasury is authorized specifically to promulgate regulations modifying the DOE regulations to the extent "necessary or appropriate" to carry out the purposes of the WPT.[16] Under this broad regulatory authority, the Treasury has issued proposed regulations defining *property* for purposes of the WPT.[17]

The proposed regulations follow the DOE's definition of *property*[18] in defining the term by reference to the geographical boundaries of the right to produce crude oil (an operating or working interest arising from a lease or fee interest) as that right existed on January 1, 1972.[19] However, the proposed regulations provide that a property is created for WPT purposes as of January 1, 1972, only if the right was in production of crude oil in commercial quantities *(see Case 212)* on that date.[20] If the right (i.e., the property) was not producing crude oil in commercial quantities on January 1, 1972, a WPT property is created at the time of first commercial production after January 1, 1972.[21]

The DOE's property definition,[22] as amended, permitted certain separate and distinct producing reservoirs to be treated as separate properties for purposes of the DOE price regulations. The amended definition is as follows:

> *'Property'* means the right to produce domestic crude oil which arises from a lease or from a fee interest. A producer may treat as a separate property each separate and distinct producing reservoir subject to the same right to

12. I.R.C. Sec. 4991(e)(1)(A); I.R.C. Sec. 4991(e)(2); Prop. Reg. Sec. 51.4996-4(a)(1); Prop. Reg. Sec. 51.4996-4(b).
13. Prop. Reg. 51.4996-4(a).
14. I.R.C. Sec. 4991(d)(1)(A); Prop. Reg. Sec. 51.4991-1(b)(3)(i).
15. I.R.C. Sec. 4991(d)(1)(A); I.R.C. Sec. 4991(e)(2); I.R.C. Sec. 4996(b)(8); Reg. Sec. 51.4991-1(b); Reg. Sec. 51.4996-1(f).
16. I.R.C. Sec. 4997(b).
17. Prop. Reg. Sec. 51.4996-4.
18. 10 CFR Sec. 212.72.
19. Prop. Reg. Sec. 51.4996-4(a); Prop. Reg. Sec. 51.4996-4(b).
20. Prop. Reg. Sec. 51.4996-4(l).
21. *Ibid.*
22. 10 CFR Sec. 212.72.

produce crude oil, provided that such reservoir is recognized by the appropriate governmental regulatory authority as a producing formation that is separate and distinct from, and not in communication with, any other producing formation.

The Treasury commentary accompanying the proposed regulations indicates that the rules regarding the creation of separate properties from a single right to produce crude oil generally follow principles developed in two 1977 DOE rulings,[23] but will be mandatory rather than permissive.[24]

The proposed regulations provide that a single instrument such as a lease or deed shall be treated as transferring more than one right to produce crude oil if:

(1) The instrument specifically identifies portions of the acreage;

(2) The instrument creates significantly different rights and duties with respect to the specifically identified portions;

(3) The holders of the rights transferred have in good faith relied upon such differences in their exploration and development efforts;

(4) The holders of the rights have consistently and historically accounted for such portions separately; and

(5) The holders of the rights have consistently and historically treated each such portion as a separate right to produce crude oil.[25]

On the other hand, in limited situations a single right to produce crude oil that would be a single property under the rules above shall be treated as more than one property.[26] These situations involve noncontiguous tracts,[27] separate accountability to royalty owners,[28] separate accountability for severance tax purposes,[29] very large tracts[30] and separate reservoirs.[31]

To illustrate one situation, assume the facts of the case are changed to have Producer B sublease the entire 640-acre tract to Producer F, with the provision that a well must be drilled in the upper 320-acre half of the tract first and then in the lower 320-acre tract. To the extent this is not accomplished, any 320-acre tract without a producing well reverts back to Producer B at the end of the five-year lease. If Producer F treats each of the specifically identified tracts as separate properties and consistently accounts for each tract as a separate right to produce, then each tract may also be a separate WPT property.[32]

The operator of a single right to produce crude oil may elect to treat as separate properties each separate and distinct producing reservoir subject to the same right to produce crude oil that is not in communication with any other producing reservoir subject to the same right to produce crude oil.[33] If the operator makes this election, each reservoir is treated as a separate property. Once made,[34] the election is irrevocable and applies to all current producers and all producers that later acquire an interest

23. FEA Ruling 1977-1, 42 F.R. 3682 (1977); FEA Ruling 1977-2, 42 F.R. 4409 (1977).
24. 51 F.R. 34095 (September 25, 1986).
25. Prop. Reg. Sec. 51.4996-4(c).
26. Prop. Reg. Sec. 51.4996-4(d)(1).
27. Prop. Reg. Sec. 51.4996-4(d)(2).
28. Prop. Reg. Sec. 51.4996-4(d)(3).
29. Prop. Reg. Sec. 51.4996-4(d)(4).
30. Prop. Reg. Sec. 51.4996-4(d)(5).
31. Prop. Reg. Sec. 51.4996-4(d)(6).
32. Prop. Reg. Sec. 51.4996-4(f), Example 12.
33. Prop. Reg. Sec. 51.4996-4(d)(6)(i)(A).
34. Prop. Reg. Sec. 51.4996-4(d)(6)(ii).

in the properties. The election also applies to each separate and distinct newly discovered producing reservoir that is not in communication with any other producing reservoir subject to the same right to produce.

In certain situations, separate distinct rights to produce may be combined and treated as a single WPT property.[35] Examples of these situations include voluntary or state required aggregations[36] and unitizations.[37] *(See Cases 214 and 215.)*

Case 214
Windfall Profit Tax Treatment of Stripper Well Crude Oil Production from Unitized Properties

Producers A and B each own an undivided 50% working interest in Property X. Both A and B are independent producers. Property X is a stripper well property with one well. The average daily production of Property X for the 12-month period before unitization is eight barrels.

Producers C, D and E own, respectively, an undivided 40%, 25% and 35% working interest in Property Y. Producers C and D are integrated producers, while Producer E is an independent producer. Property Y is a single well, tier-1 Property. The average daily production of Property Y for the 12-month period before unitization is 12 barrels.

Effective June 1, 1987, Producers A, B, C, D and E enter into an agreement to unitize Properties X and Y so that a secondary water-flood project may be started. The unitization agreement among the producers provides that production from the resulting unit will be allocated one-third to the Property X producers and two-thirds to the Property Y producers. In addition, the imputed stripper well crude oil will be allocated 80% to Property X and 20% to Property Y.

In June 1987, the unit produces (net to the working interest) an average of 18 barrels per day (nine barrels per well) of crude oil (540 barrels). In July 1987, the unit produces (net to the working interest) an average of 30 barrels per day (15 barrels per well) of crude oil (930 barrels).

Producers A, B, C, D and E share in production from the unit (based on the terms of the unitization agreement) as follows:

Property	Gross Production Allocation	Producer	% Working Interest in X or Y	Net % Working Interest in Unit*
X	33⅓	A	50	16⅔
		B	50	16⅔
Y	66⅔	C	40	26⅔
		D	25	16⅔
		E	35	23⅓
Totals	100%			100%

* Computed by multiplying the gross production allocation percentage on a property by the producer's percentage working interest in that respective property.

35. Prop. Reg. Sec. 51.4996-4(e).
36. Prop. Reg. Sec. 51.4996-4(e)(1).
37. Prop. Reg. Sec. 51.4996-4(e)(2).

Producers A, B, C, D and E, therefore, are allocated (based on the terms of the unitization agreement) the following crude oil production (in barrels) from the unit during June and July of 1987:

Producer	June	July
A	90	155
B	90	155
C	144	248
D	90	155
E	126	217
Totals	540	930

The House and Senate Reports[38] that accompanied the enactment of the windfall profit tax (WPT) authorize the Treasury to promulgate regulations to implement effectively the WPT as that law pertains to unitizations. The Department of Energy (DOE) had developed elaborate rules that provided for the imputation of stipulated volumes of crude oil production from properties of different pricing categories (i.e., stripper well crude oil and newly discovered oil) on the advent of unitization.[39] These rules ("hold harmless rules") were designed to place producers in essentially the same position after unitization with respect to the pricing make-up of the aggregate production of the properties as had existed before unitization. To facilitate the undertaking of enhanced recovery projects (which typically are conducted in the form of unitizations), the DOE designed imputation rules with the objective of making the formation of those units "neutral" from the perspective of crude oil pricing.

The House and Senate[40] Reports indicate that WPT regulations governing unitizations can adopt or modify, where appropriate, the unitization rules established for price control purposes. Under this authority, the Internal Revenue Service (IRS) has proposed regulations[41] covering these imputation principles, which closely follow the DOE rules. When the unitization occurs after February 29, 1980, the imputed stripper well crude oil for a particular month is the greater of:

(1) The total number of barrels of crude oil removed from the premises during that particular month multiplied by a fraction, the numerator of which is the total barrels produced and sold during the 12 months immediately preceding the formation of the unit from all properties forming the unit that constitute stripper properties before inclusion in the unit and the denominator of which is the total barrels produced and sold during that period from all properties making up the unitized property, or

(2) The total number of barrels of crude oil produced and sold during the 12-month period preceding formation of the unit from all properties making up the unit that were stripper properties prior to formation of the unit multiplied by a fraction, the numerator of which is the number of days in that month and the denominator of which is the number of days in that 12-month period.[42]

38. House Report No. 96-304, 1980-3 C.B. 114; Senate Report No. 96-394, 1980-3 C.B. 170.
39. 10 CFR Sec. 212.75.
40. House Report No. 96-304, 1980-3 C.B. 114; Senate Report No. 96-394, 1980-3 C.B. 170.
41. Prop. Reg. Sec. 51.4996-5.
42. Prop. Reg. Sec. 51.4996-5(b)(2).

This approach is illustrated in the following table:

Month	Formula	Imputed Stripper Well Crude Oil
June - Greater of: or	(1) $540 \times \frac{2920}{7300} = 216$ (2) $2920 \times \frac{30}{365} = 240$	240
July - Greater of: or	(1) $930 \times \frac{2920}{7300} = 372$ (2) $2920 \times \frac{31}{365} = 248$	372

It also is necessary to determine in what manner the monthly volume of imputed stripper well crude oil should be allocated among Producers A, B, C, D and E. A crude oil pricing case[43] held that pre-unitization properties lose their separate identity when unitized (i.e., one property is thereafter created), such that producers contributing the stripper well properties to a unit lost their ability to claim unilaterally 100% of the imputed stripper well production as part of (or in full satisfaction of) their full share of crude oil production allocable under the unitization agreement. The court noted that the allocation of the unit's imputed stripper well crude oil production could be apportioned among the participants of the unit agreement in any way those participants may negotiate as part of the terms of the unit agreement. The proposed regulations[44] give effect to the unitization agreement, but are very specific as to how the respective classes of production are allocated. For months after November 30, 1986, the imputed stripper well crude oil (determined by use of the formula illustrated above) shall not exceed the number of barrels of crude oil removed from the premises of the unitized property during that month allocated by the unitization agreement to the constituent properties.

In this example, the imputed stripper well crude oil for June was determined to be 240 barrels, but the total production allocated by the unitization agreement to Property X (the only stripper property before the unitization) is only 180 barrels (540 × 33⅓%). Therefore, even though the imputed stripper well crude oil production could be 240 barrels based upon historical production levels prior to unitization, the terms of the unitization agreement are respected and, in this case, limit the qualified production to the total production from Property X.[45] The terms of the agreement also further allocate only 80% of the imputed stripper well crude oil to Property X (Producers A and B) and 20% to Property Y (Producers C, D and E). The balance of the production from the unit would be tier-1 production. The results of these calculations and the allocations to the producers would be as follows for June and July:

Producer	June			July		
	Tier 1	Stripper	Total	Tier 1	Stripper	Total
A	18	72	90	31	124	155
B	18	72	90	31	124	155
C	130	14	144	223	25	248
D	81	9	90	139	16	155
E	113	13	126	196	21	217
Total	360 bbls.	180 bbls.	540 bbls.	620 bbls.	310 bbls.	930 bbls.

43. Francis Oil and Gas, Inc. v. Exxon Corporation, 687 F.2d 484 (TECA 1982).
44. Prop. Reg. Sec. 51.4996-5(e).
45. Prop. Reg. Sec. 51.4996-5(e)(1); Prop. Reg. Sec. 51.4996-5(e)(7), Example 1.

In this situation the qualified stripper production is limited to an amount which is less than the limitation determined by reference to historical production levels. This result would have been different if Property X had been allocated a larger share of the total unit production. The agreed allocation or sharing of gross production between Property X and Property Y is presumably a reflection of the expected total future production from each respective property. While this is a negotiated allocation based upon expected economics, the calculation of the imputed stripper production limitation should be considered in both the gross production allocation and the stripper production allocation if the producers are to obtain the maximum WPT benefit. Contractually agreed allocations of the imputed stripper crude oil among the constituent properties will be respected by the IRS, provided the allocation is not being made primarily to avoid WPT.[46] If all the properties making up the unit were qualified stripper well properties before the unitization, all the production from the unit will be considered to be stripper crude oil.[47]

Similar calculations are required to determine imputed heavy crude oil and imputed newly discovered crude oil whenever the unit is comprised of these WPT property types.[48]

In the instant case, it would be economically attractive from a WPT perspective for Producers A, B *and* E to be allocated 100% of the imputed stripper well production because that production (in the hands of Producers A, B and E) presumably will otherwise be exempt from WPT.[49] Producers C and D, on the other hand, will experience a WPT rate shift of only 10% (difference between tier-1 rate (70%) and tier-2 rate (60%)) with respect to their crude oil production from the unit categorized as imputed stripper crude oil.[50] The illustration above presumed the production on Property Y was shared pro rata by Producers C, D and E. If the agreement among these producers allocated all stripper crude oil to Producer E, the maximum WPT savings would be realized. The regulations do not discuss whether this type of allocation would be respected.

When rights to produce from which no crude oil was produced before the unitization are combined with qualified stripper properties, the determination of the imputed stripper crude oil is further complicated. First, the imputed newly discovered crude oil is determined. Then the imputed stripper crude oil is calculated and, in some cases, a portion of the newly discovered crude oil can also be treated as imputed stripper crude oil. The regulations contain a series of examples illustrating the steps to be taken in making this calculation.[51]

The projected impact of the WPT net income limitation (NIL) *(see Case 221)* attributable to unit production may also influence the participants' negotiations of their respective WPT tier classification share of crude oil production from the unit. For example, a producer may be virtually indifferent to an allocation of the highest WPT tier rate category for crude oil production provided he may "shelter" the incremental WPT rate differential through the WPT NIL. This may be the case when a producer has: (1) a higher relative "as-if" cost depletable basis *(see Case 222)* or (2) considerable overhead to apportion to his economic interest in that property.

46. Prop. Reg. Sec. 51.4996-5(e)(6)(ii).
47. Prop. Reg. Sec. 51.4996-5(e)(1).
48. *Ibid.*
49. I.R.C. Sec. 4994(g).
50. I.R.C. Sec. 4987(b)(1).
51. Prop. Reg. Sec. 51.4996-5(d)(1); Prop. Reg. Sec. 51.4996-5(g)(3); Prop. Reg. Sec. 51.4996-5(g)(4); Prop. Reg. Sec. 51.4996-5(e)(7), Example 3; Prop. Reg. Sec. 51.4996-5(e)(7), Example 4; Prop. Reg. Sec. 51.4996-5(e)(7), Example 5.

It is unclear how the WPT transfer rules *(see Cases 219, 224 and 228)* would operate in the context of the imputed crude oil production rules that apply to unitizations. Conceptually, Producers A, B and E should be able to preserve their independent-producer status under the unit agreement such that any tier-1 production allocable to them under that agreement is taxed at a 50% WPT rate and any imputed stripper well production is exempt from WPT.[52] This approach is consistent with percentage depletion[53] concepts that essentially view the contributing participants to a unitization agreement as maintaining their pre-unitization percentage depletion independent-producer status through an economically comparable percentage share of oil and gas production under the unitization agreement. Presumably, a "cash equalization payment" to equalize relative pre-unitization development expenses *(see Case 148)* will necessitate a fractional application of both sets of WPT transfer rules *(see Cases 219, 224 and 228)* to the extent the payor effectively is "purchasing" a partial interest in the unit. This approach is consistent with the percentage depletion rules.[54] Application of the WPT transfer rules *(see Cases 219, 224 and 228)* is unclear in situations where equalization of relative pre-unitization development expenses is accomplished through temporary "special allocations" of initial production or simply delayed participation in the production from the unit.

A more difficult technical issue regarding the WPT transfer rule ramifications of a unitization agreement may exist if Producers A and B, the contributors of the stripper well property, were integrated producers, and Producers C, D and E, the contributors of the tier-1 property, were independent producers. In this case, it is not clear whether a full (or even partial) allocation of imputed stripper well crude oil to Producers C, D and E as part of (or in full consideration of) their allocable share of crude oil production under the unitization agreement could be made because a direct transfer of a stripper well property from an integrated producer to an independent producer would render the WPT stripper well exemption ineffective to that property for the independent producer.[55]

Attribution of stripper well crude oil production is made on the basis of the crude oil production volume of the actual wells from the stripper well property physically located within the boundaries of the unit.[56] If the XY property subsequently produces less than 10 barrels per day of crude oil for any consecutive 12-month measuring period, the entire crude oil production from that property thereafter will qualify as stripper well crude oil production. Under the DOE rules, once a property qualifies as a stripper well property, the property permanently retains that status irrespective of the fact that crude oil production may subsequently exceed 10 barrels per day or that new reservoirs may be discovered.[57] Presumably, the same principle should apply for the WPT. Unfortunately, in issuing proposed regulations[58] defining stripper well properties, the IRS specifically provided that whenever a new reservoir is discovered on a stripper property, the eligibility for stripper status must be redetermined unless an election is made to treat the new reservoir as a separate property. It is uncertain whether this provision will be removed before the regulations are finalized, but if the IRS stays with this approach, it would eliminate some of the incentives for operating and continuing to produce stripper properties that might otherwise be abandoned.

52. I.R.C. Sec. 4987(b); I.R.C. Sec. 4994(g).
53. Prop. Reg. Sec. 1.613A-7(o).
54. *Ibid.*
55. I.R.C. Sec. 4994(g)(2).
56. Prop. Reg. Sec. 51.4996-5(e)(4).
57. 10 CFR Sec. 212.54; Rustex Oil, Inc., Interpretation 1978-5, 45 F.R. 12852 (Mar. 28, 1978).
58. Prop. Reg. Sec. 51.4991-1(b).

Should the XY property subsequently qualify as a stripper well property, it is not clear whether Producers A and B could claim their full unit crude oil production allocation as exempt stripper well oil because of the transfer rules.[59] Producer E should be able to claim his full unit crude oil production allocation as exempt stripper well oil provided Producers A and B were independent producers at all times after July 22, 1981.[60] Producers C and D would be taxed on their full unit crude oil production allocation as tier-2 oil.[61]

Case 215
Forced Pooling Agreements — Determination of Windfall Profit Tax Property Classification for Newly Discovered Crude Oil

Producers A and B own 100% of the working interest in Property X, a 290-acre oil and gas lease. The property has one producing well, which has produced from the N Reservoir, a tier-1 property, since 1975.

Producers C and D own 100% of the working interest in Property Y, a 400-acre oil and gas lease. Property Y is contiguous to Property X. Property Y has three producing wells, all of which have produced from the N Reservoir, a tier-1 property, since 1973.

Producers A and B propose to drill a second well on Property X to Reservoir N at a location that is on the boundary of Lease Y. Producers A and B apply to Z, the state conservation commissioner, for a spacing unit designation covering the proposed well. Commissioner Z includes 80 acres from Property X and 80 acres from Property Y in the spacing unit for the proposed well. None of the acreage contained in Commissioner Z's proposed spacing unit contains a producing well.

Under applicable state law, Producers C and D have three courses of action:

(1) Participate with Producers A and B in the drilling of the proposed well on a basis proportionate to the relative acreage each contributes to the spacing unit.

(2) Sell their working interest in the 80 acres from Property Y to Producers A and B at a price set by Commissioner Z.

(3) Retain a proportional (based on acreage contributed to the unit) reversionary working interest in the proposed well that becomes effective once Producers A and B recover a multiple (i.e., 200%, 300%, etc.) of their costs to drill, equip and operate the proposed well.

Producers C and D decide to drill the proposed well with Producers A and B. Producers A, B, C and D execute a pooling agreement, with the royalty owners holding the royalty interests underlying the spacing unit. A producing well is completed in 1987 on the pooled acreage to the N Reservoir. Producers A, B, C and D want to determine if the production from the proposed well will be categorized as newly discovered oil for windfall profit tax (WPT) purposes.

59. I.R.C. Sec. 4994(g)(2).
60. *Ibid.*
61. I.R.C. Sec. 4987(b)(1).

Under the authority granted Treasury to prescribe regulations,[62] including changes in the application of the Department of Energy (DOE) regulations, as may be necessary or appropriate to administer and implement effectively the WPT, the Internal Revenue Service (IRS) has announced its position with respect to the treatment of poolings and unitizations for purposes of WPT property determinations.[63] The DOE generally defined *property* by reference to the right to produce crude oil, but with certain exceptions to this general rule. One such exception was the aggregation of several separate rights to produce into a single pooling or unitization. Without referring to any specific DOE rulings, the preamble to these proposed regulations states that exceptions to the general definition of *property* are similar to those provided by the DOE but are mandatory rather than permissive.[64]

The statute[65] provides that post-1978 transfers of any portion of a property do not permit classification of subsequent crude oil production from that property (or portion thereof) as, for example, newly discovered crude oil if that production would not have so qualified absent the transfer. Whether a pooling or unitization constitutes a "transfer" for this purpose is not absolutely clear. In a 1980 DOE administrative ruling,[66] it was held that a producer forming a voluntary pooling agreement with the royalty owners of portions of two properties had formed a new separate property eligible for uncontrolled pricing. Although the pooled acreage did not have a producing well, the original properties had several wells producing since 1972.

Later in 1980, the DOE issued a ruling "clarifying" certain aspects of the June 1979 definition of *newly discovered crude oil* for price control purposes.[67] This ruling provided that rearrangements of a property by unitization or pooling, for example, that occur after 1978 do not permit production from the rearranged property to qualify as newly discovered crude oil if the physical premises of the rearranged property was part of a property that had crude oil production in 1978. Since the WPT statute defines *newly discovered crude oil* by reference to the June 1979 energy regulations, the 1980 ruling may be technically inapplicable as it was issued after the cut-off date. Nevertheless, the preamble referred to above[68] embraces this ruling in that it states that all the production from a unit cannot be considered newly discovered if any portion of a property included in the unit had production during 1978. Also, another proposed regulation[69] defines the term *newly discovered crude oil property* to include a unitized property made up *entirely* of properties that did not produce crude oil in commercial quantities in 1978. *(See Case 212.)*

If this definition is strictly applied by focusing on the historical crude oil production make-up of the entire property (before pooling) even though only an unproductive portion of a property is contributed in the pooling, the production from Reservoir N under the acreage pooled by Producers A, B, C and D will not constitute newly discovered crude oil. Although the unit itself has never produced, the acreage comprising the unit is from rights to produce that are classified as tier-1 properties.

However, this definitional approach was not followed in a recent District Court decision[70] involving very similar facts. In that case, 40 acres from a tier-1 property

---

62. I.R.C. Sec. 4997(b).
63. Prop. Reg. Sec. 51.4996-4(e).
64. 26 CFR Part 51, 51 F.R. 34093 (Sept. 25, 1986).
65. I.R.C. Sec. 4996(e); Reg. Sec. 51.4996-3(b).
66. Hunt Oil Company, Interpretation 1980-17, 45 F.R. 46787 (July 11, 1980). *See also* L. O. Ward, Interpretation 1979-17, 44 F.R. 60264 (Oct. 19, 1979); Depco, Inc., 2 DOE Para. 80, 167 (1978); Fain Porter Production Company, 3 DOE Para. 80,123 (1979).
67. FEA Ruling 1980-3, 45 F.R. 48577 (1980).
68. 26 CFR Part 51, 51 F.R. 34653 (Sept. 30, 1986).
69. Prop. Reg. Sec. 51.4996-1(m)(2)(iii).
70. George v. U.S., 657 F. Supp. 32 (E.D. Mich. 1986), 87-1 USTC 9197; Reg. Sec. 1.614-8(b)(6).

were combined under state order with 40 acres from a property that had never produced. The 80-acre unit itself did not include any wells, but a successful well was subsequently completed in 1979. After analyzing the legislative history of the *property* definition adopted by the Crude Oil Windfall Profit Tax (COWPT) Act, the court concluded the production from the well was entirely newly discovered oil despite the fact that the reservoir under the unit was quite possibly the same reservoir as that in production on the tier-1 property. The court believed that the IRS's approach of classifying the production in this case was similar to the reservoir approach, which had been considered and dropped during the drafting of the COWPT Act, and should not now be resurrected. Congress had rejected that approach, and the court, therefore, should do likewise. The court, without making reference to the preamble, considered the *property* definition contained in the currently proposed regulations to be consistent with its holding.[71]

Determining the WPT tier classification of production from the pooled acreage becomes more complicated if the acreage from Property X, for example, included a well with production classified as newly discovered crude oil and the acreage from Property Y included a well with production classified as tier-1 crude oil. The DOE regulations[72] *(see Case 214)* provide elaborate rules to impute crude oil production from properties of different classifications into a resulting unit. These rules have been adopted, for the most part, under the proposed regulations dealing with unitized properties.[73]

For situations where a right to produce is unitized before production has begun, a special rule is provided for determining the classification of the production. In this case, the surface acreage within the unitized property on which there has been no production as compared to the total surface acreage of the unitized property yields a fraction which is used to calculate the share of production that is deemed to be newly discovered crude oil.[74] For this purpose, unitized surface acreage that is not underlain by proven, developed or undeveloped oil and gas reserves shall be disregarded.[75] The production in excess of this determination is then imputed based on historical production levels.[76]

If the well on the pooled acreage is completed in a different producing reservoir with no production in 1978, that production clearly should be eligible for newly discovered crude oil classification under the amended DOE *property* definition *(see Case 213)* provided a separate reservoir election is made.[77]

For purposes of the WPT 90% net income limitation (NIL) *(see Case 221)*, the pooled acreage of Producers A, B, C and D will be considered to be a separate property. The income tax definition of *property*[78] *(see Section III)*, which is used for computing the WPT NIL,[79] treats a pooling as a separate property.[80]

71. Prop. Reg. Sec. 51.4996-4(e)(1)(iv).
72. 10 CFR Sec. 212.75.
73. Prop. Reg. Sec. 51.4996-5.
74. Prop. Reg. Sec. 51.4996-5(e)(3).
75. Prop. Reg. Sec. 51.4996-5(d)(1)(ii).
76. Prop. Reg. Sec. 51.4996-5(d)(1)(i).
77. Prop. Reg. Sec. 51.4996-4(d)(6); Prop. Reg. Sec. 51.4996-4(f), Example 21; Prop. Reg. Sec. 51.4996-4(f), Example 22.
78. I.R.C. Sec. 614(a).
79. Reg. Sec. 51.4988-2(b)(1)(i).
80. I.R.C. Sec. 614(b)(3)(A); Reg. Sec. 1.614-8(b)(6).

Case 216
Independent-Producer Definition

> Corporation X is a publicly held corporation with two subsidiaries, Corporation Y and Corporation Z. Corporation Y is the owner of various working and royalty interests in oil and gas leases located throughout the United States. All its oil and gas sales are made to unrelated parties at or near the wellhead. Neither Corporation X nor Y is a refiner or retailer, and Corporation Y is considered an independent producer standing alone. Corporation Z purchases petroleum or derivative products from unrelated third parties and resells these products at retail.
>
> Corporation Z does not sell under any trademark or trade name but sells more than $5 million in a given calendar year to end users. Corporation Y does not produce any of the products sold by Corporation Z. Corporations X, Y and Z join in the filing of a calendar-year, consolidated federal income tax return.

In this situation, Corporations Y and Z are related because Corporation X owns 100% of the outstanding stock of both corporations. However, Corporation Y, the producer, has no direct or indirect ownership interest in Corporation Z, the retailer, and, therefore, does not benefit from the retail sales of Corporation Z. Corporation Y will not lose the benefit of the reduced windfall profit tax (WPT) rates for independent-producer oil because a related sister company, through which it does not sell its production, is a retailer.[81]

For WPT purposes, an *independent producer* is defined by reference to the rules for percentage depletion,[82] except that the de minimis rules prescribed for determining whether a person is a retailer or refiner are applied on a calendar-year basis rather than a tax-year basis. Generally, a producer may not avail himself of the reduced WPT rates for independent-producer oil during any calendar year during which he is a retailer or refiner.[83] *(See Case 217.)* Qualification as an independent producer also is one of the requirements that must be satisfied for oil production to qualify as exempt stripper well oil.[84] *(See Case 228.)*

The proposed regulations regarding percentage depletion define a *retailer* as any taxpayer who has gross receipts, directly or through a related person, from the sale of oil, natural gas or derivative products in excess of $5 million per year.[85] For this purpose, the taxpayer is deemed to be selling oil or natural gas through a related person in any case where the taxpayer may benefit from the sale by reason of this direct or indirect ownership in the related person.[86]

A producer is related to a retailer if either owns 5% or more in value of the outstanding stock of the other, or if a third person owns 5% or more in value of the outstanding stock in both.[87] *(See Case 113.)*

If Corporation X or Z were a refiner, Corporation Y would not be entitled to the independent-producer WPT rates. For purposes of the WPT, a taxpayer is a refiner

81. IRS Letter Ruling 8204217; IRS Letter Ruling 8250014 (Technical Advice Memorandum); IRS Letter Ruling 8330001 (Technical Advice Memorandum); IRS Letter Ruling 8336088; IRS Letter Ruling 8340019.
82. I.R.C. Sec. 4992(b).
83. I.R.C. Sec. 4992(b)(2).
84. I.R.C. Sec. 4994(g).
85. Prop. Reg. Sec. 1.613A-7(r).
86. *Ibid.*
87. I.R.C. Sec. 613A(d)(3); Prop. Reg. Sec. 1.613A-7(m).

if he and related persons engage in the refining of crude oil in excess of 50,000 barrels on any day during a calendar year.[88] Even if Corporation Y does not engage in refining activities and does not sell its production to Corporation X or Z, it still will not be considered an independent producer for any calendar year during which Corporation X or Z is considered a refiner.

Unlike the exclusion under the retailer rules, Corporation Y does not have to receive any direct or indirect economic benefits from the refining activities to lose its independent-producer status under the refiner rules. *(See Case 114.)*

Case 217
Independent-Producer Oil

During the quarter ending June 30, 1987, Producer A had 95,000 barrels of qualifying tier-1 oil production and 35,000 barrels of tier-2 oil production. The 35,000 barrels of tier-2 oil production consist of 5,000 barrels of production from an interest in a Naval Petroleum Reserve, 10,000 barrels of production from properties purchased from an integrated oil company in 1986 and 20,000 barrels of exempt stripper well production. Producer A is an independent producer and uses the calendar year for federal income tax purposes. All the production is attributable to working interests in properties owned by Producer A.

When an independent producer's combined daily production of qualifying tier-1 and tier-2 oil exceeds 1,000 barrels, the 1,000-barrel limitation must be allocated between these tiers in the same proportion that these quantities make up the producer's total qualifying tier-1 and tier-2 production.[89] For the calendar quarter ending June 30, 1987, the independent-producer amount for Producer A is computed as follows:

	Barrels of Qualified Production	Percentage	Independent-Producer Amount*
Tier 1	95,000	95%	86,450
Tier 2	5,000	5%	4,550
Total	100,000	100%	91,000

* 91 days in the period April 1 through June 30, at 1,000 barrels per day.

Independent-producer oil is defined as that portion of the qualified production of an independent producer not exceeding the independent-producer amount for the quarter.[90] The independent-producer amount is determined by multiplying the number of days in the calendar quarter by 1,000.[91] The total number of barrels of crude oil so determined qualifies for the lower independent-producer windfall profit tax (WPT) rates.

For purposes of the WPT, an *independent producer* is defined in the same way as when computing percentage depletion, except that the tests for determining whether a person is a retailer or refiner are applied on a calendar-year basis rather than a tax-year basis.[92] A calendar-year taxpayer always has the same status for depletion and WPT purposes. A fiscal-year taxpayer, however, actually could have a "dual status," whereby it is eligible for percentage depletion for its tax (fiscal) year but loses its

88. I.R.C. Sec. 4992(b); I.R.C. Sec. 613A(d)(4); Prop. Reg. Sec. 1.613A-7(s).
89. I.R.C. Sec. 4992(c)(2)(A); Reg. Sec. 51.4992-1(c).
90. I.R.C. Sec. 4992(a).
91. I.R.C. Sec. 4992(c)(1).
92. I.R.C. Sec. 4992(b).

WPT independent-producer status for a calendar year that includes a portion of the taxpayer's fiscal year. *(See Case 216.)*

Only the portion of an independent producer's tier-1 and tier-2 production that qualifies for the lower independent-producer WPT rates is considered in allocating the 1,000-barrel amount.[93] Therefore, both the production from the transferred properties and the exempt stripper well production are disregarded in calculating the appropriate allocation.[94]

Producer A should allocate the independent-producer amount for each tier to the barrels with the highest removal price. The remaining 8,550 barrels of tier-1 production and the remaining 450 barrels of tier-2 production will be subject to the rates for oil that is not independent-producer oil, i.e., 70% and 60%, respectively.[95] This method of allocation is mandatory and, for the most part, will represent a decided advantage because the production with the highest removal prices ordinarily will yield the largest amount of windfall profit and the highest WPT. This method may not yield the best results, however, in situations where a property with higher-priced production is subject to the 90% net income limitation.

Allocation of the production within a tier presumably is determined solely by comparing the removal price of each barrel of production without regard to any particular property. For an independent producer with more than 1,000 barrels per day of combined qualifying tier-1 and tier-2 production, it may be necessary to include a portion of the production from each property in the independent-producer amount, even though this allocation procedure is inconsistent with the rules relating to certification of production for withholding purposes.[96] In addition, a portion will be subject to the regular WPT rates.

The allocation of the 1,000-barrel amount between qualifying tier-1 and tier-2 production has been of limited application since the exemption for stripper well oil became effective beginning in 1983. Most independent producers no longer have any tier-2 production that qualifies for the lower 30% WPT rate. The only production that qualifies for the lower rate, but that is not exempt, is production from an economic interest in a Naval Petroleum Reserve and a limited number of transferred stripper well properties. An example of such a transferred stripper well property is one that was transferred after July 22, 1981, from an individual who was not an independent producer upon his death to an individual who was an independent producer.[97]

Case 218
Allocation of 1,000-Barrel-Per-Day Windfall Profit Tax Independent-Producer Amount Within Related Group

Individuals A and B are married and have a minor child, C. Individuals E and F are not related to Individuals A, B or C or to each other. Individuals A and F each own 50% of the outstanding stock of Corporation D on January 1, 1987. Individual E acquired 40% of Corporation D's outstanding stock from Individual F on March 1, 1987. Individuals A, E and F also own 10%, 60% and 30%, respectively, of Corporation G.

The producers, all of which qualify as independent producers, had the following respective average daily amounts of qualified production during the first quarter of 1987:

---

93. I.R.C. Sec. 4992(c)(2).
94. I.R.C. Sec. 4992(d).
95. I.R.C. Sec. 4987(b).
96. Reg. Sec. 51.4995-2(c).
97. I.R.C. Sec. 4992(d)(3)(C)(i); I.R.C. Sec. 4994(g)(2).

Producer	January*	February*	March*	Total
A (individual)	800	900	700	2,400
B (individual)	300	400	300	1,000
C (individual)	100	200	100	400
D (corporation)	500	700	500	1,700
E (individual)	400	500	400	1,300
F (individual)	1,000	1,100	1,000	3,100
G (corporation)	1,300	1,400	1,200	3,900
	4,400	5,200	4,200	13,800

*Production occurs pro rata during the month.

The producers ask for guidance as to the allocation of the 1,000-barrel-per-day windfall profit tax independent-producer amount for the first quarter of 1987.

For any calendar quarter, the 1,000 barrels per day of qualified production subject to the lower windfall profit tax (WPT) rates must be allocated among persons who are members of the same related group at any time during the calendar quarter.[98] The 1,000-barrel-per-day amount is allocated among members of the group in proportion to their respective qualified production for that quarter.[99] The proposed regulations[100] provide that if a person is a member of a related group for only a portion of a calendar quarter, the allocation of the 1,000-barrel-per-day amount is made only for each day during the quarter in which that person is a member of the related group. For purposes of applying these statutory allocation rules, an S corporation is treated as a partnership and the shareholders of the S corporation are treated as partners in a partnership.[101]

The allocation of the 1,000-barrel-per-day amount is based on each member's respective share of "qualified production."[102] Accordingly, if a member has royalty production or is the transferee of crude oil production for which the small-producer transfer exemption[103] is not applicable, that nonqualifying production is not considered in apportioning the 1,000-barrel-per-day amount. Similarly, an independent producer's interest in exempt stripper well production is not considered.[104] Allocation of the 1,000-barrel-per-day amount is made first to members of the related group, based on each member's relative qualified production, prior to further apportionment of a member's share of the related group allocation between qualifying tier-1 and tier-2 production at the member level.[105] *(See Case 217.)* As a practical matter, independent producers generally will not have any qualified tier-2 production that does not otherwise qualify as exempt stripper well oil. Thus, the mandatory allocation between tier-1 and tier-2[106] is of limited significance after December 31, 1982. *(See Case 217.)*

The 1,000-barrel-per-day amount is subject to allocation in any of the following situations:

☐ Members of a family, which includes spouses and minor children (as determined under state law).[107]

☐ A controlled group of corporations, using a 50% ownership test.[108]

98. I.R.C. Sec. 4992(e)(1); Reg. Sec. 51.4992-2(a)(1).
99. Reg. Sec. 51.4992-2(a)(2)(i).
100. Reg. Sec. 51.4992-2(a)(2)(ii).
101. I.R.C. Sec. 4992(f).
102. I.R.C. Sec. 4992(e)(1); I.R.C. Sec. 4992(d); Reg. Sec. 51.4992-2(a)(2)(i).
103. I.R.C. Sec. 4992(d)(3)(B); Reg. Sec. 51.4992-1(d)(3)(ii).
104. I.R.C. Sec. 4991; I.R.C. Sec. 4992(c).
105. Reg. Sec. 51.4992-2(a)(2)(ii).
106. I.R.C. Sec. 4992(c)(2); Reg. Sec. 51.4992-1(c).
107. I.R.C. Sec. 4992(e)(2)(A); I.R.C. Sec. 4992(e)(3)(C); Reg. Sec. 51.4992-2(c)(1).
108. I.R.C. Sec. 4992(e)(2)(B); I.R.C. Sec. 4992(e)(3)(A); Reg. Sec. 51.4992-2(c)(2).

□ A group of entities under common control.[109]

□ Corporations, trusts or estates in which 50% or more of the beneficial interest is owned by the same family,[110] using constructive ownership principles.[111]

The statutory rules governing the allocation of the 1,000-barrel-per-day independent-producer amount for WPT purposes are similar (but not identical) to the percentage depletion provisions.[112] *(See Cases 106 and 107.)*

A controlled group of corporations includes a parent-subsidiary controlled group, brother-sister controlled group and a combined group determined under the principles of I.R.C. Section 1563. For purposes of applying the I.R.C. Section 1563 principles in this context, however, "more than 50%" is to be used in lieu of "at least 80%" and I.R.C. Section 1563(b)(2) will not apply.[113]

A group of entities under common control includes a parent-subsidiary group,[114] a brother-sister group[115] or a combined group.[116] The rules applying to a group of entities under common control are applicable to estates and trusts, as well as corporations.[117] For corporations, ownership of stock possessing more than 50% of the total combined voting power or more than 50% of the total value of all classes of stock is required in determining whether a "controlling interest" exists.[118] For estates and trusts, ownership of more than 50% of the "actuarial interest" in those entities is required in determining whether a "controlling interest" exists.[119] Special rules define what constitutes an "actuarial interest."[120] Thus, for example, if an estate owns 50% of the only class of outstanding stock of a corporation, the estate and the corporation must share the 1,000-barrel-per-day amount.

If 50% or more of the beneficial interest in one or more corporations, trusts or estates is owned by the same family, all those entities and that family are required to share the 1,000-barrel-per-day WPT independent-producer amount.[121] It should be noted that, for percentage depletion purposes, the 1,000-barrel-per-day amount is not required to be allocated between individuals and thcir controlled corporations. Fifty percent or more of the beneficial interest means, in the case of a corporation, 50% or more in value of the outstanding stock (excluding treasury stock).[122] Fifty percent or more of the beneficial interest means, in the case of a trust or estate, an "actuarial interest" of 50% or more of that trust or estate, determined on the basis of all the property owned by the estate or trust, not solely on crude oil property interests.[123] In making the 50% test, special constructive ownership rules apply. In general, these rules treat an interest owned by or for a corporation, partnership, trust or estate as owned by the entity and proportionately by its shareholders, partners or beneficiaries.[124]

The statute[125] provides that if an independent producer is a member of more than one related group under the rules discussed above, that person's allocation of the 1,000-barrel-per-day amount is made by reference to the related group allocation that yields the smallest allocation of the 1,000-barrel-per-day amount to that person. The

109. I.R.C. Sec. 4992(e)(2)(C); I.R.C. Sec. 4992(e)(3)(B); Reg. Sec. 51.4992-2(c)(3).
110. I.R.C. Sec. 4992(e)(2)(D); Reg. Sec. 51.4992-2(c)(4).
111. I.R.C. Sec. 4992(e)(3)(D); Reg. Sec. 51.4992-2(d).
112. I.R.C. Sec. 613A(c)(8); Prop. Reg. Sec. 1.613A-3(g).
113. I.R.C. Sec. 4992(e)(3)(A); Reg. Sec. 51.4992-2(c)(2).
114. Reg. Sec. 51.4992-2(c)(3)(i).
115. Reg. Sec. 51.4992-2(c)(3)(ii).
116. Reg. Sec. 51.4992-2(c)(3)(iii).
117. Reg. Sec. 51.4992-2(c)(3).
118. Reg. Sec. 51.4992-2(c)(3)(iv)(A).
119. Reg. Sec. 51.4992-2(c)(3)(iv)(B).
120. Reg. Sec. 51.4992-2(c)(3)(v).
121. I.R.C. Sec. 4992(e)(2)(D); Reg. Sec. 51.4992-2(c)(4).
122. Reg. Sec. 51.4992-2(c)(4)(i).
123. Reg. Sec. 51.4992-2(c)(4)(ii); Reg. Sec. 51.4992-2(c)(3)(v).
124. I.R.C. Sec. 4992(e)(3)(D); Reg. Sec. 51.4992-2(d).
125. I.R.C. Sec. 4992(e)(3)(E); Reg. Sec. 51.4992-2(e)(1).

requirement to apportion the 1,000-barrel-per-day amount by reference to the allocation that results in the smallest allocation to the independent producer in more than one related group, however, does not serve to reallocate the unused allocation of that independent producer's share of the 1,000-barrel-per-day amount to the other members of the related group(s) in which the independent producer has a larger (but not fully utilized) share of the 1,000-barrel-per-day amount.[126]

Applying the foregoing rules relating to the required allocation of the 1,000-barrel-per-day amount yields the following groups of producers that must share the 1,000-barrel-per-day amount for the first quarter of 1987:

Related Group	Producers in Related Group	Type of Related Group	Period in Related Group
1	A, B, C and D	Family and 50%-or-more owned corporation[127]	January, February and March
2	D and F	Family (individual) and 50%-or-more owned corporation[128]	January and February**
3	D and G*	Controlled group of corporations (brother-sister group)[129]	March**
4	E and G	Family (individual) and 50%-or-more owned corporation[130]	January, February and March

*	January and February			March		
	D	G	Identical Ownership	D	G	Identical Ownership
A	50%	10%	10%	50%	10%	10%
E	0%	60%	0%	40%	60%	40%
F	50%	30%	30%	10%	30%	10%
Totals	100%	100%	40%	100%	100%	60%
	(not brother-sister group—less than 50% identical ownership)			(brother-sister group—more than 50% identical ownership)		

** In allocating the 1,000-barrel-per-day amount to producers that were members of these related groups for less than the entire quarter, the following computations assume the average daily production in any month occurred pro rata during the month.

Computation of total production for the first quarter of 1987 is:

Producer	January	February	March	Total Production
A	800 × 31 days = 24,800	900 × 28 = 25,200	700 × 31 = 21,700	71,700
B	300 × 31 = 9,300	400 × 28 = 11,200	300 × 31 = 9,300	29,800
C	100 × 31 = 3,100	200 × 28 = 5,600	100 × 31 = 3,100	11,800
D	500 × 31 = 15,500	700 × 28 = 19,600	500 × 31 = 15,500	50,600
E	400 × 31 = 12,400	500 × 28 = 14,000	400 × 31 = 12,400	38,800
F	1,000 × 31 = 31,000	1,100 × 28 = 30,800	1,000 × 31 = 31,000	92,800
G	1,300 × 31 = 40,300	1,400 × 28 = 39,200	1,200 × 31 = 37,200	116,700

Allocation of each group's 1,000-barrel-per-day amount depends on whether the producers were members of the group for the entire quarter. If so, the allocation is based on the ratio of each producer's total production for the quarter to total

126. Reg. Sec. 51.4992-2(e)(1).
127. I.R.C. Sec. 4992(e)(2)(A); I.R.C. Sec. 4992(e)(2)(D).
128. *Ibid.*
129. I.R.C. Sec. 4992(e)(2)(B); I.R.C. Sec. 4992(e)(2)(C).
130. I.R.C. Sec. 4992(e)(2)(A); I.R.C. Sec. 4992(e)(2)(D).

production for the quarter by all producers that were members of the group for the entire quarter. (See computation for Groups 1 and 4 below.)

If the producer is not a member of a group for the entire quarter, the allocation must be done on a daily basis. (See computation for Groups 2 and 3 below.)

These allocations can be illustrated as follows:

Allocation of 1,000-barrel-per-day Amount

	Group 1	
Producer	**First Quarter**	
A	$\frac{71,700}{163,900} \times 1,000 =$	437
B	$\frac{29,800}{163,900} \times 1,000 =$	182
C	$\frac{11,800}{163,900} \times 1,000 =$	72
D	$\frac{50,600}{163,900} \times 1,000 =$	309
Totals		1,000

	Group 2				
Producer	**January**		**February**		**March**
D	$\frac{500}{1,500} \times 1,000 =$	333	$\frac{700}{1,800} \times 1,000 =$	389	
F	$\frac{1,000}{1,500} \times 1,000 =$	667	$\frac{1,100}{1,800} \times 1,000 =$	611	N/A
Totals		1,000		1,000	

	Group 3			
Producer	**January**	**February**	**March**	
D			$\frac{500}{1,700} \times 1,000 =$	294
G	N/A	N/A	$\frac{1,200}{1,700} \times 1,000 =$	706
Totals				1,000

	Group 4	
Producer	**First Quarter**	
E	$\frac{38,800}{155,500} \times 1,000 =$	250
G	$\frac{116,700}{155,500} \times 1,000 =$	750
Totals		1,000

The following table summarizes each producer's independent-producer amount for the calendar quarter.

Actual Barrel Allocation for January, February and March

Producer	January	February	March	Total Barrels
A	437 × 31 = 13,547	437 × 28 = 12,236	437 × 31 = 13,547	39,330
B	182 × 31 = 5,642	182 × 28 = 5,096	182 × 31 = 5,642	16,380
C	72 × 31 = 2,232	72 × 28 = 2,016	72 × 31 = 2,232	6,480
D	309* × 31 = 9,579	309* × 28 = 8,652	294* × 31 = 9,114	27,345
E	250 × 31 = 7,750	250 × 28 = 7,000	250 × 31 = 7,750	22,500
F	667 × 31 = 20,667	611 × 28 = 17,108	1000 × 31 = 31,000	68,775
G	750* × 31 = 23,250	750* × 28 = 21,000	706* × 31 = 21,886	66,136

* Because Producers D and G were members of more than one related group during the calendar quarter, the allocation that yields the smallest allocation of the 1,000-barrel-per-day amount is required.

It is important to note that Producers A, B and C will not have to share the 1,000-barrel-per-day depletable oil quantity with Producer D under the percentage depletion rules. *(See Case 107.)* Likewise, Producer F will not be required to share the depletable oil quantity (for percentage depletion purposes) with Producer D, and Producer E will not be required to share the depletable oil quantity (for percentage depletion purposes) with Producer G. This situation occurs because, under the percentage depletion rules, the 1,000-barrel-per-day amount is not required to be allocated between individuals and their controlled corporations, as is required under the WPT rules. Producers D and G, however, will be required to share the depletable oil quantity for percentage depletion purposes during the period March 1-March 31 because they constitute a brother-sister group.[131] *(See Case 106.)*

The regulations[132] provide for a daily allocation of the 1,000-barrel-per-day amount in cases where an independent producer is a member of a related group for only a portion of a calendar quarter. In the facts of the instant case, Groups 2 and 3 make an allocation based on only a portion of the calendar quarter. Because the ownership of Producer D changed on March 1, 1987, a one-month allocation of the 1,000-barrel-per-day amount was used for the last month in the calendar quarter. If the ownership of Producer D had changed on, for example, March 7, a daily allocation of the 1,000-barrel-per-day amount during March would have been required. If the average daily production in March was not produced pro rata over the days in that month, the regulations provide that a separate allocation of the 1,000-barrel-per-day amount must be made, based on each member's relative production for each separate day within the month. For related groups not subject to partial quarterly allocation of the 1,000-barrel-per-day amount, the computation of average daily production should be based on total production for the entire calendar quarter.

The statute and regulations[133] provide that if a member of a related group is not an independent producer, that member is not required to be allocated a portion of the 1,000-barrel-per-day amount shared by the related group.

The requirement that the 1,000-barrel-per-day amount be allocated among members of a related group (based on relative qualified production) is a mandatory allocation and cannot be selectively allocated to minimize the related group's overall WPT

131. I.R.C. Sec. 613A(c)(8); Prop. Reg. Sec. 1.613A-3(g).
132. Reg. Sec. 51.4992-2(a)(2)(ii).
133. I.R.C. Sec. 4992(e)(1); Reg. Sec. 51.4992-2(a)(3), Example 2.

liability, by, for example, allocating the 1,000-barrel-per-day WPT independent-producer amount to members of the related group that cannot generate a net income limitation. *(See Case 221.)*

Case 219
Independent-Producer Transfer Rules

> Corporation A has been newly formed for acquisitions. Corporation B is engaged primarily in the exploration, development and production of oil and gas. Included in the assets owned by Corporation B are interests in proven oil and gas properties. Corporation C is the parent of a group of corporations engaged in the exploration, development and production of oil and gas. The assets of Corporation C and the other members of the group also include interests in proven oil and gas properties. Corporation A proposes to acquire all the assets and assume all the liabilities of Corporation B through a statutory merger in which the Corporation B stock will be exchanged for stock in Corporation A followed by the merger of B into A. Corporation A also intends to exchange its stock for 80% or more of the outstanding stock of Corporation C. Certain of Corporation B's and C's oil production qualifies for the reduced windfall profit tax rates on tier-1 and tier-2 oil because both corporations are independent producers.

Immediately after the exchange of stock between Corporation A and the shareholders of Corporation B, the two corporations will be members of the same controlled group of corporations.[134] If the subsequent merger of Corporation B into Corporation A is accomplished pursuant to an exchange that qualifies under I.R.C. Section 351, the transfer of the oil and gas properties from Corporation B to Corporation A should not be a disqualifying transfer for purposes of computing the independent-producer amount.[135]

The transfer of Corporation C stock to Corporation A should not disqualify any of the properties owned by the C group because only the C stock has been transferred and the independent-producer transfer rules relate to the transfer of properties. The new group, with Corporation A as the parent and Corporation C and its related group as subsidiaries, will be required to allocate the 1,000-barrel-per-day independent-producer amount among the corporations based on relative tier-1 and tier-2 production.[136] *(See Case 218.)*

Generally, an independent producer is entitled to the lower independent-producer windfall profit tax (WPT) rates on up to 1,000 barrels a day of combined tier-1 and tier-2 production.[137] *(See Case 217.)* However, production from tier-1 or tier-2 properties transferred on or after January 1, 1980, generally will not qualify for the reduced rates unless the transfer meets certain exceptions to this general rule.[138]

Although the law does not define a *transfer* specifically, the regulations define it as "any sale, exchange, lease, sublease, gift, bequest, devise, or other disposition (including a distribution by an estate or a contribution to or a distribution by a corporation, partnership or trust, whether or not a taxable event) of rights (including rights less

---

134. I.R.C. Sec. 613A(c)(8)(D)(i); Prop. Reg. Sec. 1.613A-7(l).
135. I.R.C. Sec. 613A(c)(9)(B)(ii); IRS Letter Ruling 8216045.
136. I.R.C. Sec. 4992(e)(1).
137. I.R.C. Sec. 4987; I.R.C. Sec. 4992; Reg. Sec. 51.4992-1.
138. I.R.C. Sec. 4992(d)(3); Reg. Sec. 51.4992-1(d)(3)(i).

than fee simple) with respect to the property."[139] This definition is similar to the definition of *transfer* used to calculate the net income limitation; however, there are differences. The most notable difference is that the independent-producer transfer rules apply to the transfer of any tier-1 or tier-2 property, regardless of whether it is proven, while the transfer rules applicable to the net income limitation apply only in situations where there is a transfer of a proven property. *(See Case 224.)*

The Internal Revenue Code (the Code) makes exceptions in the transfer rules for independent producers in case of transfers of property at death, certain changes in beneficiaries of a trust, certain small producers and any transfer where the transferor and transferee are required to share the 1,000-barrel-per-day independent-producer amount.[140]

The final regulations provide a de minimis rule whereby a partnership may transfer a property to an independent producer and have the property retain its eligibility for independent-producer rates if less than 2% of the partnership is owned by persons who are "disqualified transferors."[141] A disqualified transferor is any person other than an independent producer or an independent producer with qualified production in excess of that person's independent-producer amount.[142]

The Internal Revenue Service (IRS) has ruled that when three subsidiaries are merged into the common parent pursuant to a statutory merger (type-A reorganization), the transferred properties with tier-1 and tier-2 production will continue to qualify for the reduced WPT rates applicable to independent producers because the transferor and transferee previously were required to share the 1,000-barrel amount and, thus, specifically were excluded from the independent-producer transfer rules.[143] The IRS also has issued a similar ruling with respect to a tax-free liquidation of two subsidiaries into the parent corporation.[144]

Generally, in a tax-free reorganization or merger involving unrelated corporations with proven oil and gas properties, the transferee corporation will not be entitled to percentage depletion or the lower independent-producer rates on the transferred properties after the transfer. To be exempt from the transfer rules, the Code requires corporations to be members of a controlled group sharing a single depletable oil quantity.[145] However, the IRS has held that a parent corporation can merge into its newly created subsidiary and the transferred properties still will qualify for percentage depletion, even though the group exists only temporarily and one of the corporations ceases to exist.[146] *(See Case 109 for a discussion of exceptions to the transfer rules for purposes of percentage depletion.)*

Fact situations similar to the above case also have been considered by the IRS in private rulings[147] dealing with whether transferred proven properties qualify for percentage depletion after a statutory merger of an existing corporation into a newly created corporation. The IRS concluded that, in a statutory merger, if the oil and gas properties are transferred in an exchange to which I.R.C. Section 351 applies, they are eligible for percentage depletion, even though the corporations have not shared the 1,000-barrel limitation other than immediately before the merger. The significant point in this determination apparently is that the exception to the transfer rule

139. Reg. Sec. 51.4992-1(d)(3)(i); Reg. Sec. 51.4996-3(b).
140. I.R.C. Sec. 4992(d)(3)(C); Reg. Sec. 51.4992-1(d)(3)(iii).
141. Reg. Sec. 51.4992-1(d)(3)(ii); IRS Letter Ruling 8405092.
142. Reg. Sec. 51.4992-1(d)(3)(ii)(B).
143. IRS Letter Ruling 8126061.
144. IRS Letter Ruling 8337022.
145. I.R.C. Sec. 613A(c)(9)(B)(iv).
146. IRS Letter Ruling 7945095; IRS Letter Ruling 8216045.
147. IRS Letter Ruling 8216045; IRS Letter Ruling 8229072.

provided by the Code[148] does not require an allocation of the depletable oil quantity for any period before the exchange provided the exchange qualifies for tax-free treatment under I.R.C. Section 351 and the depletable oil quantity is allocated between the transferor and transferee as of the effective date of the merger. The fact that the transferor corporation goes out of existence following the exchange apparently is not a significant issue.

In a private letter ruling[149] dealing with WPT and the transfer of stock and oil properties to a newly formed corporation pursuant to an exchange offer, the IRS ruled that: (1) the transfer of a corporation's stock is not a transfer for WPT purposes and (2) if all the parties to the exchange are independent producers and not disqualified transferors before the exchange, the tier-1 and tier-2 properties will continue to be eligible for the independent-producer rates after the exchange. This conclusion was reached because the transfer rule[150] generally is meant to apply to only the actual transfer of an interest in crude oil property. Also, the transfer rule does not apply to the transfer of an interest in property if it can be demonstrated that the transferred property was not owned after December 31, 1979, by a person who was a disqualified transferor for any quarter during the period beginning with the quarter ending after September 30, 1979, and ending with the quarter ending before the date the property interest is transferred.[151]

Case 220
Severance Tax Adjustment

State T imposes a severance tax on oil at the rate of 5% of the gross value of oil removed and an additional severance tax of $.015 per barrel removed. These taxes were imposed prior to March 31, 1979. Effective January 1, 1987, the state increased its severance tax from 5% of gross value to 8% of the gross value of oil removed.

The 8% severance tax imposed by State T will qualify for the severance tax adjustment. Even though the rate has been increased subsequent to March 31, 1979, the new rate applies equally to all portions of the gross value of each barrel of oil subject to that tax.[152]

The severance tax of $.015 per barrel does not qualify for the severance tax adjustment because it is unrelated to the gross value of the extracted oil.[153]

In computing the windfall profit per barrel, a producer is allowed to reduce the gross sales price per barrel by the adjusted base price and the severance tax adjustment.[154]

The severance tax adjustment is that portion of the severance tax applicable to the excess of the removal price over the adjusted base price of each barrel of taxable crude oil.[155] The tax does not have to be identified as a severance tax, but it must be imposed by a state and must be based on the gross value of the oil produced.[156]

148. I.R.C. Sec. 613A(c)(9)(B)(ii).
149. IRS Letter Ruling 8230166.
150. I.R.C. Sec. 4992(d)(3)(A).
151. Reg. Sec. 51.4992-1(d)(3)(ii)(A).
152. Reg. Sec. 51.4996-2(c)(2).
153. I.R.C. Sec. 4996(c)(2); Reg. Sec. 51.4996-2(b).
154. I.R.C. Sec. 4988(a).
155. I.R.C. Sec. 4996(c); Reg. Sec. 51.4996-2(a).
156. Reg. Sec. 51.4996-2(b).

The facts stated here allow a fairly easy determination of whether the tax will qualify for the severance tax adjustment. However, the states assess taxes on crude oil in a variety of ways.The Internal Revenue Service (IRS) has issued a number of rulings on whether the severance tax adjustment is allowed for:

☐ Idaho, Louisiana, Mississippi and Texas[157]

☐ Alabama, Indiana, Kentucky, Michigan, Nebraska, North Dakota, Oklahoma, South Dakota, Tennessee and Utah[158]

☐ Wyoming[159]

☐ California, Nevada and Ohio[160]

☐ Alaska[161]

☐ Arkansas[162]

☐ West Virginia[163]

☐ Colorado[164]

☐ Montana[165] and

☐ New Mexico.[166]

The IRS has not considered in a published ruling taxes imposed on crude oil by several other states. Producers with oil production in these states may have their severance tax adjustment challenged if it is not clear that the tax is imposed by the state or if its computation is not based on gross value.

Several states impose certain conservation and/or occupational taxes that are levied on the basis of the gross value of the production but are not withheld at the wellhead by the purchaser. These taxes, nevertheless, qualify for the severance tax adjustment and should be considered by the producer in determining his liability for windfall profit tax (WPT). Producers paying these taxes should compute their WPT, taking these taxes into account in detemining the windfall profit on each barrel of oil. A cash-basis taxpayer will match the tax with barrels removed, regardless of whether payment of the tax is made in the same year as production. The statute[167] discusses the severance tax adjustment in terms of the "tax imposed with respect to such barrels" and, therefore, implies a direct matching of the tax with the appropriate barrels.

Case 221
Net Income Limitation

During 1987, Producer B received $15,000 for qualified newly discovered crude oil production from Property X, representing 3% of the estimated recoverable reserves on the property. Lease operating expenses, production taxes and overhead for the year amounted to $4,000. Producer B

157. Rev. Rul. 82-86, 1982-1 C.B. 188.
158. Rev. Rul. 82-87, 1982-1 C.B. 189.
159. Rev. Rul. 82-87, 1982-1 C.B. 189, *as amplified by* Rev. Rul. 86-45, 1986-1 C.B. 340.
160. Rev. Rul. 82-88, 1982-1 C.B. 190.
161. Rev. Rul. 82-167, 1982-2 C.B. 351, *revoking* Rev. Rul. 82-89, 1982-1 C.B. 191.
162. Rev. Rul. 82-90, 1982-1 C.B. 192. *See also* Rev. Rul. 82-194, 1982-2 C.B. 355, *which modifies* Rev. Rul. 82-90 *with respect to salt water-producing oil wells.*
163. Rev. Rul. 82-91, 1982-1 C.B. 193.
164. Rev. Rul. 82-92, 1982-1 C.B. 194; G.C.M. 38848.
165. Rev. Rul. 83-92, 1983-1 C.B. 303.
166. Rev. Rul. 86-46, 1986-1 C.B. 341.
167. I.R.C. Sec. 4996(c)(1)(A).

paid a $25,000 lease bonus to acquire the property and $175,000 to drill the initial well. The cost recovery allowance on the lease and well equipment for the year was $3,500. The windfall profit tax withheld was $590. Producer B, an independent producer and cash-basis taxpayer, files his tax returns on a calendar-year basis.

The taxable windfall profit realized on a barrel of crude oil is limited to 90% of the net income attributable to the barrel. This limitation is intended to encourage the continued production of less profitable oil. The appropriate tax rate is applied to the lesser of the windfall profit or 90% of the net income attributable to the barrel of crude oil to determine the producer's windfall profit tax (WPT).[168]

The net income attributable to a barrel of oil is determined by dividing the taxable income, as defined, from the property attributable to taxable crude oil by the number of barrels of taxable crude oil sold (as defined for depletion purposes) within the tax year. In this situation, the property is the same as the unit of property determined for percentage depletion purposes.[169] Similarly, taxable income from the property is determined for WPT in the same way it is determined for percentage depletion purposes, except that no deduction is allowed for productive intangible drilling and development costs (IDC), qualified tertiary injectant expenses (when capitalized) or WPT.[170] Although no deduction is allowed for percentage or regular cost depletion in determining net income, a deduction is allowed for "as-if" cost depletion.[171] *(See Case 222.)*

A precise matching of the windfall profit realized on specific barrels with the net income realized from those same barrels is not required.[172] The computation of the 90% net income limitation (NIL) uses the same income and expense data and information as used for percentage depletion purposes. Thus, in the case of a cash-basis, calendar-year taxpayer, the NIL computation will be based on revenues received and expenses paid in one year that are attributable in part to production during the preceding year. Similarly, the income and expense information used for the NIL computation normally will not include the revenues and expenses attributable to production during the last month of the year because they typically are not received or paid until the following year. Items of income and expense are properly considered in the computation of the NIL for the year they are recognized according to the taxpayer's method of accounting for income tax reporting purposes.

The application of these regulatory principles by a cash-basis producer to properties that have commenced production before yearend but with respect to which no production proceeds actually were received before yearend will result in the producer's receiving a refund of the entire amount of the WPT that actually is withheld from the payments for the initial year's production. The producer's net income is zero because he recognizes no current-year income under his cash-basis method of accounting.[173] This treatment results in the correct NIL computation even when part of the sales proceeds is escrowed awaiting settlement of a title dispute.[174] The escrowed sales proceeds are excluded from the NIL computation for the year during which the oil was removed because they properly are excluded from the computation of taxable income for that year.

168. I.R.C. Sec. 4988(b)(1).
169. Reg. Sec. 51.4988-2(d)(1).
170. I.R.C. Sec. 4988(b)(3)(A); I.R.C. Sec. 4988(b)(3)(B); Reg. Sec. 51.4988-2(b).
171. I.R.C. Sec. 4988(b)(3)(C); Reg. Sec. 51.4988-2(b)(3).
172. Reg. Sec. 51.4988-2(b)(1)(iii); Rev. Rul. 83-185, 1983-2 C.B. 200.
173. IRS Letter Ruling 8346003 (Technical Advice Memorandum).
174. G.C.M. 38963. *See also* IRS Letter Ruling 8410005 (Technical Advice Memorandum).

When revenue is placed in escrow due to a price dispute, the NIL can become distorted. In that case, the number of barrels removed from the property during the year is not affected by the escrow requirement. Instead, the sales price per barrel is reduced by the disputed amount, which causes a reduction in the net income per barrel for the year of removal. If the producer loses the pricing dispute, he has calculated the proper net income limitation and has paid the proper amount of WPT. On the other hand, if the producer wins his pricing dispute, even partially, he will receive the proceeds held in escrow and include them in taxable income for the year received. There is no provision, however, for recomputing the NIL for the original removal year. As a result, the producer may pay a lesser amount of WPT than he would have paid absent the pricing litigation.

Producer B's WPT for 1987 is computed as follows:

Gross income	$15,000
Less:	
Lease operating expense, production taxes and overhead	4,000
Cost recovery allowance	3,500
"As-if" cost depletion [($25,000 + $175,000) × 3%]	6,000
Net income	$ 1,500
WPT ($1,500 × 90% × 22.5%)	$ 304

Producer B can claim a WPT refund of $286 ($590 − $304) because the tax computed under the NIL is less than the cumulative WPT withheld on the barrels produced. Technically, the WPT is based on the lesser of the windfall profit realized on a barrel of crude oil or 90% of the net income attributable to a barrel of crude oil. Accordingly, the preceding computation should be performed on a barrel-by-barrel basis rather than in the aggregate. However, when the NIL per barrel is in all cases less than the windfall profit per barrel, the tax liability will be the same whether the computation is made in the aggregate or on a barrel-by-barrel basis.

The statute refers to "the taxable income from the property" concept under the percentage depletion rules *(see Case 87)* as a starting point in the computation of the WPT NIL. The percentage depletion provisions require that an aliquot portion of lease bonus paid with respect to the property be excluded in computing "gross income from the property" and in determining "taxable income from the property." *(See Case 87.)* The statute, therefore, allows Producer B to exclude $750 (3% × $25,000) of the lease bonus under the "bonus exclusion rule" and also to consider $750 as part of his "as-if" cost depletion in computing his net income limitation. The Internal Revenue Service (IRS) has issued a technical advice memorandum[175] confirming this result. However, after reconsideration, the IRS has issued more recently another technical advice memorandum[176] holding that taxpayers are not permitted to exclude from gross income from the property an allocable portion of the lease bonus paid in respect of the property. This holding was based on the fact that reference by the WPT NIL provisions to the percentage depletion computation is only for purposes of adopting the general definition of gross income and does not require the adoption of a "bonus

175. IRS Letter Ruling 8412004 (Technical Advice Memorandum).
176. IRS Letter Ruling 8543005 (Technical Advice Memorandum); G.C.M. 39423.

exclusion rule" having limited applicability to the computation of percentage depletion. In addition, it was held that allowing an exclusion of the bonus was essentially equivalent to a deduction for depletion, which is forbidden in determining the NIL.[177]

The facts in this case do not discuss the method used in determining the proper amount of overhead to allocate the Property X. *(See Case 90 for a discussion of the allocation of indirect expenses for depletion purposes.)* The IRS has previously ruled[178] that WPT should not be considered to be a direct expense for purposes of the direct expense method of allocating overhead. In a recent decision,[179] the Tax Court refused to follow this ruling and agreed with the taxpayer that the amount of WPT incurred, albeit an imperfect approach, was, nonetheless, a reasonable factor to consider in the allocation formula.

The IRS recently has begun to take the position that an allocable portion of indirect or overhead expenses must be treated as IDC for purposes of computing the WPT NIL.[180] *(See Case 90.)* This position is consistent with a similar IRS position with respect to the amount of IDC that constitutes a tax preference item.[181] This recharacterization also will have the effect of increasing the amount of potential IDC recapture. Specifically, the IRS's position is that certain indirect expenses that have been apportioned to a property (pursuant to the percentage depletion regulations) may be considered incident to and necessary for drilling and, therefore, are properly treated as IDC. Producers confronted with determining their position on this issue should consider the "benefits" as well as the "costs" that can result from the recharacterization of allocated overhead costs. At least with respect to the calculation of the WPT NIL, the benefits can, in many situations, exceed the costs. For example, although the capitalization of the overhead as IDC will reduce the impact of the NIL in the year the well is drilled, the additional "as-if" depletion in later years will increase the beneficial impact of the NIL in those later years. In many cases, there will be little or no detriment in the tax year the well is drilled as there may be minimal, if any, revenue received during that initial tax year. Further, with respect to wells drilled before the enactment of the WPT, the capitalization of the overhead incurred in those years will increase the "as-if" basis for all succeeding years. (*See Case 187 for discussion of the uniform cost-capitalization provisions.)*

Case 222
"As-if" Cost Depletion

Producer A paid a bonus of $10,000 to Landowner Z for a lease covering 160 acres. Producer A incurred $55,000 of intangible drilling and development costs (IDC) ($45,000 attributable to the lease and $10,000 attributable to the equipment) and $25,000 of equipment costs in drilling and completing a well on the lease.

"As-if" cost depletion is the cost depletion that would have been allowed for the tax year if all productive IDC and all qualified tertiary injectant expenses (if an election is made to capitalize those expenses for this purpose) incurred by the taxpayer had been capitalized and taken into account in computing cost depletion, and if cost depletion

177. I.R.C. Sec. 4988(b)(3)(B)(i).
178. Rev. Rul. 85-79, 1985-1 C.B. 337.
179. Shell Oil Co. 89 T.C. No. 33 (1987).
180. IRS Letter Ruling 8406006 (Technical Advice Memorandum); IRS Letter Ruling 8622005 (Technical Advice Memorandum); IRS Letter Ruling 8640006 (Technical Advice Memorandum).
181. Internal Revenue Manual Audit Sec. 4232.8, Para. 620(1)(b)(5) (April 18, 1985).

had been used by the taxpayer with respect to the property for all tax years.[182] If the taxpayer had deducted percentage depletion in prior years' income tax returns, it will have no effect on the computation of "as-if" cost depletion.

Producer A should compute "as-if" cost depletion for this property based on $65,000 ($10,000 lease cost plus $55,000 IDC). Producer A must deduct depreciation or cost recovery allowances on the $25,000 equipment cost and on an allocable portion of his overhead and other indirect expenses in determining taxable income from the property for purposes of the net income limitation (NIL). *(See Case 221.)*

The election to expense IDC for federal income tax purposes permits a taxpayer to deduct amounts that, absent the election, would be capitalized as leasehold cost or equipment costs and recovered through deductions for depletion and depreciation or cost recovery allowances. Had Producer A not elected to expense IDC, he would have capitalized $45,000 of the IDC as additional basis in the lease and $10,000 as additional basis in the equipment. For oil and gas properties placed in service after 1986, the law regarding recapture upon disposition requires all IDC and depletion (to the extent the depletion reduces basis) to be recaptured in full, limited to the amount of gain.[183] For properties placed in service prior to 1987, the proposed regulations require segregation of the IDC between the amounts that would have been capitalized as leasehold cost and those that would have been capitalized as depreciable costs. Then depreciation and depletion are recomputed each year as though IDC had been capitalized, and IDC subject to recapture may be reduced.[184] However, the law relating to the computation of the net income limitation clearly provides that "as-if" cost depletion is determined by capitalizing as cost basis in the property all the productive IDC that may be deducted as expenses pursuant to an election to treat those costs as expenses.[185] Accordingly, Producer A will not be required to analyze current or prior years' IDC to segregate the amount that would have been capitalized as depreciable cost, regardless of the time the property was placed in service.

For tax years beginning after 1986, taxpayers may elect to amortize rather than deduct currently all or a portion of their productive IDC.[186] (Note that for tax years prior to 1987, individual taxpayers also had this option, including the availability of a five-year amortization period.) One interpretation of the statute indicates that any IDC deferred by reason of this election is no longer considered IDC required to be capitalized for purposes of computing the "as-if" cost depletion deduction. Thus, if this interpretation is correct, it is possible to accelerate the deduction of the IDC for purposes of the windfall profit tax (WPT) NIL in any case where the amortization rate (10%) exceeds the otherwise applicable cost depletion rate.

Only 70% of the domestic IDC paid or incurred after December 31, 1986, by an integrated oil company may be deducted currently.[187] The remaining 30% is to be deducted ratably over a 60-month period beginning with the month in which those expenditures are paid or incurred.[188] *(See Case 24.)* This deferred IDC similarly may not be required to be capitalized for purposes of computing the "as-if" cost depletion deduction.

A taxpayer can deduct tertiary injectant expenses in computing net income from the property, or he may elect to capitalize them in determining his "as-if" basis.[189] The

182. I.R.C. Sec. 4988(b)(3)(C).
183. I.R.C. Sec. 1254.
184. Prop. Reg. Sec. 1.1254-1(a)(2).
185. I.R.C. Sec. 4988(b)(3)(D).
186. I.R.C. Sec. 59(e).
187. I.R.C. Sec. 291(b)(1).
188. I.R.C. Sec. 291(b)(2).
189. I.R.C. Sec. 4988(b)(3)(C); I.R.C. Sec. 4988(b)(3)(E).

treatment of tertiary injectant expenses elected for the WPT NIL has no effect on the treatment of these costs for federal income tax purposes.[190]

The IDC required to be capitalized to compute "as-if" cost depletion do not include any costs incurred in drilling a nonproductive well.[191] Thus, to determine the net income from the property, dry-hole costs are deducted from gross income in the tax year the costs are paid or incurred. *(See Case 221 for a discussion concerning possible capitalization of a portion of indirect expenses as additional "as-if" basis.)*

For WPT purposes, a *nonproductive well* is defined as any well that has been abandoned or is reasonably expected never to produce oil or gas in commercial quantities.[192] The Internal Revenue Service (IRS) has ruled that, even though a well has been abandoned, the IDC related to it must remain in the property's "as-if" cost basis if the well was completed as a producing well.[193] A direct writeoff of the IDC of a nonproductive well can be taken, but only if the well was abandoned before being completed as a producing well. This definition differs from that included in Committee Reports on the classification of IDC as a tax preference item. That definition refers to production for a "substantial period of time" and compares the amount of production to the costs of drilling the well. Thus, it is possible that a particular well may be treated as a productive well for WPT purposes and as a nonproductive well for tax preference purposes.

IDC commonly is incurred in drilling a well to a depth below known producing mineral deposits to test for other deposits. When these efforts are successful, the IDC incurred clearly should be considered as recoverable costs in the "as-if" depletion computation; when these efforts are unsuccessful and no well is completed, the costs incurred should not be considered. In some cases, however, an unsuccessful well may be plugged back and completed in the known producing deposit. The IRS has ruled that in these cases only, the IDC reasonably allocable to the producing mineral deposit may be used to determine cost depletion in the WPT "as-if" depletion computation; the remaining costs must be considered nonproductive IDC.[194] *(See Cases 174, 175 and 176 for determination of productive IDC for alternative minimum tax purposes.)* According to this ruling, the allocation between productive and nonproductive IDC must be made regardless of whether the taxpayer has elected to treat each operating mineral interest in a tract or parcel of land as a separate property for depletion purposes. Thus, to the extent those costs must be considered nonproductive IDC, a taxpayer derives no future benefit in the form of "as-if" cost depletion in the WPT NIL. These costs must be deducted from gross income in the tax year they are paid or incurred.

The IRS has ruled that costs incurred in drilling injection wells must be capitalized into the taxpayer's "as-if" cost basis.[195] The IRS reasoned that injection well costs cannot be deducted as costs of drilling a nonproductive well because the well was not drilled for the purpose of producing oil or gas.

In a technical advice memorandum,[196] the IRS has held that proven undeveloped reserves must be included in the determination of total estimated recoverable reserves for use in computing the "as-if" cost depletion deduction,[197] notwithstanding the fact

190. I.R.C. Sec. 193; I.R.C. Sec. 4988(b)(3)(E).
191. I.R.C. Sec. 4988(b)(3)(D).
192. Reg. Sec. 51.4988-2(b)(3)(iii).
193. Rev. Rul. 83-5, 1983-1 C.B. 298.
194. Rev. Rul. 82-71, 1982-1 C.B. 185.
195. Rev. Rul. 84-65, 1984-1 C.B. 229.
196. IRS Letter Ruling 8328004 (Technical Advice Memorandum).
197. Reg. Sec. 1.611-2(c)(1); Reg. Sec. 51.4988-2(b)(3)(ii).

that expenditures required to develop those reserves cannot be included in the "as-if" basis until they actually are incurred.[198]

Case 223
Net Income Limitation on Properties Producing Both Oil and Either Gas or Exempt Oil

> **Producer A received $360,000 from the sale of oil and $100,000 from the sale of gas produced from Property X during 1987. Producer A's expenses attributable to Property X for lease operating expense, depreciation, overhead, production and severance taxes and ad valorem taxes for the year were $237,500. Of this amount, $160,000 clearly was identified as relating directly to the production of oil, and $27,500 was clearly identified as relating directly to the production of gas. Producer A is a cash-basis, calendar-year taxpayer.**

To compute the net income limitation for 1987, Producer A must determine the allowable deductions attributable to the production of taxable crude oil.[199]

The regulations provide that in situations where taxable oil and either gas or exempt oil are produced from the same property, the amount of expenditures attributable to taxable crude oil is the sum of the expenses that can be clearly identified as relating solely to the production of taxable crude oil and a proportionate amount of any remaining expenditures that cannot be identified as relating solely to the production of the gas or the exempt oil.[200] The proportionate amount is determined by prorating the expenses on the basis of the relative gross income from taxable crude oil and gas or exempt oil. Producer A will consider the $160,000 of directly related expenses and $39,130 of the other expenses (($237,500 − $27,500 − $160,000) × ($360,000 ÷ $460,000)) as expenses solely for the production of taxable crude oil in computing the net income limitation.

This case, like the example in the regulations,[201] makes reference to certain costs that can be identified clearly as relating solely to the production of either oil or gas. The regulations, however, do not give any guidance as to what types of expenses can be considered "clearly identified." For example, will a taxpayer be expected to identify depreciation or cost recovery allowances on equipment such as tank batteries as relating solely to oil and depreciation or cost recovery allowances on gas-separating facilities as relating solely to gas? This direct identification concept is inconsistent with the proposed regulations dealing with the computation of percentage depletion,[202] which provide that all expenditures are to be allocated between oil and gas production from the same property based on relative gross income. The Treasury commentary accompanying the final net income limitation regulations implies that the regulations covering the determination of expenditures attributable to crude oil are in response to comments from producers that requested that, if an expense can be specifically attributed to gas, exempt oil or taxable crude oil, they should be able to allocate the expense directly to that production.[203] Clearly, when there is sufficient information to determine the amount of severance taxes, trucking, depreciation on tank batteries, pumping units or other equipment, etc., costs can be allocated specifically to the oil or

198. I.R.C. Sec. 4988(b)(3)(C).
199. Reg. Sec. 51.4988-2(b)(1)(ii).
200. Reg. Sec. 51.4988-2(b)(2).
201. Reg. Sec. 51.4988-2(b)(4)(i).
202. Prop. Reg. Sec. 1.613A-3(d)(3).
203. T.D. 7790, 1981-2 C.B. 220.

gas produced. However, many producers do not now have sufficient information to make these types of specific allocations and may be unable to obtain the necessary information economically. In these situations, the producer necessarily must prorate the unidentifiable costs (typically, the costs other than production and severance taxes) on the basis of relative gross income.

The "as-if" cost depletion for each year (including years ending before March 1, 1980) is computed by first taking total "as-if" basis as of the end of the year and dividing that amount by total estimated recoverable reserves at the beginning of the year (including gas reserves converted to equivalent barrels of oil) to determine a unit cost. The unit cost then is multiplied by the production during the year (including gas production converted to equivalent barrels of oil) to determine "as-if" cost depletion, which then is prorated for purposes of the net income limitation between the oil and gas production based on relative gross income.[204] For each succeeding year, the producer will reduce his "as-if" cost basis by the full amount of the prior years' "as-if" cost depletion (including the amounts attributable to both oil and gas) and will increase his basis by any current-year expenditures that must be capitalized as "as-if" cost basis before computing that year's "as-if" cost depletion deduction.[205]

Case 224
Transfer of Proven Property and the Net Income Limitation

During 1987, Company C purchased a proven property from Producer A for $200,000. Producer A originally paid $25,000 for the property and incurred $150,000 of intangible drilling and development costs (IDC) to develop the property. The property had estimated recoverable reserves of 40,000 barrels of oil when Company C acquired the property, and Producer A previously has deducted $5,000 of "as-if" cost depletion. The property produced 2,000 barrels of oil during 1987 after Company C acquired the property. During 1988, Company C spent $350,000 in additional drilling costs to develop the property further. Producer A also owns another property that he purchased for $100,000, and he incurred $500,000 of IDC in drilling a successful well. For estate and business planning reasons, Producer A transferred this property to B, a new corporation owned 100% by Producer A, in a tax-free incorporation on which no gain or loss was recognized.

Special transfer rules apply for purposes of determining the basis to be used for computing "as-if" cost depletion in situations where property has been transferred from one taxpayer to another. These rules are necessary to prevent taxpayers from obtaining an increase in basis and thus reducing the windfall profit tax (WPT). Without these rules, the owner of a producing property with a low basis could sell the property for an amount that would increase its basis in the hands of the transferee. That new basis would increase the "as-if" cost depletion deduction, lower the net income limitation and possibly permit the avoidance of a significant portion of the WPT that otherwise would be due. These transfer rules apply to transfers of proven oil or gas properties after 1978.[206]

If Company C was allowed to use its acquisition cost for purposes of computing "as-if" cost depletion, the depletion deduction would be $10,000 ($200,000 ÷ 40,000) ×

204. Reg. Sec. 51.4988-2(b)(4)(ii).
205. *Ibid.*
206. I.R.C. Sec. 4988(b)(4).

2,000). Had Producer A retained the property, his "as-if" cost depletion deduction for the same period would have been only \$8,500 ((\$170,000 ÷ 40,000) × 2,000). Because the transfer otherwise will result in an increase in the "as-if" cost depletion deduction, C Company must compute its "as-if" deduction by taking into account only those costs that would have been allowable for the transferor and costs incurred after the transfer.[207] In this case, C Company is allowed a deduction of \$8,500 for "as-if" cost depletion for 1987. C Company will be allowed to increase its "as-if" cost basis in 1988 for the expenditure of \$350,000 of additional IDC.

In this situation, when only one property is transferred and the information regarding acquisition cost and IDC is readily available, it is a simple matter to determine whether the transferor's "as-if" cost depletion is less than the amount determined by the transferee. However, there probably are numerous cases in which the information cannot be obtained so easily. A taxpayer that purchases producing properties should consider whether the transferor should be required to furnish this information as a condition of closing, particularly if substantial properties are involved. There may be situations in which the necessary records have been destroyed, are inadequate or simply are not available. In these cases, the transferee may have to reconstruct adequate support for each element of the "as-if" cost depletion deduction. A cost depletion deduction based on this type of reconstruction should be acceptable, as long as the evidence accumulated supports the reasonableness of the results.[208] Extreme care, however, must be used in situations where the actual data are not available. Careful attention should be given to the economics of prior drilling arrangements to determine their effect on the transferor's "as-if" basis. For example, the effect of carried interests, tax partnerships or production payments involved in the development of the property must be considered in developing the necessary information. The transferee also should be prepared to meet resistance from the Internal Revenue Service (IRS) when the actual data are not available.

To determine whether a property is a proven property and, thus, subject to the transfer rules that limit the amount of "as-if" cost depletion allowable to a transferee, the definition of a *proven property* is the same as that used in determining whether percentage depletion is allowable to a transferee.[209] The term *transfer* means "any change in legal or equitable ownership by sale, exchange, gift, bequest, devise, lease, sublease, assignment, contract or other disposition (including creation of a production payment that gives the transferee an economic interest in the property, a distribution by an estate, and any contribution to or any distribution by a corporation, partnership or trust)."[210] Because the transfer rules apply only when the transferee is entitled to a larger "as-if" cost depletion deduction than the transferor, they have no effect on a transferee that is entitled to a smaller "as-if" cost depletion deduction than the transferor. Neither do they affect the transferee's "as-if" deduction in certain nontaxable transactions in which the basis of the property to the transferor carries over to the transferee.

In a general counsel memorandum and a related private letter ruling, the IRS considered these transfer rules in a situation involving the consolidation of numerous partnerships into one partnership.[211] In analyzing the IRS's conclusions, it is important to recognize that the factual situation involved in the memorandum and ruling is unusual in that the income tax basis and the "as-if" basis of the partnership properties apparently were equal in amount. Thus, the memorandum and ruling do not address

207. I.R.C. Sec. 4988(b)(4)(A).
208. T.D. 7790, 1981-2 C.B. 220.
209. I.R.C. Sec. 4988(b)(4)(B).
210. Reg. Sec. 51.4988-2(c).
211. IRS Letter Ruling 8313019; G.C.M. 39172.

the appropriate treatment of "as-if" basis, in excess of the related income tax basis, in a partnership "rollup" or consolidation.

The definition of a *proven property* apparently includes a property that produced only gas before its transfer but that, as a result of additional drilling and development by the transferee, later begins producing oil. To limit the transferee's "as-if" basis to the transferor's "as-if" basis plus expenditures incurred after the transfer under these circumstances seems unduly harsh. Relief may be secured by an election to treat the oil as a separate property. *(See Case 58.)*

Under a literal interpretation of the law, new Corporation B will be limited to an "as-if" basis of only $100,000 (the transferor's and the corporation's tax basis in the property), even though Producr A's "as-if" basis, had he not transferred the property, would have been $600,000. Similar results will occur in most situations involving nontaxable transfers in which the transferor's tax basis of the properties transferred carries over to the transferee. Other examples include gifts, pro-rata current distributions from a partnership, transfers between members of a consolidated corporate group, and certain types of corporate reorganizations. It is possible that Congress never intended to cause a reduction in the "as-if" cost basis to be used in computing the "as-if" cost depletion in these situations.

Case 225
Windfall Profit Tax on Partnership Properties

> **Investor L is a limited partner in ABC 1987 Ltd., a federally registered limited partnership formed under Texas law. The partnership owns three leases producing taxable crude oil, the production of which is being sold to three different purchasers. The partnership and Investor L both use the calendar year; however, the partnership uses the accrual method of accounting, while Investor L uses the cash method for federal income tax purposes.**

The partners, not the partnership, are the producers of the partnership's taxable crude oil production.[212] Therefore, the partners of ABC 1987 Ltd., not the partnership, are liable for windfall profit tax (WPT) on their proportionate shares of the partnership income.[213] Each of the partners is required to determine his respective WPT liability or overpayment. In doing so, he must take into account the tier classification of the partnership's properties; his producer status (i.e., whether or not independent); his proportionate share of the partnership's production; his proportionate share of the partnership's items of income and costs entering into the calculation of the 90% net income limitation *(see Cases 221 and 226)*; and his proportionate share of the WPT withheld by either the first purchaser of the production or by the partnership.

Notwithstanding the fact that the partners, as the producers, are liable for the WPT on their share of partnership production, the Internal Revenue Code provides for "partnership level" administrative and judicial proceedings to determine the proper treatment of "partnership items" for WPT purposes.[214] Generally, *partnership items* are items that more appropriately are determined at the partnership level rather than at the partner level.[215] These consist of: (1) the removal price, (2) the adjusted base price, (3) the tax tier, (4) the severance tax adjustment, (5) the quantity of oil removed

212. I.R.C. Sec. 4996(a)(1)(C).
213. I.R.C. Sec. 4986(b).
214. I.R.C. Sec. 6221; Conference Committee Report No. 97-760, 1982-2 C.B. 663.
215. I.R.C. Sec. 6232(a); Reg. Sec. 51.6232(a)-2(a).

from the premises, (6) the determination of whether the oil qualifies as exempt Alaskan oil, (7) the determination of when removal from the premises occurs and what constitutes the property, (8) the percentage interest of each partner in the oil removed, (9) both the total amount and each partner's share of WPT withheld or paid by the partnership for oil removed during the taxable period, (10) the WPT liability of each partner for that partner's share of the partnership oil removed during the tax period and (11) the net income limitation to the extent that it can be computed at the partnership level.[216] Items that depend on the status of the partner, such as the independent-producer amount and certain exemptions, are not partnership items.[217] In the computation of the partner's WPT liability specified in item (10) above, the partnership disregards the net income limitation and assumes that the information furnished to the partnership by the partner regarding his status as an independent producer or exempt status is correct.[218]

In addition, the partnership, acting through its tax matters partner, may act on behalf of its partners for purposes of the determination, assessment and collection of the WPT.[219] However, the authority of the partnership to act on behalf of any particular partner may be negated by an appropriate individual partner election.[220] Further, if one or more partners with a combined interest of at least 5% in partnership income so elect, the authorization of the partnership to act on behalf of its partners ceases to apply for the entire partnership.[221]

The purpose of giving the partnership the option of electing to act on behalf of the partners for purposes of the determination, assessment and collection of the WPT is to provide the partnership an opportunity to reduce the amount of information that must be delivered to the partners and to simplify the overall WPT reporting process. For example, if the election is made, it will not be necessary to provide information needed to compute the net income limitation or Form 6248 to each partner[222] (although individual Form 6248s still must be provided to the Internal Revenue Service (IRS)).[223] However, it will be necessary for the partnership to provide to the partners before March 31 of the year following the removal year a statement indicating the partners' allocable share of the WPT paid or withheld during the removal year.[224] Further, the partnership can file a single claim for refund, if applicable, due to overwithholding or the net income limitation on behalf of all the partners.[225] If the partnership is required to prepare 250 or more Form 6248s for 1987, such "forms" are required to be submitted to the IRS via magnetic media.[226]

It must be noted that these provisions do not alter the fact that each partner remains primarily liable for the WPT on his allocable share of the taxable crude oil produced by the partnership.[227] Each partner still is required to certify to the partnership his status as an independent producer and his eligibility for exemption for independent stripper wells, qualified royalty production and other producer-related provisions. The partnership is to assume that the certifications are correct and then will use this information in computing and paying the WPT.[228] A partner's liability for WPT will

216. Reg. Sec. 51.6232(a)-2(b).
217. Conference Committee Report No. 97-760, 1982-2 C.B. 663.
218. Reg. Sec. 51.6232(a)-2(b)(9).
219. I.R.C. Sec. 6232(c)(1); Reg. Sec. 51.6232(c)-1(a).
220. I.R.C. Sec. 6232(c); Reg. Sec. 51.6232(c)-1(a)(3).
221. I.R.C. Sec. 6232(c)(2); Reg. Sec. 51.6232(c)-1(a)(2).
222. Reg. Sec. 51.6232(c)-1(b)(2).
223. Reg. Sec. 51.6232(c)-1(b)(3).
224. Reg. Sec. 51.6232(c)-1(b)(2).
225. Reg. Sec. 51.6232(c)-1(b)(4)(ii).
226. Reg. Sec. 301.6011-2(c)(1)(i)(B).
227. Conference Committee Report No. 97-760, 1982-2 C.B. 663.
228. Reg. Sec. 51.6232(c)-1(b)(4)(iii).

be abated to the extent of any WPT paid by the partnership, but, in determining the partner's liability, the partner is precluded from filing a claim for refund if the WPT overpayment arises from partnership items.[229]

As a federally registered partnership, ABC 1987 Ltd. can elect to assume the responsibilities of the first purchaser regarding the withholding and payment of the WPT on the partnership's production.[230] *(See Case 235.)* Partnerships that are not federally registered can elect to assume these responsibilities only if they distribute 10% or more of the entire proceeds from the sale of oil from a property.[231]

The advantages gained from an election to be a "qualified disburser" include keeping all WPT calculations and reporting obligations "in house"; the partnership then is not dependent on first purchasers for information necessary to meet the annual reporting requirements at the partnership and partner levels. A slight cash flow benefit also is realized when a WPT liability is generated because the partnership generally will receive production revenues a few weeks before the related WPT must be deposited. However, qualified disburser elections probably should be deferred on new properties when division of interest problems may delay revenue distributions because the partnership can be required to make a deposit of WPT before receiving the gross revenues from which the WPT must be withheld.

The WPT is not deductible by the partnership for federal income tax purposes. The WPT actually withheld from payments received by the partnership during the year is treated as a distribution from the partnership to the partners.[232] WPT then is deducted by the partner to whom the partnership's oil income is allocated under the provisions of the partnership agreement.[233] The amount of the WPT deduction allowable to Investor L, a limited partner, in this case should be determined under his method of accounting[234] and should be considered an expense of the appropriate property for depletion purposes.[235] His deduction for WPT on the partnership's properties is his proportionate share of the WPT withheld from remittances by the first purchaser or his proportionate share of the WPT actually paid during the year by ABC 1987 Ltd. if it is the qualified disburser on the property.

Case 226
Windfall Profit Tax 90% Net Income Limitation of Partners

Under the provisions of the ABC 1987A Ltd. partnership agreement, the general partner is allocated all capital costs and 1% of all exploration, drilling and development costs that are deductible for federal income tax purposes. The limited partners are allocated 99% of all exploration, drilling and development costs deductible for federal income tax purposes. Revenues and operating expenses are allocated 40% to the general partner and 60% to the limited partners. In view of the provisions of the agreement regarding distribution of the partnership's assets upon liquidation or termination, these allocation provisions have the requisite substantial economic effect and, consequently, are recognized for federal income tax reporting purposes. ABC 1987A Ltd. follows the accrual basis method of accounting for tax reporting purposes.

229. Reg. Sec. 51.6232(c)-1(b)(4)(iv).
230. Reg. Sec. 51.4995-5(b)(3).
231. Reg. Sec. 51.4995-5(b)(1).
232. House Report No. 96-817, 1980-3 C.B. 266.
233. I.R.C. Sec. 164(a)(4); Reg. Sec. 51.6232(a)-1(c).
234. Rev. Rul. 81-99, 1981-1 C.B. 312; Rev. Rul. 82-174, 1982-2 C.B. 99; IRS Letter Ruling 8240013 (Technical Advice Memorandum).
235. Reg. Sec. 1.613-5(a).

It is clear that partners are the producers of their proportionate shares of the partnership production of taxable crude oil and, thus, liable for windfall profit tax (WPT) on that production. As producers, they also are entitled to any overpayment credit or refund resulting from the application of the 90% net income limitation on the amount of windfall profit subject to WPT. For oil removed in tax periods beginning before January 1, 1983, these determinations were made at the partner level rather than the partnership level, but usually using data and information furnished to the partners by the partnership. Now the partnership may elect to act on behalf of its partners for purposes of the determination, assessment and collection of the WPT.[236] *(See Case 225.)* The effect of such an election is to allow the partnership to act on behalf of the partners with regard to administrative filings with the Internal Revenue Service (IRS). The ultimate WPT liability should be exactly the same for each partner's share of production, whether or not this election is made.

If ABC 1987A Ltd. does not make the election for 1987, or to the extent the partners elect to negate the partnership election *(see Case 225)*, each of the partners of ABC 1987A Ltd. should calculate his WPT liability and 90% net income limitation for each of the partnership's properties,[237] taking into account his proportionate share of the partnership's production and items of income and costs allocated to him under the provisions of the partnership agreement (and any other items separately incurred by the partner that are properly includable in the partner's net income limitation computation).[238] Therefore, the general partner, in making his 90% net income calculation for each property, will consider 40% of the partnership's revenues and operating expenses, 100% of the cost recovery allowances on the partnership's equipment and the "as-if" cost depletion allowable (taking into account 100% of lease costs and 1% of the partnership's deductible expenditures for exploration, drilling and development). *(See Case 222.)* Each limited partner, in making his net income calculation for each property, will consider his share of 60% of the partnership's revenues and operating expenses and his "as-if" cost depletion allowable (taking into account his share of 99% of the partnership's deductible expenditures for exploration, drilling and development). *(See Case 222.)* Neither the general partner nor the limited partners should consider any deduction for WPT in the calculation of their 90% net income limitation.[239]

If ABC 1987A Ltd. makes an effective election for 1987, the net income limitation of both the general and limited partners will be calculated in the same manner as explained above, but the calculations and actual filing of applicable claims for refund, etc., will be prepared and filed by ABC 1987A Ltd. rather than by the individual partners. *(See Case 225.)*

The WPT on the partnership's production is not deductible by the partnership for income tax reporting purposes. Instead, it is treated by the partnership as a distribution of money to the partners, who are entitled to a deduction for the WPT because they are considered to be the producers of the partnership's production.[240] Although the ABC 1987A Ltd. partnership uses the accrual method of accounting for income tax reporting purposes *(see Case 225)*, it is probable that many of the partners, particularly the individuals, use the cash method. Their allowable deduction for WPT must be determined pursuant to their method of accounting.[241] Accordingly, the

236. I.R.C. Sec. 6232(c)(1); Conference Committee Report No. 97-760, 1982-2 C.B. 663; Reg. Sec. 51.6232(c)-1(a).
237. Reg. Sec. 51.4988-2(b)(1)(i).
238. Reg. Sec. 51.4988-2(c)(3).
239. I.R.C. Sec. 4988(b)(3)(B)(ii).
240. House Report No. 96-817, 1980-3 C.B. 266.
241. Rev. Rul. 81-99, 1981-1 C.B. 312; Rev. Rul. 82-174, 1982-2 C.B. 99; IRS Letter Ruling 8240013 (Technical Advice Memorandum).

partnership, in preparing its income tax return, should eliminate the WPT expense shown on its books by reclassifying the WPT withheld during the year under the cash method of accounting as a cash distribution to the partners. The difference between the accrual-basis WPT amount and the cash-basis WPT deemed to be distributed apparently should be treated as a deferred item for income tax reporting purposes. (Any partners on the accrual basis should treat the deferred item as a deduction on their own tax returns.) The instructions issued by the IRS for use in filing partnership tax returns for years before 1987 state that a partner's allowable WPT deduction for the partnership's tax year should be reflected in the partnership tax return as an unallowable deduction (as opposed to a distribution). The appropriateness of these instructions is questionable because they appear to conflict with the applicable legislative history[242] and the difference in treatment appears to affect the taxable income of certain partners that have basis limitations.

Although all other items of income and expense considered in the percentage depletion calculation are properly and correctly stated on an accrual basis, the WPT expense should be shown on either the cash or accrual basis, depending on each partner's individual method of accounting.

Presumably, any WPT refund received by the partnership on behalf of the partners will be treated as a capital contribution to the partnership by the partners (or as nontaxable partnership income as provided for by the IRS partnership return instructions). The taxable income resulting from the receipt of the WPT refund apparently should be recognized by the partners in accordance with their individual accounting method. Transfers of partnership interests will complicate the reporting process because the taxpayers who were partners at the time the related production occurred presumably will recognize the income and receive credit for the capital contribution, even if they no longer are partners at the time the partnership actually receives the refund.

Case 227
Royalty-Owner Exemption

> **During 1981, Lessor R, an individual, executed two leases to Operator A for cash and retained a 1/16 overriding royalty interest in each lease. Operator A drilled and completed an oil well on each lease during 1982. Lessor R's share of production from the well on Lease X for 1987 was 913 barrels, and his share of the production from the well on Lease Y for 1987 was 365 barrels. There are no other producing wells on the leases or in the immediate vicinity. Lessor R uses the calendar year and the cash method of accounting for federal income tax reporting purposes.**

For 1985 and thereafter, Lessor R will be exempt from windfall profit tax (WPT) on his share of production from both Leases X and Y, up to a maximum of three barrels per day. For 1982 through 1984, Lessor R had been exempt from WPT on up to two barrels per day. The maximum qualified production amount actually is computed separately for each calendar quarter, with the limit being the number of days in the quarter multiplied by three barrels per day.[243]

To realize the cash flow benefits from this exemption as soon as possible, Lessor R can certify to the first purchaser his qualification for this exemption and the estimated

242. House Report No. 96-817, 1980-3 C.B. 266.
243. I.R.C. Sec. 4994(f); Reg. Sec. 51.4994-1(f).

amount of his production that qualifies for the exemption.[244] In certifying for 1987, Lessor R can certify that production from either Lease X or Lease Y, but he cannot certify both leases.[245] Lessor R's share of the production is 2½ barrels per day from Lease X and one barrel per day from Lease Y, which in total exceeds the limitation on exempt royalty oil.[246]

Normally, Lessor R should certify the production on the lease for which the highest amount of WPT is being withheld. However, there may be other factors influencing the selection of the lease on which to apply the exemption. For example, Lessor R may want to apply his exemption to the production from Lease Y if, because of other expenses, his percentage depletion deduction on Lease Y is limited to 50% of net income. Judicious use of this exemption at the end of the year, irrespective of prior certification, can maximize the federal income tax and WPT benefit.

Lessor R must obtain the remainder of his exemption for 1987 that cannot be certified to the first purchaser as a credit or refund when filing his income tax return for the respective years, or Lessor R can claim it as an overpayment of WPT by filing a claim for refund.

A *royalty owner* must be an individual, an estate or a qualified family farm corporation to qualify for the royalty-owner exemption.[247] In addition, the applicable barrel limitation must be allocated between certain related royalty owners.[248] For purposes of the royalty-owner exemption, qualified royalty production includes production attributable to all types of nonoperating interests, including overriding royalty interests, net profits interests and production payments.[249] The exemption generally does not apply to interests created out of an operating mineral interest or transferred after June 9, 1981. There are, however, several exceptions to the transfer restriction.[250]

Assuming Lessor R transfers the overriding royalty interest to a grantor trust, he will continue to be eligible for the royalty-owner exemption with respect to production attributable to that interest. Generally, the transfer of a royalty interest to a trust will not disqualify the production from that interest as qualified royalty production if the transfer is made between persons who share a single exemption amount.[251] The trust, however, will not be able to certify its production as exempt from withholding. Instead, the trust will prepare a Form 6248 showing Lessor R his allocable share of trust production for the calendar year. (Lessor R's share of trust production is based on his share of the trust's adjusted distributable net income for the calendar year.)[252] Lessor R then will use this information in preparing a claim for refund of WPT withheld on exempt production.

Case 228
Stripper Well Crude Oil Production Exempt from Windfall Profit Tax

Operator A, an independent producer, has a working interest in three leases. Lease X was acquired via a drill-and-produce-to-earn farmout from Company B in 1972. Operator A drilled and completed a producing

244. I.R.C. Sec. 4995(a)(9).
245. Reg. Sec. 51.4995-2(b)(2); T.D. 7811, 1982-1 C.B. 186.
246. I.R.C. Sec. 4994(f)(2)(A).
247. I.R.C. Sec. 4994(f)(3)(A); Reg. Sec. 51.4994-1(f)(2); I.R.C. Sec. 6429(d)(1).
248. I.R.C. Sec. 4994(f)(3)(B); I.R.C. Sec. 6429(c)(2); I.R.C. Sec. 6429(c)(4); Reg. Sec. 51.4994-1(f)(4)(iii).
249. I.R.C. Sec. 4994(f)(3)(A); I.R.C. Sec. 6429(d)(2); Reg. Sec. 51.4994-1(f)(3).
250. Reg. Sec. 51.4994-1(f)(3).
251. I.R.C. Sec. 6430(c)(3); Reg. Sec. 51.4994-1(f)(3)(iii)(C).
252. I.R.C. Sec. 6430(c)(2).

oil well on Lease X in 1973. Lease Y was obtained from the landowner in 1980, and Operator A drilled and completed a producing oil well on this lease during that year. Lease Z was purchased from Company C, an integrated oil company, in 1982. Lease Z had four producing oil wells (drilled and completed by Company C in 1976) located on it when purchased by Operator A. All three leases have been producing not more than 10 barrels per well per day for more than a year and have been certified as stripper well properties.

Operator A's crude oil production from Lease X is exempt from windfall profit tax (WPT), effective for oil removed from the premises after December 31, 1982.[253] For oil removed before that date, Operator A's production from Lease X is subject to WPT at the independent-producer rates prescribed for tier-2 properties[254] to the extent of 1,000 barrels per day of combined tier-1 and tier-2 production. *(See Case 217.)*

Operator A's crude oil production from Lease Y similarly is exempt from WPT, effective for oil removed from the premises after December 31, 1982, even though the property is classified as tier 3.[255] Before that date, Operator A's production from Lease Y was subject to WPT at the rates prescribed for tier-3 properties.

Operator A's crude oil production from Lease Z after December 31, 1982, is not exempt from WPT because the lease was owned by a person other than an independent producer (i.e., an integrated oil company) after July 22, 1981.[256] Therefore, Operator A's production from Lease Z is subject to WPT at the nonindependent-producer rates prescribed for tier-2 properties (i.e., 60%).[257] Furthermore, in Operator A's calculation of the 90% net income limitation, his "as-if" cost depletion will be limited to an amount not greater than the deduction Company C would have been entitled to before the transfer. *(See Case 224.)*

Under the June 1979 Department of Energy regulations, properties that had an average daily production of not more than 10 barrels per well for any consecutive 12-month period after 1972 generally were classified as stripper well properties. These properties were not subject to the previously existing price controls.

Production from stripper wells is exempt from the WPT only if the producer qualifies as an independent producer *(see Case 216)* and only to the extent the production is attributable to the independent producer's working interest in the stripper well property. There are also certain limitations with respect to proven properties transferred after July 22, 1981.[258]

The transfer rule prescribed for exempt stripper properties appears to have been designed to prevent nonindependent producers on July 22, 1981, from transferring their stripper well properties to independent producers and thereby avoiding the WPT on that production after 1982. Independent-producer status, however, occasionally is lost for a calendar year, sometimes inadvertently, and later reestablished. Such a producer loses his stripper exemption beginning with the calendar year during which his status changes to a nonindependent producer and is not eligible for the stripper exemption until the calendar year in which he regains his independent-producer status. For purposes of determining whether a qualified stripper property has been owned by a nonindependent producer after July 22, 1981, the current owner

253. I.R.C. Sec. 4991(b)(6); I.R.C. Sec. 4994(g)(1).
254. I.R.C. Sec. 4991(d)(1)(A); I.R.C. Sec. 4987(b)(2).
255. I.R.C. Sec. 4991(b)(6); I.R.C. Sec. 4991(d)(2); I.R.C. Sec. 4994(g).
256. I.R.C. Sec. 4994(g)(2).
257. I.R.C. Sec. 4987(b)(1); I.R.C. Sec. 4992(d)(3).
258. I.R.C. Sec. 4994(g).

is not considered.[259] This prevents a producer from losing forever the exempt stripper status due to a temporary classification as a nonindependent producer. If a qualified stripper property is transferred, however, the transferee producer will not be eligible for exempt stripper status if any of the preceding owners ever have been nonindependent producers at any time after July 22, 1981. It does not matter that this status may have been only temporary. The stripper-property transfer rule does not apply if the property is not a "proven" property at the date of transfer.[260] The definition of *proven property* for this purpose follows the definition used for depletion purposes. *(See Case 108.)*

Proposed regulations[261] issued by the Internal Revenue Service on January 20, 1983, regarding stripper well properties have been criticized soundly because they appear to undermine the intent of Congress in granting the stripper exemption by limiting its availability. Consequently, it is expected those proposed regulations will be revised substantially before they are finalized.

Case 229
Incremental Tertiary Oil

> On March 21, 1986, Operator C submits an application to the State Commissioner for self-certification of a tertiary recovery project on Unit X. At the same time, a copy of the self-certification report is submitted to the Internal Revenue Service (IRS). On April 13, 1986, the State Commissioner having jurisdictional authority over Unit X certifies the project. During June 1986, Operator C purchases $5 million worth of organic polymers, all of which are injected during 1986. Operator C owns 100% of the working interest and begins a tertiary recovery project using a polymer-augmented water-flood method on August 7, 1986. The average monthly amount of crude oil removed from Unit X for the six-month period ended March 31, 1979, is 25,500 barrels. In January 1987, Unit X produces 65,100 barrels of crude oil. Unit X is a tier-1 property. Operator C uses the calendar year and cash method of accounting for federal income tax reporting purposes.

All of the crude oil produced from Unit X in January 1987 is incremental tertiary oil and, therefore, qualifies as tier-3 oil since, through the application of the statutory formula, the base level is reduced to zero (as discussed below).

If the production in this case had been for January 1986 and all the other events had occurred one year earlier, the calculation of the incremental tertiary oil for Unit X for January 1986 would have been computed as follows:

Average base level at 3/31/79	25,500 bbls.
Less: 25,500 x 80% (1% per month for 1/1/79 through 8/7/85)[262]	(20,400)
25,500 x 10% (2½% per month for 9/1/85 through 12/31/85)[263]	(2,550)
Base level for January 1986	2,550 bbls.
January 1986 production	65,100 bbls.
Less: January base level	(2,550)
Incremental tertiary oil	62,550 bbls.

259. I.R.C. Sec. 4994(g)(2).
260. *Ibid.*
261. Prop. Reg. Sec. 51.4991-1(b).
262. I.R.C. Sec. 4993(b)(1)(A).
263. I.R.C. Sec. 4993(b)(1)(B).

Crude oil determined to be incremental tertiary oil will be treated for windfall profit tax (WPT) purposes as tier-3 oil.[264] Therefore, production of this oil by both independent and nonindependent producers from tier-1 properties will be taxed at the lower 30% rate, which offsets some of the higher costs incurred to maximize ultimate recovery. This production from tier-2 properties also yields nonindependent producers substantial benefits from the lower WPT rate. The only benefit derived by independent producers on tier-2 properties is in the form of a higher base price because they were taxed already at the 30% rate for years before 1983 and they are exempt from WPT on qualified stripper well oil for oil removed after 1982. *(See Case 228.)*

A qualified tertiary recovery project is one that was certified and approved pursuant to the June 1979 energy regulations or one that meets the statutory requirements.[265] New projects can be qualified only under the statute. The statute and regulations require that the injection of liquids, gases or other matter must have begun after May 1979, that the portion of the property to be affected be adequately delineated and that the project involve the application (according to sound engineering principles) of one or more tertiary recovery methods that reasonably can be expected to increase the amount of crude oil ultimately recovered.[266] In addition, the operator must submit certification either from a petroleum engineer[267] or the proper jurisdictional agency[268] that the project meets these requirements. The operator also is required to submit certification from a petroleum engineer that the project continues to meet these requirements in accordance with guidelines established by regulations.[269]

Operator C has fulfilled the statutory requirement for certification of the tertiary recovery project.[270] He may request a ruling that the project is a qualified tertiary recovery project.[271] Because a jurisdictional agency certified Operator C's tertiary recovery project, the IRS is required to issue a ruling within 180 days after receipt of the information necessary to approve the ruling request.[272] The tertiary method adopted by Operator C is one of nine methods listed in the June 1979 energy regulations[273] (miscible fluid displacement, steam-drive injection, microemulsion, in-situ combustion, polymer-augmented water-flooding, cyclic-steam injection, alkaline flooding, carbonated water-flooding and immiscible carbon-dioxide displacement), but a different method could have been used if approved by the Associate Chief Counsel (Technical).[274] In two separate private rulings,[275] the IRS approved a tertiary recovery project using an immiscible nitrogen drive, a method that is not listed in the June 1979 energy regulations. However, the IRS later reconsidered its conclusion and revoked at least one of these rulings.[276]

For a project (other than a Department of Energy-certified project or a significant expansion of a pre-June 1979 project) to be a qualified project, the injection of the liquids, gases or other matter must have begun after May 1979.[277] The project's date of inception is important not only to demonstrate that it began after May 1979 but also because it is used to compute the base level described below. Operator C's tertiary recovery project is deemed to have begun August 7, 1986, which is the date the injection of the tertiary injectants began.[278]

---

264. I.R.C. Sec. 4991(e)(1)(C).
265. I.R.C. Sec. 4993(c)(1); Prop. Reg. Sec. 51.4993-1(b).
266. I.R.C. Sec.4993(c)(2); Prop. Reg. Sec. 51.4993-1(c)(2).
267. I.R.C. Sec. 4993(c)(2)(D)(i).
268. I.R.C. Sec. 4993(c)(2)(D)(ii); I.R.C. Sec. 4993(d)(5); Rev. Proc. 83-83, 1983-2 C.B. 598; G.C.M. 39089; IRS Letter Ruling 8346026.
269. I.R.C. Sec. 4993(c)(2)(E); Prop. Reg. Sec. 51.4993-1(e)(6).
270. I.R.C. Sec. 4993(c)(2)(D); Prop. Reg. Sec. 51.4993-1(c)(2)(iv).
271. Reg. Sec. 51.4993-4(a).
272. I.R.C. Sec. 4993(d)(7); Reg. Sec. 51.4993-4(c).
273. 10 CFR Sec. 212.78(c).
274. I.R.C. Sec. 4993(d)(1)(B); Prop. Reg. Sec. 51.4993-1(e)(5).
275. IRS Letter Ruling 8226152; IRS Letter Ruling 8235055.
276. IRS Letter Ruling 8410029. *See also* Rev. Rul. 85-141, 1985-1 C.B. 277.
277. Rev. Rul. 81-309, 1981-2 C.B. 225; IRS Letter Ruling 8150111; I.R.C. Sec. 4993(c)(2)(B).
278. I.R.C. Sec. 4993(d)(2); Prop. Reg. Sec. 51.4993-1(d)(2).

Operator C has described its project as covering all of Unit X. Presumably, this will meet the necessary requirements for delineation. In some cases, only a portion of the property qualifies as a tertiary project if only a portion of the property's production will be enhanced.[279]

Because this is a qualified tertiary project, Operator C is entitled to the lower WPT rates for the incremental tertiary oil. *Incremental tertiary oil* is defined as the increased production achieved from the initiation or significant expansion of a qualified tertiary recovery project. The amount of increased production is measured by comparing the production from the property for the month in question to the base level for the property for that month.[280]

The *base level* for a property is defined as the average monthly amount of crude oil removed from the property for the six-month period ended March 31, 1979, reduced (but not below zero) by two amounts: (1) 1% of the beginning average monthly amount for each month after 1978, up to and including the month that the qualified tertiary project begins and (2) 2.5% of the beginning average monthly amount for each full month after the project begins and ending with the month preceding the month for which the base level is being determined.[281]

Operator C determines his WPT on all barrels produced in January 1987, using the tier-3 rates and base prices. He uses these rates and prices because the base level calculated as described in the preceding paragraph exceeds the average monthly production for the six-month period ended March 1979. For January 1986, he determined his WPT on 2,550 barrels, using the tier-1 rates and base prices, and he determined the WPT with respect to 62,550 barrels, using the 30% WPT rate and the tier-3 base prices. Had the unit produced both tier-1 and tier-2 oil, the incremental tertiary oil would have been allocated pro rata to each tier, based on total barrels produced within each tier during the month. Once this allocation is made, the barrels with the highest selling price within each tier then are considered to be incremental tertiary oil.[282]

For purposes of the 90% net income limitation, Operator C can elect to capitalize the qualified tertiary injectant expenses as additional "as-if" cost basis *(see Cases 221 and 222)*, even though these costs are expensed for federal income tax purposes.[283] This election is made on a property-by-property basis. The election is irrevocable and applies to all qualified tertiary injectant expenses for the year of the election and all subsequent years.[284]

Operator C, as a cash-basis taxpayer, claims a deduction in 1986 for the $5 million worth of injectants purchased in June 1986. For federal income tax purposes, Operator C will expense the qualified tertiary injectant costs in either the tax year during which the injectant is injected or the tax year in which the expenses are paid or incurred, whichever is later.[285] In this case, the proper year for the deduction is 1986, the year the injectants were purchased and injected. Had the injection been delayed until 1987, Operator C could not have claimed a deduction until 1987. A deduction for the tertiary injectant costs could have been limited had recoverable hydrocarbons (natural gas or crude oil, including condensate or oil from other sources such as oil shale)[286] constituted 25% or more of the value of the injectant.[287] If the value of the recoverable hydrocarbons is 25% or more of the value of the injectant, the deductible cost is limited to the value of the nonhydrocarbon component of the injectant plus the

279. I.R.C. Sec. 4993(d)(3); Prop. Reg. Sec. 51.4993-1(c)(2)(ii); IRS Letter Ruling 8208198.
280. I.R.C. Sec. 4993(a).
281. I.R.C. Sec. 4993(b).
282. I.R.C. Sec. 4993(b)(3).
283. I.R.C. Sec. 4988(b)(3)(C)(i)(II); I.R.C. Sec. 4988(b)(3)(E).
284. Reg. Sec. 51.4988-2(c)(6).
285. I.R.C. Sec. 193; Reg. Sec. 1.193-1(a).
286. Reg. Sec. 1.193-1(c)(4).
287. I.R.C. Sec. 193(b); Reg. Sec. 1.193-1(c)(3).

value of the nonrecoverable hydrocarbon. (Hydrocarbon injectants are considered recoverable except to the extent the taxpayer can demonstrate them to be nonrecoverable.)[288] If the recoverable hydrocarbons make up less than 25% of the value of the injectant, the entire cost of the injectant may be expensed.[289] *(See Case 120.)*

Case 230
Pledged and Carved-Out Production Payments

> Operator A owns the working interests in two producing leases. Lease X is fully developed because several producing wells were drilled on it in prior years.
>
> Lease Y has only one well drilled on it, and there are three more possible locations for wells that would develop the property completely. Operator A sells P a production payment of $3 million on Lease Y, under the terms of which he is obligated to spend the proceeds drilling and completing the three additional wells. At the same time, Operator A sells R a production payment of $5 million on Lease X which he plans to spend on acquisition, exploration, drilling and development of new leases. The principal, plus interest at the rate of 2% above the prime rate charged by Operator A's bank (net of all taxes other than income), on each of the production payments is payable out of 65% of the gross proceeds from sales of production from each of the leases. Operator A drills and completes the three additional wells on Lease Y at a cost of $3.25 million.

With respect to Operator A, the gross income from sales of crude oil produced on Lease X will be the same for percentage depletion purposes and for windfall profit tax (WPT) purposes. Carved-out production payments (except those pledged for development of the burdened property)[290] and retained production payments (except those retained in a leasing transaction) created on or after August 7, 1969,[291] are treated as mortgage loans and purchase-money mortgage loans, respectively, and do not constitute an economic interest (subject to percentage depletion) in the property.[292] *(See Case 135 for a discussion of the imputed interest rules as they relate to carved-out production payments, and see Case 138 for a discussion of the original-issue discount rules.)* Therefore, R is not liable for WPT because he is not the producer of that oil.[293] *(See Case 212.)* Instead, Operator A, who holds the only economic interest in Lease X, is liable for WPT on both his share of the production and the production used to discharge the production payment and interest.[294]

Operator A will not recognize any gross income at the time of sale of the production payment on Lease X but will recognize gross income, in accordance with his method of accounting, as the oil is produced, even though a portion of the proceeds from the sale of production goes directly to R to discharge the production payment and to pay interest.[295] *(See Case 135.)* Operator A is entitled to a deduction for the interest. A part or all of the interest expense is treated as an indirect or overhead expense allocable to all Operator A's producing properties for purposes of calculating the 50% of net income limitation on percentage depletion[296] and for purposes of calculating the 90% of net income limitation on the amount of profit subject to WPT.[297]

---

288. Reg. Sec. 1.193-1(c)(2).
289. Reg. Sec. 1.193-1(e), Example 2.
290. I.R.C. Sec. 636(a).
291. P.L. 91-172 (Tax Reform Act of 1969), Sec. 503(c)(1)-(3).
292. I.R.C. Sec. 636(a); I.R.C. Sec. 636(b).
293. I.R.C. Sec. 4986(b); Rev. Rul. 84-16, 1984-1 C.B. 229; IRS Letter Ruling 8531059.
294. I.R.C. Sec. 4986(b); I.R.C. Sec. 4996(a)(1)(A); Rev. Rul. 84-16, 1984-1 C.B. 229; IRS Letter Ruling 8531059.
295. Reg. Sec. 1.636-1(a)(1)(ii).
296. Reg. Sec. 1.636-1(a)(1)(ii); I.R.C. Sec. 613(a); Reg. Sec. 1.613-5(a).
297. I.R.C. Sec. 4988(b)(3); Reg. Sec. 51.4988-2(b)(1)(ii).

The gross income recognized by Operator A from sales of crude oil produced on Lease Y will be different, as discussed below, for purposes of percentage depletion and the calculation of the 90% net income limitation for WPT.[298] Also, Operator A will consider only the excess expenditures of $250,000 (i.e., $3,250,000 - $3,000,000) incurred by him in drilling and completing the three additional wells on the lease for both federal income tax and WPT purposes.[299] The purchaser of a production payment pledged for development of the burdened property[300] is considered to own an economic interest (subject to depletion) in the property. Therefore, P is liable for WPT because he is the owner of an economic interest (a pledged production payment) in the property and considered to be the producer of the oil used to discharge the production payment.[301]

Although not considered in the facts of this case, presumably, P will not be willing to enter into the pledged production payment arrangement on Lease Y if he is not also entitled to be reimbursed for his WPT expense out of production. It is not clear how any such reimbursements are to be treated by either P or Operator A. It appears this reimbursement may be treated as an additional amount due under the production payment arrangement. If so, the reimbursement will be excluded from Operator A's depletable gross income on Lease Y (similar to the interest element of the production payment). P, on the other hand, will include the reimbursement in his gross income and deduct an equal and offsetting amount for the WPT expense paid by him. Resolution of this issue must await further developments in this area.

The creation of P's production payment pledged to develop Lease Y is considered a "transfer" for purposes of computing the WPT 90% net income limitation because Lease Y was proven when P acquired his interest.[302] *(See Case 224.)* It is unclear under the WPT transfer rules[303] how P is to calculate his "as-if" cost depletion deduction because it is uncertain what portion (if any) of Operator A's "as-if" basis he may consider in making this computation. *(See Case 224.)* It may be appropriate, pending resolution of the issue, for P to consider a proportionate part of Operator A's "as-if" basis equal to the number of estimated barrels required to discharge the production payment, divided by total estimated barrels attributable to Operator A's working interest, then multiplied by Operator A's remaining "as-if" basis.

If this approach is used, P's calculation of the 90% net income limitation may result in an overpayment credit or refund of the WPT paid. In this situation, the pledged production payment agreement probably should provide that any overpayment credit or refund of WPT received by P will be treated as a payment on the production payment obligation.

Operator A is not required to include the income from production used to discharge the production payment and interest in his depletion calculation, but he is required to include this production and income in the calculation of his 90% net income limitation for WPT purposes.[304] In view of this requirement, it seems that Operator A should be permitted to consider all his expenditures for drilling and completing the three additional wells on Lease Y in the calculation of his 90% net income limitation. However, the statute does not authorize this treatment apparently because, at the time of enactment of the WPT, consideration was not given to the fact that pledged production payments are treated differently from other carved out production payments and retained production payments. Without corrective legislation or regulations, an inequitable WPT may result on Operator A's 35% share of the production from Lease Y.

298. I.R.C. Sec. 4988(b)(5); Reg. Sec. 51.4988-2(c)(2); I.R.C. Sec. 636(a); Reg. Sec. 1.636-1(b)(1).
299. G.C.M. 22730, 1941-1 C.B. 214.
300. I.R.C. Sec. 636(a); Reg. Sec. 1.636-1(b).
301. I.R.C. Sec. 4986(b); I.R.C. Sec. 4996(a)(1)(A); Rev. Rul. 84-16, 1984-1 C.B. 229.
302. I.R.C. Sec. 4988(b)(4)(B); Reg. Sec. 51.4988-2(c)(1).
303. I.R.C. Sec. 4988(b)(4)(A); Reg. Sec. 51.4988-2(c)(1).
304. I.R.C. Sec. 4988(b)(5); Reg. Sec. 51.4988-2(c)(2); I.R.C. Sec. 636(a); Reg. Sec. 1.636-1(b).

Operator A will not recognize any gross income at the time of sale of the pledged production payment on Lease Y,[305] nor will he be allowed any basis, deductions or credits for his expenditures in drilling and completing the three additional wells on Lease Y, except for the $250,000 excess expenditures. Similarly, Operator A will not recognize any gross income as the oil that is used to discharge the production payment and interest is produced and sold. Consequently, his income tax calculations will exclude the pledged production payment income, both at the time of sale and at the time of actual production. Operator A will exclude the basis, deductions and credits arising from the expenditure of the proceeds received from the sale of the pledged production payment. *(See Cases 150 and 151.)*

Case 231
Net Profits Interest

In 1983, Lessor R sold an unproven lease to Operator A, an independent producer, for $10,000 and retained a 15% net profits interest. The agreement provided that Lessor R would receive 15% of the net profits realized by Operator A, defined as gross income from the sale of oil and gas produced from the lease, less all Operator A's costs of acquisition, exploration, development, operation and taxes (other than income and windfall profit). Before 1987, Operator A drilled and completed an oil well on the lease and recovered from production all costs he incurred.

During 1987, the property produced 10,000 barrels, attributable to the interests of Operator A and Lessor R, which sold for $300,000.* Operator A incurred operating expenses of $100,000 and workover costs of $50,000. Thus, Lessor R is entitled to receive $22,500 [($300,000 − $100,000 − 50,000) × 15%)] for his net profits interest before consideration of windfall profit tax (WPT).

* $30/barrel average sales price assumed for illustration purposes only.

The WPT is imposed on the *producer of the crude oil,*[306] defined as the holder of the economic interest of the crude oil produced,[307] and it is a firmly established judicial principle that the owner of a net profits interest holds an economic interest in the oil produced.[308] The WPT rate for Lessor R will be the same as for other nonoperating interest owners.[309]

Because the net profits agreement was entered into after March 31, 1982, Lessor R is liable for windfall profit tax on 1,500 barrels of taxable crude oil produced from the lease during 1987 and Operator A is liable for WPT on the remaining 8,500 barrels. This is determined by attributing to Lessor R his net profits interest percentage of the barrels produced without considering any WPT expense-sharing provision in the net profits interest agreement or any deduction for WPT expense.[310] Lessor R has a net income per barrel of $15, while Operator A similarly has a net income per barrel of $15 (($300,000 − $45,000 − $85,000 − $42,500) ÷ 8,500 = $15), before considering any "as-if" cost depletion, depreciation or overhead expenses attributable to the property. This method of determining Lessor R's share of the gross production is consistent with the determination of his share of the production for depletion purposes, whereby Lessor R is deemed the producer of 1,500 barrels (i.e., 15% × 10,000).[311]

305. I.R.C. Sec. 636(a); Reg. Sec. 1.636-1(b).
306. I.R.C. Sec. 4986(b).
307. I.R.C. Sec. 4996(a)(1); Reg. Sec. 51.4996-1(b).
308. Burton-Sutton Oil Co. v. Comm'r, 328 U.S. 25 (1946), 34 AFTR 1017, 46-1 USTC 9243; Comm'r v. Southwest Exploration Co., 350 U.S. 308 (1956), 48 AFTR 683, 56-1 USTC 9304.
309. I.R.C. Sec. 4987(b).
310. I.R.C. Sec. 4996(a)(1)(B); Reg. Sec. 51.4996-1(b)(3).
311. Prop. Reg. Sec. 1.613A-7(f)(3).

If the net profits interest agreement had been entered into before March 31, 1982, Lessor R's share of the production for 1987 would have been 750 barrels, determined by dividing his net profits amount ($22,500) by the $30-per-barrel gross sales price, without considering any WPT expense-sharing provision in the agreement or any deduction for WPT expense.[312] In that case, Operator A would have been liable for WPT on the remaining 9,250 barrels. Operator A's net income per barrel would be $13.78 (($300,000 - $45,000 - $85,000 - $42,500) ÷ 9,250).

Technically, returning to the facts given, Lessor R is being allocated 750 barrels, representing a pro-rata share of the "cost recovery oil" (crude oil, representing reimbursement of qualified costs), as well as his pro-rata 750-barrel share of the net profits.[313] This method arrives at the gross income and gross barrels of production necessary to produce Lessor R's net profits. Lessor R's pro-rata share of gross income, costs and production is generally equal to his percentage share of the net profits realized from the property. The costs, income and production thus attributed to the net profits interest owner are "taken away" from the working interest owner to calculate his 90% net income limitation. The following computation illustrates how Lessor R is allocated his pro-rata share of the cost recovery oil (the 750 barrels of production effectively paying his pro-rata share of operating and workover costs) and how Lessor R and Operator A each have the same $15 net income per barrel amount before considering any "as-if" cost depletion, depreciation or overhead expenses attributable to the property:

	Amount	Barrels**
Lessor R's net profits interest	$22,500	750
Add gross-up for expenses:		
Operating ($100,000 × 15%)	15,000	500
Workover ($50,000 × 15%)	7,500	250
Total deemed gross income **	$45,000	1,500
Less deemed expenses:		
Operating	15,000	
Workover	7,500	
Lessor R's net income	$22,500	
Net income per barrel* ($22,500 ÷ 1,500)	$ 15	

	Total		Attributable to R		Attributable to A	
	Amount	Barrels	Amount	Barrels	Amount	Barrels
Gross income/ production**	$ 300,000	10,000	$ 45,000	1,500	$ 255,000	8,500
Less:						
Operating expenses	(100,000)		(15,000)		(85,000)	
Workover costs	(50,000)		(7,500)		(42,500)	
Net income	$ 150,000		$ 22,500		$ 127,500	
Net income per barrel* ($150,000 ÷ 10,000)	$ 15					
($22,500 ÷ 1,500)			$ 15			
($127,500 ÷ 8,500)					$ 15	

* Before considering any "as-if" cost depletion, depreciation or overhead expenses attributable to the property.

** $30/barrel sales price assumed for illustration purposes only.

The allocation of the cost recovery oil to the owner of the net profits interest is not made until the first tax period (i.e., calendar quarter) with respect to which the owner

312. IRS Letter Ruling 8109064.
313. I.R.C. Sec. 4996(h)(2); Reg. Sec. 51.4996-1(b)(3)(iv).

of the net profits interest receives a share of production remaining after that cost recovery. However, the allocation is made for all subsequent tax periods, regardless of whether the property later shows a profit or a loss.[314] The allocation of a loss to the owner of the net profits interest will affect the calculation of the 90% net income limitation because the cost recovery oil will be allocated in a year subsequent to the allocation of the corresponding costs. The allocation of a loss to the owner of the net profits interest seems to assume that the working interest owner will recoup the loss out of future payments otherwise payable to the net profits interest owner.

An apparent exception is a net profits interest arrangement requiring an annual determination of the amount of net profits to be shared that does not permit carryover deductions of the prior years' losses by the working interest owner. This type of arrangement results in an inequitable sharing of production and WPT expenses, unless the prescribed allocation method limits the production, expenses and income of the net profits interest owner to amounts that result in zero net income for the net profits interest owner for the year of the loss. The net profits interest owner will be allocated his pro-rata share of production, income and costs only to the extent of this gross income. The excess costs will be reallocated to the working interest owner, who in reality has borne the economic burden of the costs and should be entitled to consider the excess costs in his own 90% net income limitation. Although the regulations do not contain such a detailed explanation,[315] this should be the result in this situation, as cost recovery oil is defined to exist only to the extent the property has sufficient revenues to reimburse for the expenses. To the extent the expenses will not be reimbursed, there is no cost recovery oil to allocate to the net profits interest holder.

The rules with respect to net profits interests are applicable only for persons owning an economic interest in the burdened property.[316] The definition of *net profits agreement* is not intended to include carried-interest arrangements.[317]

If Lessor R is an individual, an estate or a qualified family farm corporation,[318] its share of the production qualifies as exempt royalty oil and would be exempt from WPT to the extent of three barrels per day.[319] *(See Case 227.)*

Case 232
Windfall Profit Tax Relating to Gas Well Condensate

> Producer X sells natural gas produced from Lease M to pipeline Company ABC. Before the purchase of the gas by ABC, Producer X recovers some crude oil through the use of a field separator and he sells the oil separately to Purchaser P. Company ABC takes title to the gas after this process is completed and subsequently recovers drip condensate at various points along the pipeline. This condensate appears in the system due to the temperature and pressure changes involved in normal pipeline operation. The contract between Producer X and Company ABC does not require ABC to reimburse or make settlement with X for the sale of drip condensate, so Company ABC sells it to Purchaser Q and retains all the proceeds.

The assessment of windfall profit tax (WPT) on condensate from natural gas wells has been a controversial subject since the WPT originally was enacted. The controversy has centered around whether condensate produced from a gas well is subject to WPT and, if so, who is considered to be the producer. Congress resolved this

314. I.R.C. Sec. 4996(a)(1)(B)(ii); Reg. Sec. 51.4996-1(b)(3)(ii).
315. Reg. Sec. 51.4996-1(b)(3)(iv).
316. I.R.C. Sec. 4996(h)(4); Reg. Sec. 51.4996-1(b)(3)(vi).
317. Senate Report No. 97-592, 1983-1 C.B. 491; Reg. Sec. 51.4996-1(b)(3)(vii), Example 6.
318. I.R.C. Sec. 6429(d)(1).
319. I.R.C. Sec. 4991(b)(5); I.R.C. Sec. 4994(f).

controversy in 1982 by clarifying the statutory language and by including explanatory comments in the related Committee Reports.[320] The definition of *taxable crude oil* was amended, effective as of the original date of the enactment of the WPT, to clarify that condensate recovered from a gas well is subject to the WPT. Although the term *taxable crude oil* still is defined as all "domestic crude oil" other than exempt oil, *domestic crude oil* now is defined simply as crude oil produced from a well located in the United States or a U.S. possession.[321] The definition of *crude oil* for WPT purposes now follows the definition developed by the Department of Energy in its pricing regulations. Therefore, the statute now clearly provides that natural gas liquids, including condensate recovered from gas production by mechanical separators at any point at or before the inlet side of the gas-processing plant, are subject to the WPT.

After clarifying that condensate is, in fact, subject to the WPT, Congress also addressed the question of who is liable for payment of the WPT, and the related administrative issues concerning withholding and deposit procedures. The issues involved can be illustrated by the factual situation presented in this case. Producer X owns the economic interest in the property and ordinarily would be responsible for the WPT; however, Company ABC received the drip condensate sales proceeds from which the WPT should be withheld. Irrespective of who is treated as the producer, Purchaser Q was confronted with the question of whether to withhold WPT because it was not required to do so with the removal of crude oil from the property occurring before its sale.

The Committee Reports[322] confirm that only the producer that holds the economic interest in the crude oil in place can be liable for the WPT. Thus, a pipeline or gas processor that recovers condensate produced by another will not be liable for the WPT other than as a withholding agent with respect to the tax owed by the producer. The Committee Reports also provide that WPT will not be imposed on incidental liquids recovered in pipeline operations (unless those liquids or the proceeds therefrom are allocated to the producer) if the producer applied standard separation technology before delivery of the gas to the pipeline.

In recognition that the condensate often is recovered after the production has been removed from the premises, the statute was amended to provide that condensate recovered off the premises by mechanical separation is deemed to be removed, for WPT purposes, on the date on which it is so recovered.[323]

Although the question of when withholding is required apparently has been resolved, problems may arise if the seller is not the actual producer. The Committee Reports[324] explaining the changes made to this section recognized these problems and suggested that the Secretary of the Treasury may wish to modify the present WPT withholding with respect to the removal of condensate recovered off the premises. For example, the first purchaser may be responsible for withholding only on payments made for condensate sold for the account of the producer, and the gas processor could be responsible for withholding WPT with respect to the portion of recovered condensate he is entitled to take as compensation for his services.

There still are no formal rules concerning the determination of the removal price of condensate. Although the removal price will depend on the facts and circumstances in each situation, its determination generally should follow the same guidelines used for

320. Conference Committee Report No. 97-986, 1983-1 C.B. 492.
321. I.R.C. Sec. 4996(b)(3).
322. Senate Report No. 97-592, 1983-1 C.B. 492.
323. I.R.C. Sec. 4996(b)(1).
324. Senate Report No. 97-592, 1983-1 C.B. 492.

determining the amount of gross income for depletion purposes.[325] *(See Case 87.)* Therefore, the removal price should not include any value for transportation or processing.[326] For example, if the producer is not compensated for condensate recovered after gas is removed from the premises, no WPT will be imposed on the producer because the removal price of the condensate will be zero. A producer also may not be liable for WPT if his contractually defined removal price is determined to be less than the base price for that crude oil. However, these arrangements must be scrutinized carefully to make certain that the value of the gas is not being overstated while the value of the condensate is being understated in an effort to reduce the amount of WPT imposed.[327]

The Internal Revenue Service (IRS) has held that condensate recovered as the result of ambient ground temperatures and normal atmospheric pressure affecting the net gas in the pipeline, i.e., causing the heavier hydrocarbon portion of the gas to form liquids, is subject to the WPT where such condensate is recovered at or before the inlet side of the taxpayer's gas-processing plant.[328] On the other hand, natural gas liquids recovered within a processing plant by absorption, adsorption or extraneous refrigeration processes are not subject to WPT.[329]

In the fact situation involved in this case, the crude oil recovered by Producer X with the field separator will fall under the normal withholding rules for crude oil because it never leaves the premises before its sale. Thus, Purchaser P should withhold WPT from the payments made to Producer X for this crude oil. The drip condensate that is recovered at various points along the pipeline by Company ABC probably will not be subject to WPT because it is likely the removal price is zero in the facts presented. Even if some allocation of the gas purchase price were made, such price is probably less than the applicable adjusted base price. As these liquids arise primarily due to changes in temperature and pressure, they are taxable crude oil if recovered before being processed in a gas-processing plant. Producer X must be prepared to demonstrate he is not somehow being indirectly compensated for the liquids at a price which would create a taxable windfall profit.

How to determine whether and when WPT should be withheld is much less clear if certain facts in this case are changed. Who has responsibility, if any, to withhold if there is no separator on Lease M, but rather the gas is sold directly into the Company ABC pipeline? The gas is often transported under pressure to the gas plant where processes are applied before any mechanical separation takes place to recover natural gas liquids. Based on an annual test, the producer is then allocated the barrels of condensate he would have received had a field separator been used. This process can be a more efficient means of recovering greater quantities of condensate and was in use long before the WPT law became effective. Additionally, the inlet side of a gas plant may not be as easy to identify as it seems. There does not seem to be a so-called "standard" gas plant that every company uses. Each plant tends to be a custom application.

In situations involving "skim oil," the IRS held that the person recovering the oil actually is a first purchaser required to withhold WPT.[330] In that case, the taxpayer (R) was engaged in the business of disposing of saltwater that was a byproduct of oil production. During this disposal process, the saltwater was transported from the

325. Senate Report No. 97-592, 1983-1 C.B. 492.
326. Reg. Sec. 1.613-3(a).
327. Senate Report No. 97-592, 1983-1 C.B. 492.
328. IRS Letter Ruling 8621002 (Technical Advice Memorandum).
329. *Ibid.*
330. IRS Letter Ruling 8321069; IRS Letter Ruling 8404051; IRS Letter Ruling 8404088.

respective leases to a central facility. There, a certain amount of oil (referred to as skim oil) was recovered. The disposal agreement gave R title to any oil thus recovered. R sold the skim oil to a purchaser, who was withholding WPT from its payments to R. R did not believe WPT should be withheld and asked the IRS to rule. The IRS held that R was not the producer of the oil because he did not own an economic interest in the properties but that he actually was the first purchaser and should have deposited the required WPT. R had paid (with services) a price equal to the fair market value (FMV) of his services rendered in recovering the crude oil in excess of the compensation (other than the skim oil) he received for recovering that crude oil. The FMV of R's services was deemed to be the FMV of the crude oil recovered, plus any compensation paid for removing the crude oil. As a first purchaser, R had to withhold and deposit the tax and file certain information statements.[331] The base price and tier of the crude oil recovered had to be certified by the operator of the property. (If no certification had been received, the rule regarding incomplete information would have applied.[332]) The oil was deemed to be removed when the saltwater containing the skim oil was transported.

The IRS has reached a similar conclusion with respect to a situation involving the recovery of crude oil from tank bottoms by an independent service contractor.[333]

Case 233
Deductibility of Windfall Profit Tax

> **Individual A owns a working interest in Lease M. During 1987, $48,000 of windfall profit tax should have been withheld with respect to oil removed from this lease, but due to a clerical error $50,000 actually was withheld. After making his 90% net income computation, Individual A determines that his actual liability for windfall profit tax is only $40,000. The amount of windfall profit tax withheld from paid production during 1987 was $44,000. Individual A is an independent producer using a calendar year and cash method of accounting for federal income tax purposes.**

Individual A should deduct $44,000 of windfall profit tax (WPT) in his 1987 income tax return[334] and consider $44,000 of WPT expense for percentage depletion purposes.[335]

Had the $2,000 overwithholding error been discovered during the year, the first purchaser would have been required to adjust for the error by underwithholding from subsequent payments for oil removed during the same calendar year.[336] The first purchaser may correct the $2,000 overwithholding error by reducing the WPT withheld from subsequent payments for oil removed during 1988 if the adjustment also can be reflected in the annual information statement provided by the purchaser for 1987.[337] Because the annual information statement is required to be furnished by the first purchaser to the producer on or before March 31 following the calendar year during which the oil is removed, the overwithholding error must be corrected by the purchaser before the following March 31.[338] If the first purchaser pays more than the WPT required to be deposited for oil removed during a tax period, the first purchaser

331. Reg. Sec. 51.4997-2; Reg. Sec. 51.4995-3.
332. Reg. Sec. 51.4995-1(b)(2).
333. IRS Letter Ruling 8336007 (Technical Advice Memorandum).
334. I.R.C. Sec. 164(a)(5); Rev. Rul. 81-99, 1981-1 C.B. 312.
335. I.R.C. Sec. 613(a); Reg. Sec. 1.613-5.
336. Reg. Sec. 51.4995-1(c)(1)(ii).
337. *Ibid.*
338. Reg. Sec. 51.4997-2(c)(4).

can file a claim for refund after the due date of the return for that tax period, which is the last day of the second month following the end of the calendar quarter.[339]

If, instead of an actual withholding error, there is merely an error in the preparation of the Form 6248 received by Individual A from the first purchaser on March 31, the first purchaser will be required to file a new Form 6248.[340] Because the error exceeds $100, if it is discovered after March 31, 1988, but before July 1, 1988, the purchaser will be required to furnish to Individual A and file with the Internal Revenue Service (IRS) a corrected Form 6248 for 1987 on or before July 31, 1988.[341] If the error is discovered on or after July 1, 1988, the purchaser will be required to furnish to Individual A and file the corrected Form 6248 on or before March 31, 1989 (the time the next original yearly statement is required to be furnished and filed).[342] If the error is less than $100, the corrected statement will be required to be furnished and filed on or before March 31, 1989, regardless of when it is discovered.[343] A corrected yearly statement is not required to be filed if the corrected statement will reflect a change of less than $1.00 (one dollar) in each of the following: WPT liability, WPT withheld, and the amount of underwithheld or overwithheld tax.[344]

If the first purchaser does not correct the $2,000 overwithholding error, Individual A can file a claim for refund or credit of the overpayment but only after February 28, 1988, (the time the tax is deemed to have been paid by Individual A) and before the expiration of the statute of limitations.[345]

Individual A may file a second claim for refund or credit of the $8,000 overpayment of WPT due to the application of the net income limitation only after the end of his tax year, but not before February 28, 1988.[346] Alternatively, Individual A may file a single claim for refund or credit of the overpayment attributable both to the withholding error and the 90% net income limitation. The claim for credit can be incorporated into Individual A's income tax return for 1987.

As a practical matter, Individual A will not be able to file a complete claim for refund or a tax return claiming credit for the overpayment until he receives the annual statement from the first purchaser because the statement is required to be attached to either the claim for refund or his income tax return.[347] As stated above, the first purchaser is required to furnish the producer this statement on or before March 31 following the year during which the oil is removed, and a copy of this statement must be filed with the IRS on or before April 30 of that same year.[348]

Individual A should include his WPT refund of $10,000 in his gross income for the year in which the refund actually is received.[349] The refund also should be included in self-employment income to the extent the original deduction of the WPT had reduced self-employment income in the previous year.[350] However, all or a portion of the refund may not be included in income if the deduction of the WPT expense in 1987 did not result in any tax benefit,[351] or to the extent Individual A's depletion deduction for 1987 would have been increased had the refunded WPT not been deducted in a

---

339. Reg. Sec. 51.6402-1(b)(1).
340. Reg. Sec. 51.4997-2(c)(5).
341. Reg. Sec. 51.4997-2(c)(5)(i).
342. Reg. Sec. 51.4997-2(c)(5)(iii), Example 2.
343. Reg. Sec. 51.4997-2(c)(5)(i).
344. Reg. Sec. 51.4997-2(c)(5)(ii).
345. I.R.C. Sec. 4995(a)(4); Reg. Sec. 51.6402-1(c)(1).
346. Reg. Sec. 51.6402-1(c)(2).
347. Reg. Sec. 51.6402-1(c)(1).
348. Reg. Sec. 51.4997-2(c)(4).
349. Rev. Rul. 83-102, 1983-2 C.B. 198.
350. Rev. Rul. 83-102, 1983-2 C.B. 198; G.C.M. 39024.
351. Rev. Rul. 83-102, 1983-2 C.B. 198.

1987 percentage depletion computation.[352] In the latter event, the net amount of the refund required to be included in income is not to be considered in the percentage depletion computation of that year.[353] A possible alternative would be to reduce the WPT expense deduction on Lease M in the year the refund is received for purposes of computing the year's percentage depletion.[354] In that case, no changes would be made to the depletion computation on Lease M for 1987.

The timing of the recognition of the income is not clear if the overpayment is claimed as a credit on Individual A's 1987 federal income tax return. The instructions to the 1986 Forms 6249 and 1040 (Schedules C and E) state that the amount of any credit or refund of overpaid WPT received in 1986 for tax year 1985, based on either overwithholding or the net income limitation, is reportable as income in 1986. Thus, it appears that Individual A should include the $10,000 in gross income in 1987, even if the amount is applied against the balance of the tax due rather than actually being refunded. This treatment seems to be consistent with normal cash-basis accounting rules.

The uncertainty as to the timing of recognition is created by at least two developments. First, the IRS concluded in a technical advice memorandum[355] that, if the taxpayer claims the overpayment of WPT as a credit against his federal income taxes, he must include the amount of the overpayment as income in that same tax return. This conclusion, however, does not appear to be adequately supported by the discussion included in the memorandum and appears to be contrary to normal cash-basis accounting rules. In any event, the IRS's position with regard to this issue is unclear.

The second development that creates uncertainty is the 1982 amendment to the statute,[356] which provides that a WPT overpayment can be used to reduce the amount of estimated tax payments that otherwise would be required. *(See Case 236.)* It seems reasonable that Individual A should report the overpayment as income in 1987, at least to the extent the overpayment was used to reduce estimated tax payments that were otherwise due and payable during 1987.

If Individual A is an accrual-basis taxpayer, he will be required to reduce his 1987 WPT expense deduction by the amount of the overpayment due to both the withholding error and the application of the net income limitation to state properly and correctly the expense on an accrual basis at $40,000. He will not be required to make any further adjustments in 1988.[357]

Case 234
Claims for Refund of Overpaid Windfall Profit Tax by Fiscal-Year Taxpayers

> Corporation C files its federal income tax returns based on a fiscal year ending April 30. It owns a direct interest in several oil and gas properties and an indirect interest in several oil and gas properties through ABC Partnership, which files its returns on a calendar-year basis. For calendar year 1987, Corporation C determines that several purchasers have overwithheld $15,000 of windfall profit tax (WPT) due to various clerical

352. I.R.C. Sec. 111(a); Rev. Rul. 77-79, 1977-1 C.B. 34.
353. Rev. Rul. 77-79, 1977-1 C.B. 34.
354. Reg. Sec. 1.613-5(a).
355. IRS Letter Ruling 8240013 (Technical Advice Memorandum).
356. I.R.C. Sec. 6654(f)(3)(B).
357. Rev. Rul. 82-174, 1982-2 C.B. 99; Russell E. Logan, 86 T.C. 1222 (1986).

errors. Corporation C also will be entitled to a refund of additional WPT, due to the 90% net income limitation.

Corporation C may file a refund claim after February 28, 1988, for the $15,000 of overwithheld WPT and the refund due to the application of the net income limitation for the first four months of 1987 on directly held properties.[358] Corporation C may file an additional claim for refund (or take credit on its income tax return) as a result of the 90% net income limitation any time after April 30, 1988. However, Corporation C can include only production from directly held properties for the months of May and June and the last two quarters of 1987 and none of the production for the first four months of 1988.[359] Corporation C cannot claim a refund for the first four months of 1988 because the WPT for these months is not deemed to be paid until February 28, 1989. *(See Case 233 for a further discussion of when WPT is deemed to be paid and when a refund can be claimed for calendar-year taxpayers.)* Because a producer is not deemed to have paid the WPT on the oil removed until the last day of the first February following the calendar year in which the oil is removed, a fiscal-year taxpayer will have to file more than one claim for refund to receive WPT refunds as soon as possible.

A taxpayer must wait to claim a refund of WPT attributable to the 90% net income limitation for any tax period (calendar quarter) until either February 28 following the tax period or the last day of its tax year, whichever is later.[360]

To compute the 90% net income limitation on the properties in ABC Partnership, the partnership's tax year and method of accounting for income tax purposes are to be used.[361] Because ABC Partnership is on the calendar year, Corporation C will be permitted to file a claim for refund of WPT for 1987 resulting from the net income limitation computed by Partnership ABC any time after February 28, 1988, when the WPT for 1987 is deemed to be paid.[362] Partnership ABC may elect, with the requisite consent of the partners, to compute and file any claim for refund of WPT on behalf of the partners.[363] *(See Case 226 for a further discussion.)* The election to assume this responsibility must be filed on or before September 30 of the removal year.[364]

On the other hand, if the partnership is on a fiscal year ending April 30 and if Corporation C uses the calendar year for income tax reporting purposes, there would be slight changes in the times when claims for refund can be filed.[365] In that case, with respect to the partnership properties, Corporation C can file a claim for refund for the first four months of 1987 after February 28, 1988, using the partnership's net income limitation based on production, income and expense for its tax year ending April 30, 1987. However, even though the WPT for the last eight months of 1987 is deemed to be paid on February 28, 1988, a claim for refund from application of the 90% net income limitation cannot be filed at least until after April 30, 1988, when the production, income and expense for the partnership for that tax year can be determined.

If Corporation C is producing crude oil not subject to withholding and thereby depositing its own WPT, it can file claims for refund due to overpayments for any tax period (calendar quarter) any time after the end of the second month following the

358. Reg. Sec. 51.6402-1(c).
359. Reg. Sec. 51.6401-1(c)(2).
360. *Ibid.*
361. Reg. Sec. 51.4988-2(c)(3).
362. I.R.C. Sec. 4986(b); I.R.C. Sec. 4996(a)(1)(C); Reg. Sec. 51.6402-1(c)(2); Reg. Sec. 51.6402-1(d).
363. I.R.C. Sec. 6232(c)(1); Reg. Sec. 51.6232(c)-1.
364. Reg. Sec. 51.6232(c)-2(b)(2).
365. Reg. Sec. 51.6402-1(d).

close of the tax period.[366] Claims for refund due to the application of the 90% net income limitation can be filed by Corporation C only after the end of its tax year.[367]

Case 235
Qualified Disburser Election

P is the first purchaser of the production from Lease X, which is operated by A. Purchaser P pays 100% of the sales proceeds for the production from Lease X to Operator A. Operator A retains 30% of the payment attributable to his interest in the property and distributes the remaining 70% to the other interest owners. To speed up the preparation and improve the accuracy and reliability of annual statements of windfall profit tax (WPT) withheld, Operator A would like to assume the responsibilities of Purchaser P for the withholding, payment and reporting of windfall profit tax.

Operator A should file a statement with Purchaser P (signed and dated) that establishes: (1) Operator A is a "qualified disburser"[368] for Lease X and (2) Operator A assumes complete responsibility for meeting all the withholding, depositing and reporting requirements with respect to sales of oil on that property that normally would be the responsibility of the first purchaser.[369] The election normally will be effective for oil removed after the date on which the election is received by Purchaser P. Purchaser P is required to file a copy of the election with the Internal Revenue Service (IRS) Center in Austin, Texas.[370] Purchaser P then will no longer withhold any windfall profit tax from the sales proceeds remitted to Operator A. Operator A will withhold and deposit WPT from the 70% that it disburses to other interest owners based on the certifications, just as Purchaser P would have been required to do as first purchaser. With respect to the 30% that Operator A retains, he must comply with the same depository requirements that are imposed on producers of oil that is not subject to withholding.[371]

A qualified disburser generally is a disburser that: (1) distributes at least 10% of the entire proceeds from the sale of oil on a property (excluding the disburser's own production), (2) is an integrated oil company required to make semimonthly payments or (3) is a federally registered partnership.[372] *(See Case 225 for a further discussion of when a partnership is considered to be federally registered and when a qualified disburser election should be made.)*

In addition to the advantages noted in Case 214, Operator A also will be able to consider the 90% net income limitation in determining the amount of WPT to be deposited on his own share of the production.

In this situation, Operator A is a qualified disburser because he distributes more than 10% of the production from Lease X, excluding his own production. Any one of the interest owners to whom Operator A disburses also could be a qualified disburser provided the same tests are met at that level. Note that at least 10% of the total production on the property must be distributed and not just 10% of the amount received. If one of the other interest owners is a qualified disburser, Operator A will not withhold any WPT on that production.

---

366. Reg. Sec. 51.6402-1(b)(1).
367. Reg. Sec. 51.6402-1(b)(2).
368. Reg. Sec. 51.4995-5(b).
369. Reg. Sec. 51.4995-5(c).
370. Reg. Sec. 51.4995-5(d).
371. Reg. Sec. 51.4995-5(e); Reg. Sec. 51.4995-3(f).
372. Reg. Sec. 51.4995-5(b).

In this case, P was the first purchaser. There are times when the identity of the first purchaser is not always clear. *(See Case 232 regarding the first purchaser of "skim oil.")* In certain situations, the IRS considers the holder of a division order to be the actual first purchaser.[373] Generally, if the division order provides that the holder is to take title to the oil produced and then arrange for the sale and distribution of proceeds, the holder will be deemed to be a first purchaser. On the other hand, if the division order merely appoints the holder as an agent, he is not considered to be the first purchaser. The identity of the first purchaser is significant since that person has reporting requirements and is liable for withholding WPT.[374] Also, when the holder of the division order is the actual first purchaser, certain elections (such as the qualified disburser election) must be filed with him to be effective.

Additionally, a first purchaser must be careful when recognizing a qualified disburser election or any other election in which he would be giving up his responsibility for withholding and depositing WPT. If, for any reason, the election were invalid, the first purchaser would be liable for the amount of WPT that should have been withheld.[375] The first purchaser is liable not only for withholding but also for the correct amount.[376]

Case 236
Windfall Profit Tax Overpayment Reduces Estimated Tax Payments Required

> A, an individual oil producer, owns a working interest in a lease, the production from which is subject to windfall profit tax (WPT) withholding. In 1986, Producer A had a total income tax liability of $10,000 before consideration of a $4,000 WPT overpayment (due to overwithholding and the net income limitation). For 1987, Producer A has an estimated tax liability of $25,000 and a projected WPT overpayment of $3,000.

The statute provides that regulations are to be prescribed to establish the extent to which individual[377] and corporate[378] taxpayers will be allowed to consider windfall profit tax overpayments in computing their estimated tax and any related underpayment penalties. Corporate taxpayers should consider a WPT overpayment attributable to WPT withheld in excess of the aggregate WPT liability as a credit or reduction of the amount of the underpayment to tax.[379] The February 28 deemed payment date has no effect in determining the amount of the WPT overpayment.[380] Although the mandated regulations have not yet been proposed for individuals, Internal Revenue Service (IRS) Publication 505 (Rev. Dec. 86) contains a discussion explaining the manner in which a WPT overpayment can be taken into account in calculating any penalty for underpayment of estimated tax.

The publication provides that only the portion of the WPT overpayment that is due to a withholding error or the portion of the overpayment attributable to the net income limitation that is computed with respect to payments for crude oil that were subject to

373. Rev. Rul. 82-205, 1982-2 C.B. 350.
374. I.R.C. Sec. 4995(a); Reg. Sec. 51.4995-3; Reg. Sec. 51.4997-2.
375. I.R.C. Sec. 4995(a); IRS Letter Ruling 8309003 (Technical Advice Memorandum).
376. IRS Letter Ruling 8323008 (Technical Advice Memorandum); IRS Letter Ruling 8323010 (Technical Advice Memorandum).
377. I.R.C. Sec. 6654(f)(3)(B).
378. I.R.C. Sec. 6154(c); I.R.C. Sec. 6655(f)(2)(B).
379. Prop. Reg. Sec. 1.6655-1(b)(5)(ii)(B).
380. *Ibid.*

withholding can be used to reduce the amount of any required estimated tax payments. Thus, any WPT overpayment attributable to properties that are not subject to withholding will not have any impact on the amount of the required estimated tax payments or any related underpayment penalties.

The qualifying portion of any WPT overpayment is treated in the same manner as a credit (i.e., foreign tax credit) as opposed to being treated as a payment. Therefore, the qualifying portion of the WPT overpayment for the prior year reduces the amount of the prior-year tax liability for purposes of computing the required estimated tax installment payment based on 100% of the prior-year tax liability. The qualifying portion of the current-year overpayment also constitutes a reduction of the current-year tax liability for purposes of computing the "90% of the total tax" amount, which is needed to determine whether there is an underpayment. In the absence of regulations to the contrary, it appears that a WPT overpayment for the current year is not to be considered if the required installment payment is based on the taxpayer's annualized taxable income, alternative minimum taxable income and adjusted self-employment income.[381]

Applying these principles to Producer A's factual situation leads to the conclusion that Producer A should make estimated tax payments of $6,000. The prior-year tax liability ($6,000) exception is less than 90% of the current-year estimated tax liability ($22,000) and, thus, constitutes the minimum amount of estimated tax payments that must be made to avoid any underpayment penalties. The factual information provided is not sufficient to allow for a determination of whether the installment payments could be less if they were based on Operator A's annualized income.

Case 237
Windfall Profit Tax Concepts of Removed from the Premises and Removal Price — Offshore and Onshore Operations

Corporation A is the operator of three contiguous offshore oil leases (blocks) located 80 miles offshore. There are no on-site storage facilities on the single production platform for any of the blocks. All the production that is not consumed on site for production operations is transferred into a pipeline owned by Corporation X. The production from the three blocks is sold and billed to the various purchasers of the crude oil at an onshore terminal facility from which crude oil is continuously delivered to the purchasers' barges and/or pipelines. Because the working interest ownership in the three blocks varies, the crude oil production is separately metered at the point the crude oil enters Corporation X's pipeline from the various wells on the production platform such that an accurate accounting to each owner may be made. The $1-per-barrel transportation charge levied by Corporation X is paid out of the gross sales proceeds received when Corporation A sells the crude oil production at the onshore terminal facility to the purchasers on behalf of the various owners or producers.

Corporation A also is the operator of an onshore tertiary recovery project that produces heavy oil by injecting steam into the producing crude oil formation. The tertiary recovery project is conducted on a unitized property. Corporation A uses crude oil recovered from operations as fuel to power the steam generators for the tertiary recovery project. Rather than acquire additional crude oil or residual fuel oil from third parties to power

381. I.R.C. Sec. 6654(d)(2).

the steam generators, Corporation A occasionally transfers crude oil from certain contiguous and noncontiguous leases that produce crude oil from conventional means to power the steam generators. To the extent the ownership interests in the unitized tertiary recovery property and the other leases from which crude oil is transferred are not identical, cash payments are made to account for differences in ownership.

If crude oil is removed (or deemed removed) from the property before it is sold, the removal price is considered to be the amount that results (or would result) from application of the constructive sales price principles in determining gross income from the property for percentage depletion purposes on the date the crude oil is removed or deemed removed from the premises.[382] For purposes of determining gross income from the property for percentage depletion purposes,[383] *premises* is defined to mean "in the immediate vicinity of the well."[384] There are no specific guidelines that establish the geographical parameters of "the immediate vicinity of the well." Thus, this determination occasionally must be based on the particular facts and circumstances of each case.[385]

Crude oil that is produced and injected (without leaving the property and before manufacture or conversion) into a well on the property or used to power a production process or production equipment is not considered to be removed for purposes of imposition of the windfall profit tax (WPT).[386] It is not completely clear what constitutes the full scope of the term *production process.* Examples given in the regulations include crude oil used to power a production process, such as a tertiary injection process or a water flood, and crude oil used to power production equipment such as an artificial lift device.[387] Presumably, other uses such as crude oil burned on the premises to power a heater treater would also constitute a "production process." If crude oil production is used on the lease in a capacity other than to power a "production process" or "production equipment," that crude oil is deemed removed (for purposes of imposition of the WPT) when that crude oil is used.

For purposes of imposition of the WPT, transportation of crude oil a distance of five miles or less to a first storage facility where it is held until later sale is not considered removed from the premises. Instead, such oil is considered removed from the premises when it is removed from the first storage facility.[388] The proposed regulations[389] had originally provided for a storage facility located no more than two miles away (10 miles from the point crude oil comes onshore in the case of offshore properties). When the regulations were finalized, a common five mile rule was adopted for both onshore and offshore (measured from the point that crude oil first comes onshore) properties.[390]

If the manufacture or conversion of crude oil into refined products begins before the crude oil is removed from the premises, the crude oil is considered (without exception) removed from the premises on the day that manufacture or conversion begins. The "removal price" is the constructive sales price for purposes of determining gross income from the property for percentage depletion purposes.[391] For purposes of determining constructive sales price, "premises" is the property from which the crude

382. I.R.C. Sec. 4988(c)(3); Reg. Sec. 51.4988-1(b)(1).
383. Reg. Sec. 51.4996-1(d)(1); Reg. Sec. 1.613-3(a).
384. Reg. Sec. 1.613-3(a).
385. IRS Letter Ruling 8246023.
386. Reg. Sec. 51.4996-1(d)(2).
387. *Ibid.*
388. Reg. Sec. 51.4996-1(d)(3)(ii).
389. Reg. Sec. 51.4996-1(d)(3)(ii); Notice of Proposed Rulemaking, LR-227-81, 1983-1 C.B. 1000.
390. T.D. 8103, 51 F.R. 33741 (Sept. 23, 1986).
391. I.R.C. Sec. 4988(c)(4).

oil was produced, not the location of the crude oil at the time manufacture or refining begins.

In the instant case, the production from the three offshore blocks is considered "removed from the premises" on the first date that any of the following occurs: (1) withdrawal from the first storage facility (2) sale or exchange or (3) manufacture or conversion.[392] The onshore terminal facility operates as a terminal for immediate delivery of the crude oil and has no significant storage facility; therefore, the exception to the removal-from-the-premises rule when crude oil is moved a short distance from the premises to storage is not applicable.[393] Instead, the oil will be considered removed at the time the sale takes place. Corporation A's use of crude oil on site for production operations is not an event that triggers imposition of the WPT.[394] *(See Case 92 for income tax implications of using crude oil or gas production for production operations.)* The "removal price" used to compute the WPT for the crude oil produced from the three blocks should be equal to the representative market or field price of the oil before transportation. Given that no actual market or field price exists, a reasonable method of estimating that price generally will be to use the sales price to the purchaser at the onshore terminal facility, less the transportation costs charged by Corporation X.[395] The producers will be required to deposit their own WPT for the three blocks because the crude oil production is not subject to withholding.[396]

Transportation of crude oil from a producing tract or parcel of land (as defined for depletion purposes)[397] to a contiguous tract or parcel of land (or a group of contiguous tracts or parcels) is not considered to be removed from the premises provided the following conditions are met:

- ☐ The crude oil has not been manufactured or converted;
- ☐ The crude oil is used on the transferee tract or parcel of land to power a production process or production equipment or is injected into a well and
- ☐ The same person or group of persons holds 100% of the operating mineral interests in each of the tracts or parcels of land.[398]

The term *contiguous* for this purpose means "actually touching along a substantial common border." The physical touching must be with respect to the underlying mineral interest; physical touching of the surface is not necessary.[399]

If crude oil is transported from one producing tract or parcel of land to another contiguous tract or parcel of land (or a group of contiguous tracts or parcels of land) when a producer's interests in those tracts or parcels of land are not identical, the number of barrels of crude oil, the constructive sales price of which equals the fair market value of the money or other consideration received, is considered removed for purposes of the imposition of the WPT.[400]

If crude oil is transported from one tract or parcel of land and injected in a contiguous tract or parcel of land (or a group of contiguous tracts or parcels of land) such that it is not considered removed for purposes of the imposition of the WPT, the crude oil that

392. Reg. Sec. 51.4996-1(d)(3)(ii).
393. *Ibid.*
394. Reg. Sec. 51.4996-1(d)(2).
395. I.R.C. Sec. 4988(c)(3); Reg. Sec. 51.4988-1(b)(1); Rev. Rul. 83-161, 1983-2 C.B. 202; James P. Evans, 11 T.C. 726 (1948).
396. Reg. Sec. 51.4995-1(a)(1).
397. Reg. Sec. 1.614-1(a)(3).
398. Reg. Sec. 51.4996-1(d)(3)(i); IRS Letter Ruling 8246023.
399. Reg. Sec. 51.4996-1(d)(3)(i)(C); Reg. Sec. 51.4996-1(d)(3)(i)(E), Example 2.
400. Reg. Sec. 51.4996-1(d)(3)(i)(B).

is first recovered after injection is deemed to be of the same tier category as the injected oil.[401]

In the instant case, the transportation of crude oil from contiguous leases to the unitized property subject to the tertiary recovery process will not be a constructive transfer for WPT purposes, except to the extent that consideration (other than certain crude oil production adjustments) is used to adjust for the ownership differential between the two properties.[402] Crude oil production from the contiguous leases or the unitized property used to power the steam generators is not considered removed for purposes of the WPT.[403] Crude oil transported from the noncontiguous leases that are not part of the same group of leases contiguous to the producing lease used to power the steam generators on the unitized property is considered removed when transported from the lease and, thus, is subject to WPT based on the constructive sales price rules for determining removal price.[404] The producers will be required to deposit their own WPT because the crude oil production is not subject to withholding.[405] If Corporation A should "exchange" crude oil produced from the unitized property for residual fuel to power the steam generators, the crude oil is considered removed from the premises on the day of transportation and the producers will be liable for the deposit and payment of their own WPT.[406]

401. Reg. Sec. 51.4996-1(d)(4).
402. Reg. Sec. 51.4996-1(d)(3)(i).
403. Reg. Sec. 51.4996-1(d)(2).
404. Reg. Sec. 51.4996-1(d)(3).
405. Reg. Sec. 51.4995-1(a)(1).
406. Rev. Rul. 82-160, 1982-2 C.B. 349.

Glossary

Advance Royalty: A royalty payment made in advance of production (includes lease bonus payments).

Alaskan North Slope Crude Oil: Crude oil that was subject to the upper-tier ceiling prices when crude oil prices were controlled prior to January 28, 1981. For windfall profit tax purposes, this production is tier-1 oil.

Base Price: For windfall profit tax purposes, a price per barrel of crude oil that depends on the tier in which the oil is classified. This base price is adjusted for inflation and added to the severance tax adjustment; these items are used to determine the windfall profit per barrel.

Bonus: Consideration for the grant or assignment of an oil and gas lease.

Bottom-Hole Contribution: Money or property given to an operator for the drilling of a well on property in which the payor has no interest. The contribution is payable whether the well is productive or nonproductive.

Carried Interest: A fractional interest in an oil and gas lease that, by its terms, relieves the holder from personal liability for a portion or all of the development and operating costs and permits the co-owner or co-owners who assume those liabilities to recoup their expenditures out of the proceeds from the oil and gas produced and sold.

Carved-Out Drill Site: An interest in an immediate drill site earned as a result of drilling a well. The drilling also earns an interest, usually fractional, in surrounding acreage.

Carved-Out Production Payment: A production payment assigned by the owner of an interest in oil and gas, which is to be paid from a fractional part of the owner's continuing interest.

Casing: Pipe inserted into the well during the drilling process to prevent water seepage and cave-ins.

Christmas Tree: An assembly of valves and fittings located at the casing head of an oil well to control the flow from the well to storage tanks and pipelines.

Complete Payout: The time at which the gross income attributable to all the operating mineral interests in a well equals all expenditures for the drilling and development of that well plus the cost of operating the well during the payout period.

Constructive Sales Price: For windfall profit tax purposes, the minimum removal price that may be used for sales of crude oil between related persons. This amount is equivalent to the representative market or field price of the oil (see Reg. Sec. 1.613-3).

Contiguous Leases: Leases that have a common boundary line.

Continuing Property Interest: An interest in oil and gas (i.e., working interest or royalty interest) that is not limited in amount or duration.

Cost Depletion: A deduction based on recovery of the taxpayer's basis in the oil and gas property in proportion to the production and sale of minerals.

Crude Oil: Petroleum crude and other hydrocarbons that exist as liquids in underground reservoirs and remain in a liquid state at standard atmospheric pressure. For windfall profit tax purposes, this term also includes certain types of condensate and natural gas liquids. However, this term does not include synthetic fuels such as shale oil.

Cycling Plant: A plant for the removal of distillate and condensate from wet gas and the injection of the residue dry gas into the reservoir.

Deferred Bonus: A lease bonus paid to the grantor of an oil and gas lease over a period of years.

Delay Rentals: Amounts paid to a lessor subsequent to the payment of the bonus for the privilege of deferring the commencement of a well on a lease.

Dry-Hole Contribution (or Money): Money or property given to an operator for drilling a well on property in which the payor has no interest. Such a contribution is payable only if the well is found to be nonproductive.

Economic Interest: Any interest in oil or gas in place that entitles the holder to a deduction for depletion on income derived from that interest (see Reg. Sec. 1.611-1(b)).

Farmout: The transfer of an oil and gas lease to secure development. The assignor usually retains an overriding royalty but may retain any type of interest or adjoining acreage.

First Purchaser: The party that is responsible for withholding the windfall profit tax from the amounts payable to producers, depositing the tax and filing quarterly tax returns.

Footage Drilling Contract: A well-drilling contract that provides for payment at a specific price per foot drilled.

Geological and Geophysical Costs: Expenditures an operator incurs in making surveys with such devices as gravity meters, seismographs, magnetic meters, etc., to locate possible oil-bearing structures in areas of interest.

Gross Income from the Property: For depletion purposes, the amount for which the taxpayer sells oil or gas in the immediate vicinity of the well site. If the oil or gas is not sold in the immediate vicinity, the gross income shall be assumed to be the equivalent representative market or field price before conversion or transportation (see Reg. Sec. 1.613-1).

Injection or Input Well: A well used to inject gas, water, propane, steam, etc., under high pressure into a producing formation to maintain sufficient pressure to produce the recoverable reserves.

Intangible Drilling and Development Costs (IDC): All expenditures for wages, fuel, repairs, hauling, supplies, etc., that, in and of themselves, do not have a salvage value but are incident to and necessary for the drilling of wells and the preparation of wells for the production of oil and gas.

Lease: A transaction in which the owner of the operating rights in an area of interest assigns all or part of those rights and retains a continuing nonoperating interest in production.

Limited Overriding Royalty: A royalty interest that is limited in duration and that, for tax purposes, is treated as a carved-out production payment.

Mineral Rights: The total rights to oil and gas in place, which usually include the reasonable use of the surface of the land to develop and produce oil and gas. These rights are made up of two separate types of rights, the royalty and the operating (or working) interest.

Minimum (Guaranteed) Royalty: A lessee's obligation to pay a lessor during the term of the lease either a fixed sum of money periodically or an agreed share of the proceeds of the oil and gas produced and saved, whichever is greater.

Miscible Drive: Injecting a miscible material into a reservoir to increase the specific gravity of the heavier reservoir fluids by mixing or dilution to facilitate production of heavier hydrocarbons.

Net Income Limitation: The windfall profit tax on a barrel of oil may not exceed 90% of the net income attributable to that barrel.

Net Profits Interest: A type of overriding royalty interest in production created by contractual arrangement with a lessee and measured by a certain percentage of the net profits from the operation of the property. (The definition of *net profits* may not be identical in every case. For example, some arrangements may exclude development costs in computing net profits. Others may charge gross capital costs, while others charge only depreciation, etc.)

Obligation Well: Any well that is drilled in consideration for the assignment of an operating or royalty interest in property.

Oil, Gas or Geothermal Property: For purposes of the intangible drilling and development costs (IDC) recapture provisions, each operating interest with respect to which any intangible drilling costs are properly chargeable. Also, nonoperating interests retained by a lessor if he held, before the lease, an operating interest on which IDC were charged.

Operator: One who holds all or a fraction of the working or operating rights in an oil and gas lease and is obligated for the cost of production either as a fee owner or under a lease or any other form of contract that creates working or operating rights (see Reg. Sec. 1.612-4(a)(1)).

Overriding Royalty: An interest carved out of the lessee's working interest that entitles the holder to receive a fraction of production, or the proceeds therefrom, free of any production or operating costs but not production and severance taxes.

Percentage Depletion: A statutory allowance of a deduction of specified percentages of the gross income from the property but not to exceed 50% of the net income from the property.

Production (Oil) Payment: A right to receive in cash or in kind a specific share of the production from a property up to an agreed amount.

Reserved (Retained) Production Payment: A production payment of an interest in an oil or gas property, reserved or retained by the transferor.

Royalty: The fraction of the oil or gas owned by the landowner or the possessor of royalty rights. It entitles the holder to receive proceeds from the sale of that oil or gas free of any production or operating costs but not of any production and severance taxes.

Removal Price: For windfall profit tax purposes, the amount for which a barrel of crude oil is sold, including any adjustments to the sales price made after the sale. If the crude oil is removed from the premises before it is sold or is sold to related parties, the removal price is the constructive sales price. In addition, the removal price for Alaskan North Slope Crude Oil is specially defined.

Secondary Production: Oil or gas production obtained by injecting liquids or gases into a reservoir.

Severance Tax: A state or local tax on the removal of minerals from the ground, usually levied at some number of cents per barrel of oil or per MCF of gas but sometimes based on a percentage of value.

Severance Tax Adjustment: For windfall profit tax purposes, the state severance or production tax levied on the windfall profit element of the price of a barrel of crude oil, up to a maximum rate of 15%. This adjustment is added to the adjusted base price and offset against the removal price of a barrel of oil to determine the windfall profit on that barrel of oil.

Sharing Arrangement: A transaction in which one party makes a contribution to the burden of developing an oil and gas property as consideration for receiving an interest in that property.

Shut-In Royalty: A payment to keep a lease alive, even without production, from a well capable of production in paying quantities. Relates primarily to gas wells that are shut in for a lack of market.

Spudding In: The beginning of drilling operations of a well.

Stripper Well Properties: Generally, properties for which average daily production per well has been 10 barrels or less of crude oil per day during any consecutive 12-month period after 1972. For windfall profit tax purposes, this type of production is tier-2 oil.

Take-or-Pay Contract: A gas purchase contract that requires the purchaser to take a minimum annual volume of gas that the producer has available for delivery, or to pay for that minimum amount even if not taken.

Term Royalty: A royalty interest with a clause that fixes the duration of the interest granted. Such a clause may cause this type of interest to be treated as a production payment.

Tertiary Production: Oil and gas production obtained through enhanced recovery methods such as injecting heat or carbon dioxide and other hydrocarbons into a formation to increase efficiency. Similar to secondary production.

Tier: A term used for setting price controls on oil and gas in applying the crude oil windfall profit tax.

Tier-1 Oil: Any taxable crude oil other than tier-2 oil or tier-3 oil.

Tier-2 Oil: Any oil, other than tier-3 oil, that was produced from a stripper well property or from the National Petroleum Reserve.

Tier-3 Oil: Newly discovered oil, heavy oil and incremental tertiary oil.

Top Lease: The granting of a new oil and gas lease prior to termination of an existing lease, with the new lease becoming effective upon expiration of the old lease.

Turnkey Drilling Contract: A well drilling contract that requires the driller, if he obtains commercial production, to equip the well to such a stage that the lessee or operator may turn a valve and the oil will flow into a tank.

Unit of Property: For depletion purposes, each separate interest owned by the taxpayer in each mineral deposit in each separate tract or parcel of land.

Unitization: An arrangement whereby various royalty and working interests on each tract or lease comprising an oil or gas reservoir are pooled or joined so that each interest party acquires an undivided interest in the entire reservoir.

Windfall Profit: The excess of the removal price of a barrel of crude oil over the sum of the adjusted base price and the severance tax adjustment.

Working Interest (Operating Rights): The interest in a mineral property evidenced by lease or other form of contract (*see Operator*).

Several excellent books on oil and gas industry terminology are available. This glossary is not intended to be a complete listing.

Table of Citations

Case Citations

A

B

C

H

I

M

	Page
McCahill v. Helvering, 75 F.2d 725 (8th Cir. 1935), 15 AFTR 304, 35-1 USTC 9100	140
McFaddin, James L. C., 2 T.C. 395 (1943)	24
McLean v. Comm'r, 120 F.2d 942 (5th Cir. 1941), 27 AFTR 544, 41-2 USTC 9553	248,256,277
Megert v. Campbell (N.D. Tex. 1963), 12 AFTR2d 5913, 63-2 USTC 9800	297
Mel Dar Corp., T.C. Memo Dec. (Mar. 30, 1960)	243,244
Mel Dar Corp. v. Comm'r, 309 F.2d 525 (9th Cir. 1962), 10 AFTR2d 5845, 62-2 USTC 9793	55
Merrill v. Comm'r, 336 F.2d 771 (9th Cir. 1964), 14 AFTR2d 5703, 64-2 USTC 9771	267
Mesa Petroleum Co., 58 T.C. 374 (1972)	161
Miller, Robert H., T.C. Memo Dec. (Feb. 23, 1961)	255
Miller v. U.S. (E.D. Okla. 1969), 24 AFTR2d 69-5363, 69-2 USTC 9578	253
Miller v. U.S. (C.D. Cal. 1977),41 AFTR2d 78-376, 78-1 USTC 9127	41
Mirabel Quicksilver Co., 41 B.T.A. 401 (1940)	155
Missouri River Sand Co. v. Comm'r, 774 F.2d 334 (8th Cir. 1985), 56 AFTR2d 85-6115, 85-2 USTC 9732, *aff'g* 83 T.C. 193 (1984)	35
Mohawk Petroleum Co. v. Comm'r, 148 F.2d 957 (9th Cir. 1945), 33 AFTR 1226, 45-1 USTC 9265	122
Moline Properties v. Comm'r, 319 U.S. 436 (1943), 30 AFTR 1291, 43-1 USTC 9464	329
Moncrief v. U.S., 730 F.2d 276 (5th Cir. 1984), 53 AFTR2d 84-1479, 84-1 USTC 9417	329
Montreal Mining Co., 2 T.C. 688 (1943)	155
Morgan, U.S. v., 321 F.2d 781 (5th Cir. 1963), 12 AFTR2d 5404, 63-2 USTC 9653	248,256,268, 277,291,296
Morrissey v. Comm'r, 296 U.S. 344 (1935), 16 AFTR 1274, 36-1 USTC 9020	331
Mountain Fuel Supply Co. v. U.S., 449 F.2d 816 (10th Cir. 1971), 28 AFTR2d 71-5833, 71-2 USTC 9681	161
Murphy Oil Co. v. Burnet, 55 F.2d 17 (9th Cir. 1932), 10 AFTR 1028, 3 USTC 1002	5
Murphy Oil Co. v. Burnet, 287 U.S. 299 (1932), 11 AFTR 1095, 3 USTC 1002	181,250,368

Page

Q

R

S

T

Z

Page

Internal Revenue Code Citations

Page

Session Law Citations

Regulation Sections

Temporary Regulations

Proposed Regulations

Page

Revenue Rulings

Revenue Procedures

Chief Counsel's Memoranda

Private Letter Rulings

	Page
IRS Letter Ruling 7808253250D (Technical Advice Memorandum)	53
IRS Letter Ruling 7824062	210
IRS Letter Ruling 7831003 (Technical Advice Memorandum)	43
IRS Letter Ruling 7834002 (Technical Advice Memorandum)	40
IRS Letter Ruling 7837004 (Technical Advice Memorandum)	40
IRS Letter Ruling 7838107	209
IRS Letter Ruling 7842008 (Technical Advice Memorandum)	155
IRS Letter Ruling 7902021 (Technical Advice Memorandum)	233,234,235
IRS Letter Ruling 7908005 (Technical Advice Memorandum)	161
IRS Letter Ruling 7913012	210
IRS Letter Ruling 7925011 (Technical Advice Memorandum)	384
IRS Letter Ruling 7931034	472
IRS Letter Ruling 7937015 (Technical Advice Memorandum)	190
IRS Letter Ruling 7937057	210
IRS Letter Ruling 7938028	211,218
IRS Letter Ruling 7945095	209,519
IRS Letter Ruling 7949013 (Technical Advice Memorandum)	2,251
IRS Letter Ruling 7951080	50
IRS Letter Ruling 7952066	136,209
IRS Letter Ruling 7952161	270
IRS Letter Ruling 8002016 (Technical Advice Memorandum)	383
IRS Letter Ruling 8005008 (Technical Advice Memorandum)	223
IRS Letter Ruling 8005042	210
IRS Letter Ruling 8009001 (Technical Advice Memorandum)	222
IRS Letter Ruling 8012060	60,61
IRS Letter Ruling 8014024 (Technical Advice Memorandum)	31
IRS Letter Ruling 8015047 (Technical Advice Memorandum)	164
IRS Letter Ruling 8026071	210,375
IRS Letter Ruling 8031082	209
IRS Letter Ruling 8041015 (Technical Advice Memorandum)	164
IRS Letter Ruling 8042011 (Technical Advice Memorandum)	48
IRS Letter Ruling 8042070	225
IRS Letter Ruling 8042080	225
IRS Letter Ruling 8043098	369
IRS Letter Ruling 8047005 (Technical Advice Memorandum)	31
IRS Letter Ruling 8049078	262,263
IRS Letter Ruling 8102027	211
IRS Letter Ruling 8104176	377
IRS Letter Ruling 8106045	184
IRS Letter Ruling 8107136	370
IRS Letter Ruling 8109064	543
IRS Letter Ruling 8111055	59,60,61
IRS Letter Ruling 8113044	379
IRS Letter Ruling 8115094	379
IRS Letter Ruling 8116041	377
IRS Letter Ruling 8125001	269,307
IRS Letter Ruling 8126061	209,519
IRS Letter Ruling 8127017 (Technical Advice Memorandum)	442
IRS Letter Ruling 8127060	136
IRS Letter Ruling 8128096	211,218

Treasury Decisions

Income Tax Unit Rulings

Committee Reports

Other Pronouncements

Index

A

B

C

D

H

I

J

L

M

N

P

Q

R

T

V

W

The Arthur Andersen Worldwide Organization

The Arthur Andersen Worldwide Organization includes separate practice entities, many of which use the Arthur Andersen name (Member Firms), Arthur Andersen & Co., Société Coopérative (the administrative coordinating entity with offices in Geneva, Switzerland, and Chicago, Illinois, USA) and other practice entities with which Member Firms have exclusive representation agreements, all of which are authorized under the laws of the countries in which they are located. The extensive interchange of personnel training and practice programs provides a worldwide organization of many individuals of many nationalities who adhere to uniform objectives of professional leadership and client service while complying with the laws, regulations and professional ethics of the countries in which they operate.

Argentina
Buenos Aires

Australia
Adelaide
Brisbane
Canberra
Melbourne
Perth
Sydney

Bahrain
Manama

Belgium
Antwerp
Brussels

Bermuda
Hamilton

Brazil
Belo Horizonte
Campinas
Rio de Janeiro
Salvador
São Paulo

Canada
Calgary
Mississauga
Montreal
Ottawa
Toronto
Vancouver
Winnipeg

People's Republic of China
Beijing
Shanghai

Colombia
Bogotá
Calí

Denmark
Århus
Copenhagen

Ecuador
Guayaquil
Quito

Egypt
Cairo

Federal Republic of Germany
Cologne
Düsseldorf
Frankfurt am Main
Hamburg
Hannover
Munich
Stuttgart

Finland
Helsinki

France
Lyon
Paris
Strasbourg

Greece
Athens

Guatemala
Guatemala City

Hong Kong
Hong Kong

India
Bombay
New Delhi

Indonesia
Bandung
Jakarta
Medan
Surabaya
Ujung Pandang

Republic of Ireland
Dublin

Italy
Bologna
Genoa
Milan
Naples
Rome
Treviso
Turin
Verona

Ivory Coast
Abidjan

Japan
Nagoya
Osaka
Tokyo

Jordan
Amman

Republic of Korea
Seoul

Luxembourg
Luxembourg

Malaysia
Kuala Lumpur

México
Guadalajara
México City
Monterrey

The Netherlands
Amsterdam
Eindhoven
The Hague

Nigeria
Lagos

Norway
Oslo
Stavanger
Trondheim

Oman
Muscat

Peru
Lima

Philippines
Bacolod City
Baguio City
Bataan
Cagayan de Oro
Cebu City
Cotabato City
Davao City
Dumaguete City
Iligan City
Iloilo City
Manila
Tacloban City
Zamboanga City

Portugal
Lisbon

Puerto Rico
San Juan

Saudi Arabia
Al Khobar
Jeddah
Riyadh

Republic of Singapore
Singapore

Republic of South Africa
Cape Town
Durban
Johannesburg
Pretoria

Spain
Barcelona
Bilbao
La Coruña
Madrid
Malaga
Oviedo
San Sebastián
Seville
Valencia
Vigo
Zaragoza

Sweden
Göteborg
Malmö
Stockholm

Switzerland
Geneva
Lugano
Zurich

Taiwan
Kaohsiung
Taichung
Taipei

Thailand
Bangkok
Chiengmai
Songkhla

Turkey
Istanbul

United Arab Emirates
Abu Dhabi
Dubai

United Kingdom
Aberdeen
Birmingham
Bristol
Cambridge
Cardiff
Edinburgh
Glasgow
Leeds
London
Manchester
Newcastle upon Tyne
Nottingham
Reading
St. Helier

United States
Albuquerque, NM
Ann Arbor, MI
Atlanta, GA
Austin, TX
Baltimore, MD
Bellevue, WA
Birmingham, AL
Bloomfield Hills, MI
Boise, ID
Boston, MA
Charlotte, NC
Chattanooga, TN
Chicago, IL
Cincinnati, OH
Cleveland, OH
Columbia, SC
Columbus, OH
Dallas, TX
Dayton, OH
Denver, CO
Detroit, MI
Fort Lauderdale, FL
Fort Worth, TX
Grand Rapids, MI
Greensboro, NC
Hartford, CT
Honolulu, HI
Houston, TX
Indianapolis, IN
Jackson, MS
Jacksonville, FL
Kansas City, MO
Lafayette, LA
Las Vegas, NV
Little Rock, AR
Long Beach, CA
Long Island, NY
Los Angeles, CA
Louisville, KY
Manchester, NH
McLean, VA
Memphis, TN
Miami, FL
Milwaukee, WI
Minneapolis, MN
Nashville, TN
New Jersey (Roseland)
New Orleans, LA
New York, NY
Oakland, CA
Oklahoma City, OK
Omaha, NE
Orange County, CA
Orlando, FL
Philadelphia, PA
Phoenix, AZ
Pittsburgh, PA
Portland, OR
Princeton, NJ
Raleigh, NC
Richmond, VA
Rochester, NY
Sacramento, CA
St. Louis, MO
Saint Paul, MN
St. Petersburg, FL
Salt Lake City, UT
San Antonio, TX
San Diego, CA
San Francisco, CA
San Jose, CA
Sarasota, FL
Seattle, WA
Stamford, CT
Tallahassee, FL
Tampa, FL
Toledo, OH
Tucson, AZ
Tulsa, OK
Washington, DC

Venezuela
Caracas